Commercial
DIVING
Manual

Commercial
DIVING
Manual

Richard Larn &
Rex Whistler

DAVID & CHARLES
Newton Abbot   London   North Pomfret (Vt)

British Library Cataloguing in Publication Data

Larn, Richard
  Commercial diving manual.
  1. Diving, submarine
  I. Title   II. Whistler, Rex
  627'.72   GV840.S78

ISBN 0-7153-8414-7

Printed in Great Britain
for David & Charles (Publishers) Limited
Brunel House Newton Abbot Devon

Published in the United States of America
by David & Charles Inc
North Pomfret Vermont 05053 USA

CONTENTS

Acknowledgements

Foreword

ACKNOWLEDGEMENTS

The authors extend their grateful appreciation and thanks to the many
individuals, companies and organisations, who have contributed effort,
times, material or permission to reproduce material, towards this manual.
In particular, the office and diving staff of Prodive Limited, the
Commerical Diving Centre at Falmouth, Cornwall, including David Ryeland,
Tom Norman and the instructors for their technical advice and comments;
Dr Mike Haywood, for his NDT material, Eileen Caton for preparation of
a great deal of the draft material, Falmouth Technical College and
Mrs J. Perry, who helped put the very first edition together, and Bridget
Larn, who made a considerable contribution towards this edition.

Acknowledgement is also made to the following, who represent diving
companies, manufacturers, organisations and authors of technical books
and manuals, to which reference was made in the preparation of this
diving manual, or who have given permission to reproduce material, or
made a contribution; the Controller of Her Majesty's Stationery Office,
regarding BR 2806; U.S. Department of Navy, for illustrations and other
extracts from the U.S. Navy Diving Manual; the British Sub Aqua Club;
General Aquadyne Inc; U.S. Divers; Helle Engineering; Kirby Morgan Inc;
Diving Unlimited; Underwater Instrumentation; ICI, Nobel Division;
N.B. Zinkowski, 'Commercial Oilfield Diving' (Cornell Maritime Press);
W.G. Newberry, 'Handbook for Riggers'; J. Strykowski, 'Divers and Cameras';
D.E. Hewitt, 'Engineering Drawing and Design'; Reed's Nautical Almanac '
(1982 edition), Thomas Reed Publications; Consolidated Pneumatics (Gordon
Railton and Co); Dive Dynamics; Harbens Ltd; Tirfor Ltd; Stanley Tools
Ltd; and many others who may not have been acknowledged individually
but to whom we extend our gratitude.

Additionally, we wish to thank the Manpower Services Commission,
Training Division, for permission to reproduce the greater part of their
publication, Basic Air Diving Training Standard (September 1981).

FOREWORD

The concept of this diving manual was born out of a need for a single
publication, which embraced all the relevant aspects of basic diving
theory and practice, required by those being trained to the relatively
new Health and Safety at Work (Diving Operations) Regulations 1981.

There are of course many professional diving manuals and publications
on the market, but generally speaking, these all have a high degree of
specialisation, as with the RN Diving Manual (BR 2806), or the U.S. Navy
Diving Manual. Other publications are orientated towards the offshore
diving industry, or sport diving for example, and whilst excellent and
very necessary in their particular field, again they do not meet the
needs of a trainee diver entering the commerical diving world.

Such a manual has been a personal ambition of mine since 1971 when,
on leaving the Royal Navy, I became intimately involved with the training
of commercial divers. Developments in equipment, the introduction of
the Manpower Services Commission's Standard for Basic Diver & Underwater
Worker, as well as other legislation regarding diver safety, training
and employment caused the project to be shelved until 1980 when Rex
Whistler joined my staff, initially as Training Manager and later as a
fellow director. With considerable drive and initiative, he compiled
the first draft. With suitable changes and revision from time to time,
this manual has been in daily use by trainee divers for almost four years,
and has proved its worth.

With British diving standards being slowly accepted throughout
Europe, and other parts of the world, the content of this manual is
international, and hopefully will be instrumental in raising the
standards of diver training in other countries.

                    Richard Larn   Rex Whistler

CHAPTER 1

DIVING HISTORY

In the warmer waters of the world, it would appear that men have always speared fish for food, harvested sponges, pearls and coral as barter goods, and generally recovered items from sunken boats and ships. It is therefore impossible to even guess at what period in pre-history men first learnt to swim, and then to hold their breath underwater, but it is known that the profession of diving dates back over 5,000 years.

It was in northern Europe during the Middle Ages, that men first made serious endeavours to remain underwater long enough to perform useful work, and then only in connection with salvage. Little or no underwater construction work was carried out using divers until the late 1700s. Perhaps the biggest stumbling block of all to the progress of diving was the total inability to produce a successful 'force-pump', so that the majority of devices were only variations of diving-bells, or else 'inventions' for devices with an open breathing tube to the surface. Although the principle of the diving-bell may seem very basic today, it was not so to even the keenest scientific brains of the time. Perhaps the earliest successful excursion underwater in a bell was that undertaken in the River Tagus, before Emperor Charles V in 1538, when two Greeks were lowered to the river bed in an inverted, weighted vase, and survived.

The first recorded use of the word 'diver' in this context in England can be found in the Calendar of Domestic State Papers. This relates to one Jacob Johanson, a Dutchman who specialised in the recovery of ships' anchors around the Goodwin Sands in 1616, and went on to work on many shipwrecks recovering cannon, anchors and treasure. By 1624 "Jacob the dyver" was well known in the best of Court circles, working for the King or the Duke of Buckingham. His equipment remains a mystery, but must be assumed to have been a diving bell.

William Phipps has a place in diving history, not for his famous excursions to the West Indies to recover over £200,000 of treasure from sunken Spanish galleons, but because he devised a method of supplying additional but small amounts of air in weighted upturned buckets, which were "bled" into the bell. In 1690, Edmund Halley improved on this method by using weighted, sealed barrels, each fitted with a short leather pipe. If hung lower than the mouth of the bell, on opening the cock at the end of the pipe, the barrel's content of fresh air entered the bell, replenishing the contents to some small degree.

Figure 1-1 A diving bell of 1678

No further developments took place in bell diving until the middle of the eighteenth century, when a Scotsman named Spalding made great improvements to this device by including a sealed compartment at the top of the bell, controlled by valves, which allowed the bell to rise or sink. The inventor also became the victim of the first known diving bell accident, since in 1783 Spalding and his nephew both asphyxiated whilst working on a wreck on the Irish coast.

The first development of any form of "atmospheric " diving dress is attributed to John Lethbridge, of Newton

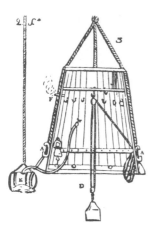

Figure 1-2 Spalding's diving bell, showing suspended weight lowered to the bottom to adjust working height.

Abbot. His device took the form of a tapered wooden barrel, into which he was sealed when the lid was placed in position. His arms protruded from two leather covered seals, which gave him a degree of restricted and painful movement, and a small glass port for a degree of vision. He would remain sealed in this device for eight or ten hours at a time, the foul air being replenished by means of a pair of bellows every time he returned to the surface, and the ventilation bungs were removed. He could remain at a depth of 60ft for up to twenty minutes.

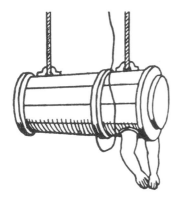

Figure 1-3 Lethbridge's diving barrel

This invention was quickly followed by Captain Rowe's 'barrel' which was made of copper entirely, and proved less troublesome in tropical climates where Lethbridge's wooden device tended to warp if allowed to become too dry. Both men worked all over the world for both the Dutch and English East India Companies, salvaging cargo and specie from shipwrecks.

The 'standard' diving helmet, often accredited to Augustus Siebe, was in fact the invention of John and Charles Deane, brothers from Whitstable, in Kent. In 1823 they invented and patented a breathing apparatus for use at the scene of fires, and developed it for eventual use under-water. This helmet, with improvements in its sealing and the associated diving dress, went on to be used internationally for the next 150 years, and in fact is still used.

Closed circuit apparatus was then followed in 1942 by Cousteau's 'aqualung', better known today as SCUBA, which has opened up the depths of the sea to everyone, and a long way from the days when there was but one diver in the whole of England!

DECOMPRESSION SICKNESS (the Bends)

As the potential for the use of divers to assist in underwater construction work was appreciated, so others were devising methods whereby the time honoured diving bell could be adapted to allow labourers who were not divers to work beneath the surface. Chambers large enough to accept several men were built, and when connected to a surface air pump, could keep all traces of water out simply by using air pressure to combat that of the water, which was related to depth. Such devices were known as Caissons, in French, literally 'big-box', and were particularly suitable for work on bridge footings, or excavations where masons were employed.

In order to hold back the water, then the air pressure had to equal the water pressure, which sometimes meant that the men were working at the equivalent of several atmospheres, and in point of fact they were of course being subjected to all the problems

(opposite) Fig 1-4 WASP

of a diver, only they were not getting wet. It became noticeable that many of the workers, on returning to the surface, complained of dizziness, pains in their limbs or joints, difficulty in breathing, and that in later life were often crippled with what was assumed to be rheumatism.

The complaint became known as Caisson disease, which became more generally called the 'Bends', after the general similarity of the forward leaning position of fashion-conscious ladies known as the 'Grecian Bend', and the poor contorted workers returning from a day under pressure.

Today the physiology of decompression sickness is well understood, but still requires lengthy and not always successful treatment, depending on the length of exposure and pressure, plus other factors such as the amount of work preformed, previous dives, and age and fitness. It is surprising that so little work was done in this field until the early 1900s, when the Englishman Professor Haldane commenced his long series of experiments, which eventually led to the Royal Navy producing the first decompression tables.

Regulations within the United Kingdom relating to diving practice now make it mandatory for all commerical divers to undergo annual medical examinations, at which it may be necessary for the examining doctor to satisfy himself that no permanent damage has resulted from long exposures, or deep diving. It is now an accepted practice for divers to have regular 'long-bone' X-ray examinations, which will show up any deformities in the major joints of the body, the points where 'bone-necrosis' become apparent.

This is particularly necessary in cases where divers are employed on more ambitious underwater tasks, possibly at great depths, using the technique of 'saturation diving'. Compressed-air diving uses normal atmospheric air, pressurised to suit the application; deep-diving employs mixtures of oxygen and the inert gas helium, an innovation first used in the United States before the Second World War. This has proven that men can live and work at depths of up to 2,000ft (600m), although the actual deep working dive record is still around 1,500ft (450m).

Such diving is confined almost exclusively to the offshore oil and gas industry, but interest is being shown in its use for certain types of salvage work.

CHAPTER 2

PHYSICS OF DIVING

INTRODUCTION

The effects of diving on the human body are caused by the operation of certain physical laws, in particular the physical properties possessed by liquids and gases. The human body under water is operating in a completely different environment, in which it is exposed to much greater pressures than it experiences at the surface. It is necessary, therefore, to consider carefully the meanings of the terms 'force, pressure and density' as applied to liquids and gases.

Figure 2-1 The physical forces affecting a diver

FORCE, PRESSURE AND DENSITY

FORCE equals that which changes or attempts to change the state of rest or uniform motion of an object. In other words a force will move or try to move an object, or if the object is already moving, will increase or decrease its velocity. Usually given in terms of weight, i.e., kgf or gf.

PRESSURE equals force applied to a unit area of surface. In diving, unit area of surface is one square metre.

Formula - $\text{Pressure} = \dfrac{\text{Force}}{\text{Area}}$

Unit of pressure = 1 bar

NOTE: 1 bar approximates to 1 atmosphere 14.5 lbs per square inch. 1 kilogram centimetre squared, or the pressure experienced at the depth of 10 metres.

DENSITY equals a measure of the degree of packing of molecules in a substance.

Formula - $\text{Density} = \dfrac{\text{Mass}}{\text{Volume}}$

Unit of Density = $\dfrac{\text{kg}}{\text{m}^3}$

LIQUIDS AND GASES

To the diver water is, of course, the most important liquid. It has volume and weight or 'density' and will take the shape of its container. For all practical purposes water can be considered as being incompressible and the effects of temperature changes on volume and density disregarded.

LIQUIDS

Density of fresh water equals -

$$1000 \ \frac{\text{kg}}{\text{m}^3}$$

Density of sea water varies in different oceans of the world, depending on the amount of dissolved matter (mainly salt) in it. For all practical purposes, the average density can be used. Density of sea water equals -

$$1030 \ \frac{\text{kg}}{\text{m}^3}$$

GASES

All gases have some weight and occupy space and have no definite volume or shape. Compared with liquids they are very light and compressible. Atmospheric air, the air we normally breathe, is a natural mixture of approximately 21% oxygen and 79% nitrogen, with a trace of carbon dioxide and other rare gases. It also contains water vapour in an amount depending upon the weather conditions. Since gases are compressible, the density of a gas varies according to the pressure applied. Thus, the density of the gas the diver breathes varies according to the depth at which he is working.

MEASURE OF GAS AND WATER PRESSURE

WATER PRESSURE. The pressure with which the diver is most directly concerned is the pressure of the surrounding water at his diving depth (ambient pressure). Pressure in liquids conforms to certain basic laws, which **are** as follows -

a) The pressure on an object in a liquid is produced by the weight of liquid above the object and atmospheric pressure.

b) The pressure produced acts on the object from all directions (Figure 2-1).

c) The pressure will act at right angles to any surface of the object.

CALCULATIONS OF PRESSURE AT ANY DEPTH IN SEAWATER

EXAMPLE:

What weight is exerted on a one metre square plate at a depth of ten metres in seawater?

Formula = weight of water above plate equals volume of water above plate x density of seawater.

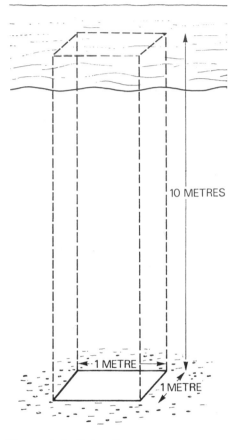

Figure 2-2 Water Pressure

Formula:

Volume of water above plate =

10 metres x 1 metre x 1 metre = $10m^3$

therefore weight of water above plate =

$10m^3$ x 1030 $\frac{kg}{m^3}$ (density of seawater) =

10 300kg

Answer: Pressure on plate = $10\ 300\ \dfrac{kg}{1m^2}$

= $10\ 300\ \dfrac{kg}{m^2}$ at a depth of 10 metres

Pressure in water is directly proportional to depth. Therefore for pressure at any depth:

Formula =

Pressure = depth (metres) x $1030\ \dfrac{kg}{m^2}$

NOTE: For most practical purposes it can be considered that water pressure

increases by $1030\ \dfrac{kg}{m^2}$ for every metre of descent.

ATMOSPHERIC PRESSURE

The atmosphere exerts a pressure on the earth's surface in the same way as water exerts pressure, i.e., it is produced by the weight of air above the earth. However, unlike water, the atmosphere, being gaseous, is compressible. Therefore its density varies with height, the greatest density being at the earth's surface, i.e., sea level. This means that the maximum atmospheric pressure is experienced at sea level at heights above sea level, the pressure would be less, depending on height.

Atmospheric pressure = pressure exerted by the weight of atmospheric gas on the earth's crust. This actual pressure will vary slightly due to changes in barometric pressure but can be considered in the terms of calculations as 14.5 lbs per square inch.

Atmospheric pressure = $10\ 300\ \dfrac{kg}{m^2}$

Atmospheric pressure will support a column of seawater 10 metres in height. Therefore it can be seen that atmospheric pressure exerts the same pressure as a 10m head of seawater.

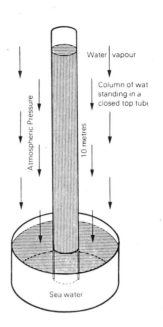

Figure 2-3 Water column supported by atmospheric pressure

ABSOLUTE AND GAUGE PRESSURE

GAUGE PRESSURE:- a pressure gauge is normally graduated to read zero when the gauge is at atmospheric pressure. Indicates pressure exerted by water alone, i.e., 20m = 2 bars gauge.

ABSOLUTE PRESSURE:- before a diver leaves the surface he is already subject to a pressure of 1 bar or

$10\ 300\ \dfrac{kg}{m^2}$

for every metre he descends the pressure will increase 0.1 of a bar. The total pressure is known as the absolute pressure.

Absolute pressure = gauge pressure + atmospheric pressure. (i.e., 20m = 3 bars absolute.)

Since pressure is directly proportional to depth, it is often convenient, in diving calculations, to work in depth rather than pressure.

GASES

Gases are the most elusive and intangible of substances, but a knowledge of the properties and behaviour of gases - especially those used for breathing - is of vital importance to a diver.

OXYGEN = O_2

This colourless, odourless, tasteless and active 'gas' readily combines with other elements. Fire cannot burn without oxygen and man cannot live without oxygen. It can also be a diver's worst enemy.

NITROGEN = N_2

Colourless, odourless and tasteless gas; unlike oxygen it will not support life. Nitrogen in the air is inert and is essentially a carrier gas.

HELIUM = He

Also colourless, odourless and tasteless. But it is monatomic; that is, it exists as a single atom; in its free state; is also inert. Helium is a rare element first discovered in 1868. Since helium is seven times lighter than air, its primary use in the 20th century was to inflate balloons. Helium co-exists with natural gas in certain wells in the South Western United States, Canada and the U.S.S.R. Present average cost 10p per cubic foot, used exclusively, mixed with oxygen for diving in excess of 50m. Because it does not have the narcotic effect of nitrogen. Helium tremor occurs in depths of 200m plus.

HYDROGEN = H_2

Hydrogen is diatomic, colourless, odourless and tasteless, and is so active that it is rarely found in free state on earth. The sun and stars are almost pure hydrogen. Hydrogen is the lightest of all elements, i.e. hydrogen balloons, etc. It is violently explosive when mixed with air, as the flaming crash of the Hindenburg airship.

Used for underwater cutting with oxygen. It has also been used for experimental diving, replacing helium.

CARBON DIOXIDE = CO_2

Colourless, odourless and tasteless, when found in small percentages in air. Greater concentrations have an acid taste and odour. Chemically active, commonly found in soda pop and fire extinguishers because it is nonflammable. Natural by-product of respiration in animals and humans.

Oxidisation of carbon in the body to produce energy. Carbon dioxide is the main cause of respiration. For divers, the two major concerns with CO_2 are control of the exhaust after breathing and contamination of the breathing supply.

CARBON MONOXIDE = CO

A man-made gas which is the product of an internal combustion engine. It is highly poisonous to man; colourless, odourless and tasteless. Hence difficult to detect. Carbon monoxide is chemically highly active and seriously interferes with the blood's ability to carry oxygen, forming carboxy haemoglobin. A typical cause of carbon monoxide poisoning in divers is contamination of the air supply from improper placing of the compressor engine exhaust, close to the pump inlet.

WATER VAPOUR = H_2O

Air always contains some percentage of water vapour which must be considered as a gas. This is the 'humidity' that sometimes makes the weather - especially hot weather - uncomfortable.

UNITS OF MEASUREMENT

The science of physics relies heavily
upon standards of comparison of one state
of matter or energy to another. Understanding and applying the principles of
physics requires that the diver be able
to employ a variety of units of measurement.

METRIC and ENGLISH SYSTEM OF MEASUREMENT

Two systems of measurement of force,
length and time are in wide use throughout the world, English and Metric. The
English system based upon the pound (lb),
and foot, is commonly used in the United
States, but is being replaced throughout
the rest of the world with the Metric
system. The Metric system, originally
developed in Continental Europe, employs
the kilogramme, and metre as a fundamental unit of measurement.

METRIC SYSTEM

The metric unit of length is the metre
(39.37 inches). For measuring smaller
lengths, the millimetre or centimetre are
used.

1 metre = 100 centimetres (cm)
        = 1,000 millimetres (mm)

1 millimetre = 0.10 centimetres
             = 0.001 metre

For longer distances, the metric system
uses the kilometre (about six-tenths of a
mile).

1 kilometre = 1,000 metres

1 metre   = 0.001 kilometre

AREA

The metric system uses its units of
length squared to measure area, as does
the English system. As in converting
from one metric unit of length to another,
converting units of area is merely a

matter of moving the decimal point. In
this case it is moved twice as many
places as in measures of length. For
example, 1.0 metre = 100.0 cm;
1.0 square metres = 10,000 square centimetres. (Compare this operation with
that of multiplying by 144 to convert
from square feet to square inches.

VOLUME OR CAPACITY

Volumes are expressed as units of length
cubed.

1 litre = 1,000 cubic centimetres
        = 0.001 cubic metre

WEIGHT

The kilogramme (kg) is the standard
metric unit of mass or weight. One
kilogramme is approximately the mass of
one litre of water or about 2.2 pounds
at 4^oC. For smaller masses the gram (g)
and milligram (mg) are used.

1 kilogramme = 1,000 g
             = 1,000,000 mg

1 gram = 0.001 kg
       = 1,000 mg

1 milligramme = 0.001 g

PRESSURE

The standard metric unit of pressure is
the Newton per square metre (N/m^2).
However, the most commonly used metric
unit of pressure is kilogrammes per
square centimetre (Kg/cm^2).

$1 \ Kg/cm^2$ = 1,000 g/cm^2
       = 1,000 cm H_2O
       = 10 metres H_2O
       = (approx.) 1 atmosphere

1 Bar   = 1.02 Kg/cm^2
        = 0.99 atm
        = 750 mm Hg
        = 10.21 metres H_2O

1 mm Hg = 1.35 g/cm^2
       = 13.5 Kg/m^2
       = 133.32 N/m^2
       = 1/760 atm

TEMPERATURE

Countries using the English system of
weights and measures generally employ
the Fahrenheit (^{o}F) temperature scale.
Countries that use the metric system,
and most scientific laboratories, use
the Celsius (formerly centigrade) scale
(^{o}C). This scale is based upon the
temperature of melting ice (32°F) as 0°C
and the temperature of boiling water
(212°F) as 100°C.

Conversion from one temperature scale to
another may be accomplished by the alge-
braic solution of the following equa-
tions:-

To convert from Fahrenheit to Celsius

   ^{o}C = 5/9ths x (^{o}F - 32)

To convert from Celsius to Fahrenheit

   ^{o}F = (9/5ths x ^{o}C) + 32

ABSOLUTE TEMPERATURE

Absolute temperature values are used
when making certain types of calculations, such as when employing the
ideal gas laws. The absolute temperature
scales are based upon absolute zero -
the lowest temperature that could possibly be reached - at which all molecular
motion would cease. On the Fahrenheit
scale this temperature is -459.72^{o}F, in
Celsius it is -273.12^{o}C. These numbers
are normally rounded off to -460°F and
-273°C.

To convert from Fahrenheit to absolute
temperature (called degrees Rankine - ^{o}R)

^{o}R = ^{o}F + 460

To convert from Celsius to absolute temperature (called degrees Kelvin - ^{o}K)

^{o}K = ^{o}C + 273

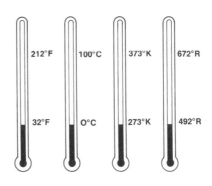

Figure 2-4 Fahrenheit, Celsius, Kelvin
          and Rankin temperature
          scales showing the freezing
          and boiling points of water

GAS LAWS

BOYLES LAW

Because gases are compressible their
volumes can be altered by a change of
pressure. The amount by which the volume changes depends on the change of
pressure and is explained fully in
Boyle's Law, which states:

IF THE TEMPERATURE IS KEPT CONSTANT, THE
VOLUME OF A GIVEN MASS OF GAS WILL VARY
INVERSELY AS ITS ABSOLUTE PRESSURE.

PV = C

From this law it follows that the density varies directly as the absolute
pressure. In other words, if the pressure of a gas is doubled the density is
also doubled. But the volume is decreased to one half of the original
volume. It is most important that the
diver should clearly understand this
relationship between volume and pressure.

It is not necessary to complicate this
simple rule by taking into account the
exact effect of changes in temperature,
but it should be observed that if the
temperature of a confined gas is
increased there will be a resultant rise

in pressure and that if the temperature is decreased there will be a corresponding fall in pressure.

CHARLES' LAW

CHARLES' LAW STATES THAT THE AMOUNT OF CHANGE IN EITHER VOLUME OR PRESSURE IS DIRECTLY RELATED TO THE CHANGE IN THE ABSOLUTE TEMPERATURE.

Boyle had shown that pressure and volume were inversely related. However, since his experiments were conducted at relatively low pressures and at whatever the temperature happened to be on the day of his experiments, they provided no clues as to the influence of temperature. A French scientist, Jacques Charles, found that if the pressure was kept constant - as in some sort of freely-expanding container - the volume of gas would increase as the temperature increased. Conversely, if the volume was restrained in a rigid container, the pressure would increase with the temperature. This is all in accordance with the kinetic theory of gases - higher temperatures, higher molecular speeds.

For example:- an aqualung cylinder filled too quickly, causing a rise in temperature, when cooled will contain less pressure.

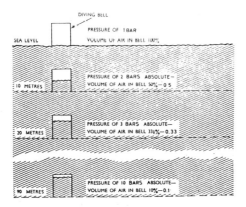

Figure 2-5 Relationship between depth, pressure and volume

Note the greatest change at the surface.

PARTIAL PRESSURES

It is important in air and mixture diving to know the values of the partial pressures of the gases present, because if they are too high or, for oxygen, too low or too high, a diver may suffer from a variety of ill effects as a result.

DALTON'S LAW OF PARTIAL PRESSURES - IN A MIXTURE OF GASES, EACH CONSTITUENT GAS EXERTS A PRESSURE. THE SUM OF THESE PRESSURES IS THE ABSOLUTE PRESSURE OF THE MIXTURE. In other words, "the whole is equal to the sum of its parts". Partial pressure is expressed as Pp and always as an absolute pressure.

For example - Pp of O_2 = PpO_2 bars abs.

Parts of a bar can be expressed as a millibar

For example - 1 bar = 1000 millibars.

When dealing with very small quantities of gas such as measuring CO_2, etc., PARTS PER MILLION may be used.

To convert millibars to PPm = millibars x 1000 ÷ absolute pressure

For example - 2 millibars of CO_2 at 50m
$$= \frac{2 \times 1,000}{6} = 333PPm$$

To convert percentage multiply this percentage at a given depth by 10,000.

For example - maximum CO_2 at 158m
= 0.036%

To obtain PPm - 0.036 X 10,000 = 360PPm

As an introduction to understanding the working of Dalton's Law, three main formulas can be employed to find any of the following, providing the other two are known:-

1) To find the Pp of a gas,

$$Pp = percentage \times \frac{(BA)}{100}$$

2) To find the percentage of a gas,

$$Percentage = Pp \times \frac{100}{(BA)}$$

3) To find the Bars Absolute of a gas,

$$BA = Pp \times \frac{100}{percentage}$$

An operation example will best illustrate the use of and importance of Dalton's Law.

When a diver puts on a helmet, having just before taken a normal breath of air. That breath contains millions of molecules of various gases mixed freely in the atmosphere. Pressure of the gas he has just taken in is normal atmospheric pressure = 1.0 bar absolute.

Since the composition of the air is almost constant we know that for every 10,000 molecules of gas in that breath, 2,100 will be oxygen, 7,800 will be nitrogen, 97 will be of all the other gases except carbon dioxide which will comprise approximately 3 molecules.

In accordance with Dalton's Law:-

$$PpO_2 = \frac{21\%}{100\%} \times 1 \ BA = 0.21 \ BA \ or$$
$$210 \ millibars.$$

Inert gas partial pressure:-

$$PpN_2 = \frac{79\%}{100\%} \times 1 \ BA = 0.79 \ BA \ or$$
$$790 \ millibars.$$

Carbon Dioxide partial pressure:-

$$PpCO_2 = \frac{0.03\%}{100\%} \times 1 \ BA = 0.0003 \ BA \ or$$
$$3 \ millibars.$$

Now let's see what happens to the breathing mixture at the operating depth of 40m. The composition of the air has not changed, but the quantity being delivered to the diver is 5 times what he was

breathing at the surface. More molecules are compressed into the same volume. Employing Dalton's Law to determine the partial pressure at depth:-

$$PpO_2 = \frac{21\%}{100\%} \times 5 \ BA = 1.05 \ BA \ or$$
$$1,050 \ millibars.$$

$$PpN_2 = \frac{79\%}{100\%} \times 5 \ BA = 3.95 \ BA \ or$$
$$3,950 \ millibars.$$

$$PpCO_2 = \frac{0.0003\%}{100\%} \times 5 \ BA = 0.0015 \ BA \ or$$
$$150 \ millibars.$$

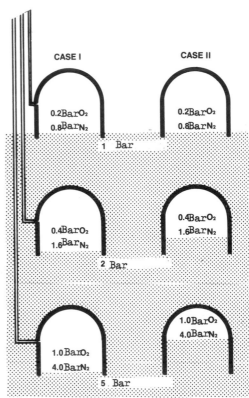

Figure 2-6 Partial Pressure:

In cases similar to the situation in a diver's lungs, the partial pressures of the two gases (at constant volume) increase because of the addition of more gas molecules.

In case II, similar to an open-bottom diving bell, partial pressures of the two gases increase due to compression.

In both cases the sum of the partial pressures equals the hydrostatic pressure, and individual partial pressures increase in direct proportion to absolute pressure.

From the previous calculations it can be seen that the partial pressure increased relative to pressure. Although, the percentages stay the same. When we are considering Gas Toxicity of dangerous levels it is important that we understand the partial pressure. For example, we know that oxygen can become toxic at 2 BA and we should not exceed this level.

QUESTION

At what depth does oxygen exceed a partial pressure of 2 BA in normal breathing air?

$$BA = Pp \times \frac{100\%}{\text{Percentage}} \text{ therefore}$$

$$BA = 2 \times \frac{100}{21} = 9.5 \; BA = 85m$$

(Remember that the answer is given in BA)

High and low danger levels can be applied to oxygen mixtures -

HYPOXIA (Low Level) is between 0.2 and 0.16 BA.

ANOXIA A total lack of oxygen in the body.

HYPEROXIA (High Level) 2.0 BA. (Oxygen can be breathed in excess of this if in a chamber environment).

NITROGEN Levels in excess of 3.0 BA have toxic effects giving symptoms similar to drunkeness. (Nitrogen narcosis) British

regulations limit the use of compressed air to 50m due to the toxicity of this gas.

HYPERCAPNIA - CO_2 Poisoning. At atmospheric pressure up to about 0.3%. Carbon dioxide can be breathed with no ill effects on the body. As the percentage increases a higher respiration and pulse rate will be observed.

HYPOCAPNIA A condition resulting from low levels of carbon dioxide in the blood leaving the lungs. Symptoms of hypocapnia range from lightheadedness and a tingling sensation to muscular spasms and perhaps even loss of consciousness.

CARBON MONOXIDE Carboxy haemoglobin is formed due to the intrusion of this gas into the blood stream, effectively causing Hypoxia.

SURFACE EQUIVALENT - levels are generally referred to surface equivalent limits.

NB. For further information on gas poisonings, see Physiology.

GAS ABSORPTION IN LIQUIDS

HENRY'S LAW states:- AT A CONSTANT TEMPERATURE THE MASS OF A GAS THAT DISSOLVES IN A GIVEN MASS OF LIQUID WITH WHICH IT IS IN CONTACT IS ALMOST DIRECTLY PROPORTIONAL TO THE PARTIAL PRESSURE OF THAT GAS.

Practical effects on a diver:- at atmospheric pressure, about 1.25 GM (1 litre) of nitrogen is dissolved in the body liquid, i.e., blood, fatty tissue, watery tissue, etc.

An increase in pressure will cause more nitrogen to be absorbed, proportional to the increase, i.e., at 2 BA, 2.5 GM (2 litres). This is roughly true providing the time of exposure is long enough (an explanation of saturation is given later). If the pressure on a

diver is released too quickly, i.e., he
comes up too quickly from depth, not
observing his decompression obligations.
Bubbles will form, this can be compared
to a soda pop. These bubbles can be
repressurised into solution. But if
they are not, they will circulate in the
blood stream until obstructed, i.e., by
a joint, small blood vessels, etc.,
eventually causing a bend. (Bubble formation and decompression requirements
are dealt with in Physiology.)

BUOYANCY

Buoyancy - the force which makes objects
float, whether pieces of cork or ships
with steel hulls. It was first defined
by the Greek mathematician Archimedes
who established that WHEN AN OBJECT IS
WHOLLY OR PARTIALLY IMMERSED IN A
LIQUID, THE UPTHRUST IT RECEIVES IS
EQUAL TO THE WEIGHT OF LIQUID DISPLACED.
This is known as Archimedes' principle,
and it applies to all objects and fluids.

The tendency of a substance to float - or
not to float - in water is indicated by
its specific gravity. For a solid or a
liquid, this is a number assigned on the
basis and ratio of the density of the
substance to the density of fresh water.
Water is given a specific gravity of
1.0. Whether an object floats or not depends on the relative magnitude of the
weight and upthrust. There are three
possible cases. These terms are frequently used in diving to describe the
different stages of buoyancy.

1. Positive buoyancy - indicates a tendency to float.

2. Negative buoyancy - which denotes a
tendency to sink.

3. Neutral buoyancy - which reflects a
condition of balance wherein an object
will tend to neither rise nor sink but
will remain suspended at any particular
level.

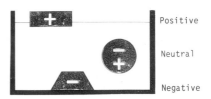

Figure 2-7

The human body has a specific gravity
of approximately 1. This will vary
slightly from one person to the next;
the average man will experience little
difficulty in floating in water, a fat
person will readily float, and a person
with a thin, lean body may experience
trouble floating. The natural buoyancy
of any swimmer can temporarily be
increased by his taking a deep breath
of air. This inflates the chest cavity,
displacing more water and thereby increasing the upward, buoyant force.

A diver can vary his buoyancy in several
ways. By adding weights to his gear,
he can cause himself to sink. He can
increase or decrease the amount of air
in the suit, thus changing his displacement and thereby his buoyancy.
Applying the principle of Archimedes,
it is readily determined that one-half
cubic foot (14.2 litres) of added displacement will provide a lifting force
of 32 lbs (14.5 kg).

Divers usually seek a condition of
slightly negative buoyancy. For a diver
in a helmet and dress, it gives him a
better foothold on the bottom. For a
diver using SCUBA a situation of neutral
buoyancy is preferred when it enhances
his ability to swim easily, change depth
and 'hover'.

During a dive the changing displacement
means that he must control his buoyancy
to counter the changes. For example; if
ascending, he does not vent the air

sufficiently to offset the increased volume in his suit, his situation will become increasingly critical.

The faster he rises, the more the air expands, causing an even faster ascent until he pops to the surface, out of control and with possibly serious consequences from decompression sickness or from colliding with the bottom of his ship or other surface object. This condition is known as BLOWING UP.

A condition opposite to BLOWING UP can also pose a problem for the diver. That is, as he descends and the air in his suit becomes compressed, he displaces less water and sinks faster. This can lead to the same sort of chain reaction and to the danger of SQUEEZE unless he adds sufficient air to keep his displacement at a balanced value.

CHANGE OF BUOYANCY WITH DEPTH

A self-contained diver wearing scuba is buoyant because of the air in his lungs, air trapped in the suit and any natural buoyancy of his breathing apparatus. To assist his descent he vents his suit at the surface before swimming down. As the water pressure increases and compresses the air in his suit, his displacement is reduced, and he is made more negatively buoyant and his speed of descent is increased.

EMERGENCY ASCENT

In an emergency there are two methods of increasing buoyancy -

a. Decreasing the diver's weight by slipping weights.

b. Increasing the upthrust by using suit inflation.

The former is the preferred method as it gives a more controllable rate of ascent.

MISCELLANEOUS PHYSICAL PHENOMENON

Since water is a medium of much greater density than air, a number of other physical phenomenon occur, mainly connected with - HEAT, LIGHT and SOUND.

LIGHT

The human eye needs light to see, because what it sees is actually an image created by the reflection of light from various surfaces, objects or particles in the water. Underwater, light is affected by some factors not usually encountered on the surface.

1. Diffusion - scattering of light.

2. Turbidity - which blocks the light.

3. Absorption - which alters the colour and intensity of the light.

4. Refraction - which bends the light.

DIFFUSION and TURBIDITY

Light that does penetrate the water decreases in intensity with depth, as the light rays are scattered and absorbed; impurities such as silt, algae and chemical pollution can effectively block the penetration of light into water. Causing in some cases nil visibility close to the surface. In this situation a torch is of very little use due to diffusion. Hence the expression 'a diver's eyes are very often his fingers'.

ABSORPTION

Just as the level of light is changed, so is the colour quality of the light. Colours underwater are modified with depth, because wave length of the visible spectrum are progressively absorbed by the water. This happens at very shallow depths at the red end of the light spectrum. As depth increases yellow light disappears and at this point most objects take on a blue colour,

red objects appear black. The use of
artificial light for photography, at
depth is necessary to replace the filtered colours.

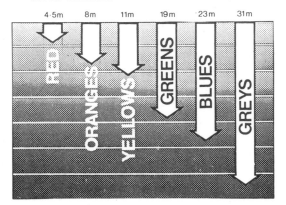

Figure 2-8 Light Absorption

REFRACTION

When a light ray passes from one medium
to the other at an angle, it will actually change direction as it either slows
down or speeds up. The diver is mostly
concerned with the effect of the <u>bending</u>
of the light rays passing from the surrounding water to the less dense medium
of the air in the face mask or helmet.
This <u>refraction</u> will give a false impression of the position of underwater
objects, which will appear to be larger
than their true size and only about three
quarters of their true distance. Also
refraction reduces the diver's effective
form of vision, and considerably distorts
objects viewed through the visor at an
oblique angle, and outside an angle of
48.6 degrees from the normal objects will
not be observed at all because of the
total internal refraction.

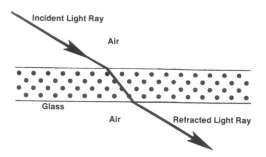

Figure 2-9 Refracted Light - as light
rays pass through mediums of different
density, they are refracted (bent) and
displaced.

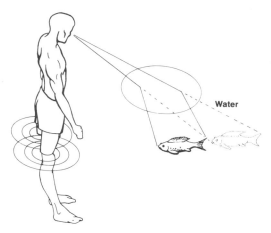

Figure 2-10 Light rays are refracted
as they enter water. The fish above is
actually in the location shown by the
solid outline, but the man observing it
sees it to the rear of its actual location.

SOUND

Sound is produced by the vibration of
an object, which sets up a pattern of
waves of moving molecules in the air,
water or other medium. These waves,
in turn, cause a sympathetic vibration

in a detector such as an eardrum or the diaphragm of a microphone. Sound travels best in a dense medium, since the more closely packed the molecules the more efficiently they transmit the waves, and sound will not travel at all in a vacuum because there are no molecules.

Water which is fairly dense, is an excellent sound conductor and will transmit at a rate of about 3,240 mph (1,500 metres per second). This is approximately four times the speed of sound in air. The fact that sound, in water, travels so much faster makes it almost impossible to pinpoint the source of sound underwater.

Talking underwater is impossible, man's vocal chords are designed to operate in the environment of air, and sound cannot cross from air to water, or from water to air to any major extent.

Two divers wearing helmets can put them together and carry out a conversation, since the metal easily conducts the sound of their voices. However, if they are separated by only a few inches of water, vocal communication is impossible.

Since water is a better conductor of sound than air, we must always consider this characteristic when conducting underwater operations which could produce damaging noise, i.e. explosives, pneumatic tools, etc.

COMMUNICATIONS

Voice communication through a surface telephone has been in operation for many years. Mixed gas diving has presented a new problem of helium voice distortion (Donald Duck) which increased with pressure. A new type of communications set has been developed to reduce this problem by slowing down the sound which has been speeded up by the less dense medium. Developments are at present continuing into through water (no wires) communications; several sets are commercially available and seem to have an application in free swimming situations, such as those experienced by the Police, or emergency communication with a diving bell.

(Communications are dealt with in more detail in Chapter 7 and 9)

Figure 2-11 Water, being a much better sound conductor than air, permits ships to hear submerged shore warnings from as far as 15 miles away.

HEAT

Heat, or the absence of it, is critical to man's environmental balance. The human body functions only within a very narrow range of internal temperature (which will be examined in detail in Physiology). A diver may lose his body heat by CONDUCTION, CONVECTION OR RADIATION. But mostly by conduction and least by radiation.

CONDUCTION

An unprotected or inadequately protected diver, ie., bad fitting wetsuit or leaky drysuit, will lose heat to the surrounding water by direct conduction, through the skin. The rate at which he loses the heat depends on the difference in the temperature between the body and water.

At water temperatures below 20°C some protective clothing must be worn. In the North Sea where the temperatures are approximately 3°-4°C, the insulation of a diver against cold has been of prime importance to diving contractors, hence the development of several types of heated suits, i.e. hot water, electrical, and chemical.

Material of very low conductivity placed between body and the surrounding water will insulate it. The insulation provided by woollen clothing comes mainly from the fact that they contain a series of air pockets that place a layer of air between the body and the colder water.

Some substances are excellent conductors of heat, i.e. iron, helium and water.

Some, like air, are very poor conductors; a poor conductor, if placed between a source of heat and another substance, will insulate the substance and appreciably slow the transfer of heat. When water temperature is very low, and the diver loses insulation perhaps because of a leaky suit, his body temperature may fall drastically, causing eventual unconsciousness. This condition is known as **hypothermia**. Helium is a good conductor of heat; divers using this gas at depth require specially heated suits and at depths in excess of 100 metres gas heating is recommended.

Several factors contribute to the problem of maintaining a diver's body temperature, including suit compression, increased gas denisty, thermal conductivity of breathing gases and respiratory heat loss.

The cellular neoprene wet suit loses a major proportion of its insulation quality as depth increases and the material is compressed. A normal wet suit loses 60% of its insualting quality when it is used at 50 metres. As a consequence it is often necessary to employ a thicker suit, a dry suit, or a hot water suit for extended exposures at great depth.

RADIATION

Radiation is the transfer of heat by invisible waves as experienced when standing in sunlight or in from of an eletric radiator.

SUMMARY

These principles of physics provide the keystone in understanding the reasons for employing various diving techniques and procedures, and the operation of associate equipment. They also assume particular significance in studying the effects of the underwater environment upon the human body.

CHAPTER 3

UNDERWATER PHYSIOLOGY

PHYSIOLOGY is the study of the functions and vital processes of living organisms. ANATOMY is the study of the organisation and structures of the body - the housing in which the processes of physiology are carried on. It is important for the diver to have a basic understanding of his body and its vital processes so that he will respect the increased demands that the underwater environment imposes upon him. This chapter presents a general discussion of the physiology and anatomy necessary for this understanding.

STRUCTURE OF THE BODY

The human body is a combination of interdependent systems, each with certain specialised functions. Those major systems which are of particular importance to a diver are:-

1. Skeletal
2. Muscular
3. Nervous System
4. Circulation
5. Respiratory
6. Digestive Excretory

1. SKELETAL

The SKELETAL system provides the basic structure around which the body is formed. It gives strength to the body and protection to the vital organs.

2. MUSCULAR

MUSCLES make the body move - every movement from the blinking of an eye to the raising of a leg. Additionally, they offer protection to the vital organs. Some muscles are controlled by conscious effort, while others perform their functions automatically while the body is sleeping or awake. Whether we are aware of their function or not.

3. NERVOUS SYSTEM

The NERVOUS SYSTEM includes the brain, the spinal cord and a complex network of nerves. It coordinates all the body functions and activities. The basic unit of the nervous system is the NEURON, a particular type of cell which has the ability to transmit electrochemical signals, which relay data to and from the brain at speeds as great as 350 feet per second. There are about 10 billion neurons in the body, the smallest of which is microscopic and the largest of which have fibres which reach all the way from the spinal cord to the big toe.

All parts of the body - all of the bones, muscles, nerves and vital organs - are made up of CELLS and tissue fluids. There are many types of cells, but most have a common characteristic: the ability to utilise the energy derived from food.

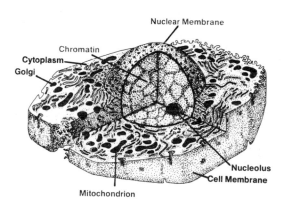

Figure 3-1 Cutaway of a typical cell - Although cells vary greatly in shape all have three basic components: nucleus, cytoplasm and cell membrane.

The process of converting food into energy can best be described as a slow flameless burning (oxidisation).

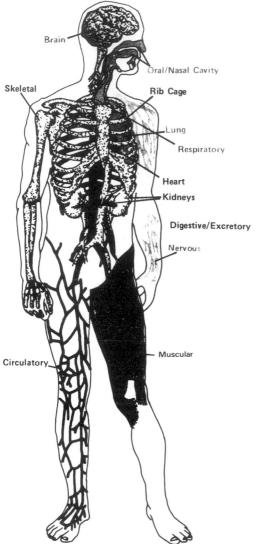

Figure 3-2 Man's physiological systems - included in this partial cutaway view are elements of the various body systems.

Food when combined with oxygen in the cell produces CARBON DIOXIDE as a waste product. The general term which is applied to the processes by which the cells work is METABOLISM.

4. CIRCULATORY SYSTEM

The centre of the system is the heart. The blood moves through a network of blood vessels, the largest being about one inch in diameter while the smallest are so slender that ten together would not equal the thickness of a single human hair.

These blood vessels are called ARTERIES, VEINS and CAPILLARIES, the capillaries being the smallest, marking the end of the outward flow of blood and also marking the beginning of the return flow towards the heart.

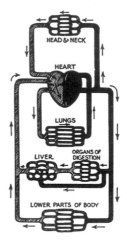

Figure 3-3 Circulatory System

HEART

The heart can be thought of as two pumps. The right side of the heart pumps at a low pressure to the microscopic vessels in the lungs, called capilliaries. The left side of the heart pumps at high pressure through the AORTA and arteries to the capillaries in the rest of the body. Each side of the heart comprises of an upper and a lower chamber or VENTRICLE. Between the upper and lower chambers of each side and on the output side of each main chamber are flap valves, which act as non-return valves, preventing back flow and so keeping the blood flowing in the right direction.

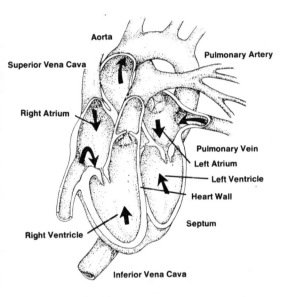

Aorta

Pulmonary Artery

Superior Vena Cava

Right Atrium

Pulmonary Vein

Left Atrium

Left Ventricle

Heart Wall

Septum

Right Ventricle

Inferior Vena Cava

Figure 3-4 The Heart - A cutaway view illustrating the major components and blood flow.

BLOOD

Blood has four main components:-

50% Fluid Plasma
45% Red Cells (Erythrocytes)
 5% White Cells (Leukocytes)
and Platelets (Thrombocytes)

Plasma is a yellowish solution, 92% water that carries the red and white

cells, as well as a number of other substances. These include basic nutrients, various chemicals, special proteins and hormones, and some quantity of dissolved gas. The 25 trillion red cells in the blood carry the bulk of the oxygen to the body cells, where they exchange it for carbon dioxide.

Some oxygen is dissolved in the plasma but the quantity is so small that it cannot support the needs of the body. The oxygen transport is made possible because of a substance containing the red cells which has a particular affinity for oxygen. This is HAEMOGLOBIN, an iron-rich compound which forms a loose chemical bond with oxygen in the lungs and releases the oxygen to the cells of the body as required. When the haemoglobin is enriched with oxygen, it is bright red in colour. As the oxygen level is reduced, the colour changes to a dark, dull and almost bluish hue.

CARBON DIOXIDE is carried by the blood in several different ways. About one half of it is dissolved in the plasma and the remainder enters into a chemical combination with the haemoglobin. Upon reaching the lungs, the haemoglobin instantly gives up its share of carbon dioxide in exchange for oxygen.

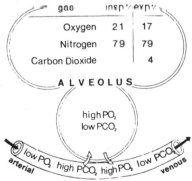

gas	insp.	exp.
Oxygen	21	17
Nitrogen	79	79
Carbon Dioxide		4

ALVEOLUS

high PO₂
low PCO₂

low PO₂ high PCO₂   high PO₂ low PCO₂
arterial   venous

Figure 3-5 The diffusion of gases through the alveolar capillaries.

There are several types of white cells, but each type works to keep the body free of infection by attacking and consuming invading bacteria. The white cells are outnumbered by the red cells in the order of 700 to 1. However, when faced with an infection, the body produces additional white cells so rapidly that the number in the system may double within a few hours. The third type of cells in the blood are the PLATELETS, which are involved in the clotting process.

CARDIAC OUTPUT

Cardiac output is a measure of the amount of blood pumped by the heart in a stated period of time, usually expressed in litres per minute. With the body at rest the heart may beat 60-80 times per minute, and the cardiac output might be five litres per minute. With the body engaged in hard work, the rate may reach 150 beats per minute, with a cardiac output of 35 litres per minute. The heart does not only beat faster, but it also enlarges to handle a greater volume with each beat. The heart beat rate is controlled by a small section of the nervous tissue located in the right ATRIUM, called the SINUS NODE. This is the pacemaker of the heart, regularly sending a small electrical impulse through the heart muscle, causing it to contract.

The average human being has about five litres of blood in his body. In an average day, the heart may actually pump more than 7,200 litres of blood around the body.

BLOOD PRESSURE

Every beat of the heart sends a surge of pressure through the circulatory system, a surge which is greater at the heart and gradually diminishes in force as it spreads through the body. This surge can be seen or felt as the PULSE, in those arteries which are near the surface of the skin.

This pressure is measured in millimetres of mercury and is expressed as SYSTOLIC over DIASTOLIC. A normal reading for a young man at rest might be about 120/80.

5. RESPIRATORY SYSTEM

Respiration is usually thought of in terms of BREATHING only, but actually includes the utilisation of oxygen and the various exchanges of gas which take place throughout the body as part of the METABOLIC process. For clarification, breathing is sometimes called EXTERNAL RESPIRATION, and the other aspects are identified as INTERNAL RESPIRATION.

The respiratory system is comprised of those parts of the body which are involved in the process of breathing. The LUNGS, the air passages leading to the lungs, the RIB CAGE, DIAPHRAGM and other muscles which help produce the movement of air in and out of the lungs.

The LUNGS can be thought of as being two elastic bags containing about 3 million distendable air sacs or ALVEOLI. The area over which gas exchange takes place is approximately the size of a tennis court.

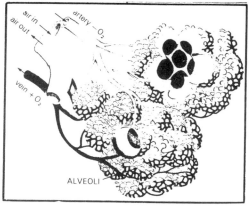

Fig 3-6 THE LUNGS

The alveoli present a large moist surface area to facilitate the exchange of gas between the blood in the lung capillaries, and the breathing mixture in the alvioli The breakdown of gases during breathing can be described as:-

IN - inspired air = 21% Oxygen
                    79% Nitrogen
       with traces of Carbon Dioxide

OUT - expired air = 17% Oxygen
                    79% Nitrogen
                     4% Carbon Dioxide

Breathing is a result of combined movement of the rib cage and the diaphragm, which increases or decreases the volume of the chest cavity. For inspiration, the ribs are raised and the diaphragm (which forms the bottom of the chest cavity), is lowered. In accordance with Boyle's Law, the pressure in the chest is decreased and air from the outside of the body - since it is at a relatively higher pressure - will move into the lungs.

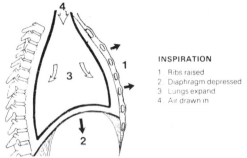

INSPIRATION

1. Ribs raised
2. Diaphragm depressed
3. Lungs expand
4. Air drawn in

Figure 3-7 Chest movement during
            inspiration.

When the rib cage is lowered and the diaphragm raised, the volume is decreased and the air is forced out of the lungs.

However, no matter how hard a person might try, he will not be able to expel all of the air present in his lungs.

A RESIDUAL VOLUME of 1 to 1.5 litres will always remain.

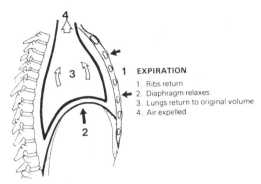

EXPIRATION

1. Ribs return
2. Diaphragm relaxes
3. Lungs return to original volume
4. Air expelled

Figure 3-8 Chest movement during
            exhalation.

The terms for measuring the capacity of the lungs with which the diver should be familiar are as follows:-

TIDAL VOLUME

Tidal volume is the amount of air moved in and out of the lungs during a single breathing cycle.

VITAL CAPACITY

Vital capacity is the greatest amount of air which can be moved in and out of the lungs in a single breath. (This is measured during a commercial diving medical.)

RESPIRATORY RATE

The number of breathing cycles in one minute, a normal average rate would be between 12 and 14 cycles per minute.

RESPIRATORY DEAD SPACE

Respiratory dead space is that fraction of a breath which does not reach the alveoli and therefore does not participate in the gas exchanges in the lungs. The respiratory dead space is extended when wearing breathing apparatus.

Certain parts of a diver's apparatus, such as mouth pieces or full facemasks, can substantially add to the dead space reducing the portion of the tidal volume which can effectively be used in respiration.

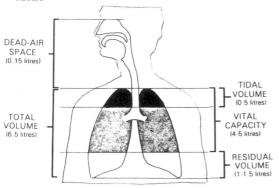

DEAD-AIR SPACE (0.15 litres)

TOTAL VOLUME (6.5 litres)

TIDAL VOLUME (0.5 litres)

VITAL CAPACITY (4-5 litres)

RESIDUAL VOLUME (1-1.5 litres)

Figure 3-9 Lung capacities.

CONTROL OF BREATHING

Respiratory centres in the brain, sensitive to the levels of carbon dioxide and acid in the blood, control the rate and volume of breathing. If these levels become too high, the centre will trigger an increase in breathing which will move a greater volume of air through the lungs until the carbon dioxide and acid levels are returned to normal.

BREATH-HOLDING AND HYPERVENTILATION

Most people can hold their breath for between one and two minutes, but usually not much longer without training or special preparation. At some point during a breath-holding attempt, the desire to breathe will become so intense that it can no longer be forestalled. This demand, as

mentioned earlier, is signalled by the respiratory centre responding to the increased level of carbon dioxide and acids in the blood.

In order to increase the "breath-holding-diver's" endurance underwater, the practice of HYPERVENTILA-TION is sometimes employed, but it is emphasised that this is a dangerous procedure.

Hyperventilation is breathing more than is necessary to eliminate the carbon dioxide produced by the metabolism. By over-ventilating the lungs, the free diver reduces the partial pressure of carbon dioxide in the blood below a normal level, and can therefore hold his breath longer while the carbon dioxide level is built up to the point at which the respiratory centre will force resumption of breathing. If the carbon dioxide stores are ventilated below the stimulus level, there is little stimulus to breathe. While the period of breath-holding is being prolonged because the diver experiences no discomfort, the oxygen partial pressure will progressively fall. Since low levels of oxygen do not force a powerful demand to resume breathing, the level of oxygen in the blood may reach the point at which the diver will lose consciousness before he feels the demand to breathe.

Hyperventilation can be unintentional as well as voluntary. It may be triggered by anxiety, and it can be experienced by normal individuals in any stress situation. For example, a diver using scuba for the first time is likely to hyperventilate to some extent because of his natural anxiety.

Hyperventilation can also cause HYPOCAPNIA, a condition resulting from low levels of carbon dioxide in the blood leaving the lungs. Symptoms of hypocapnia range from light-headedness and a tingling sensation to muscular spasms and perhaps even loss of consciousness. The opposite condition to hypocapnia is HYPERCAPNIA, resulting from an excess of carbon dioxide when ventilation is inadequate. An excess of carbon dioxide can result in symptoms similar to HYPOXIA, confusion, an inability to think clearly, loss of consciousness and generalised convulsions which may be confused with oxygen poisoning but have an altogether different chemical effect on the brain. Serious and longlasting damage is not likely with carbon dioxide poisoning, as with hypoxia, and a diver who has lost consciousness solely because of excess carbon dioxide can usually be revived by adequate ventilation with fresh air. Breathing an excess of carbon dioxide may also increase the possibility of decompression sickness, and will speed up the onset of oxygen poisoning. The most common source of carbon dioxide poisoning is from the diver's own metabolic processes. The most common cause is the failure to properly ventilate the breathing apparatus. A diver can even poison himself by the inadequate ventilation of his own lungs. For example, when a diver, trying to conserve his breathing supply, reduces his breathing rate below a safe level. (See excessive carbon dioxide.)

6. DIGESTIVE/EXCRETORY

The digestive system converts food to a form that can be transported to, and utilised by, the cells. Through a combination of mechanical, chemical and bacteriological actions, the digestive system reduces food into soluble basic materials such as amino acids, fatty acids, sugars and water. These materials diffuse into the blood and are carried by the CIRCULATORY SYSTEM to all of the cells in the body.

Metabolism produces certain waste materials which must be removed from the cells. Solid and liquid wastes are dissolved in the blood as it flows past the cells, and are carried to the kidneys where they are filtered out. These wastes are then passed to the bladder for temporary storage as urine. Carbon dioxide and other gaseous wastes are carried by the blood to the lungs, where they are passed out of the body as part of the exhaled breath.

The metabolism is influenced by the rate at which the body needs energy. When a person sleeps, for instance, his metabolic rate is low and respiration and circulation proceed at a matching low level. When body activity is increased, the respiratory and circulatory level must also increase to supply more food and more oxygen to the cells, and to remove the greater quantity of waste material.

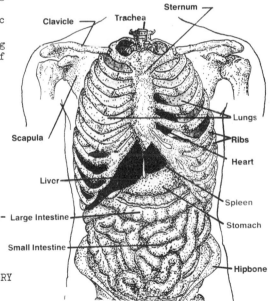

Figure 3-10 Thoracic and abdominal viscera shown in relation to the skeleton.

THE INTERDEPENDENCE OF THE BODY SYSTEMS

An interruption or disruption of one of the systems will have some effect upon the rest of the body, but in most cases the effect can be tolerated while the problem is being corrected. A broken bone or cut muscle, for instance, may impair locomotion, but the body will usually continue to function in an acceptable manner while the basic metabolic processes work to repair the damage. An injury to the nervous system might be permanent, causing paralysis or blindness, but the unaffected parts of the body may continue to function normally. The average person can live for several weeks without taking in any new food supplies, provided that the body is supplied with water to carry off chemical wastes of metabolism. The body cells will extract energy as necessary from stored food materials already in the body.

However, the body is not very successful in handling interruptions of the respiratory and circulatory systems. A person can function for only a few minutes without breathing before the cells, deprived of a fresh supply of oxygen, will begin to die. Those most immediately affected will be the cells of the brain, which normally use 20% of the entire blood's oxygen supply. Brain cells will begin to die in about four minutes. If performed promptly, mouth-to-mouth resuscitation or the administration of 100% oxygen with a resuscitator may restore respiration before cellular damage becomes too widespread.

Major disruption of the circulatory system can have an even more drastic and immediate effect on the body. If the heart should stop beating, thus halting the circulation of the blood, the cells in the brain will suffer damage almost immediately. With this occurrence, all the systems of the body are threatened. The pumping action of the heart can sometimes be restored by heart massage, or electrical and chemical stimuli, which to be effective, must be administered immediately. (See Chapter Ten, DIVING EMERGENCIES)

The respiratory and circulatory systems are so vital to the body that anything which interferes with them can result in serious problems. By its very nature, the underwater environment poses continuing hazards to respiration and circulation. A diver must have a particularly thorough understanding of both the anatomy and physiology of these two systems.

EFFECTS OF PRESSURE ON THE BODY

The tissues of the body can withstand tremendous pressure. Men have made actual sea dives of 400 metres, and in experimental situations, have been exposed to pressure equivalent to a dive of 600 metres. Small animals such as mice, goats and monkeys, have withstood pressures equivalent to dives as great as 1,700 metres. The majority of the body is composed of vitually incompressible liquids, permitting external pressures to be evenly transmitted throughout all of the tissues. If air is supplied at approximately the same pressure as that surrounding the diver, then natural air spaces in the body, the LUNGS, MIDDLE EAR, SINUSES and sometimes the STOMACH and INTESTINES, will be in pressure balance with the body tissues and external pressure.

The pressure related problems which may arise as a diver descends in water, will manifest themselves in one or more of these natural air spaces, or equipment which places an air space next to the diver's body and then cannot be equalised. Natural air spaces have vents which normally allow pressure to equalise. The lungs are ventilated by breathing, the middle ear and all the sinuses are connected by air passages with the throat and nose. If these passages should become blocked - by the congestion of a head cold, for example - air trapped in the spaces cannot be equalised as the diver descends.

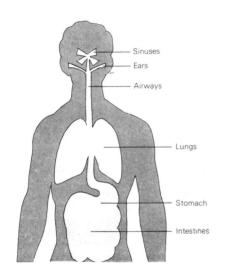

Figure 3-11 Natural Air Spaces

EARS AND SINUSES

SINUSES

These are cavities usually 6 or 7 in number in the bony structure of the skull. Their main function is to lighten the skull, but they also give resonance to the voice, as can be noticed by the change in voice of a person with a severe cold or catarrh. The sinus cavities are lined with mucous membrane similar to that in the nose and, to provide means of equalisation of pressure between the cavities and the mouth, are connected to the back of the nose and throat by narrow canals through the bone of the skull.

This means that normally there is a free flow of air to the sinuses from the back of the nose and throat. However, if the canal through the bone becomes blocked by mucous or swelling of the tissues, the flow will not occur. In these circumstances, the volume of air in the sinuses contracts on increase in external pressure, causing pain in the form of headaches or possibly damage to the sinus linings as a result. These may burst causing the cavities to fill with blood. Diving should be avoided when suffering from a cold, catarrh or throat infection, otherwise sinus trouble can be expected.

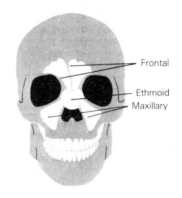

Figure 3-12 Sinuses.

EARS

The diagram shows the construction of the ear, and it will be seen that the ear drum separates the middle ear space from the outside, while this space is connected to the back of the throat by the EUSTACHIAN tube. Sounds received from the outside cause vibrations of the eardrum that are transmitted by a chain of small bones, the OSSICLES, to the nerves of hearing contained in the inner ear.

The Eustachian tube is only lightly closed and usually opens, in the healthy individual, during the act

of swallowing. Its function is to allow
air in or out of the middle ear to maintain
an equal pressure. However, under large
pressure differences, the tube does not
open freely and discomfort is felt as the
drums are stretched inwards. This discomfort is overcome by opening the

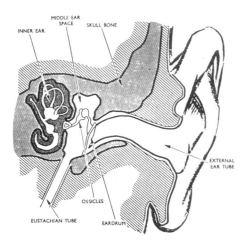

Figure 3-13 Diagram of Human Ear

Eustachian tube and allowing air to pass
into the middle ear to equalise the pressure
on each side of the drum; this can usually
be done by using what is called the VAL-
SALVA manoeuvre. This consists of pinching
the nose and swallowing or blowing against
the closed nose, which opens the Eustachian
tube, which forces the air through the
tube, equalising the pressure. The act of
clearing is evident either as a feeling of
relief or as an audible click in the ear.

EAR IN NORMAL STATE
Pressure in the Middle
Ear is normally the same
as that in the throat and
Outer Ear Canal. There is
no imbalance of pressure
on the drum.

Figure 3-14

During ascent the air escapes on its
own and clearing is not usually
necessary. A blocked Eustachian tube
can bring about problems ranging from
severe pain to severe ear injuries.

"EARS"

If the Eustachian tube becomes blocked
by swelling or mucous, the pressure
on the inside and outside of the ear-
drums does not balance. When this
happens the drum bulges inwards and
the stretching causes pain. "Ears"
is usually caused by catarrh or a
cold, but sometimes clearing the ears
too late brings it on; and not using
the correct procedure. In this case,
ascending a few feet may clear the
ears and allow the descent to be
continued.

EXTERNAL PRESSURE ON EAR
Increased ambient press-
ure pushes the drum in-
wards, causing pain. Rel-
ieved by admitting air from
throat via eustachian tube
— if it is not blocked

Figure 3-15

"REVERSED EARS"

This condition can occur on both
descent and ascent.

ON DESCENT – If the external ear is
blocked, ie by a hood, or an earplug,
because the eardrum is held from
inside it cannot move outward to
equalise the pressure, and, as the
tissue fluids transmit the pressure,
blood blisters tend to form in the
external ear canal to equalise the
pressure. These may involve the
eardrum and may also burst, causing
bleeding from the external ear.

ON ASCENT - If the Eustachian tube blocks off at a depth, then as external pressure decreases on ascent, the gas in the middle ear will expand to produce a positive pressure effect within the middle ear, sometimes resulting in dizziness.

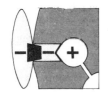

REVERSED EAR
Ear plugs seal off the outer ear canal; an increase in pressure in the middle ear could cause the drum to bulge outward and suffer damage.

Figure 3-16

PREVENTION

(a) Clear ears on descent before pain is felt.

(b) Do not dive with a cold or catarrh.

(c) Do not wear earplugs or block the external ear in any way.

NOTE: A perforated eardrum usually heals fairly rapidly, but a diver is unfit for diving until healing has taken place, which could be approximately 3 weeks.

TOOTH SQUEEZE

This results when a small pocket of trapped gas has been generated by decay or is lodged under a poorly fitted or cracked filling. If this pocket of gas is completely isolated, the pulp of the tooth or the tissues in the tooth socket can be squeezed into place.

This can on occasions cause the tooth to explode on ascent.

LUNG SQUEEZE

When a diver descends, the increase in pressure causes a decrease in volume of the air in the lungs. At about 30m the volume of air will have decreased to the residual capacity. It can occur only when a diver on surface supply has a sudden fall in pressure and the non-return valve fitted to the gas supply line fails to operate. It is prevented by supplying gas at the same pressure as the surrounding water and by checking non-return valves before diving.

BURST LUNG AND AIR EMBOLISM

As the diver ascends, gas in his body or apparatus will expand in accordance with Boyle's Law. If this expansion is not accommodated or controlled, the diver might encounter any of several serious and painful disabilities. These include:

(a) Gas Embolism
(b) Emphysema
(c) Pneumothorax
(d) Intestinal or stomach cramps.

(a) GAS EMBOLISM - is caused by excess gas pressure inside the lungs. It is most likely to develop during an improperly executed rapid ascent, as in a case of blow-up or when making an emergency free ascent. Additionally, if the diver should try to hold his breath during the ascent, the increasing gas pressure in the lungs can rupture the alveoli and lung capillaries, forcing bubbles of gas directly into the blood stream. These bubbles may then be carried throughout the circulatory system, and will continue to expand. If any become too large to pass through the blood vessels, an obstruction, or EMBOLUS will form and block the proper flow of blood.

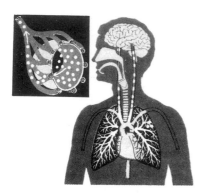

Figure 3-17 Gas Embolism

(b) INTERSTITIAL EMPHYSEMA - involves an
entry of gas into the interstitial tissue
in the lungs and, like gas embolism, it
can arise as a tear of lung tissue if the
diver fails to adequately exhale during
an ascent.

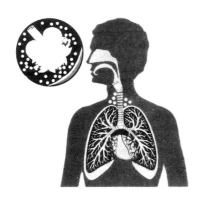

Figure 3-18 Interstitial Emphysema

SUBCUTANEOUS EMPHYSEMA - results
from the expansion of gas which has
leaked from torn tissue into the
subcutaneous tissues.

MEDIASTINAL EMPHYSEMA - is a
condition whereby a gas has been
forced through torn lung tissue into
the loose mediastinal tissues in the
middle of the chest.

(c) PNEUMOTHORAX - results from gas
being forced between the lungs and
the lining of the chest cavity. Its
increasing volume as the diver
ascends collapses the lung and may
displace the heart thus compromising
circulation.

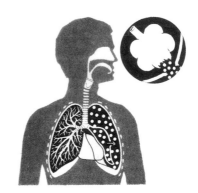

Figure 3-19 Pneumothorax

(d) INTESTINAL OR STOMACH CRAMPS -
pockets of gas may form in the
intestines as a result of normal
digestive processes, or the diver
may swallow gas which becomes
trapped in his stomach. These conditions could result in painful
cramps during ascent, but in most

cases the expending gases will purge themselves through the natural body vents.

FACE SQUEEZE

This is a result of rapid descent in the water and not allowing any gas to bleed through into the facemask or helmet. The volume of gas in the mask will contract leaving the partial vacuum. Because of its rigid walls, it is the face that is sucked out, resulting in a swollen face, haemorrhages and bloodshot eyes.

EFFECTS OF ABNORMAL GAS LEVELS

HYPOXIA

The term Hypoxia applies to any situation in which the tissue cells fail to receive or utilize enough oxygen. Hypoxia can result from such factors as:-

(a) Blockage or restriction of breathing as in obstruction of airway or asthma.

(b) Inadequate oxygen in the breathing mixture.

(c) Diseases of the lungs which inhibit diffusion of oxygen from the Alveoli to the blood.

(d) Conditions in the blood (such as anaemia or carbon monoxide poisoning) which interfere with the transport of oxygen.

(e) Circulatory impairment.

(f) Toxic conditions which prevent the cells from properly using the oxygen they receive.

The partial pressure of oxygen in the breathing mixture must remain above 0.16 bars or hypoxia will be likely. The probable symptoms experiences with lower partial pressures are:-

0.14 bar - first symptoms (drowsiness, inability to think clearly, lack of fine muscle control).

0.12 bar - discomfort, rapid breathing.

0.10 bar - some people will lose consciousness.

0.06 bar - anyone will be unconscious, below this level, death may quickly ensue.

The shortage of oxygen in the haemoglobin produces one visible sign of hypoxia, a general blueness (CYANOSIS) of the lips, nail beds and skin. Unfortunately, this is not likely to be notices by the diver while at work and is not a reliable indicator of hypoxia even for the trained observer at the surface. The same sort of signs could be caused merely by prolonged exposure in cold water, and, conversely, if the hypoxia is caused by carbon monoxide poisoning these parts of the body will tend to be redder in colour than normal.

A diver can be supplied with a breathing mixture that has a lower percentage of oxygen than air, if the partial pressure of the oxygen at the operating depth will be maintained at 0.16 bars or higher. Breathing a mixture with 5% oxygen at 30 metres (4 bars) would be almost equivalent to breathing air at the surface (5% x 4 bars = 0.20 bars pp O_2). However, when a diver breathing such a mixture starts to ascend, the oxygen percentage must be increased to maintain an acceptable partial pressure or he will quickly become hypoxic, might lose consciousness and could die.

Since a particular danger of hypoxia is the inability to detect and diagnose the problem, prevention is an essential measure.

Hypoxia is treated in the same manner as any serious interruption of the breathing process:-

(a) Administer oxygen or provide sufficient fresh air.

(b) Clear any obstructions from the air-way, if necessary.

(c) Administer appropriate resuscitation, if necessary.

If treatment is timely, recovery is usually prompt and complete. If treatment is delayed or insufficient, damage to the brain cells may be permanent and death may result. (For more detailed information on treatment see Chapter 10 - Resuscitation.)

NITROGEN NARCOSIS

Most divers who breathe air under pressure will at some depth experience NITROGEN NARCOSIS (sometimes called RAPTURE OF THE DEEP). Symptoms of this problem generally begin to appear at about 30m and progress rapidly beyond that depth. However, there is a wide range of individual susceptibility and some divers, particularly those experienced in deep operations with air, can often work as deep as 60m without serious difficulty.

The symptoms, although quite specific, are not always apparent to the individual. The nitrogen produces an intoxicating effect similar to that of alcohol. The narcosis is characterized by a slowing of mental activity, amnesia, fixation of ideas, slowing of reaction time and general euphoria. The greatest hazard of nitrogen narcosis is that it may cause the diver to disregard the job or particularly his personal safety.

Because of the problems of nitrogen narcosis diving in excess of 50m is done on mixed gas (oxy-helium) - because this gas has no narcotic effect. The mechanism by which nitrogen, under pressure, produces the narcotic effect is not known. Narcotic potency of nitrogen and other inert gases may be correlated with their relative solubility in fat.

OXYGEN POISONING

The susceptibility to central nervous system oxygen poisoning varies somewhat from person to person. The use of an 'oxygen tolerance test' for diving training candidates is intended to identify those whose sensitivity to oxygen is unusually high. Individual susceptibility will also vary from time to time. A major external factor contributing to the development of oxygen poisoning is the presence of a high level of carbon dioxide in the breathing mixture from a contaminated gas supply, or as a consequence of heavy exertion or inadequate ventilation.

The diver is at risk of oxygen poisoning when the partial pressure of oxygen exceeds 2 bars absolute. The air diver seldom encounters oxygen partial pressures above this level since it represents a depth of 90m. The problems of CO_2 retention and nitrogen narcosis tend to limit the maximum air depth. His greatest opportunity for being exposed to the potential of oxygen poisoning is during recompression treatment or surface decompression using oxygen. For this reason, it is essential that the diver is constantly monitored inside the chamber for the related symptoms of oxygen poisoning.

Sometimes early evidences of oxygen poisoning appear before convulsions. If recognised, these symptoms may provide sufficient warning to permit reduction in oxygen partial pressure and prevent the onset of more serious symptoms. The warning symptoms most often encountered, in the approximate order of their likelihood of occurrence, include:-

1 MUSCULAR TWITCHING - this usually appears first in the lips or elsewhere in the face, but it may affect any muscle.

2 NAUSEA - this may come and go periodically.

3 DIZZINESS.

4 ABNORMALITIES OF VISION OR HEARING - tunnel vision (loss of the ability to see things to the sides) is one of the more frequent visual symptoms.

5 DIFFICULTY IN BREATHING - the diver may have air hunger, may sense an increase in breathing resistance for no apparent reason, or may have trouble taking a full breath into his lungs.

6 ANXIETY AND CONFUSION.

7 UNUSUAL FATIGUE.

8 INCOORDINATION, CLUMSINESS, ETC.

Not all of these symptoms will always appear and most of them are not exclusively symptoms of oxygen poisoning. Twitching is the clearest warning of oxygen toxicity, but it may occur too late. The appearance of any one of these symptoms, however, usually represents a bodily signal of distress of some kind and should be heeded.

Convulsions are the most important consequence of oxygen poisoning due to excess oxygen. Treatment consists of the following procedures:-

1 Do not restrain the man except to prevent him from harming himself against the chamber.

2 Remove the oxygen breathing mask.

3 Insert a soft object (other than a finger) between the teeth to prevent tongue chewing.

4 Wait. The convulsion will almost always cease in a few minutes.

EXCESSIVE CARBON DIOXIDE

In diving operations, an excess of carbon dioxide in the tissues (HYPERCAPNIA) is generally the result of a build up of carbon dioxide in the breathing supply or in the body as a result of:-

1 Inadequate ventilation.

2 Increased CO_2 production during work or while under stress.

3 Contamination of the breathing mixture.

The most common source of hypercapnia is the diver's own metabolic processes, and the most common cause is the failure to properly ventilate the breathing apparatus.

SYMPTOMS

1 Breathlessness and panting.

2 Dizziness, nausea, headaches, anxiety.

3 General distress, sweating and palpitations.

4 Loss of consciousness.

5 Death will ensue quickly.

The warning signals of approaching hypercapnia are likely to be more serious to the diver than the usual symptoms of hypoxia. The increasing level of carbon dioxide in the blood stimulates the respiratory centre to increase the breathing rate and volume, and the rate of heartbeat is often increased. However, variables such as work-rate, depth and the composition of the breathing mixture may produce changes in breathing and blood circulation which could mask any changes caused by hypercapnia.

CARBON MONOXIDE POISONING

Carbon monoxide is not found in any sig-nificant quantity in fresh air. When it does pollute the breathing supply (usually from engine exhaust in proximity to the compressor intake), even a concentration as low as .002 bars can be fatal. Carbon monoxide is so highly toxic because it combines with haemoglobin 200 times more readily than does oxygen, displacing large quantities of oxygen and rapidly bringing about hypoxia. A concentration of carbon monoxide as low as .001 bars will replace one half of the oxygen which would normally be carried by the haemoglobin, even though the lungs may contain a normally ample supply of oxygen.

SYMPTOMS

The symptoms of carbon monoxide poisoning are almost identical to those of hypoxia, since it is in fact a condition of hypoxia, caused by an interference with the normal transport of oxygen in the blood. One major difference, however, is that the victim will not display the blueness (cyanosis) that is typical of hypoxia. When haemoglobin is combined with carbon monoxide it is an even brighter red than when combined with oxygen, bringing an unnatural redness to the LIPS, NAIL BEDS and SKIN.

If theonset of the poisoning is gradual, the diver may experience a TIGHTNESS ACROSS THE FOREHEAD, HEADACHE and pounding at the temples, and, occasionally, nausea and vomiting. The usual symptoms of hypoxia - including confusion and disorientation -

are not likely to be apparent to the diver.

A particularly treacherous factor in carbon monoxide poisoning is that conspicuous symptoms may be delayed until the diver begins to surface. This is because, while at depth, the greater partial pressure of oxygen in the breathing supply will force more oxygen into solution in the blood plasma, which will forcibly displace carbon monoxide from the haemoglobin. During ascent, as the partial pressure of oxygen diminishes, the full effect of the carbon monoxide will be felt.

TREATMENT

Carbon monoxide poisoning is treated in much the same manner as any respiratory problem; by providing fresh, clean air. However, if avail-able, the patient should be given oxygen at 2 bars absolute and this should be the treatment of choice.

This will help the haemoglobin to purge the carbon monoxide and return to normal as quickly as possible.

Breathing fresh air should eliminate most of the carbon monoxide from the blood, in a moderate case, in a few hours. Breathing oxygen at an increased pressure may substantially reduce this time.

ASPHYXIA AND STRANGULATION

If a diver stops breathing entirely, or if he is breathing an atmosphere that is low in oxygen and high in carbon dioxide, he will soon become both hypoxic and hypercapnic. The term used to describe the presence of both conditions is ASPHYXIA.

Hypoxia and hypercapnia do not always occur together. However, when hypoxia becomes severe enough to halt breathing, carbon dioxide will rapidly build up in the body and the resulting condition will be asphyxia.

A stoppage of breath due to injury or obstruction of the air passages is known as STRANGULATION. This is a condition which has little to do with the nature of the breathing mixture, and can be caused by such factors as a crushing injury to the trachea or a laryngeal spasm. The tongue of an unconscious person may fall back into his throat, causing an obstruction. Other causes include inhaled water, saliva or vomitus, or an airway obstructed by a foreign body such as food, seaweed or false teeth.

A strangulation victim will often struggle violently, even if unconscious, in an attempt to breathe.

BODY TEMPERATURE AND HEAT LOSS (HYPOTHERMIA)

The human body only functions effectively within a very narrow range of internal or CORE temperatures. The average, or "normal" level of 98.6 $^{\circ}$F (37 $^{\circ}$C) is maintained by natural mechanisms of the body, aided by artificial measures such as the use of protective clothing or air conditioning when external conditions tend towards extremes of cold or heat. A drop of as little as 1 $^{\circ}$C in core temperature causes shivering and discomfort. A 2 $^{\circ}$C fall causes the body to maximise its efforts to prevent further heat loss, and shivering is extreme. Any further drop in deep body temperatures will be accompanied by reduced efforts by the body to protect itself, and the drop in core temperature accelerates.

The following table gives an indication of the progressive symptoms and effect of a fall in deep body temperature:-

DEEP BODY TEMPERATURE - EFFECT

$^{\circ}$C

36-35	Rise in metabolism and respiration, sensation of severe cold.
35	Metabolism begins to decrease.
34.5	Respiration begins to decrease.
34	Heart rate begins to decrease, blood pressure falls.
33	Shivering gives way to muscle rigidity, mental confusion, semi-consciousness, speech is impaired.
30	Unconsciousness, respiration becomes irregular, pupils dilate.
28	Respiration ceases.
25	Death.

Normally the metabolic processes of the body constantly generate enough heat each hour to warm 2 litres of ice cold water to body temperature (37 $^{\circ}$C) and if doing hard work may generate as much as 10 times this amount. If this heat were allowed to build up inside the body, it would soon reach a high enough level to damage the cells - approximately 41 $^{\circ}$C. In order to maintain equilibrium the body must lose heat at the same rate as it produces it.

This is accomplished in several different ways. The blood circulating through the body picks up excess heat and carries it to the lungs, where some of it is lost with the exhaled breath. Heat is also transferred to the surface of the skin, where most of it is dissipated through a combination of CONDUCTION, CONVECTION and RADIATION. Moisture, released by the sweat glands in the skin, cools the surface of the body as it evaporates. During hard work the sweat glands will increase their activity in an attempt to dissipate the increased internal temperature. The maintenance of proper body temperature is particularly difficult for a diver working underwater.

At extremely low temperatures, or with prolonged immersion, body heat loss will reach a point at which death will occur. In water of 42 ^{O}F (6 ^{O}C), an unclothed man of average build will become helpless within 30 minutes and will probably die within an hour. He could withstand immersion at 60 ^{O}F (16 ^{O}C) for about 2 hours. If he were wearing heavy, conventional clothing, these times could be more than doubled. A diver, wearing appropriate dress and thermal underwear or an exposure suit, can greatly offset the effects of heat loss under normal diving conditions and can work in very cold water for reasonable periods of time.

WIND CHILL is another factor which has to be considered. A wet body even wearing a couple of thick wet sweaters or a diving suit will quickly loose body heat if exposed to wind. If the diver is wearing a wet suit, or his dry suit has become wet during a dive, he should wear a windproof garment while on deck.

With exceptionally deep diving certain aspects of heat loss problems are aggravated and require special consideration. With air diving the pressure at depth compresses the insulating materials and reduces their effectiveness. Also, as the density of the breathing medium is increased, the heat loss from the body with each exhalation becomes significant.

During mixed gas diving using oxy-helium mixtures, a diver may lose as much if not more heat purely through breathing as he is generating. In order to permit diving at great depths, gas heating is recommended below 100 m and the diver will wear special diving suits, heated by circulating hot water.

TREATMENT

Let us first review the symptoms in order of severity:-

1   Complaints of cold.

2   Mental and physical lethargy.

3   Mental confusion (so that the symptoms escape notice in oneself.

4   Slurred speech.

5   Shivering.

6   Stiffness and/or pain, and/or cramp in the muscles.

7   Abnormal vision.)
)   Very serious
8   Collapse and   )   symptoms.
    unconsciousness.)

Treatment of hypothermia commences by removing the subject from cold and preventing further heat loss. This can be accomplished by placing the subject in an 'exposure bag', or space blanket - if practical, with other bodies to increase rewarming. Where practical, the subject should be stripped of wet clothing, dried and dressed in dry clothes. The subject should then be taken ashore as quickly as possible and, if possible, taken to hospital for subsequent treatment.

The treatment which is given is to immerse the trunk of the subject body in hot water (42 $^{\circ}$C) until deep body temperature improves. Monitoring of this really requires special equipment, hence the need for medical care. The arms and legs are not immersed in order to prevent a rush of cold blood from these extremities to the body core.

This could cause an AFTER DROP in which the core temperature drops further. If the victim's core temperature is already low this could have a disastrous effect.

The rewarming process must be gradual and overall. The application of local heat (eg hot water bottles, rubbing to stimulate circulation) must be avoided. Giving alcohol to a hypothermic patient is like putting a nail in his coffin - alcohol opens up the blood capillaries and encourages cold blood from the body surface to return to the core.

Once the subject has responded to treatment he should be placed in a warm bed and given warm, high-energy food and drink.

Hypothermia is clearly a condition to be avoided, and one which, with forethought, IS easy to avoid.

HYPERTHERMIA

Heat exhaustion or HYPERTHERMIA is caused when the body is unable to cool the core temperature sufficiently by sweating, etc.

SYMPTOMS

1 Dizziness, restlessness and headaches.

2 Difficulty in breathing.

3 Rapid pulse and excessive sweating.

4 Cold, clammy appearance of the skin.

5 High temperature.

6 Twitching and cramp.

7 Loss of consciousness.

TREATMENT

Allow the patient to rest in a cool place and give the subject plenty of water to drink with some salt added.

In serious cases pack ice around the patient.

NITROGEN ABSORPTION

Nitrogen is an almost inert gas which combines with other elements only with difficulty. However, when air or oxy-nitrogen mixture is inhaled, the nitrogen comes into contact with the blood while passing through the walls of the alveoli in the same way as oxygen. The average human body, at sea level, contains about 1 litre of dissolved nitrogen. The amount of gas contained in solution varies relative to the pressure acting upon it. This it does in accordance with HENRY'S LAW. Henry's Law states that:

"At a constant temperature the mass of gas that dissolves in a given mass of liquid with which it is in contact is always directly proportional to the partial pressure of that gas."

Since the amount of nitrogen dissolved in a fluid depends upon the pressure, at 2 bars absolute the body should contain about 2 litres of nitrogen, at 3 bars absolute 3 litres and so on. This is roughly true, providing the time of exposure is long enough.

Of the nitrogen in the body, approximately half the amount at atmospheric pressure is contained in the blood and watery tissues, while the remainder is held in the fatty tissues. However, although there is less fat than water in the body, nitrogen is 5 times more soluble in fat than in water, so the presence of excess fat in the body predisposes a person to decompression sickness.

Inert gas dissolves in the body at first quickly and then more slowly, until no more gas will dissolve. This condition of equilibrium is called SATURATION and the time taken to reach this state the SATURATION TIME. The saturation time for a man is not accurately known but is thought to be about 8 hours (nitrogen). The rate at which portions of the body become saturated will vary; some areas have a relatively poor blood supply, and will become saturated more slowly than others, like fatty tissues, which will absorb about 5 times as much inert gas as will watery tissues.

It should be noted that nitrogen and helium have significantly different saturation and DESATURATION rates, helium being much quicker than nitrogen, hence requiring less decompression.

The use of nitrogen mixtures for saturation are generally restricted to shallow depths, mainly for hyperbaric welding habitats, etc.

Saturation is only relative, since if after spending 8 hours at 8 bars absolute (70 m) a person goes quickly to 15 bars absolute (140 m), that person is now only half saturated at the new depth.

DESATURATION

The process of desaturation is the reverse of saturation. If the partial pressure of the gas in the lungs is reduced, either through a change in pressure or the breathing medium, the new pressure gradient will induce the inert gas to diffuse from the tissues to the blood, from the

blood to the gas in the lungs and then out of the body with the expired breath. Some parts of the body will desaturate more slowly than others, for the same reason they saturate more slowly - poor blood supply, or a greater ability to absorb gas.

There is a major difference between saturation and desaturation. The body will accommodate relatively large increases in the partial pressure of the inspired gas without any ill effect. However, the same is not true for desaturation, where a high pressure gradient (towards the lower outside) can lead to serious problems.

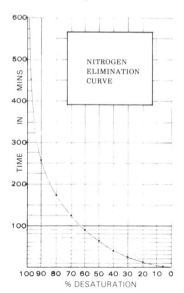

Figure 3-20   Nitrogen Elimination Curve

DECOMPRESSION

If the pressure of a liquid, which has been partly or completely saturated with gas, is reduced, some of the gas comes out of solution.

In the process, bubbles of gas are produced in the liquid. An illustration of this is the removal of the crown cap on a bottle of fizzy lemonade.

The blood and tissues of the body can apparently hold gas in a super-saturated degree before bubbles will form. This allows a diver to ascend a few metres without experiencing decompression sickness, while allowing some of the excess gas to defuse out of the tissues and be passed out of his body. By progressively ascending in increments, and then waiting for a period of time at each level, the diver will eventually reach the surface without experiencing decompression sickness.

In actual air diving practice, a diver will not remain at depth long enough to become fully saturated with nitrogen. In a short dive only those tissues which saturate quickly will absorb any appreciable quantity of gas, and they will desaturate easily. The amount of time that a diver must spend at these predetermined STOPS is laid down clearly in a DECOMPRESSION TABLE. These tables have been developed through research and experimentation by commercial diving companies and naval test programmes. They have been composed to provide guide lines for controlled decompression for a wide range of diving circumstances. The factors involved include such considerations as DEPTH and BOTTOM TIME of the dive, and whether or not the diver has made more than one dive within a **time** period, all of which will have some influence upon the quantity of nitrogen which will have been absorbed. Established decompression tables must be rigidly followed to ensure maximum diver safety.

Not all decompression is carried out by staged ascent to the surface; if the depth of the dive is less than 10 metres no stops or stage decompression are required. Also, within certain limits,

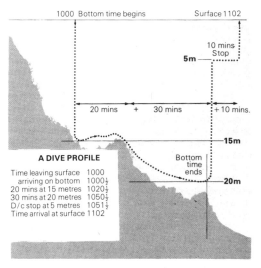

A DIVE PROFILE

Time leaving surface 1000
arriving on bottom 1000½
20 mins at 15 metres 1020½
30 mins at 20 metres 1050½
D/c stop at 5 metres 1051½
Time arrival at surface 1102

Figure 3-21   A Dive Profile

the diver can be brought out of the water, repressurised in a chamber, and then decompressed on the surface. The use of pure oxygen during surface decompression can reduce the time which will be required for controlled decompression. If used, pure oxygen will significantly reduce the partial pressure of the nitrogen in the alveoli, creating a higher pressure gradient than would otherwise be present.

A common practice for decompression in oxy-helium diving is the LINEAR decompression. The divers undergo a slow bleed to the surface maintaining a slightly higher partial pressure of oxygen. This slow bleed may be in the order of 25 minutes per metre, becoming as long as 50 minutes per metre near the surface.

Although decompression procedures have been thoroughly tested in the laboratory and field, adherence to procedures and compliance with the standard tables does not guarantee that a diver will avoid decompression sickness. There are a number of individual differences and environmental factors which may influence development of decompression problems in spite of all precautions.

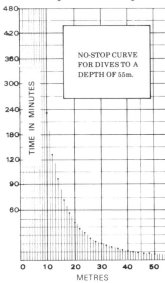

NO-STOP CURVE FOR DIVES TO A DEPTH OF 55m.

Figure 3-22   No-Stop Curve for Dives to a Depth of 55 m.

These include age, degree of obesity, excessive fatigue, lack of sleep, alcoholic indulgence, impure oxygen being used for decompression (this can be a common problem overseas and all oxygen used for decompression should be checked for purity before use), or anything which, in general, contributes to a poor physical condition or poor cirulatory efficiency.

Professor Haldane, working in the early 1900s, advanced the hypothesis that bubbles will form in the body only if the pressure of gas inside was more than $2\frac{1}{4}$ times the pressure outside. Thus it is safe to ascend directly from 10m (2 Bars absolute) to the surface (1 Bar absolute) since bubbles do not form. This is also true for greater depths, eg 50m (6 Bars absolute) to

20 m (3 bars absolute). This is usually known as the FIRST STOP WITH SAFETY and may be stated as follows:- A diver may always be allowed to ascend safely to half his absolute depth.

This is useful if it is necessary to bring up a diver in an energency, since while he is ascending, his correct stops may be determined.

DIVING AND ALTITUDE

To take account of the reduced surface pressure when carrying out dives at altitude, for instance in a mountain lake, adjustments must be made to decompression tables.

BONE NECROSIS

DYSBARIC OSTEONECROSIS, ASEPTIC BONE NECROSIS is a long-term condition which is generally assumed to be caused by the blockage of nutrient vessels of the bones by bubbles formed during decompression, and can result in a weakening in the mechanical strength of the affected bone. Bone necrosis in the compressed air worker or diver begins as a symptomless LESION detectable only by radiography. It occurs typically in the HUMERUS, FEMUR or TIBIA, although lesions in other bones have been detected. Commercial divers are generally susceptible to necrosis because of their increased durations and decompression tables used. Necrosis is common to both air and mixed gas diving.

Current medical practice offshore requires a diver to have periodic LONG BONE X-rays in order to detect any symptoms of the disease.

CHAPTER 4
AIR DECOMPRESSION

AIR DECOMPRESSION - U.S. NAVY

When air is breathed under pressure, as discussed in Chapter 3, the inert nitrogen diffuses into the various tissues of the body. Nitrogen uptake by the body continues, at different rates for the various tissues, as long as the partial pressure of the inspired nitrogen is higher than the partial pressure of the gas absorbed in the tissues. Consequently, the amount of nitrogen absorbed increases with the partial pressure of the inspired nitrogen (depth) and the duration of the exposure (time).

When the diver begins to ascend, the process is reversed as the nitrogen partial pressure in the tissues exceeds that in the circulatory and respiratory systems. The pressure gradient from the tissues to the blood and lungs must be carefully controlled to prevent too rapid a diffusion of nitrogen. If the pressure gradient is uncontrolled, bubbles of nitrogen gas can form in tissues and blood which results in the development of decompression sickness.

To prevent the development of decompression sickness, special decompression tables have been established. These tables take into consideration the amount of nitrogen absorbed by the body at various depths for given time periods. They also consider allowable pressure gradients which can exist without excessive bubble formation, and the different gas elimination rates associated with various body tissues.

Stage decompression, requiring stops of specific durations at given depths, is used in air diving because of its operational simplicity. It will be found that the decompression tables require longer stops at more frequent intervals as the surface is approached due to the higher gas expansion ratios which occur at shallow depths.

The USN decompression tables are the result of years of scientific study, calculation, animal and human experimentation, and extensive field experience. They represent the best overall information available, but as depth and time increases, they tend to be less accurate and require careful application. Lacking the presence of a trained Diving Medical Officer or someone otherwise qualified, the tables must be rigidly followed to ensure maximum diving safety. Variations in decompression procedures are permissible only with the guidance of a qualified diving medical officer in emergency situations.

Five different tables are discussed in this chapter, and each has a unique application in air diving. Four of these tables provide specific decompression data for use under various operating conditions. The remaining table is employed in determining decompression requirements for situations in which more than one dive will be performed in a 12-hour period.

DEFINITION OF TERMS

Those terms which are frequently used in discussions of the decompression tables are defined as follows:

DEPTH - when used to indicate the depth of a dive, means the maximum depth attained during the dive, measured in feet of seawater.

BOTTOM TIME - the total elapsed time from when the diver leaves the surface in descent to the time (next whole minute) that he begins his ascent, measured in minutes.

DECOMPRESSION STOP - specified depth at which a diver must remain for a specified length of time to eliminate inert gases from his body.

DECOMPRESSION SCHEDULE - specific decompression procedure for a given combination of depth and bottom time as listed in a decompression table; it is normally indicated as feet/minutes.

SINGLE DIVE - any dive conducted after 12 hours of a previous dive.

RESIDUAL NITROGEN - nitrogen gas that is still dissolved in a diver's tissues after he has surfaced.

SURFACE INTERVAL - the time which a diver has spent on the surface following a dive; beginning as soon as the diver surfaces and ending as soon as he starts his next descent.

REPETITIVE DIVE - any dive conducted within a 12-hour period of a previous dive.

REPETITIVE GROUP DESIGNATION - a letter which relates directly to the amount of residual nitrogen in a diver's body for a 12-hour period following a dive.

RESIDUAL NITROGEN TIME - an amount of time, in minutes, which must be added to the bottom time of a repetitive dive to compensate for the nitrogen still in solution in a diver's tissues from a previous dive.

SINGLE REPETITIVE DIVE - a dive for which the bottom time used to select the decompression schedule is the sum of the residual nitrogen time and the actual bottom time of the dive.

TABLE SELECTION

The following tables are actual decompression tables:

Standard Air Decompression Table
No Decompression Limits and Repetitive Group Designation Table
Surface Decompression Table Using Oxygen
Surface Decompression Table Using Air

They present a series of decompression schedules which must be rigidly followed during an ascent following an air dive. Each decompression table has specific conditions which justify its selection. These conditions are basically depth and duration of the dive to be conducted, availability of a recompression chamber, availability of an oxygen breathing system within the chamber, and specific environmental conditions such as sea state, water temperature, etc.

THE RESIDUAL NITROGEN TIMETABLE FOR REPETITIVE AIR DIVES provides information relating to the planning of repetitive dives.

The 5 air tables and the pertinent criteria for the selection and application of each are listed. General instructions for using the tables and special instructions applicable to each table are discussed.

OMITTED DECOMPRESSION

Omitted decompression is considered an emergency situation requiring recompression treatment.

GENERAL USE OF DECOMPRESSION TABLES

VARIATIONS IN RATE OF ASCENT. With the exception of the Surface Decompression Table Using Oxygen, the rate of ascent for all dives is 60 feet per minute. If the diver is to decompress according to the Surface Decompression Table Using Oxygen, his rate of ascent should be 25 feet per minute. Since conditions sometimes prevent these ascent rates from being maintained, a general set of instructions has been established to compensate for any variations in rate of ascent. These instructions, along with examples of their application, are listed below:

Example No 1 -

Condition - Rate of ascent less than 60 fpm, delay occurs greater than 50 fsw.

Procedure - Increase BOTTOM TIME by the difference between the actual ascent time and the time if 60 fpm were used.

A dive was conducted to 120 feet with a bottom time of 60 minutes. According to the 120/60 decompression schedule of the Standard Air Decompression Table, the first decompression stop is at 30 feet. During the ascent the diver was delayed at 100 feet and it actually took 5 minutes for him to reach his 30 foot decompression stop. If an ascent rate of 60 fpm were used, it would have taken him one minute 30 seconds to ascend from 120 feet to 30 feet. The difference between the actual and 60 fpm ascent times is 3 minutes 30 seconds. Increase the bottom time of the dive from 60 minutes to 63 minutes 30 seconds and continue decompression according to the schedule which represents this new bottom time ... the 120/70 schedule. (Note from the Standard Air Decompression Table that this 3 minute 30 second delay increased the diver's total decompression time from 71 minutes to 92 minutes 30 seconds - an increase of 21 minutes 30 seconds.)

Example No 2 -

Condition - Rate of ascent less than 60 fpm delay occurs less than 50 fsw.

Procedure - Increase TIME OF FIRST DECOMPRESSION STOP by difference between the actual ascent time and the time if 60 fpm were used.

A dive was conducted to 120 feet with a bottom time of 60 minutes. From the Standard Air Decompression Table the first decompression stop is at 30 fsw. During the ascent, the diver was delayed at 40 feet and it actually took 5 minutes for him to reach his 30-foot stop. As in the preceding example, the correct ascent time should have been one minute 30 seconds causing a delay of 3 minutes 30 seconds. Increase the length of the 30 foot decompression stop by 3 minutes 30 seconds. Instead of 2 minutes, the diver must spend 5 minutes 30 seconds at 30 feet. (Note that in this example, the diver's total decompression time is increased by only 7 minutes; the 3 minute 30 second delay in ascent plus the additional 3 minutes 30 seconds he had to spend at 30 feet.)

Example No 3 -

Condition - Rate of ascent greater than 60 fpm, no decompression required, bottom time places the diver within 10 minutes of decompression schedule requiring decompression.

Procedure - Stop at 10 feet for the time that it would have taken to ascend at a rate of 60 fpm.

A dive was conducted to 100 feet with a bottom time of 22 minutes. During ascent, the diver momentarily lost control of his buoyancy and increased his ascent rate to 75 fpm. Normally, the 100/25 decompression schedule of the Standard Air Decompression Table would be used, which is a no-decompression schedule. However, the actual bottom time of 22 minutes is within 10 minutes of the 100/30 dive schedule which does require decompression. The diver must stop at 10 feet and remain there for one minute and 40 seconds, the time that it would have taken for him to ascend at 60 fpm.

Example No 4 -

Condition - Rate of ascent greater than 60 fpm, decompression required.

Procedure - Stop 10 feet below the first decompression stop for the remaining time that it would have taken if a rate of 60 fpm were used.

A diver ascending from a 120/50 scheduled dive takes only 30 seconds to reach his 20-foot decompression stop. At a rate of 60 fpm his ascent time should have been one minute 40 seconds. He must return to 30 feet and remain there for the difference between one minute 40 seconds and 30 seconds, or one minute 10 seconds.

The rate of ascent between stops is not critical, and variations from the specified rate require no compensation.

SELECTION OF DECOMPRESSION SCHEDULE

The decompression schedules of all the tables are given in 10 or 20-foot depth increments and, usually, 10-minute bottom time increments. Depth and bottom time combinations from actual dives, however, rarely exactly match one of the decompression schedules listed in the table being used. As assurance that the selected decompression schedule is always conservative - (a) always select the schedule depth to be equal to or the next depth greater than the actual depth to which the dive was conducted, and (b) always select the schedule bottom time to be equal to or the next longer bottom time than the actual bottom time of the dive. **(Continued overleaf)**

AIR DECOMPRESSION TABLES SELECTION CRITERIA

TITLE	APPLICATION
US Navy Standard Air Decompression Table	No locally available decompression chamber. Conditions dictate in-water decompression permissible. Normal and exceptional exposure dive schedules. Repetitive dives - normal decompression schedules only.
No-Decompression Limits and Repetitive Group Designation Table for No-Decompression Air Dives	Decompression not required. Repetitive dives.
Residual Nitrogen Time Table for Air Dives	Repetitive Group Designations after surface intervals greater than 10 minutes and less than 12 hours. Residual Nitrogen Times for repetitive air dives.
Surface Decompression Table Using Oxygen	Available recompression chamber with oxygen breathing system. Conditions dictate in-water decompression undesirable. No repetitive dives.
Surface Decompression Table Using Air	Available recompression chamber without an oxygen breathing system - or - Diver forced to surface prior to completing decompression. Conditions dictate in-water decompression undesirable. No repetitive dives.

If the Standard Air Decompression Table, for example, was being used to select the correct schedule for a dive to 97 feet for 31 minutes, decompression would be carried out in accordance with the 100/40 schedule.

NEVER ATTEMPT TO INTERPOLATE BETWEEN DECOMPRESSION SCHEDULES

If the diver was exceptionally cold during the dive, or if his work load was relatively strenuous, the next longer decompression schedule than the one he would normally follow should be selected. For example, the normal schedule for a dive to 90 feet for 34 minutes would be the 90/40 schedule. If the diver were exceptionally cold or fatigued, he should decompress according to the 90/50 schedule.

RULES DURING ASCENT

After the correct decompression schedule has been selected, it is imperative that it be exactly followed. Without exception, decompression must be completed according to the selected schedule unless the directions to alter the schedule are given by a diving medical officer.

Ascend at a rate of 60 fpm when using all tables except the Surface Decompression Table Using Oxygen. This table uses a rate of 25 fpm. Any variation in the rate of ascent must be corrected in accordance with the earlier instructions. The diver's chest should be located as close as possible to the stop depth. A pneumofathometer is the most practical instrument for ensuring proper measurement.

The decompression stop times, as specified in each decompression schedule, begin as soon as the diver reaches the stop depth. Upon completion of the specified stop time, the diver ascends to the next stop, or to the surface, at the proper ascent rate. DO NOT INCLUDE ASCENT TIME AS PART OF STOP TIME.

EXCEPTIONAL EXPOSURE

The exceptional exposure air decompression schedules presented in the Standard Air Decompression Table are for dives which expose the diver to oxygen partial pressures and environmental conditions considered extreme. The prolonged decompressions, which must be carried out in the water, impose exceptional demands on the diver's endurance. Because of this, decompressions conducted according to these schedules have limited assurance that they will be completed without an incidence of decompression sickness. For this reason, the Diving Officer must fully justify the need for conducting an exceptional exposure dive.

REPETITIVE DIVES

During the 12-hour period after an air dive, the quantity of residual nitrogen in a diver's body will gradually reduce to its normal level. If, within this period, the diver is to make a second dive - called a repetitive dive - he must consider his present residual nitrogen level when planning for the dive.

The procdures for conducting a repetitive dive are summarized. Upon completing his first dive, the diver will have a Repetitive Group Designation assigned to him by either the Standard Air Table or the No-Decompression Table. This designation relates directly to his residual nitrogen level upon surfacing. As nitrogen passes out of his tissues and blood, his repetitive group designation changes. The Residual Nitrogen Table permits this designation to be determined at any time during the surface interval.

Just prior to beginning the repetitive dive, the residual nitrogen time should

be determined using the Residual Nitrogen
Table. This time is added to the actual
bottom time of the respective dive to give
the bottom time of the equivalent single
dive. Decompression from the repetitive
dive is conducted using the depth and
bottom time of the equivalent single dive
to select the appropriate decompression
schedule. Equivalent single dives which
require the use of exceptional exposure
decompression schedules should, whenever
possible, be avoided.

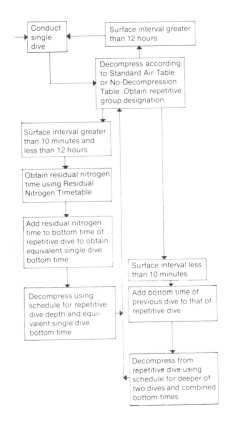

Figure 4-1 Repetitive Dive Flowchart

To assist in determining the decompression schedule for a repetitive
dive, a systematic repetitive dive
worksheet should always be used. (Fig. 4.4)

If still another dive is to follow the
repetitive dive, the depth and bottom
time of the first equivalent single
dive should be inserted in part 1 of
the second repetitive dive worksheet.

SURFACE DECOMPRESSION

Surface decompression is a technique
for fulfilling all or a portion of
the diver's decompression obligation
in a recompression chamber. By using
this technique, the time which the
diver must spend in the water is significantly reduced, and when oxygen is
breathed in the recompression chamber,
the diver's total decompression time
is reduced.

Surface decompression offers many
advantages, most of which enhance the
diver's safety. Shorter exposure time
to the water keeps him from chilling
to a dangerous level. Inside the
recompression chamber, he can be maintained at a constant pressure, unaffected by surface conditions of the
sea. Observed constantly by the
chamber operator, and monitored inter-
mittently by medical personnel, any
signs of decompression sickness can
be readily detected and immediately
treated.

If an oxygen breathing system is
installed in the recompression chamber,
surface decompression should be conducted according to the Surface
Decompression Table Using Oxygen.
If air is the only breathing medium
available, the Surface Decompression
Table Using Air must be used.

There is no surface decompression table
for use following an exceptional

exposure dive. Additionally, repetitive diving tables for dives following surface decompression have not been calculated.

DIVE RECORDING

Under British regulations divers are required to record all dives or exposures to pressure in an approved log book. Figure 4-3 shows a Prodive Log Book sheet.

AIR DECOMPRESSION TABLES

US NAVY STANDARD AIR DECOMPRESSION TABLE

This manual has combined the Standard Air Table and the Exceptional Exposure Air Table into one table as titled above. To clearly delineate between the standard and exceptional exposure decompression schedules, a line has been drawn between them.

The USN decompression tables are the result of years of scientific study, calculation, animal and human experimentation, and extensive field experience. They represent the best overall information available, but as depth and time increases, they tend to be less accurate and require careful application. Lacking the presence of a trained Diving Medical Officer or someone otherwise qualified, the tables must be rigidly followed to ensure maximum diving safety. Variations in decompression procedures are permissible only with the guidance of a qualified diving medical officer in emergency situations.

These limits are not to be exceeded without the approval of the Diving Officer in charge of the operation, and then, only after careful consideration of the potential consequences involved.

If the bottom time of a dive is less than the first bottom time listed for its depth, decompression is not required. The diver may ascend directly to the surface at a rate of 60 fpm. The repetitive group designation for no-decompression dives is given in the No-Decompression Table.

As will be noted in the Standard Air Table, there are no repetitive group designations for exceptional exposure dives. Repetitive dives following an exceptional exposure dive are not permitted.

Figure 4-2 Deep-sea divers undergoing in-water decompression.

Example -

Problem - Diver Bowman has just completed a salvage dive to a depth of 143 feet for 37 minutes. He was not exceptionally cold or fatigued during the dive. What is his decompression schedule and his repetitive group designation at the end of the decompression?

Solution - Select the equal or next deeper and the equal or next longer

DATE ....7...7..80........ SERIAL NUMBER ....1....

EMPLOYERS NAME ....OCEANSERVE INTERNATIONAL......

EMPLOYERS ADDRESS ....BRIDGE OF DON ABERDEEN......

GEOGRAPHIC LOCATION .....PRODIVE LTD. FALMOUTH DOCKS. CORNWALL....

AIR TABLE - USN

Dive No	Left Surface	Arrived Bottom	Left Bottom	Max Depth	Bottom Time	Time to First	Time left First	Time to Second	Time left Second	Time to Third	Time left Third	Time to Surface	Arrived Surface	Total Ascent	TTUP	R	G
(1)	09 00	0903	09·30	130	30m	1·50	20' M 09 34 30	10m 10m 09 53	10' M	-	N/A M -	10m 09 54 10	23·10	53·10		M

SURFACE DEC'N — CHAMBER STOPS — AIR ☐ O₂ ☐

Dive No	Chamber Bottom	Time left First	Time to Second	Time left Second	Time to Surface	Total Ascent	Arrive Surface	TTUP
		M	M	M				

U/W VIS: 3'

PLATFORM: PRODIVER

WEATHER: FINE

DEC'N SCHEDULES: 130/30 USN

SUPERVISOR: D. RYLAND

SEA STATE: CALM

H.W: 1202   TIDE: 15'2"

TASK: CONSTRUCTION OF SBM MANIFOLD

EQUIPMENT: KMB 10. BAND MASK SDDE.

DIVER .... D. PRODIVER

SUPERVISOR ....

COMPANY ....

Figure 4-3 Prodive Log Book Sheet

REPETITIVE DIVE WORKSHEET

I. PREVIOUS DIVE:

_____ minutes   ☐ Standard Air Table

_____ feet   ☐ No-Decompression Table

_____ repetitive group designation

II. SURFACE INTERVAL:

_____ hours _____ minutes on surface.

Repetitive group from I _____

New repetitive group from surface

Residual Nitrogen Timetable _____

III. RESIDUAL NITROGEN TIME:

_____ feet (depth of repetitive dive)

New repetitive group from II. _____

Residual nitrogen time from

Residual Nitrogen Timetable _____

IV. EQUIVALENT SINGLE DIVE TIME:

_____ minutes, residual nitrogen time from III.

+ _____ minutes, actual bottom time of repetitive dive.

= _____ minutes, equivalent single dive time.

V. DECOMPRESSION FOR REPETITIVE DIVE:

_____ minutes, equivalent single dive time from IV.

_____ feet, depth of repetitive dive

Decompression from (check one):
☐ Standard Air Table ☐ No-Decompression Table
☐ Surface Table Using Oxygen ☐ Surface Table Using Air
☐ No decompression required

	Decompression Stops:	_____ feet _____ minutes
		_____ feet _____ minutes
		_____ feet _____ minutes
Schedule used _____		_____ feet _____ minutes
Repetitive group _____		_____ feet _____ minutes

Figure 4-4   Repetitive Dive Worksheet

decompression schedule. This would be the 150/40 schedule.

ACTION	TIME (min:sec)	TOTAL ELAPSED ASCENT TIME (min:sec)
Ascend to 30 feet at 60 fpm	1:53	1:53
Remain at 30 feet	5:00	6:53
Ascend to 20 feet	0:10	7:03
Remain at 20 feet	19:00	26:03
Ascend to 10 feet	0:10	26:13
Remain at 10 feet	33:00	59:13
Ascend to surface	0:10	59:23

Repetitive Group Designation   "N"

NO DECOMPRESSION LIMITS AND REPETITIVE GROUP DESIGNATION TABLE FOR NO-DECOMPRESSION AIR DIVES

The No-Decompression Table serves two purposes. First it summarizes all the depth and bottom time combinations for which no decompression is required. Secondly, it provides the repetitive group designation for each no-decompression dive. Even though decompression is not required, an amount of nitrogen remains in the diver's tissues after every dive. If he dives again within a 12-hour period, the diver must consider this residual nitrogen when calculating his decompression.

Each depth listed in the No-Decompression Table has a corresponding no-decompression limit given in minutes. This limit is the maximum time that a diver may spend at that depth without requiring decompression. The columns to the right of the no-decompression limits column are used to determine the repetitive group designation which must be assigned to a diver subsequent to every dive. To find the repetitive group designation enter the table at the depth equal to or next greater than the actual depth of the dive. Follow that row to the right to the bottom time equal to or next greater than the actual bottom time of the dive. Follow that column upward to the repetitive group designation.

Depths above 35 feet do not have a specific no-decompression limit. They are, however, restricted in that they only provide repetitive group designations for bottom times up to between 5 and 6 hours. These bottom times are considered the limitations of the No-Decompression Table and no field requirement for diving should be extended beyond them.

Any dive below 35 feet which has a bottom time greater than the no-decompression limit given in this table is a decompression dive and should be conducted in accordance with the Standard Air Table.

Example -

Problem - In planning a dive, the Master Diver wants to conduct a brief inspection of the work site, located 160 feet below the surface. What is the maximum bottom time which he may use without requiring decompression? What is his repetitive group designation after the dive?

Solution - The no-decompression limit corresponding to the 160 foot depth in the No-Decompression Table is 5 minutes. Therefore, the Master Diver must descend to 160 feet, make his inspection and begin his ascent within 5 minutes without having to undergo decompression.

NO-DECOMPRESSION LIMITS AND REPETITIVE GROUP DESIGNATION TABLE FOR NO-DECOMPRESSION AIR DIVES

Depth (feet)	No-decompression limits (min)	A	B	C	D	E	F	G	H	I	J	K	L	M	N	O
10		60	120	210	300											
15		35	70	110	160	225	350									
20		25	50	75	100	135	180	240	325							
25		20	35	55	75	100	125	160	195	245	315					
30		15	30	45	60	75	95	120	145	170	205	250	310			
35	310	5	15	25	40	50	60	80	100	120	140	160	190	220	270	310
40	200	5	15	25	30	40	50	70	80	100	110	130	150	170	200	
50	100		10	15	25	30	40	50	60	70	80	90	100			
60	60		10	15	20	25	30	40	50	55	60					
70	50		5	10	15	20	30	35	40	45	50					
80	40		5	10	15	20	25	30	35	40						
90	30		5	10	12	15	20	25	30							
100	25		5	7	10	15	20	22	25							
110	20			5	10	13	15	20								
120	15			5	10	12	15									
130	10			5	8	10										
140	10			5	7	10										
150	5			5												
160	5				5											
170	5				5											
180	5				5											
190	5				5											

Following the 160 foot depth row to the 5 minute column, the repetitive group designation at the top of this column is D.

RESIDUAL NITROGEN TIMETABLE FOR REPETITIVE AIR DIVES

The quantity of residual nitrogen in a diver's body immediately after a dive is expressed by the repetitive group designation assigned to him by either the Standard Air Table or the No-Decompression Table. The upper portion of the Residual Nitrogen Table is composed of various intervals between 10 minutes and 12 hours, expressed in hours:minutes (2:21 = 2 hours 21 minutes). Each interval has 2 limits; a minimum time (top limit) and a maximum time (bottom limit).

Residual nitrogen times, corresponding to the depth of the repetitive dive, are given in the body of the lower portion of the table. To determine the residual nitrogen time for a repetitive dive, locate the diver's repetitive group designation from his previous dive along the diagonal line above the table. Read horizontally to the interval in which the diver's surface interval lies. The time spent on the surface must be between or equal to the limits of the selected interval.

Next, read vertically downwards the new repetitive group designation. This designation corresponds to the present quantity of residual nitrogen in the diver's body. Continue downwards in this same column to the row which represents the depth of the repetitive dive. The time given at the intersection is the residual nitrogen time, in minutes, to be applied to the repetitive dive.

RESIDUAL NITROGEN TIMETABLE FOR REPETITIVE AIR DIVES

*Dives following surface intervals of more than 12 hours are not repetitive dives. Use actual bottom times in the Standard Air Decompression Tables to compute decompression for such dives.

Repetitive group at the beginning of the surface interval

Surface interval credit table (times shown as H:MM, lower/upper bounds of each interval; entries end at 12:00° = more than 12 hours):

A — 0:10 / 12:00°

B — 0:10 2:11 / 2:10 12:00°

C — 0:10 1:40 2:50 / 1:39 2:49 12:00°

D — 0:10 1:10 2:39 5:49 / 1:09 2:38 5:48 12:00°

E — 0:10 0:55 1:58 3:23 6:33 / 0:54 1:57 3:22 6:32 12:00°

F — 0:10 0:46 1:30 2:29 3:58 7:06 / 0:45 1:29 2:28 3:57 7:05 12:00°

G — 0:10 0:41 1:16 2:00 2:59 4:26 7:36 / 0:40 1:15 1:59 2:58 4:25 7:35 12:00°

H — 0:10 0:37 1:07 1:42 2:24 3:21 4:50 8:00 / 0:36 1:06 1:41 2:23 3:20 4:49 7:59 12:00°

I — 0:10 0:34 1:00 1:30 2:03 2:45 3:44 5:13 8:22 / 0:33 0:59 1:29 2:02 2:44 3:43 5:12 8:21 12:00°

J — 0:10 0:32 0:55 1:20 1:48 2:21 3:05 4:03 5:41 8:41 / 0:31 0:54 1:19 1:47 2:20 3:04 4:02 5:40 8:40 12:00°

K — 0:10 0:29 0:50 1:12 1:36 2:04 2:39 3:22 4:20 5:49 8:59 / 0:28 0:49 1:11 1:35 2:03 2:38 3:21 4:19 5:48 8:58 12:00°

L — 0:10 0:27 0:46 1:05 1:26 1:50 2:20 2:54 3:37 4:36 6:03 9:13 / 0:26 0:45 1:04 1:25 1:49 2:19 2:53 3:36 4:35 6:02 9:12 12:00°

M — 0:10 0:26 0:43 1:00 1:19 1:40 2:06 2:35 3:09 3:53 4:50 6:19 9:29 / 0:25 0:42 0:59 1:18 1:39 2:05 2:34 3:08 3:52 4:49 6:18 9:28 12:00°

N — 0:10 0:25 0:40 0:55 1:12 1:31 1:54 2:19 2:48 3:23 4:05 5:04 6:33 9:44 / 0:24 0:39 0:54 1:11 1:30 1:53 2:18 2:47 3:22 4:04 5:03 6:32 9:43 12:00°

O — 0:10 0:24 0:37 0:52 1:08 1:25 1:44 2:05 2:30 3:00 3:34 4:18 5:17 6:45 9:55 / 0:23 0:36 0:51 1:07 1:24 1:43 2:04 2:29 2:59 3:33 4:17 5:16 6:44 9:54 12:00°

(Z) — 0:10 0:23 0:35 0:49 1:03 1:19 1:37 1:56 2:18 2:43 3:11 3:46 4:30 5:28 6:57 10:06 / 0:22 0:34 0:48 1:02 1:18 1:36 1:55 2:17 2:42 3:10 3:45 4:29 5:27 6:56 10:05 12:00°

NEW → GROUP DESIGNATION: Z O N M L K J I H G F E D C B A

RESIDUAL NITROGEN TIMES (MINUTES)

REPETITIVE DIVE DEPTH	Z	O	N	M	L	K	J	I	H	G	F	E	D	C	B	A
40	257	241	213	187	161	138	116	101	87	73	61	49	37	25	17	7
50	169	160	142	124	111	99	87	76	66	56	47	38	29	21	13	6
60	122	117	107	97	88	79	70	61	52	44	36	30	24	17	11	5
70	100	96	87	80	72	64	57	50	43	37	31	26	20	15	9	4
80	84	80	73	68	61	54	48	43	38	32	28	23	18	13	8	4
90	73	70	64	58	53	47	43	38	33	29	24	20	16	11	7	3
100	64	62	57	52	48	43	38	34	30	26	22	18	14	10	7	3
110	57	55	51	47	42	38	34	31	27	24	20	16	13	10	6	3
120	52	50	46	43	39	35	32	28	25	21	18	15	12	9	6	3
130	46	44	40	38	35	31	28	25	22	19	16	13	11	8	6	3
140	42	40	38	35	32	29	26	23	20	18	15	12	10	7	5	2
150	40	38	35	32	30	27	24	22	19	17	14	12	9	7	5	2
160	37	36	33	31	28	26	23	20	18	16	13	11	9	6	4	2
170	35	34	31	29	26	24	22	19	17	15	13	10	8	6	4	2
180	32	31	29	27	25	22	20	18	16	14	12	10	8	6	4	2
190	31	30	28	26	24	21	19	17	15	13	11	10	8	6	4	2

If the surface interval is less than 10 minutes, the residual nitrogen time is the bottom time of the previous dive. All of the residual nitrogen will be passed out of the diver's body after 12 hours, so a dive conducted after a 12-hour surface interval is not a repetitive dive.

There is one exception to this table. In some instances, when the repetitive dive is to the same or greater depth than the previous dive, the residual nitrogen time may be longer than the actual bottom time of the previous dive. In this event, add the actual bottom time of the previous dive to the actual bottom time of the repetitive dive to obtain the equivalent single dive time.

Example -

Problem - A repetitive dive is to be made to 98 fsw for an estimated bottom time of 15 minutes. The previous dive was to a depth of 102 fsw and had a 48 minute bottom time. The diver's surface interval is 6 hours 28 minutes (6:28). What decompression schedule should be used for the repetitive dive?

Solution - Using the repetitive dive worksheet - (see opposite column)

REPETITIVE DIVE WORKSHEET

I. PREVIOUS DIVE:
_48_ minutes   ☑ Standard Air Table
_102_ feet   ☐ No-Decompression Table
_M_ repetitive group designation

II. SURFACE INTERVAL:
_6_ hours _28_ minutes on surface.
Repetitive group from I _M_
New repetitive group from surface
Residual Nitrogen Timetable _B_

III. RESIDUAL NITROGEN TIME:
_98_ feet (depth of repetitive dive)
New repetitive group from II. _B_
Residual nitrogen time from
Residual Nitrogen Timetable _7_

IV. EQUIVALENT SINGLE DIVE TIME:
_7_ minutes, residual nitrogen time from III.
_15_ minutes, actual bottom time of repetitive dive.
_22_ minutes, equivalent single dive time.

V. DECOMPRESSION FOR REPETITIVE DIVE:
_22_ minutes, equivalent single dive time from IV.
_98_ feet, depth of repetitive dive

Decompression from (check one):
☐ Standard Air Table ☐ No-Decompression Table
☐ Surface Table Using Oxygen ☐ Surface Table Using Air
☑ No decompression required

Decompression Stops: ____ feet ____ minutes
   ____ feet ____ minutes
   ____ feet ____ minutes
   ____ feet ____ minutes

Schedule used ____   ____ feet ____ minutes

Repetitive group ____

SURFACE DECOMPRESSION TABLE USING OXYGEN

The application of the Surface Table Using Oxygen requires a recompression chamber with an oxygen breathing system.

The ascent rate to the first decompression stop, or to the surface if no stops are required, is 25 feet per minute. The ascent time between each stop, and from the 30 foot stop to the surface, is one minute.

Once the diver is on the surface, his tenders must remove his breathing apparatus and his weight belt and assist him into the recompression chamber within $3\frac{1}{2}$ minutes.

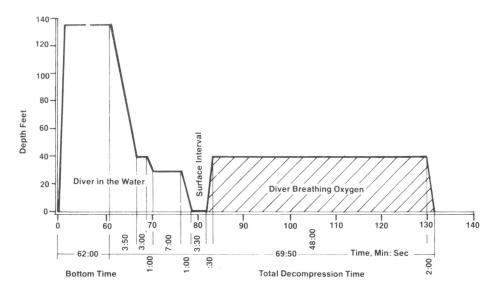

Figure 4-5 Decompression profile for a dive to 136 feet for 62 minutes using the Surface Table Using Oxygen.

Pressurization of the chamber with air should take about 30 seconds. This means that the total elapsed time from when the diver leaves the 30 foot water depth to when he reaches the 40 foot recompression depth MUST NOT EXCEED 5 MINUTES.

As soon as the diver enters the chamber he must begin breathing pure oxygen via an approved mask breathing system. He is to remain on oxygen down to and throughout the designated 40 foot stop time. While the diver is breathing oxygen, the chamber must be ventilated, as prescribed in Chapter 6.

Upon completion of the designated 40 foot chamber stop, the chamber should be depressurized to atmospheric pressure at a constant rate over a 2 minute period. During ascent, the diver is to remain on oxygen.

Should the diver develop oxygen toxicity problems, or the oxygen breathing system fail, the diver should be decompressed according to the Surface Decompression Table Using Air, disregarding all time spent breathing oxygen.

Example -

Problem - Determine the decompression schedule for a dive to 136 feet for 62 minutes using the Surface Table Using Oxygen.

Solution - The correct decompression schedule for a dive to 136 feet for 62 minutes is the 140/65 schedule. The decompression profile is illustrated above.

SURFACE DECOMPRESSION TABLE USING AIR

The Surface Table Using Air should be used for surface decompression after an air dive when a recompression chamber without an oxygen breathing system is available. Also, if oxygen

breathing must be stopped at any time when
decompressing on the Surface Table Using
Oxygen, the applicable chamber stops listed
in the Surface Table Using Air must be
carried out in their entirety.

The total ascent times of the Surface Table
Using Air exceed those of the Standard Air
Decompression Table. The advantages of
using this table are strictly those of
maintaining the diver in a controlled,
closely observed environment during
decompression.

When employing the Surface Table Using Air,
the diver should ascend from the last
water stop at 60 fpm. The time spent on
the surface should not exceed $3\frac{1}{2}$ minutes
and the rate of descent to the first chamber
stop should be 60 fpm. The total elapsed
time for these three procedures must not
exceed 5 minutes.

U.S. NAVY STANDARD AIR DECOMPRESSION TABLE

Depth (feet)	Bottom time (min)	Time first stop (min:sec)	Decompression stops (feet) 50	40	30	20	10	Total ascent (min:sec)	Repetitive group
40 (12m)	200						0	0:40	*
	210	0:30					2	2:40	N
	230	0:30					7	7:40	N
	250	0:30					11	11:40	O
	270	0:30					15	15:40	O
	300	0:30					19	19:40	Z
	360	0:30					23	23:40	**
	480	0:30					41	41:40	**
	720	0:30					69	69:40	**
50 (15m)	100						0	0:50	*
	110	0:40					3	3:50	L
	120	0:40					5	5:50	M
	140	0:40					10	10:50	M
	160	0:40					21	21:50	N
	180	0:40					29	29:50	O
	200	0:40					35	35:50	O
	220	0:40					40	40:50	Z
	240	0:40					47	47:50	Z
60 (18m)	60						0	1:00	*
	70	0:50					2	3:00	K
	80	0:50					7	8:00	L
	100	0:50					14	15:00	M
	120	0:50					26	27:00	N
	140	0:50					39	40:00	O
	160	0:50					48	49:00	Z
	180	0:50					56	57:00	Z
	200	0:40				1	69	71:00	Z
	240	0:40				2	79	82:00	**
	360	0:40				20	119	140:00	**
	480	0:40				44	148	193:00	**
	720	0:40				78	187	266:00	**
70 (21m)	50						0	1:10	*
	60	1:00					8	9:10	K
	70	1:00					14	15:10	L
	80	1:00					18	19:10	M
	90	1:00					23	24:10	N
	100	1:00					33	34:10	N
	110	0:50				2	41	44:10	O
	120	0:50				4	47	52:10	O
	130	0:50				6	52	59:10	O
	140	0:50				8	56	65:10	Z
	150	0:50				9	61	71:10	Z
	160	0:50				13	72	86:10	Z
	170	0:50				19	79	99:10	Z

* **See No Decompression Table for repetitive groups**
****Repetitive dives may not follow exceptional exposure dives**

AIR DECOMPRESSION

U. S. NAVY STANDARD AIR DECOMPRESSION TABLE

Depth (feet)	Bottom time (min)	Time first stop (min:sec)	Decompression stops (feet)					Total ascent (min:sec)	Repetitive group
			50	40	30	20	10		
80 (24m)	40						0	1:20	*
	50	1:10					10	11:20	K
	60	1:10					17	18:20	L
	70	1:10					23	24:20	M
	80	1:00				2	31	34:20	N
	90	1:00				7	39	47:20	N
	100	1:00				11	46	58:20	O
	110	1:00				13	53	67:20	O
	120	1:00				17	56	74:20	Z
	130	1:00				19	63	83:20	Z
	140	1:00				26	69	96:20	Z
	150	1:00				32	77	110:20	Z
	180	1:00				35	85	121:20	**
	240	0:50			6	52	120	179:20	**
	360	0:50			29	90	160	280:20	**
	480	0:50			59	107	187	354:20	**
	720	0:40		17	108	142	187	455:20	**
90 (27m)	30						0	1:30	*
	40	1:20					7	8:30	J
	50	1:20					18	19:30	L
	60	1:20					25	26:30	M
	70	1:10				7	30	38:30	N
	80	1:10				13	40	54:30	N
	90	1:10				18	48	67:30	O
	100	1:10				21	54	76:30	Z
	110	1:10				24	61	86:30	Z
	120	1:10				32	68	101:30	Z
	130	1:00			5	36	74	116:30	Z
100 (30m)	25						0	1:40	*
	30	1:30					3	4:40	I
	40	1:30					15	16:40	K
	50	1:20				2	24	27:40	L
	60	1:20				9	28	38:40	N
	70	1:20				17	39	57:40	O
	80	1:20				23	48	72:40	O
	90	1:10			3	23	57	84:40	Z
	100	1:10			7	23	66	97:40	Z
	110	1:10			10	34	72	117:40	Z
	120	1:10			12	41	78	132:40	Z
	180	1:00		1	29	53	118	202:40	**
	240	1:00		14	42	84	142	283:40	**
	360	0:50	2	42	73	111	187	416:40	**
	480	0:50	21	61	91	142	187	503:40	**
	720	0:50	55	106	122	142	187	613:40	**
110 (33m)	20						0	1:50	*
	25	1:40					3	4:50	H
	30	1:40					7	8:50	J
	40	1:30				2	21	24:50	L
	50	1:30				8	26	35:50	M
	60	1:30				18	36	55:50	N
	70	1:20			1	23	48	73:50	O
	80	1:20			7	23	57	88:50	Z
	90	1:20			12	30	64	107:50	Z
	100	1:20			15	37	72	125:50	Z

* See No Decompression Table for repetitive groups
**Repetitive dives may not follow exceptional exposure dives

U.S. NAVY STANDARD AIR DECOMPRESSION TABLE

120 (36m)

Bottom time (min)	Time to first stop (min:sec)	70	60	50	40	30	20	10	Total ascent (min:sec)	Repetitive group
15								0	2:00	*
20	1:50							2	4:00	H
25	1:50							6	8:00	I
30	1:50							14	16:00	J
40	1:40						5	25	32:00	L
50	1:40						15	31	48:00	N
60	1:30					2	22	45	71:00	O
70	1:30					9	23	55	89:00	O
80	1:30					15	27	63	107:00	Z
90	1:30					19	37	74	132:00	Z
100	1:30					23	45	80	150:00	Z
120	1:20				10	19	47	98	176:00	**
180	1:10			5	27	37	76	137	284:00	**
240	1:10			23	35	60	97	179	396:00	**
360	1:00		18	45	64	93	142	187	551:00	**
480	0:50	3	41	64	93	122	142	187	654:00	**
720	0:50	32	74	100	114	122	142	187	773:00	**

130 (39m)

Bottom time (min)	Time to first stop (min:sec)	70	60	50	40	30	20	10	Total ascent (min:sec)	Repetitive group
10								0	2:10	*
15	2:00							1	3:10	F
20	2:00							4	6:10	H
25	2:00							10	12:10	J
30	1:50						3	18	23:10	M
40	1:50						10	25	37:10	N
50	1:40					3	21	37	63:10	O
60	1:40					9	23	52	86:10	Z
70	1:40					16	24	61	103:10	Z
80	1:30				3	19	35	72	131:10	Z
90	1:30				8	19	45	80	154:10	Z

140 (42m)

Bottom time (min)	Time to first stop (min:sec)	90	80	70	60	50	40	30	20	10	Total ascent (min:sec)	Repetitive group
10										0	2:20	*
15	2:10									2	4:20	G
20	2:10									6	8:20	I
25	2:00								2	14	18:20	J
30	2:00								5	21	28:20	K
40	1:50							2	16	26	46:20	N
50	1:50							6	24	44	76:20	O
60	1:50							16	23	56	97:20	Z
70	1:40						4	19	32	68	125:20	Z
80	1:40						10	23	41	79	155:20	Z
90	1:00					2	14	18	42	88	166:20	**
120	1:30					12	14	36	56	120	240:20	**
180	1:20				10	26	32	54	94	168	386:20	**
240	1:10			8	28	34	50	78	124	187	511:20	**
360	1:00		9	32	42	64	84	122	142	187	684:20	**
480	1:00		31	44	59	100	114	122	142	187	801:20	**
720	0:50	16	56	88	97	100	114	122	142	187	924:20	**

* See No Decompression Table for repetitive groups
**Repetitive dives may not follow exceptional exposure dives

AIR DECOMPRESSION

U.S NAVY STANDARD AIR DECOMPRESSION TABLE

Depth (feet)	Bottom time (min)	Time to first stop (min:sec)	Decompression stops (feet)									Total ascent (min:sec)	Repetitive group
			90	80	70	60	50	40	30	20	10		
150 (45m)	5										0	2:30	C
	10	2:20									1	3:30	E
	15	2:20									3	5:30	G
	20	2:10								2	7	11:30	H
	25	2:10								4	17	23:30	K
	30	2:10								8	24	34:30	L
	40	2:00							5	19	33	59:30	N
	50	2:00							12	23	51	88:30	O
	60	1:50						3	19	26	62	112:30	Z
	70	1:50						11	19	39	75	146:30	Z
	80	1:40					1	17	19	50	84	173:30	Z
160 (48m)	5										0	2:40	D
	10	2:30									1	3:40	F
	15	2:20								1	4	7:40	H
	20	2:20								3	11	16:40	J
	25	2:20								7	20	29:40	K
	30	2:10							2	11	25	40:40	M
	40	2:10							7	23	39	71:40	N
	50	2:00						2	16	23	55	98:40	Z
	60	2:00						9	19	33	69	132:40	Z
	70	1:50					1	17	22	44	80	166:40	Z

Depth (feet)	Bottom time (min)	Time to first stop (min: sec)	Decompression stops (feet)											Total ascent (min: sec)	Repetitive group
			110	100	90	80	70	60	50	40	30	20	10		
170 (51m)	5												0	2:50	D
	10	2:40											2	4:50	F
	15	2:30										2	5	9:50	H
	20	2:30										4	15	21:50	J
	25	2:20									2	7	23	34:50	L
	30	2:20									4	13	26	45:50	M
	40	2:10								1	10	23	45	81:50	O
	50	2:10								5	18	23	61	109:50	Z
	60	2:00							2	15	22	37	74	152:50	Z
	70	2:00							8	17	19	51	86	183:50	Z
	90	1:50						12	12	14	34	52	120	246:50	**
	120	1:30				2	10	12	18	32	42	82	156	356:50	**
	180	1:20			4	10	22	28	34	50	78	120	187	535:50	**
	240	1:20			18	24	30	42	50	70	116	142	187	681:50	**
	360	1:10			22	34	40	60	98	114	122	142	187	873:50	**
	480	1:00	14	40	42	56	91	97	100	114	122	142	187	1007:50	**
180 (54m)	5												0	3:00	D
	10	2:50											3	6:00	F
	15	2:40										3	6	12:00	I
	20	2:30									1	5	17	26:00	K
	25	2:30									3	10	24	40:00	L
	30	2:30									6	17	27	53:00	N
	40	2:20								3	14	23	50	93:00	O
	50	2:10							2	9	19	30	65	128:00	Z
	60	2:10							5	16	19	44	81	168:00	Z

* See No Decompression Table for repetitive groups
**Repetitive dives may not follow exceptional exposure dives

U. S. NAVY STANDARD AIR DECOMPRESSION TABLE

190 (57m)

Bottom time (min)	Time to first stop (min:sec)	110	100	90	80	70	60	50	40	30	20	10	Total ascent (min:sec)	Repetitive group
5												0	3:10	D
10	2:50										1	3	7:10	G
15	2:50										4	7	14:10	I
20	2:40									2	6	20	31:10	K
25	2:40									5	11	25	44:10	M
30	2:30								1	8	19	32	63:10	N
40	2:30								8	14	23	55	103:10	O
50	2:20							4	13	22	33	72	147:10	Z
60	2:20							10	17	19	50	84	183:10	Z

Decompression stops (feet)

EXCLUSIVELY EXCEPTIONAL EXPOSURE TABLES:-

200 (60m)

Bottom time (min)	Time to first stop (min:sec)	130	120	110	100	90	80	70	60	50	40	30	20	10	Total ascent (min:sec)
5	3:10													1	4:20
10	3:00												1	4	8:20
15	2:50											1	4	10	18:20
20	2:50											3	7	27	40:20
25	2:50											7	14	25	49:20
30	2:40										2	9	22	37	73:20
40	2:30									2	8	17	23	59	112:20
50	2:30									6	16	22	39	75	161:20
60	2:20								2	13	17	24	51	89	199:20
90	1:50					1	10	10	12	12	30	38	74	134	324:20
120	1:40				6	10	10	10	24	28	40	64	98	180	473:20
180	1:20		1	10	10	18	24	24	42	48	70	106	142	187	685:20
240	1:20		6	20	24	24	36	42	54	68	114	122	142	187	842:20
360	1:10	12	22	36	40	44	56	82	98	100	114	122	142	187	1058:20

Decompression stops (feet)

210 (63m)

Bottom time (min)	Time to first stop (min:sec)	130	120	110	100	90	80	70	60	50	40	30	20	10	Total ascent (min:sec)
5	3:20													1	4:30
10	3:10												2	4	9:30
15	3:00											1	5	13	22:30
20	3:00											4	10	23	40:30
25	2:50										2	7	17	27	56:30
30	2:50										4	9	24	41	81:30
40	2:40									4	9	19	26	63	124:30
50	2:30								1	9	17	19	45	80	174:30

SURFACE DECOMPRESSION TABLE USING OXYGEN

Depth (feet)	Bottom time (min)	Time to first stop or surface (min:sec)	Time (min) breathing air at water stops (ft)				Surface interval	Time at 40-foot chamber stop (min) on oxygen	Surface	Total decompression time (min:sec)
			60	50	40	30				
70 (21m)	52	2:48	0	0	0	0		0		2:48
	90	2:48	0	0	0	0		15		23:48
	120	2:48	0	0	0	0		23		31:48
	150	2:28	0	0	0	0		31		39:48
	180	2:48	0	0	0	0		39		47:48
80 (24m)	40	3:12	0	0	0	0		0		3:12
	70	3:12	0	0	0	0		14		23:12
	85	3:12	0	0	0	0		20		29:12
	100	3:12	0	0	0	0		26		35:12
	115	3:12	0	0	0	0		31		40:12
	130	3:12	0	0	0	0		37		46:12
	150	3:12	0	0	0	0		44		53:12
90 (27m)	32	3:36	0	0	0	0		0		3:36
	60	3:36	0	0	0	0		14		23:36
	70	3:36	0	0	0	0		20		29:36
	80	3:36	0	0	0	0		25		34:36
	90	3:36	0	0	0	0		30		39:36
	100	3:36	0	0	0	0		34		43:36
	110	3:36	0	0	0	0		39		48:36
	120	3:36	0	0	0	0		43		52:36
	130	3:36	0	0	0	0		48		57:36
100 (30m)	26	4:00	0	0	0	0		0		4:00
	50	4:00	0	0	0	0		14		24:00
	60	4:00	0	0	0	0		20		30:00
	70	4:00	0	0	0	0		26		36:00
	80	4:00	0	0	0	0		32		42:00
	90	4:00	0	0	0	0		38		48:00
	100	4:00	0	0	0	0		44		54:00
	110	4:00	0	0	0	0		49		59:00
	120	2:48	0	0	0	3		53		65:48
110 (33m)	22	4:24	0	0	0	0		0		4:24
	40	4:24	0	0	0	0		12		22:24
	50	4:24	0	0	0	0		19		29:24
	60	4:24	0	0	0	0		26		36:24
	70	4:24	0	0	0	0		33		43:24
	80	3:12	0	0	0	1		40		51:12
	90	3:12	0	0	0	2		46		58:12
	100	3:12	0	0	0	5		51		66:12
	110	3:12	0	0	0	12		54		76:12
120 (36m)	18	4:48	0	0	0	0		0		4:48
	30	4:48	0	0	0	0		9		19:48
	40	4:48	0	0	0	0		16		26:48
	50	4:48	0	0	0	0		24		34:48
	60	3:36	0	0	0	2		32		44:36
	70	3:36	0	0	0	4		39		53:36
	80	3:36	0	0	0	5		46		61:36
	90	3:12	0	0	3	7		51		72:12
	100	3:12	0	0	6	15		54		86:12

Surface interval column: SURFACE INTERVAL NOT TO EXCEED 5 MINUTES

Middle annotation: TOTAL TIME FROM LAST WATER STOP TO FIRST CHAMBER STOP NOT TO EXCEED 5 MINUTES

Surface column: 2-MINUTE ASCENT FROM 40 FEET IN CHAMBER TO SURFACE WHILE BREATHING OXYGEN

SURFACE DECOMPRESSION TABLE USING OXYGEN

Depth (feet)	Bottom time (min)	Time to first stop or surface (min:sec)	Time (min) breathing air at water stops (ft)				Surface interval	Time at 40-foot chamber stop (min) on oxygen	Surface	Total decompression time (min:sec)
			60	50	40	30				
130 (39m)	15	5:12	0	0	0	0		0		5:12
	30	5:12	0	0	0	0		12		23:12
	40	5:12	0	0	0	0		21		32:12
	50	4:00	0	0	0	3		29		43:00
	60	4:00	0	0	0	5		37		53:00
	70	4:00	0	0	0	7		45		63:00
	80	3:36	0	0	6	7		51		75:36
	90	3:36	0	0	10	12		56		89:36
140 (42m)	13	5:36	0	0	0	0		0		5:36
	25	5:36	0	0	0	0		11		22:36
	30	5:36	0	0	0	0		15		26:36
	35	5:36	0	0	0	0		20		31:36
	40	4:24	0	0	0	2		24		37:24
	45	4:24	0	0	0	4		29		44:24
	50	4:24	0	0	0	6		33		50:24
	55	4:24	0	0	0	7		38		56:24
	60	4:24	0	0	0	8		43		62:24
	65	4:00	0	0	3	7		48		70:00
	70	3:36	0	2	7	7		51		79:36
150 (45m)	11	6:00	0	0	0	0		0		6:00
	25	6:00	0	0	0	0		13		25:00
	30	6:00	0	0	0	0		18		30:00
	35	4:48	0	0	0	4		23		38:48
	40	4:24	0	0	3	6		27		48:24
	45	4:24	0	0	5	7		33		57:24
	50	4:00	0	2	5	8		38		66:00
	55	3:36	2	5	9	4		44		77:36
160 (48m)	9	6:24	0	0	0	0		0		6:24
	20	6:24	0	0	0	0		11		23:24
	25	6:24	0	0	0	0		16		28:24
	30	5:12	0	0	0	2		21		35:12
	35	4:48	0	0	4	6		26		48:48
	40	4:24	0	3	5	8		32		61:24
	45	4:00	3	4	8	6		38		73:00
170 (51m)	7	6:48	0	0	0	0		0		6:48
	20	6:48	0	0	0	0		13		25:48
	25	6:48	0	0	0	0		19		31:48
	30	5:12	0	0	3	5		23		44:12
	35	4:48	0	4	4	7		29		57:48
	40	4:24	4	4	8	6		36		72:24

Surface interval column note: TOTAL TIME FROM LAST WATER STOP TO FIRST CHAMBER STOP NOT TO EXCEED 5 MINUTES

Surface column note: 2-MINUTE ASCENT FROM 40 FEET IN CHAMBER TO SURFACE WHILE BREATHING OXYGEN

AIR DECOMPRESSION

SURFACE DECOMPRESSION TABLE USING AIR

Depth (ft)	Bottom time (min)	Time to first stop (min:sec)	Time at water stops (min)			Surface Interval	Chamber stops (air) (min)		Total ascent time (min:sec)
			30	20	10		20	10	
40 (12m)	230	0:30			3			7	14:30
	250	:30			3			11	18:30
	270	:30			3			15	22:30
	300	:30			3			19	26:30
50 (15m)	120	:40			3			5	12:40
	140	:40			3			10	17:40
	160	:40			3			21	28:40
	180	:40			3			29	36:40
	200	:40			3			35	42:40
	220	:40			3			40	47:40
	240	:40			3			47	54:40
60 (18m)	80	:50			3			7	14:50
	100	:50			3			14	21:50
	120	:50			3			26	33:50
	140	:50			3			39	46:50
	160	:50			3			48	55:50
	180	:50			3			56	63:50
	200	:40		3			3	69	80:10
70 (21m)	60	1:00			3			8	16:00
	70	1:00			3			14	22:00
	80	1:00			3			18	26:00
	90	1:00			3			23	31:00
	100	1:00			3			33	41:00
	110	:50		3			3	41	52:20
	120	:50		3			4	47	59:20
	130	:50		3			6	52	66:20
	140	:50		3			8	56	72:20
	150	:50		3			9	61	78:20
	160	:50		3			13	72	93:20
	170	:50		3			19	79	106:20
80 (24m)	50	1:10			3			10	18:10
	60	1:10			3			17	25:10
	70	1:10			3			23	31:10
	80	1:00		3			3	31	42:30
	90	1:00		3			7	39	54:30
	100	1:00		3			11	46	65:30
	110	1:00		3			13	53	74:30
	120	1:00		3			17	50	81:30
	130	1:00		3			19	63	90:30
	140	1:00		26			26	69	126:30
	150	1:00		32			32	77	146:30
90 (27m)	40	1:20			3			7	15:20
	50	1:20			3			18	26:20
	60	1:20			3			25	33:20
	70	1:10		3			7	30	45:40
	80	1:10		13			13	40	71:40
	90	1:10		18			18	48	89:40
	100	1:10		21			21	54	101:40
	110	1:10		24			24	61	114:40
	120	1:10		32			32	68	137:40
	130	1:00	5	36			36	74	156:40

Surface Interval column (vertical): TOTAL TIME FROM LAST WATER STOP TO FIRST CHAMBER STOP NOT TO EXCEED 5 MINUTES

SURFACE DECOMPRESSION TABLE USING AIR

Depth (ft)	Bottom time (min)	Time to first stop (min:sec)	50	40	30	20	10	Surface Interval	Chamber stops (air) 20	Chamber stops (air) 10	Total ascent time (min:sec)
100 (30m)	40	1:30					3			15	23:30
	50	1:20				3			3	24	35:50
	60	1:20				3			9	28	45:50
	70	1:20				3			17	39	64:50
	80	1:20				23			23	48	99:50
	90	1:10			3	23			23	57	111:50
	100	1:10			7	23			23	66	124:50
	110	1:10			10	34			34	72	155:50
	120	1:10			12	41			41	78	177:50
110 (33m)	30	1:40					3			7	15:40
	40	1:30				3			3	21	33:00
	50	1:30				3			8	26	43:00
	60	1:30				18			18	36	78:00
	70	1:20			1	23			23	48	101:00
	80	1:20			7	23			23	57	116:00
	90	1:20			12	30			30	64	142:00
	100	1:20			15	37			37	72	167:00
120 (36m)	25	1:50					3			6	14:50
	30	1:50					3			14	22:50
	40	1:40				3			5	25	39:10
	50	1:40				15			15	31	67:10
	60	1:30			2	22			22	45	97:10
	70	1:30			9	23			23	55	116:10
	80	1:30			15	27			27	63	138:10
	90	1:30			19	37			37	74	173:10
	100	1:30			23	45			45	80	189:10
130 (39m)	25	2:00					3			10	19:00
	30	1:50				3			3	18	30:20
	40	1:50				10			10	25	51:20
	50	1:40			3	21			21	37	88:20
	60	1:40			9	23			23	52	113:20
	70	1:40			16	24			24	61	131:20
	80	1:30		3	19	35			35	72	170:20
	90	1:30		8	19	45			45	80	203:20
140 (42m)	20	2:10					3			6	15:10
	25	2:00				3			3	14	26:30
	30	2:00				5			5	21	37:30
	40	1:50			2	16			16	26	66:30
	50	1:50			6	24			24	44	104:30
	60	1:50			16	23			23	56	124:30
	70	1:40		4	19	32			32	68	161:30
	80	1:40		10	23	41			41	79	200:30
150 (45m)	20	2:10				3			3	7	19:40
	25	2:10				4			4	17	31:40
	30	2:10				8			8	24	46:40
	40	2:00			5	19			19	33	82:40
	50	2:00			12	23			23	51	115:40
	60	1:50		3	19	26			26	62	142:40
	70	1:50		11	19	39			39	75	189:40
	80	1:40	1	17	19	50			50	84	227:40

Surface Interval note (vertical): SURFACE INTERVAL NOT TO EXCEED 5 MINUTES — TOTAL TIME FROM LAST WATER STOP TO FIRST CHAMBER STOP

AIR DECOMPRESSION

SURFACE DECOMPRESSION TABLE USING AIR

Depth (ft)	Bottom time (min)	Time to first stop (min:sec)	Time at water stops (min)					Surface Interval	Chamber stops (air) (min)		Total ascent time (min:sec)
			50	40	30	20	10		20	10	
160 (48m)	20	2:20				3			3	11	23:50
	25	2:20				7			7	20	40:50
	30	2:10			2	11			11	25	55:50
	40	2:10			7	23			23	39	98:50
	50	2:00		2	16	23			23	55	125:50
	60	2:00		9	19	33			33	69	169:50
	70	1:50	1	17	22	44			44	80	214:50
170 (51m)	15	2:30				3			3	5	18:00
	20	2:30				4			4	15	30:00
	25	2:20			2	7			7	23	46:00
	30	2:20			4	13			13	26	63:00
	40	2:10		1	10	23			23	45	109:00
	50	2:10		5	18	23			23	61	137:00
	60	2:00	2	15	22	37			37	74	194:00
	70	2:00	8	17	19	51			51	86	239:00
180 (54m)	15	2:40				3			3	6	19:10
	20	2:30			1	5			5	17	35:10
	25	2:30			3	10			10	24	54:10
	30	2:30			6	17			17	27	74:10
	40	2:20		3	14	23			23	50	120:10
	50	2:10	2	9	19	30			30	65	162:10
	60	2:10	5	10	10	44			44	81	216:10
190 (57m)	15	2:50				4			4	7	22:20
	20	2:40			2	6			6	20	41:20
	25	2:40			5	11			11	25	59:20
	30	2:30		1	8	19			19	32	86:20
	40	2:30		8	14	23			23	55	130:20
	50	2:20	4	13	22	33			33	72	184:20
	60	2:20	10	17	19	50			50	84	237:20

Surface Interval: SURFACE INTERVAL NOT TO EXCEED 5 MINUTES — TOTAL TIME FROM LAST WATER STOP TO FIRST CHAMBER STOP

CHAPTER 5

THERAPEUTIC RECOMPRESSION

DECOMPRESSION SICKNESS

Decompression sickness results from the formation of bubbles in the blood or body tissues and is caused by inadequate decompression following a dive or other exposure to high pressure.

Inadequate decompression may occur even though normal precautions are followed. Abnormal conditions in the diver or his surroundings may cause him to absorb an excessive amount of inert gas or may inhibit the natural elimination of the dissolved gas during normal controlled decompression. Also any alteration of the gas mixture will effect the amount of inert gas absorbed during a dive, and for this reason, different decompression requirements are provided, for different sets of circumstances. EQUIVALENT AIR TABLES or tables calculated for the mixture used at the depth required.

DIAGNOSIS OF DECOMPRESSION SICKNESS

Decompression sickness normally causes symptoms to appear within a short period of time following a dive or other exposure to pressure.

If a controlled decompression procedure during ascent, has been shortened, or by-passed, a diver could be suffering from decompression sickness even before he reaches the surface. In a large sampling of cases, the timing after surfacing to the onset of symptoms was as follows:-

50% occur within 30 minutes
85% occur within 1 hour
95% occur within 3 hours
1% delayed more than 6 hours.

Symptoms which occur 24 hours or more following a dive are normally not caused by decompression sickness.

Other factors for evaluating symptoms include depth and duration of the dive, the decompression tables used, and the possibility of other conditions such as GAS EMBOLISM.

The best qualified person available should make the diagnosis. Evaluation should not be delayed pending the arrival of a better qualified person. A wide range of symptoms may accompany the initial stages of an attack (or HIT) of decompression sickness. The diver may also exhibit certain signs which a trained observer will identify with decompression sickness. Some of the symptoms will be so pronounced that there will be little doubt as to the cause. Others may be subtle, and even some of the more important could be overlooked in a cursory examination of the patient.

Various symptoms of decompression sickness have been found to occur with the following frequency -

Local pain	89%
- Leg	30%
- Arm	70%
Dizziness (the staggers)	5.3%
Paralysis	2.3%
Shortness of breath (the chokes)	1.6%
Extreme fatigue and pain	1.3%
Collapse with unconsciousness	.5%

MILD SYMPTONS OF DECOMPRESSION SICKNESS

As will be noted above, the most common sympton is pain in an arm or a leg. These may occur together, of course, or pain may appear in some other part of the body. The pain is usually slight when first noticed, but may grow progressively worse until unbearable. It may seem to come from deep in a bone and will often become centred in a joint. It is sometimes easy to misinterpret pain as a sympton, assuming it to be the result of a muscle sprain or bruise.

If there is any doubt as to the origin of the pain, assume that the diver is suffering from mild decompression sickness and treat him accordingly.

Among the more usual symptoms of mild decompression sickness, the diver might notice a prickling, tingling, itching or burning of the skin, any of which could start in a small area, then spread, and then once again become localized. A sensation of this sort is often the first noticed symptom An observer should also watch for any skin rash or mottling indicative of skin bends.

Pain may mask other, frequently more significant, symptoms. However, pain should not be treated with drugs in an effort to make the patient more comfortable because it may well be the only means for localizing the problem and monitoring the progress of any treatment.

SERIOUS SYMPTOMS OF DECOMPRESSION SICKNESS (CNS)

Serious problems which effect the central nervous system (CNS) require immediate treatment, even before a full examination and diagnosis can be performed. If there are any signs that the nervous system is affected, the diver should be recompressed immediately. The examination may be completed in the chamber at treatment pressure. Since CNS treatment is for the most severe possibility, any symptoms which may go unnoticed will probably not be significant.

Abdominal pain (which can easily be confused with a 'gas pain') should be regarded as a serious symptom, as it may signal involvement of the spinal cord. With this, or with any other possible nervous system involvement, immediate recompression must be instituted.

The symptoms of serious decompression sickness
are:-

SPINAL BEND

Weakness or paralysis
Tingling or numbness of the limbs
Girdle pain of the body
Difficulty in passing urine

CEREBRAL BEND

Unconsciousness
Visual Disturbances
Convulsions
Headache
Loss of speech or hearing
Depression
Confusion
Unusual behaviour or other neuro-logical signs

STAGGERS

Staggering gait
Inability to balance
Giddiness and vomiting

CHOKES

Pain or tightness in the chest
Breathlessness
Shallow, rapid respiration
Collapse
Shock
Serious symptoms may occur either with or without mild symptoms.

Many of these are easily overlooked, or passed off by the victim as being of no consequence. For this reason, they must be particularly watched for during the immediate post-dive activi-ties of the diver. He may just think he has been working too hard. He may also experience shortness of breath, coughing, or wheezing, or may notice pain when taking a deep breath. In rare instances (about one case in 200), the victim may suddenly lose consciousness and collapse.
A symptom of this sort is more usually linked with gas embolism, and treat-ment should proceed accordingly.

Many of the symptoms of decompression sickness are the same as those for gas embolism, and since the treatment for gas embolism will at the same time be appropriate treatment for decompression sickness, any such confusion of symptoms will not be too important.

GAS EMBOLISM AND RELATED CONDITIONS

Gas embolism is caused by the expansion of gas which has been taken into the lungs while breathing under pressure and held in the lungs during an ascent. The gas might have been retained in the lungs by choice (voluntary breathholding) or by accident (as when the air passages become blocked). The gas could have become trapped in an obstructed portion of the lung which was the result of damage from some previous disease or accident. Or the diver, reacting with panic to a difficult situation, may hold his breath without realizing that he is doing so.

However the gas may have become trapped in the lungs, it will expand as the diver rises. If there is enough gas, and if it expands sufficiently, the pressure will tend to force gas through the alveolar walls and into the bloodstream and surrounding tissues.

The gas thus forced into the blood may be carried by arteries throughout the body. These gas bubbles may lodge in the arteries, the spinal cord or the brain, cutting off blood circulation. Gas which has been forced into the lung tissues may also flow under the skin and collect around the heart or in the chest causing collapse of a lung.

SYMPTOMS

Difficultly in breathing
Pain behind the breastbone
Unconsciousness
Blood froth around the lips
Possible distension below rib cage
Death

The term GAS EMBOLISM, as used in diving refers to gas which has been forced into the bloodstream. The related conditions which result when the gas is forced into the tissues are:-
- mediastinal emphysema, gas trapped in the tissues of the chest around the heart, great vessels and lungs.

SYMPTOMS

The symptoms of MEDIASTINAL EMPHYSEMA may include pain under the breastbone, shortness of breath and faintness. These latter two would be the result of the trapped gas pressing against the lungs, heart and large blood vessels, thereby interfering with the breathing and/or blood circulation. This might also be evidenced by blueness (cyanosis) of the skin, lips or fingernails.

- Subcutaneous emphysema, gas trapped under the skin (often in the area of the neck, having moved up from the point of rupture or 'leaking' in the lungs.

SYMPTOMS

SUBCUTANEOUS EMPHYSEMA may not be noticed by the victim except in extreme cases, although he might experience a feeling of fullness around the neck and may have difficulty in swallowing. The sound of his voice may change, and an observer may also note a marked swelling or inflation of the neck. Movement of the skin near the collar bone may produce a crackling or crunching sound (crepitation).

- Pneumothorax, where the gas is caught between the lungs and chest wall.

SYMPTOMS

PNEUMOTHORAX is usually accompanied by a sharp pain in the chest which is aggravated by deep breathing. To minimize this pain, the victim will be breathing in a shallow rapid manner. He may show signs of hypoxia and may

exhibit a tendency to bend the chest toward the side involved. If a lung has in
fact been collapsed by the trapped gas,
it may be detected by listening to both
sides of the chest. A collapsed lung will
not produce audible sounds of breathing,
depending upon the degree of collapse.

The potential hazard of gas embolism may
be prevented or substantially reduced by
careful attention to the following -

A. Medical selection of diving personnel
with particular attention to elimination
of men who show evidence of lung disease
or who have a past history of respiratory disorders.

B. Evaluation of Physical condition immediately before a dive - any impairment
of respiration, as from a cold, bronchi-
tis, etc., must be considered to be potentially disqualifing.

C. Every diver must be given proper training in diving physics and physiology as
well as in the correct use of various
diving equipment. Particular attention
must be given to the training of SCUBA
divers because of the comparatively high
incidence of embolism accidents experienced in SCUBA operations.

D. A diver must never hold his breath
during ascent from a dive in which breathing apparatus has been used.

E. When making an emergency ascent, the
diver must EXHALE CONTINUOUSLY.

F. Other factors in the prevention of
gas embolism include good planning, and
adherence to the established dive plan.
Trying to stretch a dive to finish a task
can too easily lead to the exhaustion of
the air supply and the need for an emergency ascent. Further, the diver must
know and follow good diving practices,
must keep himself in good physical condition, and must not hesitate to report
any symptoms whatsoever, no matter how
trivial they might seem to the Diving
Supervisor.

A case of gas embolism must be diagnosed

quickly and correctly. The supply of
blood to the brain or spinal cord is
almost always involved, and unless
promptly and properly treated (by recompression), gas embolism is likely to
result in death or permanent brain damage. By the same token, since the brain
is so rapidly affected, definite symptoms of gas embolism are likely to show
up within a minute or two after surfacing. Any serious decompression sickness
symptom, other than unconsciousness,
which develops much later should not be
regarded as the result of gas embolism.
This does not rule out, however, the
possibility of other medical conditions
which are related to gas embolism.

As a basic rule, any diver who may have
obtained a breath from any source at
depth - whether from diving apparatus
or from a diving bell - and who is
unconscious or soon loses consciousness
upon reaching the surface, must be assumed to be suffering from a gas embolism
and recompression treatment must be
started immediately. If the diver re-
gains consciousness before recompression
has started, and shows no signs of brain
injury, gas embolism is probably not
involved.

DIAGNOSIS OF DECOMPRESSION SICKNESS

SIGNS & SYMPTOMS	DECOMPRESSION SICKNESS: MILD: Skin	MILD: Pain Only	SERIOUS: CNS	SERIOUS: Chokes	GAS EMBOLISM: CNS SYMPTOMS: Brain Damage	CNS SYMPTOMS: Spinal Cord Damage	Pneumo-Thorax	Mediastinal Emphysema
Pain-Head					■			
Pain-Back			□					
Pain-Neck								■
Pain-Chest			□	■		□	■	□
Pain-Stomach			■			□		
Pain-Arms/Legs		■				□		
Pain-Shoulders		■				□		
Pain-Hips		■				□		
Unconsciousness			■	□	■	□	□	
Shock			■	□	■	□	□	
Vertigo			■					
Visual Difficulty			■		■			
Nausea/Vomiting			■		■			
Hearing Difficulty			■		■			
Speech Difficulty			■		■			
Balance Lack			■		■			
Numbness	□		■		■	□		□
Weakness		□	■		■	□		
Strange Sensations	□		■		■	□		
Swollen Neck								■
Short of Breath			□	□	□	□	□	□
Cyanosis				□	□	□	□	□
Skin Changes	■							

■ Probable
□ Possible Cause

Figure 5-1

Figure 5-1 contains a guide for non-medical personnel to use in forming a diagnosis of decompression sickness. However, one point must always be kept in mind:- <u>IF IN ANY DOUBT RECOMPRESS</u>

Figure 5-2 contains symptom and injury report forms to be completed in the event of a decompression accident.

5.6

SYMPTOM LIST -- DECOMPRESSION ACCIDENT

Date:..

1   Barge/Rig: ....   2 Patient's Name: ....

3   PRINCIPAL SYMPTOM
    or MAIN INJURY:

4   Type of dive: 5   Depth: ....

6   Time of accident: 7   Time of surfacing:.........................

8   Bottom time: 9   Ascent time: ....

10 Gas mix used: .... 11 Dive procedure: ....

12 Decompression shortened?............. 13 By how much? ....

14 Explosive ascent? .... 15 Therapeutic table
                                     in use: ....

16 Previous dive depth: .... 17 Previous dive time: ....

18 FIRST SIGNS:

		YES	NO
19	PAIN, in joints or muscles		
20	FATIGUE – more or less intense		
21	DEAFNESS – hearing problems		
22	LOSS OF BALANCE – standing with eyes closed impossible............		
23	VERTIGO, NAUSEA, VOMITING		
24	PAIN – in the lumbar region, around waist		
25	VISUAL PROBLEMS		
26	SHOCK – paleness, weakness anxiety		
27	SPEECH PROBLEMS		
28	PINS & NEEDLES		
29	STANDING UPRIGHT – impossible or difficult		
30	PARALYSIS – muscles without strength		
31	Inability to urinate		
32	LOSS OF CONSCIOUSNESS		
33	DIFFICULT OF PAINFUL BREATHING – 'Chokes'		
34	RESPIRATORY DISTRESS – worsening with decompression		
35	CYANOSIS		

36 Present status ....

37 Medical Treatment given ....

38 FORM COMPLETED BY ....

39 DATE OF COMPLETION ....

40 TIME OF COMPLETION ....

Fig 5-2

RECOMPRESSION TREATMENT U.S.N.

When the diver has received inadequate decompression or falls victim to gas embolism, the first treatment procedure is to return the diver to a pressurized environment where the expanded gases will be recompressed to a manageable volume. This will relieve any local pressure caused by the bubbles, will restore normal blood flow and will frequently relieve the patient of many, if not all, of the subjective symptoms. After recompression treatment is underway, additional treatment may be administered.

Certain facets of recompression treatment cannot be overstressed –

1. Treat promptly and adequately.

2. Do not delay treatment for the arrival of medical personnel.

3. The effectiveness of treatment decreases with the length of time between the onset of symptoms and the treatment.

4. Do not ignore seemingly minor symptoms, they can quickly become major.

5. Follow the selected treatment table accurately and completely.

6. If a symptom – or group of symptoms seems to be relieved, do not assume that the treatment is finished. Follow the tables to completion, and keep the diver in the immediate vicinity of the chamber (or the diving station) for at least 6 hours following recompression and within half an hour travel time to the chamber for 24 hours.

NO RECOMPRESSION CHAMBER. In the event that the diving facility is not equipped with a recompression chamber, the Diving Supervisor has two alternatives. If recompression of the patient is not immediately necessary, he may be transported to the nearest recompression chamber for treatment. (The location of the nearest recompression chamber must be included in the data collected during the planning phase of the dive).

If immediate recompression treatment is necessary, the patient must be treated in the water. The hazards involved in this procedure must be carefully weighed against the complications which may result if treatment is delayed.

Except in grave emergencies, seek the nearest recompression chamber, even if it is at a considerable distance.

TRANSPORTING THE PATIENT. Not all patients will require immediate recompression – that is, a certain delay may be acceptable while the patient is transported to a recompression chamber. While preparing a patient for recompression (when a delay is necessary) and while moving him to a chamber, he should be kept lying down, feet slightly higher than his head, with his body tilted 20° to the left side. This position may help to keep bubbles away from the more critical sites. Additionally, the patient should be kept warm, and his condition must be constantly monitored for signes of a blocked airway, fainting, cardiac arrest, cessation of breathing or sudden massive internal bleeding.

Always keep in mind that the most obvious symptoms may not actually be related to the most serious problem – a number of conditions may well exist at the same time. For example, the victim may be suffering from both decompression sickness and severe internal injuries.

If the patient must be transported, the initial arrangements should have been made well in advance of the actual diving operations. These arrangements – which would include an "alert" notification to the recompression chamber and a determination of the most effective means of transportation – should be posted on

" Job-Site Emergency Check List "
for instant referral.

If the patient is moved by air, the
helicopter or other aircraft should be
flown as low as possible. An unnecessary altitude means an additional reduction in external pressure and possible additional symptoms severity or
complications. While in transit, oxygen (if available) should be administered to the patient.

Ambulances normally carry Nitrous
Oxide. This should not be administered to a patient suffering from
decompression sickness.

Have someone call ahead to ensure that
the chamber will be ready, and that
qualified medical personnel will be
standing by. If two-way communications can be established, obtain
consultation with the doctor while in
transit.

IN-WATER RECOMPRESSION (U.S.N. ONLY)

A. If water recompression must be
used and the diver is conscious and
able to care for himself -

   1. Use either a full face mask or,
       preferably a rigid helmet or
       handmask. Never recompress a
       diver in the water using
       SCUBA with a mouthpiece.

   2. Follow treatment tables as
       closely as possible.

   3. Maintain constant communication.

 B. If the diver is unconscious or
incapacitated, send another diver down
with him to control his valves and
otherwise assist him.

C. If a lightweight diving outfit or
SCUBA (with full face mask) must be
used, keep at least one diver with the
patient at all times. Plan carefully
for shifting rigs or cylinders. Have
an ample number of tenders topside and
at intermediate depths.

D. If the depth is inadequate for
full treatment according to the tables

   1. Take the patient to maximum
       available depth.

   2. Keep him there for 30 minutes.

   3. Bring him up according to Table
       2A of the Treatment Table using
       air. Do not use stops shorter
       than those of Table 2A.

TREATMENT TABLES. Extensive research
and field experience have shown the
therapeutic value of oxygen administration during recompression treatment.
The Oxygen Treatment Tables are the preferred procedure for recompression
treatment. When employing the Tables
be particularly conscious of the early
signs of O_2 toxicity which can be readily remembered by the acronym, VENTID -
Vision, Ears, Nausea, Twitching,
Irritability, Dizziness.

The Air Treatment Tables are not nearly
as effective as the Oxygen Treatment
Tables and should be employed only when
oxygen is not available in the recompression chamber, if in-water recompression is necessitated, or in situations
in which treatment using the Oxygen
Treatment Tables are unsuccessful.

The maximum recompression depth employed
in treatment is based upon the response
of the patient's signs and symptoms to
increasing pressure. Symptoms of
decompression sickness and gas embolism
normally respond quickly to repressurization, and a depth is reached (depth
of relief - DOR) at which primary
symptoms have subsided. Pressurization
is continued until the shallowest

standard recompression depth is reached -60' or 165'- depending upon the table selected.

Following arrival at the required recompression depth, the patient's condition should be closely monitored. The patient is maintained at depth for the time period required on the applicable table. If symptoms persist, it may be necessary to extend the time period on the bottom or consider repressurization to greater depth. Either action will require selection of an alternate treatment table. Recompression below 165' should not be attempted except upon the direct advice of a diving medical officer since specialized decompression procedures will be required. Following the required time on the bottom, decompression is initiated following the specific schedule given in the appropriate table. During the decompression phase, the patient should be closely observed for a recurrence of symptoms which may necessitate immediate repressurization to relief depth and an alternate decompression procedure.

RULES FOR RECOMPRESSION TREATMENT

ALWAYS

1. Follow the Treatment Tables accurately.

2. Have qualified tender in chamber at all times during recompression.

3. Maintain the normal descent and ascent rates.

4. Examine patient thoroughly at depth of relief or treatment depth.

5. Treat an unconscious patient for gas embolism or serious decompression sickness unless the possiblity of such a condition can be ruled out without question.

6. Use oxygen if available.

7. Have a qualified diver accompany the patient in the chamber during treatment.

8. Be alert for oxygen poisoning if oxygen is used.

9. In the event of oxygen convulsion remove the oxygen mask and keep the patient from harming himself.

10. Maintain oxygen usage within the time and depth limitations.

11. Check patient's condition before and after coming to each stop and during long stops.

12. Observe patient for at least 6 hours after treatment for recurrence of symptoms.

13. Maintain accurate timekeeping and recording.

14. Maintain a well stocked medical kit at hand.

NEVER

1. Permit any shortening or other alteration to the tables except under the direction of a trained Diving Medical Officer.

2. Exceed descent rate tolerated by the patient.

3. Let patient sleep between depth changes or for more than one hour at any one stop.

4. Continue ascent if patient's condition worsens.

5. Wait for a bag resusitator. Use mouth-to-mouth immediately if breathing ceases.

6. Break rhythm during resuscitation.

7. Permit the use of oxygen below 60'.

8. Fail to report symptoms early (diver).

9. Fail to treat doubtful cases.

10. Allow personnel in the chamber to assume any cramped position which may interfere with complete blood circulation.

NOTE: The utilization of an He-O_2 breathing medium is an option to be considered at the discretion of the cognizant medical officer as determined by the circumstances of the individual case.

OMITTED DECOMPRESSION

Certain emergencies may interrupt or prevent specified decompression. Blowup, exhausted air supply, bodily injury and the like constitute such emergencies. If the diver shows any symptoms of decompression sickness or gas embolism, immediate treatment using the appropriate oxygen or air recompression treatment table is essential. Even if the diver shows no symptoms of ill effects, omitted decompression must be made up in some manner to avert later difficulty.

USE OF SURFACE DECOMPRESSION TABLES

The Surface Decompression Table Using Oxygen or the Surface Decompression Table Using Air may be used to make up omitted decompression only if the emergency surface interval occurs at such a time that water stops are not required by these tables, or if required, have already been completed.

SURFACE DECOMPRESSION TABLES NOT APPLICABLE

When the conditons which permit the use of the surface decompression tables are not fulfilled, the diver's decompression has been compromised. Special care must be taken to detect signs of decompression sickness, regardless of what action is initiated. The diver must be returned to pressure as soon as possible. The use of a recompression chamber is strongly preferred over in-water recompression.

WHEN A RECOMPRESSION CHAMBER IS AVAILABLE

Even if the diver show no ill effects from his omitted decompression, he needs immediate recompression. Take him to depth as appropriate for Recompression Treatment Table 1A or 5. If he shows no ill effects, decompress him in accordance with the Treatment Table. Consider any decompression sickness developing during or after this procedure as a recurrence.

WHEN NO CHAMBER IS AVAILABLE

Recompress the diver in the water following as nearly as possible Recompression Treatment Table 1A. Keep the diver at rest, provide a standby diver, and maintain good communication and depth control.

When this course of action is impossible, use the following procedure which is based on the Standard Air Decompression Table with 1 minute between stops-

- Repeat any stops deeper than 40ft.

- At 40ft, remain for one-fourth of of the 10ft stop time.

- At 30ft, remain for one-third of the 10ft stop time.

- At 20ft, remain for one-half of the 10ft stop time.

- At 10ft, remain for 1-½ times the scheduled 10ft stop time.

DECOMPRESSION SICKNESS TREATMENT   GAS EMBOLISM TREATMENT

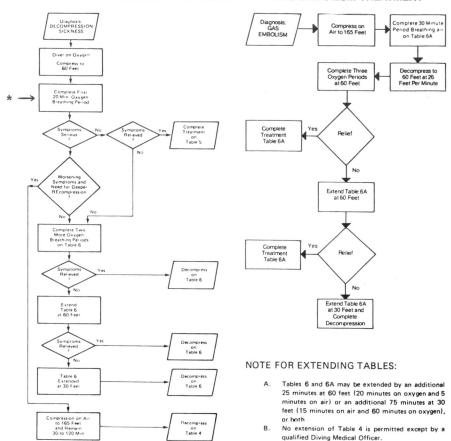

NOTE FOR EXTENDING TABLES:

A. Tables 6 and 6A may be extended by an additional 25 minutes at 60 feet (20 minutes on oxygen and 5 minutes on air) or an additional 75 minutes at 30 feet (15 minutes on air and 60 minutes on oxygen), or both

B. No extension of Table 4 is permitted except by a qualified Diving Medical Officer.

* The patient's condition should be reviewed after 10 minutes of the first 20 minutes oxygen breathing cycle. If symptoms are relieved, complete oxygen breathing cycle and continue treatment on Table 5. If symptoms are not relieved after 10 minutes but are relieved within 20 minutes, complete oxygen breathing cycle and continue treatment on Table 6.

Decompression Sickness Treatment and Gas Embolism charts.

RECURRENCE DURING TREATMENT   RECURRENCE FOLLOWING TREATMENT

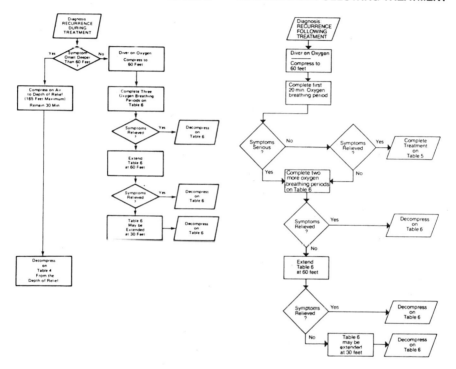

Recurrence During Treatment and Recurrence Following Treatment charts.

LIST OF U.S. NAVY RECOMPRESSION TREATMENT TABLES

TABLE	USE
5 - Oxygen Treatment of Pain-only Decompression Sickness	Treatment of pain-only decompression sickness when symptoms are relieved within 10 minutes at 60 feet.
6 - Oxygen Treatment of Serious Decompression Sickness	Treatment of serious decompression sickness or pain-only decompression sickness when symptoms are not relieved within 10 minutes at 60 feet.
6A - Air and Oxygen Treatment of Gas Embolism	Treatment of gas embolism. Use also when unable to determine whether symptoms are caused by gas embolism or severe decompression sickness.
1A - Air Treatment of Pain-only Decompression Sickness - 100-foot Treatment	Treatment of pain-only decompression sickness when oxygen unavailable and pain is relieved at a depth less than 66 feet.
2A - Air Treatment of Pain-only Decompression Sickness - 165-foot Treatment	Treatment of pain-only decompression sickness when oxygen unavailable and pain is relieved at a depth greater than 66 feet.
3 - Air Treatment of Serious Decompression Sickness or Gas Embolism	Treatment of serious symptoms or gas embolism when oxygen unavailable and symptoms are relieved within 30 minutes at 165 feet.
4 - Air Treatment of Serious Decompression Sickness or Gas Embolism	Treatment of worsening symptoms during the first 20-minute oxygen breathing period at 60 feet on Table 6, or when symptoms are not relieved within 30 minutes at 165 feet using air treatment Table 3.

TABLE 5—MINIMAL RECOMPRESSION, OXYGEN BREATHING METHOD FOR TREATMENT OF DECOMPRESSION SICKNESS AND GAS EMBOLISM

1. Use—treatment of pain-only decompression sickness when oxygen can be used and symptoms are relieved within 10 minutes at 60 feet. Patient breathes oxygen from the surface.
2. Descent rate—25 ft/min.
3. Ascent rate—1 ft/min. Do not compensate for slower ascent rates. Compensate for faster rates by halting the ascent.
4. Time at 60 feet begins on arrival at 60 feet.
5. If oxygen breathing must be interrupted, allow 15 minutes after the reaction has entirely subsided and resume schedule at point of interruption.
6. If oxygen breathing must be interrupted at 60 feet, switch to TABLE 6 upon arrival at the 30 foot stop.
7. Tender breathes air throughout. If treatment is a repetitive dive for the tender or tables are lengthened, tender should breathe oxygen during the last 30 minutes of ascent to the surface.

Depth (feet)	Time (minutes)	Breathing Media	Total Elapsed Time (minutes)
60	20	Oxygen	20
60	5	Air	25
60	20	Oxygen	45
60 to 30	30	Oxygen	75
30	5	Air	80
30	20	Oxygen	100
30	5	Air	105
30 to 0	30	Oxygen	135

TABLE 5 DEPTH/TIME PROFILE

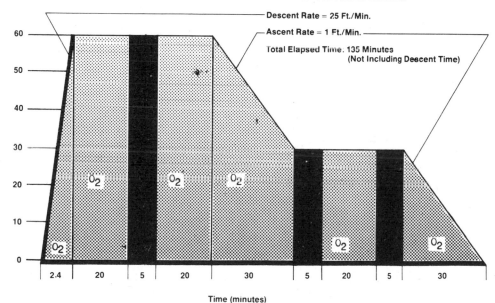

Descent Rate = 25 Ft./Min.

Ascent Rate = 1 Ft./Min.

Total Elapsed Time. 135 Minutes
(Not Including Descent Time)

Depth (feet)

Time (minutes)

TABLE 6—MINIMAL RECOMPRESSION, OXYGEN BREATHING METHOD FOR TREATMENT OF DECOMPRESSION SICKNESS AND GAS EMBOLISM

1. Use—treatment of decompression sickness when oxygen can be used and symptoms are not relieved within 10 minutes at 60 feet. Patient breathes oxygen from the surface.

2. Descent rate—25 ft/min.

3. Ascent rate—1 ft/min. Do not compensate for slower ascent rates. Compensate for faster rates by halting the ascent.

4. Time at 60 feet—begins on arrival at 60 feet.

5. If oxygen breathing must be interrupted, allow 15 minutes after the reaction has entirely subsided and resume schedule at point of interruption.

6. Tender breathes air throughout. If treatment is a repetitive dive for the tender or tables are lengthened, tender should breathe oxygen during the last 30 minutes of ascent to the surface.

7. Table 6 can be lengthened by an additional 25 minutes at 60 feet (20 minutes on oxygen and 5 minutes on air) or an additional 75 minutes at 30 feet (15 minutes on air and 60 minutes on oxygen), or both.

Depth (feet)	Time (minutes)	Breathing Media	Total Elapsed Time (minutes)
60	20	Oxygen	20
60	5	Air	25
60	20	Oxygen	45
60	5	Air	50
60	20	Oxygen	70
60	5	Air	75
60 to 30	30	Oxygen	105
30	15	Air	120
30	60	Oxygen	180
30	15	Air	195
30	60	Oxygen	255
30 to 0	30	Oxygen	285

TABLE 6 DEPTH/TIME PROFILE

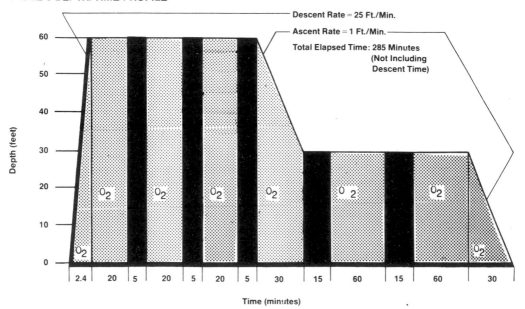

Descent Rate = 25 Ft./Min.
Ascent Rate = 1 Ft./Min.
Total Elapsed Time: 285 Minutes (Not Including Descent Time)

Depth (feet)

Time (minutes)

TABLE 6A—MINIMAL RECOMPRESSION, OXYGEN BREATHING METHOD FOR TREATMENT OF DECOMPRESSION SICKNESS AND GAS EMBOLISM

1. Use—treatment of gas embolism when oxygen can be used and symptoms moderate to a major extent within 30 minutes at 165 feet.

2. Descent rate—as fast as possible.

3. Ascent rate—1 ft/min. Do not compensate for slower ascent rates. Compensate for faster ascent rates by halting the ascent.

4. Time at 165 feet—includes time from the surface.

5. If oxygen breathing must be interrupted, allow 15 minutes after the reaction has entirely subsided and resume schedule at point of interruption.

6. Tender breathes air throughout. If treatment is a repetitive dive for the tender or tables are lengthened, tender should breathe oxygen during the last 30 minutes of ascent to the surface.

7. Table 6A can be lengthened by an additional 25 minutes at 60 feet (20 minutes on oxygen and 5 minutes on air) or an additional 75 minutes at 30 feet (15 minutes on air and 60 minutes on oxygen), or both.

Depth (feet)	Time (minutes)	Breathing Media	Total Elapsed Time (minutes)
165	30	Air	30
165 to 60	4	Air	34
60	20	Oxygen	54
60	5	Air	50
60	20	Oxygen	79
60	5	Air	84
60	20	Oxygen	104
60	5	Air	109
60 to 30	30	Oxygen	139
30	15	Air	154
30	60	Oxygen	214
30	15	Air	229
30	60	Oxygen	289
30 to 0	30	Oxygen	319

TABLE 6A DEPTH/TIME PROFILE

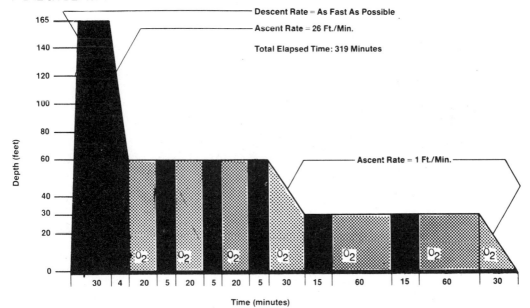

Descent Rate = As Fast As Possible

Ascent Rate = 26 Ft./Min.

Total Elapsed Time: 319 Minutes

Ascent Rate = 1 Ft./Min.

TABLE 1A—RECOMPRESSION TREATMENT OF DECOMPRESSION SICKNESS AND GAS EMBOLISM USING AIR

TABLE 1A NOTES—

1. Use—treatment of pain-only decompression sickness when oxygen cannot be used and pain is relieved at a depth less than 66 feet.
2. Descent rate—25 ft/min.
3. Ascent rate—1 minute between stops.
4. Time at 100 feet—includes time from the surface.
5. If the piping configuration of the chamber does not allow it to return to atmospheric pressure from the 10 foot stop in the one minute specified, disregard the additional time required.

TABLE 1A

Depth (feet)	Time (minutes)	Breathing Media	Total Elapsed Time (minutes)
100	30	Air	30
80	12	Air	43
60	30	Air	74
50	30	Air	105
40	30	Air	136
30	60	Air	197
20	60	Air	258
10	120	Air	379
0	1	Air	380

TABLE 1A DEPTH/TIME PROFILE

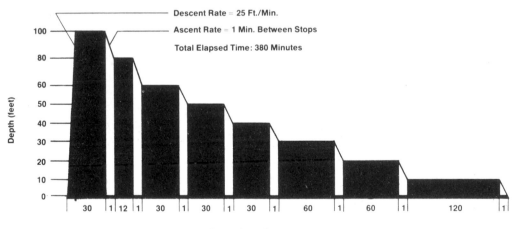

Descent Rate = 25 Ft./Min.

Ascent Rate = 1 Min. Between Stops

Total Elapsed Time: 380 Minutes

TABLE 2A—RECOMPRESSION TREATMENT OF DECOMPRESSION SICKNESS AND GAS EMBOLISM USING AIR

1. Use — treatment of pain-only decompression sickness when oxygen cannot be used and pain is relieved at a depth greater than 66 feet.
2. Descent rate — 25 ft/min.
3. Ascent rate — 1 minute between stops.
4. Time at 165 feet — includes time from the surface.
5. If the piping configuration of the chamber does not allow it to return to atmospheric pressure from the 10 foot stop in the one minute specified, disregard the additional time required.

Depth (feet)	Time (minutes)	Breathing Media	Total Elapsed Time (minutes)
165	30	Air	30
140	12	Air	43
120	12	Air	56
100	12	Air	69
80	12	Air	82
60	30	Air	113
50	30	Air	144
40	30	Air	175
30	120	Air	296
20	120	Air	417
10	240	Air	658
0	1	Air	659

TABLE 2A DEPTH/TIME PROFILE

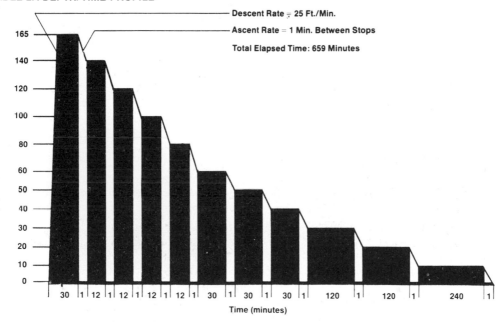

TABLE 3—RECOMPRESSION TREATMENT OF DECOMPRESSION SICKNESS AND GAS EMBOLISM USING AIR

1. Use—treatment of serious symptoms when oxygen cannot be used and symptoms are relieved within 30 minutes at 165 feet.

2. Descent rate—as fast as possible.

3. Ascent rate—1 minute between stops.

4. Time at 165 feet—includes time from the surface.

5. If the piping configuration of the chamber does not allow it to return to atmospheric pressure from the 10 foot stop in the one minute specified, disregard the additional time required.

Depth (feet)	Time	Breathing Media	Total Elapsed Time (hrs:min)
165	30 min.	Air	0:30
140	12 min.	Air	0:43
120	12 min.	Air	0:56
100	12 min.	Air	1:09
80	12 min.	Air	1:22
60	30 min.	Air	1:53
50	30 min.	Air	2:24
40	30 min.	Air	2:55
30	12 hr.	Air	14:56
20	2 hr.	Air	16:57
10	2 hr.	Air	18:58
0	1 min.	Air	18:59

TABLE 3 DEPTH/TIME PROFILE

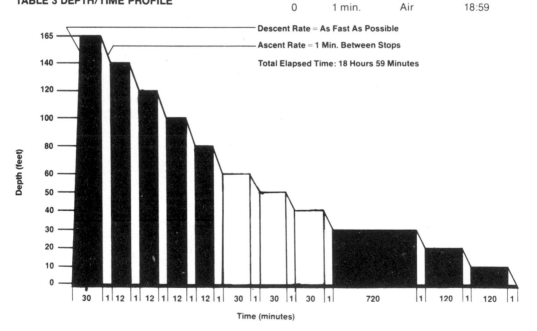

Descent Rate = As Fast As Possible

Ascent Rate = 1 Min. Between Stops

Total Elapsed Time: 18 Hours 59 Minutes

TABLE 4—RECOMPRESSION TREATMENT OF DECOMPRESSION SICKNESS AND GAS EMBOLISM USING AIR

1. Use—treatment of serious symptoms or gas embolism when oxygen cannot be used or when symptoms are not relieved within 30 minutes at 165 feet.

2. Descent rate—as fast as possible.

3. Ascent rate— l minute between stops.

4. Time at 165 feet— includes time from the surface.

5. No modification or extension of this table is permitted except by a Diving Medical Officer.

6. If the piping configuration of the chamber does not allow it to return to atmospheric pressure from the 10 foot stop in the one minute specified, disregard the additional time required.

Depth (feet)	Time	Breathing Media	Total Elapsed Time (hrs:min)
165	½ to 2 hr.	Air	2:00
140	½ hr.	Air	2:31
120	½ hr.	Air	3:02
100	½ hr.	Air	3:33
80	½ hr.	Air	4:04
60	6 hr.	Air	10:05
50	6 hr.	Air	16:06
40	6 hr.	Air	22:07
30	11 hr.	Air	33:08
30	1 hr.	Oxygen (or air)	34:08
20	1 hr.	Air	35:09
20	1 hr.	Oxygen (or air)	36:09
10	1 hr.	Air	37:10
10	1 hr.	Oxygen (or air)	38:10
0	1 min.	Oxygen	38:11

TABLE 4 DEPTH/TIME PROFILE

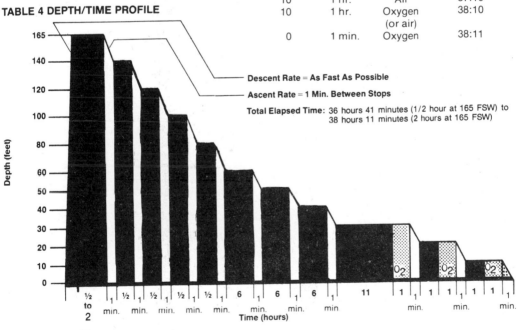

Descent Rate = As Fast As Possible

Ascent Rate = 1 Min. Between Stops

Total Elapsed Time: 36 hours 41 minutes (1/2 hour at 165 FSW) to 38 hours 11 minutes (2 hours at 165 FSW)

THERAPEUTIC DECOMPRESSION   R.N. BR2806

INTRODUCTION

The advent of advanced diving equipments with increased performances in respect of both depth and endurance has brought about an increase in the incidence of decompression and associated sicknesses.

Decompression sickness may be mild, can maim for life or even prove fatal. It is often extremely painful.

The dangers of decompression sickness must never be ignored, and its onset must be treated promptly for a complete cure to stand a chance of being effected.

(It should be noted that injury to a diver during a dive or on surfacing may produce decompression sickness in the region of the injury).

Clinical conditions attributable to other than decompression sickness are not as a rule aggravated by recompression and are not, therefore, to be regarded as a reason for delaying treatment.

Treatment can be conducted satisfactorily only in a compression chamber capable of holding two or more people and fitted with an inner and outer compartment. Such treatment is dealt with in this section, as well as treatment under less favourable conditions.

FIRST-AID TREATMENT

Until the patient arrives at the compression chamber, he should be kept as comfortable as possible. If available, oxygen may be beneficial.

Morphia, nitrous oxide (as available in many ambulances) and other pain killing drugs or alcohol are not to be administered, as they may mask the symptoms and prevent correct diagnosis. In addition, nitrous oxide may actually worsen decompression sickness.

PREPARATION OF THE CHAMBER

Since the patient and attendants may have to spend many hours in the chamber, much thought must be given to making them as comfortable as possible in the limited space available. (Refer to Chapter 6 for the chamber preparation and practical operation).

EXAMINATION

If a diving Doctor is available and no serious symptoms are present, the patient is to be examined before recompression. The diving Doctor may sometimes decide to delay recompression in serious cases also, in order to carry out procedures such as intravenous infusion, drawing blood, or insertion of catheters. If no diving Doctor is available, the patient is to be placed in a compression chamber, with an attendant whenever possible, and the chamber pressurised without delay.

UNUSUAL OR DIFFICULT CASES

Although the majority of cases of decompression sickness will respond to the treatment laid down, there are occasions when the advice of a specialist diving Doctor is to be sought. This procedure will apply to unusual or difficult cases, which are to be regarded as emergencies. In such cases an immediate telephone call (even from overseas) is to be made through the Portsmouth Dockyard Exchange (Portsmouth (0705) 22351), asking for:

In working hours: The Superintendent of Diving, HMS VERNON.

Out of working hours: The Duty Lieutenant Commander, HMS VERNON.

These officers are responsible for locating one of the specialist diving Doctors on the staff of the Institute of Naval Medicine.

TREATMENT IN A TWO-COMPARTMENT COMPRESSION CHAMBER

The treatment for all forms of decompression sickness and arterial gas embolism involves recompression of the patient at the earliest opportunity and subsequent decompression at a rate depending on the patient's condition. The various treatments are described below. The choice of recompression procedures is summarised in (Fig. 1)

TREATMENT OF MILD SYMPTOMS

If the symptoms are joint pains only, even though severe, and there is no evidence of a more serious condition, the patient is to be treated as shown below:

A. Oxygen available

    a. If oxygen is available proceed as follows:

        1. The patient starts breathing oxygen at the surface.
        2. Descend to 18m in one to two minutes.
        3. Do not stop to verify any report of symptom relief.

    b. If symptoms are fully relieved within 10 minutes at 18m, decompress in accordance with Table 61.

    c. If symptoms are not fully relieved within 10 minutes at 18m, and it is certain that no serious symptoms are present, follow Table 62. Table 62 may be extended on specialist advice. Do not compress to 50m in the absence of serious symptoms.

B. Oxygen not available

    d. If oxygen is not available proceed as follows:

        1. Descend to 50m at a steady rate of 10m per minute-
        2. Do not stop to verify any report of symptom relief.

    e. If symptoms are relieved upon reaching 50m, follow Table 52.

    f. If symptoms are relieved within the first 25 minutes at 50m, follow Table 53. If not, follow Table 55 or 73, after 2 hours at 50m.

    f. Contact a diving medical specialist whenever symptoms are not fully relieved at treatment depth.

TREATMENT OF SERIOUS SYMPTOMS

If the illness appears life-threatening, or in cases of definite arterial gas embolism, the chamber is to be pressurised without delay with air to 50m at the fastest rate that can be tolerated by the patient. Time must not be wasted on the assessment of the causes, as the sooner the patient is recompressed the better the chance of recovery. If pain increases during the descent, the descent must be halted and then continued at a slower rate more tolerable to the patient. This is normally of the order of 30m per minute.

    a. If the diagnosis is arterial gas embolism, the patient is free of signs and symptoms after 25 mins, and O_2 is available, then decompression according to Table 63 may be commenced after 30 mins at 50m.

    b. For all others decompress according to Table 54, 55 or 73.

    c. Contact a diving medical specialist when symptoms are not relieved within 25 minutes at 50m.

For illnesses not lift-threatening, but consisting of serious symptoms, proceed as follows:

A. Oxygen available

a. If O_2 is available, proceed as follows:

　　1. The patient starts breathing O_2 at the surface.
　　2. Descend to 18m in one or two minutes.
　　3. Do not stop to verify any report of symptom relief

b. If symptoms are fully relieved within 10 minutes at 18m, decompress according to Table 62.

c. If symptoms are not cured but improving, follow Table 62. The Table may be extended at 18m, and 9m. Contact diving medical specialist.

d. If after 10 minutes there has been no improvement, take the patient off oxygen and compress the chamber to 50m, on air (if less than 5 hours since onset of symptoms).

e. If symptoms are fully relieved within 25 minutes at 50m, decompress on Table 53 after 30 mins.

f. If symptoms are not relieved within 25 minutes at 50m, follow Table 54 or 73 after 2 hours at 50m.

B. Oxygen not available

If O_2 is not available, compress to 50m on air and follow the procedure in paras. e and f above, substituting Table 55 for Table 54.

DELAY IN SYMPTOMS

When there is a delay of more than 5 hours between the time of onset of symptoms of decompression sickness and treatment, use only Tables 61 and 62. Table 61 is then used only for mild symptoms which are relieved within 10 minutes at 18m.

RECURRENCE OF SYMPTOMS

a. If symptoms return or worsen during decompression on Table 61 or 62, return to 18m and repeat the stops of Table 62.

b. If symptoms return or worsen on an air treatment table, compress to the depth of relief, not exceeding 50m. After 30 minutes at the depth of relief, reduce pressure to the next stoppage and follow Table 73, 54 or 55.

c. In the case of blow up from deep diving, if symptoms persist at 50m recompress to maximum depth of chamber or 70m and decompress in accordance with Table 71.

d. For recurrence on Table 63, follow para (a) above if the recurrence occurs after leaving 18m, or para (b) if at 18m or deeper.

e. For recurrences after completion of the treatment table, use Table 62 if O_2 is available, otherwise Table 55 or 73.

f. For all recurrences, diving medical specialist advice is to be sought.

ALTERNATIVE THERAPEUTIC TABLES

The diving supervisor is not to deviate from the foregoing except on specialist medical advice.

Some of the alterations to treatment that may be recommended by such a specialist diving Doctor include the following:

a. Repetitions of oxygen therapies.

b. Periods of oxygen breathing during air tables.

c. Continuous bleed (saturation) decompression as in Tables 71 or 72.

d. Extension of Table 62.

e. Use of oxygen-enriched mixture.

f. Use of prolonged compression and
    saturation decompression, when
    equipment is available.

OMITTED DECOMPRESSION

When a diver has surfaced without completing all of his decompression stoppages, action must be taken to prevent
decompression sickness. If he is free
of signs and symptoms of decompression
sickness or gas embolism, proceed as
follows:

a. If the diver surfaces early and
    without problems and can be recom-
    pressed within the decompression
    rules then act accordingly, other
    wise use the treatments given in
    the succeeding paragraphs.

b. If the diver has only missed stops
    at 18m or less, recompress to 18m,
    on oxygen and follow Table 61.

c. If the diver has missed stops from
    deeper than 18m, recompress to 50m
    and follow Table 52.

d. If at any time the diver shows signs
    or symptoms of decompression sick-
    ness or gas embolism, treat as des-
    cribed for recurrences.

CLINICAL TREATMENT

Clinical treatment is continued throughout the decompression therapy; particular
care should be taken to prevent dehydrat-
ion or shock, and appropriate intravenous
fluids should be given as soon as possible if the later diagnosis is made.

The Doctor   if not present when the
therapeutic treatment started, should
question and examine the patient as soon
as possible. He should advise recompression or a change to a longer table if

he suspects any residual or new lesion.
In consideration of the difficulties of
making a satisfactory physical examination of a patient while under pressure
in a chamber, it needs to be emphasised
that, in the absence of abnormal signs,
the patient should be treated symptom-
atically.

The following checks are to be made by
the Doctor or, in his absence, the
attendant:

a. On reaching maximum depth, the pat-
    ient is to be questioned and examined
    as completely as possible to detect
    incomplete relief or the presence
    or symptoms previously unnoticed.

b. The patient must at least be made
    to stand and walk the length of the
    chamber.

c. Rechecking is to be carried out
    periodically, eg. before commencing
    each ascent.

d. The patient is to be asked how he is
    on arrival at each stop and period-
    ically during the longer stops.

e. The patient must be woken from sleep
    during changes in depth and at four-
    hourly intervals during stops, as
    symptoms can recur during sleep.

ACTION IN THE ABSENCE OF A COMPRESSION
CHAMBER

If a diver develops decompression sickness when away from the vicinity of a
chamber, action must be taken to transfer him to a chamber as soon as possible.

The following steps must be taken:

a. Contact by telephone or signal the
    nearest authority controlling a
    chamber and request the chamber be
    made available.

Treatment of Decompression Sickness following
air or N₂O₂ mixture diving.

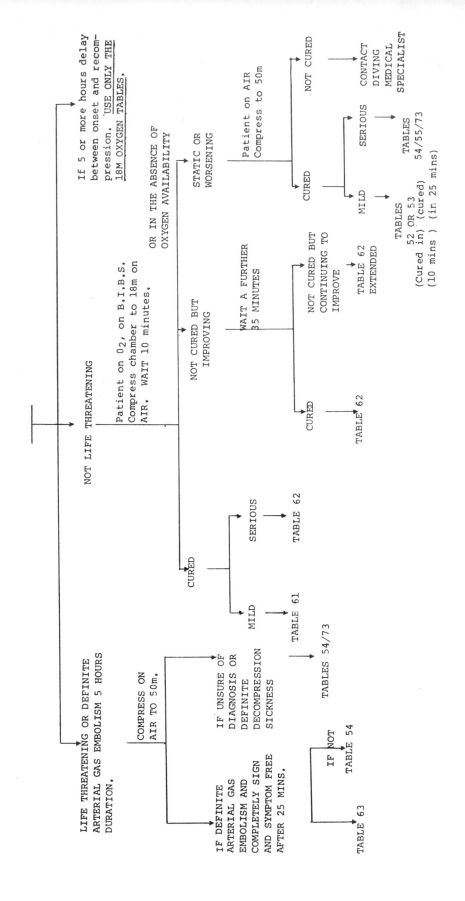

Fig 5-3

b. Dispatch the patient by the quickest available means. If he has to be sent by air, the aircraft cabin pressure should not be less than that for a height of 1000ft.

c. If available, oxygen should be breathed during transfer.

d. The patient should be accompanied by the diving supervisor who was in charge of the diving operation and, if available, a Doctor. If it is not possible for the diving supervisor to attend, the patient must be accompanied by another diver who knows the full details of the case.

POST-TREATMENT RESTRICTIONS

Decompression sickness leads to many difficulties in assessing the degree of recovery, even after therapeutic treatment. The restrictions outlined below, which are considered the minimum acceptable, are to be applied after all cases of decompression sickness.

SURFACING AFTER THERAPEUTIC TREATMENT

The patient is to be kept close to a chamber for six hours and within one hour's travelling time for the next 18 hours.

MILD CASES

If the symptoms were joint pains only and the treatment described in Table 51 or Table 61 was successful, the patient is not to be allowed to dive for 24 hours and no deeper than 10m for a further two days.

SERIOUS CASES

If the symptoms were serious or, if the symptoms were mild but required recompression on any routine other than Tables 51 or 61, the casualty must be seen by a Doctor experienced in diving medicine before diving again. The examining

Doctor would normally consider seven days to be the minimum desirable period of lay-off for a case who has made a complete recovery as assessed by a full diving medical examination.

MISCELLANEOUS COMPLICATIONS

If any symptoms or signs of decompression sickness persist and further recompression is not advised, no diving is to be allowed until the patient has been re-examined for fitness to dive as for the annual medical examination.

AIDE MEMORIE

The following errors are to be avoided:

a. Divers failure to report symptoms early.

b. Failure to treat dubious cases.

c. Failure to treat promptly.

d. Failure to recognise serious symptoms.

e. Failure to treat adequately.

f. Failure to keep patient close to chamber after treatment.

APPLICATION OF THERAPEUTIC TABLES

Different therapeutic tables are provided for different sets of circumstances and are applied as described in the preamble to each series.

Additionally there are some common factors, which are outlined below:

a. Descent time. Descent time, which varies between tables, is not included in the elapsed time-

b. Elapsed time. The timing of each table starts when maximum pressure is reached, and is given in hours and minutes opposite each step of the table.

c. Stoppages. The duration of stoppages is given, oxygen being breathed as indicated.

d. Ascent. The rate of ascent varies
between tables, but with all tables
the ascent becomes critical near the
surface, where the rate of change of
pressure is greatest. If, as the
compression chamber nears the surface, air begins to escape round the
door seal, compensations by admitting more compressed air may be needed. In addition, the gauges may
indicate that the surface has been
reached when there is still some
pressure in the chamber. If this
occurs the chamber must continue to
be vented at the established rate
until the pressure is equalised.

e. Surfacing. On arrival at the surface both patient and attendant must
remain in the chamber for one minute
in case of return of symptoms.

TABLES 61, 62: OXYGEN-RECOMPRESSION
THERAPY

Tables 61 and 62 are employed when oxygen
is available and is required for the
greater part of the therapy.

These tables are applied as described
in Application of Therapeutic Tables,
but with the following modifications:

a. Descent. The descent is to take
one to two minutes.

b. Ascent. The ascent is to be conducted as follows:

1. It is to be at a continuous
bleed rate of three metres in
10 minutes.

2. If the rate is slowed it is not
to be compensated for by subsequent acceleration.

3. The ascent should be halted if
the rate is exceeded, or if the
ascent cannot be controlled
accurately during flushing of
the chamber.

c. Oxygen. Oxygen is to be breathed
before descent. The attendant may
remain on air unless it is a repetitive dive, when he must breathe
oxygen for the final nine-metres
ascent.

To help prevent O_2 poisoning, the
patient is to be kept at rest,
lying down, during all oxygen breathing periods at nine-metres or
deeper.

Oxygen poisoning is not likely to
occur with these tables, but the
Supervisor must be prepared and
take the following action:

1. If ascending, halt the ascent
and maintain depth.

2. Instruct the attendant to
remove the oxygen mask and
protect the tongue of the
convulsing patient and prevent him from injuring himself

3. Wait until 15 mins after all
symptoms of O_2 poisoning have
subsided, then resume the O_2
treatment table at the point
of interruption. In the unlikely event of a second
episode of O_2 poisoning, act
as in 2 above, then change to
decompression on Table 55 or
73 from the same depth. However, if the patient is free
of decompression sickness
symptoms, and the depth is
less than nine metres, continue to bleed to the surface
on air.

TABLE 61
Oxygen Recompression Therapy

GAUGE DEPTH (metres)	STOPPAGES/ ASCENT (minutes)	ELAPSED TIME (hours and minutes)	RATE OF ASCENT (metres/minute)
18	20 (O₂)	0000–0020	—
18	5	0020–0025	—
18	20 (O₂)	0025–0045	—
18–9	30 (O₂)	0045–0115	3 m in 10 mins
9	5	0115–0120	—
9	20 (O₂)	0120–0140	—
9	5	0140–0145	—
9–0	30 (O₂)	0145–0215	3 m in 10 mins
Surface		0215	

TABLE 62
Oxygen Recompression Therapy

GAUGE DEPTH (metres)	STOPPAGES/ ASCENT (minutes)	ELAPSED TIME (hours and minutes)	RATE OF ASCENT (metres/minute)
18	20 (O₂)	0000–0020	—
18	5	0020–0025	—
18	20 (O₂)	0025–0045	—
18	5	0045–0050	—
18	20 (O₂)	0050–0110	—
18	5	0110–0115	—
18–9	30 (O₂)	0115–0145	3 m in 10 mins
9	15	0145–0200	—
9	60 (O₂)	0200–0300	—
9	15	0300–0315	—
9	60 (O₂)	0315–0415	—
9–0	30 (O₂)	0415–0445	3 m in 10 mins
Surface		0445	

TABLE 63: DEEP AIR-OXYGEN RECOMPRESSION THERAPY

In cases of definite arterial gas embolism, when the patient is completely relieved of symptoms within 25 minutes at 50 metres, this table may be used-

The table is applied as in Application of Therapeutic Tables.

a.   Rate of descent - as fast as tolertolerable.

b.   Rate of ascent.

1.   From 50m to 18m in 4 minutes.

2.   From 18m to 9m and 9m to the surface: at 3m in 10 minutes.

c.   The oxygen part of the schedule is conducted as in Table 62, except that the attendant must always breathe O_2 during the final 9m of ascent.

TABLE 63
Air-Oxygen Recompression Therapy

GAUGE DEPTH (Metres)	STOPPAGES/ ASCENT (Minutes)	RATE OF ASCENT (Metres/Minute)
50	30	—
50–18	4	—
18	20 (O₂)	8m in 1 min
18	5	—
18	20 (O₂)	—
18	5	—
18	20 (O₂)	—
18	5	—
18–9	30 (O₂)	—
9	15	3m in 10 mins
9	60 (O₂)	—
9	15	—
9	60 (O₂)	—
9–0	30 (O₂)	3m in 10 mins
Surface		

TABLES 52 to 55: AIR-RECOMPRESSION THERAPY

Tables 52, 53 and 55 are the air tables normally employed for therapeutic decompression. Table 54 may be employed instead of Table 55 when oxygen is available.

NOTE: Oxygen therapy should always be used where possible.

These tables are applied as described in Application of Therapeutic Tables, but with the following modifications:

a. Rate of descent.

1. In mild cases - at a rate of approximately 10 metres per minute.

2. In serious cases - as fast as can be tolerated by the patient. This is normally in the order of 30 metres per minute.

b. Ascent. Ascent between stoppages is to take five minutes. This is not included in the stoppage times, but has been allowed for in the elapsed times.

c. Oxygen. Both patient and attendant are to breathe oxygen as indicated in Table 54.

TABLE 52
AIR RECOMPRESSION THERAPY

GAUGE DEPTH (metres)	STOPPAGES (hours (h) and minutes (min))	ELAPSED TIME (hours and minutes)	RATE OF ASCENT
50	30 min	0000–0030	5 minutes be-
42	12 min	0035–0047	tween stoppages
36	12 min	0052–0104	throughout
30	12 min	0109–0121	
24	12 min	0126–0138	
18	30 min	0143–0213	
15	30 min	0218–0248	
12	30 min	0253–0323	
9	2 h	0328–0528	
6	2 h	0533–0733	
3	2 h	0738–0938	
Surface		0943	

TABLE 53
AIR RECOMPRESSION THERAPY

GAUGE DEPTH (metres)	STOPPAGES (hours (h) and minutes (min))	ELAPSED TIME (hours and minutes)	RATE OF ASCENT
50	30 min	0000–0030	5 minutes be-
42	12 min	0035–0047	tween stoppages
36	12 min	0052–0104	throughout
30	12 min	0109–0121	
24	12 min	0126–0138	
18	30 min	0143–0213	
15	30 min	0218–0248	
12	30 min	0253–0323	
9	12 h	0328–1528	
6	2 h	1533–1733	
3	2 h	1738–1938	
Surface		1943	

TABLE 54
AIR RECOMPRESSION THERAPY

GAUGE DEPTH (metres)	STOPPAGES (hours (h) and minutes (min))	ELAPSED TIME (hours and minutes)	RATE OF ASCENT
50	2 h	0000–0200	5 minutes be-
42	30 min	0205–0235	tween stoppages
36	30 min	0240–0310	throughout
30	30 min	0315–0345	
24	30 min	0350–0420	
18	6 h	0425–1025	
15	6 h	1030–1630	
12	6 h	1635–2235	
9	11 h	2240–3340	
	1 h (02)	3340–3440	
6	1 h	3445–3545	
	1 h (02)	3545–3645	
3	1 h	3650–3750	
	1 h (02)	3750–3850	
Surface		3855	

TABLE 55
AIR RECOMPRESSION THERAPY

GAUGE DEPTH (metres)	STOPPAGES (hours (h) and minutes (min))	ELAPSED TIME (hours and minutes)	RATE OF ASCENT
50	2 h	0000–0200	5 minutes be-
42	30 min	0205–0235	tween stoppages
36	30 min	0240–0310	throughout
30	30 min	0315–0345	
24	30 min	0350–0420	
18	6 h	0425–1025	
15	6 h	1030–1630	
12	6 h	1635–2235	
9	12 h	2240–3440	
6	4 h	3445–3845	
3	4 h	3850–4250	
Surface		4255	

TABLES 71, 72, 73: MODIFIED AIR-RECOMPRESSION THERAPY

Tables 71 and 72 can be used instead of the air recompression therapies, Tables 51 to 55, on the advice of a specialist diving Doctor.

Table 73 may be used in place of Tables 54 and 55. Although somewhat more difficult to accomplish, the smaller step size in the final 18m is preferred, especially in cases of gas embolism or incomplete relief of decompression sickness. The table approximates the bleed rate of the final 18m of Tables 71 and 72.

These Tables are applied as described in Application of Therapeutic Tables, but with the following modifications for Tables 71 and 72:

a. Ascent. The ascent is to be conducted as follows:

    1. It is to be a continuous bleed at the rates indicated.

    2. If the rate is slowed it is not to be compensated for by subsequent acceleration.

    3. The ascent should be halted if the rate is exceeded or if the ascent cannot be controlled accurately during flushing of the chamber.

b. Oxygen. Oxygen may be administered periodically to selected cases as advised by the diving Doctor.

TABLE 71
MODIFIED AIR RECOMPRESSION THERAPY

GAUGE DEPTH (metres)	STOPPAGES/ ASCENT (hours (h) and minutes (min))	ELAPSED TIME (hours and minutes)	RATE OF ASCENT (metres/hour)
70	30 min	0000–0030	—
70–63	7 min	0030–0037	60 m/h
63–51	2 h	0037–0237	6 m/h
51–39	4 h	0237–0637	3 m/h
39–29	5 h	0637–1137	2 m/h
29–20	6 h	1137–1737	1·5 m/h
20–10	10 h	1737–2737	1 m/h
10–0	20 h	2737–4737	0·5 m/h
Surface		4737	

TABLE 72
MODIFIED AIR RECOMPRESSION THERAPY

GAUGE DEPTH (metres)	STOPPAGES/ ASCENT (hours (h) and minutes (min))	ELAPSED TIME (hours and minutes)	RATE OF ASCENT (metres/hour)
50	2 h (see NOTE)	0000–0200	—
50–39	3 h 40 min	0200–0540	3 m/h
39–29	5 h	0540–1040	2 m/h
29–20	6 h	1040–1640	1·5 m/h
20–10	10 h	1640–2640	1 m/h
10–0	20 h	2640–4640	0·5 m/h
Surface		4640	

TABLE 73

MODIFIED AIR RECOMPRESSION THERAPY

GAUGE DEPTH (Metres)	STOPPAGES (hours (h) (minutes (min)		RATE OF ASCENT
50	2h		–
42		30 mins	5 mins
36		30 mins	between
30		30 mins	stoppages
24		30 mins	throughout
18	6h		
17		55 mins	
16		55 mins	
15		55 mins	
14		55 mins	
13		55 mins	
12		55 mins	
11		55 mins	
10	1h	55 mins	
9	1h	55 mins	
8	1h	55 mins	
7	1h	55 mins	
6	1h	55 mins	
5	1h	55 mins	
4	1h	55 mins	
3	1h	55 mins	
2	1h	55 mins	
1	1h	55 mins	
Surface			

GLOSSARY OF TERMS

ALVEOLI — Thin walled sacs in the lung where exchange between breathing gas and dissolved gas in the blood occurs.

BEND — Decompression accident occurring primarily in joints and muscles.

CEREBRAL EMBOLISM — Bubble of gas in the blood stream reaching the brain and interfering with central nervous action.

CORTICOIDS — Drugs with a strong anti-inflamatory action.

CYANOSIS — Blue colour of the skin resulting from lack of oxygen in blood.

EMBOLISM, GAS — Bubble of gas in the blood stream forming a blockage.

EMBOLISM, FAT — Small mass of fatty material blocking blood stream. Fat embolisms can occur in severe decompression accidents if not treated quickly.

EQUIVALENT DECOMPRESSION — Lengthened decompression carried out when normal decompression is halted for any reason.

HEMIPLEGIA — Paralysis of one side of the body.

HYPEROXIC CRISIS — Seizure caused by breathing high partial pressure of O_2. First signs are twitching of lips and facial muscles leading to visual, hearing and sensory difficulties and finally an attack resembling epilepsy.

LUDION — A deep excursion dive from saturation requiring a decompression stop or stops to return to living depth.

NAUSEA — The _feeling_ of being about to vomit.

NEUROLOGICAL — To do with the nervous system. Nervous communication carries sensory message inwards to brain and spinal cord, and outwards to "effector organs" such as muscles.

PARAPLEGIA — Paralysis of lower half of the body.

PLATELETS — Particles in the blood much smaller than corpuscles, which clump

VERTIGO — The _feeling_ of motion, often spinning or tumbling when stationary.

VESTIBULAR — To do with the vestibular system or semi-circular canals in the inner ear. The system is the sense-organ of balance and perception of motion.

together and stick to
site of injury; also
caused to clump by
bubbles of gas.

PLEURAL   – Spaces within each side
CAVITIES   of chest totally
                   occupied by each lung.

PNEUMOTHORAX   – Gas bubble occupying
                   the pleural cavity
                   resulting from rupture
                   of the lung.

PULMONARY   – Damage to the lung
BAROTRAUMA   caused by difference
                   of pressure.

QUADRIPLEGIA   – Paralysis of all four
                   limbs.

RESPIRATORY   – To do with respiration.
                   Respiratory symptoms
                   can result from pul-
                   monary barotrauma or
                   from a neurological
                   accident.

CHAPTER 6

RECOMPRESSION CHAMBERS

The two compartment recompression chamber (or twin lock chamber as it is sometimes referred to, each compartment being a pressure lock) is the one most commonly used in air diving operations for surface decompression and therapeutic treatment. Twin lock chambers are required because they allow tending or medical personnel to enter and leave the chamber while maintaining pressure in the main compartment. Single lock chambers are no longer permitted under U.K. commercial regulations, except for emergency evacuation under pressure, most chambers are provided with a medical lock for passing in and out small objects, such as food and medical supplies. The basic components of a recompression chamber are much the same from one model to another, and certain design specifications apply to all commercially available air chambers.

They must be able to impose and maintain a pressure equivalent to 50 MSW (6 bars absolute). All piping and valving should be arranged to permit control of the air supply and exhaust (for both compartments) from either the inside or the outside of the chamber. All lines should be identified and labelled to indicate, function, content, maximum pressure and direction of flow. Chamber doors should be fitted with DOGS or STRONG BACKS to prevent the doors opening while under pressure.

The optimum chamber ventilation requires maximum separation of the inlet and exhaust ports in the chamber. Exhaust ports should be guarded to prevent accidental body contact or objects being drawn into them when they are open. All chambers must be fitted with appropriate pressure guages outside the chamber. These gauges should be calibrated to read in metres of sea water (MSW), or feet of sea water (FSW) depending on the depths indicated in the tables being used. These gauges should be periodically calibrated by a competent person to ensure accuracy.

Chamber communications should be provided to both compartments by either an approved divers amplifier or a sound powered telephone. Because of the possibility of fire or explosion when working in an oxygen or compressed air atmosphere, all electrical wiring and equipment used must meet rigid specifications i.e. all wiring must be heavy duty, armoured or in a conduite. All switches must be located outside the chamber, internal lighting fixtures must be pressure proof, maximum 24v and should be permanently installed, flourescent tubes should never be used.

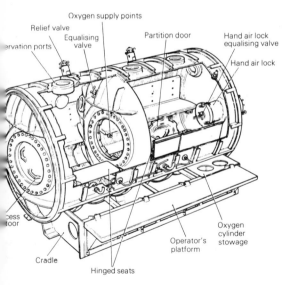

Fig. 6 -1 General view of a recompression chamber.

Both compartments of the chamber should be fitted with pressure relief valves set to the maximum working pressure of the chamber. The recompression chamber should be examined and tested according to current legislation. A specification plate should be affixed to the chamber indicating its maximum working pressure, test pressure and last date of hydrostatic test.

In order to achieve this in chambers which are regularly used for therapeutic recompression, the chamber should be fitted with an oxygen analysor. There are a number commercially available including, Servomex, and Beckman. They work by using oxygen's magnetic properties to measure the percentage of oxygen in a given mass of gas.

Chamber Gas Supply

A recompression treatment facility must have a primary and secondary air supply system which satisfies the following requirements:-

1. Primary - sufficient air to pressurise the chamber twice to 50 M.S.W., and ventilate throughout the treatment.

2. Secondary - sufficient air to pressurise the chamber once to 50 M.S.W., and ventilate for one hour.

Either system must consist of an air bank or suitable compressor, or both, providing air to diving purity standards (see chapter 7).

The recompression chamber should be equipped with a means of delivering breathing oxygen to a patient in the main compartment. It may be useful if the oxygen can also be provided to the outer lock where it will help with the decompression of tenders who are leaving the chamber before the patient has been fully decompressed. The inner lock should be provided with connections for three or four demand type oxygen inhalators, (B.I.B.S., Built In Breathing System). In some chambers this system is fitted with an overboard dump for this exhaled gas.

When breathing oxygen in a chamber the percentage of oxygen in the atmosphere of the chamber must not exceed 25%.

Fig 6-2 A diver carrying out decompression, note the B.I.B.S. system.

If this is not available the chamber should be ventilated with fresh air approximately 5 minutes in every 15 minutes when using air. 3 minutes in every 5 minutes when using oxygen.

Preperation of the Chamber

The recompression chamber, like any piece of emergency equipment, must be kept in immediate readiness. The chamber must be in good repair, well maintained, in test and equipped with all necessary ancillary equipment. A chamber is not a spares compartment for use as a dormitory or dry store.

The chamber and the air and oxygen supply should be checked prior to use and on a regular basis in accordance with current regulations. A chamber check list has been compiled for your use Fig. 6-4.

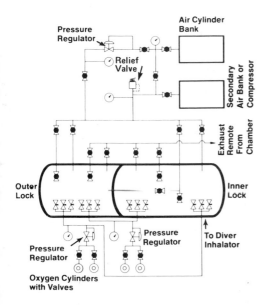

Fig. 6-3 Recompression chamber gas supply schematic.

All diving personnel must be trained in the operation of the chamber.

The greatest single hazard in the use of a recompression chamber is from explosive fire. Fire will propagate more than 2 to 6 times faster under hyperbaric conditions due to the high partial pressures of oxygen in the chamber atmosphere.

The following precautions must be taken to minimise fire hazard:-

1. Remove any fittings or equipment which do not conform with the standard requirements for electrical systems (as previously described) or which are made of any flammable materials. Permit no wooden deck grating or shelving in chamber. Replace them with metal or other fire proof materials.

2. Equip the chamber with flame proof bedding, if a mattress is used, ensure it is completely enclosed in a flame proof cover. Do not put any more bedding in a chamber than is necessary for the comfort of the occupants, and never use blankets of nylon or synthetic fibre because of the possibility of sparks from static electricity.

3. Only fire retardent paint may be used in a chamber and the minimun coats applied for satisfactory maintenance. If there is any doubt as to the type of paint that has previously been used, the chamber should be cleaned down to base metal and repainted. After painting, do not use the chamber until it is thoroughly dry and all volatile vapours have been removed.

4. Keep oil and volatile materials out of the chamber. If any have been used ensure that the chamber is thoroughly ventilated before pressurisation. Do not put oil on or in any fittings or high pressure line: and if for any reason oil is spilled in the chamber or soaked into any chamber surface or equipment, it must be completely removed. If lubricants are required i.e. for door seals etc., only approved lubricants such as MS4 silicone compound should be used.

TABLE Fig. 6-4

RECOMPRESSION CHAMBER CHECKOUT PROCEDURE

Prior to each recompression treatment, and at monthly intervals, the following checkout should be conducted:

CHAMBER

1. ☐ Clean

2. ☐ Free of all extraneous gear

3. ☐ Free of noxious odours and/or contaminants

4. ☐ Medical kit stocked and accessible

5. ☐ Doors and door seals undamaged, properly installed and lubricated

VENTILATION SYSTEM

1. ☐ Valves checked

AIR SUPPLY

1. ☐ Primary supply; enough air to pressurize chamber to working pressure twice.

2. ☐ Secondary supply operational

3. ☐ Fittings tight, filters clean, valves properly positioned, gauges calibrated.

OXYGEN SUPPLY

1. ☐ Cylinders full and identified as "breathing oxygen"

2. ☐ Masks installed; inhalators functioning

3. ☐ Fittings tight, filters clean, valves properly positioned, gauges calibrated

4. ☐ Oxygen elimination system, if installed, operational. (overboard dump)

ELECTRICAL SUPPLY

1. ☐ Lights operative

2. ☐ Properly grounded; wiring approved

3. ☐ Monitoring equipment calibrated and operational

COMMUNICATION SYSTEM

1. ☐ Primary system operational

2. ☐ Secondary system operational

FIRE PREVENTION SYSTEM

1. ☐ Extinguishing system, if installed, charged and operational

2. ☐ Water and sand buckets in chamber

3. ☐ All combustile material enclosed in fireproof jackets

4. ☐ No chemical fire extinguishers inside chamber

Regularly inspect and clean air filters and accumulators in the air supply lines to protect against the introduction of oil or other vapours into the chamber. Permit no one to wear oily clothing into the chamber.

5. No toxic chemicals must be allowed into the chamber or equipment containing them i.e. mercury thermometers.
No toxic chemicals should be used to clean the chamber i.e. Vim, Domestos etc., only Panacide or other odourless cleaners should be used.

6. Never permit anyone to carry smoking materials, matches or lighters into the chamber, even if he does not intend to use them. A warning sign (Fig. 6-5) should be posted inside and outside the chamber.

7. The chamber must be equipped with appropriate fire-fighting materials such as buckets of water and sand. Fire extinguishers containing carbon tetrachloride, CO_2, or dry powder must never be used. These chemicals are toxic in confined, pressurised atmospheres.

**WARNING
FIRE/EXPLOSION HAZARD**
No matches, lighters,
electrical appliances
or flammable materials
permitted in chamber

Fig. 6-5 Fire/Explosion Warning Sign for recompression chamber.

Chamber Ventilation

Where no regeneration equipment is fitted to the chamber it must be flushed through periodically in order to keep the level of carbon dioxide to a minimum and top up the consumed oxygen. Where oxygen is being used by the patient, flushing through removes again excess carbon dioxide and also keeps the oxygen percentage below 25%.

Flushing Through

Air is allowed to enter the chamber through the inlet valve. While a constant pressure is maintained in the chamber by allowing the same amount of gas to escape through the exhaust valve. As mentioned earlier, for this to be most effective, the inlet and outlet valves should be seperated as much as possible inside the chamber. Care must be taken to ensure no alteration of chamber depth occurs during this operation.

Notes on Chamber Ventilation-

1. Ventilation should take place to assure that the effective concentration of carbon dioxide will not exceed 1.5 percent (11.4 mmHg) and that when oxygen is being used, the true percentage of oxygen in the chamber will not exceed 25 percent. If continuous analysis of oxygen is available, the chamber should be ventilated to keep the oxygen percentage below 22.5 percent in order to reduce fire hazard.

2. Determine the necessary valve settings for the selected flows and depths by using the chamber itself as a measuring vessel with the help of a stopwatch.

3. There is seldom any danger of having too little oxygen in the chamber. Even with no ventilation and a high carbon dioxide level, the oxygen present would be ample for a long time.

4. Coming up to the next stop reduces the standard cubic metres of gas in the chamber and proportionally reduces the quantity of air required for ventilation.

5. Continuous ventilation is by far the most efficient method of ventilation in terms of the amount of air required for ventilation. However, it has the disadvantage of exposing the men in the chamber to a constant source of noise. At the very high ventilation rates required for oxygen breathing, this noise can reach the ranges where hearing loss becomes a real hazard to the men in the chamber. If high sound levels do occur, especially during exceptionally high ventilation rates, the men in the chamber must wear ear protectors similar to those used in aviation on flight decks. The only modification which these items require is a small hole drilled into the central cavity so that they do not produce a seal which could cause an ear squeeze.

6. Note that the size of the chamber does not influence the amount of air required for ventilation.

7. Note also that increasing depth increases the actual mass of air required for ventilation; but when the amount of air is expressed in volumes as measured as chamber pressure, increasing depth **does** not change the number of actual cubic metres required.

Overboard Dump

The term overboard dump refers to a means of evacuating the divers expired air from the B.I.B.S. system without introducing it into the chamber atmospheres.

This is used extensively in chambers requiring long oxygen therapies where continual flushing through to limit the amount of oxygen in the chamber atmosphere is undesirable.

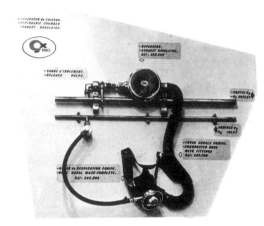

Fig. 6-6 Comex pro overboard dump assembly.

Chamber Pressure Test

Under British regulations chambers must undergo a pressure test upon the following:-

1. Its initial installation.
2. After it has been altered or repaired.
3. In any event not more than three months before it is used.
4. Every two years it must be subjected to a complete survey and air pressure leak test.
5. Every five years it must be hydrostatically tested and the chamber must be stamped with the test date.

RULES FOR CHAMBER OPERATION

ALWAYS

1. Take all precautions against fire.

2. Provide water and sand buckets.

3. Use fire retardant paint and materials in the chamber.

4. Ventilate the chamber according to specified rates.

5. Assure proper decompression of all personnel entering the chamber.

6. Ensure that the chamber and its auxilliary equipment is in operational condition at all times.

7. Ensure that all personnel are trained in operation of equipment and are able to do any job required in treatment.

8. Prepare the chamber for immediate re-use following a treatment.

NEVER

1. Use oil on any oxygen fitting or piece of equipment.

2. Allow **air** supply tanks to be depleted or reach low capacity.

3. Allow damage to door seals and dogs.

4. Allow open flames, matches, cigarette lighters or pipes to be carried into the chamber.

5. Permit electrical appliances to be used in the chamber.

CHAPTER 7

AIR DIVING EQUIPMENT

Figure 7-1 Commerical diver dressed in neoprene dry-suit, safety harness, heavy-duty weight belt, shallow water boots, and neck ring, dam and jocking strap for surface supply helmet, with inverted bale-out cylinder.

The selection of the correct equipment for the completion of any underwater task is of paramount importance.

Considerations such as depth, duration, location of worksite and tools to be used should be carefully considered.

Outlined in this chapter are two main categories of air diving equipment, which are:-

(1) S.C.U.B.A. (Self contained under-
    water breathing apparatus).
(2) Surface supplied.

Surface supplied diving may be further categorised as:-

(a) Surface supplied, free flow equipment.
(b) Surface demand equipment.

BREAKDOWN OF EQUIPMENT (SCUBA)

Every Scuba set will include the following basic components:-

1. Demand regulator assembly.

2. One or more air cylinders.

3. Cylinder valve, and reserve manifold.

4. Back pack or harness.

DEMAND REGULATOR ASSEMBLY

The purpose of the regulator is to reduce the high pressure air in the cylinders to a pressure which can be used by the diver, and to deliver the air as required at a sufficient flow rate.

The specific operation of the demand unit may vary from one type of regulation or to another, but the basic principle is the same for all.

There are three main types of regulator commercially available, these are:-

1. Single stage, twin hose regulator.

2. Two stage, twin hose regulator.

3. Two stage, single hose regulator.

The last of these, the two stage, single hose regulator is the one most commonly used today.

This is the regulator used by Prodive, and this will be the only one dealt with in this manual.

In the first stage, high pressure air from the cylinder passes through a regulator, which reduces the pressure to a level approximately 8 to 11 bars above ambient (this figure varies between manufacturers).

In the second stage, water at ambient pressure acts directly on one side of a moveable diaphragm. A low pressure air chamber is situated on the other side.

The diaphragm is directly linked to a low pressure valve, by a lever mechanism. When the air pressure in the low pressure chamber equals the ambient water pressure, the diaphragm is in its central position and the valve is closed. When the diver "demands" air, the suction produced by his lungs reduces the pressure in the low pressure chamber, causing the diaphragm to be pushed inwards by the now higher ambient water pressure. The diaphragm actuates the low pressure valve, which opens and permits air to flow to the diver, the larger the breath the wider the low pressure valve is opened, allowing more air to flow.

When the diver stops inhaling, the pressure on either side of the diaphragm is again balanced and the low pressure valve closes. As the diver exhales, the exhaust air passes through one or more "mushroom" valves and vents into the water.

SINGLE HOSE REGULATOR

In the single hose, two stage regulator the first stage is mounted on the air cylinder just after the cylinder valve. The second stage unit is located at the diver's mouth. The two stages are connected by a length of durable, flexible medium pressure hose, which passes over the diver's right shoulder.

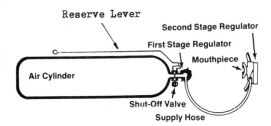

Figure 7-2. Schematic of single hose, two-stage demand regulater SCUBA.

The second stage also contains a purge valve, which when pressed passes the medium pressure air through the stage and the mouth piece, blowing out any water which may have entered the system. This "purging" feature is one of the several advantages which the single hose system has over the double hose. Other advantages include reduced drag in the water from the single, smaller, hose and less likelihood of it being damaged if snagged, also Buddy Breathing, whereby one diver provides air from his SCUBA set to another diver in an emergency is more easily accomplished using a single hose regulator.

The principle disadvantage of the single hose unit is that the exhaust bubbles may rise in front of the diver's face, interfering with his vision. Another disadvantage is that when using it in arctic conditions it is susceptible to freezing up. Some manufacturers, including 'Poseidon' have overcome this by fitting a 'silicone' filled cap over the first stage, but it is not recommended that single hose regulators be used for sub-zero diving without modification.

FIRST STAGE VALVE ASSEMBLY (UNBALANCED)

There are two main methods of achieving medium pressure air from high pressure via the first stage, these are:-

1. Diaphragm.
2. Piston.

SECOND STAGE VALVE ASSEMBLY

There are two main types of second stage valve assembly which differ in the direction in which they operate, they are:

1. Upstream.
2. Downstream.

Figure 7-3 shows a single hose demand valve with a diaphragm-action, first stage and an upstream 'tilt valve', second stage.

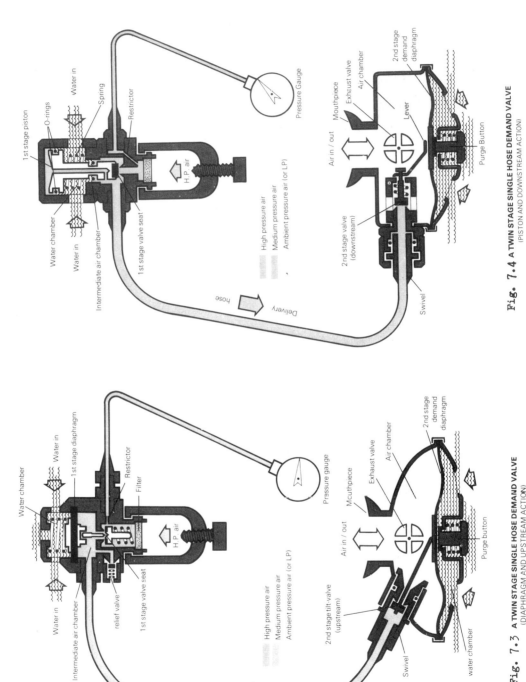

Fig. 7.3 A TWIN STAGE SINGLE HOSE DEMAND VALVE
(DIAPHRAGM AND UPSTREAM ACTION)

Fig. 7.4 A TWIN STAGE SINGLE HOSE DEMAND VALVE
(PISTON AND DOWNSTREAM ACTION)

The tilt valve is so named because movement of the second stage diaphragm does not lift the valve head off its seat, but instead tilts it to one side.

Figure 7-4 shows a single hose valve which has a piston action first stage with a downstream second stage. The piston is the only moving part within the first stage. The spring plus water pressure pushes on the underside of the piston head, lifts the stem off the valve seat. Air then flows through the orifice and into the hose. The piston stem is hollow and so air pressure is also transmitted to the top of the piston head. When the pressure has reached a pre-set level, it will overcome the combined spring and water pressure and the piston will move down to close the valve.
(NOTE: The intermediate pressure working over the large diameter of the piston head will easily overcome the much higher pressure trying to flow through the small diameter orifice).
The piston head and stem are sealed with "O"-rings and may also incorporate plastic wiper rings.

The downstream second stage consists of a spring-loaded valve sealing against the valve seat. Movement of the lever, initiated by the diaphragm, lifts the valve to admit air to the mouthpiece.
NOTE: For ease of breathing, the air flow from the demand valve should be self-sustaining to minimise effort. Valves are constructed so that the incoming air is blown into the delivery hose as a fast moving "jet", thus creating a Venturie effect. The velocity of the air causes a partial vacuum which sucks more air from the chamber thus sustaining the flow. Without the venturie effect the diver would have to suck for the entire inhalation.

BALANCED DEMAND VALVES

To achieve a balanced condition it is essential that both ends of the valve head be exposed to identical pressure.

Figure 7-5 shows a balanced first stage valve. Cylinder pressure is introduced at the side of the control valve. The valve head seals against the orifice, and that portion of the valve head actually over the orifice is exposed to the interstage pressure. To counteract this, the stem of the valve head is led back into a small chamber which is also open to the interstage pressure. The effect of cylinder pressure on the valve head has been neutralised.

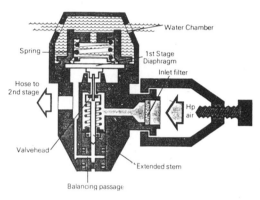

Figure 7-5. A BALANCED (diaphragm) FIRST STAGE.

Figure 7-6 shows a through piston balanced first stage. Characteristically the high pressure air from the cylinder

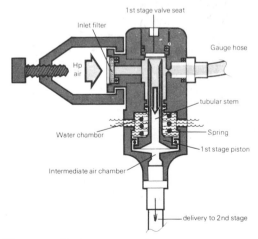

Figure 7-6. A BALANCED (piston) FIRST STAGE

enters at the side of the piston stem, rather than "end-on" as in the unbalanced version already described.

MOUTHPIECE

The size and design of the Scuba mouthpiece differs little between manufacturers. Figure 7-7 shows how it should be held in the mouth.

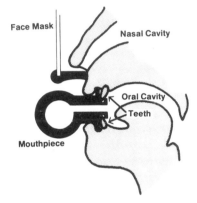

Fig 7-7

AUXILLIARY PRESSURE TAPPING

It is usual for two or sometimes three hose outlets to be tapped into the chamber cap to supply intermediate air to ancilliary devices such as dry suit inflation of life jacket and H.P. air to a contents gauge.

The majority of these buoyancy compensating devices are designed to be supplied with air be means of an intermediate pressure take-off from the demand valve first stage. The supply hose will have some form of quick-release coupling which operates successfully even though the hose is pressurised and these couplings will in reach of the diver should he wish to disconnect it without assistance. The hose is also fitted with a non-return valve which will prevent air from escaping while disconnected.

POROSINT OR SINTERED FIRST STAGE FILTER

A sintered filter which is measured in microns (usually 50 micron) and is constructed of welded bronze balls which are sintered onto a mesh backing is situated in the first stage inlet and is used to filter the H.P. air from the cylinder. They are easily replaceable and should be regularly inspected and changed if necessary.

MAINTENANCE

A diver's life depends upon efficient performance of his demand valve. This finely engineered device is sensitive to wear and tear and corrosion of its internal parts. It is, therefore, imperative that it receives care and regular servicing. ALWAYS wash a regulator in fresh water after use and hang it up to dry.

AIR CYLINDERS

The Scuba set consists of one or more H.P. cylinders. If more than one is used they are joined together using a manifold.

A high pressure air cylinder is a potentially dangerous piece of equipment and is subject to regulations of specification during manufacture.

All countries have regulations affecting the use of high pressure cylinders, and these can vary from country to country. Anomalies can arise where a cylinder is perfectly acceptable in its country of origin but not in another. Whilst international discussions are being held to rationalise this situation, it will be some time before a state of uniformity is reached.

Until this situation is rectified cylinders must adhere to the regulations in force in the country in which they are being used.

U.K. REGULATIONS

In the United Kingdom, the health and safety executive (H.S.E.) (Explosives Branch) is responsible for the approval of specifications to which all types of gas cylinders are manufactured, and for regulations concerning their use. The regulations affecting the use of diving cylinders are:-

The gas cylinder (conveyance) regulations Numbers 679 (1931), 1594 (1947) and 1919 (1959).

These regulations permit only cylinders manufactured to the following specifications to be used for the conveyance of compressed air in the U.K.

(1) British Standards Institute Specification 399,400 and 1045.

(2) Air Ministry Specification 0.133 (exemption order).

(3) H.S.E. specification, H.O.S. and H.O.T. (steel cylinders).

(4) H.S.E. specification, H.O.A.L 1, 2, and 4 aluminium cylinders.

The three British Standards Institute specifications (1) are intended for heavy industrial cylinders and are not likely to be encountered in diving sets, although they may appear in storage banks. The exemption order on Air Ministry specification 0.133 is a wartime relic and H.S.E. no longer approves their use.

Acceptable specifications for steel diving cylinders are the H.S.E., H.O.S. and H.O.T. specifications.

Aluminium cylinders are covered by H.S.E. specifications, H.O.A.L. 1, 2 and 4. 3 is not suitable for diving sets.

Confirmation that a cylinder has been manufactured to an approved specification is a guarantee of its soundness at the time of manufacture.

These specifications stipulate the composition of the metal and define the minimum wall thickness of the cylinder in relation to the pressure and diameter. Stringent tests are laid down, which must be carried out during the manufacture of each batch of cylinders, culminating in an hydraulic stretch test for every cylinder.

All cylinders carry the following markings:-

(1) Manufacturer's marks and serial number.

(2) Specification (e.g. H.O.S. or H.O.A.L 2).

(3) Date of manufacture and test.

(4) Water capacity (W.C.) and cylinder weight. (not normally shown on aluminium cylinders).

(5) Working pressure (W.P.) and test pressure (T.P.).

(6) Marks and dates of subsequent tests.

These markings may be on the shoulder of the cylinder or on a brass collar around its neck. The charging and testing pressures are determined at the time of manufacture, and cannot be altered subsequently. The water capacity is a measurement of the internal volume of the cylinder expressed as the weight or volume of water it will contain.

CARE AND MAINTENANCE

Corrosion is the main enemy of cylinders and yet simple precautions will avoid most of the ill effects. Most diving is carried out in salt water and all diving equipment should be thoroughly washed in fresh water.

Remove cylinder boots periodically and wash out the accumulated salt and silt; do the same with localised corrosion to the cylinder by trapping mineral particles in contact with the cylinder. Aluminium cylinders are especially susceptible to electrolytic corrosion if a stainless steel harness band is left in place for long periods.

Figure 7-8 A diver undergoes a checkout just prior to a dive.

Keep cylinders painted to identify their contents. British H.S.E. regulations require compressed air cylinders to be painted grey with black and white quaters. Zinc spraying of steel cylinders is a very good pre-treatment for painting, some American cylinders are even hot dipped galvanised.

Dry, pure air and regular inspection are the surest protection against internal corrosion. It is recommended that all cylinders undergo internal visual inspection once a year. Cylinders should not be stored in a fully charged state for long periods. The high partial pressure of oxygen can lead to accelarated corrosion if there is any water present. Neither should they be left completely with the valve open, the cylinder will "breath" and any changes in temperature will result in condensation inside the cylinder.

CYLINDER TESTING

In the United Kingdom it is a health and safety executive requirement that all cylinders used for the conveyance of high pressure gases be subjected to periodic inspection and hydraulic testing. While the law requires tests at five year intervals, in the case of aqualung cylinders, the H.S.E. recommends a test interval of three years from the date of manufacture and every two years thereafter.

The test pressure for a cylinder is deter-mined at the time of manufacture and is stamped on the cylinder. The precise value varies according to the specification, type and size of the cylinder, but is approximately $1\frac{1}{3}$ (steel) to $1\frac{2}{3}$ (aluminium) times the working pressure.

During its statutory test the cylinder is first inspected externally for damage, corrosion or unauthorised repair - such as welding. The cylinder markings are checked to establish the specification and its correct test pressure.

After removal of the pillar valve, the cylinder is internally inspected. A light bloom of rust in steel is not in itself casue for rejection, but heavy pitting or localised pitting may be. Light rust may be removed by rumbling, i.e. partially filling the cylinder with cracked shot and them rotating it continuously for several hours.

HYDRAULIC STRETCH TEST

For the hydraulic stretch test the cylinder is completely filled with water and connected to a high pressure hydraulic pump. It is then pressurised to its stamped test pressure, and its volumetic pressure is released, and if the cylinder is in good condition it will return to its original size. As the cylinder ages the metal becomes less "elastic" and does not return to its original size. This residual expansion - known as <u>permanent set</u> - is also measured, and the H.S.E. regulations state that the permanent set must not exceed 10% of the expansion measured at the test pressure. If it exceeds this it indicates that the metal has lost its <u>ductility</u>, or perhaps because of **corrosion**, has developed a **weakness**.

The main method of hydraulically testing a cylinder is by <u>jacketed testing</u> Figure 7-9 shows a typical jacketed testing rig.

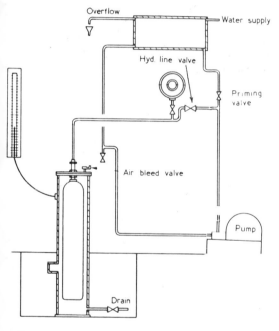

Figure 7-9. Water-jacket volumetric expansion test (fixed burette method)

In this method the water filled cylinder is immersed in another water filled container. This is the <u>jacket</u>. The jacket is not pressurised and, although sealed with a lid, is open to atmospheric pressure via a calibrated sight tube.

The cylinder is pressurised via the pump. As the cylinder expands it displaces water from the jacket which is measured on the <u>sight tube</u>. When the pressure is released the sight tube reading will indicate any permanent set in the cylinder.

CERTIFICATE AND STAMPING

The inspection company should issue a test certificate for each cylinder. This certificate should identify the cylinder by specification and serial number. It should show the relevant charging and test pressures, the amount of permanent set encountered, and comment on the internal condition of the cylinder.

The cylinder must be stamped with the date of the test which may be shown as month and year or quarter and year. The stamping should be <u>only</u> on the <u>shoulder</u> or <u>neck ring</u> of the cylinder, never on the side.

INFLATION CYLINDERS

No regulations at present require cylinders used for suit inflation or adjustable buoyancy life jackets (A.B.L.J's) to be tested, although they possibly have the hardest life of all air cylinder. Because of constant filling and decanting they quickly become corroded internally and externally. It is recommended that they should be subjected to the same inspection and testing procedures as aqualung cylinders.

PILLAR VALVES

Pillar valves are generally of three types, these are:-

(1) Unbalanced
(2) Glandless
(3) Balanced

The pillar valve can be secured into the bottle by either a <u>taper thread</u> or a <u>parallel thread</u> sealed with an "O" ring.

TAPER THREADS

At right angles to surface of cone At right angles to axis of cone

PARALLEL THREADS

Chamfer or recess for 'O' ring seal

Figure 7-10.

(a) Unbalanced

This is generally the commonest pattern of pillar valve. With this type the spindle and valve are in one piece and the spindle screws directly into the valve body.

The term 'unbalanced' means that the high pressure air is attempting to blow the valve head through the valve body.

This force has to be registered by the actual thread and hence will wear relatively quickly. Lack of lubrication will aggravate the condition. Once the screw thread is worn the complete pillar valve assembly must be replaced.

(b) Glandless

Although still an unbalanced valve, this type is more complex and has some advantages. In the first place the valve head does not rotate with the spindle, so there is less wear on the valve seat. Secondly, the high pressure air is prevented from escaping up the spindle by a 'bell' shaped diaphragm which is attached to the valve head. The actuating screw thread is contained in the cap nut, and being of larger diameter than in the design previously described, is not prone to wear. Even if the thread did seize it would only be necessary to replace the cap nut and spindle, not the whole valve. Thirdly, the top 'O' ring does not seal H.P. air, but serves as a wiper ring to prevent ingress of salt etc. into the screw thread.

(c) Balanced

Figure 7-12 shows the third type, the 'Balanced' valve. The valve head although separate from the spindle, still rotates

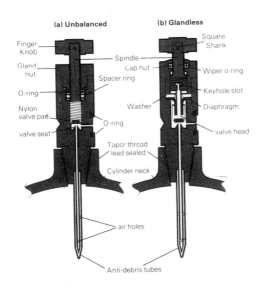

Figure 7-11.

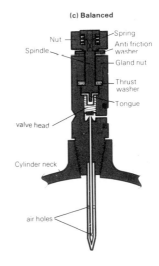

Figure 7-12

with it, being driven by a tongue and groove connection. This rotates the valve head but also allows it to move axially along the screw thread without the spindle following it. When the valve is 'open', the high pressure air flows past the thread of the valve head so that it is completely surrounded, with the result that there is no extra thrust exerted on the thread. Instead, this thrust is taken on a P.T.F.E.(Poly Tetra fluro ethylene) washer, situated behind the shoulder on the spindle. Since there is axial thrust on the valve head it is considered to be in a 'Balanced' condition.

ANTI-DEBRIS TUBE

This small tube extends from the base of all pillar valves into the cylinder. Its purpose being to prevent any loose debris or water present in the cylinder from entering the pillar valve should the cylinder be inverted. Any foreign matter present in the cylinder will lie harmlessly in the shoulder, while the air is drawn from a point above it.

RESERVE VALVES

For all commercial diving operations, the pillar valve unit (other than those used for surface supplied 'Bail out bottles' - see chapter 9) must contain an air reserve mechanism.

The most commonly used is a manually activated valve. There are other types, including an 'Automatic' design integral to the demand regulator, but these are not permitted because they do not provide a proper physical reserve function.

The air reserve mechanism serves two purposes:-

(1) It gives warning to the diver that his air supply is almost exhausted.

(2) Provides the diver with a quantity of reserve air, sufficient to enable him to reach the surface.

The usual air reserve mechanism contains a spring loaded check valve which will begin to close as the air pressure in the cylinder falls to a pre-determined level. On a single cylinder this is usually 30-50 bars, on twin cylinders 60-80 bars. (A reserve mechanism is normally only fitted to one cylinder of a 'twin set', hence when the reserve is activated the air will decant into both cylinders, causing a subsequent drop in pressure.)

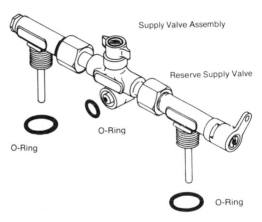

Figure 7-13. High pressure manifold.

As this valve slowly closes, the air flow is reduced and the diver will soon find breathing increasingly more difficult. As soon as he notices this increased resistance to breathing, he should locate the reserve lever on the side of his Scuba set and 'pull' it into the down position which will open the reserve valve, making the reserve air available to him.
Note: Care must be taken throught the dive to ensure the reserve lever is not accidentally displaced.

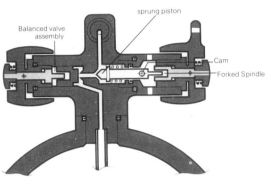

Figure 7-14. Reserve valve.

BACKPACK SCUBA HARNESS

A variety of 'Back Pack' or cylinder harnesses used to hold the Scuba bottle(s) on the diver's back have been developed. The harness may include a light weight frame with the cylinder(s) held in place with clamps or straps (not of quick release type). The most common system for holding the unit on the diver uses shoulder and waist straps. All straps have a quick release feature, easily operated by either hand.

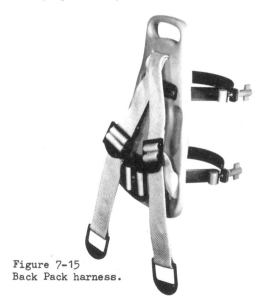

Figure 7-15
Back Pack harness.

SURFACE DIVING HARNESS

Another type of cylinder harness which also incorporates a safety harness and weight 'pockets' is one which has become increasingly popular for commerical use. Figure 7-16 shows a typical surface diving harness showing the parachute safety harness and 'quick' release weight pockets.

Figure 7-16 Bell diving harness with weights held in pockets.

SAFETY HARNESS

The diver's safety harness contructed of webbing and provided with welded 'D' ring attachment points for the diver's life line should be worn under all other diving equipment. There are a number of designs currently in use, but, however they are constructed they must be able to lift the diver 'bodily' from the water. Fig. 7-17 shows the diver's safety harness used by Prodive.

Figure 7-17 Surface diving harness

FACE MASK

The face mask or half mask primarily protects the diver's eyes and nose from the water. As a secondary function it provides maximum visibility by putting a layer of air between the lens of the eye and the water, thus permitting the eye to focus on the transmitted images. This feature, however, is only minor in comparison to the psychological value of protecting the eyes and nose from the water.

Figure 7-17a Two types of diving half-masks.

Face masks are available in a variety of shapes and sizes. A diver should select the style which makes a seal and feels comfortable on his face.

Proper fit can be checked in two steps -

(1) Holding the mask in place with one hand, inhale gently through the nose and let go of the mask. It should stay in place, held by the suction.

(2) Put the mask on as it will be worn, with the head strap properly adjusted, and again inhale gently through the nose. If the mask seals, it should provide a good seal in the water.

Some masks are equipped with a one-way purge valve to aid in clearing the mask of water, and some masks have 'indents' at the nose or a neoprene nose pad to allow the diver to pinch off his nostrils to equalize the pressure in his ears and sinuses. Several models are available for divers who wear eyeglasses. One type provides a prescription-ground faceplate, while another type has special holders for separate lenses. Selection of a mask with 'special features' is a matter of personal preference or need. There is, however, one firm requirement which must be met in any face mask: the faceplate must be constructed of tempered or shatter-proof safety glass. Faceplates made of ordinary glass are a serious hazard to the eyes. Plastic faceplates, which are shatter-proof, are generally unsuitable because they fog too easily in use and are easily scratched.

The size or shape of the faceplate is another matter of personal choice, but the diver should seek a mask which provides the widest clear range of vision. Note: It should be emphasised that the provision of a 'purge valve' in the face mask should not override the requirement to teach the diver the basic skill of clearing the face mask of water.

FULL FACE MASK

This type of mask encloses the whole face giving the diver more protection from contaminated water, cold, and allows the use of communications.

The demand valve mouth piece penitrates through the front of the mask and is held in the diver's mouth in the same way as for normal Scuba, except that when communications are fitted, the diver is able to remove the mouthpiece for short periods to talk.

There are two types used by Prodive:-

(1) Navy pattern "Avon" full face mask.

(2) Cressi full face mask.

AVON: Constructed of rigid rubber is held on the diver by a rubber "spider".

The mask has a glycerine filled face seal and perspex face plate which also forms part of the sides of the mask.

Figure 7-18 Comex-Pro band mask.

The mask can be fitted with either a single or twin hose regulator as required.

Ear equalisation is achieved using a detachable nose clip.

CRESSI:

A derivation of the 'Cressi sub' half mask. With the face seal extended to cover the mouth and chin.

The mask will accept most types of regulator mouth pieces.

The face plate is made of toughened glass and is interchangeable with the "Cressi Sub" half mask.

It is held on the diver's face using a "spider" in a similar manner to the Avon.

Ear equalisation is achieved using the contoured nose piece.

Figure 7-19 Cressi full face-mask.

WEIGHT BELT

A Scuba set is designed to have nearly neutral buoyancy when in the water. In general, a unit with full tanks tends to have negative buoyancy, becoming slightly positive as the air supply is consumed. Most divers are positively buoyant and need to add extra weight to achieve neutral or slightly negative status.

Figure 7-20 Typical weight-belts fitted with quick-release pins.

This extra weight is furnished by the use of a weighted belt, worn outside of all other equipment and strapped so that it can be easily ditched in the event of an emergency. The buckle must have a quick-release feature, easily operated by either hand; the weights (normally made of lead) should have smooth edges so as not to damage any protective clothing; the belt itself should be made of a rot and mildew resistant fabric, such as nylon webbing, or rubber.

As mentioned earlier this weight can alternatively be held in weight pockets attached to the diving harness. This allows more even distribution of weight over the shoulders and is much favoured by divers using neoprene dry suits because of the extra weight required with this type of suit.

KNIFE AND SCABBARD

A multitude of different types of knives are available. When choosing bear in mind that a diver's knife should be heavy and robust because it may be used for anything from a toothpick to a crowbar.

Knives are generally constructed of stainless steel to avoid corrosion. They may have single or double edged blades, the most useful type is one which has a normal knife edge on one side and a saw blade

on the other. All knives of whatever style must be kept sharp.

Figure 7-21 Two types of diving knife.

The knife, if not of the closing type, must be carried in a suitable scabbard, worn on the diver's safety harness or calf. The position being a matter of personal preference providing the knife is readily accessable. The scabbard should hold the knife in a positive, but easily released manner. Security of the knife can be augmented by the use of a neoprene knife band and the provision of a suitable landyard.

SWIMFINS

Fins increase the efficiency of the swimming diver, allowing him to move faster, further, and to swim with a low expenditure of energy.

Fins are manufactured from a variety of materials and in several styles. There are, however, two basic types:

1 Shoe Fitting. Soft braided type which are generally used by amateur divers over wet suit booties.

Figure 7-22 Full foot swim fins.

2 'Jetfins' or professional which
  are of much heavier construction and
  more robust. These are held in place
  by adjustable heel straps and are
  designed in larger sizes to fit over
  commercial diving suits. The type
  that is chosen is a matter of personal
  preference, although fins with small
  or very soft blades should be avoided.

LIFE JACKETS

For use only with 'wet suits' or dry
suits not fitted with suit inflation.
Life preservers used in diving generally
fall into two categories:

1 Surface life jacket (SLJ) A CO_2
  cartridge or orally inflated jacket.

  This type must only be used for
  additional surface bouyancy as no
  pressure relief valve is fitted to
  the jacket.

2 Adjustable Buoyancy Life Jacket (ABLJ)

  This type of jacket is designed
  primarily for diving and is inflated either by a small compressed

air cylinder attached to the jacket
or by a low pressure inflation
hose from the Scuba cylinder, or
in some cases both.

The jacket is fitted with an
automatic relief valve which can,
on some models, be manually operated.

Figure 7-23 This ABLJ has an air cylinder
mounted behind the jacket. An automatic
mouthpiece enables the air from the
cylinder to be breathed om an emergency
failure of the main air supply. A direct-
feed can easily be fitted for routine
bouyancy adjustment.

This type of life jacket is used
almost exclusively with wet suits for
commercial diving and unlike the Co2
cartridge type are designed to be
inflated underwater either in an
emergency or as a buoyancy aid.

NOTE: The jacket should be fitted to
the diver underneath all other equipment. The air cylinder should be
checked before every dive.

Buoyancy Compensator Pack (BCP) This is a life jacket/buoyancy compensator which is integrated with the harness back pack. It comprises a horseshoe-shaped buoyancy bag attached to the periphery of an aqualung. Inflation is either by direct feed or mouth, and the buoyancy bag has a pressure relief valve.

Most BCP's have an integral weight system similar to that mentioned under harnesses earlier.

DIVING SUITS

There are a considerable number of manufacturers producing suits in a variety of designs and materials to accommodate differing water temperatures and times of immersion. They follow, however, the following basic principles:

"WET" SUIT

This is a form fitting suit, usually made of closed cell neoprene. It is designed to permit a thin layer of water to be trapped next to the diver's skin where it is warmed by the heat of the body. Wet suits are available in a variety of thicknesses and generally the thicker the material, the better the insulation. However, as the diver descends and is subject to Boyle's Law, the gas in the neoprene will be compressed, considerably reducing the suit thickness and hence effectively reducing insulation.

Standard size suits, as well as custom fitted are available, the fit is of paramount importance for affording the diver protection. Although wet suits are useful for short durations at shallow depths they have disadvantages, which are:-

(1) Reduced thermal insulation at depth.

(2) They offer very little surface insulation from the elements.

(3) A bad fitting suit will be subject to a "flushing through" of cold water.

DRY SUIT

There are two main types of dry suit available. The object of both is to encase the diver's body in a warm, insulated environment.

"AVON" DRY SUIT

This suit which was originally developed for Navy use is constructed of canvas backed rubber and sealed at the wrist by a soft rubber "cuff", and at the neck by a detachable "neck seal".

Entry into the suit is achieved either through the neck's soft rubber "yoke" or by means of a waterproof zip fitted across the back of the shoulders.

Warm woollen underwear should be worn to increase thermal protection. This generally is in the form of a "woolly bear" one-piece undergarment.

Inflation of the suit either to prevent "squeeze" which occurs as the diver descends and the air in the suit is compressed, or, for surface support, can be achieved by either direct feed inflation via the Scuba set of a suit inflation cylinder (see Neoprene Dry Suits).

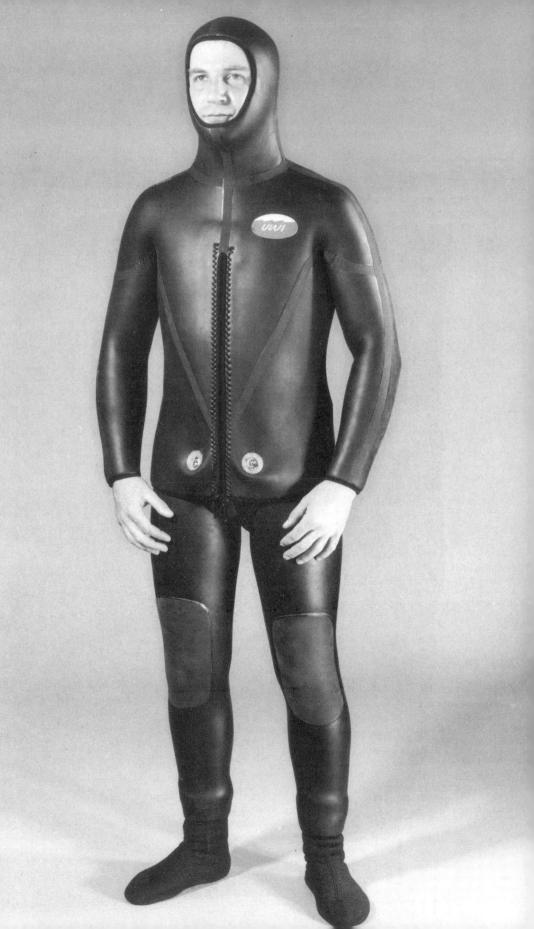

The disadvantages of this type of suit are:-

(1) The suit rubber has a limited life and eventually becomes porous.
(2) Should the suit become flooded it offers little thermal protection.
(3) Suits fitted with neck rings are uncomfortable to wear for long periods.

Figure 7-25. The Navy dry suit has a neck entry apperture, which is sealed with a neck seal, ring and clamp band.

NEOPRENE DRY SUIT ("UNISUIT")

The neoprene dry suit performs the same function as the Avon Dry Suit, except that the suit is constructed of closed cell neoprene which has a nylon lining on both sides. Neck and wrist seals are of single lined neoprene. The suit is entered by means of a waterproof, pressure proof zipper which either runs

(opposite) Figure 7-24 "WET SUIT"

from the chest level down around the crutch and up to the back of the neck, or across the back of the shoulders.

Figure 7-26 Neoprene dry-suit, with bale-out cylinder harness.

Inflation is controlled using an "inlet" and "outlet" valve normally fitted to the chest of the suit. Air is supplied from either a low pressure take-off from the first stage of the regulator or from a suit inflation cylinder mounted on the diver.

This type of suit offers greater protection from cold than do the other two suits previously mentioned. However, it does have certain disadvantages:-

(1) Because of its thick neoprene construction the amount of buoyancy given by the suit is significantly more. Therefore the diver must carry more weight to achieve neutral buoyancy.
(2) Again because they are constructed of neoprene and the seams are glued and

stitched they are generally more
difficult to maintain watertight.
Continual care and regular maintenance
are necessary.

All dry suits can be worn with hoods,
gloves, boots or fins as conditions
require. If the diver is working
in conditions where his suit could
become torn or punctured, he should be
provided with some additional protection in the form of coveralls or heavy
chaffing gear.

HOT WATER SUIT (OPEN CIRCUIT)

The hot water suit system comprises a
surface heat exchange unit to heat sea
or fresh water at temperatures up to
80 $^{\circ}$C and at flow rates up to 8 gallons
per minute. A supply hose to the diver
and a hot water suit constructed from
6mm chemically blown neoprene.

Hot water enters a supply manifold
located on the right hip of the suit
and is routed through tubes for even
distribution. The manifold normally
consists of three valves: A master
flow valve that also includes a bypass
feature to permit the diver to "dump"
water which is either too hot or too
cold, and two valves that permit
individual flow control to the front
and back torso. Hot water to the arms
and legs is controlled by the master
flow valve.

See following diagram.

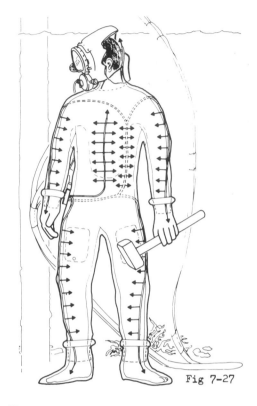

Fig 7-27

The suit is normally one piece and is
fitted with zippers on the front and
lower legs for ease of entry.

The booties are not integral with the
suit as hot water must be allowed to
escape to prevent an excessive amount
building up in the legs while out of the
water.

Tubes are provided to the wrists, feet
and neck to supply hot water to the
gloves, booties and hood as required.

Fig 7-27a. Hot water suit, with hose connection detail.

The suit is loose fitting to achieve the even distribution of water, and to allow the diver to wear a thin neoprene or nylon undersuit to protect him to some degree from excessively hot water, and in the event of hot water failure, offer him some thermal protection. This type of equipment is widely used for mixed gas diving and is very effective. However it does have some disadvantages:-

(1) High initial cost of equipment - the burner alone costs in excess of £10,000.
(2) Should the hot water supply fail the diver becomes chilled very quickly.
(3) Basic requirement for this suit is a large diameter hot water supply hose, which can be combersome in surface supplied diving.

(4) If the surface unit is not properly maintained and controlled the possibility of burning the diver may occur.
(5) Hot water contained within the suit makes the diver more susceptible to skin infections.

SUIT MAINTENANCE AND REPAIR

WET SUIT

Wet suits should be washed thoroughly in fresh water after use and hung up to dry. Zips should be greased with MS 4 silicone compound. For prolonged periods of storage, suits should not be hung on hangers - neatly fold and store out of direct sunlight.

REPAIR

Wash thoroughly in fresh water. Allow to dry. Repair using neoprene cement, trimming away old glue where possible. Repair should be allowed to cure for at least 24 hours. Repair should be taped with unbacked wet suit tape and lining stitched where possible.

"AVON" DRY SUIT

Dry suits should be washed thoroughly in fresh water after use and hung up to dry inside out if interior is also wet. Zips (where fitted) should be lubricated with beeswax or paraffin wax. Cuffs and neck seals should be dusted with french chalk. For prolonged periods of storage, suits should not be hung on hangers - neatly fold and store out of direct sunlight.

POROSITY TEST

If the suit is suspected of being _porous_ or has holes which are undetectable by normal immersion. A porosity test should be carried out as follows:-

- fit mandrels into the cuffs and neck and close waterproof zips if fitted.

- inflate suit using inflation cylinder or direct feed hose.
  NOTE: Do not over-inflate the suit as this could cause damage.

- cover suit in diluted washing-up liquid.

- examine suit carefully and mark any holes or areas of porosity with chalk.

- deflate suit, wash area to be repaired carefully and allow to dry thoroughly.

REPAIR

Repair suit using car inner tube patches and cement or proprietory "Avon" repair kit.

The area to be repaired must be cleaned using a degreasant and the suit material roughened. Two coats of adhesive should be applied and allowed to dry before attaching the patch. Once on the patch should be rolled.

Repair should be allowed where possible to cure for 24 hours.

NEOPRENE DRY SUIT

Neoprene dry suits should be washed thoroughly in fresh water after use and hung up to dry inside out if interior is also wet. Zips should be lubricated with beeswax or paraffin wax. Cuffs and neck seals should be sprayed with silicone compound or dusted with French chalk. For prolonged periods of storage suits should not be hung on hangers - neatly fold and store out of direct sunlight.

If the suit is suspected of being porous or has holes which are undetectable, a porosity test should be carried out as outlined in "Avon" dry suits.

REPAIR

Wash thoroughly in fresh water and allow to dry. Repair using neoprene cement, trimming away old glue where possible and stitch lining. Repair should be allowed to cure for at least 24 hours.
NOTE: Due to the problem experienced in some neoprene dry suits of leaking feet, it is advised that "overshoes" are worn whenever possible to reduce wear to this particularly vulnerable area.

HOT WATER SUITS

(As for wet suits)

Care should be taken to ensure the correct functioning of the manifold and condition of the coupling for the hot water hose.

HEATED UNDERSUITS

Electrical. Used extensively in the early seventies for short duration mixed gas diving. The suit consisted of a one piece under-garment normally worn under an "Avon" type dry suit and fitted with a matrix of small electrical resistance wires which cover the diver's body.

Power at approximately 14 volts D.C. is supplied via the diver's umbilical.

Experiments are continuing to improve the effeciency for modern application, however, their main disadvantages are:-

(1) They only provide a superficial heat over the diver's body.
(2) Where resistance wires become bunched, especially around the stomach, localised hot spots can develop.

CLOSED CIRCUIT HOT WATER UNDERSUITS

Originally designed for use from lock-out submersibles requiring independence from the surface. The suit which is similar to the electrical undersuit is fitted with a matrix of small tubes within which hot water is circulated.

The pump can either be mounted in the submersible and the suit fed via a supply and return hose, or, mounted on the diver. This type of suit although not as efficient as the open circuit hot water suit does have the advantage that should the hot water supply fail, the water within the suit will be retained.

Due to incidents where the open circuit hot water supply has been lost for many hours and the diving bell has remained on the seabed. This type of system has attracted much attention.

OPTIONAL EQUIPMENT

WRIST WATCH

Diving watches must be waterproof, pressureproof and equipped with a rotating bezel outside the dial which can be set to indicate the elapsed time of a dive. A luminous dial with large numerals is also necessary. Additional features such as automatic winding, non-magnetic components and stop watch action can be obtained.

A diver may select from a number commercially available, but there is no such thing as a cheap diving watch, and if a watch is to go underwater or in a recompression chamber, it must specifically be designed for this purpose.

The wrist watch should be worn on the same arm as the depth gauge since the functions of the two are so closely related in depth, time consideration of the dive.
NOTE: Watches for use in a helium environment must be specifically designed for this purpose. Some like Rolex are fitted with a helium relief valve, as this gas will find its way into even the best instruments.

DEPTH GAUGE

The depth gauge measures the pressure created by the water column above the diver, and is calibrated to provide a direct reading of the depth of water in either feet or meters. Depth gauges are designed to be read in conditions of limited visability, and should be worn on the wrist along side the watch. Three types are most commonly available, these are:-

(1) Capillary gauge or bathymeter
(2) Bourdon Tube
(3) Diaphragm Gauge

Capillary. A capillary or bathymeter is the simplest of all the gauges. It is a thin column of air, sealed at one end with the other end open to the water. When the gauge is submerged water enters the tube and subject to Boyle's Law the air contained in the tube is compressed. As can be seen from the diagram Figure 7-28 that the scale on the gauge is non-linear and the graduations at depth become small. It is, however, useful at shallow depths, and very accurate.

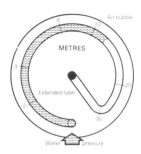

Fig 7-28 Capillary Gauge

BOURDON TUBE This is a curved metal
tube, sealed at one end, which attempts
to straighten itself as pressure is
increased within it. A linkage is
attached to its closed end, thus moving
a needle over a dial, indicating
pressure/depth.

There are three main types of depth
gauges incorporating this principle
these are:-

Open Bourdon Tube The Bourdon Tube
is fitted into a rigid and sealed case,
one end of which is fixed and open to
the water, the other is free to move as
water pressure is transmitted along it.

Being open to the water, this gauge can
be susceptible to internal corrosion
and silting and must be washed in fresh
water after use.

Sealed Bourdon Tube The sealed Bourdon
Tube was developed to overcome the
problems of silting and corrosion
experienced with the open tube variety.

This gauge is fundamentally the same,
but the tube is oil-filled and
separated from the water by a rubber
diaphragm. The pressure from the
water is transmitted through the
diaphragm into the oil and the
pressure of oil in the tube begins to
straighten it and moves the pointer.

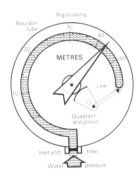

Fig 7-29 Open Bourdon Tube Gauge

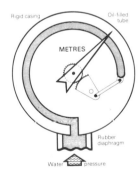

Fig 7-30 Sealed Bourdon Tube Gauge

NOTE: Do not mistake the gauge for a
diaphragm gauge, it is primarily a
Bourdon Tube.

Enclosed Bourdon Tube. This gauge is sometimes referred to as an "oil-filled" gauge and is probably the most popular type currently in use.

The Bourdon Tube is air-filled at atmospheric pressure and is sealed at both ends. The tube and mechanism are mounted in a pliable case which is filled with oil. When submerged pressure is applied through the rubber case to the Bourdon Tube, causing it to move the pointer.

Figure 7-31. Enclosed Bourdon Tube Gauge.

Diaphragm Gauge. The gauge comprises a thin metal diaphragm mounted in a rigid hermetically sealed case with most of the air surrounding the mechanism and face having been removed to create a partial vacuum.

When submerged the water enters through large holes in the back of the case and presses on the diaphragm. This is transmitted to a toothed quadrant which moves the pointer.

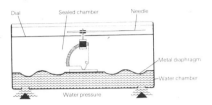

Figure 7-32. Diaphragm gauge.

"Micro chip" technology has produced the latest addition to the range of depth gauges available. As yet comparatively new and expensive it has a pressure sensor giving a digital read-out and is battery powered.

Whichever type of gauge is chosen, it must be accurate over all depth ranges. Decompression, especially using U.S.N. tables relies heavily on accurate speed of ascent and stop depth.

A secondary method of checking the diver's depth such as a lead line, lazy shot or pneufathomometer is recommended.

THE MAGNETIC COMPASS

A small magnetic compass, worn on the wrist or attached to a swim board is commonly used as an aid to underwater navigation. Such a compass is not particularly accurate, but can be of great value, especially under conditions of poor visability.

Wrist compasses must be pressure proof and preferably "oil" filled to dampen the needle sufficiently to remove undue movement.

It should have a clearly marked direction of travel and some means of
ensuring that the predetermined course
is followed. This facility is normally
provided by a rotating "bezel" with
prominent marks or "lubber" lines.

Compasses usually have an outer scale
which is calibrated through 0° - 360°.
It should be noted that on some
compasses the calibrations are in
reverse, i.e. instead of going clock-
wise from 0° - 360° the figures are
set anti-clockwise. Thus, the magnetic
north pointer will indicate the bearing
on which the diver is travelling
(Figure 7-33) rather than the bearing
from which he has come.

Figure 7-33a **Underwater compass**
Figure 7-33b **Depth gauge**

Figure 7-34.   Swim board instrument panel.

SURFACE MARKER FLOAT

The surface marker float consists of a
200mm expanded polystyrene sphere with a
wooden stave passed through the centre
extending approximately 150mm each side.

The float line of small (4-5mm) diameter
terylene or nylon rope, is also passed
through the float and made fast to its
own part. Its length can then be adjusted
by figure-of-eight turns round the float,
the rope being finally secured at the
required length by a clove hitch on the
protruding stave.

Figure 7.35 Surface marker float, with
method of stowing line.

The diver's end of the float line should
be secured to the left chest "D"-ring of
the safety harness.

For recognition purposes, floats should be
brightly coloured and at night should be
fitted with an indicating light.

BUDDYLINES

When two or more divers are being prepared
to operate as a pair on a single surface
marker float or life line, a Buddyline is
used to join them together.

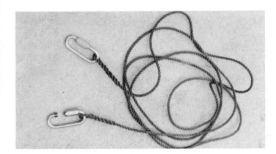

Figure 7-36. Buddyline Span.

The Buddyline is constructed of 5mm line, approximately 2-4 metres in length and provided with an inglefield clip at each end to secure the line to the diver's safety harness, in this way two or three divers may retain in physical contact and life line signals may be relayed.

INDICATING LIGHT

A diving indicating light, operated by the diver is to be worn during all night diving operations.

The light should be securely fixed to the divers safety harness and turned on while the diver is on the surface.

Those commercially available are normally battery powered and are of the flashing type (Strobe light).

Figure 7-36b Diver's hand-held lamps, with waterproof switch and sealed beam unit. Suitable for the air range only.

Figure 7-36c KMB-16 Superlite diving helmet

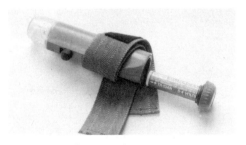

Figure 7-36a Diver's indicating strobe, showing internal battery.

AQUADYNE HELMET A.H. 2

PRINCIPLE OF OPERATION:

The Aquadyne diving helmet is designed to provide work support for the individual performing tasks under-water which require good communications, head protection and may require pro-longed working in cold or contaminated water.

The Helmet is of open circuit design, that is the diver receives a constant flow of air while the free flow valve is open and a surface supply of breathing gas is connected and supplied at adequate pressure.

No regulator or mouthpiece is used to meter gas to the diver.

The exhaust valve acts as a port for the circulating gas to escape into the water.

Figure 7-37 Aquadyne AH-2 air helmet, with neck-ring, dam and harness.

Exhausting of the breathing medium takes place automatically whenever the internal helmet pressure exceeds the ambient water pressure plus the spring pressure holding the exhaust mushroom valve closed.

The diver can adjust the internal pressure within the helmet by use of the exhaust valve handle, located on the end of the exhaust valve on the right hand side of the helmet. This is especially useful when the helmet is used with a variable volume dry suit.

The internal pressure can be reduced quickly by the use of the internal head button located inside the helmet. A push of the head automatically unseats the exhaust valve to vent down the helmet/suit pressure without having to alter the automatic exhaust valve setting.

DESCRIPTION:

The main body of the helmet is constructed from polyester reinforced fibreglass, hand laid in a mould to form one piece body. The fibreglass body, in addition to providing a protective housing and an air environ-ment for the diver's head and neck, serves as a base to which all other helmet components are attached.

PORTS:

The two helmet ports are cut from poly-carbonate (Lexan) plate. Port thickness for the front port and top port is $\frac{3}{8}$" and $\frac{1}{4}$" respectively.

Figure 7-38 Fibreglass shell for the AH-2 diving helmet.

NON RETURN/CHECK VALVE:

A brass cartridge "check valve" is employed in the aquadyne helmet to prevent a reverse flow of air from the helmet should an air hose failure occur.

The cartridge valve incorporates an O-ring body seal and is inserted into the air inlet manifold opening and at the rear of the helmet.
NOTE: These two non return valve cartridges are NOT interchangeable.

Figure 7-39 Check valve, showing air flow direction 'arrow'.

FREE FLOW VALVE:

This valve is of forged brass construction and has a rated working pressure of 200 Bars. Both the inlet port and outlet are machined to $\frac{3}{8}$" male swaglok to accommodate the $\frac{3}{8}$" tube connections inside the helmet.

Figure 7-40 Free-flow valve, showing directional 'arrow'

AIR MUFFLER/DIFFUSER:

The purpose of the air muffler/diffuser is to provide a means of reducing the noise level caused by air entering the helmet from the free flow valve and direct the air across the inner face of the front port, preventing fogging.

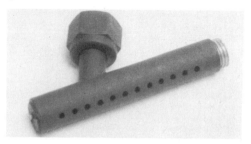

Figure 7-41 Air muffler/diffuser unit.

EXHAUST VALVE:

The exhaust valve has a variable force spring arrangement which is controlled by the exhaust valve knob at the outer end of the valve body. The adjustable range is $\frac{1}{4}$ to $1\frac{1}{2}$ Psig over ambient water pressure.

A manual over-ride exhaust control is provided by means of a head button attached to the stem of the poppet valve which protrudes into the helmet. The head button may be utilised to reduce the helmet pressure below a given adjustment setting or below the $\frac{1}{4}$ Psig minimum setting.

Figure 7-42 Exhaust valve assembly.

Fig 7.43 Air muffler/Diffuser, stripped to show
various components.

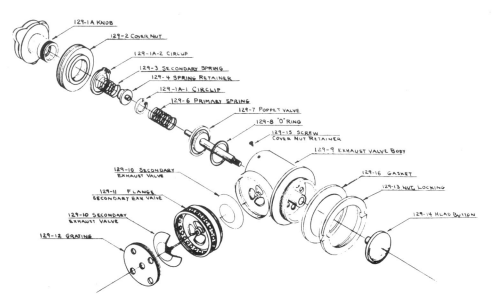

129-1A KNOB
129-2 COVER NUT
129-1A-2 CIRCLIP
129-3 SECONDARY SPRING
129-4 SPRING RETAINER
129-1A-1 CIRCLIP
129-6 PRIMARY SPRING
129-7 POPPET VALVE
129-8 'O' RING
129-15 SCREW
COVER NUT RETAINER
129-9 EXHAUST VALVE BODY
129-16 GASKET
129-13 NUT LOCKING
129-10 SECONDARY
EXHAUST VALVE
129-11 FLANGE
SECONDARY EXH VALVE
129-14 HEAD BUTTON
129-10 SECONDARY
EXHAUST VALVE
129-12 GRATINE

Fig 7.44 Exhaust valve, exploded view

Fig. 7.45 Free Flow Valve, exploded view

Two secondary exhaust valves of the neoprene mushroom type are installed in
series with, and downstream of, the primary exhaust valve outlet. The
secondary valves prevent water from
entering the helmet through the open
primary valve during the exhaust mode
regardless of diver orientation.

COMMUNICATIONS:

Two way communications are provided as
standard equipment. A microphone located
at the left side of the helmet interior
and two ear phones, one located in each
ear pod.

Internal wiring consists of a two-wire
system with the microphone and two ear
pieces wired in parallel.

NECK RING AND LATCHING MECHANISM:

The neck ring assembly is designed to
provide a quick connect/disconnect helmet
coupling whereby a positive mechanical
connection and watertight seal are
obtained.

The neck ring assembly consists basically
of two stainless steel rings, a hinged
V-ring clamping mechanism to hold the two
rings together and an over-centre latch
and locking device to tension and secure
the clamps. The upper neck ring, consti-
tuting the male half of the coupling is
bonded onto the base opening of the helmet
and is an integral part of the helmet
body. A groove is machined in the upper
neck ring for installation of an O-ring
which seals against the top face of the
lower neck ring. The upper neck ring
also has two bayonet slots machined on
its lower surface 180 Degrees apart.

The lower neck ring is the female half of
the helmet coupling and to it are welded
the brackets and fixtures for mounting
the hinge assembly, latching device and
the jocking cable. The skirt of the

lower neck ring is machined with a lip
at the bottom and a ribbed band above
the lip over which the neck seal or
neck opening of a dry suit (constant
volume attachment) is installed and
clamped.

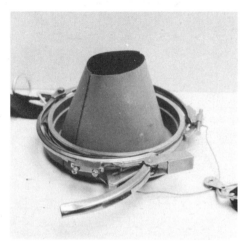

Figure 7-46 Lower neck-ring assembly
plus neoprene neck dam in position.

Two pins are welded inside the lower
neck ring to mate with the bayonet
slots of the upper neck ring. The
pins and mating bayonet slots orient
the two neck rings and achieve a mech
anical lock.

NECK SEAL:
The neckseal is constructed from double
nylon lined foam neoprene and is fabricated in a conical shape. The
large diameter of the neck seal is fitted
over the ribbed base of the lower neck
ring where it is clamped in place with
a single band clamp.

JOCKING SYSTEM
The 'Jocking' system is the means by
which the helmet is held in position

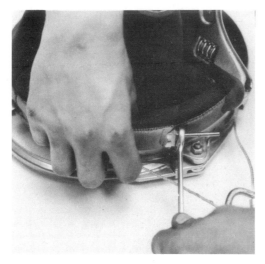

Figure 7-47 Neck seal dam installation

The lower neck ring jocking
assembly and the jocking belt provide
this capability.   A crotch strap,
permanently attached at the back of the
belt, is utilised to prevent upward
movement of the belt.

Figure 7-48 Jocking assembly from rear,
with diver connecting snap-hook.

RESERVE MANIFOLD:

The reserve manifold block serves
as the distribution point for both
the primary gas supply and the

reserve supply.   The manifold block
is designed to be worn on the belt
portion of the diver's back pack
harness providing a reserve system
control point which is readily accessible
to the diver.   A hose is furnished at
the reserve inlet port for connecting
to the first stage regulator of a
standard single hose scuba unit.
NOTE: This first stage regulator must
be provided with a pressure relief valve.

A cartridge check valve inserted into
the primary inlet port and retained by
the inlet fitting prevents loss of
reserve air in the event of a primary
air hose failure.   A shut-off valve
on the manifold isolates the reserve
air from the common passage until
opened by the diver.

Figure 7-49 Waist belt mounted, air
reserve manifold, type RM-1.

RESERVE BACK PACK

The back pack assembly consists
essentially of a standard scuba back
pack, a high pressure scuba reserve
cylinder with pillar valve, a first
stage scuba regulator (scuba single
hose unit), an Aquadyne reserve
manifold assembly and the necessary

hardware to assemble the package. The reserve bottle is mounted in the inverted position in the back pack in order to provide diver access to the pillar valve and to reduce the hose length required between the regulator and the reserve manifold.

NOTE: It is recommended that the hose from the manifold to the helmet should be constructed of SAE 100 R3 hose to prevent kinking while in use.

VARIABLE VOLUME SUIT ATTACHMENT

A variable volume suit is achieved by removing the neoprene neck dam from the lower halmet ring and attaching the ring to the yoke of a rear entry dry suit.

The volume of the suit is controlled by the inlet and exhaust valves on the helmet.

Figure 7-51 Constant-volume back-entry dry suit, showing zip fastener.

Figure 7-50 Diver fully dressed in Aquadyne AH-2 air helmet, with bale-out cylinder worn in an inverted position.

WEIGHT BELT/HARNESS

The Aquadyne diver requires significantly more weight underwater because of the large volume of air contained in his helmet and the need for a stable working attitude.

The Aquadyne diver may carry weights
by any of the following methods:-

- conventional weight belt, as for scuba.

- weight harness with quick release
weight pockets (see surface diving harness)

- combination weight belt harness (Fig 7-51)

WEIGHTED SHALLOW WATER BOOTS

Weighted Boots are an individual preference of the diver but can be useful in
reducing back strain and increases the
diver's stability.

The boot is of heavy rubber construction
laced above the ankle and fitted with a lead
insole as required.

Figure 7-52 Industrial over-boots,
with rope lacing and a lead 'sole'
fitted inside, make ideal shallow-water
diving boots.

AQUADYNE AH-2 AIR HELMET - PARTS LIST
FEBRUARY 1980

PART NUMBER	DESCRIPTION
102	Valve, Free flow complete, less knob
102-1	Nut, free flow valve
103	Knob, free flow valve
103-3	Set screw (2)
104	Washer
105	Gasket
106	Manifold assembly, Inlet
106-3*	Check-Valve, - non-return
106-4*	'O' Ring, Check Valve
106-5*	Adapter, oxygen thread
106-6	'O' Ring, Adaptor
106-7*	Gasket, Manifold
106-8*	Washer, Manifold
106-9*	Nut, Manifold locking (2)
108	Air Muffler Assembly
108-1	End Cap, Muffler (2)
108-2	Body, Muffler
108-3	Ferrule, Muffler (2 parts) (2)
108-4	Pack nut, Muffler (2)
109	Silence material, Muffler
110	Screen, Muffler
112	Feedthrough, communications
113	Gland nut, feedthrough
114	Washer Feedthrough
115	Gasket, Feedthrough
116	Nut, Feedthrough
117	Communications 4 pin connector Assembly. Male
117-1	Connector only, 4 pin male
117-2	Connector only, Female
118	Communications assembly complete (comprising - 117 + 118-1 + 4/118-2 + 3/118-5 + 3/118-4 + 2/119)
118-1	Wire, helmet communications assembly
118-2	Knife disconnect terminals (4)
118-4	Cup, Transceiver (3)
118-5	Transceiver (3)
119	'O' Ring, Feedthrough (2)
124	Frame, Top Port
125	Port, Top
126	Frame, Front Port
127	Port, Front
128	Screw, Port Frames (20)
129	Exhaust valve Assembly complete
129-1B	Knob, Exhaust Valve
129-1A-1	Circlip, Internal
129-1A-2	Circlip, External
129-2A	Cover Nut, Valve body
129-3	Spring, Secondary
129-4	Retainer, Spring
129-6	Spring, Primary
129-7	Poppet Valve
129-8	'O' Ring, Poppet Valve
129-9	Body, Exhaust Valve
129-10	Neoprene Exhaust Valve (2)

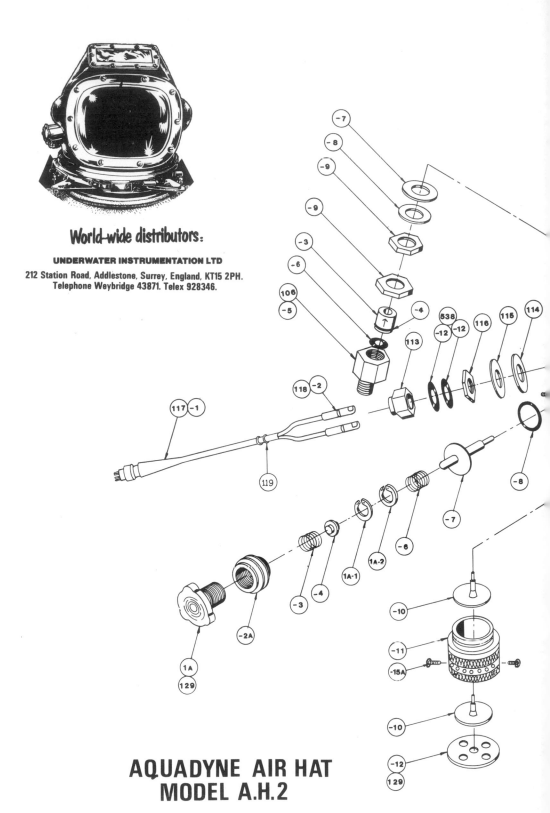

World-wide distributors:

UNDERWATER INSTRUMENTATION LTD

212 Station Road, Addlestone, Surrey, England, KT15 2PH.
Telephone Weybridge 43871. Telex 928346.

AQUADYNE AIR HAT
MODEL A.H.2

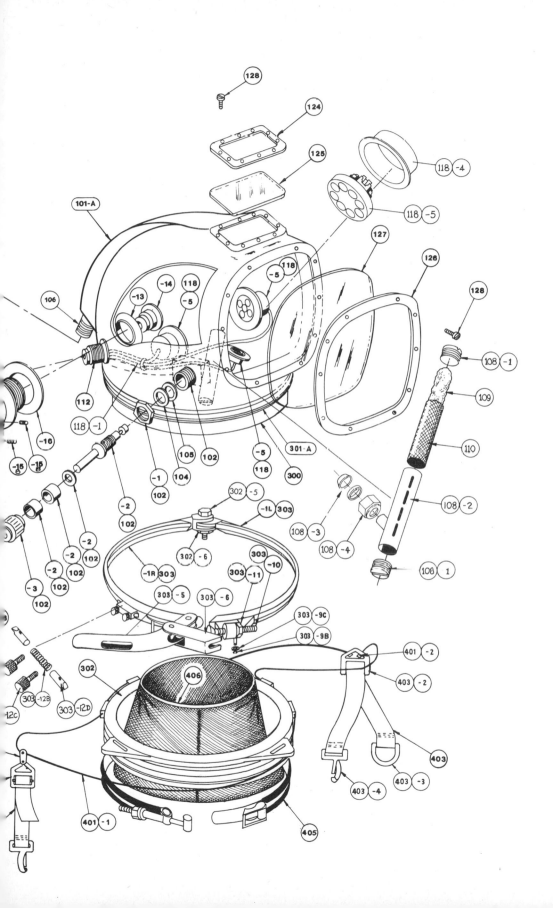

129-11	Flange, Exhaust Valve Secondary
129-12	Grating, Exhaust Valve Secondary
129-13	Nut, Locking, Exhaust Valve body
129-14	Head Button
129-15A	Screw, Grating Retainer
129-15B	Screw, Cover Nut and Flange Retainer (4)
129-16	Gasket, Exhaust Valve Body
301A	'O' Ring, Upper Neck Ring
302	Neck Ring Assembly lower (-with clamps, without jocking harness)
-	Lower Neck Ring Assembly only without clamps
302-5	Screw, rear hinge
302-6	Nut, rear hinge locking
303-1L	Clamp Ring Left
303-1R	Clamp Ring Right (without cam + clasp)
303-5	Cam Arm
303-6	Clasp
303-7	Rivet, Cam Arm - Clamp Ring
303-8	Rivet, Clasp - Cam Arm
303-9B	Circlip, Guide Pin (2)
303-9C	Washer, Guide Pin (2)·
303-10	Screw, Clasp
303-11	Nut, Clasp Screw, Locking
303-12B	Spring Latch
303-12C	Knob, Latch (2)
303-12D	Catch Latch (2)
401	Jocking Cable Assembly (401-1 + 4/401-2)
401-1	Cable
401-2	Sleeve, Cable Stops (4)
402	Jocking Strap Assembly Front with pulley
402-2	Adjustable 'D' Ring
402-3	Pulley Assembly
403	Jocking Strap Assembly Rear
403-2	Adjustable 'D' Ring
403-3	'D' Ring (also used in 404A) (5)
403-4	Snap Connector (also used in 402) (2)
404A	Light Parachute Harness
404-4	Snap Connector Adjustable (3)
405	Clamp Neck Seal
406	Neck Seal
	Tube - plastic rubber sealant

NOTE: Figures in bracket ( ) indicate quantity used in helmet.

           *   Early models of AH-2 were fitted with a circle-seal check valve part no. C2949B-6Q.15 which was a different physical size from Circle Seal check valve part no. P84-180 now fitted. When ordering parts marked with * please also advise the part no. of check valve fitted - stamped into the body. This will allow us to select the correct spare parts for your helmet.

KIRBY MORGAN KmB - BAND MASK - 10

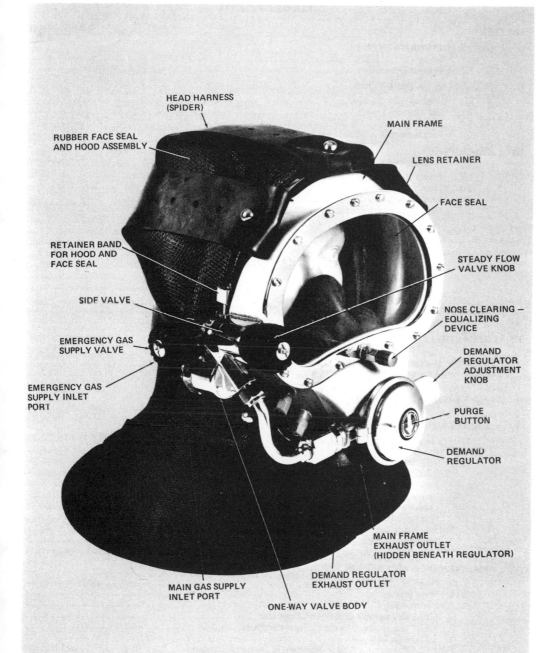

HEAD HARNESS (SPIDER)

MAIN FRAME

RUBBER FACE SEAL AND HOOD ASSEMBLY

LENS RETAINER

FACE SEAL

RETAINER BAND FOR HOOD AND FACE SEAL

STEADY FLOW VALVE KNOB

SIDE VALVE

NOSE CLEARING — EQUALIZING DEVICE

EMERGENCY GAS SUPPLY VALVE

DEMAND REGULATOR ADJUSTMENT KNOB

EMERGENCY GAS SUPPLY INLET PORT

PURGE BUTTON

DEMAND REGULATOR

MAIN FRAME EXHAUST OUTLET (HIDDEN BENEATH REGULATOR)

MAIN GAS SUPPLY INLET PORT

DEMAND REGULATOR EXHAUST OUTLET

ONE-WAY VALVE BODY

PRINCIPLE OF OPERATION

This section describes the principle of operation of the Model KMB-Band Mask-10. Numbers in parentheses correspond to the item numbers on the "exploded drawing" on page 7.50 of this manual. Refer to the parts list to obtain the correct part numbers for ordering replacement parts. The exploded drawing may be opened out to view while reading manual.

LIFE SUPPORT SYSTEM

The diver's breathing medium (air or mixed gas) is supplied by the umbilical to the side valve (84). The umbilical hose is attached to the one-way valve body (68) through the one-way valve (69). A passageway in the side valve body (68) allows the gas to pass without obstruction to the demand regulator (85). Therefore, when the umbilical is pressurized, the demand regulator is also pressurized. The steady flow handwheel (60) located on the front of the side valve (84) provides the diver with an adjustable gas flow to the interior or the mask through the muffler-deflector (7 and 8). In addition to supplying the diver with a steady flow of breathing gas, the deflector (8) directs the flow onto the viewing lens which will prevent any lens fogging.

Figure 7-53 Band-mask controls.

The demand regulator, similar to a

standard SCUBA regulator incorporates an adjustment knob system (21) which protrudes from the left side of the regulator body. This adjustment knob system allows the demand regulator to be adjusted for gas pressures up to 12 bars over ambient bottom pressure. The exhaust gases from the diver exit the demand regulator through the exhaust valve (43). When the steady flow system is in use, excess gas exits through the main exhaust valve (48), located at the bottom of the main frame (11). This valve also purges any water that may enter the interior of the mask.

An emergency supply valve is incorporated in the side valve body. A tank of compressed gas ("bail out bottle") corresponding to the main breathing mixture should be carried with the diver throughout the dive. If for any reason, the main gas supply fails, the emergency supply valve can be opened and the diver can utilize the "bail out" system.

An oral nasal mask (80) is located on the interior of the main frame (11). Its function is to reduce the dead air space, eliminating any possible CO_2 buildup, while improving mask communications.

DESCRIPTION

FRAME (11)

The main frame of the band mask is made of injection molded ABS (Acrylonitrile Butadiene Styrene) plastic. This frame provides a rigid shell for mounting the face seal, breathing gas, and the communication components. The frame is designed to allow easy replacement of any damaged or worn parts. The use of O-ring and gasket seals on all main components increases mask servicability while reducing down time.

LENS (14)

The lense is made of $\frac{1}{2}$inch acrylic plastic

which fits into a molded recess in the main frame (11). It seals off against an "O" ring (13) and is held in place by the lens retainer assembly (15). The frame has been redesigned to incorporate a new O-ring groove for the lens O-ring. The new groove reduces the stress concentration on the frame, caused by the installation of the lens retainer, while maintaining proper O-ring squeeze. The lens can be quickly and easily removed and should be replaced whenever visibility becomes restricted due to extensive scratching. However, scratches on the exterior of the lens tend to disappear underwater.

LENS RETAINER (15)

The lens retainer is secured to the main frame by fifteen slotted screws (16) which thread into metal inserts molded into the main frame. A male fitting with a packing nut protrudes from the lower centre section of the lens retainer (15). This fitting aligns and seals the nose clearing device assembly (2, 17, 18, and 19), to the frame.

NOSE CLEARING DEVICE ASSEMBLY (2, 17, 18, and 19)

The nose clearing device is made up of a neoprene pad cemented to a rod assembly (2). This assembly extends from the interior of the oral nasal mask (80) through the O-ring (17), main frame (11) and lens retainer (15), where two O-rings (18) and a packing nut (15) form a seal on the rod. The rod is tipped with a knurled knob (19) for easy manipulation.

SIDE VALVE ASSEMBLY (84)

The side valve functions as a breathing gas mainfold providing an unobstructed passage for the flow of gas to the demand regulator and constant flow defogger control valve from the umbilical

or emergency gas supply systems.

The passage to the demand regulator is never closed and is unaffected by the steady flow system. The steady flow defogger valve is operated by the side valve handwheel (60) which protrudes from the front of the valve body (68). Two mounting bolts (10 and 12) extend through the main frame (11) and thread into the side valve body (68) to secure it to the main frame. One of these bolts (10) also retains the muffler (7) and the deflector (8). When the side defogged handwheel valve (60) is turned on, gas passes from the side valve body (68) through the muffler and deflector, then onto the lens (14) to eliminate fogging. From the mask's interior, the gas will pass into the oral nasal mask (80) through the one-way valve (79). The side valve body also houses the umbilical one-way valve and the components of the emergency supply shut-off valve.

ONE-WAY VALVE (69)

This Circle Seal one-way valve is a cartridge type valve which may be quickly and easily replaced. This valve has been designed to provide large gas flow rates with negligible pressure drop. (See Figures 70 and 71) The one-way valve (69) fits inside the one-way valve body (71), which is, in turn, screwed into the side-valve body (68).

DEMAND REGULATOR (85)

The demand regulator is supplied with gas from the side valve (84). As the gas enters the demand regulator body through the inlet seat (41), the flow is opposed by the seat disc retainer (39) away from the inlet seat (41) which allows the gas to flow to the interior of the demand regulator body (29), and then through to the interior of the oral nasal mask (80). The demand valve spring (38) is assisted by the spring set (27) mounted in the adjustment knob side of the regulator body. These springs operate in unison, exerting a force which tends to hold the demand valve closed. The magnitude of this closing force may be controlled through the use of the adjustment knob (21). Turning the adjustment knob (21) clockwise will compress the spring set (27), which increases the opening effort of the demand regulator. Coversely, turning the adjustment knob (21), counter clockwise will relax the spring set (27) and the opening effort will decrease. With both standard springs in place, the demand regulator will handle a range of inlet pressures (umbilical hose pressures) of up to 12 bars above ambient bottom pressure. This is ideal for surface supply pressures of 10-12 bars as when using a compressor or bottled air supply with a regulator. Most SCUBA first stage regulators are set at approximately 8.5 bars; therefore, they may be used to regulate both the main gas supply and an emergency gas cylinder. Actual testing has revealed that when using both standard springs (27 and 38) the regulator will handle an inlet pressure of up to 14 bars before free flow occurs; however, the manufacturer only guarantees a maximum pressure of 12 bars.

If higher supply pressures are needed, such as in deeper dives where additional pressure is required due to increased gas density and flow losses through the umbilical, the spring arrangement in the demand regulator may be altered to achieve a higher operating pressure range of from approximately 12-20 bars. This alteration may be accomplished by replacing the demand valve spring (38) with a standard U.S. Divers' second stage demand valve spring (Part No. 1085-04). It should be noted that the adjustment knob (21) will not operate without the spring set (27) installed. The demand regulator body (29) is held in place on the main frame (11) by the

oral nasal fitting (81), which is installed from the inside of the mask. An O-ring (82) assures a watertight seal between the regulator (85) and main frame (11).

MAIN EXHAUST (46, 47 and 48)

The main exhaust valve (48) is located at the bottom of the mask under the demand regulator. Gas discharging from this valve automatically purges water from the interior of the mask as it is the lowest point in the mask during normal working conditions. The main exhaust cover (47) may be removed by unscrewing the main exhaust screws (46). Removal of this cover permits access to the rubber mushroom valve (48). The seat for this valve is molded into the frame (11) of the mask.

HEAD AND FACE SEAL RETAINER BANDS (6 and 50)

The top band (6) and bottom band (50) fit around the hood and face seal combination (1), and clamp it firmly to the main frame (11). Two screws (49) hold these bands in place. Five "spider" hooks, consisting of brass balls mounted on small rods are attached to the top and bottom bands.

HOOD AND FACE SEAL (1)

The hood and face seal is fabricated from foam neoprene and open cell foam. The open cell foam forms a comfortable cushion which pushes the sealing surface of the foam neoprene against the diver's face. The face seal is designed to fit a narrow face and may be modified to fit the individual diver, if desired. This may be done by trimming the face seal with either a knife or a razor blade to fit a wider face contour. The hood incorporates built-in pockets which are open to the interior of the main frame (11).

These pockets retain the earphones. Gas from the main body is allowed to flow into the pockets so that the pressure on the earphones can be equalized. The pockets provide easy access to the earphones to facilitate repair or replacement. Two 1/4 inch diameter holes have been punched in the upper rear portion of the hood to allow any gas that may leak past the face seal, to escape.

Be sure that the holes are not covered when the spider is in place. If these holes are sealed, the gas trapped in the hood will increase the mask's buoyancy and will make the spider uncomfortably tight. If additional holes are desired, be careful not to punch holes in the earphone pockets or communication wiring.

COMMUNICATIONS (3, 4, 5, 51, 52, 53, 54, 55, 56 and 36)

The communication system of the KMB-10 Band Mask has been redesigned to improve the frequency response at depth. This is accomplished by employing bone vibrator transducers which are hermetically encapsulated in a urethane compound and which are unaffected by the water pressure, or shock encountered during normal usage. The system consists of two earphones (3 and 4), a microphone (5), two communication posts (51), washers (52) and nuts (53). The communication wires can be attached to the communication posts directly or a Marsh Marine four terminal waterproof connector (92), may be utilized. When using the Marsh Marine connector, the communication wires, with front and back ferrule (90 and 91) and the nut (92) in place, should be threaded through the body (55) and nut (89) to the mask interior where they are attached to the backside of the binding posts. The O-ring seal on the body (55) prevents any leakage into the interior. The umbilical can then be fitted with the

Marsh Marine female connector (56). When the Marsh Marine is not to be used, the plug (54) and O-ring (94) will screw into the jam nut (89) to seal the hole in the frame. A slight loss of signal will result when using bare wire posts as the waterproof connector has a stronger signal output.

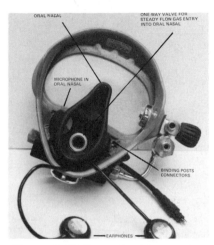

Figure 7-54 Communication system components of the band-mask.

HEAD HARNESS OR "SPIDER" (83)

The head harness or "spider", is a quickly adjustable strap for holding the mask firmly to the divers face. It is a simple piece of rubber with holes punched into it which correspond to the protrusions on the top and bottom bands (6 and 50).

ORAL-NASAL MASK ASSEMBLY (80)

The oral-nasal mask assembly (80) reduces dead air space in the mask which prevents CO_2 buildup. Inhaled gas from the demand regulator passes through the regulator mounting tube and nut (81) on the interior of the main frame (11) to the diver. Exhaust gas from the diver goes back out through this tube and then out the regulator exhaust. Gas from the steady flow valve portion of the side-valve flows into the main frame (11) then into the oral-nasal mask through a valve (79) to the diver. During the exhalation cycle, while on steady flow, the incoming gas passes through the main exhaust valve (48).

EMERGENCY GAS SUPPLY SYSTEM

If the gas supply coming through the umbilical to the mask is interrupted for any reason, the diver should have a back-up system to supply gas for returning to safety. The size of the emergency gas supply may vary, depending on the use of the mask. Most divers use a standard cylinder and a standard SCUBA back pack for an emergency gas supply. Regardless

of the supply chosen, a first stage SCUBA regulator is attached to the gas source. This regulator reduces the pressure of the emergency cylinder to approximately 8.5 bars. A standard SCUBA intermediate pressure hose should be used between the first stage regulator and the side valve (84). Normally the emergency cylinder valve is turned on and the first stage regulator and intermediate pressure hose are pressurized. Then, in an emergency, the diver need only turn on the emergency valve knob (60) which protrudes outward from the side valve body. As a precautionary measure, the first stage regulator used on the emergency cylinders must be equipped with a safety unloader. The safety unloader acts as a relief valve in the event of high pressure seat leakage in the first stage regulator. High pressure seat leakage will cause the intermediate pressure hose to be pressurized far above its rated capacity and without the safety unloader the hose could burst. A safety unloader is available from U.S. Divers Co., SURVIVAIR Division, under Part Number 9109-20, and it will screw directly into the first stage regulator's low pressure port.

Figure 7-55 A standard 60c.ft SCUBA air cylinder used as an emergency supply.

Figure 7-56 KMB-Mk 10 Band mask, showing umbilical fitted.

MAINTENANCE AND REPAIR

This section covers the maintenance and
repair of the Model KMB-Band Mask-10. A
mask that is kept clean and in good repair will provide better service to the
user. The mask is designed for easy access to all areas and rapid replacement
of any damaged parts. Numbers appearing
in parentheses indicate the item numbers
for the illustrations in this manual.
The exploded drawing at the end of this
manual may be opened out so that it can
be viewed while reading any part of the
manual. This provides a quick reference
between the reading material and the i-
tem numbers listed on the drawing. Do
not use the item numbers when ordering
spare parts. Always refer to the parts
list for the correct part numbers.

PREVENTIVE MAINTENANCE

It is important that each diver establish minimum standards for care of the
mask. Recommendations for periodic
maintenance are offered here. The type
of diving which is being done will dictate the maintenance time tables. For
example, using the mask in water that is
contaminated with petroleum products
will require more frequent maintenance,
and replacement of rubber parts than
would using the mask in salt water or
fresh water.

DAILY MAINTENANCE

1 Visually inspect the interior and exterior of the mask.

2 If the open cell foam on the face
   seal is saturated with water, squeeze
   it out by pressing the sponge against
   the main frame (11) and drain the
   water out through the exhaust valve
   (48). If the mask is not going to be
   used for a period of time, the hood
   and face seal assembly should be removed and dried before storage.

3 Remove any sand or dirt on the interior of the face lens as it may
cause scratched when anti-fogging
solution is applied prior to the
next dive.

4 Check all moving parts such as the
   adjustment knob (21), the side valve
   handwheel (60) and the nose clearing
   device (2), to ensure smooth and
   proper operation.

5 Check the communications system for
   proper installation and adjustment.
   Test both the earphones and the
   microphone for proper operation.

MONTHLY MAINTENANCE - OR BETWEEN JOBS

1 Remove hood and face seal. Check for
   damage to the hood and other neoprene
   parts and dry if necessary.

2 Inspect and test earphones, microphone, and wire connector.

3 Remove the bolt (10) and washer (9)
   muffler-deflector (8) and plastic
   sponge muffler (7). Inspect sponge
   muffler (7) and clean or replace if
   necessary.

4 Remove nose clearing device retainer
   nut (15) and lubricate O-rings (18)
   and main shaft (2). Make sure nose
   pad is secured in place.

5 Lubricate with silicone exhaust valve
   (48.)

6 Remove exhaust tube (44) and clean
   regulator exhaust seat valve.

7 Remove demand regulator clamp (30)
   and lift off demand regulator cover
   (32) and diaphragm (33). Place a
   light coat of silicone grease on the
   plate of the deaphragm (33) before
   reassembly. Inspect diaphragm carefully for any signs of wear.

8 Remove the adjustment handle (21), by
   knocking the pin (20) our of the hole
   with a 3/32 inch diameter punch.
   Place handle (21) on a solid base to
   knock out the pin so there is no

force on the regulator body. Next, remove nut (22) and the adjustment shaft (25). Turn the mask on its side and drop out the spacer (26), spring set (27), and piston (28). Clean and lubricate with silicone grease and then reassemble.

9   If the regulator lever (36) needs re-adjustment, pressurize the breathing system and then readjust.

10 Test the one-way valve (69). This may be accomplished in one of two ways:

   (a) Detach the umbilical hose from the side valve fitting (71); close the steady flow defogger control valve handwheel (60); open the emergency supply valve and try to blow into the emergency valve inlet fitting on the side valve body (68). If any gas passes through the side valve and out through the one-way valve body (71), the one-way valve (69) must be replaced. Blowing cigarette smoke through the side valve body (68) will give a visual indication of any leaks.

   (b) The one-way valve body (71) is removed from the side valve body (68). The one-way valve assembly (69) is then removed from the one-way valve body (71). The diver now blows through the one-way valve opposite the O-ring end. Again, cigarette smoke can be used to give a visual indication of a leak. The slightest leak through the one-way valve is reason enough to replace it.

BAND MASK MAINTENANCE AND REPAIR

The following sections describe in detail the disassembly, repair and reassembly of the Model KMB-Band Mask-10 and its components.

LENS RETAINER ASSEMBLY (15)

Little or no maintenance is required for the lens retainer (15). Fifteen slotted machine screws thread into metal inserts in the main frame (11).

LENS (14)

The lens is made of $\frac{1}{4}$ inch thick acrylic plastic. Small scratches on the exterior are not important as they tend to disappear under water. However, the lens is easily replaced by removing the lens retainer (15), and pressing out the lens. This operation requires the removal of the nose clearing stud (19) and the O-rings (18). An O-ring located in a groove in the main frame (11), under the lens, acts to seal out water from the interior of the mask. A replacement lens is merely dropped into place in the main frame (11) and then the lens retainer (15) is replaced. The lens retainer screws should all be installed finger tight, then tightened an additional $\frac{1}{2}$ to $\frac{3}{4}$ turn. Tightening beyond this limit does not improve the seal and may cause stress cracking of the main frame (11). Remember to replace the O-ring (17) under the lens retainer (15) when reassembling.

HOOD AND FACE SEAL

Removing screws (49) permits the removal of the bands (6 and 50). The face seal and hood (1) can then be removed from the main frame (11). The earphones must be pulled out of the earphone pockets as the hood and face seal are withdrawn from the main frame. It is extremely important that a good glue joint be maintained between the face seal rubber and the hood. Any leaks in this area will cause gas to leak out of the interior of the mask. As the gas leaks out it is replaced by the demand regulator which will free flow at a rate that is equal to the escaping gas. If the earphone pockets are ruptured or

become detached from the hood, gas may
also escape out of these pockets. Escaping gas anywhere on the face seal or
earphone pockets will cause a great deal
of noise, which will interfere with communications. The diver may also think
that the regulator is malfunctioning
since, no matter how many turns are made
on the adjustment knob (21), the free
flow persists. Therefore, be sure that
the glued joints in the hood face seal
(1) are all secure. Any commercial
quality wet suit cement may be used to
repair the hood-face seal assembly.
Holes are punched in the upper rear
portion of the hood in position so that
they are visible when the "spider" is in
place. Holes located under the "spider",
will not allow gas to escape efficiently.
These holes are necessary to vent any gas
which may enter the hood from the exhaust
or face seal. Trapped gas will cause
ballooning which results in discomfort
and additional buoyancy. To reassemble,
the hood is slipped over the main frame
(11) and then held in place while the top
and bottom bands are screwed together.
It is suggested that black plastic elec-
trician's tape be run around the edge of
the hood where it clamps to the main
frame. The tape will hold this hood in
place during installation of the top and
bottom bands. The tape will also ensure
an air-tight seal if it is overlapped
onto the main frame.

Figure 7-58 Lifting off bands - remove hood and face seal.

Figure 7-59 Removing earphones from
hood pockets.

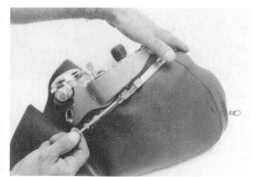

Figure 7-57 Removal of hood and face
seal retainer, top and bottom bands.

Fig 7-60 Removal of deflector and sponge muffler. The bolt also secures the side valve in place.

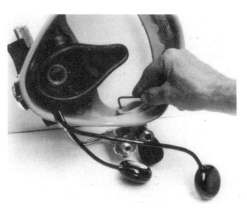

Fig 7-61 Removal of second side valve mounting bolt.

SIDE VALVE ASSEMBLY (84)

The side valve body (68) is held in place on the main frame (11) by two threaded bolts (10 and 12). These two bolts are inserted from the interior of the mask through the main frame (11) and the gasket (57), then into the side valve body (68). Removal of one of the mounting bolts (10) results in the removal of the washer (9), muffler-deflector (8), sponge muffler (7) and the spacer (93). Removal of both bolts detaches the side valve (84) from the main frame (11). To completely remove the

side valve assembly (84) from the main frame (11) and demand regulator (85), loosen the jam nut (42) and unscrew the side valve swivel fitting which is attached to the inlet seat (41). The side valve can be replaced in reverse order. Be careful to position the gasket (57) properly before tightening the side valve on the main frame. A RTV sealant may be used between body (68) and gasket (57).

The steady flow defogger control valve, the emergency valve, and the one-way valve body, can be disassembled without removing the entire side valve assembly (84) from the main frame (11). To disassemble the steady flow valve, first open the valve as far as possible, then unscrew the lock nut (58) and remove the spring (59), handwheel (60), and the washer (61). Next, using an open-end box or crescent wrench, remove the bonnet (62) and the O-ring (64). With the bonnet removed, the stem (66) washer (63) and the O-ring (65) can be lifted out of the side valve body (68). To complete the disassembly, unscrew the seat assembly (67) and remove it from the side valve. Inspect the nylon seat for wear or deep grooves and replace if necessary.

Fig 7-62 Remove side valve swivel fitting if side is to be completely removed, or pipes fitted.

The O-ring (65) and teflon washer (63)
should also be replaced, if worn.
Reassemble in reverse order of disassembly.   Thread in the seat assembly (67) until it is even with the
front of the side valve body (68).

Next, replace the stem (66) complete
with O-ring (65) and washer (63)into
the bonnet (62). Now place the stem
end into the seat assembly (67) and
rotate the valve stem (66) clockwise,
until the seat bottoms out inside the
side valve body.   Rotate the bonnet
(62) clockwise until it seats against
the side valve body (68).   At this
point, test to see if the stem rotates
freely.   If it is stiff, disassemble
and relubricate with silicone grease.
Next, tighten the bonnet with a wrench
and reassemble the washer (61) handwheel (60) spring (59) and the locknut (58).

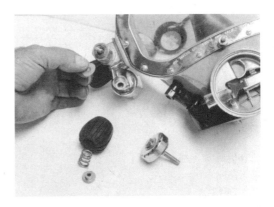

Fig 7-63   Unscrew locknut (58) and lift
off spring (59), handwheel (60) and
washer (61).

The disassembly procedure of the emergency valve is much the same as that
for the steady flow valve.   After fully
opening the valve, loosen the locknut
(58) and remove the spring (59), the
washer (61) and the handwheel (6).
Using a wrench, unscrew and remove the
bonnet (72). Next remove the O-ring
(65), back-up ring (73), gasket assembly
(76) and inspect for wear and deep grooves.
Also inspect all O-rings and gaskets for
signs of wear.   Replace any parts that
look damaged or worn.   Reassemble in
reverse order of disassembly.   Be sure
that the stem turns freely after reassembly and that the bonnet is snugly
tightened.

Fig 7-64   Remove side valve bonnet (62)

Pressurize the side valve and functionally
test both valve assemblies.

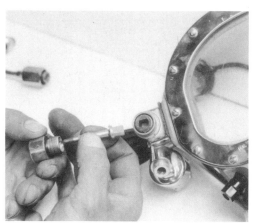

Figure 7-65 Side valve bonnett (62), washer (63), stem (66), and O-ring (65) are removed. Seat disc assembly (67) can be seen in the side valve body.

Figure 7-67 Remove one-way valve body (71) from side valve.

Figure 7-66 Remove seat disc assembly (67) next.

Figure 7-68 Remove emergency valve bonnet (72), stem (75), and unscrew disc and retainer assembly (76).

ONE-WAY VALVE (69)

The one-way valve (69) is located in the one-way valve body (71), which can be removed from the side valve body (68) with an end wrench. Once removed, the one-way valve may be pushed out with a

blunt tool. If there is any indication
of leakage, replace. Be careful on
reassembly to place the arrow on the
one-way valve in the direction of gas
flow.

Fig 7-69   One-way valve (69) can be
pushed out of valve body (71)
with blunt tool.

Fig 7-70   The circle seal cartridge
type one-way valve. Arrow
must be in direction of gas
flow.

HOW IT WORKS:

The proven principles of Circle Seal Check
Valve sealing are employed in these cartridge
type valves — instant, bubble-tight sealing
with an O-Ring. Increasing pressure makes
the seal tighter until metal-to-metal contact
is made and this withstands full system
pressures or pressure surges. The poppet
shape is different than in some Circle Seal
Check Valves, yet the principle remains the
same.

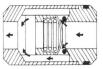

OPEN

In flow position, convex curved surface of
spring-loaded poppet permits full flow.
Cracking pressure required is governed by
the spring.

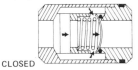

CLOSED

Closing to check position at the slightest
back pressure, dynamic O-Ring seals instantly between poppet and seat.

Fig 7-71   Principles of one-way valve

MAIN EXHAUST ASSEMBLY (46, 47 and 48)

The seat for the main exhaust is molded
into the main frame (11) of the KMB 10.
Two screws (46) hold the main exhaust
cover in place. The main exhaust
valve can be exposed by removing the
screws (46). The exhaust valve should
be removed and replaced if there are
any signs of cracking or excessive wear.
This is accomplished by bunching the
rubber together between the thumb and
forefinger and then by pulling the
exhaust valve out from the main frame
(11). A light coat of silicone grease
will improve the operation of the valve.
The valve can be reinstalled by inserting
the centre stem through the hole and
pulling from the inside of the mask
until it snaps into place in the main
frame (11).

The cover (47) should now be reinstalled. Longer screws should not be used to hold the cover on as they would protrude through the cover and interfere with the operation of the exhaust valve. The rubber face seal and hood assembly should not block the opening of the exhaust cover (47) since this too would interfere with the operation of the exhaust valve.

Any interference with the main exhaust valve (48) could cause the valve to remain open and water could then enter the interior of the mask.

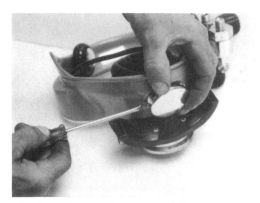

Fig 7-72 Remove 2 screws (46) to remove cover.

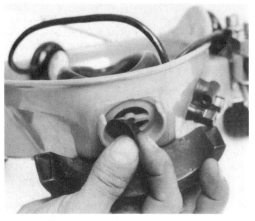

Fig 7-73 Grasp rubber exhaust valve (48) and pull to remove.

NOSE CLEARING DEVICE ASSEMBLY (2, 17, 18 and 19)

For removal of the nose clearing device main shaft (2), grasp the nose clearing stud (19) with a padded pair of pliers (use a rag). Reaching inside the mask with the other hand, grasp the nose pad and shaft and unscrew the nose clearing device (2). Next, pull the nose clearing device (2) out of the mask and remove the packing nut (15) and the two O rings (18). Check to see if the foam neoprene pad is securely attached and reglue, if necessary. Lubricate the O rings and the shaft with silicone grease before reassembly. Reassemble in the reverse order of disassembly.

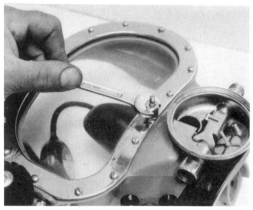

Fig 7-74 Pad the nose clearing stud (19) and hold with pliers while rotating main shaft (2) on interior of mask.

MAIN FRAME (11) (Fig 7.49/50)

The main frame is an injection molded ABS plastic unit. It is strong and extremely durable. It does not conduct electricity, which is advantageous if underwater electric arc welding is to be done by the diver. Do not use any thread sealant or thread locking fluids on the frame, as some of them promote stress cracking in the ABS plastic.

DEMAND REGULATOR ASSEMBLY (85)

The demand regulator on the Model KMB-Band Mask 10 is similar in design to a Scuba demand regulator, with the exception of the adjustment knob (21) for the control of the breathing effort. This control system permits adjustment of the breathing effort over a wide range of supply pressures.

The KMB Band Mask 10 demand regulator is equipped with two compression springs, both of which exert pressure on the demand valve, tending to hold it closed against the incoming gas pressure. Spring (38) surrounds the seat disc retainer on the left hand side of the regulator, while the spring set (27) is located in the adjustment tube on the right hand side of the regulator. The higher the inlet supply pressure, the higher the spring force required to close the demand valve and prevent free flow.

However, if there is too much spring pressure on the demand valve, the regulator will be hard to breathe. The adjustment knob (21) allows the diver to adjust the spring pressure to a point just preceding free flow, which is the easiest breathing position regardless of supply pressure. For a description of the correct spring combinations for different gas supply pressures, refer to Section "Demand Regulator"

Fig 7.76 Remove adjustment knob (21) by punching out pin (2) with 3/32 in. dia. punch. BE SURE to support the knob to prevent bending the regulator body.

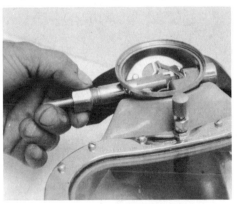

Fig 7-77 Remove adjustment shaft nut (22) and shaft (25) Unscrew counter-clockwise until they are detached from adjustment shaft tube.

Fig 7-75 Removal of Demand Regulator Cover (32) and Diaphragm (33).

Fig 7-78 Remove inlet seat (41)

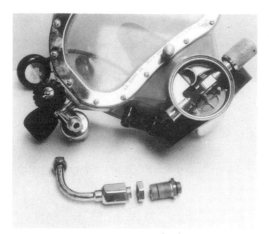

Fig 7-79 Remove the nut (34) from seat disc retainer (39) tilt mask and drop out seat disc retainer. The spacer (35) will also fall out of regulator body.

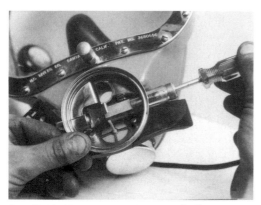

Fig 7-80 Align tip of lever (36) with tip edge of regulator body.(29)

DISASSEMBLY OF DEMAND REGULATOR (85)

1 Remove the cover clamp screw (31) and the cover clamp (3) from the demand regulator assembly. Lift the cover (32) and the diaphragm (33) from the regulator body.

2 Remove the adjustment knob (21) by punching out the pin (2) with a 3/32 in. dia. punch. Be sure to rest the handle against a solid support to prevent bending the adjustment shaft or tube. Next, remove the adjustment shaft nut (22) and the adjustment shaft (25). Both unscrew counterclockwise as they come out of the adjustment shaft tube. The O ring (23)

and washer (24) will come out along with the shaft and nut. Now tilt the mask on its side and shake until the spacer (26) spring set (27) and piston (28) fall out.

3 The regulator body may be easily removed from the main frame (11). This is accomplished by unscrewing the oral nasal mask fitting (81) which is also the nut that holds the regulator onto the main frame (11). An O ring (82) on the interior of the main frame (11) seals the regulator to the frame to prevent leakage.

4 After removing the oral nasal mask fitting (81) loosen the jam nut (42) then unscrew the fitting on the tube leading from the side valve body and separate the side valve assembly from the demand regulator. Complete side valve removal is required at this point. Next remove the inlet seat (41) from the main regulator body (29). Remove the nut (34) from the seat disc retainer (39) and washer (88) from the regulator body (29). The spacer (35) lever (36) and washer (37) will now fall out of the regulator body.

INSPECTION OF DEMAND REGULATOR PARTS

1 Seat disc retainer (39) check condition of rubber seat for wear and deep grooves.

2 Diaphragm (33). Check to determine if the rubber has separated from the metal plate.

3 O rings (40 and 23) check for irregularities in the rubber.

4 Exhaust valve (43) check for cracks and tears in the rubber.

CLEANING

All rubber and metal parts should be cleaned in warm soapy water and rinsed in fresh water.

REASSEMBLY AND ADJUSTMENT

Prior to reassembly of the demand
regulator, replace all questionable
parts with new parts. Lubricate all
O rings and threads lightly with a
silicone lubricant.

1. Place the washer (88) and the demand
valve spring (38) on the shaft of the seat
disc retainer (39) Slip this combination
into the regulator body (29) on the demand
valve end. Place the washer (37) lever (36)
and spacer (35) onto the shaft of the seat
disc retainer that protrudes through to the
interior of the regulator body (29) Screw
the nut (35) onto the threaded shaft of the
seat (39) until the seat disc retainer
protrudes about 1/16th in. past the nut (34).

2. Install the inlet seat (41) and its
O ring (4) into the regulator body (29).

3. Install the piston (28) spring set (27)
and spacer (26) into the adjustment tube
on the right hand side of the regulator body.
Generously lubricate this assembly before
reinstalling. Next thread the main
adjustment shaft (25) into the tube. Insert
the washer (24) and O ring (23) onto the
adjustment shaft. Push the adjustment
shaft nut (22) onto the adjustment shaft and
thread it into place on the regulator body (29)
Place the adjustment knob (21) onto the
adjustment shaft, making sure that the hole in
the knob aligns with the hole in the shaft. The
pin (2) is inserted into the hole to lock the
assembly together. Be sure to support the handle
(21) while inserting the pin.

4. Tighten the valve stem nut (34) until
there is no play in the lever (36). Overtightening
the nut (34) will cause the regulator to freeflow.

5. Assemble the jam nut (42) onto the inlet seat
(41) Now reinstall the side valve tube fitting onto

the inlet seat (41) Pressurize
the system to 9 bars , which is
the normal intermediate pressure
setting of a standard Scuba regulator.
Next screw in the adjustment knob
to the full "in" position, then back
off eight full turns or just prior
to freeflow. With the adjustment
knob in this position, the tip of the
lever (36) should be level with the
top of the regulator body (29).
If the lever is not in this position,
readjust by adjusting the nut (34).

6. Place the diaphragm (33) and cover
(32) in place on the regulator body
(29). The diaphragm plate should
just touch the top of the lever. Hold
the cover (32) in place and snap
the cover clamp (30) around the
regulator body. Next, install the
screw (31) and tighten to secure the
cover (32) to the regulator body

7. Depress the purge button on the
cover (32). If the purge flow seems
to be low, readjust the lever (36)
using the same method as before,
until the purge flow is satisfactory.

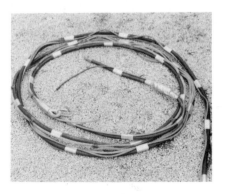

Fig. 7.81 Diving Umbilical

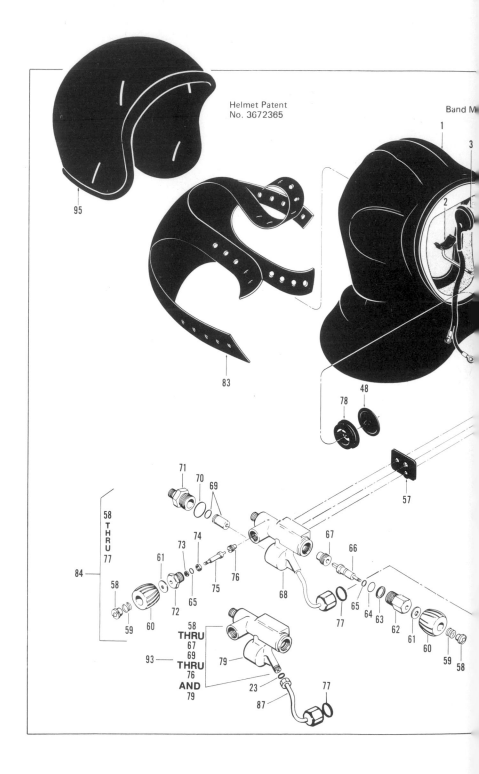

Helmet Patent
No. 3672365

Band M

95

83

1

2

3

48

78

57

71

70

69

58
THRU
77

73

74

61

67

66

84

58

72

65

75

76

68

65

64

63

62

61

60

59

59

58

60

59

58
THRU
67
69
THRU
76
AND
79

93

79

23

77

87

Exploded View
of
Kirby-Morgan Model KMB-BAND Mask-10
With Marsh Marine Connector

PARTS LIST
for
KIRBY-MORGAN MODEL KMB-BAND Mask-10
WITH MARSH MARINE CONNECTOR

Item No. Part No.	Description	Item No. Part No.	Description
1—390110	Hood & Face Seal	51—390133	Post, Communications
2—390111	Nose Clearing Device	52—845050	Washer
3—390102	Earphone, Right	53—852023	Nut
4—390103	Earphone, Left	54—390639	Plug
5—390104	Microphone	55—390635	Body, Plated
6—390112	Band, Top	56—390145	Marsh Marine, Fem.
7—390113	Sponge, Muffler	57—390136	Gasket
8—390114	Deflector, Muffler	58—052518	Locknut
9—845032	Washer	59—050107	Spring
10—390115	Bolt	60—052541	Handwheel
11—390116	Frame	61—845058	Washer
12—390117	Screw	62—390065	Bonnett
13—820259	O-Ring, Lens	63—390137	Washer
14—390083	Lens	64—820015	O-Ring
15—390118	Lens Retainer Ass'y	65—820010	O-Ring
16—834020	Screw	66—390031	Stem
17—820010	O-Ring	67—390138	Seat Disc Assembly
18—820008	O-Ring	68—390141	Block Assembly
19—390119	Stud, Nose Clearing	69—390034	Valve Ass'y, One Way
20—876007	Pin	70—820305	O-Ring
21—390120	Knob	71—390035	Body, One Way Valve
22—390121	Nut	72—050216	Bonnett
23—820011	O-Ring	73—828510	Backup O-Ring
24—106911	Washer	74—050208	Gasket
25—390122	Shaft	75—052521	Stem
26—390123	Spacer	76—390578	Disc & Retainer Assembly
27—390124	Spring Set	77—820012	O-Ring
28—390427	Piston	78—390143	Body, Oral Nasal Valve
29—390126	Box Bottom	79—390431	Side Valve Body
30—101914	Clamp, Rim	80—390032	Mask, Oral Nasal
31—834020	Screw	81—390140	Fitting, Oral Nasal
32—390127	Cover, Ass'y	82—820020	O-Ring
33—103732	Diaphragm	83—390139	Harness, Head (Spider)
34—102510	Nut	84—390153	Side Valve Ass'y
35—102517	Spacer	85—390049	Regulator
36—103729	Lever	86—390146	Marsh Marine Male
37—845022	Washer	87—390430	Tube Ass'y
38—390128	Spring	88—845001	Washer
39—104908	Seat Disc Retainer Ass'y	89—390637	Jam Nut
40—820014	O-Ring	90—390630	Ferrule, Front
41—390039	Inlet Seat	91—390633	Ferrule, Back
42—390073	Nut, Jam	92—390638	Nut, Plated
43—105139	Valve, Exhaust	93—390440	Side Valve Ass'y
44—104912	Tube, Exhaust	94—820309	O-Ring
45—833002	Screw	95—390504	Fiberglass Helmet
46—390129	Screw		
47—390130	Cover, Main Exhaust		
48—390131	Valve, Main Exhaust		
49—834021	Screw		
50—390132	Band, Bottom		

NOTE: Use only the Part No. for ordering parts. Orders should not refer to the Item No.

PARTS LIST

KEY	PART NO.	DESCRIPTION	KEY	PART NO.	DESCRIPTION
1	17-001	Adjustable Chin Strap	41a	17-041a	Nut
2	17-002	Head Cushion	41b	17-041b	Packing
3	17-003	Neck Dam	41c	17-041c	Washer
4	17-004	Neck Clamp Main Body	42	17-042	Stem
5	17-005	Nut, Neck Clamp Inner Adj.	43	17-043	Emergency Valve Body
6	17-006	Lock Washer, Neck Clamp	44	17-044	Emergency Supply Valve Complete
7	17-007	Lock Nut, Neck Clamp	45a	17-045a	Stud
8	17-008	Neck Band Complete w/rubber	*45b	17-045b	Side Valve Body
9	17-009	Screw (2)	*46b	17-046b	Side Valve Assy. Complete
10	17-010	Latch Catch	47	17-047	Microphone
11	17-011	Hinge	48	17-048	Earphone, Left
12	17-012	Hinge Sleeve	49	17-049	Earphone, Right
13	17-013	Hinge Bolt (2)	50	17-050	Communications Set, Helmet
14	17-014	Rear Hinge Tab	51	17-051	Oral Nasal Mask
15	17-015	Star Washer (4)	52	17-052	Oral Nasal Valve Body
16	17-016	Screw (4)	53	17-053	Oral Nasal Mushroom Valve
17	17-017	Yoke, Fiberglass	54	17-054	Nose Block Device
18	17-018	Washer (3)	55	17-055	Regulator Mount Nut
19	17-019	Screw (3)	56	17-056	O-Ring
20	17-020	Locknut	57	17-057	Alignment Screw
21	17-021	Spring	58	17-058	Alignment Screw
22	17-022	Handle, Main Gas Supply	59	17-059	Rear Weight
23	17-023	Washer	60	17-060	Washer
24	17-024	Bonnet	61	17-061	Screw
25	17-025	O-Ring	62	17-062	O-Ring, Helmet
26	17-026	Washer	63	17-063	Helmet, Fiberglass
27	17-027	O-Ring	64	17-064	Handle
28	17-028	Valve Stem	65	17-065	Screw (3)
29	17-029	Seat Assy.	66	17-065	Port Weight
*30b	7-030b	Bent Tube Assy. with O-Rings	67	17-067	Screw
*31b	17-031b	O-Ring	68	17-068	Screw (3)
*32b	17-032b	Bent Tube Assy.	69	17-069	Nut
33	17-033	O-Ring	70	17-070	Washer
34	17-034	Adapter, Brass	71	17-071	Deflector, Muffler
35	17-035	One-Way Valve	72	17-072	Sponge, Muffler
35a	17-035a	Body	73	17-073	Nut
35b	17-035b	Spring	74	17-074	Washer, Lock
35c	17-035c	Poppet	75	17-075	Washer, Flat
35d	17-035d	O-Ring	76	17-076	Nut (4)
35e	17-035e	O-Ring	77	17-077	Washer (2)
35f	17-035f	Wiper	78	17-078	Screw (4)
35g	17-035g	Seat	79	17-079	Washer (4)
36	17-036	Adapter S.S.	80	17-080	Starboard Weight
37	17-037	O-Ring	81	17-081	Waterproof Connector, Female
38	17-038	One-Way Valve Assy.	82	17-082	Waterproof Connector, Male
39	17-039	Locknut	83	17-083	Snap Tab (2)
40	17-040	Spring	84	17-084	Screw (2)
41	17-041	Handle, Emergency Gas Supply	85	17-085	Communications Post (2)
			86	17-086	Packing Nut
			87	17-087	Ferrule, Back

*Parts for SuperLite-17b only.

KEY	PART NO.	DESCRIPTION
88	17-088	Ferrule, Front
89	17-089	Packing Gland
90	17-090	Plug
91	17-091	O-Ring
92	17-092	Nut
93	17-093	Main Exhaust Body
94	17-094	Main Exhaust Mushroom Valve
95	17-095	Screw (2)
96	17-096	Main Exhaust Cover
97	17-097	Screw (2)
98	17-098	Exhaust Deflector
98a	17-098a	Rubber Whisker
98b	17-098b	Adapter
98c	17-098c	Plate (2)
98d	17-098d	Screws (4)
98e	17-098e	Spacer (4)
99	17-099	Exhaust Mushroom Valve
*100b	17-100b	Inlet Nipple
100c	17-100c	Jam Nut
101	17-101	O-Ring
102	17-102	Inlet Valve
103	17-103	Spring
104	17-104	Stand off Washer
105	17-105	Washer
106	17-106	Lever
107	17-107	Spacer
108	17-108	Nut
109	17-109	Diaphragm
110	17-110	Cover
111	17-111	Clamp
112	17-112	Screw
113	17-113	Regulator Body
114	17-114	Piston
115	17-115	Spring Set
116	17-116	Spacer
117	17-117	Shaft
118	17-118	Washer
119	17-119	O-Ring
120	17-120	Packing Nut
121	17-121	Adjustment Knob
122	17-122	Retaining Pin
123	17-123	Knob, Nose Block
124	17-124	Packing Nut
125	17-125	O-Ring (2)
126	17-126	O-Ring
127	17-127	Port Retainer Screw (12)
128	17-128	Port Retainer
129	17-129	Face Port
130	17-130	O-Ring, Face Port
*131b		Demand Regulator

Covers the diver's entire head. Watertight seal is formed at the neck by means of a rubber sleeve called the neck dam. The diver's entire head, ears and face remain dry.

Lined with a foam head cushion which comfortably surrounds the diver's head and upper neck, with the exception of the face and ears.

Total weight: approximately 24 pounds.

Yoke system slips around neck to secure helmet from accidental removal, and is firmly locked into place.

Helmet shell constructed of woven fiberglass and polyester resin. Very strong, resistant to cracking, and will not carry an electrical charge.

Other features include: Demand Regulator and Side Valve Assembly, major features of the life support system; and Nose Block Device which allows diver to block his nose to provide an overpressure in his sinus and inner ear, for equalization.

Helmet is an excellent combination of all factors that influence diving helmet design — a comfortable, reliable piece of equipment.

KIRBY—MORGAN HELMET — KMB-17/SUPERLITE

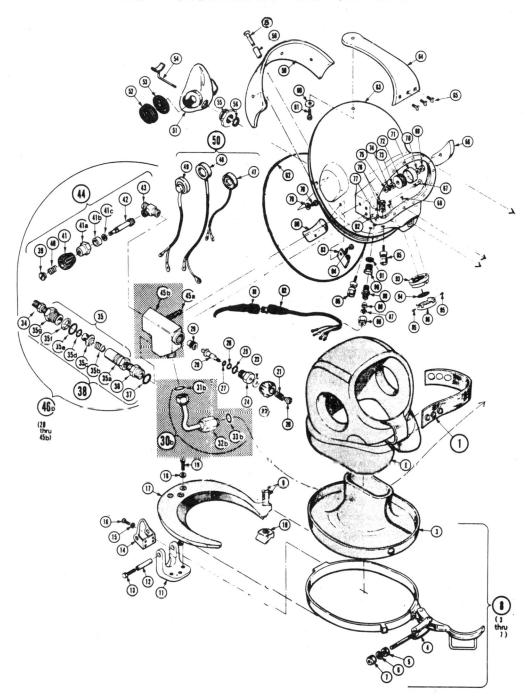

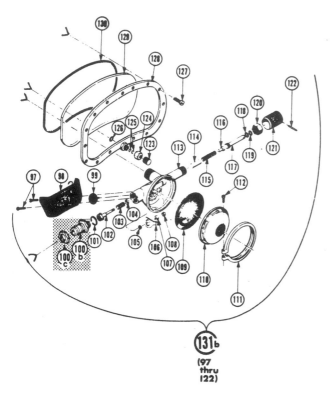

131b
(97
thru
122)

WHISKER

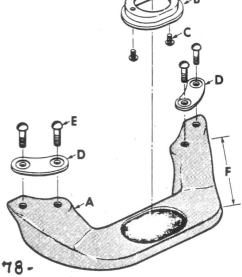

WHISKER NOT SHOWN IN DRAWING.
REPLACES EXHAUST DEFLECTOR.

KEY	PART #	DESCRIPTION
A	MS-9A-43-A	Rubber, Whisker
B	MS-9A-43-B	Adapter
C	MS-9A-43-C	Screw (2)
D	MS-9A-43-D	Plate (2)
E	MS-9A-43-E	Screw (4)
F	MS-9A-43	Whisker Kit Complete

78-

RAT HAT PARTS LIST

ITEM	PART #	DESCRIPTION	ITEM	PART #	DESCRIPTION
1	141120	1st Stage Regulator Assembly (1)	45	141131	O-Ring
2	141135	O-Ring (3)	46	141202	Valve (1)
3	140907	Pedestal Assembly (2)	47	141600	Muffler Assembly (1)
4	140905	O-Ring (2)	48	141805	Duck Bill Tie (1)
9	141419	Male Marsh & Marine Connector (1)	49	141806	Duck Bill Valve (1)
	141420	Female Marsh & Marine Connector (1)	50	141735	Lock Nut (2)
10	141424	Jam Nut (1)	52	141435	Two Wire Communication Leads (1)
11	141428	Washer (1)	53	141735	Spacer (6)
12	141426	O-Ring (1)	56	141728	Shoulder Bolt (2)
13	141425	Thru-Bulkhead Connector Body (1)	57	141732	Right Latch Handle (1)
14	140904	Jam Nut (2)	59	141294	Jam Nut (1)
16	141414	Binding Post with Two Nuts (2)	60	141206	Packing Nut (1)
17	141417	Gasket (2)	61	141216	Free Flow Knob (1)
18	141418	Washer (2)	62	141221	Set Screw (1)
21	141312	O-Ring (1)	63	141113	Washer (as required)
22	141303	Seat Base (2)	64	141112	Mounting Screw (1)
23	141308	Retaining Ring (1)	65	141105	Check Valve (2)
24	141305	Mushroom Valve (2)	66	141109	Swivel End Fitting Assembly (2)
25	141302	Exhaust Knob (2)	67	141103	O-Ring (4)
26	141309	Exhaust Knob Stop (3)	69	141111	Jam Nut (2)
27	141310	Screw (3)	70	141110	Manifold Main Body (1)
29	141313	Exhaust Pod Cover (1)	75	141807	Purge Valve Body (1)
30	141503	Gasket	79	140012	2nd Stage Regulator Tube (1)
31	140004	Medium Helmet Liner (1)	80	140016	O-Ring (1)
	140005	Large Helmet Liner (1)	81	141220	O-Ring (1)
32	141502	Face Port (1)	82	141731	Latch Handle — Left (1)
33	141501	Face Port Retainer (1)	83	141222	Disassmbly Tool (1)
34	141504	Screw (8)	85	141427	Speaker Assembly (1)
35	141401	Earphone Assembly (1)	86	141813	Seat Base (1)
36	141433	O-Ring (2)	87	141812	Mushroom Valve (1)
37	140020	Adjustment Screw (1)	88	141407	Collar (1)
38	140018	Mouthpiece	89	141311	Retaining Ring (1)
39	140017	Hose Assembly (1)			
40	141128	O-Ring (1)			
41	140010	2nd Stage Regulator (1)			
42	141729	O-Ring (1)			
43	140023	Velcro Strip (1)			
44	141227	Air Supply Tube (1)			

RAT HAT – OCEANEERING INTERNATIONAL

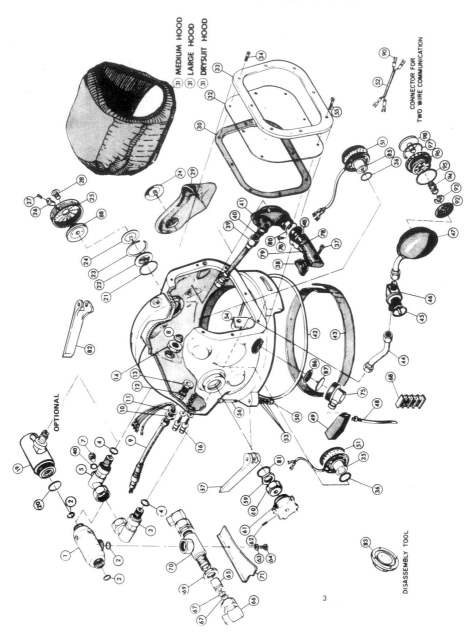

3

DIVERS SUPPLY PANEL

Certain basic requirements are essential in a well constructed panel:-

-a "non-return" valve must be fitted to the inlet side of the panel to avoid draining the divers supply hose in the event of a panel supply hose failure.
-all pipe work should be pressure rated and easily accessible for repair or inspection.
-ON/OFF valves should be lockable in the ON position and this position easily identified.

Fig 7-82

-an inlet pressure gauge should be fitted.
-divers individual supply pressure gauges should be fitted.
-reserve supply should be easily identified and pressure shown.

DIVERS UMBILICAL

An umbilical is so called because it consists of a number of elements taped and whipped together to form the life support line for the diver. It consists of the following element:-

Air Hose

The air hose must be fitted in one continuous length and conform to British Standards SAE 100 R3, normally $\frac{3}{8}$in internal diameter.

Fig 7-83 Terylene braided SAE 100 R3 Hose

End Fittings

End fittings should be of brass and are normally of the re-usable type. Most american diving equipment ie Kirby Morgan, General Aquadyne etc. use 9/16 AF umbilical connections. Prodive panel end fittings are $\frac{3}{8}$ BSP and divers end 9/16 AF.

ASSEMBLY

The hose should be parted off as squarely as possible using a knife of fine toothed hacksaw. Remove dirt particles from bore of hose. Lubricate sparingly with MS4 silicone compound.

1 Screw the hose into the ferrule (left hand thread) until the hose barely touches the bottom of the fitting.

2 lubricate the insert and the inside of the hose to avoid twisting or tearing the tube and to ease assembly.

3 Screw the insert into the ferrule until the hexagon on the insert shoulders on to the ferrule.
NOTE: any tendency for the hose to rotate in the ferrule should be resisted.

Figs 7-84 Assembly of re-usable end
           fittings

COMMUNICATIONS CABLE

The electrical wire element in a divers umbilical, associated with voice communication, normally consists of a four or six wire, water-blocked and screened cable (see page 7.59 for details).

LIFE LINE

A life line should be provided as an element of the complete umbilical to prevent weight being placed on the air hose or communications cable.

Whichever type of line is chosen it must be of sufficient strength to lift the fully dressed diver bodily from the water in an emergency.

It should be taped and whipped with the other elements to the air hose and be provided with non quick release connections for the divers harness and inboard end.

Some types of communciations cable are manufactured with a steel outer casing which is sufficiently strong to be used as a life line. In this case the life line is not necessary and the umbilical connections are attached to the communications cable and adjustment is then made so as to relieve any weight from the air hose.

Fig 7-85 Typical life line connection

PNEUMOFATHOMETER

The final component of the hose group (if no hot-water suit is being used) is the pneumofathometer. This is a simple, but accurate, depth measuring device which provides the surface with a method of constantly monitoring the diver's depth. One end of a 6 mm internal diameter non-collapsible flexible tube is connected at the surface to an air supply and pressure gauge calibrated to read in depth of sea water. The other end which is open to the sea water is fastened to the diver at chest level. The depth is determined by the air pressure required to blow and keep water out of the tube. If the diver is standing, one and a half metres must be added to the gauge reading to determine the actual depth.

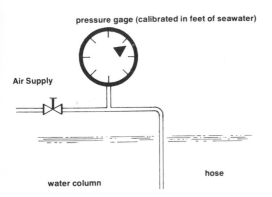

pressure gage (calibrated in feet of seawater)

Air Supply

hose

water column

Fig 7-86 Pneumofathometer

DIVERS VOICE COMMUNICATIONS SYSTEM

"HELLE" WIRE DIVER PHONE

This system provides hardwire communications between the tender and up to three divers. It is designed to give clear, reliable communications for all surface supplied helmets and masks.

Some units are also fitted with voice corrections circuitry which compensates for the distortion caused by divers speaking in a helium-oxygen atmosphere.

Figure 7-87 Two diver communications unit, suitable for air diving only.

The AMPLIFIER is the basic power unit and control panel for the intercom system. It includes a combination speaker/microphone (Tranceiver), selector switches permitting communications with as many as three divers and level controls.

The amplifier can be powered by 12 volt DC batteries or 220 or 110 volt transformer. To 12 volt ONLY ONE POWER SOURCE MAY BE USED AT A TIME.

Two wires are connected via either the front or rear panel connector or from the surface unit to the communications equipment in each diver's helmet. The diver's voices are continually being received on the surface. Should the surface tender wish to speak with any or all of the divers, he can do so by depressing the "press to talk" switch on the front panel. The surface tender can actuate switches on the front panel which also allows one diver to communicate with the other(s). All communications controls are located at the surface. It is necessary, therefore, for a surface tender to monitor and control the divers intercommunication set at all times.

The Communications Cable normally consists of a four or six wire water blocked and screened cable. Although only two wires are normally used at any one time.

Screening is provided to reduce outside interference from engine alternators etc.

Connections to the diving helmet/mask and surface amplifier are normally of two types:-

1 Bare wire to terminal posts
2 Patent under water connectors ie Marsh Marine, Prodive etc.

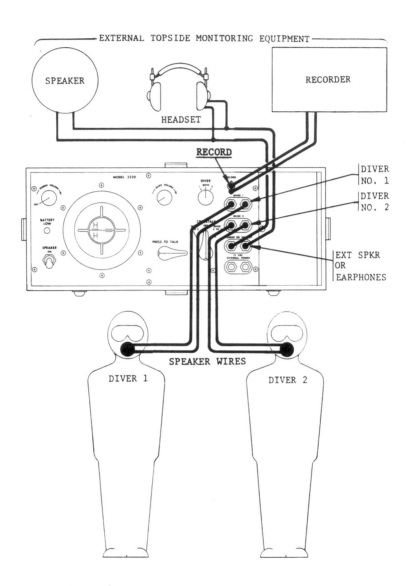

Fig 7-88 Two Wire Speaker-to-Speaker Interconnect

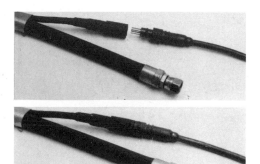

Figure 7-89a Marsh Marine 4-pin waterproof comm's. connector.
Figure 7-89b Marsh Marine connector in
the assembled condition.

The communications Harness which consists
of normally two ear pieces and a mocro-
phone are available for most modern
helmets and masks. Those designed for
use with band-masks are completely watertight but due to "potting" lose some
of their sensitivity, every transceiver
has a certain "impedance" (resistance to
flow) which must be compatible with the
amplifier.

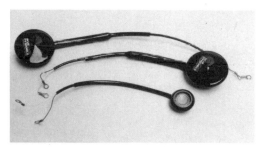

Figure 7-90 Typical replacement receivers
and microphone units.

Another type of communications harness
widely used is one made up of cheap
stereo headset receivers. These are
usually sealed using a contraceptive

condom. These give improved clarity
for short periods but require constant
maintenance.

THROUGH WATER COMMUNICATION

Through water communications work in
the same way as a radio telephone.
There are a number of systems in use
and under evaluation at the present
time.

Their main advantage is for the
untethered diver ie Navy or Police and
are finding a very real application
for emergency communication with
diving bells.

Their main disadvantage at present is
that they cannot fuction effectively
outside of a limited area and the
signal is obstructed if the diver
moves behind anything.

ACCESSORY EQUIPMENT

These items include -

- hand LEAD-LINE for measuring depth.

- SHOT LINE OR
  DESCENDING LINE to guide the diver to
  the bottom and for use in passing
  tools and equipment. This 3-inch line
  is cable-laid to prevent twisting and
  to facilitate easy identification by
  the diver on the bottom. In use, the
  end of the line may be fastened to a
  fixed underwater object, or it may be
  anchored with a weight heavy enough to
  withstand the force of the current.

- DISTANCE LINE made of 18 m of 15-thread
  cable-laid manila. The distance line
  is attached to the bottom end of the
  descending line and is used by the
  diver as a guide for searching as well
  as a means for relocating the
  descending line.

- DECOMPRESSION STAGE, constructed to
  carry one or two divers, is used both
  for putting divers into the water and
  for bringing them to the surface,
  especially when decompression stops
  must be made. The stage platform is
  made in an open grillwork pattern to
  reduce resistance from the water and
  may include seats. Guides for the
  descending line, and several eyebolts
  for attaching tools, steadying lines
  or weights are provided. The frames
  of the stages are collapsible for
  easy storage.

- STAGE LINE for raising and lowering
  the decompression stage. It is made
  up from 8 to 10 mm manila, nylon or
  polypropylene rope and marked-off at
  3 m intervals to assist in placing
  the stage at the proper decompression
  stops. The first 3 m mark is placed
  such that the diver's chest will be
  maintained at an average depth of
  3 m at his 3 m stop. The stage will
  have to be adjusted slightly

depending on the surface conditions
at the time of each dive.

Figure 7-91 Lazy-shot arrangement.

- LAZY SHOT. A lazy shot is a weighted
  line which is attached to the main
  descending line by a shackle which is
  free to run.

  The line is marked in 3 m intervals
  to correspond with the decompression
  stops and may be raised and lowered
  as required. It is used in the same
  manner as the stage line.

- "WET" BELL. The wet bell is a more
  sophisticated form of diving stage
  used for transportation to and from
  the work site, and may be used in
  the event of an emergency.

  The bell is normally provided with an
  air compartment equipped with an
  emergency or decompression breathing
  supply. Maximum permissible working
  depth under UK regulations is 50 m,
  although this type of bell is often

granted dispensation to 70m as an emergency back-up to an S.D.C. (Submersible Decompression Chamber)

Fig 7-92 "WET" BELL

- DIVING LADDER used when entering the water from the side of a small boat. The ladder is made of galvanised steel, and when in use it is held at the correct angle by a pair of struts which hold the ladder out from the side of the boat. These struts may be folded for storage.

- Cast iron WEIGHTS are provided in two sizes: 25 kilo and 50 kilo. Both sizes are used as descending line weights.

- Canvas TOOLBAG for carrying tools. The bag may be looped over the diver's arm, or it may be sent down the descending line.

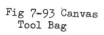

Fig 7-93 Canvas Tool Bag

- A STOPWATCH for timing the total dive time, decompression stop time, travel time, etc.

- UNDERWATER LIGHTS, if working conditions permit, these will greatly improve a diver's work capability and range of vision. A normal 100 watt photoflood type, sealed beam lamp in a suitable housing is satisfactory for use down to a depth of 45 metres.

- A WELDING FACEPLATE, fits over the regular faceplate and reduces the excessive glare produced by welding apparatus. The faceplate has a metal frame with interchangeable lenses and a spring clip for holding the lens in an "open" and "closed" position. The lenses are supplied in three degrees of increasing density designated as 4, 6 or 8. The selection of lens is determined primarily by the degree of turbidity of the water. Relatively clear water will require the use of darker lens than will muddy water.

DIVING

During all diving operations, while a diver is in the water, flag ALFA is to be flown in a prominent position.

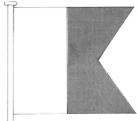

INTERNATIONAL CODE FLAG "A"
"I have a diver down; keep well clear at slow speed".

During night diving operations the diving vessel should display the lights which indicate, under International Code of signals, that the vessel is engaged in "Special Operations". This signal is two all round red lights separated by one all round white light, in a vertical position and approximately 18 inches to 2 feet apart.

AIR COMPRESSORS

Most air supply systems used in diving operations include at least one air compressor as a primary source of air. To properly select such a compressor it is essential that the diver has a basic understanding of the principles of gas compression. Generally, two types of air compressor are available. These are:-

1. DYNAMIC (CENTRIFUGAL)

2. POSITIVE DISPLACEMENT

The centrifugal compressor has, to date, been limited to special applications where high capacities of air are required. Its compact design combined with its high RPM suggests that any significant field repairs to this type of compressor would be difficult.

Positive displacement compressors may be further categorised as ROTARY and RECIPROCATING compressors. Rotary compressors usually have only one stage in which air is compressed by the action of a rotor in an eccentric stator.

The air is normally contained by sliding vanes, but in the case of the liquid ring rotary compressor water forms the containing seal.

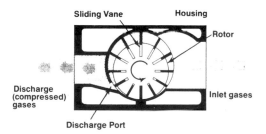

Fig 7-94 The Sliding Vane Rotary Compressor is a positive displacement, constant-volume unit with variable discharge pressure.

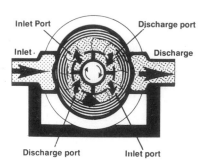

Fig 7-95   A Liquid Piston Rotary Compressor.

Rotary compressors are normally limited to pressures less than 6.8 bars and therefore, although they have very high output in the order of 8 to 9 cu metres per minute, are only adaptable to very shallow diving operations. This type of compressor normally has a diesel prime mover and is used to power air tools.

Reciprocating compressors are the most common compressors found in air diving operations. They are capable of providing capacities sufficient to support almost any surface-supplied air diving operation and recompression chamber. This type of compressor is also capable of attaining pressures high enough to charge SCUBA cylinders and high pressure cylinder banks.

The prime mover of this type of compressor is normally a diesel engine or three phase electric motor. The latter being more suitable for a fixed installation.

The compressor will consist of one or more compression cylinders dependent on the final pressure rating of the compressor. A typical HP compressor (Fig 7-96) will have three stages and be air or water cooled.

If not directly provided, capacity may be approximated from the displacement data provided on the compressor. Since

the capacity is the volume of air at
defined atmospheric conditions, compressed per unit of time, it will be

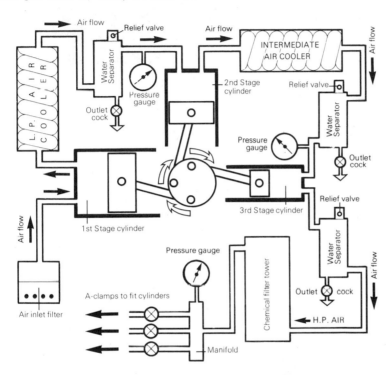

Fig 7-96 A three-stage air-cooled basic compressor layout

effected <u>only</u> by the first stage, as all
other stages serve only to increase the
pressure and reduce temperature.
All industrial compressors are stamped
with a code, consisting of at least two
but usually 4-5 numbers, which specify
the bore and stroke. Using this code
the displacement per revolution on the
compressor is equal to the volume of the
first stage cylinder(s).
The actual capacity of the compressor
will always be less than the displacement because of the CLEARANCE VOLUME of
compression. Compressors having a first
stage piston diameter of 10cms or larger

will normally have an actual capacity
of about 85% of their displacement.
The smaller the first stage piston the
lower the capacity will be (because
the clearance volume represents a
greater percentage of the cylinder
volume).

Other features of reciprocating compressors which should be understood by
those who operate and use them include:
LUBRICATION, INTERCOOLING, CONDENS-
ATION COLLECTION AND FILTRATION.

The lubricant serves four functions -

- to prevent wear between rubbing surfaces

- to seal close clearances

- to protect against corrosion

- to transfer heat and minute particles produced from wear, away from points of contact.

Unfortunately, this lubricant will vapourize into the air supply and, if not condensed or filtered out, will reach the diver's lungs.

Although every attempt should be made to limit the amount of lubricant in the air, the only assured prevention against harming the diver is to use non-toxic mineral based lubricants.

INTERCOOLERS are heat exchangers which are placed between the stages of a compressor to control the air temperature. The heat exchanger can be either air or water cooled.

During the cooling process, water vapour is condensed out of the air and is collected in condensation drains which must be periodically discharged.

Finally, as the air is discharged from the compressor, it must pass through an oil separator and a filter to remove lubricant, aerosols and particulate before it enters the accumulator.

FILTER SYSTEM:

The most efficient air filtering media are manufactured from absorbent materials whose granular form offers a high surface area to attract particles of contamination. The most common materials used are:-

SILICA GEL or ACTIVATED ALUMINA: for removing moisture.

ACTIVATED CHARCOAL: for removing oil mist and odours.

A rather more efficient filtering medium than those described above is MOLECULAR SIEVE (activated zeolites) with a granule type 13x. This material will remove both water vapour and oil mist but has the disadvantage of high cost.

The composition of a typical filter for an average-size h.p. compressor could be described as follows and is shown in Fig 7-97.

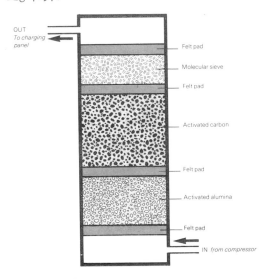

Fig 7-97   Filter tower

12.5 mm thick felt pad at inlet; and separating each chemical. Silica gel (self indicating type) at least 100 mm depth; or activated alumina, at least 100 mm depth; activated charcoal, at least 100 mm depth; 13x molecular sieve about 50 mm depth; 12.5 mm thick felt pad at outlet.

In some cases an oil/water centrifugal separator may be installed before the filter tower to remove excessive amounts of contaminate, prior to filtration which will extend the main filters operational life, and in some cases remove the necessity for silica gel.

Regular maintenance is essential. The simplest way to assess the time interval between replacement of the filter elements is by using self indicating si silica gel which changes colours as it becomes saturated with water, and regular air sampling.

Note: Silica gel can be re-used after drying.

Special considerations which apply to the use of air compressors are as follows:-

1 The compressor must deliver air at the established standards of purity.

2 The compressor should be fitted with filters to remove impurities from the air. These should be regularly checked and cleaned.

3 The engine driven compressor must always be mounted so that there is no danger of taking exhaust fumes (carbon monoxide) from the engine, or other contaminated air from local sources.

4 Only approved lubricants should be used.

STANDARDS FOR AIR

Compressed air for diving operations must meet standards of purity laid down by the BRITISH STANDARDS INSTITUTES (BS 4001).

These standards are:-
- Oxygen concentration 20-22% by volume.
- Carbon dioxide 0.05%(500ppm) maximum

- Water vapour 0.5 Grams per cubic metre maximum.

- Carbon monoxide 0.001% (10ppm) maximum.

- Oil-mist or vapour 1 milligram per cubic metre maximum.

- Solid and liquid particles not detectable except as noted above under oil-mist or vapour.

- Odour not objectionable.

To ensure that the source of the diver's breathing air, whether a compressor or h.p. cylinders, does satisfactorily meet the standards established above, it must be checked at intervals NOT exceeding six months. Preferably, testing equipment such as "Draeger" tubes and pump should be available for this periodic check.

DRAEGER MULTI -GAS DETECTOR:

These are available as complete kits, which are operated by means of a hand pump, draw a measured volume of air from a sample bag, through a calibrated glass tube containing reagent chemicals. If the contaminent for which the air is being tested is present, it reacts with these chemicals to produce a coloured stain. The length of stain thus produced is read off against calibration marks on the tube. The kit contains tubes to test approximately ten samples completely.

Air samples can alternatively be taken using evacuated sampling cylinders. These cylinders must then be taken to a qualified laboratory for analysis.

CHAPTER 8

SCUBA DIVING PROCEDURES

S.C.U.B.A. (Self Contained Underwater Breathing Apparatus).

The use of Scuba diving equipment for commercial work is sometimes underrated and, in some cases, abused as a cheap alternative to surface supplied equipment.

Scuba diving equipment affords the diver great mobility over a wide operational area and different depths but his duration underwater is limited by the air supply he carries with him.

Because of its limited duration the use of Scuba for commercial work is not recommended below 35m.

Formal training and experience combine to give the diver confidence in his ability. Beyond this, carefully established procedures as presented in this chapter, will provide maximum assurance that each dive will be carried out safely and efficiently.

PREPARATION FOR SCUBA DIVING

A certain minimum of equipment is required for every Scuba dive. This minimum may be augmented, as indicated by the nature of the work to be carried out, by items of optional accessary equipment.

Minimum Equipment

1. Scuba set - either single or twin fitted with a reserve mechanism.
2. Demand valve with contents guage.
3. Suit and hood.
4. Safety Harness.
5. Weight Belt.
6. Face Mask.
7. Swim Fins.
8. Knife.

In a free swimming situation on a surface marker float certain mandatory extras are required.

1. Wrist Compass
2. Depth Guage.

Fig 8-1 Scuba diver with minimum equipment listed above.

Diving

Before any diving operation can begin three basic steps must be taken.

1. The air supply must be provided.
2. All equipment must be assembled and thoroughly checked.
3. The diver must be dressed and given his final briefing.

Air Supply

The air used in any diving operation must meet THREE basic requirements.

1. it must meet air purity standards.
2. A sufficient quantity must be available to meet planned requirements plus an allowance for an adequate reserve.
3. The delivery system must provide a sufficient fow of air to the diver at the required pressure.

Duration of Air Supply

The duration of any cylinder, or combination of cylinders, is dependent upon the diver's consumption rate, depth of dive and capacity of the cylinders.

The effect of temperature is not usually significant when computing the duration.

Diver's Air Consumption on Surface

(a) At rest - 25 litres per minute.
(b) Doing moderate work - 25-40 litres per minute.
(c) Doing hard work - 40-70 litres per minute.

Example:

How long should a 1,700 litre (60cu ft.) cylinder last a diver doing moderate work at 18m (Absolute Pressure 2.8.) The higher rate i.e. 40 for moderate work should be used.

$$1700 \div (2.8 \times 40) = 15 \text{ mins}$$

Note: These consumption rates and subsequent calculations should only be used as a rough guide.

Methods for Charging Air Cylinders

A diving team will usually charge its own cylinders by one of two methods:-

1) Decanting - Sometimes called "Cascading":
   Transfering air from banks of large cylinders into the cylinder requiring filling.

2) High Pressure Air Compressor.

Decanting or Cascading is the fastest and most efficient method for charging air cylinders. The normal system will include a minimum of THREE large storage cylinders (designated A, B, C etc) manifolded together and feeding into a high pressure "whip" with an "A" clamp or other pillar valve attachment, contents guage and bleed valve to release the pressure in the line after charging.

Cylinders should be charged in the following manner:-

a) Check the existing pressure in the cylinders using a reliable pressure gauge.
b) Connect the cylinder to the charging whip, checking the "O" ring is in good condition and that the "A" clamp is secure.

It is advisable, when the facility is available, to immerse the cylinder in a tank of water. This will help to disapate heat generated during charging and contain an explosion should the cylinder fail.

c) Check that all fittings in the system are tight.
d) Close the bleed valve, open the cylinder air reserve mechanism (reserve lever in the DOWN position) and the cylinder valve which should be opened completely, then returned one quarter turn.
e) Slowly open the valve on cylinder "A". The sound of the air flowing into the cylinder will be noticeable. Control the flow so that the pressure in the cylinder increases at the rate which will prevent overheating; the cylinder should never be allowed to become too hot.
f) After a period of time the pressure in both cylinders will equalise and the audible flow of air will

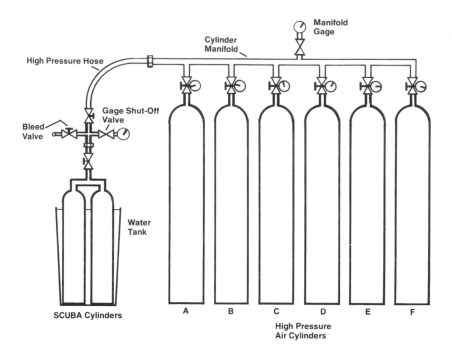

Fig 8-2 Decanting system for charging
        SCUBA

cease. Close the valve on cylinder
'A' and now open the valve on
cylinder 'B'. Again control the rate
of flow to limit the pressure change.

g) The pressure gauge should be closely
watched, and when the reading
approaches the rated pressure of the
cylinder, the valve on cylinder 'B'
should be closed and an accurate
reading taken.

h) If the pressure between cylinder 'B'
and the cylinder being charged has
equalised before the rated pressure
has been achieved, close the valve

on cylinder 'B' and slowly open the
valve on cylinder 'C' until the
required pressure is reached.

i) Close the valve on the charging
cylinder. Close the ON/OFF valve on
the charged cylinder. Check to see
that ALL valves in the system are
firmly closed.

j) If time will allow, leave the
cylinder to cool and top-up as
necessary.

k) When charging is completed and all
valves are closed, open the bleed
valve on the charging whip.

When ALL the air has been removed, disconnect the cylinder, close the air

reserve mechanism (lever in the UP position).

Additionally, it is a good practice to place a piece of masking tape over the cylinder valve. This helps to keep out dirt, retain the 'O' ring and is a means of identifying the cylinder as full.

These procedures can be repeated for additional cylinders. Eventually the pressure in cylinder 'A' will reach a level which is of no further use for charging purposes, at which time that cylinder must be removed from the system and recharged. Cylinder 'B' now replaces cylinder 'A' and cylinder 'C' likewise replaces 'B'. A new cylinder is put on line, taking the place of cylinder 'C'.

The charging of a storage bank by a suitable H.P. compressor 'in situ' is preferable to the removal and replacement of heavy cylinders.

Air Compressors

Can be used to directly charge Scuba cylinders, but because of the high pressures required few portable compressors are of any use for charging large quantities of cylinders. For example, the capacities of various portable compressors range from 9-43 litres per minute. At these rates it could take as long as two hours to fill one 1700 litre cylinder.

If a SUITABLE compressor is available, the basic charging procedure will be the same as that outlined for decanting except that the compressor will replace the bank of the cylinders. Special considerations which apply to the use of air compressors are:-
The compressor must deliver air at the established standards of purity.
The compressor should be equipped with filters to remove impurities from the air. These should be regularly checked and cleaned.
Standards for inspection and maintenance

must be carefully met.
An engine driven compressor must always be mounted so that there is no danger of taking exhaust fumes (carbon monoxide) from the engine or other contaminated air from local sources.
Only approved lubricants are to be used.

Additional information on the use of air compressors will be found in Chapter 7.

Notes on Charging Cylinders too Quickly

1) As a cylinder is charged, according to CHARLE'S LAW the air as it is compressed will increase in temperature and the cylinder will become warm. When the cylinder subsequently cools condensation can form on the interior of the cylinder and give rise to corrosion.

2) Again according to CHARLE'S LAW, as the temperature of the air in the cylinder rises its pressure will also rise. Therefore, if a cylinder is filled to its working pressure too quickly causing heat, as it cools this pressure will drop and the cylinder will have a less than maximum charge.

3) A sudden increase in pressure on a cylinder, as would occur with rapid charging, places stress on the cylinder which will reduce its life and increase the possibility of it failing.

Equipment Preparation

Prior to any dive, all equipment must be carefully inspected for signs of deterioration, damage or corrosion and must be tested for proper operation where required. Pre-dive preparation procedures must be standardized, must never be altered in the interests of 'convenience', and must be the personal concern of each diver. Every diver must always check his own equipment and must never assume that any piece of equipment is ready for use unless he has personally verified that readiness, even if other personnel have been assigned to prepare and check-out the equipment.

EQUIPMENT PREPARATION (SCUBA)

GENERAL CHECKLIST

Air Cylinders

Inspect for rust, cracks, dents or any other evidence of weakness or fault. Pay particular attention to loose or bent valves.

Check cylinder markings and verify suitability for use. Check that the hydrostatic test date has not expired.

Remove masking tape and inspect 'O' ring. Verify that the reserve mechanism is in a closed position signifying a filled cylinder ready for use.

Back-Pack Harness Straps

Check for signs of rot or excessive wear. Adjust straps for individual use, and test quick-release mechanisms.

Regulator

Attach regulator to the cylinder on/off valve, making certain that the 'O' ring is properly sealed. Open the cylinder valve all the way and then back off $\frac{1}{4}$ turn. Check for any leaks in the regulator by listening for the sound of escaping air. Check the contents using the H.P. gauge. If a leak is suspected determine the exact location by submerging the valve assembly and the regulator in a tank of water and looking for bubbles. Frequently the problem can be traced to an improperly sealed regulator. This is corrected by closing the valve, bleeding

the regulator, detaching and reseating. If leak is at the 'O' ring, and reseating does not solve the problem, replace the 'O' ring.

With single-hose unit, the hose supplying air should come over the diver's RIGHT shoulder. Inhale and exhale SEVERAL TIMES through the mouth-piece, making sure that the demand stage and mushroom valves are working correctly. Depress and release the purge button at the mouthpiece and listen for any sound of leaking air. Breathe in and out several times. Close the cylinder on/off valve. During this period the suit inflation hose, if fitted, should be tested.

Life Preserver (Wet suit only)

Orally inflate to check for leaks, and then squeeze all of the air out. The final amount of remaining air in the vest should be sucked out so that the preserver is completely empty. Whichever type of inflation is fitted i.e. H.P. cylinder, CO_2 cartridge or direct feed, check its operational condition.

Face Mask

Check the seal of the mask and the condition of the head strap. Check for cracks in the skirt and faceplate.

Fins

Check straps and inspect blades for any signs of cracking.

Diving Knife

Test the edge of the knife for sharpness, and make sure that the knife is fastened securely in the scabbard. Verify that the knife can be removed without difficulty.

Weight Belts

Check that the belt is in good condition
and that the proper number of weights
are in place and secure. Verify that
the quick-release buckle is functioning
properly.

Wristwatch

Check that watch is wound and set to the
correct time. Inspect the pins and strap
of the watch for wear.

Depth Gauge and Compass

Inspect pins and straps on each. Make
sure depth gauge is properly calibrated.
If possible, check compass against
another compass.

General

Inspect any other equipment which will
be used on the dive as well as any
spare equipment that MAY be used during
the dive. This would include spare
regulators, cylinders, and gauges.
Also check all lines, tools, and other
optional gear. Finally, lay all equipment in a place where it will be out of
the way of deck traffic and ready for
use.

DIVER PREPARATION

When the diver has completed inspecting
and testing his equipment, he reports
his readiness to the diving supervisor.
When the diving supervisor and the
divers are all satisfied that the requirements of the operation are FULLY understood and the divers are in good health
and otherwise ready to proceed, the
divers may dress for the dive.

Dressing

Every Scuba diver must be able to put
all his gear on by himself, although the
assistance of a tender or buddy is
encouraged.

The dressing sequence is only important
with regard to the following items of
equipment:

SAFETY HARNESS must be worn under all
other equipment.
LIFE JACKET must be worn over the
safety harness but under all other
equipment.
WEIGHT BELT must be OUTSIDE of all back-
pack harness straps, or other equipment
which could prevent its quick release in
the event of an emergency.

During training at Prodive it is mandatory that the tender or buddy go through
a set 'check list' to ensure that the
diver has been dressed correctly which
will be given to the supervisor prior
to the dive.

Scuba Equipment Read-Out (including full face mask)

1. Life Line secure.
2. Main Valve 'open'.
3. Contents Reading(Bars).
4. Demand Valve checked ('purged').
5. Diver has been seen to locate,
   operate and return reserve.
   Reserve is now closed.
6. Diver has been seen to locate his
   weight release pin.
7. Diver (number) ready for the water.

The diver is now ready to enter the
water, at the discretion of the diving
supervisor who will have made sure that
all diving signals are being displayed
and regulations adhered to.

Water Entry

There are several methods of water entry, with the choice usually determined by the nature of the diving platform. Several basic rules apply to all methods of entry -
-LOOK before jumping or pushing off from the platform or ladder.
-TUCK chin into chest and hold the cylinders with one hand to prevent them from hitting the back of the head.
-HOLD the mask in place with the fingers and the mouthpiece in place with the heel of the hand.

The Front Jump or Step In is the most frequently used method and is best used from a stable platform or vessel which is not easily disturbed by the diver's movements. To make the entry, the diver should not actually "jump" into the water but simply take a large step out from the platform.

Techniques differ for actually entering the water after the jump according to the diver's height from the water. Up to 1.5 meters the diver should keep his legs in an open stride. Above 1.5 meters the legs should be brought together and fins pointed. He should try to enter the water with a slightly-forward tilt of the upper body so that the force of entry will not drive his tanks up to hit the back of his head. At all times the diver should be looking straight ahead.

The Rear Roll is the normal method for entering the water from a small boat. A fully-outfitted diver, standing on the edge of a boat, would unnecessarily upset the stability of the craft and the diver himself would be in danger of falling either into the boat, or unprepared into the water. To execute a rear roll, the diver sits on the gunwhale of the boat, facing inboard. With chin on chest and one hand holding his mask and mouthpiece in place (just as in all other methods of entry), he rolls backward, essentially moving through a full backward somersault.

If working from the beach, the diver will make a choice of entry depending upon the condition of the surf and the slope of the bottom. If the water is calm and the slope gradual, the diver can walk out, carrying his fins until he reaches water deep enough for swimming. If moderate to high surf is running (but not high enough to cause postponement of the operation), the diver, wearing his fins, should walk backwards into the waves, until he has enough depth for swimming. He should gradually settle into the waves as they break around him.

If diving as a BUDDIED PAIR on a distance line each diver will be responsible for the checking and subsequent read-out of the others equipment. Entry into the water can be achieved in any of the previously mentioned ways. At no time must one or other of the divers disconnect themselves from the surface marker or buddy line.

Whichever method of entry is adopted the divers and their attendants or buddies must be aware of the potential hazzards involved in jumping into unknown water. The attendant must pay special attention to the amount of life line required to allow the diver to enter the water safely.

PRE-DESCENT SURFACE CHECK

In the water and prior to descending to operating depth, the diver and his attendant make a final check of his equipment-

-make a breathing check of the Scuba set and its contents.
-the attendant should visually check his diver's equipment for leaks.
-check his face mask seal (a small amount of flooding may have occurred on water entry).
-check bouyancy. A Scuba diver should strive for neutral bouyancy (if carrying extra equipment or heavy tools, he might easily be negatively bouyant and

and adjustment may be necessary).

If wearing a dry suit either "avon" or unisuit types check for leaks; vent the air from the suit as necessary by opening the cuff; adjust suit inflation as necessary for proper buoyancy.

It is important that the diver orientates himself before leaving surface in order to give himself some direction when reaching sea bed. If the diver is wearing a compass he should check this before leaving surface.

DESCENT

Immediately prior to descending the diver(s) signal their attendant and the bottom time begins.

When using dry suit the diver should always leave surface "feet first" in order to prevent a build up of air in the feet of the suit which could push off the fins.

Descent should always be made down the shot line where one is provided. The diver(s) may swim down, or they may pull themselves down the shot line. The rate of descent will generally be governed by the ease with which the diver(s) will be able to equalise the pressure in their ears and sinuses but it should never exceed 30m per minute. If difficulty is experienced in clearing the diver(s) should stop and ascend slightly until the pressure is relieved. The descent should then continue at a slower rate. If a problem still persists after several attempts to equalise, the dive should be aborted.

DIVING TECHNIQUES AND PROCEDURES

BREATHING

When using SCUBA for the first time, a diver is likely to experience a natural anxiety to breathe more rapidly and deeply than normal. He must learn to breathe in an easy, slow rhythm, at a steady pace. The rate of work should be paced to the breathing cycle, rather than changing the breathing to support the work rate. If the diver finds himself breathing too hard, he should pause in his work until his breathing returns to his normal level. Some divers, knowing that they have a finite air supply which must govern the length of the dive, will attempt to conserve air by holding their breath. One common technique is to skip-breathe - to insert an unnatural, long pause between each breath. BREATH-HOLDING and SKIP-BREATHING ARE DANGEROUS and frequently lead to shallow-water blackout. Divers must not use these techniques in an effort to increase bottom time.

Every diver will note some increased resistance to breathing caused by the design of his equipment. For normal diving, the level of resistance should not change until the primary air supply has been almost depleted. A marked increase in breathing resistance is the signal to the diver to activate his air reserve and to immediately begin his ascent. A diver can check on the status of his air supply by taking a sudden, deep breath. If there is a marked pinching off of the air, the supply is approaching exhaustion.

RESERVE PROCEDURE

Single Sets

On entering the water the reserve lever should be in the "up" position and its operation checked during the diver's read-out.

The reserve lever should not be pulled until either -

-the contents gauge reads zero.
-the diver experienced difficulty in breathing from the demand valve.

After the reserve lever has been pulled
the diver then checks the contents of
his set using the H.P. contents gauge,
which should read between 30-50 bars.
The diver should then surface.

Twin Sets

As for single sets, except that

-after the reserve lever has been pulled,
time should be allowed for the set to
decant before checking the contents
gauge. Because the reserve mechanism
is only fitted to one cylinder and
decanting occurs when the lever is
pulled the following procedure can, at
the supervisor's discretion, be adopted
in depths SHALLOWER THAN 10 METERS.

After equalisation the diver may return
his reserve lever and continue the dive
until either -

-again the contents gauge reads zero.
-again he experiences difficulty breathing from the demand valve.

After the reserve lever has been pulled
for the second time the diver should
surface.

Mask Clearing

Some water seepage into the face mask is
a normal condition and is often useful
in defogging the lens. From time to time
the quantity may build up to a point where
it must be removed. Also, on occasion,
a mask may become dislodged and flooded.

To clear a flooded mask not equipped with
a purge valve, the diver should roll on
his side or look upward, so that the
water will collect at the side or bottom
of the mask. Using either hand, the
diver applies a firm direct pressure on
the opposite side or top of the mask,
and exhales firmly and steadily through
the nose. The water will be forced out
under the skirt of the mask.

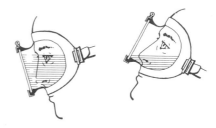

Figure 8-3 To clear a flooded face-
mask, push gently on the upper portion
of the mask and exhale through the nose
into the mask. As water is forced out,
tilt the head backward until the mask
is clear.

When using a full face mask the technique is the same except with the "avon"
a nose clip is worn. In this case air
must either be forced past the nose
clip or allowed to escape from the side
of the mouthpiece.

Mouthpiece Clearing

If the mouth piece is accidentally
pulled from the mouth and becomes flooded
while underwater. With single hose
SCUBA this is not too serious a problem
since the hose (carrying air at medium
pressure) will not flood and the mouthpiece can quickly be cleared by depressing
the purge button as the mouthpiece is
being replaced.

Underwater Swimming Technique

For underwater swimming all propulsion
comes from the action of the legs. The
hands are used only for manoeuvring.
The leg kick should be through a large
easy arc with the main thrust coming
from the hips. The knees and ankles
should be relaxed. The rhythm of the
kick should be maintained at a level that
will not unduly tire the legs or bring on
muscle cramps.

Buddy Breathing

If a diver runs out of air or his SCUBA malfunctions, he can obtain air from his buddy on a sharing basis. Buddy breathing is stictly an emergency procedure, which must be practiced in advance of need so that each diver will be thoroughly familiar with the procedure.

The steps to be followed in buddy breathing are -

A. Remain calm, and signal the problem to the buddy by pointing at your mouthpiece.
B. DO NOT grab for the buddy's mouthpiece. The diver places his hand on the hand which the buddy is using to hold the mouthpiece. The buddy and the diver should hold on to each other by grasping a strap or the free arm.
C. The buddy must make the first move by taking a breath and passing it to the other diver. The other diver will then guide it to his mouth. Both divers will maintain direct hand contact on the mouthpiece.
D. The mouthpiece may have flooded during the transfer. In this case it must be cleared either by use of the purge button or by exhaling before a breath can be taken.
E. The diver should take two full breaths (exercising caution in the event that all of the water has not been purged) and hand the mouthpiece back to the buddy. The buddy should then take two breaths, and the cycle is repeated.
F. The diver taking the breaths may become more bouyant than the other. The divers must be careful not to drift away from each other.
G. The divers should repeat the breathing cycle and establish a smooth rhythm. No attempt should be made to surface until the cycle is stabilised and the proper signals have been exchanged.
H. During ascent the diver without the mouthpiece must exhale slowly to offset the effect of decreasing pressure on their lungs.

Diver Communications

The primary form of underwater communication between divers is by hand signal; primary communication between the surface and a diver is accomplished through line-pull signals. If divers are operating under conditions of low visibility, the buddy pairs will at times be forced to communicate with line-pull signals on the buddy line.

Hand signals and line-pull signals should be delivered in a forceful, exaggerated manner so that there can be no ambiguity about the signal and so that it is obvious that a signal is in fact being given.

VISUAL SIGNALS

The following hand signal code is used widely throughout the diving industry with some small variations to suit individual circumstances i.e. the signal used in the code to signify that the diver is "well" is often replaced by the "thumbs up".

This variation is acceptable providing all diving team members are aware of the signals being used.

DIVER TO DIVER AND TO THE SURFACE

NUMBERS

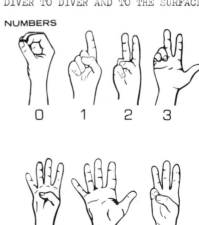

0   1   2   3

4   5   6

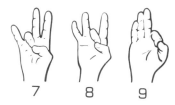

7   8   9

**OK
all is well**

This can be either a question from one diver to another, or an affirmative reply to this question. Keep the fingers straight.

**Stop
stay
where
you
are**

Often followed by another signal explaining why — unless the reason is obvious.

You or me

Diver points to himself or another diver, indicating the person referred to in the signal which follows.

**Go up
I am going up**

An instruction to ascend. Upward movement of the hand adds emphasis.

**Go down
I am going down**

An instruction to descend, normally made only at the start of a dive.

Something wrong

Not an emergency, but an indication that all is not well. Usually followed by an indication of the source of trouble.

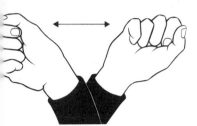

Distress

A signal which elicits immediate action to rescue the diver giving it.

I am on reserve

Indicates that air supply is low, and the dive should be terminated. Give 'oooond' signal in response.

I cannot pull my reserve

Use in event of reserve valve failure. Buddy should check action of reserve and be ready to share if necessary.

LIFELINE SIGNALS

Manual Signals

1 In the absence of any alternative method, manual signals by line are employed for all communications in which two divers or an attendant and a diver are physically in contact, whether it be by lifeline, foatline, or buddyline.

2 Signals are of two kinds:

(a) Long, steady and distinct PULLS
(b) Short, sharp BELL PULLS made with the same timing as striking a ship's bell.

3 PULLS AND BELLS must never be made violently as this may embarrass the diver.

Signalling Procedure

4 All signals from attendant to diver are to be preceded by one pull to attract attention; the signal is then made after the diver has answered with one pull.

5 All signals received must be acknowledged by repeating the signal, but not unless the signal is clearly understood. If a signal is not acknowledged or is acknowledged incorrectly, the person making the signal should then go on repeating the signal until a correct acknowledgement is received. When a signal is being acknowledged incorrectly, the diving supervisor may decide to surface the diver to clarify the situation.

6 It must be remembered that a diver at work may not always be able to acknowledge a signal immediately, and the attendant must wait a few moments before repeating the signal.

7 FOUL LINES. If the lifeline gets turned around an obstruction it may be impossible to get signals through and the turns must be taken out from the surface as soon as practicable.

8 INTERPRETATION OF SIGNALS. The attendant must use his judgment in the interpretation of signals and must consider the most likely meaning of each signal; for instance, when a diver is descending and the attendant knows the diver is near his depth or job, one pull on the line means the diver has reached his depth or job. On the other hand, a single pull while the diver is on his way down means 'Hold on'. As it would be difficult to distinguish a single bell from one pull, one pull is included in the direction and working signals, which are otherwise bell signals.

9 If the attendant receives two bells immediately after the diver has reached the bottom, it means the diver wants slack on the shot rope taken up; and when it is properly adjusted the diver signals 'Hold on' to signify that the rope can be secured inboard. On the other hand, two bells given immediately after the diver has signalled he is coming up means he wants to be pulled up.

EMERGENCY PULL-UP

This signal, a succession of pulls, is to be used only in great emergency; it is not to be answered but obeyed - IMMEDIATELY

FLOAT LINE SIGNALS

1 Divers attached to floats make their signals by pulling on the float line and causing the float to bob up and down.

2 To signal back to the diver a boat must close the float and the float line must be taken in hand to pass the signals in the normal manner.

3 Care must be taken, however, especially when working in a tideway, that the diver is not pulled away from his task by allowing any undue strain to come on the float line owing to drift of the attendant boat.

BUDDYLINE SIGNALS

1 Communication between a pair of divers underwater is by the single-lifeline code of signals on the buddyline.

2 This code may be supplemented by special prearranged signals, but to avoid confusion these should be kept to a minimum.

3 A diver requiring help from his companion in an emergency gives the emergency signal - a rapid succession of pulls.

SINGLE-LIFELINE CODE - ATTENDANT TO DIVER (see overpage)

ATTENDING

Prior to, and during dressing the following should be observed:-

-the lifeline must be secured to the harness using a bowline knot.
-the inboard end of the lifeline must be secured inboard at all times.
-divers should be referred to by number i.e. diver one, diver two etc.
-attendants should assist the diver during dressing to check the equipment.

When a diver is being tended by either a line from the surface or a buddyline several basic considerations apply:-

SINGLE-LIFELINE CODE - ATTENDANT TO DIVER

General Signals

1 pull	To call attention Are you well?
2 pulls	Am sending down a rope's end (or as pre-arranged)
3 pulls	You have come up too far Go down slowly till we stop you
4 pulls	Come up
4 pulls followed by 2 bells	Come up, hurry up, or Come up, surface decompression
4 pulls followed by 5 bells	Come up your safety float

Direction signals

1 pull	Search where you are
2 bells	Go to the end of distance line or jack-stay
3 bells	Face shot then go right
4 bells	Face shot then go left
5 bells	Come into your shot, or turn back if on a jackstay

SINGLE-LIFELINE CODE - DIVER TO ATTENDANT

General Signals

1 pull	To call attention Made bottom Left bottom Reached end of jackstay I am well
2 pulls	Send me down a rope's end (or as pre-arranged)
3 pulls	I am going down
4 pulls	May I come up?
4 pulls followed by 2 bells	I want to come up Assist me up
Succession of pulls (must be more than four)	EMERGENCY SIGNAL Pull me up IMMEDIATELY
Succession of 2 bells	Am foul and need the assistance of another diver
Succession of 3 bells	Am foul but can clear myself if left alone
4 pulls followed by 4 bells	Attend telephone

Working Signals

1 pull _ _ _ _ _ _ _ _ _ _ _ _ _ _ _ _ _ _ _ Hold on or stop

2 bells _ _ _ _ _ _ _ _ _ _ _ _ _ _ _ _ _ _ _Pull up

3 bells _ _ _ _ _ _ _ _ _ _ _ _ _ _ _ _ _ _ _Lower

4 bells _ _ _ _ _ _ _ _ _ _ _ _ _ _ _ _ _ _ _Take up slack lifeline, or You are
holding me too tight

5 bells _ _ _ _ _ _ _ _ _ _ _ _ _ _ _ _ _ _ _Have found, **started**, or completed
work.

ATTENDING (Continued)

-lines should be kept free of slack.
-any signal via the line must be
 acknowledged by returning the same signal
 except the emergency signal which should
 be acted upon immediately.
-the attendant should signal the diver
 with a single pull every five or six
 minutes to determine if the diver is
 'well'. A return signal of one pull
 from the diver will communicate that he
 is alright.
-the diver and attendant must be particularly aware of the possibilities for
 snagging lifelines or for becoming
 entangled.
-if the use of a lifeline is likely to
 inhibit the diver while underwater he
 may at the supervisors descretion be
 attached to a surface marker float.
 (This is a dispensation awarded to
 Prodive for training purposes and is
 not admissable under normal regulations.)

The divers while buddied together will be
attached to a surface marker buoy. This
buoy (or witness float) must be kept in
close observation at all times. Should
weather conditions deteriorate the divers
must be called up.

Signals may be passed to and from the
divers while underwater through the
surface float. Communication between
divers can either be hand or line signals.

WORKING WITH TOOLS

The near-neutral buoyancy of a SCUBA
diver poses certain problems when working
with tools. The diver is virtually
unable to bring any leverage to bear.
When he tries to apply force to a wrench,
for example, he will push himself away
from the wrench and very little force
will be applied to the work. When using
any tool which requires such leverage
or force (including pneumatic or
hydraulic power tools), the diver should
try to brace himself in some way with
his feet, a free hand, or a shoulder.
If both sides of the work are accessible,
two wrenches - one on the nut and one on
the bolt - should be used. By pulling
on one wrench and pushing on the other,
the counter force will permit most of
the effort to be transmitted to the
work.

Any tools to be used should be organized
in advance, and the diver should carry
as few items with him as possible. If
many tools are required, a canvas tool
bag should be used to lower them to
the diver as needed.

The SCUBA diver where possible should
avoid the use of pneumatic tools and
H.P. water-jetting equipment due to
the high noise levels created.

ADAPTING TO UNDERWATER CONDITIONS

Through careful and thorough planning, the divers will be prepared for the underwater conditions at the diving site and will have been provided, as necessary, with appropriate auxiliary equipment, protective clothing, and tools. Adaptation to certain conditions, however, cannot be facilitated by accessory gear and the diver will have to employ particular operational techniques to offset the effects of these conditions.

For example-

-stay two or three feet above a MUDDY BOTTOM, use a restricted kick and avoid stirring up the mud. A diver should position himself so that the current will carry any clouds of mud away from the work site.
-over a wreck, coral or rocky bottom, be careful to avoid cuts and abrasions.
-avoid abrupt changes of depth.
-DO NOT MAKE SIGHT-SEEING EXCURSIONS to explore "interesting" sites away from the dive site unless such excursions have been included in the dive plan.
-be aware of the peculiar properties of LIGHT underwater. Depth perception is altered on a basis of 3 to 4 (an object that seems to be three feet away is actually four feet away), and objects tend to appear larger than they really are.
-be aware of unusually STRONG CURRENTS.

Ascent (Normal)

When it is time to return to the surface, either diver or attendant may signal the end of the dive. When the signal has been acknowledged, the divers must start for the surface.

For normal ascent, from a dive with no decompression requirements, the divers will breathe steadily and naturally, and ascend to the surface at a rate of 18 m per minute. The divers MUST NEVER HOLD THEIR BREATH DURING ASCENT, because of the danger of an air embolism.

If decompression is required, the divers will ascend according to the appropriate decompression schedule.

While ascending, keep a watch overhead for objects-especially those which may be floating on the surface. A good practice is to spiral slowly while rising to provide a full 360 degree scan. The diver should keep an arm extended over his head to prevent striking his head on any unseen object.

Decompression

Whenever possible, SCUBA operations must be conducted so that no decompression will be required. This is not always feasible, but a requirement for decompression should be known well in advance of a given dive and appropriate preparations must be made.

While the Diving Supervisor is planning the operation, he will determine the required bottom time for each dive. Based upon the time and depth of the dive, he will compute the required decompression profile from the tables presented in Chapter Four. The breathing supply required to support the total time in the water must then be calculated. If the air supply is not sufficient, a back-up SCUBA will have to be made available to the diver. The back-up unit can be strapped to a a decompression stage or tied off on a lazy shot (see equipment).

When the diver has completed his assigned task, or has reached the maximum allowable bottom time prescribed in the diveplan, he must ascend to the decompression stage or the lazy shot, and signal the surface that he is ready to begin decompression. With a stage being handled from the surface, the diver will be taken through the appropriate stops while the timekeeper controls the progress. Before each move of the stage, the tender will signal the diver to prepare for the lift and the diver will signal back when prepared. When using a lazy shot, the tender will signal when each stop has been completed, at which point the lazy shot will be raised to his next stop and the diver will swim up, signalling his arrival at the next stop. Stop times will always be regulated by the tender.

In determining the levels for the decompression stops, the sea state on the surface must be taken into consideration. If large swells are running, the decompression stage or lazy shot will be constantly rising and falling with the movements of the surface support craft. The depth of each decompression stop should be calculated so that the diver's chest will never be brought above the depths prescribed for the stops in the decompression tables.

In the event of an accidental surfacing or an emergency, the Diving Supervisor will have to determine if decompression should be resumed in the water or if the services of a recompression chamber are required. The possibility of having to make such a choice should be anticipated during the planning stages of operation.

SURFACING AND LEAVING THE WATER

When approaching the surface, a diver must make certain that he is not coming up underneath the support craft or any other object on the surface. He should listen for the sound of propellers of other boats etc.

Arriving on surface he should immediately come to the diving ladder or support craft and come out of the water through The "splash" zone as quickly as possible. Any divers following him inboard should stay well clear of the ladder until the diver is secured inboard.

On being secured inboard (one metre clear of the ladder) the diver should give his name and report "well".

When diving on a surface marker float sometimes it is necessary to recover the divers inboard of the support craft. This is best accomplished after removing the divers SCUBA set and weight belt. The diver should at all times remain on his lifeline until he is secure.

POST-DIVE PROCEDURES

Physiological problems may not be evident until some time after a dive. The diver and all other members of the diving team must constantly be alert for the possibility of such problems as decompression sickness and embolism. Injuries sustained during a dive - such as cuts or animal bites - may not be noticed at first because of shock or the numbing effect of cold water. For these reasons diving personnel should remain under the observation of the Diving Supervisor for as long as possible after a dive.

If satisfied with his apparent physical condition, the diver's first responsibility after the dive is to check his equipment for damage and get it out of the way of the on-deck activity.

The Diving Supervisor should de-brief each returning diver as soon as practical while the experience of the dive is still fresh in the diver's mind. The Diving Supervisor should determine if the assigned tasks were completed, if any problems were encountered, if any changes to the over-all dive plan are indicated, and if the divers have any suggestions for the next divers.

Post-Dive Maintenance and Stowage

Each diver is responsible for the immediate post-dive maintenance and proper disposition of the equipment he used during the dive.

The following procedures should be followed:-

A. Turn off the cylinder on/off valve and depress the reserve lever even if the tank has only been partially used. This will serve as a warning that the tank has been used and must be checked and refilled. It is also a good practice to place it in a specially designated area to avoid any possible mix-up.

B. Bleed the regulator by inhaling through the mouthpiece, or pressing the purge button, and remove the regulator.

C. Be sure that the protective cone is clear of water or dirt, check the 'O' ring, and secure the cone in place over the regulator inlet. This will keep foreign particles out of the regulator and also permit submerging the regulator in fresh water for cleaning without permitting water to enter the first stage of the regulator.

D. If the regulator - or any other equipment - has been damaged, it should be tagged "damaged" and separated from the rest of the equipment. Damaged equipment should be repaired, inspected, and tested as soon as possible. Irreparable equipment must be destroyed and discarded.

E. Wash all equipment with fresh water and be sure to remove all traces of salt. The salt will not only speed corrosion of the materials but may also plug up vent holes in the regulator and the depth gauge. All parts of the equipment must be free to move.

F. When all equipment has been washed and rinsed, it should be hung up to dry and then placed in appropriated stowage. Regulators should be stowed separately and never left mounted on cylinders. When dry, suits should be carefully folded or hung. The suits should never be hung from a hook or a wire hanger since they will stretch out of shape or be torn. Masks, depth gauges, life vests and any other equipment which can be damaged or scuffed by rough handling should be individually stored and never dumped collectively in a box or drawer. Batteries should be removed from lights, tested, and stored separately. All lines should be dried, coiled and properly stowed.

H. A fully-charged cylinder may be stored for months without harm. The quality of the air will not deteriorate. However, it is a good practice to change the air in a cylinder if it has been in storage for over a year.

Complete maintenance of SCUBA regulators, valving, tanks and accessory equipment should only be performed by trained personnel in properly equipped facilities. Specific instructions for such maintenance are found in the technical manuals provided by the equipment manufacturers.

The diver, however, will frequently find it necessary to perform simple field maintenance and repair. Such first-line care will do much to ensure the continued safe and efficient operation of the equipment.

Each diving facility should assemble or have access to a basic "Field Repair and Maintenance Kit"

ALL REPAIR AND MAINTENANCE SHOULD BE FOLLOWED BY A THOROUGH INSPECTION AND TESTING OF THE EQUIPMENT TO ENSURE ITS FULL OPERABILITY AND SAFETY. IF THERE IS ANY QUESTION ABOUT A PARTICULAR PIECE OF EQUIPMENT, DO NOT DIVE WITH IT UNDER ANY CIRCUMSTANCE.

CHAPTER 9

SURFACE SUPPLIED DIVING PROCEDURES

Surface supplied air diving involves those forms of diving in which a breathing mixture is supplied from the surface to the diver by a flexible hose.

This equipment may be further categorised as :-
a) Surface supplied, free flow.
b) Surface demand.

SURFACE SUPPLIED FREE FLOW

This type of equipment does not contain a "Demand" air system. Air is supplied to the diver through an "inlet" valve, circulated around the helmet and then exhausted to the water through an adjustable exhaust valve, both of these valves are controlled by the diver.

A direct development from the original standard diving dress, the modern "rigid helmet" is constructed from a fibreglass moulding and is either attached to a diving suit to form a "constant volume" or sealed around the neck by a neoprene "dam".

Figure 9-1 Diver, dressed, on the ladder

This type of helmet has to a certain extent been superseded by the new types of "demand" helmets such as the Kirby Morgan 17 Superlite, Miller, Ratcliff and Savoie; however, their suitability for heavy construction work due to a constant volume facility and lack of breathing resistance have made them a firm favourite with many construction divers.

The main advantage of rigid helmet equipment over Scuba are :-

- Surface supplied air
- Harder working capability due to no mechanical disadvantage
- Protection from water pollution
- Head protection
- Head insulation

Figure 9-2.   Divex air helmet

Because of the amount of different types of rigid helmets commercially available, it is only intended to deal specifically with the dressing and use of the Aquadyne A.H.2 (Air Hat) but the principles outlined can be applied to most surface supplied free flow equipment.

PREPARATION FOR RIGID HELMET DIVING

A certain minimum of equipment is required for every rigid helmet dive. This minimum may be augmented, as indicated by the nature of the work to be carried out by items of accessory equipment.

MINIMUM EQUIPMENT

1. A suitable main supply of breathing air.
2. A reserve supply of breathing air.
3. Surface supply panel
4. Air supply "umbilical"
5. Communications
6. Pneumofathometer

Diver:-

1. Suit and underwear
2. Safety harness
3. Rigid helmet complete
4. "Bail out" bottle
5. Weight belt
6. Boots
7. Knife

PREPARATION FOR DIVING

Before any diving operation can begin, three basic steps must be taken.

1. The air supply must be provided

2. All equipment must be assembled and thoroughly checked

3. The diver must be dressed and given his final briefing.

Figure 9-3 Diver dressed in AH-2.

MAIN AIR SUPPLY

Air for surface supplied diving is generally provided by a suitable L.P. compressor situated in the support craft or dock side (see Chapter 7 - Air Compressors) from H.P. storage bank reduced in pressure.

Whatever the source of breathing air it must conform to the British Standard B.S. 4001 (see Chapter 7 - Air Purity Standards).

L.P. COMPRESSOR SUPPLY

Proper design of the air supply system leading into and out of the compressor is essential if the compressor is to perform according to its rating. Unfortunately, these areas are often overlooked.

The air supplied from the compressor will enter an accumulator. As the pressure builds up in the accumulator, it will eventually reach the relief pressure of the compressor at which time the excess air will simply be discharged to the atmosphere.

Figure 9-4 A large air supply bank, fed direct from an HP compressor, with a cylinder charging panel between the 4th and 5th cylinder.

All piping in the system must be designed and installed to minimize pressure drops. Intake ducting, especially, must be of sufficient diameter that the rated capacity of the compressor will not be limited. All joints and fittings must be checked for leaks using soapy water; all filters, strainers and separators must be kept clean; lubricant, fuel and coolant levels must be periodically checked.

Any diving air compressor, if not permanently installed, must be firmly lashed in place. Most portable compressors are provided with lashing rings for this purpose.

The accumulator serves two purposes:-

1. It acts as a final water separator.

2. In the event of a compressor failure it allows a breathing "space" in which to bring into operation the reserve supply.

The compressor is generally fitted with the following filters:
- water separator
- charcoal or alumia filter
- silica gel (this is sometimes omitted if the air is too dry)

See Compressors - Chapter 7.

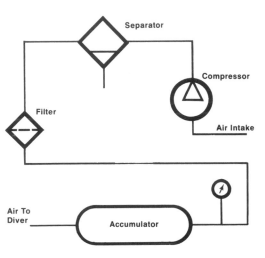

Figure 9-5. Schematic of major components of a compressor-equipped air supply system.

HIGH PRESSURE AIR CYLINDERS

Submarine high-pressure air cylinders are designed to hold air at a rated pressure of 200 Bars. A convenient and satisfactory diving air supply system can be achieved with the use of four or more of these flasks. A suitable system can also be set up using other cylinders which are suited to diving applications.

The complete air supply system includes the necessary piping and manifolds, a high-pressure strainer, a pressure reducing valve, and at least a 30 litre volume tank. A high-pressure gauge must be located ahead of the reducing valve, and a low-pressure gauge must be connected to the volume tank.

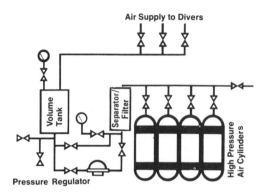

Air Supply to Divers

Volume Tank

Separator/Filter

High Pressure Air Cylinders

Pressure Regulator

Figure 9-6. Typical High Pressure Cylinder Bank Air-Supply System Schematic.

In using this system, one tank must be kept in reserve, and no more than two divers may be supplied at one time. The divers take air from the volume tank in which the pressure is regulated to conform to the air supply requirements of the dive. The duration of the dive will be limited to the length of time the cylinders will provide air before being depleted to a level that is 3 Bars above the divers' working pressure. As this level is approached the divers must be brought up from the bottom. The reserve tank may be put on the line once the divers are on their way to the surface and must be of sufficient capacity, determined in advance, to support their decompression requirements.

If cylinder banks are used to back-up a compressor supply, the bank must be manifolded with the primary source so that an immediate switch from primary to secondary air is possible.

As with SCUBA operations, the quantity of air which can be supplied by a system using cylinders is determined by the initial capacity of the cylinders and the depth of the dive. The duration of the air supply must be calculated in advance, and must include any provisions for decompression stops.

AIR REQUIREMENT

The Air requirement of a surface-supplied free flow diver is significantly higher than that required by a demand system.

When calculating the <u>minimum</u> air requirement for a surface-supplied free flow helmet, the following formula should be used:-

Supply Pressure = 2 Bars above ambient

Air Requirement = 70 litres/per bar/
                              per minute.

<u>Example</u>

You are required to purchase a compressor capable of supporting a rigid helmet diver at 50m.

<u>Formula:</u> 50m = 6 Bars absolute
2 Bars over-
pressure +
6 Bars absolute
pressure   = 8 Bars
8 x 70 litres = 560 litres/per minute

<u>Answer:</u> The compressor must supply a <u>minimum</u> of 560 litres per minute at 8 Bars.

RESERVE SUPPLY

A reserve supply of air capable of
bringing the diver(s) safely to
surface observing any decompression
obligation should be available.

This is usually in the form of H.P.
cylinders which are connected to the
panel via a reducer. This air is
subject to all the purity tests
B.S.4006.

The system should be fully tested
after installation to ensure that it
will support the diving operations
for which it is required.

EQUIPMENT PREPARATION

Prior to any dive, all equipment must
be carefully inspected for signs of
deterioration, damage or corrosion and
must be tested for proper operation
where required. Pre-dive preparation
procedures must be standardized, must
never be altered in the interests of
"convenience," and must be the personal
concern of each diver. Every diver
must always check his own equipment and
must never assume that any piece of
equipment is ready for use unless he has
personally verified that readiness, even
if other personnel have been assigned to
prepare and check-out the equipment.

EQUIPMENT PREPARATION- AQUADYNE AH2

GENERAL CHECKLIST - DIVER'S INDIVIDUAL
EQUIPMENT

BAIL-OUT CYLINDER: Inspect for rust,
cracks, dents or any other evidence of
weakness or fault. Pay particular
attention to loose or bent valves.
Check cylinder markings and verify
suitability for use. Check that the
hydrostatic test date has not expired.
Remove masking tape and inspect O-ring.
Check contents using a reliable pressure
gauge.

BACK-PACK HARNESS STRAPS: Check for
signs of rot or excessive wear. Adjust
straps for individual use, and test
quick release mechanism.

SAFETY HARNESS: Check for signs of
rot or excessive wear.

BAIL-OUT BOTTLE REGULATOR: Attach
regulator to the cylinder pillar valve,
making certain that the O-ring is
properly seated and that the manifold
is closed. Open the cylinder valve
all the way and then back off $\frac{1}{4}$ turn.
Check for leaks in the regulator by
listening for the sound of escaping
air. Check the contents using the
H.P. gauge. If a leak is suspected,
determine the exact location by submerging
the valve assembly and the regulator
in a tank of water and looking for
bubbles. Frequently the problem
can be traced to an improperly seated
regulator. This is corrected by
closing the valve, bleeding the
regulator by opening the bail-out
manifold, detaching and reseating.

If the leak is at the O-ring and
reseating does not solve the problem
replace the O-ring.

BAIL-OUT MANIFOLD: Check the main
supply inlet non-return valve, by
sucking and blowing on the inlet.
Check the hand wheel for ease of
operation and all connections for
tightness.

HELMET: Check the main supply inlet
non-return valve, by sucking and
blowing on the inlet. Check condition of
supply hose from manifold to helmet.
Check inlet and exhaust valves for
correct functioning. Check Helmet
body for damage or loose fittings.
Check neck dam and locking mechanism
for condition and correct functioning.
Check communications. Check locking
mechanism for signs of excessive wear.
Check nose clearing pad.

SUIT: Check suit for obvious damage and check correct functioning of suit inflation.

WEIGHTED SHALLOW WATER BOOTS: Examine boots for excessive wear and broken laces. Check weighted insoles are present if required.

DIVING KNIFE: Test the edge of the knife for sharpness, and make sure that the knife is fastened securely in the scabbard. Verify that the knife can be removed without difficulty.

WEIGHT BELT: Check that the belt is in good condition and that the proper number of weights are in place and secure. Verify that the quick-release buckle is functioning properly.

GENERAL: Inspect any other equipment which will be used on the dive as well as any spare equipment that may be used during the dive. Also check all lines, tools and other optional gear. Finally, lay all equipment in a place where it will be out of the way of deck traffic and ready for use.

Having completed the previously mentioned individual divers equipment checks, the surface attendant must ensure that

- a suitable main supply of air is present at the panel

- a suitable reserve supply is available at the panel

- the inboard end of the umbilical is secure

- the diver's number conforms with his communications number and the communications have been checked

- the umbilical has been blown through before connecting the helmet and bailout manifold.

DIVER PREPARATION

When the diver and attendant have completed inspecting their equipment, they report their readiness to the diving supervisor.

When the diving supervisor and the divers are all satisfied that the requirements of the operation are fully understood and the divers are in good health and otherwise ready to proceed, the divers may dress for the dive.

DRESSING

Fasten the jocking belt around the waist with the crotch strap centred at the diver's back. Connect the adjustable belt clip to the belt "D"-ring at the divers right side and adjust for comfort.

Fig 9-7 Jock strap adjustment

Position the slide buckle to the front and centre of the belt.

Connect the crotch strap to the bottom of the slide buckle and adjust.

Put the neck ring on over the diver's head with the latching mechanism to the front.

Place the helmet over the diver's head and mate it with the lower neck ring. Note that the bayonet pins in the neck ring are located at each shoulder and that the helmet locks onto the pins by rotating the helmet to the diver's LEFT. With the helmet bayonet slots mated with the lower neck ring pins and the helmet rotated to the diver's left, close the neck ring clamps. Engage the clasp over the ball end screw and push the cam arm across centre until it is closed and latched. Verify the lock by pulling on the cam arm.

Fig 9-8   Placing neck ring over
          diver's head

Connect the front neck ring jocking strap to the top of the slide buckle and the back neck ring jocking strap to the "D"-ring at the back centre of the belt and adjust the straps so that the back of the neck ring is about $\frac{1}{2}$" lower than the front.

Put on and fasten the bail-out bottle back-pack with the reserve manifold positioned at the diver's right front. Verify that the reserve valve on the reserve manifold is closed

Open pillar valve on the reserve bottle and confirm there are no leaks. Verify primary and reserve air supply to helmet.

Adjust free flow valve to allow a sufficient quantity of air into the helmet to prevent CO_2 build up.

Adjust exhaust valve as required.

Verify that the lower neck ring catching mechanism is open.

Figure 9-9 Placing helmet on head.

Attendants should ensure during dressing that –

- the umbilical carbine clip is secured to the LEFT chest "D" ring on the safety harness and that no load is taken on any element of the umbilical, other than the life line.

- the weight belt is secured firmly around the diver's waist and that the release mechanism, (if one is fitted), is working correctly. (The weight belt may be attached before the bail-out bottle to ease dressing, but, the attendant must ensure that it can be released in an emergency).

- the helmet is locked on air at the panel before placing the helmet on the diver's head and adjusted for comfort.

- the bail-out bottle is open and is fully charged.

- the bail-out manifold can be located and operated by the diver.

During training at Prodive it is mandatory that the attendant go through a set "Check List" to ensure that the diver has been dressed correctly, which will be given to the supervisor prior to entering the water.

AQUADYNE A H 2 RIGID HELMET READ-OUT

1. Umbilical secure

2. Helmet secure

3. Communications tested (see voice procedures)

4. Bail-out bottle open

5. Contents reading

6. Diver has been seen to locate and operate bail-out manifold. Manifold is now closed

7. Diver has been seen to locate weight belt release pin/flap

8. Diver (number) is ready for the water

Prior to and during diving operations the panel operator will be required to give a read-out of the panel status as follows:-

1. Main supply pressure (minimum of 2 bars above ambient)

2. Reserve H.P. contents

3. Diver (number) locked on air (minimum of 2 bars above ambient)

4. Diver (number) has reported well.

The diver is now ready to enter the water, at the discretion of the diving supervisor who will have made sure that all diving signals are being displayed and regulations adhered to.

SURFACE DEMAND EQUIPMENT

Air is supplied from the surface via a flexible air hose to the diver where it is taken on demand (in its normal operating mode) through a regulator, similar to that of an ordinary scuba demand valve.

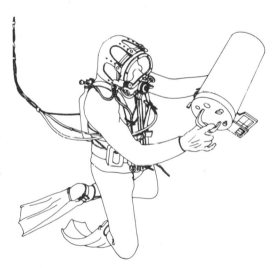

Fig 9-10   KMB 10 Band Mask

The "Band-mask", or "Demand" helmet has become by far the most popular form of surface supplied diving equipment. Its advantages over scuba are -

- surface supplied gas with unlimited duration

- communications

- mask offers better visibility and more protection from contaminated water

- has a facility for an independant bail-out supply

- in the event of a diver becoming unconscious his mouth will be surrounded by gas which will be given on demand

- if the unbilical is fitted with a pneumo-fathometer line his depth can be monitored independently

Its advantages over rigid helmets are -

- more manoeuvrability

- oral nasal which prevents CO_2 build-up

- requires less air than a rigid helmet

- independent bail-out hose (Aquadyne AH2)

Because of the variety of demand helmets and bandmasks currently available it is only intended to deal the Morgan Systems, Inc. MARK 10 BANDMASK in detail, but the general principles outlined can be applied to most types of demand equipment.

PREPARATION FOR SURFACE DEMAND DIVING

A certain minimum of equipment is required for every surface demand dive. This minimum may be augmented, as indicated by the nature of the work to be carried out by items of accessory equipment.

Figure 9-11 Surface control panel, with controls and depth 'pneumo'.

MINIMUM EQUIPMENT

1. A suitable main supply of breathing air

2. A reserve supply of breathing air

3. Surface supply panel

4. Air supply "umbilical"

5. Communications

Diver:-

1. Suit and underwear

2. Safety Harness

3. Kirby/Morgan band-mask Mk 10 complete including "spider"

4. Bail-out bottle

5. Weight belt

6. Fins/boots

7. Knife

PREPARATION FOR DIVING

Before any diving operation can begin, three basic steps must be taken

1. The air supply must be provided

2. All equipment must be assembled and thoroughly checked

3. The diver must be dressed and given his final briefing.

MAIN SUPPLY

The equipment required to supply air to the surface demand diver is fundamentally the same as that required for free flow helmets.(See main air supply and L.P. compressor supply free flow rigid helmets). However, a demand system uses significantly less air because air is only taken on demand (in its normal operational mode) therefore, a different air requirement should be used to calculate the minimum output of a compressor.

AIR REQUIREMENT

The equipment functions in a similar manner to a single hose demand valve. The air supply hose from the surface represents the medium pressure hose, and the demand regulator the second stage.

The Kirby/Morgan range of band-masks and helmets are designed to function with a variation of supply pressure between 3-11 bars above ambient, with an optimum of 8-10 bars, however, higher supply pressure limits are obtainable, following additional regulator adjustment.

The variation in medium pressure is adjusted for breathing comfort by an external adjustment of the second stage regulator.

When calculating the MINIMUM air requirement, the following formula should be used:-

Minimum supply pressure = 3 bars above ambient.

Divers air consumption on surface:-

A) at rest - 25 litres per min.

B) doing moderate work - 25-40 litres per min.

C) doing hard work - 40-70 litres per min.

EXAMPLE

What is the minimum air requirement from a compressor to support one surface demand diver at 50 m doing moderate work.

(The higher rate of 40 for moderate work should be used)

Supply pressure = 3 bars above ambient

Air requirement = 40 litres/per bar/ per minute.

50 m = 6 bars absolute + 3 bars minimum over pressure = 9 bars.

9 x 40 litres = 360 litres/per minute.

ANSWER - The compressor must supply a MINIMUM of 360 litres per minute at 9 bars.

RESERVE SUPPLY

A reserve supply of air capable of bringing the diver(s) safely to surface observing any decompression obligation should be available. This is usually in the form of H.P. cylinders which are connected to the panel via a reducer. This air is subject to all the purity tests B.S. 4006.

The system should be fully tested after installation to ensure that it will support the diving operations for which it is required.

EQUIPMENT PREPARATION

Prior to any dive, all equipment must be carefully inspected for signs of deterioration, damage or corrosion and must be tested for proper operation where required. Pre-dive preparation procedures must be standardized, must never be altered in the interests of "convenience" and must be the personal concern of each diver. Every diver must always check his own equipment and must never assume that any piece of equipment is ready for use unless he has personally verified that readiness, even if other personnel have been assigned to prepare and check-out the equipment.

EQUIPMENT PREPARATION K.M.B. MK 10 BAND MASK

GENERAL CHECKLIST (DIVER'S INDIVIDUAL EQUIPMENT)

BAIL-OUT CYLINDER: Inspect for rust, cracks, dents or any other evidence of weakness or fault. Pay particular attention to loose or bent valves. Check cylinder markings and verify suitability for use. Check that the hydrostatic test date has not expired.

Remove masking tape and inspect O-ring.

Check contents using a reliable pressure gauge.

BACK-PACK HARNESS STRAPS: Check for signs of rot or excessive wear. Adjust straps for individual use, and test quick release mechanism.

SAFETY HARNESS: Check for signs of rot or excessive wear.

BAIL-OUT BOTTLE REGULATOR: Attach regulator to the cylinder pillar valve, making certain that the O-ring is properly seated and that the manifold is closed. Open the cylinder valve all the way and then back off $\frac{1}{4}$ turn. Check for leaks in the regulator by listening for the sound of escaping air. Check the contents using the H.P. gauge. If a leak is suspected, determine the exact location by submerging the valve assembly and the regulator in a tank of water and looking for bubbles. Frequently the problem can be traced to an improperly seated regulator. This is corrected by closing the valve, bleeding the regulator by opening the bail-out manifold, detaching and reseating.

If the leak is at the O-ring and reseating does not solve the problem, replace the O-ring.

BAIL-OUT/FREE FLOW MANIFOLD: Check the main supply inlet non-return valve, by sucking and blowing on the manifold inlet and that the manifold is secure to the mask frame.

Check the hand wheels for ease of operation and all connections for tightness.

MASK: All rubber, metal and moulded plastic components should be visually inspected for excessive wear and proper attachment.

Rubber components should be free of

cracks or signs of fatigue. The face seal and oral nasal mask should be securely attached to the frame.

Fig 9-12 KMB MK 10

The nose clearing device should slide in and out easily.

Check demand regulator for correct functioning and adjust as necessary using the adjustment knob on the left side of the regulator. Check the condition of the "wet" hood and securing band.

Check condition of "spider".

Check communications and that ear receivers are in correct position.

SUIT: Check suit for obvious damage and check correct functioning of suit inflation.

BOOTS/FINS: Examine boots for excessive wear and broken laces.

Check weighted insoles are present if required.

Swim fins - check straps and inspect blades for any sign of cracking.

DIVING KNIFE: Test the edge of the knife for sharpness, and make sure the knife is fastened securely in the scabbard. Verify that the knife can be removed without difficulty.

WEIGHT BELT: Check that the belt is in good condition and that the proper number of weights are in place and secure. Verify that the quick-release buckle is functioning properly.

GENERAL: Inspect any other equipment which will be used on the dive as well as any spare equipment that may be used during the dive. This would include spare regulators, cylinders and gauges. Also check all lines, tools and other optional gear. Finally, lay all equipment in a place where it will be out of the way of deck traffic and ready for use.

Having completed the previously mentioned individual diver's equipment checks, the surface attendant must ensure that:-

- a suitable main supply of air is present at the panel

- a suitable reserve supply is available at the panel

- the inboard end of the umbilical is secure

- the diver's number conforms with his communications number and communications have been checked

- the umbilical has been blown through before the mask is connected.

DIVER PREPARATION

When the diver has completed inspecting and testing his equipment he reports his readiness to the diving supervisor. When the diving supervisor and the divers are all satisfied that the requirements of the operation are fully

understood and the divers are in good
health and otherwise ready to proceed,
the divers may dress for the dive.

DRESSING

Prior to placing the mask on the diver
a thin film of anti-fogging solution
should be applied to the interior of
the face plate. Any dishwashing liquid
may be used. The umbilical gas supply
should be turned on and the demand
regulator adjusted to a slight free flow
by turning the adjustment knob.

Fig 9-14. The tender secures the
head harness (spider) on the diver.

It should be ensured during dressing
that -

- the umbilical carbine hook is secured
to the left chest D-ring on the safety
harness and that no load is taken on
any element of the umbilical other than
the life line.

- the weight belt is secured firmly
around the diver's waist and that the
release mechanism is working correctly.
(The weight belt may be attached before
the bail-out bottle to ease dressing
but the attendant must ensure that it
can be released in an emergency).

- the mask is locked on air at the
panel before placing it on the diver.

- the bail-out is fully charged and
open to the manifold and that the diver
can locate and operate the manifold.

During training at Prodive it is
mandatory that the attendant go through
a set "checklist" to ensure that the

Fig 9-13 Placing the mask on the
diver's head.

The diver now slips the hood over his
head so that his face is in the proper
position in the hood face seal. The
attendant now closes the zipper and
places the head harness, or "spider",
on the diver's head, securing it to the
top and bottom posts. The "spider"
should be as low as possible on the neck
so that a pressure is put on the base of
the skull by the lower two legs of the
"spider". The amount of tension will
vary with individual preference and can
only be determined by practice.

diver has been dressed correctly, which will be given to the supervisor prior to entering the water.

Fig 9-15. A strain relief snap is secured to the diver's harness to prevent umbilical pull on the mask.

K.M.B. MK 10 READ-OUT

1) Umbilical secure

2) Mask secure

3) Communications tested (see voice procedures

4) Bail-out bottle open

5) Contents reading

6) Diver has been seen to locate and operate bail-out manifold. Manifold is now closed.

7) Diver has been seen to locate weight belt release pin/flap

8) Diver (number) is ready for the water.

Prior to and during diving operations the panel operator will be required to give a read-out of the panel status as follows:-

1) Main supply pressure (minimum of 3 Bars above ambient)

2) Reserve H.P. Contents

3) Diver locked on air at (minimum of 3 Bars above ambient)

4) Diver (number) has reported well

The diver is now ready to enter the water, at the discretion of the diving supervisor who will have made sure that all diving signals are being displayed and regulations adhered to.

ENTERING THE WATER

When entering the water by ladder, the diver must be assisted by the tenders. His movements must be cautious, especially when nearing the water, to guard against being pushed or lifted off the ladder by wave action.

If entering by stage, the diver should centre himself on the platform or seat and have a good grip on the rails. Upon signal from the Diving Supervisor, the winch operator and line handlers should take a strain on the stage line; then, following appropriate signals, they should lift, guide and lower the stage to the water, using the stage line and steadying lines. Visual signals for winch operators are illustrated overleaf.

Should a diver in a lightweight KMB jump into the water, he must maintain a grip on the facemask and the tender must be sure to provide sufficient slack in the lifeline and air hose.

WINCH HAND SIGNALS

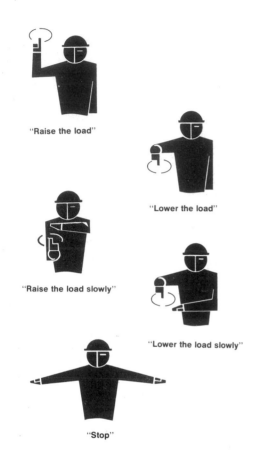

"Raise the load"

"Lower the load"

"Raise the load slowly"

"Lower the load slowly"

"Stop"

Fig 9-16. Winch Signals

As the diver enters the water, he checks
for leaks. The tender can be of
assistance by looking for any tell-tale
bubbles. A communications and time-
check is made. This is the time to
report any malfunctions or deficiencies
not previously noted. When satisfied
that he is ready in all respects to
begin the dive, the diver notifies the

Diving Supervisor. At this point, the
tenders haul the diver over to the
descending line.

When on the down line the diver vents
his suit and adjusts his buoyancy ready
for descent. He then signals his
readiness to the attendant who notifies
the Diving Supervisor.

DESCENT

When using a dry suit the diver should
always leave surface feet first to
avoid a build-up of air in the feet of
the suit.

Descent may be accomplished with the aid
of a DESCENDING LINE or as a passenger
on the stage. By whatever method,
topside personnel must ensure that the
diver only has sufficient umbilical with
which to descend. Too much "slack" in
his umbilical will not only be a hindrance
to him but will also increase the risk of
him becoming foul, or, in the event of
him loosing the shot and falling, could
damage the divers ears.

While descending, the diver should
adjust his air supply as required so
that he breathes easily and comfortably.

The diver should equalise the pressure
in his ears and sinuses, as necessary
on descent using the nose clearing pads
provided.

The rate of descent will normally be
controlled by the ease with which the
diver is able to equalise but should
never exceed 30 m per minute. If
difficulty is experienced in clearing the
diver(s) should stop and ascend slightly
until the pressure is relieved. The
descent should then continue at a slower
rate. If a problem still persists after
several attempts to equalise, the dive
should be aborted.

During the descent the panel attendant
should monitor the divers. Progress
using the pneumofathometer.

Fig 9-17. Correct method for descending on a descending line

PNEUMOFATHOMETER

During the divers descent, air should be "purged" through the pneumo at over the divers ambient pressure. Approximately every 30 seconds the air supply valve to the pneumo should be closed and the divers depth noted. In this way the divers progress during the descent may be monitored.

UNDERWATER PROCEDURES

The diver should signal his arrival on the bottom and quickly check bottom conditions, location, etc.

The panel operator should note the divers depth and report the depth to the diving supervisor.

If conditions are radically different than expected, he will report his observations to the diving supervisor and if there is any doubt about the safety of the diver, the dive should be aborted.

Upon reaching the bottom, and before leaving the area of the stage or descending line, the diver should pause to adjust his buoyancy and to make certain that his air supply is adequate.

The diver should also check his physical condition, to satisfy himself that his helmet or mask is being properly ventilated. While at rest, he should feel comfortable and be breathing normally. If he is experiencing rapid breathing, panting or shortness of breath, abnormal perspiration or undue sensation of warmth, dizziness, unclear eyesight or if the helmet ports have become cloudy, there is probably an accumulation of excess CO_2 in his helmet. He should immediately increase the flow of air by simultaneously opening the air control and the exhaust valves. Proper ventilation of the helmet is usually obtained with the exhaust valve opened $2\frac{1}{2}$ or 3 turns, and the air control valve adjusted accordingly.

Next, the diver must orient himself to the bottom and the work site, using such clues as the lead of the umbilical, natural features on the bottom, the direction of current. He must always keep in mind, however, that bottom current may not match the surface current, and in any event, the direction of current flow may change significantly during the period of the dive. If he has any trouble in determining his orientation the tender can guide him by use of the communication in a similar manner to life line direction signals. The diver is now ready to move off to the work site, and to begin his assignment.

MOVEMENT ON THE BOTTOM

- before leaving the descending line or stage, insure that the umbilical is not fouled with the lines.

- loop one turn of the umbilical over an arm; this will act as a buffer against a sudden surge or pull.

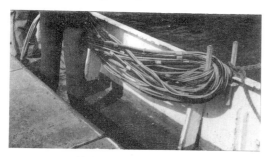

Figure 9-18 A diver's shot-line and sinker. Note that the shackle would normally be 'moused'.

The diver should proceed with caution always being aware of the possibility of fouling his umbilical. If obstructions are encountered, pass over the obstruction, rather than under or around. If

you pass around an obstruction, make sure that you later return to the same side to avoid fouling.

- moving on a wreck or rocky bottom, take care that lines do not become fouled on outcroppings; guard against tripping and getting feet caught in crevices. Watch out for sharp projections which can cut hoses, diving dress or unprotected hands. The tender must be part-icularly careful to take up any slack in the umbilical to avoid fouling.

DIVING TECHNIQUES AND PROCEDURES

KMB MK 10 BANDMASK

FLOODING

There are two methods of clearing a flooded mask:

1. Depressing the purge button located in the centre of the front cover of the demand regulator, or

2. Turning on the steady flow valve handwheel.

Both of these methods allow breathing gas to enter the interior of the mask, which in turn will rapidly blow out any water through the exhaust valves. It is unlikely that the mask will ever flood out during use, as any break in the face seal will cause the demand regulator to free flow. This is due to the greater pressure at the lower part of the mask. This action assumes that the diver is in a normal working position where the demand regulator is lower than the rest of the mask.

FACE SQUEEZE

One of the major problems that occurs in most face masks is when the hose breaks near the surface and the one-way valve on the mask fails to operate. A suction is thus created in the face cavity which could result in serious injury to the diver. The KMB-10 mask is designed to eliminate this possibility of injury. If both the hose and one-way valve fail, the soft face seal will be pulled into the interior of the mask away from the divers face making a squeeze impossible. While this would result in immediate flooding of the unit, no physical injury to the diver from a squeeze would occur. In spite of this safety feature, the diver should be very careful to frequently check the one-way valve to make sure it is operating properly. A faulty one-way valve could also result in a depletion of the emergency gas supply following a surface hose break.

AQUADYNE AH.2 HELMET

FLOODING

There are two methods of evacuating water which has entered the helmet through the neck seal.

1. Increasing the air into the helmet and opening the neck seal with a finger, or

2. Leaning to the diver right and evacuating the water through the exhaust valve.

Water in the helmet is normally a sign of incorrect valve adjustment.

MAIN SUPPLY FAILURE

AQUADYNE AH.2

In the event of a main supply failure, the diver must open the bail out manifold and adjust the helmet valves for minimum air consumption. Notify the surface and terminate the dive IMMEDIATELY.

If after turning on the bail out manifold the diver still does not receive air to the helmet, he should immediately check his bail out contents and open his inlet

free flow valve which may have been inadvertently closed by an obstruction leading the diver to believe his main supply had failed.

KMB MK 10

In the event of a main supply failure the diver must open the bail out supply valve situated behind the steady flow valve on the mask manifold and adjust the mask for minimum air consumption. Notify the surface and terminate the dive IMMEDIATELY.

If after turning on the bail out manifold, the diver still does not receive air to the demand regulator he should immediately check his bail out contents and open his steady flow valve.

In the event of a demand regulator failure, the diver may surface using the mask in a "free flow" mode.

VOICE COMMUNICATIONS

The surface-supplied diver has one or two means of communicating with the surface support team. He has both voice communications which should be as the primary method, and life line signals using the umbilical as an emergency back-up.

Direct diver to diver conversations are possible with the rigid helmet, since the helmet body serves as a sound conductor. Two divers need only touch helmets to talk with each other. Other diver communications may be the same as used in SCUBA operations. Diver to diver hand signals, slate boards etc.

DIVERS COMMUNICATIONS VOICE PROCEDURE.

All conversation on Surface/Diver communications should be kept to a minimum to avoid mistakes, and to ensure that the line is open for any urgent messages. Unnecessary talk is not to be permitted.

BASIC RULES

(a) Conversation to either Diver or
Surface is generally preceded by
saying who is being called and who
is calling.

    eg When the Surface is calling
        Diver 1 -
        "Diver 1 Surface"
        Which is answered with -
        "Surface, Diver 1" from the
        diver.

(b) In the case of an extreme emergency
the above rule is not followed.
When the diver's distress call is
heard it is acted upon immediately.

(c) If a message is not heard clearly
the receiver should request that the
message be repeated in the following
way:-

Diver 1 - "Message ...."
Surface - "Diver 1, Surface, come
back"

(d) To check a diver's wellbeing the
following procedure is used:-

Surface - "Diver 1, Surface"
Diver 1 - "Surface, Diver 1"
Surface - "Are you well?"
Diver 1 - "Well" or "Negative"
           (Reason)

(e) A dive using communications should
be carried out in the following
manner:-

Prior to the dive the diver or
communications attendant should
check for correct functioning of
the telephone equipment.

Surface - "Diver 1, Surface"
Diver 1 - "Surface, Diver 1"
Surface - "Communication's check,
          how do you hear me?"
Diver 1 - "Loud and clear, how me?"
Surface - "Loud and clear also"
Diver 1 - "Understood"

When the diver is fully dressed and
ready to enter the water he rechecks
the communications. Upon successful
completion of his test the supervisor will order the diver into the
water. When the diver has carried
out any necessary diving checks the
supervisor will order him to leave
surface.

Surface - "Diver 1, Surface"
Diver 1 - "Surface, Diver 1"
Surface - "Leave surface"
Diver 1 - "Understood - left surface"

Upon reaching the bottom the diver
reports:-

Diver 1 - "Surface, Diver 1"
Surface - "Diver 1 - Surface"
Diver 1 - "Made bottom"
Surface - "Understood"

When the diver is ready to leave
bottom the supervisor will tell the
diver to "Stand-by to leave bottom",
in the following manner:-

Surface - "Diver 1, Surface"
Diver 1 - "Surface, Diver 1"
Surface - "Stand-by to leave bottom"
Diver 1 - "Ready to leave bottom"
Surface - "Understood"

To call the diver up the following
routine should be used:-

Surface - "Diver 1, Surface"
Diver 1 - "Surface, Diver 1"
Surface - "Leave bottom"
Diver 1 - "Left bottom"
Surface - "Understood"

Upon reaching the surface the diver
reports:-

Diver 1 - "Surface, Diver 1"
Surface - "Diver 1, Surface"
Diver 1 - "On surface, reports well"
Surface - "Understood"

If wet stops are to be carried out the surfacing procedure must be modified to the following:-

Surface - "Diver 1, Surface"
Diver 1 - "Surface, Diver 1"
Surface - "Leave bottom, come up to first stop"
Diver 1 - "Left bottom"
Surface - "Understood"

Upon reaching first stop the diver reports:-

Diver 1 - "Surface, Diver 1"
Surface - "Diver 1, surface"
Diver 1 - "Made first stop"
Surface - "Understood"

The above procedure is following throughout all of the "stops" until the surface is reached, where the diver gives the appropriate report.

During the dive if "working orders" are being used there is no need for the formality of calling "Surface, Diver 1" Etc. When using a crane for example, orders such as "up slow - down slow - stop etc" should be given direct. (The inconvenience of following the call up routine except for initial identification is obvious). The message should still be repeated by the recipient however.

TENDING THE DIVER

The tender is directly responsible for the safety of the diver.

Before dressing the diver it should be ensured that he is a safe distance from the water edge, and that:-

- the umbilical has been secured inboard

- the non-return valves in the helmet/ mask and main supply manifold have been checked

- sufficient air is "on" to the helmet/

mask and reserve air supply to the panel

- the communications and helmet number conform to the divers number

- the carbine hook is secure to the left chest 'D'-ring of the divers safety harness

- the weight belt is secured firmly around the divers waist and that the release pin is in working order

- attendants must tend the divers at all times while he is on air

- at no time should the weight of a diver on an umbilical, be taken across an obstruction which might kink or damage the air hose

- there should be a panel/comm's operator in attendance at all times during diving operations.

The umbilical must be paid out at a steady rate to permit the diver to descend smoothly. The tender should handle the lines from a point at least 3 m from the descending line. If a stage is being used, the descent rate must be co-ordinated with the winch operator or line handlers.

Throughout the dive, the tender must keep slack out of the line while at the same time not holding it too taut. 1.5 to 2 metres of slack will permit the diver freedom of movement and prevent him from being pulled off his feet by surging of the support craft or the force of any current acting on the line. The tender should, from time to time, "fish" the diver by taking in on the short slack to make sure that movement by the diver has not resulted in excessive slack. Too much slack in the line will hinder the tender from catching a fall, and increase the possibility of fouling of the lines.

The tender also constantly monitors the diver's progress, and keeps track of his relative position. He will do this by a number of methods -

- by following the trail of bubbles. If the diver is searching the bottom, the bubbles should move in a regular pattern; if he is working in place, they should not shift position

- by feeling the pull of the umbilical

- by watching the pneumofathometer pressure gauge, to keep track of the operating depth. The gauge will provide a direct reading, without the need to add air, if the diver remains at a constant depth or rises. If he descends, the hose will have to be cleared and a new reading made

- by monitoring the gauges on the supply systems for any powered equipment. For example, the ammeter on an electric welding unit will indicate a power drain when the arc is in use; the gas pressure gauges for a gas torch will register the flow of fuel. Additionally the "pop" made by a gas torch being lighted will probably be audible over the intercom, and bubbles from the torch will break on the surface giving off small quantities of smoke

- by feeling vibration in the air-power lines of pneumatic tools.

UNUSUAL SITUATIONS

- WHEN WORKING INSIDE A WRECK. This technique applies to the tending divers as well: every diver who penetrates a deck level must have his own tending diver at the level - or levels - above him. Obviously, an operation requiring penetration through multiple deck levels will require detailed advance planning in order to provide for the proper support of the number of divers required.

- ENTER ANY CONFINED SPACE FEET FIRST and never force through an opening which is just barely large enough for entry.

- WHEN WORKING UNDER THE BOTTOM OF A SHIP, the diver should not work on the opposite side of the keel from his tender. Such movement would interfere with proper tending. In ship repair and salvage, consideration should be given to need for special rigging and staging.

- IF WORKING WITH OR NEAR LINES OR MOORINGS, some specific precautions are required -

  A. Stay away from lines under strain.
  B. Avoid passing under lines or moorings if at all possible; avoid brushing against lines or moorings which have been in the water long enough to become encrusted with barnacles.
  C. If a line or mooring is to be shifted, the diver must be brought to the surface and, if not removed from the water, moved to a position well clear of any hazard
  D. If a diver must work with several lines - as messengers, lifting lines, etc - each should be distinct in character (size or material) or marking (colour codes, tags, wrapping).
  E. NEVER CUT A LINE UNLESS IDENTIFICATION IS POSITIVE.
  F. When making preparations to lift heavy weights from the bottom, the lines selected must be of sufficient strength, and the surface platform must be positioned directly above the load.

JOB SITE PROCEDURES

The range of jobs with which a diver may become involved is wide, jobs - including such assignments as clearing fouled propellers, patching collision damage, replacing underwater valves or fittings, preparing for salvage of sunken vessels and recovery of heavy objects from the bottom.

For most underwater work, the diver will need to use appropriate tools. Many of these are standard hand-tools (preferably made of corrosion-resistant materials), and others are specially designed for underwater work. A qualified diver will become familiar with the particular considerations involved in working with tools underwater, whether the tool be a screwdriver or a welding torch. Hands-on training experience is the only way to get the necessary skills. In working with tools certain basic rules always apply -

A. Never use a tool that is not in good repair. If a cutting tool becomes dulled from use, it should be returned to the surface for sharpening.

B. Don't overburden the worksite with unnecessary tools, but at the same time, arrange to have all tools which may be needed, readily available.

C. Tools may be secured to the diving stage by lanyard, may be carried in a tool bag looped over the diver's right arm, or may be lowered on the descending line using a riding shackle and a light line for lowering. Power tools should be sent down ahead of the diver and should be returned to the surface before the diver makes his ascent. It is good practice to have lanyards attached to all tools, connectors, shackles, and shackle pins.

D. The diving stage itself may be used as a work site. Such use permits organization of tools while providing for security against loss. The stage can also help give the diver leverage or stability needed when applying

force (as to a wrench) or when working with a power tool which will tend to transmit a force back through the diver.

Figure 9-19 (top) An alert Attendant helping his diver up the ladder, keeping the umbilical short in case the diver falls.
Figure 9-20 (bottom) A twin-lock, 4-man, skid-mounted compression chamber, for deck use.

EMERGENCY PROCEDURES

The subject of emergency procedures is covered in detail in Chapter 10 of this manual. However, there are a number of problems which a diver is likely to encounter in the normal range of activity which, if not promptly solved, can lead to full-scale emergencies. These problems - and the appropriate action to be taken, are -

- LOSS OF DISTANCE LINE. First, search carefully within arm's reach. If the line is not located, DO NOT enter into an area search, but inform the surface of the loss. The tender will then attempt to guide the diver toward the descending line. The diver may make contact before too long. He should then signal to the tender and return to his work.

- FOULED LINES. As soon as a diver discovers that his umbilical has become fouled, he must stop and think. Pulling or tugging, without a plan, may only serve to increase the problem and could lead to a cut hose. The surface should be notified. (The fouling may prevent transmission of line-pull signals). If the lines are fouled on some obstruction, re-tracting steps should free them. If the lines cannot be unfouled quickly and easily, the stand-by diver must be sent down to assist. He will be sent down as normal procedure should communications be interrupted and the tender not be able to haul the diver up. The stand-by diver, following down the first diver's umbilical (as a descending line), should be able to trace the foul and release it.

- If the diver becomes fouled with the descending line, and cannot easily un-foul himself, it will be necessary to haul the diver and the line to the surface, or to cut the weight free of the line and attempt to pull it free from topside. If the descending line is secured to an object, or if the weight is too heavy, the diver may have to cut the line before he can be hauled up. For this reason, a diver

should normally not be permitted to descend on a line that he cannot cut. If job conditions call for use of a steel cable or a chain as a descending line, the Diving Supervisor must approve of such use.

The best safety factors are a positive, confident attitude about diving and careful advance planning for emergencies. When a diver finds himself in trouble underwater, he should relax, avoid panic, communicate his problem with the surface and carefully think through the possible solutions to the situation.

ASCENT See Chapter 8 - Ascent (Normal)

To prepare for a normal ascent, the diver should clear the job site of tools and equipment. These can be returned to the surface by special messenger lines sent down the descending line. If the diver cannot find the descending line and needs a special line, this can be bent onto his lifeline or umbilical and pulled down by the diver. He must take care not to foul the lifeline or umbilical as it is laid down beside him. The tender will then pull up the slack. This technique is useful in shallow water, but not too practical in deep dives.

The diving stage, if possible, should be positioned on the bottom. If for some reason, such as fouling of the diver's lifeline or air hose around the descending line prevents sending the stage to the bottom, it should be positioned below the first decompression stop. The markers on the stage line will assist the winch operator in setting the stage: however, they are NOT the primary means of determining the actual decompression stops. Readings from the pneumofathometer are the primary depth measurements

If ascent is being made using the descending line or the stage has been positioned below the first decompression stop, the tender signals the diver "Finish work, stand-by to come up" when all tools and extra lines have been cleared away. The diver acknowledges the signal and having returned to the shot (descending line) he will report that he is "Ready to leave bottom". On command he will then "Leave bottom" reporting "Left bottom" as he does so to the surface. During the ascent, the diver should vent his suit to avoid becoming too buoyant and rising too quickly, he can check his ascent by clamping his legs on the descending line and adjusting his buoyancy.

The rate of ascent is a critical factor in decompressing the diver and must be carefully controlled at 60ft per minute by the tender (25ft per minute if using the Surface Decompression Table Using Oxygen). He can most accurately monitor the progress of the ascent with the pneumofathometer. When the diver is nearing the level of the stage, he should be warned by the tender so that he will avoid colliding with it. As he reaches the stage, he climbs aboard and notifies surface that he is "on the stage" or level with lazy shot. The stage is then brought up to the first decompression stop.

Details of decompression procedure, including explanation of the tables, are presented in Chapter 4.

In moving upward during the decompression periods, the diver must satisfy himself that he is not developing any sumptoms of physical problems. If he feels any pain, dizziness, numbness, etc., he must immediately notify surface. During this often lengthy period of ascent, the diver must also check to insure that his umbilical is not becoming fouled on the stage line, the descending line, or any steadying weights hanging from the stage platform.

Upon arrival at the surface, the diver should take a firm hold on the rails of the stage and signal his readiness to the tenders. The topside personnel, timing the movement as dictated by any surface wave action, co-ordinate bringing the stage and the umbilical aboard.

If the diver must leave the water via ladder, the tenders must provide assistance. The diver will be tired, the gear is heavy, and a fall back into the water could result in serious injury. UNDER NO CONDITIONS should the helmet/mask be taken off or any equipment removed, before the diver is firmly in board.

SURFACE DECOMPRESSION. Decompression in the water is time consuming, uncomfortable and inhibits the ability of the support vessel to get underway, whether because of weather, or to meet an operating schedule. Further, the diver cannot be provided with medical treatment if needed, and there is always the possibility of a severe chilling or accident. For these reasons, decompression is often accomplished in a surface chamber when one is installed on the support craft.

However, in transferring a diver from the water to the chamber, the tenders will be allowed no more than 3.5 minutes to undress the diver. The diver may not smoke, nor can he take any smoking materials into the chamber with him. The hazards of fire, especially if oxygen is used to facilitate decompression, are extreme. A tender, or any diving medical personnel required by the nature of the dive or the condition of the diver, MUST BE in the chamber, with any necessary supplies, well ahead of the arrival of the diver. The time factor can be critical, and delays because of incomplete preparation cannot be tolerated. Undressing of a diver for surfact decompression should be practiced until a smooth, co-ordinated evolution is developed.

POST DIVE PROCEDURES The immediate
post-dive activities of the diving team
can be considered in three general areas.

SAFETY OF THE DIVER - Administer any
indicated medical treatment, as for cuts
or abrasions. Monitor the general condition of the diver until satisfied that
no problems are likely to develop. The
diver will not leave the immediate
vicinity of the diving site, and will not
be left alone, for at least six hours.
The diver will not leave the general
vicinity, and he definitely must not fly,
for at least 12 hours.

RECORDS AND REPORTS - Certain information
must be logged as soon as the diving
operations are completed, while other
record-keeping can be scheduled when
convenient. The timekeeper is responsible
for the diving log, which must be kept
as a running account of the dive. The
diver is responsible for making appropriate entries in his personal diving
record. Other personnel, as assigned,
are responsible for maintaining equipment usage logs.

INSPECTION, MAINTENANCE AND REPAIR OF
EQUIPMENT - Before stowage, items of
diving equipment must be washed with
fresh water, repaired as necessary and
lubricated where appropriate. All gear
must be dried, and given proper stowage.
Specific details of inspections, and
repair are presented in Chapter 7.

PRE-DIVE CHECKLIST

BASIC PREPARATION

1 Check that for dives in excess of
   25 m a recompression chamber is
   available.

2 Verify that the proper signals
   indicating underwater operations are
   being conducted are properly
   displayed.

3 Make sure that all personnel concerned or in the vicinity have been
   informed that diving operations are
   underway.

4 Determine that all valves, switches,
   controls and equipment components
   that influence the diving operation
   are properly "tagged-out" to prevent
   inadvertent shut-down or activation.

EQUIPMENT PREPARATION

1 Assemble all members of the diving
   team as well as support personnel
   (winch operators, boat crew, watch-
   standers, etc.).

2 Assemble and lay out all equipment
   that may be used on the dive, either
   as primary equipment or standby spares
   for the diver (or standby diver).
   This should include ALL accessory
   equipment and tools.

3 Check all equipment for superficial
   wear, tears, dents, distortion or any
   other apparent discrepancies.

4 Check all masks, helmets, viewing
   ports, faceplates, seals, and visors
   for broken glass or plastic.

5 Check all belts, laces, and lanyards
   for wear and renew as needed.

GENERAL EQUIPMENT

1 Check that all needed accessory

equipment, tools, lights, special
systems, spares, etc are on scene
and in working order. In testing
lights, all tests should be conducted with lights submerged in
water and extinguished before the
removal to prevent over-heating and
failure.

2 Erect the diving stage or attach the
   diving ladder. In the case of the
   stage, be careful to insure that the
   shackle connecting the stage line is
   securely fastened WITH THE SHACKLE
   PIN SEIZED WITH THE WIRE TO PREVENT
   OPENING.

PREPARING THE AIR SUPPLY

1 Check that a primary and suitable
   back-up supply is available with a
   capacity in terms of purity, volume,
   and supply pressure to completely
   service ALL divers and accessory
   equipment throughout all phases of
   the planned operation.

2 Determine that proper personnel are
   available to operate and stand watch
   on the air supply.

3 Compressors -

   a Determine that sufficient fuel,
      cooland, lubricants, and anti-
      freeze are available to service
      all components throughout the
      operation. All compressors
      should be fully fuelled,
      lubricated and serviced (with all
      spillage cleaned up completely).

   b Verify that the appropriate
      operating and service **manuals**
      are on hand.

   c Check maintenance and repair
      logs to insure the suitability
      of the compressor (both primary
      or back-up) to support the
      operation.

d   Verify that all compressor controls are properly marked and any remote valving is tagged-off with "Diver's Air Supply - Do Not Touch" signs.

e   Make sure that the compressor is secure in the diving craft and will not be subject to operating angles that will exceed 15 degrees.

f   Verify that the oil in the compressor is of a type that is proper for the particular compressor and is not petroleum-based. Check that the compressor oil does not overflow the "Fill" mark or contamination of the air supply could result from fumes or oil mist.

g   Check that the compressor exhaust is vented away from work areas and specifically, does not foul the compressor intake.

h   Check that the compressor intake is obtaining a free and pure suction without contamination. Use pipe to lead intake to free suction if necessary.

i   Check that compressors are not covered during operation.

j   Check all filters, cleaners, and oil separators for cleanliness.

k   Bleed off all condensed moisture from filters and the bottom of volume tanks (accumulators). All manifold drain plugs should be checked.

l   Check that all belt-guards are properly in place on drive units.

m   Check all pressure-release valves, check valves, and automatic unloaders

n   Verify that all supply hoses running to and from the compressor have proper leads, do not pass near high-heat areas such as steam lines, are free of kinks and bends, and are not exposed on deck in such a way that they could be rolled over, damaged, or even severed by machinery or other activities.

ACTIVATE THE AIR SUPPLY

1   COMPRESSORS -

a   Make sure that all run-up and warm-up procedures are completely followed.

b   Check all filler valves, filler caps, overflow points, bleed valves, and drain-plugs for leakage or malfunction of any kind.

c   Soap-test all valves and connections.

d   Verify that there is a pressure gauge on the air receiver and that it is functioning properly, and that the compressor is meeting its delivery requirements.

e   Check that the air supply is not being delivered below purity standards (smell, taste), or in excess of 95 $^{\circ}$F.

f   In all cases where compressors are used as a back-up, either to a shipboard system, cylinder bank, or another compressor - the back-up compressor will be kept running throughout the diving operation.

2   CYLINDERS -

a   Gauge all cylinders for proper safety.

b   Verify the availability and suitability of the reserve cylinders.

c   Check all manifolding and valving for operation.

d   Activate and check delivery.

AIR HOSES

1   Check that diving air hoses which form part of the diver's umbilical conform to minimum standards of construction (SAE 100 R3).

2   The air hose must have been pressure tested to 1½ times its operating pressure not more than three months before its time of use and to normal maximum operating pressure not more than twenty four hours before use.

3   Check hose and connections for damage.

4   Check that no weight will be taken by the air hose.

TEST OF EQUIPMENT WITH ACTIVATED AIR SUPPLY.

1   Hook-up all air hoses to helmets, masks, chambers, and make connections between back-up supply and primary supply manifold.

2   Verify flow to helmets and masks.

3   Check all exhaust and air control valves.

4   Hook up and test all communications.

5   Check air flow from both primary and back-up supplies to chamber.

6   Detach all hoses except that leading to chamber. Make sure chamber supply is completely shut off and no air is leaking to chamber, depleting the air supply.

RECOMPRESSION CHAMBER CHECKOUT (PRE-DIVE ONLY)

1   Check that the chamber is completely free and clear of all combustible materials. This includes paint cans, refuse, matches, lighters, etc.

2   Check primary and back-up air supply to chamber as well as all pressure gauges.

3   Check that the chamber is free of all odours or other contaminants.

4   Check the chamber oxygen supply, and that suitable numbers of oxygen masks are rigged for at least two divers, one tender, and one medical assistant.

5   Verify the presence of a sanitary bucket in the chamber in case of sickness.

6   Verify that the medical kit is completely outfitted and in close proximity to the chamber.

7   Check all doors and seals.

8   Verify that all chamber electrical fittings are fitted with armoured cable and special lighting fixtures and bulbs. All switches should be on the outside of the chamber.

FINAL PREPARATIONS

1   Verify that all necessary records, logs, and timesheets are on the diving station.

2   Check that appropriate decompression tables are readily at hand.

3   Verify that all air supply systems have a volume tank or accumulator installed in the air supply line between the supply source and the diver's hose connection. An oil separator must be installed between the tank and the connection.

CHAPTER 10

DIVING EMERGENCIES

An emergency, by definition, is an un-
foreseen combination of circumstances
or the resulting state that calls for
immediate action. Because of the
characteristics of the underwater
environment, a situation which might
only be annoying on the surface may
assume life-or-death proportions for a
working diver.

By training and experience, a diver
must be able to handle the wide range
of actual and potential emergency
situations which he may encounter. He
must be able to separate the important
from the trivial, while at the same
time recognizing the dangers which a
seemingly minor symptom or event may
foreshadow. He must be able to identify and properly react to the warning
signals of various physiological disorders, whether affecting himself or
other divers. He must have a working
knowledge of the most effective
methods for handling physical emergencies (such as entrapment or malfunctioning equipment) as well as a
basic knowledge of the correct steps
to be taken in treating medical emergencies.

And, most importantly, he must be able
to work toward solving the emergency
while he himself is under the emotional
and physical stress which is almost
certain to be one component of any
emergency situation.

Knowledge and training are vital. Men
who are well-trained, well-rested, alert
and confident, only rarely cannot cope
with an emergency. An operation that is
thoroughly planned, with a carefully
paced workload and the prior organization of all necessary personnel, equipment and supplies, tends to be a safer
operation. Equipment in good repair,
properly maintained and not jury-rigged
or "adapted" to a non-designed task, is
usually safe equipment. And finally,

while the environment of the dive
cannot be directly controlled, it can
be understood and any hazardous
elements provided for with special
training, equipment or scheduling.

This chapter does not cover every
possible situation which may cause
problems for a diver, nor will it
serve as a text on basic First Aid.
Other sections of this manual cover
general work procedures, including
some which apply in emergency situations, and other publications
present sufficient material on general medical procedures that this
information need not be repeated
here.

This chapter specifically details
those emergencies which -
- may be a matter of life or death

- are unique to diving

- may seriously interfere with the
  success of an operation

MEDICAL EMERGENCIES-
IMMEDIATE ACTION

Diving personnel who require emergency
medical treatment fall into one of two
classes: those who require recompression, and those who do not. All
members of the diving team should be
able to make this differentiation and
should have sufficient knowledge and
training to proceed with appropriate
treatment or corrective action. It may
well be that no treatment would be the
most appropriate course of action,
especially for non-medical personnel,
and the first rule of first aid is to
do nothing that will do harm to the
patient. However, there are four
medical problems which must be solved
immediately and cannot wait for the
arrival of medical personnel.

In order of priority, the immediate actions which must be taken are-

- assure clear airway

- restore breathing

- assure heart function

- stop massive bleeding

Following these four steps, a more thorough diagnosis of the problem can be made and the assistance of more-qualified personnel obtained. From that point, the person helping a severely injured man will best serve his patient by protecting him from further harm, and by striving to maintain breathing, heart beat and blood circulation in a stable condition. Other treatment, such as placement in a recompression chamber, may be concurrent with these procedures. This will be covered later.

RESUSCITATION. Resuscitation is a general term which covers all the measures taken to restore vital signs, particularly breathing and heart beat.

These measures include pulmonary resuscitation to restore breathing and cardiac resuscitation to re-establish normal heart action.

PULMONARY RESUSCITATION A cessation of breathing, leading to asphyxia, can very quickly result in cell damage and death. The problem may be the result of a number of factors which must be considered in connection with any attempts to restore breathing. These are -

1. Mechanical blockage of the air passages by water, vomitus, blood clots, or foreign bodies.

2. Blockage of the air passages by abnormal swelling and increased secretions of mucous membranes
' which may be caused by allergic reactions or severe inflamation.

3. Dysfunction of the respiratory muscle action or disruption of the chest breathing action which may be caused by chest trauma.

4. Paralysis of the respiratory system as a result of nerve injury caused by -

   a) damage to the spine or brain

   b) electric shock

The first action is to assure a clear airway before starting resuscitation. Vomitus or objects lodged in the throat, for example, can often be cleared with a finger (taking care not to push the material more firmly into place).

Once a clear airway has been established manual pulmonary resuscitation may be started. Manual resuscitation should be continued until a mechanical resuscitator is made available.

MOUTH-TO-MOUTH RESUSCITATION. Of the several methods of manual pulmonary resuscitation which have been developed - mouth-to-mouth, back pressure-armlift, chest pressure-armlift, back pressure-hiplift - the only effective, and the method of choice for initial resuscitation until a bag resuscitator is available, is the mouth-to-mouth technique. Although the other techniques may prove of value in certain situations, such as excessive vomiting or facial injuries, the mouth-to-mouth is the only successful technique in the majority of cases. Detailed instructions for performing mouth-to-mouth resuscitation will be found in Figure No. 10-1.

The use of an S-shaped plastic airway is often advantageous in conducting mouth-to-mouth resuscitation, and one should be part of every first aid kit.

Figure 10-1 Mouth-to-Mouth Resuscitation.

Lift Neck

Lift the neck and extend the head to
open air passages.

Extend Head

Draw down the victim's lower lip.
Pull chin upward until head is tilted
back fully. Pinch off the nostrils with
your other hand, this prevents air leakage when inflating the lungs.

Inflate Lungs

Place your mouth over the mouth of an
adult or large child. For a small child
place your mouth over both the nose and
mouth. Make a tight seal and blow into
the air passages until the chest rises.
Infants and small children only need
small puffs or air. Remove your mouth
and let the patient breathe out through
his nose or mouth. Continue this at
the rate of 12-14 times per minute for
an adult, and at least 20 times a minute
for a child. For Mouth to Nose Resuscitation, inflate the lungs through the
nose, keeping the mouth closed.

Use of the airway offers not only an
aesthetic advantage over direct mouth
contact, but also helps to maintain a
clear air passage. However, the airway
may cause the patient to gag and vomit
if left in place when he starts to
respond to resuscitation efforts.

Mouth-to-mouth resuscitation must be
continued without interruption. If the
principal attendant becomes fatigued,
his relief must take over without breaking the rhythm. If the patient shows
any signs of an effort to regain natural
breathing, the timing of the cycle should
be adjusted to match his effort. If the
patient starts to breathe for himself,
he should be watched closely and resuscitation resumed if his effort falters
or seems to become too feeble.

Once mouth-to-mouth resuscitation has
begun, treatment of other injuries can
be administered. The patient should be
kept lying down. He should be made as
comfortable as possible; wet clothing
should be removed, and he should be kept
warm. No attempt should be made to give
him any food, drink or medicine by mouth
until he is fully conscious. And, as
promptly as possible, he must be examined by a Doctor - even if there do not
seem to be any residual ill-effects from
the emergency.

Mechanical Resuscitation - A bag resuscitator, a simple, hand-powered device,
can be substituted for mouth-to-mouth
resuscitation when it is immediately
available (Figure 10-2). It allows the

use of oxygen to assist respiration and is readily employed in recompression chambers. All diving units should be equipped with an AMBU-type resuscitator, and all members of the diving team should be thoroughly familiar with the proper operation of the apparatus.

CARDIAC RESUSCITATION

Cardiac arrest may result from electric shock or asphyxia, or it can be caused by a combination of factors such as hypoxia, shock or embolism. There are a number of other causes; but, in the immediate emergency situation, the cause is not as important as the effort to restore - or mechanically reproduce - the heart beat. Arrest of heart action can be recognized by the absence of pulse in the major vessels. If the heart has been interrupted more than four minutes, irreversible damage to the brain and other vital organs will usually result.

Figure 10-2 Mechanical Bag Resuscitator (Modulaid).

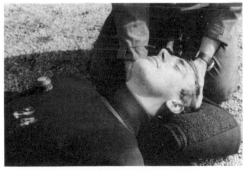

The victim is placed on his back in a comfortable position and a "pillow" (in this case a wet suit top) is positioned under his neck. His wet suit top is opened.

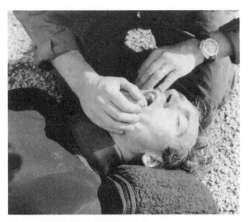

His chin is then lifted, and his mouth cleared of any foreign matter.

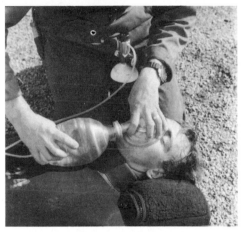

The resuscitator mask is then placed and firmly held over his nose and mouth, and the bag is squeezed and released in a rhythmic manner to simulate normal respiration. The operator should check the victim's chest movements to insure proper operation of the resuscitator.

The mechanical bag resuscitator may also be used with a pure oxygen supply. Operational procedures are identical except that oxygen rather than air is forced into the victim's lungs.

Closed-chest cardiac massage is a
method for artificially continuing
the flow of blood to the central
nervous system and vital organs.
Hopefully, the closed-chest message
will result in a spontaneous
resumption of the heart beat. If it
does not, massage is continued while
the patient is being moved to an area
of complete medical assistance.
Cardiac massage shall be continued
until directions to stop are given by
a medical officer, or until the victim's
pulse remains absent for more than
15 minutes.

Check for pulse at either side of the
windpipe on the neck. If none is present,
lift neck and extend head to open air
passage.

Go into a kneeling position on either
side of the patient. Then place the
heel of one hand on the lower third of the
breastbone with the fingers pointing
toward the patient's armpit. Now place
the other hand directly on top of the
first as shown by the illustration.

Press downward, using your body weight,
compressing the chest approximately $1\frac{1}{2}$
inches. (Always use less pressure with
children or the aged.) Release pressure

immediately. Compress the chest and
release once every second, eight
consecutive times. After eight
compressions, ventilate the lungs ONCE
using mouth-to-mouth technique.

This cycle should be maintained by
continuously alternating mouth-to-mouth
resuscitation with the heart massage.
Observe for return of spontaneous
cardiac action every 3 minutes.

Figure 10 - 3 Heart-lung resuscitation;
call doctor at once.

In closed-chest cardiac massage, the
operator applies pressure on the victim's
breastbone, which squeezes his heart and
serves to simulate the normal pumping
action. At the same time, the victim's
lungs must be ventilated using mouth-to-
mouth resuscitation, or preferably, 100%
oxygen administered with a bag resuscitator. Heart-lung resuscitation will
help to offset the asphyxia and hypoxia
which are a natural result of cardiac
arrest; without the circulation of
blood, the cells of the brain, and the
rest of the body will die due to lack of
oxygen. A detailed procedure for performing heart-lung resuscitation is described
in Figure No. 10 - 3.

CONTROL OF MASSIVE BLEEDING Massive
bleeding must be immediately controlled.
If the victim also requires resuscitation,
the two problems must be handled simultaneously. Bleeding may involve arteries,
and both the urgency and method of treatment may be determined in part by the
nature of the source.
Arterial bleeding can be identified as
follows:
-bright red blood, gushing forth in jets
or spurts which are synchronized with
the pulse.

Internal bleeding - the signs of external
are obvious, but the first aid team must
be alert for the possibility of unseen,
internal hemorrhage. Victims subjected
to crushing injuries, heavy blows or

deep puncture wounds should be carefully observed for signs of internal bleeding. Signs usually present include:

- moist, clammy, pale skin
- feeble pulse with very rapid pulse rate
- lowered blood pressure
- faintness or actual fainting
- blood in stool, urine or vomitus, or from the mouth

Internal bleeding can only be controlled by trained medical personnel and often only under hospital conditions. Efforts in the field are generally limited to replacing lost volume through infusion of saline, Ringer's lactate or other fluids.

EXTERNAL ARTERIAL HEMORRHAGE

There is only one effective measure which can be used to control external arterial hemorrhage - direct pressure on the wound. The pressure is best applied with sterile compresses, placed directly and firmly over the wound. In a crisis, almost any material can be used.

Two alternate methods of controlling bleeding, often suggested in medical texts, are by applying pressure to the various pressure points in the body and by applying a tourniquet. In almost every instance, these methods have proven to be significantly less effective than local pressure. The location of pressure points is easily forgotten in emergency circumstances. Additionally, even when the pressure point technique is properly applied, collateral circulation will usually allow the **hemmorrhage to persist.**

A tourniquet is a constricting band which, when tightened about the appendage above the wound, practically stops the flow of blood to the wound. This method of controlling bleeding often results in the later need for amputation of the damaged appendage, and for that reason a tourniquet should only be applied when amputation is judged an inevitable consequence of the wound.

EXTERNAL VENOUS HEMORRHAGE

Venous hemorrhage is not as dramatic as severe arterial bleeding, but if left unchecked, can be equally serious. Venous bleeding can almost always be adequately treated by direct pressure on the wound.

MEDICAL EMERGENCIES - NON-RECOMPRESSION TREATMENT

Any emergency in a diving situation could result in a requirement for medical treatment. Many of these emergencies are analogous to those encountered in any environment, and normal first aid measures are employed. In some circumstances, such as traumatic injuries occuring under water, the need for decompression may complicate procedures. Thus the need for adequate dive decompression may affect wound management techniques. In serious situations a judgement may be required to bypass normal decompression and risk decompression sickness in favour of rendering immediate aid to the diver.

Aside from the complications introduced by recompression considerations, this section of the Diving Manual concerns disorders which are unique to diving, require special procedures, and are not treated by recompression. For convenience these problems can be divided into two areas -

1. Respiratory emergencies, as directly related to the quantity and quality of the breathing supply.

2. In-water emergencies with direct medical involvement.

The most serious conditions which can apply to any of these categories have already been covered -

    cessation of breathing

    cardiac arrest

    massive hemorrhage.

A potentially serious sympton which may be common to these categories is loss of consciousness which may be both a warning of a severe problem and a complicating factor in any diagnosis.

Loss of consciousness can be the result of near-drowning, inadequate oxygen, an oxygen convulsion or an excess of carbon dioxide in the blood. But, in diving, loss of consciousness must be considered to be a symptom of the most dangerous problems - gas embolism and decompression sickness. Recompression should be given in almost every case of unconsciousness simply because it is seldom possible to be certain that it is not essential. If satisfied that recompression is not called for in a given case, then treatment can progress along other lines, as outlined in the following sections.

RESPIRATORY EMERGENCIES All human life is directly dependent upon the quantity and quality of it's breathing mixture. Any deviations from established standards can result in a number of respiratory problems. Because of the particular nature of the underwater environment, any such problem - which on the surface might easily be handled as a transient annoyance - must be handled as an emergency.

Not all respiratory problems must necessarily result in the termination of the dive - if they are identified and corrected soon enough. With most, however, the need to ensure the safety of the diver should be brought to the surface for treatment and thorough examination by medical personnel. Beware of the diver who reports from the bottom "I think I'm OK now" and wants to continue.

Every diver and every other member of the diving team must know the warning signs and symptoms of each of these problems:

    Oxygen deficiency (hypoxia)

    Carbon dioxide poisoning

    Carbon monoxide poisoning

    Asphyxia

    Strangulation

    Chemical irritants

    Nitrogen narcosis

    Oxygen poisoning (toxicity)

SYMPTONS/TREATMENT OF RESPIRATORY DISORDERS

A.   Oxygen Deficiency - Although the specific cause varies as discussed in Chapter Three, the following disorders all result in the same condition - a shortage of oxygen reaching the cells for normal metabolism. In summary, these disorders are -

    -Hypoxia, caused by loss or inadequacy of the air supply.

    -Carbon dioxide poisoning, resulting from inadequate ventilation of apparatus, over-exertion, controlled or "skip" breathing, excessive dead space in equipment.

-Carbon monoxide poisoning, caused by induction of exhaust fumes into the air supply compressor.

-Asphyxia, simultaneous oxygen deficiency and carbon dioxide excess usually caused by loss or inadequacy of the air supply.

-Strangulation, obstruction of the airway by a foreign object, laryngal spasm or abnormal swelling.

-Chemical irritants, presence of irritating chemicals contaminating the air supply resulting in pulmonary edema.

SYMPTOMS OF OXYGEN DEFICIENCY - The following signs and symptoms may be noted in situations involving oxygen deficiency -

Labored breathing	Lack of muscular coordination
Mental confusion	
Bad taste	Headache
Nausea	Chest discomfort
Unconsciousness	Weakness

TREATMENT OF OXYGEN DEFICIENCY - The following procedures should be followed if oxygen deficiency is suspected -

1. Abort the dive.
2. Switch to an alternate air supply
3. Send down the standby diver to assist.
4. Thoroughly ventilate the apparatus.
5. Administer 100% oxygen.

NITROGEN NARCOSIS - The narcotic effect of high partial pressures of nitrogen can produce euphoria, disorientation, lapses of rationality or judgement, and other behavior similar to that of alcoholic intoxication. Nitrogen narcosis is normally encountered below 30m and may result from exceeding established depth limits.

TREATMENT OF NITROGEN NARCOSIS - Reduction of the nitrogen partial pressure is the standard procedure for treatment. Specifically -

1. Diver should ascend to a shallower depth.

2. If mental acuity is not restored, abort the dive.

C. OXYGEN TOXICITY - As discussed in Chapter Three, oxygen toxicity (poisoning) can result from the inspiration of oxygen at partial pressures greater than 2 bars absolute. Established depth and bottom time limits normally preclude the possibility of the development of in-water oxygen toxicity in air diving. Oxygen toxicity in air diving may be encountered while administering 100% oxygen during surface decompression procedures.

SYMPTOMS OF OXYGEN TOXICITY - The following signs and symptoms may be noted in situations involving oxygen toxicity -

Muscle twitching	Abnormal vision (particularly "tunnel vision")
	Hearing abnormalities
Nausea	Convulsions
Dizziness	
Behavioral abnormalities (irritability, anxiety, confusion, unusual fatigue)	
Incoordination	Convulsions

TREATMENT FOR OXYGEN TOXICITY
Procedures for treating oxygen toxicity involve immediate reduction in oxygen partial pressure and protection of the

diver from physical injury if he begins to convulse. Specifically -

1. Stop mask breathing and breathe chamber atmosphere.

2. If symptoms persist, switch to an air decompression schedule.

3. If the diver is having convulsions, protect him from physical harm and protect his tongue with a padded depressor.

IN-WATER EMERGENCIES WITH DIRECT MEDICAL INVOLVEMENT

Emergencies discussed in this section are those which arise out of the nature of the diving environment - drowning, pressure imbalance, and problems of low temperatures and heat loss leading to emergency conditions.

DROWNING   A swimmer can fall victim to drowning because of over-exertion, panic, inability to cope with rough water, exhaustion, or the effects of cold water or heat loss. These same factors can affect a diver but, if he is properly equipped, trained and monitored by a buddy or a surface tender, drowning should be a remote possibility. Unfortunately, divers do drown - even when equipped, trained and tended.

The prevention of drowning is best insured by the establishment of, and thorough training in, safe diving practices coupled with the careful selection of diving personnel. A physically-fit, confident diver, equipped with proper gear, should not easily fall victim to drowning. At the same time, however, over-confidence - in both self and equipment - can give a feeling of security that might lead a diver to take dangerous risks.

The treatment of near-drowning falls into two phases: one, restore breathing and heartbeat, and, two call for assistance from qualified medical personnel. Regardless of the mildness or severity of a near-drowning case, all victims should be hospitalized as quickly as possible. The occurrence of pulmonary edema (accumulation of fluids in the lungs), pneumonia, and other complications may be delayed for many hours after the incident and proper medical observation is essential. Subsequent to resuscitation while awaiting transportation to medical facilities, the patient should be kept warm and rested.

SQUEEZE   Basically, squeeze or barotrauma is caused by a lack of pressure equalization between parts of the body or between the body and diving equipment. It normally occurs during descent. Cause as follows -

- Middle-ear squeeze, caused by a blocked eustachian tube.

- External-ear squeeze, caused by a hood or other piece of equipment covering the external ear passage.

- Lung (thoracic) squeeze, which may happen when the air in the lungs is compressed to less than residual volume. This could happen in an extremely deep breathhold (free) dive.

- Body squeeze, caused by a failure of the air supply to balance water pressure; can be precipitated by a fall into water of greater depth, or by the absence or failure of the safety air non-return valve.

- Face-mask squeeze, caused by a failure to equalize air in the mask by nasal exhalation.

- Suit squeeze, normally occurs in dry-type suits in which a pocket or air becomes trapped under a fold or fitting and pinches the skin in the fold area.

Treatment of Squeeze - Squeeze may be relieved by the following procedures -

1. Stop descent.
2. If efforts to equalize pressure fail, ascent to shallower depth.
3. If further efforts to equalize pressure fail, abort the dive.
4. If an ear drum rupture is suspected, send down the standby diver to assist.
5. Report any physical injury to the medic for appropriate treatment.

THERMAL CONSIDERATIONS   The problems caused by diving in cold water, or by body heat loss in water below a temperature of about 34°C are more serious than often realized and affect not only diver efficiency but threaten his life as well.

Sudden immersion in very cold water results in the diver being unable to hold his breath which causes him to lose bouyancy. He hyperventilates uncontrollably and loses his ability to co-ordinate swimming maneuvers. Prolonged immersion will result in profound heat loss (hypothermia) and rapid deterioration of mental and physical performance.

In water below 41°F (5.5°C), and unclothed man of average body will probably become helpless from hypothermia in less than 30 minutes. He can withstand immersion at 59°F (15.5°C) for up to approximately 2 hours. If wearing heavy, conventional clothing these times can be more than doubled, and for divers, wearing adequate diving dress and insulating underwear, immersion time can be significantly increased. There is, of course, a wide range of individual tolerance to immersion in cold water which occur primarily as a result of the insulating effects of body fat. Overweight personnel normally have significantly greater cold water endurance than thin people.

There are two rules which must be observed by a man who is in the water with inadequate thermal protection and finds himself becoming incapacitated by the cold -

1. If the water temperature is below 77°F (35°C) do not move any more than is absolutely necessary. At temperatures above 77°F, exercise will help increase the production of heat and help forestall hypothermia; at temperatures below 77°F, exercise will increase the loss of body heat.

2. If supported by a life preserver or a floating object, and if rescue or pick-up seems reasonably certain, do not attempt to swim for shore or a boat. Very good swimmers, in very cold water, have failed to cover distances as short as 70 metres.

Hypothermia is an emergency condition and must be quickly treated. Merely getting the victim out of the water is not enough to save his life, as the loss of heat from the inner organs will continue for some time as long as the skin temperature remains low. Putting a blanket around the victim will be of little help except in very mild cases - his body will not be generating enough heat to provide any warmth under the blanket.

Active warming must be initiated at once. This can include use of heaters, fires, hot showers or hot baths. Giving the victim hot liquids or alcoholic beverages will probably have a positive psychological effect but will usually not have much physiological benefit.

In extreme cases, where the victim is apparently dead, a hot bath combined with mouth-to-mouth resuscitation and external cardiac massage may prove successful. The bath should be as hot as 110°F (44°C) and the victim's trunk should be fully immersed, with his arms and legs out of the water. The bath must be discontinued when the heart beat and respiration are regular and increasing in frequency, accompanied by a general improvement of condition, or if his deep body temperature reaches 91°F (32.8°C) and is rising steadily. From this point, he should be wrapped in blankets and allowed to re-warm spontaneously.

Complications which may arise, such as sudden deterioration of condition or loss of blood pressure, require the immediate attention of medical personnel.

If any personnel should suffer from frozen extremities, resulting from exposure or immersion, they may be given initial treatment as follows -

1. If still actually frozen, thaw the affected extremity quickly by immersion in water at 104°F (40°C).

2. If already thawed after having been frozen, keep the limb dry, give the patient drugs to relieve pain and otherwise leave alone.

3. In the case of a non-freezing injury - where the limbs may have been kept at just above freezing temperature, in or out of the water, for several hours, give the victim a hot immersion bath (104 to 110°F, 44°C) but keep the limbs out of the water, keep them elevated and administer pain-relieving drugs.

In all such cases, the victim should be seen by a doctor as soon as possible.

Another thermal condition which may require emergency treatment is heat exhaustion - always a possibility when the diver is working in waters above 95°F (35°C). Prevention is the result of good planning and careful avoidance of over-work. Treatment consists of placing the casualty in a reclining position in a cool environment and giving cool water, containing 0.1 per cent sodium chloride, by mouth.

POLLUTION POISONING   Divers who will be operating in contaminated water, or where contamination (as from a leaking barge) is likely, should be provided with appropriate protective gear and required prophylaxis, e.g., ear washing solution, should be available at the diving station. These procedures are properly part of the planning phase of the operation; medical personnel should be consulted for the correct treatment for the type of exposure that may be encountered by the divers.

GAS EXPANSION   Occasionally, a diver may experience various types of internal gas expansion. For example, in rare instances, a middle ear or sinus that has equalized on descent may block on ascent, trapping a pocket of gas. Slowing the rate of ascent will usually permit the gas to escape without additional complications.

A more common condition results from the generation of gas in the intestines during a dive, or from the swallowing of air which becomes trapped in the stomach. These pockets of gas will usually work their way out of the system through the natural vents. If not, and if the pain begins to pass the stage of mild discomfort, ascent should be halted and the diver should descend slightly until the pain is relieved. Then he should attempt to belch or release the gas anally - with a caution, however, overzealous attempts to belch may result in swallowing more air.

Most intestinal gas expansion can be avoided by a few simple precautions - do not dive with an upset stomach or bowel, avoid eating foods which are likely to produce intestinal gas, and avoid swallowing air during a dive.

MEDICAL EMERGENCIES REQUIRING RECOMPRESSION

There are two basic classes of medical

emergency which require treatment
by recompression - gas embolism (and
several related conditions) and
decompression sickness. Gas embolism
is the most dangerous, and must be
treated as an extreme emergency. It
is an accident which can occur during
a brief, shallow dive - even a dive
made in a swimming pool with breathing
equipment. It develops rapidly, and
must be treated quickly. Decompression
sickness can be just as serious, but
may develop quite gradually up to
24 hours after the completion of a
seemingly routine and uneventful dive.
Decompression sickness is not unique
to diving - it can affect aviators or
men working in pressure chambers - but
can only occur when "decompression"
(a reduction in the pressure surrounding the body) has taken place.
(See Chapter 5. Therapeutic
Recompression).

CHAPTER 11

STANDARD DIVING EQUIPMENT

The "standard" or "hard-hat" diving
apparatus, although often considered
obsolete, is in fact still the only
dress totally suitable for prolonged
hard underwater work in shallow
depths. Its manufacture is now very
limited, but it is still in regular
use in both naval and commercial
dockyards throughout the world. Hence
a basic working knowledge of this
equipment, in particular the dressing
and general operation, should be part
of every working diver's experience.

DEVELOPMENT

Credit for the invention and subsequent development of the diving helmet,
its associated "open" and later "closed"
dress has, in the past, been mistakenly
credited to Augustus Siebe, but it is
now generally accepted that the true
inventors were John and Charles Deane,
of Whitstable, in Kent, in 1828.

In their own diving manual,
printed in 1836, the brothers claimed
"that on one occasion they remained
underwater for 5 hours, 40 minutes,
and had reached a depth of 120ft, and
did not really consider 180ft impossible".
The original apparatus consisted of a
copper helmet attached to a loose canvas
dress, which was open to the sea, which
in fact still worked very much on the
diving bell principle, and with all the
relevant limitations. The greatest single
advance in this field came when the Deane
brothers closed off the lower part of the
dress, making it a true, one-piece dry
suit, which kept the diver much warmer,
and allowed true mobility underwater.
This advance added considerably to the
buoyancy of the equipment, and additional
chest, back, and boot weighting became
necessary, but was the only real disadvantage. Apart from refinements, particularly to the inlet valve, and the introduction of helmet communications, as well
as the use of modern materials, the
dress and equipment generally as used
today, has in fact changed very little
since its inception almost 150 years ago.

Fig 11-1 Standard divers under
training

THE EQUIPMENT

The essential items of the "standard"
diving outfit, necessary to put a
man underwater are as follows:

a) Standard diving dress and its
    associated "collar"
b) Corselet and fittings, which
    includes certain special tools
c) Diver's helmet
d) Air pipe or hose
e) Breast rope, which incorporates
    the diver's telephone cable
f) Front and back lead weights
g) Waist belt and jocking strap
h) Pair of weighted boots
i) Air supply
j) Accessories

DETAILS OF THE EQUIPMENT

STANDARD DRESS AND COLLAR.

The dress is manufactured of sheet
rubber, sandwiched between two layers
of tanned twill canvas. At the neck
is attached by adhesive, a flexible
collar of thick vulcanised rubber,
to allow entry by the diver, and to
which will be clamped the corselet,
which makes a watertight joint.
Inside the collar is a canvas "bib"
piece, which when pulled up and correctly folded around the divers neck,
serves to catch any small amount of
water which may leak through the
corselet joint, or via the helmet's
"spit-cock". The suit is sealed at
the wrists by means of soft rubber
cuffs. Should a particular diver have

such small wrists that a watertight seal cannot be easily obtained, wide rubber bands, commonly known as "greys", or "reds" for very small wrists should be used, and are a standard item. These bands, made of thin sheet rubber, are worn so as to half overlap the normal wrist seal, but can equally well be worn under the cuff, to increase the diameter of the wrist as necessary. Care must be exercised when using extra wrist seals, since these may restrict or even stop blood flow to the hands, cutting off the circulation completely. Such soft rubber rings are normally supplied with each new suit on purchase, being graded as "broad" and "narrow", as well as "plain" and "ribbed".

The "horse-collar", a canvas ring filled with horse-hair, is worn around the neck, sitting down comfortably on the shoulders, to protect the diver from the weight of the combined helmet, corselet, back and front weights, which will be in the order of 54kg. It is an extremely painful process to attempt to wear full "standard" dress without this item, or suitable alternative protection. The soles of the feet of "standard" dress have only one additional thickness of canvas as additional protection, and therefore the diver should be discouraged from walking about in the dress without boots, to prevent wear and tear, which can only lead to a leak in due course.

After use, the dress should be washed off with fresh water, using a scrubbing brush if necesssary to get rid of mud etc, and then hung, upside down, on a suitable framework to dry. Suits should not be spread out in the sun to dry, since the pure rubber collar and cuffs will quickly perish, unlike the neoprene or other synthetic components of other diving dress, which are not so vulnerable.

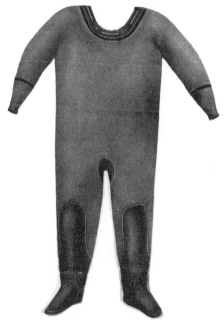

Fig 11.2   Admiralty 6 bolt "standard" diving dress

Fig 11.3   A soft material, harbour dress, designed for use with a 12 bolt diving helmet

If the suit is wet inside, or has been fouled so that scrubbing is necessary, then it must be reversed completely, washed and then dried before the outside is treated. If it was necessary for the diver to have relieved himself inside the suit, then a mixture of warm water and disinfectant should be used at the earliest opportunity. Failure to take this action quickly will usually render the suit unusable due to the smell, which may never disappear.

Additional chafing patches are normally fitted during manufacture to the knees, soles of the feet, elbows and crutch.

Variations of "standard" dress necessary to suit different helmets

a) No bolt dress, with a special flanged collar
b) 3 bolt dress, with special collar
c) 6 bolt dress, once the standard Admiralty, or Royal Navy pattern
d) 8 bolt dress, with special collar
e) 12 bolt dress, with special collar
f) 12 bolt dress, with square collar

CORSELET AND FITTINGS

The corselet or breastplate is the fitting which allows the helmet to be attached to the suit. It is normally manufactured from heavy gauge sheet copper, strehgthened around the edge and central opening, and fitted with the appropriate number of brass, threaded studs, depending on the particular model. These studs pass through the holes in the indiarubber collar of the dress, then shaped brass strips sandwich the collar itself, held down by butterfly nuts to create a watertight joint.

The open top of the corselet has an interrupted male screw thread, which is normally right-handed, designed to mate with a similar female thread on the helmet, so that when the latter is rotated one-eighth of a turn, a seal is achieved. The lower edge of the helmet bears down on a rubber gasket fitted into the corselets top flange.

Fig 11-4   An 8 bolt helmet and matching corselet

Two studs are fitted to the breastplate, usually at the front only. but with some models, both front and back, which take the clips of the jockstrap fittings, also the lanyards of the lead front and back weights. Although helmets are not supplied with lanyards fitted, it is the normal accepted practice to splice two lengths of line around the top flange of the helmet, each with a "tail" of at least 45cms of clear line, which are used to secure the breast rope and air hose in position alongside the helmet, by means of a rolling hitch knot on each.

It is important that the serial number of a corselet should match that of the helmet with which it is to be mated. These items are manufactured as mated pairs or sets, which must remain together. If items with differing serial numbers are used together, it may not be possible

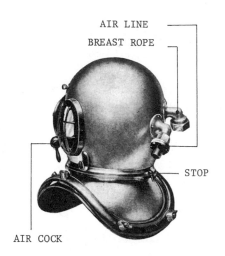

AIR LINE

BREAST ROPE

STOP

AIR COCK

Fig 11-5 A back view of a standard diver's helmet, showing the various fittings, and their use

to achieve a watertight seal, and even irreparable distortion may result if force is used.

THE HELMET

As with the corselet, the helmet is manufactured from copper sheet, usually tinned after being shaped on a mandril. The base of the helmet carries an interrupted male, right-hand thread, to mate with its matching corselet. A small hinged brass "stop", fitted at the back of the helmet, prevents its unscrewing when in use, and the lack of this simple but very necessary device caused an unfortunate number of drownings in the early days of the equipment, until the "stop" became a standard fitting.

Most helmets are fitted with three glass windows or ports, but sometimes four, all of which are manufactured of at least 12mm plate glass, the side windows and sometimes that at the top, being protected by brass guard bars. The front window is always made to open, and may be screwed or hinged to effect a seal.

Air enters the helmet from a connection at the back of the helmet, the air hose normally being tied back to the left hand side of the diver's helmet/ corselet. The hose is normally fitted with a simple screw thread and gasket connection, done up with a spanner, and the air on entering, passes immediately through a non-return inlet valve. This inlet valve consists of a spindle holding a rubber valve. The valve is normally held "shut" by a light copper spring, but air pumped down the supply hose to the diver easily overcomes this spring pressure, and the diver receives a constant supply. Should this supply fail for any reason, such as a pump defect, or the diver's air hose was severed or badly kinked, then this valve would immediately close under spring pressure, trapping whatever air was inside the helmet and suit. If such a valve were not fitted, or in an emergency situation failed to operate, then the pressure exerted by the water surrounding the diver would attempt to squeeze his body inside his helmet, and then up the air pipe to the point of least pressure, ie. the surface. Such valves have not always been fitted as a standard item, and the results of accidents need no further explanation. The cleaning and routine testing of these valves is of the greatest importance.

On the right hand side of the helmet is the exhaust valve, which can be any one of a number of different models, three variations of which are illustrated on the next page. Their function is to allow excess air to escape, and since this will alter the volume and hence the buoyancy of the divers suit, the diver has full manual control over its setting. The action of screwing "down" or closing the valve will allow less air to escape and hence increase buoyancy, and vice versa. Since exhausting air makes for considerable noise in the helmet, it is often necessary for the diver to temporarily close the valve completely when in telephone conservation with the surface or other divers. This can be achieved by screw-

Fig 11-6   12 bolt diving helmet

A

Fig 11-6(a) Exhaust valve

B

Fig 11-6(b) Exhaust valve with centre spindle, and below, internal control

C

This part inside helmet

ing down on the valve until fully closed, or on some models, by the operation of the centre spindle, pushing it inwards towards the helmet.

Fig 11-6(c) shows the Royal Navy or Admiralty pattern exhaust valve, which can be opened to allow excess air to escape by the diver "nudging" it with his head from the inside. This device has proven to be of immense value in the case of a diver becoming over inflated, and suffering what is known as a "blow-up", ie. the diver arrives on the surface with his suit so fully inflated that he is unable to bend his arms to even reach the exhaust valve. Experience in the operation pf the exhaust valve is the secret of safe and efficient use of this equipment.

On the front right side of most helmets will be found a control known as the "spit-cock". When turned by the diver, it allows the entry of a very fine jet of seawater, which can be acught in the mouth, or sucked in directly, which can then be spat over the front glass of the helmet to clear misting. An altern-ative use is to assist vent off excess air, should it prove that the exhaust valve is unable to get rid of it fast enough.

AIR HOSE

Air hose or pipe is normally supplied in 9, 13, 15 and 18m lengths. The 9m lengths are supplied from manufact-urers with a male connection at one end, and a female at the other, and will sink when pressurised with air. 13m lengths have female connections at both ends, and are buoyant. A length of this " floating" hose is normally connected to the helmet, to assist relieve the weight of the hose overall on the diver.

The physical construction of "standard" divers air hose, from the outside inwards, is as follows:

1 Layer of rubber
2 Three layers of canvas
3 Two layers of steel wire mesh
   between items 1 and 2
4 Two additional layers of canvas
5 One internal layer of rubber

Such hose is pressure tested to 272kg/mm². Rubber, fibre, neoprene or even leather washers are used in the joints between lengths of hose pipe.

BREAST ROPE

Made of plaited hemp, reinforced, contains a core of three insulated conductors connected to the divers telephone system. Tested to a breaking strain of 272kg without loss of electrical continuity, the breast rope should be capable of withstanding a pull of 590kg before parting. Supplied in 91m lengths, with male and female couplings as appropriate to the particular type of equipment. The helmet connection is normally supported by two short lengths of brass chain, to act as a restrainer and prevent undue strain on the electrical connections. The contact pins of the telephone system are such that the plug/socket arrangement cannot be incorrectly connected.

   It is recommended that breast ropes, which are in reality also lifelines, are suitably marked with coloured tape or twine whippings, to indicate the diver's depth. It is unnecessary to mark breast ropes for decompression "stop" purposes beyond 60ft (18m).

BACK AND FRONT WEIGHTS

Made of lead, weighing 18kg each, cast in a particular "heart" shape, which experience has shown to be the most suitable for the job. They are fitted with rope handles or "beckets" for carrying purposes, and the back weight with a long, double ended lanyard, which should be tied around the diver's waist. Weights are manufactured with either metal eyeplates, which are then slipped over the two studs on the front of a corselet breastplate, or else with plain lanyards, so that by slipping a "bow-hitch" knot

the diver can easily shed his weights in an emergency situation. The latter is more simple to operate, since it may be difficult underwater for the diver to physically lift off the eyeplates in order to slip the weights. The waist lanyard from the back weights should be tied in a reef-knot and not a bow, which might otherwise easily come undone.

   Alternatively, the diver may choose to wear a weight-belt or a weight-harness, as shown below.

Fig 11-7   Front and back weights

Fig 11-8 Diver's weight harness, which gives a greater flexibility of weight than those in Fig 11-7

BELT AND JOCKSTRAP

The leather belt serves two purposes:
to hold the diver's knife sheath, and
to restrict inflation of the dress below
the waist. It is important that the belt
is not omitted, otherwise the diver may
become unbalanced underwater, possibly
leading to a "blow-up" situation, ie.
his suit will become over-inflated, and
he may arrive on the surface out of
control.

The two brass eye plates on the
ends of the jock-strap, are fitted over
the breastplate studs back and front,
before the strap is pulled tight and
secured. This prevents the helmet and
corselet rising off the diver's shoulders by more than a limited amount.

BOOTS

Fig 11-9 Lead soled, brass toe capped
diving boots, of about 6kg weight each

Normally made of very stout leather,
with a wooden sole to which is screwed
or bolted a replacement lead sole. A
detachable brass toe cap protects the
end of each boot, and it may be secured
to the diver's ankles by leather straps
as shown in the above illustration, or
by means of a rope lanyard, rove through
brass eyelets. If a lanyard is used,
then a length of 38mm tarred hemp should
be centred, and an eye spliced into the
lower right eyelet on the bight, so as
to leave two free ends of some 1.2m
long, to use as laces.

DIVERS AIR SUPPLY

Air for the "standard" diver to
breathe was originally supplied
by means of a single or double
cylinder acting pump, operated by
hand, with pumps working in tandem
where considerable depths were
involved. This often required
teams of 2 or 4 men at a time, to
produce the necessary pressure and
volume. Such pumps are now
generally museum pieces, but in some
remote parts of the world or in
under-developed countries are still
in use. They do have the great
benefit of portability and are
totally self-contained, requiring
only man power.

If a diesel or petrol driven
compressor is being considered for
the provision of breathing air for
a "standard" diver, the following
points are important considerations:

1 That the cubic capacity output is
   sufficient for two divers to work
   at the maximum depth of the work
   to be undertaken. Even if only
   one diver is to be used, consideration must be given to the
   requirement of a second, stand-
   by diver, who may have need to
   enter the water at the same time.

Fig 11-10 Brass soled and toe
capped diving boots of 8kg each

Fig 11-11 A typical portable, diesel driven LP air compressor, suitable for supplying two divers using "standard" equipment to 50m.

2 The reservoir must be of sufficient volume so that one or both diver's can be surfaced, with "stops" if necessary, should the machine stop or become unserviceable.

3 The air supply must be oil free, suitable for breathing, filtered, and supplied through a suitable air control panel.

Table showing volume of air required by a "standard" diver at various depths:

Depth (ft)	Volume in cub/ft at atmospheric pressure
0	1.5
16	2.2
33	3.0
66	4.5
99	6.0
132	7.5
165	9.0

ACCESSORIES

These include many of the items normally associated with any professional dry suit diving, such as woollen undergarments, diving knife, depth gauge, telephone communications etc.

Possibly the most important item of all is the diving ladder, since with "standard" equipment, the additional weight and general bulk of the outfit makes the diver unstable out of the water. The ladder must therefore be strong enough to take the additional weight. It must also be sufficiently long for at least three rungs to be beneath the surface when rigged, and should have handrails extending at least 0.7m above the top of the ladder, to give the diver support as he steps on and off the top rung level with the deck.

On entering the water, the diver will be very buoyant, and will require a "shot-rope" to which he can cling, whilst making adjustments to his exhaust valve, venting off excess air, and testing the equipment generally before diving.

DRESSING A STANDARD DIVER

On no account should a diver be fully or even partially dressed in any form of "standard" equipment in a craft or vessel still under way. Similarly, a diver must be full undressed before a craft or vessel weighs anchor and proceeds. The reason for this is the consequence of an accident in which a boat is sinking, with a diver perhaps in his suit, possibly unable to get out in time.

The diver, assisted by his attendant, prepares the equipment to be used prior to dressing; this includes surface testing, laying out the diving dress and all the necessary accessories, preparing the air hose and breast rope. The diver then puts on what ever undergarments are considered necessary, and it is recommended that "standard" dress is never worn without some sort of protection, in order to reduce the effects of "squeeze". It will generally take two persons to comfortably dress a diver in full "standard" equipment.

After getting his legs inside the suit, and pulling it up to his waist, the remainder of the dressing procedure can be carried out whilst seated. The diver or his attendant should then lubricate his wrists, at the same time similarly treat the inside surfaces of both suit suffs. After inserting both arms inside the sleeves, the hands are forced out through the cuffs. The neck "collar" is then fitted over the head, to sit comfortably on the shoulders, followed by the corselet. Great care must be taken not to injure the diver when the corselet is being fitted, since nose and ear injury is not unusual , and it is recommended that the diver keeps one hand over the front forward lip of the corselet, in order to protect his teeth until dressing is completed.

The rubber collar of the dress is then pulled over the edge of the corselet, fitting one stud at a time through its appropriate hole, front studs forst, working over the divers shoulders to the back. The diver then stands up, so that the attendant can pull the canvas "bib" up to its full height, before the diver again becomes seated. After this the "bib" is folded neatly and comfortably around the neck, the ends being tucked out of sight.

Brass strips, marked "front" and "back", which form part of the corselet are then placed over the studs, a brass wing nut put in place, and lightly screwed down. Placing one hand inside the neck ring of the corselet, opposite each nut in turn, a special socket spanner is employed to tighten them, leaving the two shoulder nuts till last, which sit over the joints in the brass strips. The hand inside the neck ring is important, since it is possible for the socket spanner to lift up and spin off the nut, striking the diver in the face and causing serious injury.

Should any "greys" or "reds" be required over the wrist seals, they should be fitted next.

Fit the jock-strap with the diver standing and upright, followed by the waist-belt which should carry the knife and sheath. The diver then sits down again whilst his boots are fitted and the straps or laces made secure. If lanyards are being used, then when secured, the straps are done up over the top, to retain the rope ends in place.

Ensuring that the front glass is removed, or hinged back open as appropriate, the helmet is then carefully placed over the diver's head, the thread is engaged, and with a one eighth turn, locked into place. Engage the locking device at the back of the helmet, and advise the diver this has been done. Bring the air pipe under the diver's left armpit, and secure it close to, but not actually touching the corselet, by means of the lanyard, using a rolling-hitch knot. Repeat the same procedure for the breast rope, under the right armpit. It is sometimes advisable to put the waist belt on over the air and breast lines, since it will help to reduce the strain on the helmet should the knots come undone.

The air supply is now connected and tested, to ensure the diver is receiving an air supply. When all is considered satisfactory, and the diver is ready, he supports his frontweight with both hands on the edge of the corselet, whilst the attendants place the back weight in position and the lanyards are secured. The top lanyards are brought over the hooks on the rim of the helmet, through the rings on the front weight, and secured by reef bow knots. The longest end of the waist lanyard is passed around the divers waist, through the eyelet on the front weight, and secured in a sheet-bend slip knot. It now only remains to close the front glass, test the telephone, and the diver is ready for the water.

CHAPTER 12

SEARCH TECHNIQUES

The ability of a diver to locate and
mark specific underwater objects and
sites, is one which requires considerable planning. Finding an object
on the seabed frequently takes more
planning, time and labour than the
actual work on the object once it
has been located.

Efficient and effective underwater
searches, therefore, become an integral part of almost every diving
operation. There are a variety of
seabed searches appropriate under
different circumstances.

The following factors govern the
choice of search:-

1   Underwater visibility. This
    can vary from 0 to 100m.
    It can also be altered by the
    seabed over which the search
    is to be carried out.

2   Nature of Seabed

  a)In deep, soft mud an object
    may sink into the seabed.

  b)In tidal areas an object may
    become covered and uncovered
    by tidal movement of the sea-
    bed.

  c)On uneven seabeds a small
    object may lie hidden in a
    depression.

  d)Profuse seaweed and kelp may
    may conceal an object and per-
    haps prohibit the use of
    "snag-line" type searches.

  e)Debris and rocks may also
    prohibit the use of "snag-
    line" searches.

3   Adverse currents.

4   Size and shape of the area
    to be searched.

5   The accuracy of the datum, if
    any.

6   Craft, equipment, personnel and
    facilities available.

7   Sea state.

8   Size of object to be located.

SEARCH METHODS

Search methods fall into THREE main
categories:-

1   "Jackstay" searches, in which
    physical contact is made with the
    object.

2   "Visual" searches.

3   Searching by shipborne locators.

1 - JACKSTAY SEARCHES

The term "Jackstay" is used for any
line, whether it be of wire or rope
of any size, that is laid on the
seabed to guide the diver. The
diameter and length will depend upon
the task to be performed. As a general rule jackstays, large in
diameter and short in length, are used
to guide surface supplied divers.
While SCUBA divers can rely on light
lines of considerable length, whichever
type is used it is important that
once it has been laid, it is not
displaced either by the diver, surface
support or the elements. For this
reason sinkers are attached to the
jackstay at intervals, generally not
greater than 100m. With heavy jackstays these sinkers can be 25kg each,
whereas with light equipment they may
weigh only 10kg.

For most seabed searches it is the
speed with which these jackstays and
associated gear can be handled which
is the controlling factor in the time
taken for the search.

Jackstay searches, though slow, are
the most reliable and in unfavourable

seabed conditions and/or bad underwater visibility, are the only ones
which offer any chance of success.
If any area is too big to be searched
all at once, the search must be
rigged so that it may be moved to an
adjacent section without gaps or
wasteful overlaps.

There are basically THREE types of
jackstay search:-

1a) <u>Circular</u> - a diver moves around
a fixed point using a radial
distance line to guide him and
snag on any object proud of the
bottom.

b) <u>Grid</u> - the divers move along
jackstays laid on the seabed
until the object is encountered.

c) <u>Snag Line</u> - Pairs of divers tow
a line between them in such a
way that objects proud of the
bottom foul the line.

2 - VISUAL SEARCHES

When the underwater visibility is
more than 6m and there is no
dense seaweed or mud which might
conceal the object, efficient
searching can be conducted by
raising a diver clear of the bottom
so that he can observe within his
field of vision.

3 - SHIPBORNE LOCATORS

This type of search should always
be considered first because, if
effective, it is quick and vastly
reduces the diving time. Commercial locators include echo sounders,
portable high definition sonar sets
and magnetic locators i.e. magneto-
meters.

Several versions of each type of
search exist. All of them can be
modified to suit different circumstances.

CIRCULAR SEARCHES

The circular search is the simplest
form of search to undertake because
it calls for the minimum of personnel
to make it effective. It should be
used where the position of the object
to be located can be accurately given.

Searching for objects

The search is carried out by one diver
connected by a life-line to his attendant on the surface. His distance
line is secured to the diver's down
line (shot); he uses the taut
distance line as a radius. Having
descended the down line and before
moving off on the search and stirring
up any mud or silt etc., he has a
good look around from his position
on the shot. He then moves out to
a distance of 2m or the limit
of his vision from the shot, and,
keeping the line taut, searches
around in a circle. On completion of
the first circle he moves out a similar distance again along the line and
carries out another circular search
in the opposite direction. He continues this procedure until the end
of the distance line is reached or
the object is found. Each search
should be made in the opposite direction to the previous one to avoid
getting turns in the umbilical or
life line around the down line.

The diver will probably not know
when he has completed a circle, but
by watching the air bubbles, the
attendant can give him a working
signal to stop him and then send him
in the opposite direction. Each circle
should just overlap to ensure that the
area is fully covered.

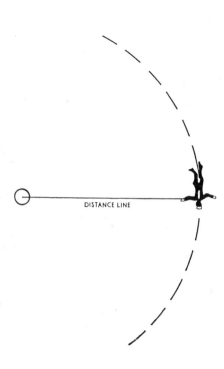

DISTANCE LINE

Fig 12.1 Circular search

ALTERNATIVE CIRCULAR SEARCH

An alternative circular search to the
one previously mentioned can be
carried out using a distance line of
approximately 30m. One diver circles
the shot at the end of the line while
the other swims to and fro between
the shot and his companion, investi-
gating any snags and carrying out a
visual or feeling search of the
bottom, depending on conditions.

Locating the object

On finding the object sought, the
diver should immediately bend his
distance line to it, after which he
may signal for a rope and have the
object hauled up or he may surface

and report. A small object may, of
course, be brought to the surface
by the diver.

ENCLOSED-WATER GRID SEARCH

This search is particularly applicable
to locks, basins and docks, where gear
can be handled ashore: otherwise long,
low pontoons can be used as platforms.
The diver usually wears boots to
carry out this search, because of the
lack of visibility and the necessity
for the diver to crawl on the bottom.

The grid is rigged between two more
or less parallel banks or platforms
up to 200m apart. Parallel jackstays
for guiding the divers are then laid
between the platforms (see Fig 12.2)

As many jackstays as possible should
be laid at the start to reduce the
number of times the grid as a whole
must be shifted and to lessen the
risk of leaving gaps. Jackstays are
stretched as taut as possible on the
bottom and laid parallel to each
other 3m or twice visibility distance
apart if divers are likely to stir
up mud or if objects are likely to
be buried in the mud.

The grid is rigged as follows:

a) Fake out all jackstays on one side
of the area. Provide two 25kg sinkers
and shot ropes per jackstay, one on
each side of the area. Space the
sinkers as requisite.

b) Pass one end of every jackstay to
the other bank and secure it to the
appropriate sinker. Lower that sinker
to the bottom.

c) Reeve the other end of every jackstay through a shackle on its appropriate sinker and lower the sinker
to the bottom, keeping the jackstay
taut.

A diver carries out the search
by moving along the bottom with
one hand touching the jackstay and
searching with the other hand, using
a bottom probe where necessary.

At the end of his first lap the diver
steps over the jackstay and returns,
keeping the same hand on the jackstay
and searching as before. At his
original starting point the diver is
tranferred to the next jackstay.

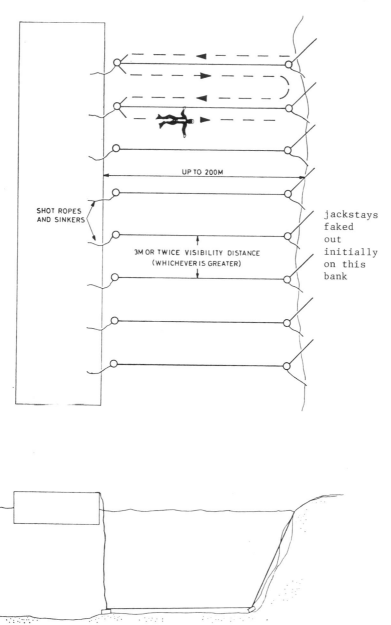

Fig 12.2 Enclosed-water grid search

The search as a whole should progress from one end of the grid to the other rather than from the ends to the middle; this eases the problem of supervision.

OPEN-WATER GRID SEARCH

If a large area has to be searched meticulously, the circular search from a shot rope is uneconomic, as it entails considerable overlapping to avoid gaps. Under these conditions a grid search can best be employed (see Fig 12.3). This type of search is worked on a rectilinear basis and entails the laying of a marker buoy at each corner. The anchor weights of these buoys are connected by light jackstays forming the sides of the rectangle, and a movable cross-connecting jackstay is also provided.

Two divers are employed. Each diver starts from a different side of the rectangle and swims along the movable jackstay, one on each side, searching his side to the maximum visibility distance. Each diver then moves his end of the jackstay along the standing jackstay to a position twice visibility distance from the old one. (In conditions of nil visibility maximum visibility is taken as the distance between the outstretched hands: 1.5m. Under these conditions the jackstay would be moved 3m after each lap.) The divers then swim back in the reverse direction.

On completion, the grid can be moved and re-laid immediately adjacent to the area covered by the first grid, and the search continued as desired, until the whole of the required areas have been completely covered by a series of adjacent rectilinear searches.

SEABED-SNAGLINE SEARCH

If a large area has to be searched, but not as thoroughly as with the grid search, and the seabed is reasonably flat and clear of obstructions, then the bottom can be covered be a pair of divers dragging a snagline between them, as shown in Fig 12.4.

Preparing the search

A marker buoy is laid in the centre of the area to assist navigation of the craft laying jackstays. It is removed before the actual search begins.

Two craft steer uptide in line abreast so that each will pass 15m from the centre marker. If, for example, 200m jackstays are being laid, a 25kg sinker, secured both to the end of the jackstay and to a marker buoy, is laid from each craft 100m before coming abreast the centre. The jackstays are then paid out astern until the craft are 130m beyond the centre, when they both anchor and drop back to 30m.

The jacksays are hauled taut and secured to 25kg sinkers, which are then lowered to the bottom. Care must be taken to see that the craft do not disturb the jackstays.

Jackstay length is governed by the ability of the available craft to stream them accurately.

A snagline up to 35m long and weighted with 30g of lead every 4m is to be prepared.

THE DIVE

The snagline is passed between the craft and the ends are given to the divers, their lifelines attached to floats. The Divers descend simultaneously to their respective jackstays and move downtide along them. At the end of their jackstays, the divers signal to the surface and are picked up in turn, one bringing up the snagline as pre-arranged.

When the snagline fouls something, both divers bend the line to their jackstays and go along it to the snag. If it is not what they are searching for, the snag is cleared and the divers return to their respective jackstays and continue the search.

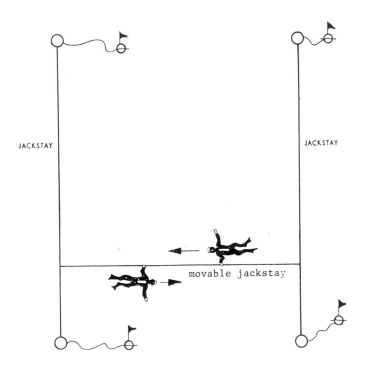

JACKSTAY   JACKSTAY

movable jackstay

Fig 12.3 Open-water grid search

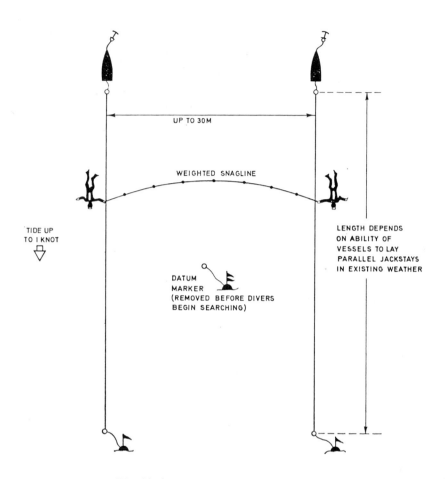

UP TO 30M

WEIGHTED SNAGLINE

TIDE UP
TO 1 KNOT

LENGTH DEPENDS
ON ABILITY OF
VESSELS TO LAY
PARALLEL JACKSTAYS
IN EXISTING WEATHER

DATUM
MARKER
(REMOVED BEFORE DIVERS
BEGIN SEARCHING)

Fig 12.4   Seabed snagline search

TOWED-DIVER SEARCH

There are two methods by which the
diver can be towed:

a) On a slightly positively buoyant
sled, controllable in depth by
the diver and fitted with a
transparent shield at the bow.
When carefully constructed
and trimmed, the sled provides
a most satisfactory method of
towing but as it is heavy and cumbersome
it is difficult to handle out

of water. It is also costly. The
ratio of length of tow to depth
of sled is 3:1.

b) By the "shot and toggle" method
which is effective and far sim-
pler. The diver is towed "free"
on the end of an 8m pendant
attached to a 25kg sinker, which
is adjusted for depth. He sits
astride the pendant on a toggle
seat, with his hands on a hand
rest, and controls his depth by
simply planing up or down with

his body. At between 2 and 3 knots he has control of his depth over a range of as much as 12m. The method is illustrated in Fig 12.5.
   in Fig 11-5.

The diver should be neutrally buoyant as for swimming. As the towed diver is not active he must wear plenty of underclothing, for he is likely to feel cold in even moderately warm water.

The diver should be secured to a floatline about 5m longer than the depth of water and with a marker float on the end.

During the towing, the marker float should be retained inboard and used as a signal line, and thrown overboard only when the diver "bales-out". Keeping the marker line in hand in the boat also prevents it causing any unnecessary drag on the diver.

The optimum performance is obtained with this search if the diver scans a 90° sector below him. This should be done as a methodical sweep followed by a quick glance over the whole sector.

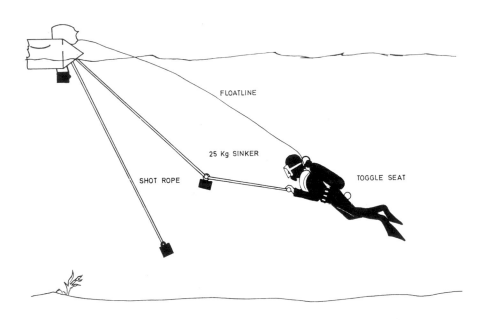

FLOATLINE

25 Kg SINKER

SHOT ROPE

TOGGLE SEAT

Fig 12.5 Towed-diver search

If the height of the diver over the bottom is 0.7 visibility distance, then the extreme swept path will be 1.4 times visibility distance.

SPEED OF ADVANCE

Because of the observer's speed of advance, however, the area towards the edge of this path will be only partially swept and the width of the wholly swept path will thus be appreciably less than the extreme width. The following table gives the ideal speeds to ensure that for given visibility distances the wholly swept width is a little over half the extreme width, successive searches being so placed that their extreme widths have a 50 per cent overlap.

VISIBILITY (m)	SPEED (kt)
6	1.5
9	2
12	3
15	3.5
18	4

Speeds of 4 knots should not be exceeded because the diver will experience control difficulty.

MARKING THE OBJECT

A buoyed shot rope should be rigged, with the sinker trailing near the bottom and within the vision of the diver. It should be ready for release at a signal from the diver. Great care must be taken to ensure that the shot rope when released does not foul the diver.

The following code may be used for passing signals by the marker float line:

SIGNAL	FROM ATTENDANT	FROM DIVER
1 Pull	Are you all right ?	Check
2 Pulls	-	Less speed
3 Pulls	-	More speed
4 Pulls	Surface	I am surfacing
2 Bells	-	Shorten tow
3 Bells	-	Lengthen tow
4 Bells	-	I am baling out
5 Bells	-	Let go the shot

UNDERWATER NAVIGATION AND ORIENTATION

Underwater navigation can broadly be divided into two sections.

1 PILOTAGE - Where direction is found by use of typical topographical features i.e. pipe line field joints, installation legs or seabed features etc.

2 NAVIGATION - Where the use of instruments such as the compass and depth gauge are employed. Often these two instruments are used together.

PILOTAGE

The senses required for direction finding are considerably impaired once the diver has left surface, and first consideration should be given to reducing the amount of direction finding to the absolute minimum. The use of a simple distance line to and from a work site will significantly improve efficiency.

If this kind of positive contact cannot be established, the tidal direction, if any, can often be a useful aid to navigation. A ship lying at anchor with the tide will have its anchor warp laying ahead and at a considerable angle. This can be used by the diver to determine his direction on reaching the bottom. The tide can also assist him during the dive giving him an indication of his direction.

Having commenced the dive at the best possible position, the problem of navigation underwater therefore entails:

1 The steering of a fairly accurate course on the bottom.

2 The ability to return to the point of departure.

The most important thing in acquiring a sense of direction underwater is always to arrive on the bottom with a static reference point established clearly, be it the down line, anchor warp, boat or shore. Once on the bottom with a sense of direction firmly established it is then possible to move away using topographical features for reference. In limited visibility the size of references must be fairly small and their frequency increased, and at each change of direction the diver must be re-orientated to his original reference point.

The use of a life line or umbilical is of great assistance in indicating direction underwater. By taking up the slack in the lines the diver is able to orientate himself with the surface. The use of life line signals by his attendant or voice communications can then direct him, provided the object's location is known by the surface crew, to the position required.

It is important that should the searching diver locate the object he should be in a position to mark it, perhaps with a distance line or a surface marker float. He should not have to return to the surface to obtain a marker and be unable to relocate his original position.

NAVIGATION

Underwater navigation, utilising instruments such as the compass and depth gauge is again subject to the same conditions as pilotage in commencing the dive at the nearest possible surface position.

Magnet Compass

Suitable compasses can be obtained for underwater use which have been adapted to resist the pressure of water. They can either be worn on the wrist, around the neck, on a lanyard or attached to a swim board (see Chapter 7 Compasses)

Cheap poor quality instruments are usually of little use. Liquid filled compasses are preferred as being more accurate due to the "dampening" effect of the liquid. They are all, however, badly affected by any steel objects, such as cylinders, other divers equipment, television cameras and sub-sea debris. These can cause wide deviation on all headings due to their magnet influence.

Some idea of the amount of deviation which may take place can be gained by placing a small piece of steel close to a compass, and watching the swing of the needle. Despite the disadvantage of metallic equipment causing deviation the compass can be extremely useful underwater. When taking a magnet reading always hold the compass in the <u>same position</u>, directly ahead of the centre line of travel at eye level. Most of the modern compasses of the oil filled type are fitted with a lubber-line on a rotating bezel. The diver, having moved away from any steel objects, selects the direction of travel required with his compass on the surface. He then rotates the bezel aligning the lubber-line with the compass needle. Having submerged he is able to re-align with magnet needle with the lubber-lines and continue on his intended course. Having continued as far along his course as required it is only necessary to turn the compass through 180° in order to return to his point of departure.

To carry out a square search using a compass in conjunction with an underwater watch, swim at a constant speed for timed periods on four headings, e.g., North - 5 mins, East - 5 mins, South - 5 mins, West - 5 mins, which should bring the diver within easy reach of the departure point. An alternative to the use of a watch can be a count of certain numbers of steps or leg strokes for each side of the square, provided they are consistent. The diver should be aware, while carrying out the compass search, of the variations of direction which can occur due to outside factors, i.e., the lifeline will tend to pull the diver off course and towards his attentant. A diver will be either left or right footed and will tend to be stronger in that leg, thus pushing the diver unknowingly off course. These alterations off course can be undetectable to the diver, but, over long distances, can be considerable.

Depth Gauge

The depth gauge is of great value for underwater navigation and is valuable in water of limited vizibility. In addition to indicating the ambient depth, it will also show if one is ascending or descending and prevent the diver losing himself in a vertical direction.

Diver's Watch

In addition to keeping a check on dive duration and cylinder endurance, the watch can be used for search schemes in calculating the length of the side of the search.

The underwater navigator has a considerable number of variables to contend with. In assessing the suitability and chances of success he must bear in mind the professional nature of his work and his cost effectiveness. Wherever possible he should establish quickly a positive link.

CHAPTER 13

RIGGING FOR DIVERS

CORDAGE - KNOTS, SPLICING AND
GENERAL ROPEWORK

The efficient and competent use of
cordage for rigging is an important
skill which should be learnt. The
ability to select and apply the
correct knot underwater, perhaps
in nil visibility or to rig blocks
and tackles, is an indication of
the ability of a working diver.

To quote Jerome K Jerome: "There is
something very strange and unaccount-
able about rope. You roll it up
with as much patience and care as
you would take to fold a new pair
of trousers and five minutes after-
wards when you pick it up, it's one
ghastly, soul revolting tangle."

TYPES OF ROPE

Rope may be constructed of Natural
Fibre such as cotton, coir, hemp,
manila and sisal, or from synthetic
fibres such as polyamide (nylon)
polyester (terylene) and polypropylene or a mixture of these synthetic
fibres.

COMPOSITION

Spun or "hawser laid" rope is generally
the most commonly available and is
composed of a number of thin yarns
spun into thicker "strands" which
are "laid up" together to form the
rope. Most rope is three stranded
and the strands are laid up right
handed. As the rope is laid up its
length contracts like a coiled
spring, giving it a certain elasticity. The elasticity in synthetic
fibre ropes is normally greater than
in natural fibre.

The selection of the correct cordage
for a specific application and the
arguments for and against natural

and synthetic fibre ropes can be
complex. Manufacturers are normally
able to advise you on the correct
application of each specific type.

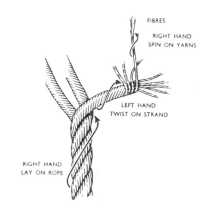

FIBRES

RIGHT HAND
SPIN ON YARNS

LEFT HAND
TWIST ON STRAND

RIGHT HAND
LAY ON ROPE

Fig 13.1   Component parts of a right
hand hawser laid rope

The majority of natural, nylon and
terylene ropes are laid up as hawser-
laid ropes. Polyethylene and polypropylene ropes are, too, but in these
the yarns may be made up of either split
fibres or monofilaments. In the latter
the yarns are extruded like thin wire.
They tend to be slippery, less strong
and difficult to handle because they
kink more readily. A common factor
among all polyethylene and polypropylene
ropes is that they all float. Most
materials can be plaited which generally
increases their flexibility, but
reduces their strength.

MEASUREMENT

Nowadays rope is generally described by
its diameter in millimetres, although
traditionally in Great Britain it has

been measured by its circumference in
inches, and reference to this system
may still be found. To convert the
circumference in inches to millimetres of diameter:-

  multipy by 8 i.e. 2in rope x 8 = 16mm

Small natural fibre cordage is measured
by ply (number of threads) or by a
number, or by weight. Small synthetic
fibre cord is measured by a number or
weight.

STRENGTH

National standards are set for various
types of rope. After samples are tested
to destruction by each manufacturer,
tables are then produced which give the
safe working load (S.W.L.) for each
type and size of cordage and its
breaking strain. It is obviously not
sensible to work near this limit, and
remember that the formulae are for
new rope.   In an emergency it is
possible to obtain a rough guide to
the breaking strain of good quality
manila rope by using the following
formula:-

$$\frac{C2}{3}$$

(The circumference in inches multiplied by itself and the answer
  divided by 3)

This will give the approximate breaking strain in tons. The safe working
load is then found quite simply by
dividing the breaking strength by a
safety factor (S.F.) of 6.

A knot will reduce the strength of a
rope by about 50% and a splice by 12%.
It is also of note that natural fibre
ropes lose almost 50% of their strength
when saturated. Always be on the look
out and watch for chafe or fraying over
the whole of a rope's length - like
chain its strength is that of its
weakest link.

HANDLING

The most important aspect of handling
and using any sort of rope is tidiness,
which in this sense refers to the
method by which the rope is to be usedm
or stowed. The art of coiling up a rope,
either its full length, or the end not
in use, is a simple but necessary skill.

Coiling should be thought about
because the 'right-hand lay' is the
cause of much twisting and tangling.
Before coiling, tangled ropes are best
laid out straight for their entire
length on land, or streamed astern
from a boat. Once laid out on land,
give them a good stretch- this helps
to remove kinks, particularly in new
natural fibre. Then work starting
with the end which is secure in the
left hand. With your right hand pull
in enough rope to make a loop about
4cm long in a CLOCKWISE DIRECTION. As
you place the loop in your left hand
roll the rope a half turn toward you
with your right thumb and forefinger.
This will counteract the twist you
put in the rope as you make the loop
and will help to eliminate kinks.

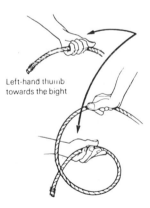

Left-hand thumb
towards the bight

Fig 13.2 Coiling a hawser-laid rope

This twist of the right hand will send potentially tangly twists down the rope until they come out at the free end, though it may prove necessary to shake the rope from time to time in order to clear them and prevent yet another tangle.

STOWAGE

There are four methods of stowing a coiled rope:

1 Holding the completed coil in your left hand take the free end in your right hand and wrap it around the coil about one-third from the top, then pass it through the top half and pull it tight. The coil then can be hung or laid down with a reasonable chance of not tangling.

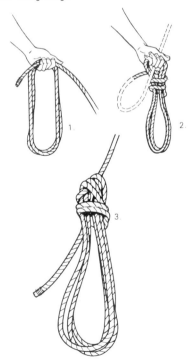

Fig 13.3 Stowing a coiled rope

2 The second method is identical to the first except where there is no free end as in the case of a distance line attached to a shot, or a line attached to a cleat.

In this case there is no free end available to pass through. Instead the last turn is looped back over the coil as shown in Fig 13.4.

Fig 13.4 Stowing a coil of rope with no loose end

3 The third way is an ideal way of stowing large coils such as life lines or those you need to use quickly. Make the coil down neatly on the ground clockwise for right hand hawser laid rope. Simply take four short lengths of small line and tie them at 90° intervals around the coil. This provides an instantly usable coil; just untie the small stuff.

4 Finally, there is one other method of stowing a rope. Just "pour" it into a box or tub. As it goes in so it should come out- provided you do not move or upset the box too much. If you do you will more than likely end up with a tangled mess.

TO FAKE DOWN A ROPE

A rope which may have to be payed out quickly, should be "faked" down as "long fakes" as stowage space allows. (A fake is one of the turns of a rope when stowed or coiled down).

a rope does not acquire as many turns as when coiled, and it will therefore run out with less chance of becoming snarled. Care should be taken that each bight at the end of a fake is laid under that immediately preceding it to ensure a clear run.

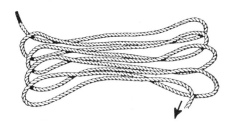

·Fig 13.5 Faking a rope

THROWING A HEAVING LINE

As its name implies a heaving line is a light flexible line that can be thrown. It is used as a messenger to pass hawsers and heavy mooring lines from ship to shore, or vice versa A heaving line consists of approximately 30m of 6mm cordage which has been well stretched. One end should be whipped and the other weighted with a monkey's fist or a heaving line knot (see Figs 13-27,28)

Fig 13.6 Throwing a heaving line

To prepare a line for throwing 20 to 25 metres should be coiled carefully in the left hand. One-third of the line is taken in the right or throwing hand, using rather small coils, the line is then thrown with the right arm straight and it must be allowed to run out freely from the coil in the left hand. The most frequent cause of bad casts is failure to have this coil properly clear for running.

WHIPPING

When using natural fibre ropes it is necessary to prevent the end from unravelling while in use. This is normally achieved by "whipping" the ends with seaming or roping twine. A considerable number of whippings are in common use each having advantages i.e. Common American, West Country and Sailmaker's. Examples of the Common and Sailmaker's are given below.

COMMON

Place the end of the twine along the rope as in (i), pass turns of the twine over the rope against its lay, working towards the end of the rope and haul each turn taut. Then lay the other end of the twine along the rope as in (ii) and pass the remaining turns over it, taking the bight of twine over the end of the rope with each turn. When the bight becomes too small to pass over the end of the rope, haul this second end of the twine through the turns which you have passed over it until taut (iii),thus completing the cast,turn round the rope and cut off the ends (iv).

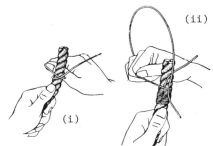

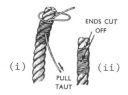

Fig 13.7 Common whipping

The whipping may then be dressed with varnish.

SAILMAKERS' WHIPPING

This whipping is the most secure - it will not work adrift under any circumstances. Unlay the end of the rope for about 50mm and hold it in the left hand pointing upwards, with the middle strand furthest away. Now take a bight in the twine about 200mm long and pass this bight over the middle strand, with the two ends towards you. Then, with the bight of twine hanging for about 50mm down the back of the rope and the ends pointing down in front, lay up the rope with the right hand. Leave the short end of twine where it is and with the long end, pass the turns of the whipping working towards the end of the rope against the lay. When sufficient turns are on take the bight of twine pass it up outside the whipping, following the lay of the strand around which it was originally put and pass it over the strand where the latter comes out at the end of the rope (Fig 13.8(i). Now haul on the short end so as to tighten the bight, then bring this end up outside the whipping, again following the lay of the rope, and then reef knot the two ends in the middle of the rope and out of sight (Fig 13.8(ii)).

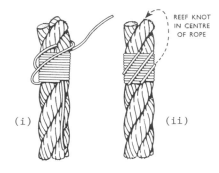

Fig 13.8 Sailmaker's whipping

In manmade fibres the same effect as whipping can be more simply obtained by wrapping the end in Sellotape, cutting through it, then melting the strands together against a hot surface or flame. It is not even vital to use adhesive tape, since the ends may be sealed with a match and moulded together with the fingers.

LASHING

Two crossed spars can be secured together either with a <u>square lashing</u> or a <u>diagonal lashing</u>. A square lashing is used when the spars are to be secured at right angles to each other, and the diagonal lashing when they are to be secured at an acute angle to each other.

SQUARE LASHING

Make fast one end of the rope to one of the spars (preferably the smaller one) with a timber hitch and haul it taut. Then cross the spars with the smaller spar lying underneath. Bring the other end of the lashing up over the larger spar, down under the smaller, up over the larger, and so on

until sufficient turns have been
taken. To avoid riding turns, the
turns on the larger spar should
lie in succession outside those
first applied, and those on the
smaller spar should lie in succession inside those first applied.
Finish by taking two or three
"frapping" turns, and make fast
with a clove hitch round all parts
or round one of the spars.

Fig 13.9 Square lashing

DIAGONAL LASHING

Make fast one end of the rope as
for a square lashing, and pass as
many turns as are required diagonally
round both spars. Then bring the end
up over one spar and take a few
more turns across the opposite
diagonal. Finish off as for a square
lashing.

Fig 13.10 Diagonal lashing

SEIZING

A seizing is a method of fastening together two parts of a rope or a life
line to an air hose in a diver's umbilical, sufficiently strongly to prevent
them from slipping while only one part
is under strain.

For seizing cordage or an umbilical
it is normal to use small 1kg line,
codline or seizing/whipping twine -
depending upon the sizes to be seized).
When seizing wire ropes flexible mild
steel wire should be used.

All seizings are begun by making a
small eye in the end of the seizing
stuff. Take the seizing round both
parts and pass the end through the
eye, taking care to keep this eye
in the centre and clear of both parts
(i).

Take the round turns very loosely round
both parts of the rope, then pass the
end back, along and between the two
parts, under the turns and through the
eye of the seizing (ii). Then heave
each turn taut and take a cross turn
round the seizing between the two parts
(iii).

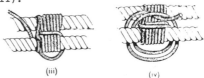

Now haul the seizing well taut and
secure its end with a clove hitch, one
part of the clove hitch being on each
side of the round turn (iv). Finally
unlay the seizing stuff and finish off
with a crown and wall close up against
the hitch (v), (Fig 13.38).

(v)

Fig 13.11 Flat seizing

BENDS AND HITCHES

ELEMENTS OF BENDS AND HITCHES

Most bends and hitches consist of
a combination of two or more of
the following elements:-

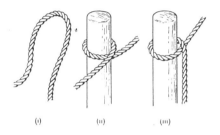

(i)   (ii)   (iii)

(i) A bight
(ii) A round turn
(iii) A half hitch
(iv) A twist
(v) An overhand knot

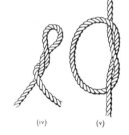

(iv)   (v)

Fig 13.12 Elements of bends
and hitches

REEF KNOT

The reef knot consists of two overhand knots made consecutively, and
is used as a common tie for bending
together two ropes of approximately
equal size. It is not liable to
come undone when there is no strain
on the knot, but it is not reliable
if the ropes are of unequal size or
very slippery unless the ends are
stopped back to the standing part.

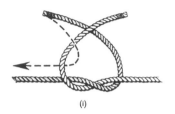

(i)

(ii)

Fig 13.13 Reef knot

BOWLINE

This is the most useful knot for
making temporary eyes in ropes of
all sizes. It is used for bending
a heaving line to a hawser, as a
lifeline round a man's waist, to
connect a diving lifeline and for a
great variety of similar purposes.
Every diver should be able to tie
a bowline round his own waist with
his eyes closed.

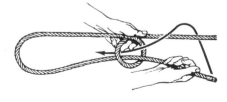

Fig 13.14 Bowline knot

FIGURE-OF-EIGHT KNOT

This knot is used to prevent a rope unreeving through an eye or a block. An overhand knot can also be used.

Fig 13.15 Figure-of-eight knot

SHEET BEND

Is used to bend a small rope to a larger one, e.g. the lazy painter of a small boat to a towing hawser. Originally used to secure a sheet to the clew of a sail.

Fig 13.16 Sheet bend

DOUBLE SHEET BEND

A more secure method of accomplishing the same purpose as a single sheet bend.

Fig 13.17 Double sheet bend

SINGLE CARRICK BEND

Used for joining two hawsers together when the join will have to pass around the capstan. The ends should be stopped to their stand part.

(i)

(ii)

Fig 13.18 Single carrick bend

DOUBLE CARRICK BEND

This is used when a more secure bend than the single carrick bend is required.

(i)

(ii)

Fig 13.19 Double carrick bend

CLOVE HITCH

A clove hitch is used to secure a rope to a spar, rail or similar fitting, also for many other purposes. It will slip along the spar or rail if subjected to a sideways pull. It can be made with the end or with the bight of the rope.

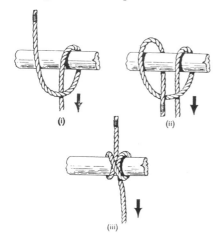

(a) On the end

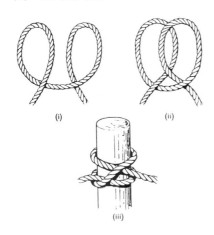

(b) On the Bight

Fig 13.20 Clove hitch knot

ROLLING HITCH

This hitch is also used for securing a rope to a spar when the pull is expected to be from one side or the other, and to another rope under strain. It is made by passing the end twice around the spar or rope, each turn crossing the standing part. A half hitch on the opposite side completes the hitch. Always pass the two turns on the side from which the pull is expected.

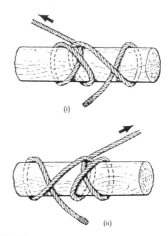

Fig 13.21 Rolling hitch knot

TIMBER HITCH

This hitch is used to secure a rope's end to a spar or bale.

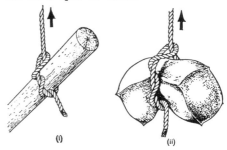

Fig 13.22 Timber hitch knot

TIMBER HITCH AND HALF HITCH

Used to tow, hoist or lower. Can be used as a substitute for a rolling hitch especially when a diver has cold hands, or in low visibility.

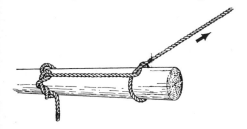

Fig 13.23 Timber hitch and half hitch

ROUND TURN AND TWO HALF HITCHES

This combination can be used to secure a heavy load to a spar, ring or shackle such as the buoy shackle of a mooring. It will never jam and can be cast off quickly. The end should be stopped to the standing part.

Fig 13.24 Round turn and two half hitches

FISHERMANS BEND

An alternative to a round turn and two half hitches, and normally used for bending a rope or hawser to the ring of an anchor. It is more suitable for a jerking pull, but will tend to jam and is not so easily cast off. The end should be stopped to the standing part.

Fig 13.25 Fisherman's bend

DOUBLE BLACKWALL HITCH

A quick means of attaching a rope to a hook (the single blackwall is not recommended).

Fig 13.26 Double blackwall hitch

MONKEYS FIST

This is used to weight the end of a heaving line so that it will carry when thrown against the wind. In appearance it is very similar to a turk's head and takes 2-2.7m of line. It is made as follows:-

1　Wind three turns round the hand.

2　Pass a second set of three turns across and around the first three in the direction indicated by the arrows.

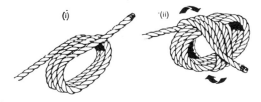

3　Pass a third three turns round and across the second three, but inside the first set and in the direction shown by the arrows. If the knot is correct the end will come out alongside the standing part.

4 To finish the knot, work all the parts taut and splice the end in the standing part.

Fig 13.27 Monkey's fist knot

HEAVING LINE KNOT

This knot is used as an alternative to the monkey's fist, and is quickly made. Form a bight about1.5mlong at the end of the line. Start frapping the end round both parts of the bight at about 200cm from the actual bend of the bight, and continue until it is all but expended. Then pass the end through the small loop left and haul on the standing part.

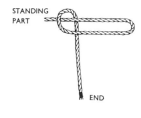

STANDING PART

END

STANDING PART

END

Fig 13.28 Heaving line knot

SLIP KNOTS

The sheet bend, the bowline and the clove hitch are the three main knots which can be released quickly by using a bight instead of an end in the last phase of making them. Such slip knots will hold a steady strain fairly well, but cannot be trusted to stand a jerking pull.

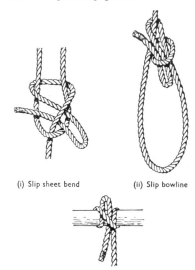

(i) Slip sheet bend   (ii) Slip bowline

(iii) Slip clove hitch

Fig 13.29 Slip knots

CORDAGE SPLICING

Every diver should be capable of making a splice in cordage, if not wire. There is nothing difficult about it and with practice splicing becomes a simple operation. It is a method of joining the ends of two ropes together or of making an eye in the end of a rope by interlocking the strands. Unless otherwise stated it should be accepted that all splices reduce

the strength of the rope by one-eighth.
Making a splice in large diameter ropes
can be assisted by the use of a wooden
'fid' which is a pointed spike made of
hardwood, and a heaving mallet for
heaving tucks into place.

TYPES OF SPLICES

BACK SPLICE

For finishing the end of a rope which
is not required to be rove through a
block - it prevents it from unlaying.

EYE SPLICE

For making a permanent eye in the end
of a rope.

SHORT SPLICE

For joining two ropes.

LONG SPLICE

For joining two ropes which are
required to pass through a block.
A well made long splice does not
increase the diameter of the rope and
should not reduce its strength.

CUT SPLICE

For making a permanent eye in the
bight of a rope.

CHAIN SPLICE

For splicing a tail into a chain
which has to be led through a block
or fairlead.

FLEMISH EYE

An ornamental eye worked in the
end of gangway and other man ropes.

The back splice, eye splice, short
splice and long splice are described
below. When reference is made to "the

left" or "the right" of a rope the
reader should imagine himself to be
looking along the rope towards the
end which is being handled.

The number of tucks required to complete a splice will vary between
natural and synthetic fibres ropes.
Natural fibre normally requires a
minimum of four tucks, whereas
manmade fibre, because of its smooth-
ness and elasticity tends to unlay
more readily. Therefore, five tucks
should be used as a minimum.

BACK SPLICE

Whip the rope at a distance from
its end equal to approximately five
times the circumference of the rope,
then unlay the strands to the whipping
and whip the end of each strand. Make
a crown knot (i), cut the whipping
and then tuck each strand over one
strand and under the next, to the left
and against the lay of the rope, as
shown (ii). After each strand is
tucked, pull the strands taut and tidy
up this first tuck, until each strand
is uniform. Repeat this tucking three
times more for natural fibre and four
times for synthetic fibre ropes (iii).

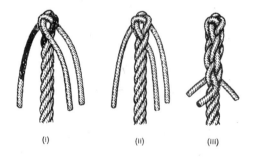

(i)   (ii)   (iii)

Fig 13.30 Making a back-splice

EYE SPLICE

Whip the rope at a distance from its
end equal to approximately five times

the size of the rope. Then unlay it to the whipping and whip the end of each strand, mark the place intended for the crown of the eye, and bend the rope back from there so as to bring the unlaid strands alongside the place where the splice is to be made, with the left and middle strands lying on the top of the rope (Fig 13.31); the set of the splice will depend on selecting this middle strand correctly.

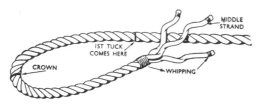

Fig 13.31 The start of an eye-splice

Now refer to Fig 13.32 in which the middle strand is marked 'A', the left hand 'B', and the right hand strand 'C', and make the splice as follows.

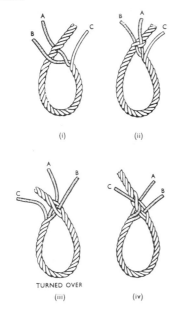

Fig 13.32 Making an eye-splice

1 Tuck 'A' from right to left, under the nearest strand of the standing part.

2 Tuck 'B' from right to left, under the next strand of the standing part.

3 Now turn the rope right over so as to bring the remaining strand 'C' on the top, and then tuck 'C' from right to left under the unoccupied strand of the standing part. Care must be taken to maintain the lay of the rope in the last strand tucked as this enables it to lie closer.

4 Now, beginning with 'C' heave each strand taut. Then tuck all three strands three times more for natural fibre and four times for synthetic fibre ropes.

SHORT SPLICE

The strands of each rope are tucked between the strands of the other rope against the lay, each strand being taken over the strand on its left, then under the next strand and emerging between this and the subsequent strand. In Fig 13.33 the ends of the ropes are lettered 'A' and 'B' and their unlaid strands 'C', 'D' and 'E' and 'F', 'G' and 'H' respectively.

1 Whip each rope at a distance from its end equal to approximately five times the size of the rope (this whipping has been omitted from rope 'A' in the illustration).

2 Unlay the strands to the whipping and whip their ends (these whippings have also been omitted).

3 Marry the two ropes so that one strand of each lies between two strands of the other (i).

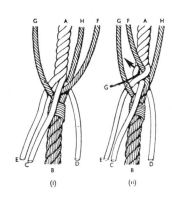

(i)   (ii)

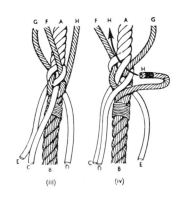

(iii)   (iv)

Fig 13.33 Making a short-splice

4   Having ensured a close marry, whip
    the strands strongly round the
    join to prevent them slipping
    and stop ends 'C', 'D' and 'E'
    to rope 'B' with a strong stop
    (whipping and stops have been
    omitted).

5   Cut the whipping on 'A'.

6   Take 'F' over 'C', under 'E', and
    bring it out between 'E' and 'D'
    (ii).

7   Take 'G' over 'E', under 'D', and
    bring it out between 'D' and 'C'
    (ii) and (iii).

8   Take 'H' over 'D', under 'C', and
    bring it out between 'C' and 'E'
    (iii).

9   Stop 'G', 'F' and 'H' to 'A', cut
    the stop and whipping on 'B', and
    tuck 'C', 'D' and 'E' in a similar
    manner.

10 Heave all six strands equally taut.

11 Again tuck each strand over the
    strand on its left and under the
    next one, and then repeat this
    operation twice more for natural
    fibre and three times more for
    synthetic fibre.

LONG SPLICE

The principle of the long splice
differs radically from that of the
short splice. One strand from each
rope is unlaid, and one from the
other rope is given a twist and laid
up in its place. The remaining strand
from each rope remains in the centre,
resulting in three pairs of strands
spaced equidistantly along the married
ropes. This method of splicing together with two ropes of similar diameter
has the advantage of not increasing
the overall diameter, thus, allowing
the rope to run through a block. To
make a long splice whip each rope at
a distance from its end equal to twelve
times the circumference of the rope,
then unlay the strands to the whippings
and whip their ends. Marry these two
ropes together, as in a short splice.
After removal of the rope whippings,
each strand is followed up by the strand
from the other rope as in Fig 13.34.

So that 'H' is unlaid and followed up by 'E', 'D' is unlaid and followed up by 'F', and 'C' and 'G' remain at the marry. Each strand is unlaid until the length of the end of the strand following it up is reduced to four times the circumference of the rope. One-third of the yarn is now taken out of all strands (not shown in Fig 12-34 (iv)), and though discarded, these yarns should not be cut off until the splice is completed.

Each pair of strands is then tied in an overhand knot (left over right for a right handed rope) and each strand is tucked over one strand and under the next as for a short splice. Half of the yarns in each strand are now taken out and the remaining yarns tucked once more to give a gradual taper.

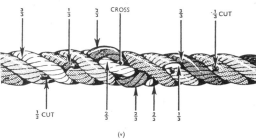

Fig 13.35 Tapering a long-splice

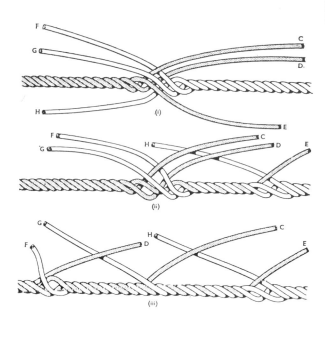

Fig 13.34 Making a long-splice

The splice is finished off by stretching it, hauling taut all ends and then cutting them off. A well made long splice will not reduce the rope's strength.

TAPERING, SERVING AND DOGGING

If a splice is to be served as shown in Fig 13.36, it must be tapered down in order to gradually reduce the splice's diameter, eventually down to the rope's normal size. Any of the previously mentioned splices may be reduced; only the long splice is reduced but not served, because it must pass through a block.

1 After the third tuck take one-third of the yarns out of each strand and tuck the remaining two-thirds once; though discarded the thirds should not be cut off until the splice is completed.

2 Halve the reduced strands, then

tuck one half of each strand and leave the other.

3 Heave all parts taut, including the discard-ends, which should now be cut off.

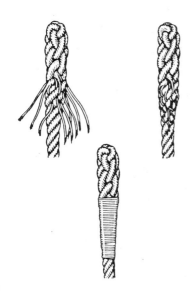

Fig 13.36 Tapering and serving a back-splice

SERVING

This consists of binding a splice or length of rope with close turns of spun yarn. Each turn should be hove taut with a special serving mallet, which has a score in its head to fit the rope and a wooden handle about 38cm long. A service is begun as for a common whipping and for an eye splice it is usual to work from the splice to the eye. The first few turns are put on by hand and hauled taut.

Possible with the use of a spike or mallet. The serving mallet is then placed on the rope and the turns of the service are passed as shown in the diagram.

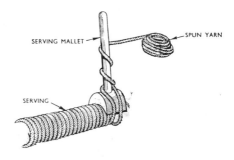

Fig 13.37 Serving a splice

Having completed the required length of service, finish it off by passing the end back under the last four turns, haul all parts taut, and make a crown and wall.

CROWN AND WALL

As described above, this knot is used to finish off the ends of seizings and servings to prevent them from unreeving. The strands are unlaid right down to the turns of the seizing or serving against which the crown is formed as close as possible. The wall is then made under it and hauled taut, thus jamming the knot in tightly.

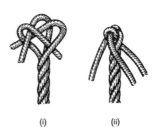

(i)   (ii)

(iii)   (iv)

Fig 13.38 Making a crown and wall

DOGGING

If the appearance of the splice is of
secondary importance or maximum
strength is required it may be
finished off by dogging the ends
by halving each of the three strands
and whipping each half to its neigh-
bour over the adjacent strand of
the main rope, as shown.

Fig 13.39 Dogged eye-splice

WIRE ROPE - CONSTRUCTION CHARACTERISTICS
AND SPLICING

CONSTRUCTION

A wire rope is constructed of a number
of small wires which extend continuously throughout its entire length.
These wires are twisted into strands
and the strands themselves are
laid up to form the rope. With
the exception of certain special
types, all wire ropes used at sea
consist of six strands. The wires
forming a strand are twisted left
handed around a jute, man-made

fibre or wire core, and the strands
forming the rope are laid up right-
handed around a hemp, man-made fibre
or jute <u>heart</u>. The heart has two
functions:

1 It acts as a cushion into which
   the strands bed, allowing them
   to take up their natural position
   as the rope is bent or subjected
   to strain.

2 In the case of jute or hemp it
   absorbs the linseed oil or other
   lubricant with which the rope
   should be periodically dressed,
   so that as the rope is stretched
   or flexed the oil is squeezed
   between the wires, thus lubricating and reducing the friction
   between them. Synthetic fibre
   hearts are normally used on
   ropes which are submerged in
   water for long periods. In this
   case any lubricant in the heart
   would be washed out leaving the
   rope unprotected. Polypropylene
   is very slippery, therefore, it
   offers the strands some lubrication.

STRAND

HEMP OR
JUTE HEART

WIRES

JUTE OR WIRE
CORE

Fig 13.40 Construction of a wire rope

A wire rope can be made flexible in
one of two ways:

1 By replacing the centre wire of
   each strand with a large core of
   jute, man-made fibre or hemp, in
   which case strength is sacrificed
   for flexibility.

2 By making each strand with a large
   number of small-gauge wires round
   a wire core, in which case the
   full strength is retained.

TYPES

As mentioned previously, steel wire
ropes are normally of six strands which
are laid up right-handed. The
number of wires per strand and the
number of strands are used to
identify the type of rope, i.e.
6-24 (F.S.W.R.) 6- is the number
or strands, 24- is the number of
wires per strand, F.S.W.R. - is the
type of rope (Flexible Steel Wire
Rope).

The examples of steel wire ropes
given below are not intended to
be comprehensive. The hearts and
cores have also been omitted from
the illustrations for clarity.

Steel Wire Rope (S.W.R.)

This is normally used for standing
rigging etc, and so is not required
to be flexible.

6 STRANDS
19 WIRES EACH

Fig 13.41 Steel wire rope (6-19 SWR.)

Its strands are made up of a small
number of large gauge wire wound round
a steel or jute core, and the strands
themselves are made up round a hemp
or jute heart.

Flexible Steel Wire Rope (F.S.W.R.)

This is used for hawsers and other
ropes in which flexibility necessitates

sacrificing a certain proportion of
its strength, and each strand consists
of a number of medium gauge wires
wound around a large jute core; the
strands themselves are made up round
a hemp or jute heart.

Extra Special Flexible Steel Wire Rope (E.S.F.S.W.R.)

This is used when strength and flexibility are both essential. The
strands are constructed of a large
number of small gauge wires which
are made of high quality steel (the
term 'extra special' refers more to
the quality of the steel than to
the flexibility of the rope). The
strands are made up round a hemp or
jute heart.

Wires which are subjected to continual
immersion in salt water can be galvanised. However, this does reduce the
ropes' flexibility. These ropes
normally have a polypropylene heart.

6 STRANDS
61 WIRES EACH

Fig 13.42 Extra special flexible steel
          wire rope (6-61 ESF.SWR.)

MEASUREMENT OF WIRE ROPE

The size of a wire rope may be measured
by its diameter. When determining the
size of a rope in this way it should
be measured, at any point throughout
its length, across its largest diameter.
Most rope gauges will also convert the
size in mm diameter to inches of circumference, which is still used for
some rope measurement.

The lengths of wire ropes are measured
in fathoms (1.8m). They:y are sold in
coils, the length of which varies with
the type and size of the rope. Usually
the smaller the size of the rope the

greater the length of a coil. The following list will give a general indication of the lengths of coils of various types of wire ropes.

S.W.R.   - 150 and 200 fathoms

F.S.W.R.   - 100, 150, 250,
                   300 and 360 fathoms

E.S.F.S.W.R.   - 100, 150, 250,
                   300 and 500 fathoms

Greater detail of the lengths can be obtained from the manufacturers.

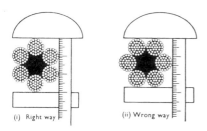

Fig 13.43 Using a wire gauge

STRENGTH

The breaking strength of wire rope differs in each type. It may be calculated approximately in tons by multiplying the square of the circumference by the figure indicated below:

F.S.W.R.   up to 114mm - 2 tons

F.S.W.R.   above 114mm - 2.5 tons

S.W.R.   - 2.75 tons

E.S.F.S.W.R.   - 3.6 tons

The safe working load (S.W.L.) of wire rope is one-sixth of its breaking strength for standing rigging, cranes, hawsers and general purpose wires, one-eighth for running rigging and slings and one-twelfth for lifts and hoists.

In some working locations such as dockyards etc, other regulations may apply to safe working loads which must be followed.

HANDLING OF WIRE ROPE

Wire rope is much less pliable than cordage. It resists being bent, does not absorb, turns readily and is therefore much more liable to kinking and snarling and tends to spring out of a coil, or off a drum or bollard. If handled correctly, however, it can be used for most of the purposes to which cordage is put, but bends and hitches cannot be made in wire rope.

To prevent crippling, a wire rope which will come under strain should never be lead through a shackle or ring bolt to alter the direction of its lead. In addition, it should not be led round a bollard or drum of a diameter less than 4 times the circumference of the rope, and if it is to run through a block the diameter of the sheave should be at least 6 times the circumference of the rope.

COILING AND UNCOILING

Wire rope, especially long lengths of it, should be stowed on reels, but where this in not practicable it must be coiled down. Wire rope is less able to absorb turns than fibre rope; when coiling down it is therefore all the more necessary to have the uncoiled portion free to revolve. Where this is impossible an alternative is to use left-handed loops, called 'frenchmen', in the coil. These 'frenchmen' serve to counteract the twists put in by coiling down right-handed.

Fig 13.44 A Frenchman

WIRE ROPE SPLICING

Wire rope is spliced in roughly the same way as fibre rope, but, wire being much less pliable, greater skill is required and particular care must be taken with whippings and seizings.

It should be remembered that the bending of the wires during splicing may injure their surface. When possible, splices should therefore be dipped in a preservative, such as mineral tar or tallow, before being served.

Splicing reduces the strength of wire rope by approximately one-eighth, but a badly made splice reduces it appreciably more. The less the strands are distorted and disturbed when tucking, the less will be their loss of strength.

There are several ways of making the first tuck of an eye splice but there appears to be little to choose between them as regards their effect on the strength of the rope, and appearance is a matter of taste. The method of splicing described here is that which is used in the Royal Navy, and is called the Admiralty Service Splice.

A marline spike with a long tapered point usually with a slight chisel end, should be used to open the strands. The correct way to use it is best demonstrated by an instructor, but proficiency will not come without practice.

The spike should be inserted before each strand is tucked and withdrawn after that tuck is complete. The tucking strand is passed through the rope in the same direction as, and beyond, the spike and it is then pulled into place in the splice.

The twisting and pulling caused in tucking the strands tend to distort their natural set and must be reduced to a minimum. Distortion is greatest when the strands are inserted close to the point at which they emerge from the last tuck, and it will be found that the strands will usually go more kindly into position if the spike is introduced under the correct strand but some inches further down the rope. The tucking strand should then be passed through, as already described, and hauled into place while working the spike back along the lay of the rope. The less the strands are distorted the neater and stronger will be the splice. In the Admiralty Splice all strands are tucked against the lay, as for cordage splicing.

When preparing wire for splicing the ends of the strands must always be firmly whipped before they are unlaid from the rope.

REDUCED TUCKING SEQUENCE

A wire splice may be reduced in much the same way as for cordage.

1　One tuck with the core in each strand.

2　Two tucks after the core of each strand has been removed.

3　One tuck with two-thirds of each strand.

4　One tuck with each remaining half.

TO MAKE AN EYE SPLICE

1　Put a stout whipping on the rope at a distance equal to 300mm for every 25mm of the circumference of the wire; for example, for a 100mm wire the whipping would be placed 1.2m from the rope's end. Whip the end of each strand, unlay the strand to the whipping and cut out the heart of the rope that is exposed (Fig 13.7(i).

2 Form the size of the eye required and stop the two parts of the wire firmly together to prevent movement during the tucking of the strands (stopping not shown).

3 Place three stands on one side of the wire and the remaining three on the opposite side of the wire (i). Note: For convenience in the following instruction the strands are numbered from 1 to 6, the top strand being No 1 as shown in Fig 13.45(i).

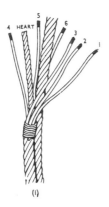

Fig 13.45(i)

The parts of the rope are distinguished by naming them the 'standing part' and the 'tucking end' (the terms are self-explanatory) and all references to the right and left apply only when looking down the rope from the crown of the eye.

4 When ready for splicing, place the eye so that the tucking end lies to the left of the standing part, as shown in (i), thus

enabling No 1 strand to be inserted from the right hand side and against the lay.

5 Tuck No 1 strand under the strand immediately below it Fig 13.45(ii).

Fig 13.45(ii) Making an eye-splice

6 Tuck No's 2,3 and 4 under successive strands of the standing part, as shown in Fig 13.46(i), (ii) & (iii).

7 Tuck No 6 under the remaining two strands of the standing part (iv).

8 Finally, tuck No 5 so that it emerges between the two strands under which No 6 lies and after passing under one strand only as shown in (v). This will result in the six strands emerging equidistantly around the standing part.

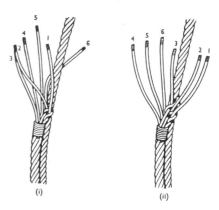

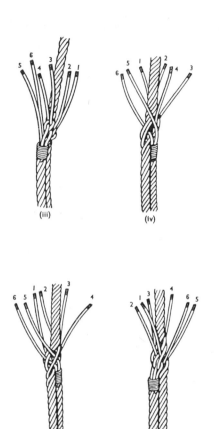

Fig 13.46 Making an eye-splice in wire(iii)

The variation in the regular sequence of tucking is necessary for a locking tuck and to make a neat splice, as shown in (vi).

9 Now pull the strands down towards the crown of the eye taking care not to cripple the wire and place a seizing outside the tucks to prevent them easing back during subsequent stages. Then if the strand cores are jute or hemp,

remove the whippings at the end of the strands, cut out the cores and then replace the whippings.

10 Tuck these coreless strands in regular sequence again, twice for rope above 100mm in circum'fce, not forgetting to place a seizing outside each series of tucks. Then take one-third of the wires out of each strand and stop them back towards the crown of the eye. Tuck the remaining two-thirds once, and then stop back half the wires in each strand again. Tuck each of the one-third strands once, remove the seizing from each tuck and then tap down all tucks with a mallet, starting from the first tuck and finishing off at the tail to remove any slack and round up the splice.

11 Then break off all ends including those stopped back, by bending each separate wire to and fro, though broken off short. A small hook is thus formed in the end of each wire which will prevent it from drawing through the holding strand.

12 The splice may now be served as described at the beginning of the Chapter.

OTHER METHODS OF MAKING AN EYE IN WIRE ROPE

TALURIT SPLICING

As a diver you will often come across this type of termination on wire. Talurit splicing saves wire because no allowance has to be made for tucking; the splice requires no serving, it is completed in one-tenth of the time taken for hand splicing and does not reduce the strength of the wire. However, it does have two main disadvantages:

1 The construction of the alloy
   ferrule can, in some circumstances, catch due to its square
   back. However, newer types are
   tapered down.

2 If used underwater for extended
   lengths of time it will act as
   a sacrificial anode to the wire,
   thus dissolving it like an anode
   on a ship's hull.

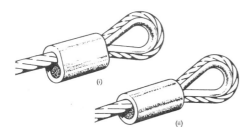

Fig 13.47 Talurit splice

To Make a Talurit Splice

One end of the rope is threaded
through an alloy ferrule of suitable
size and then threaded back on
itself through the ferrule to
so form a loop (Fig 13.47(i).
Should a thimble or other type of
fitting be required, it is placed
in the loop in the necessary
position. The ferrule is then put
in a hydraulic press between two
swages, which are of a correct
size of the wire and ferrule. Any
slack around the fitting is then
taken out by pulling the wires
standing part through the ferrule;
pressure is then applied until the
two swages meet. The pressure
exerted does not harm the rope in
any way.

Making a temporary eye using Bulldog
Grips

A temporary eye, either soft or
thimble, can be made in wire rope

by using bulldog grips, which are
screwed clamps holding the two
parts of the rope together. It is
important that the grips should be
fitted with the U-bolt over the tail
end of the rope and the bridge on the
standing part, as shown in Fig13.47
Bulldog grips are available in various
sizes to fit each size rope. Should
the correct grip for a certain rope
not be available the next largest
size should be used. Three grips
should be used on all ropes up to
75mm in circum'fce: four grips or
more should be used on larger ropes.
Their spacing should be about three
times the circumference of the rope.
Grips should not be used to join
two wires together.

Fig 13.48 Making a temporary eye with
          Bulldog grips

Modified Liverpool Salvage Splice

The strands of this splice are tucked
with the lay of the wire, each strand
being tucked the required number of
times without removing the marline
spike between tucks, and the core
remains in the strands. This allows
the splice to be tucked in a tenth
of the time of the conventional
service splice. When the tension in
the wire approaches its breaking
strength the splice will begin to
draw towards the neck of the splice,
and so give ample warning that tension
should be eased.

DISADVANTAGES

When used on the end of a tail or whip
which is free to turn the splice tends
to unlay and draw.

To make a Modified Liverpool Salvage splice

The wire is prepared as for a service splice but with reduced tucking
allowance. The wire is then hung
from a convenient fitting, with the
unlaid strands pointing downwards,
and a suitable weight is hitched
to the standing part of the wire
just clear of the deck.
When tucking each strand, its end
is entered into the standing part
of the wire above and in the
opposite direction to the marline
spike Fig 13.50

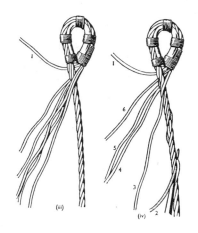

Fig 13.51 Making a modified Liverpool
salva splice (iii) & (iv)

The third strand is tucked through
the same hole, but only under one
strand and is then tucked another
three times round that strand, in
the same was as the second strand
Fig 12-52 (v). The fourth, fifth and
sixth strands are now tucked five,
four and five times respectively
round their appropriate strands.

When the sixth strand has been tucked
return to the first strand and tuck
it another three times. Fig 13.53 (vi)).

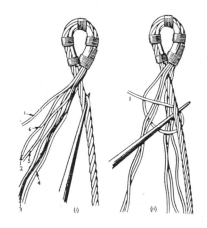

Fig 13.50 Making a modified Liverpool
salvage splice (i) & (ii)

The first strand is tucked through
three strands and is then stopped up
clear until it is finally tucked
Fig 13.51 (iii). The second strand
is tucked through the same hole, but
only under two strands and is then
tucked another four times round the
middle strand of the three under
which the first strand was placed
(making five tucks in all) without
removing the spike. Fig 13.51 (iv)).

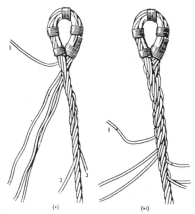

Fig 13.53 Making a modified Liverpool
salvage splice (v) & (vi)

The strands are tucked alternatively four and five times in wires
up to and including 90mm and five and
six times in wire over 90mm, thereby
giving the splice a long tapered
appearance.

Fig 13.54 Making a modified Liverpool
salvage splice (vii)

This completes the splice and the ends
can now be either cut or broken off.

Flemish or Quick Eye (Molly Hogan)

This is a method of putting an eye
in the end of a wire rope very
quickly and without the use of a
marline spike.

To make a Molly Hogan, Quick Eye or
Flemish Eye put a soft wire whipping
around the wire rope about three
times the length of the desired
eye from the end. Split the wire
down the middle into two sections
and unwind them down to the whipping. Form a loop of the desired
size crossing the two sections
at the top and lay the tails in
opposite directions back into the
wire rope, taking care to twist
the tails as necessary, so they
lay up perfectly.

After the eye has been formed, bring
the two tails together below the
throat and lay them up in a single
cable. Finish it off with either a
wire seizing or bulldog grip below
the throat. The Flemish Eye is
about 70-80% efficient and is much
favoured by professional riggers
for wire strops and slings.

RIGGING

There are very few underwater operations which do not require the divers
to carry out some rigging. Therefore,
it is of fundamental importance that
the diver has an understanding of
purchases, rigging fittings, wire
Tirfor's and pull-lifts etc, and how
to apply them to his best advantage
underwater.

The following Chapter is not intended
as a comprehensive volume on rigging
but does provide information on
basic principles, terminology and
equipment.

RIGGING FITTINGS

SHACKLES

These are coupling links used for
joining together one, or more lengths
of rope, wire or chain, provided that
in the case of wire or rope the ends
have been eye spliced. Alternatively
shackles can be used to attach these
to such fittings as eye bolts, hooks,
blocks, slings etc. Shackles are
usually made of wrought iron or mild
steel, but in the smaller sizes
stainless steel, brass and bronze are
suitable alternatives.

Those which are u-shaped are called
'straight shackles' and those which
have curved sides are called 'bow
shackles'. A bow shackle is weaker
than a straight shackle.

PARTS OF A SHACKLE

The ends of a shackle are called the 'lugs'. The space between them is called the 'jaw' and the part opposite the jaw is called the ' crown'. The inside width or length of a shackle is called the clear; the jaw is closed by a removable bolt which passes through a hole in each lug and a general purpose shackle is usually named by the manner in which its bolt is secured in place.

TYPES OF SHACKLE

1 Screw Shackle - the end of the bolt is screwed into one of the lugs, and the bolt may be fitted with a flange at its head. Screw shackle pins should always be moused with soft wire to prevent them from coming undone (Fig 13.56)

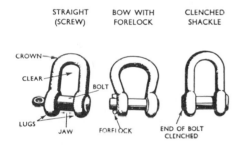

| STRAIGHT (SCREW) | BOW WITH FORELOCK | CLENCHED SHACKLE |

Fig 13.56 Straight, forelock and clenched shackles

2 Forelock Shackle - the end of the bolt projects beyond one of the lugs and a flat tapered split pin called a 'forelock' is passed through a slot in the end of the bolt; the forelock may be attached to the shackle by a keep chain, see (Fig 13.56).

3 Clenched Shackle - the end of the bolt is heated and then hammered over so that it cannot be removed thus permanently closing it (Fig 13.56).

JOINING SHACKLES, LUGLESS AND LUGGED

A tapered hole is drilled through one of the lugs and the end of the bolt, and the bolt is secured in place by a similarly tapered pin being driven into this hole and held in place by a lead pellet hammered into the mouth of the hole over the head of the pin. Sometimes referred to a a 'pin and pellet' shackle.

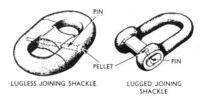

LUGLESS JOINING SHACKLE.   LUGGED JOINING SHACKLE

Fig 13.58 Joining shackles

STRENGTH OF RIGGING GEAR AND FITTINGS

The 'safe working load' (S.W.L.) of any fitting or gear is the maximum load it is designed to bear in practice and is fixed as a definite proportion of when it will break, known as the breaking strength. The ratio of the breaking strength to the safe working load is called the 'factor of safety'.

Apart from normal wear and corrosion a metal fitting which is amply strong when new may become gradually weakened by induced brittleness, sometimes called fatigue. Generally speaking fatigue is caused by suddenly applied loads, and by sharp blows such as those caused by dropping the fitting or knocking it about. Continued ill-treatment in this manner will ultimately result in the cracking and fracture of the metal.

The factor of safety and, therefore, the safe working load of a fitting is usually fixed by the designers according to the anticipated wear and fatigue between proof tests, which are normally

conducted annually. The less
frequent the tests the higher must
be the factor of safety. It must
be remembered that the proof load
stamped on each fitting is double
the safe working load, i.e. a
5 ton proof shackle has a safe working load of 2½ tons.

CALCULATING THE SAFE WORKING LOAD
OF SHACKLES

W = Tons

D = The diameter of metal at
the crown

The safe working load of a straight
shackle is found from:

$$W = 4D^2$$

and that of a bow shaped shackle
from:

$$W = 2.5D^2$$

The factor of safety for most
shackles is 6.

THIMBLES

Thimbles are classified according to
the circumference of rope for
which they are intended and also
their shape. They are manufactured
from mild steel, iron or in some
cases brass stainless steel or
gunmetal. When an eye splice is
formed at one end of a fibre or
wire rope a thimble is inserted
to take the chafe of a shackle
and also to support the eye formed
in the rope. Thimbles can be
either pre-cast or bent to shape.
They can be either round or heart
shaped and open or welded.

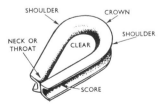

Fig 13.59 Heart-shaped thimble

HOOKS

Hooks used at sea are of many different
designs and are usually made of galvanised mild steel. They are generally
much weaker than shackles of similar
size.

The point of the hook is called the
'bill'. The body is called the 'shank'
and the bottom the 'crown'. The
part of the shank opposite the bill
is the 'back'. The 'jaw' is the space
between the bill and the shank and
the 'clear' is the inside diameter of
the crown.

Fig 13.60 Safety swivel hook

Where hooks are not fitted with spring
safety clasps, they must be moused to
prevent accidental shedding of the
load.

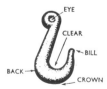

Fig 13.61 Plain hook showing the
names of the parts

MOUSING

A length of line or small wire is
rove between the point and shank
of a hook to prevent unhooking.
It is also used on screw shackles
to keep the pin in place.

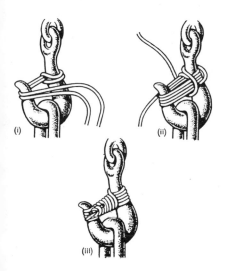

Fig 13.62 Mousing a hook

Rigging Screws and Slips

Various kinds of rigging screw
are used to adjust rigging equipment for length and tension; they
are also known as 'bottle-screws'.

RIGGING SLIP

This is a quick-release link used
for joining the end of a rope or
chain to a fitting when the end
may have to be cast off frequently
or rapidly; often used in conjunction with a bottle screw for
securing an anchor or guard rail.

Fig 13.63 Screw and slip

EYEPLATES, EYEBOLTS, DECK CLENCHES RINGBOLTS

EYEPLATES

These are of stamped steel and are
used for securing an eye to a metal
structure; they are either riveted
or welded in place.

EYEBOLTS

These are of wrought iron or mild
steel and are used for securing
an eye to a wooden structure; the
bolt is forced through a bored hole
and held in place by a nut on its
protruding end.

SCREWED EYEBOLT

EYEPLATE

Fig 13.64 Deck fittings

STROPS

A strop is a ring of cordage or wire
rope.

To Put a Strop on a Spar

If the pull is from one side so
that a strong grip is required
the strop should be attached as
in Fig 13.65.

Fig 13.65 Putting a strop on a spar

To put a strop on a rope

Middle a strop on the rope. Dog
the bights opposite ways and hook
the tackle on to both bights
(Fig 13.66). A strop will hold
on wire rope, but for a strong
pull chain must be used. The
chain can either be knotted into
a strop and used as below in
Fig 13.66, or put on as a chain
stopper as described.

Fig 13.66 Putting a strop on a rope

STOPPERS AND STOPPERING

To belay a rope which is under strain
the strain must be taken temporarily
with a stopper.

Cordage Stopper

This is used for fibre ropes only and
consists of a length of cordage made
fast to a fixture such as an eyeplate.
The stopper is laid alongside the
hawser with its tail pointing towards
the source of the strain - the tail is
half-hitched round the hawser against
the lay and then dogged round the
hawser with the lay. The end is then
held by hand or stopped to the haswer.

Chain Stopper

This is used for wire hawsers only and
is similar to a cordage stopper,
except that it consists of a length
of chain.

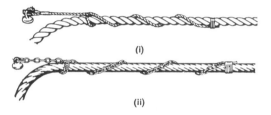

Fig 13.67 Rope and wire stoppers

Carpenters Stopper

This is used only on wire ropes and
is for temporarily holding a rope
which is under strain. It consists
of a metal block made in the form of
a thick-sided box, of which both ends
are open and the top hinged to form
a lid. The box having been closed
around the rope a wedge-piece of
the correct size for the rope is then
pushed home as far as it will go, so
that immediately any pull comes on
the rope the wedge piece is drawn
hard into the block and jams the rope.

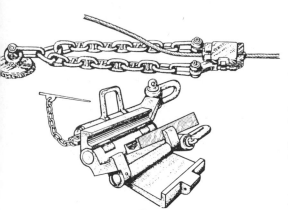

Fig 13.68 Carpenter's wire rope stopper

Its main advantage is that it does not damage the wire.

Spanish Windlass

A Spanish windlass is a means of applying force, using a bar or lever in a rotating so as to shorten a rope strop. The windlass is formed by making a strop completely round the two objects, then inserting the lever or bar and applying a twisting action as indicated.

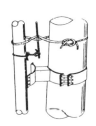

Fig 13.69 Two methods of applying a Spanish windlass

SLINGS AND SLINGING

When anything is to be hoisted, whether it is a single item or a collection of objects, it is attached to the hook of the hoisting rope by means of a sling, which may be formed by a strop. Care must always be taken when using slings, as their misuse or overloading is a frequent cause of accidents.

An important principle in slinging is illustrated in the three diagrams below (Fig 13.70). These show an object weighing 1 ton slung in three different ways, with the tension in each leg of the slings marked in each method. It will be seen that the greater the angle between the legs of the slings the greater is the tension they have to bear. For two-legged slings used in commercial practice the working load is laid down for various angles between 0° and 120°, and these slings are seldom, if ever, permitted to be used with the legs beyond this limiting angle of 120°.

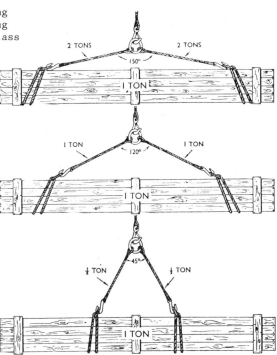

Fig 13.70 Stresses in the legs of a sling

Weights should always be slung so
that their centre of gravity is as
low as possible, and the places
where the slings are liable to be
chafed should be padded.

BLOCKS

A block is a portable pulley, made
of wood, metal, or wood and metal.

Parts of a Block

The main parts of a block are the
shell or body; the sheave or wheel
over which the rope runs; the pin
on which the sheave turns; the bush
or bearing between the sheave and
the pin; and the eye, hook, strop
or other fitting by which the block
is secured in the required position.

The top of the block where the eye
or hook is fitted is called the
crown ; the bottom of the block is
the arse or tail; the sides of the
shell are the cheeks and the grooves
made in the cheeks of some blocks
to take the strop are called the
score; the opening between the sheave
and the shell through which the rope
passes is the swallow; the eye sometimes fitted on the tail is the
becket.

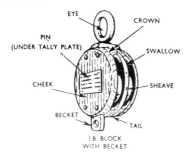

Fig 13.71 Parts of a block

Classification of Blocks

Wooden blocks are classified by their
size, which is measured around the
shell from crown to tail. An ordinary
wooden block will take a rope one-third
of its size, so that a 150mm block will
take a 50mm circumference rope.

Metal blocks are classified by the size
of rope for which they are designed,
which is marked on a plate affixed to
one cheek. Blocks may have more than
one sheave.

Types of Block

Internal Bound (I.B.) Block - this block
has a shell partly of wood and partly
of metal, and is the modern type of
wooden block. The metal portion consists of a fork-shaped steel fitting,
called the binding, which incorporates
both the eye or hook and the becket when
fitted. It also takes the pin of the
sheave. The wooden portion, which is
normally of elm, is really only a fair-
ing piece and takes no part of the load.

Fig 13.71 Internal bound (I.B.) block

Metal Blocks

Like I.B. blocks their shells have a
binding which supplies the strength but

the cheeks etc are of light plating. Some types of metal blocks however,, have their shells cast in one piece.

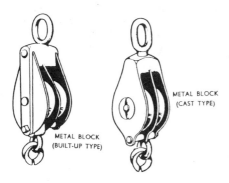

Fig 13.72 Built-up and cast types of metal blocks

Snatch Blocks

These are single blocks, either of metal or internal bound, in which part of the shell is hinged to allow a bight of rope to be inserted into the swallow from one side.

Fig 13.73 Metal snatch block

Clump Block

This block can be of wood or metal and it has an exceptionally large swallow.

It is extensively used on trawlers and is sometimes called a gantry block.

Fig 13.74 Metal clump block

Sheaves and Bearings

The sheaves of all wooden blocks are of phosphor bronze and those of metal blocks are either of phosphor bronze or mild steel. Bronze sheaves are the more expensive, but are desirable where the blocks are exposed to corrosion.

The bearing between the sheaves and the pin may be of the plain roller or self-lubrication type.

Plain bearings have a small brass bush let into their centre to form the bearing because steel bearing on steel is liable to seize. Roller bearings are fitted in a number of special blocks. Self-lubricating bearings have a perforated bronze bush next to the pin, the perforation being filled with a special lubricant.

Strength of Blocks

Generally it can be said that an I.B. (Internal Bound), a metal or a common block is about one-third of the strength of an I.B. block used for the same size of rope.

A clump block is about one quarter of the strength of such a block. Every block has its safe working load (S.W.L.) shown on a plate attached to its cheek.

PURCHASES AND TACKLES

A purchase is a mechanical device by means of which an applied pull or force is increased; it may be a system of gearing, or a combination of blocks of pulleys rove with rope or chain.

A tackle (pronounced 'tayckle') is a purchase consisting of a rope rove through two or more blocks in such a way that any pull applied to its hauling part is increased by an amount depending upon the number of sheaves in the blocks and the manner in which the rope is rove through them.

Parts of a Tackle

The blocks of a tackle are termed the standing block and the moving block The rope rove through them is called the fall which has its standing, running and hauling parts. The size of a tackle is described by the size of its fall. A 75mm luff, for example, would be rove with a 75mm fall.

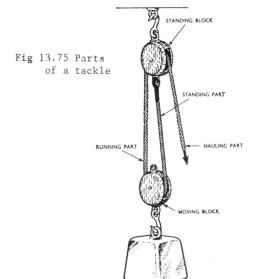

Fig 13.75 Parts of a tackle

STANDING BLOCK

STANDING PART

RUNNING PART   HAULING PART

MOVING BLOCK

Mechanical Advantages

The amount by which the pull on the hauling part is multiplied by the tackle is called its mechanical advantage (M.A.) and, if friction is disregarded, this is equal to the number of parts of the fall at the moving block. In Fig 13.76, there are two parts at the moving block, therefore, the mechanical advantage is two; in other words, a pull on the hauling part of 1cwt would, if friction were disregarded, hold a weight of 2cwt.

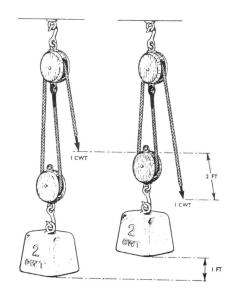

1 CWT

2 FT

1 CWT

2 CWT

2 CWT

1 FT

Fig 13.76 Mechanical advantage and velocity ratio of a tackle

Velocity Ratio

Mechanical advantage is gained only at the expense of the speed of working. In Fig 13.76 for example, the weight will only be raised 300mm for every 600mm of movement of the hauling part. The ratio between the distance moved by the hauling part and that moved by the moving block is known as the velocity ratio (V.R.) and is always equal to the number of parts of the fall at the moving block (Fig 13.76).

Reeving a Tackle to Advantage and to Disadvantage

The mechanical advantage is always greater when the hauling part comes away from the moving block. This tackle is said to be <u>rove to advantage</u>.. Conversely, a tackle in which the hauling part comes away from the standing block is said to be <u>rove to disadvantage</u>. <u>Therefore, where possible,rig a tackle so that the hauling part leads from the moving block and make the block with the greater number of sheaves the moving block.</u>

TACKLE ROVE TO DISADVANTAGE

SAME TACKLE ROVE TO ADVANTAGE

Fig 13.77 Tackles rove to advantage and disadvantage

Load on the Standing Block

The load on the standing block, and therefore on the fitting to which it is attached, is dependent upon the mechanical advantage of the tackle used. This load is calculated by adding the pull required

on the halving part to the weight which is being moved, and so for a given weight the greater the mechanical advantage the less will be the load on the standing block.

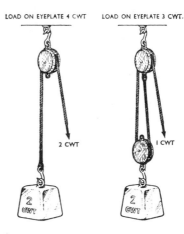

Fig 13.78 Load on the standing block

EXAMPLES OF TACKLES AND PURCHASES

LUFF

This is a purchase of 75mm in size or greater. It consists of a double and a single block, with the standing part of the fall made fast to the single block. Its V.R. is 4 if rove to advantage, and its M.A. is 3.08 and 2.3 respectively.

Fig 13.79

A luff

TWO FOLD PURCHASE

This consists of two double blocks
and is a useful general purpose
tackle. Its V.R. is 5 if rove to
advantage, and 4 if rove to disadvantage and its M.A. is 3.57 and
2.26 respectively.

Fig 13.80 Two fold purchase

THREE FOLD PURCHASE

This consists of two treble blocks;
its V.R. is 7.0 if rove to advantage
and 4 if rove to disadvantage, and
its M.A. is 3.57 and 2.26 respectively.

Fig 13.81

Three fold
purchase

MECHANICAL PURCHASES

The use of mechanical purchases for
underwater use is of considerable
advantage provided; they are reliable.
A considerable number of newly designed tools for underwater use and some
principally for surface use, are
available for the underwater rigger
to choose from. Below is a brief description of some of them.

The Lever and Ratchet purchase

In which the mechanical advantage is
gained by a simple lever working like
a pump handle. When the lever is
so worked, a pawl mounted on it revolves
a ratchet wheel, and the pawl can be
turned in either direction. It is available in a number of different sizes
which should be selected for the job in
hand. On no account should a cheater
pipe be used on come-alongs or other
lever operated pull-lifts - using one
will damage the unit. If you are unable
to jack the load with the handle supplied, use a larger sized unit or
several of them to do the job. Always
be sure the unit works in both directions
and that the chains are not kinked or
frozen before taking it underwater.
After use ensure it is properly maintained.

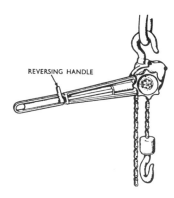

REVERSING HANDLE

Fig 13.82 Lever and Ratchet purchase

WIRE TIRFOR

The tirfor is a hand or hydraulically one-man operated machine for halving, lifting and lowering.

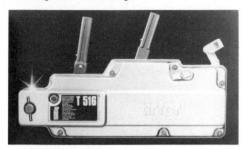

Fig 13.83 Tirfor model TU16, safe working load of 1600kg

The machine is fitted with an extendable wire which allows loads to be pulled over long distances without re-rigging.

Fig 13.84 Hand operated Tirfor

Tirfors are available in three sizes. The largest, weighing 27kg (without wire) is capable of lifting 3 tons (3000kg) and pulling 5 tons (5000 kg).

The machines are constructed with pressed steel cases and therefore require constant maintenance if used underwater.

The power-operated hydraulic Tirfor is fitted with a hydraulic ram. Patented hydraulic pump units allow power-operation of 1,2 or 4 units simultaneously by one operator. The system can work both forward (pulling or lifting) or reverse (lowering) without requiring any physical effort by the operator.

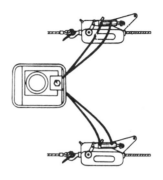

Fig 13.85 Hydraulically operated Tirfor

AIR TUGGER

The use of winches etc, which are surface operated, can if properly used, be of enormous help underwater for lifting and pulling. A type of winch commonly found on offshore drilling rigs etc, it is pneumatically powered; hence it is known as an 'air tugger'.

Fig 13.86 Air tugger

When using air tuggers underwater
ensure that they are numbered both
underwater and on the surface, to
ensure that as much as possible
no misinterpretation of instructions
can occur. Also, ensure that during
all lifting manoeuvres the diver
and his umbilical are clear.

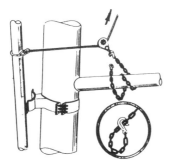

Fig 13.87 Typical application of
the use underwater of a
pneumatic tugger

CRANE SIGNALS

Whenever a crane, winch, derrick or
tugger is used to lift objects in
or out of the water a unified system
of signalling is essential apart
from ensuring that the diver is
aware of any movement by communications. The surface should move
the diver away from the immediate
area during raising and lowering.
The signal ALL STOP refers to ALL
equipment, tuggers etc, which could
affect the diver on the work site.

The following surface crane signals
should be used to direct surface
loads. The signaller should stand
in a secure position where he can
see the load and can be seen clearly
by the crane operator and diving supervisor. Each signal should be distinct
and clear.

TRAVEL TO ME   TRAVEL FROM ME

SIGNAL WITH BOTH HANDS

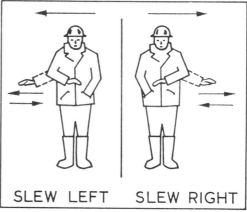

SLEW LEFT   SLEW RIGHT

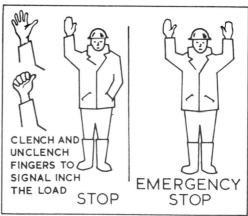

CLENCH AND
UNCLENCH
FINGERS TO
SIGNAL INCH
THE LOAD   STOP

EMERGENCY STOP

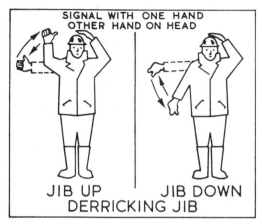

SIGNAL WITH ONE HAND
OTHER HAND ON HEAD

JIB UP   JIB DOWN
DERRICKING JIB

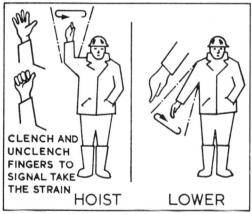

CLENCH AND
UNCLENCH
FINGERS TO
SIGNAL TAKE
THE STRAIN

HOIST   LOWER

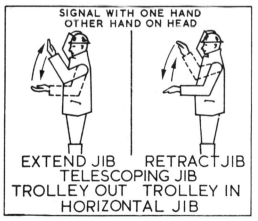

SIGNAL WITH ONE HAND
OTHER HAND ON HEAD

EXTEND JIB   RETRACT JIB
TELESCOPING JIB
TROLLEY OUT   TROLLEY IN
HORIZONTAL JIB

CHAPTER 14

HAND TOOLS UNDERWATER

The need for a commercial diver to be skilled and experienced in the use of hand tools underwater, cannot be over emphasised.

Although tool training is a mandatory requirement only for those seeking the United Kingdom qualification of HSE Part 1 diver, it is in the personal interest of all divers to become proficient in this basic but vital skill. Ideally, every diver should be a skilled fitter, but since this is not possible, those candidates for diver training without any previous tool training should at least be competent in the use of all the tools mentioned in this chapter; knowing how to identify, use and maintain them to the best effect.

There is no such thing as a hand tool that cannot be used underwater, but this does not mean that all the tools devised for surface use are equally suitable for use by divers. Corrosion presents the greatest problems, and tools such as ratchet screwdrivers, certain impact and torque wrenches, drill braces, micrometers etc. would all require a complete strip down , followed by meticulous cleaning, lubrication and re-assembly after each use, with no guarantee that they would remain serviceable. In the same way, certain surface measuring devices are totally unsuitable for use underwater, either because they are intended solely for use in a dry situation, and hence in the reduced visibility conditions encountered by divers, would be unreadable or totally inaccurate.

As with any trade or profession, the condition of the tools used by a diver reflect not only his personal attitude to the job, but also the degree of professionalism of the actual company. Rusting, broken or blunt tools will not go un-noticed by clients visiting a work site.

In the past, many divers have entered the profession with no idea how to sharpen a drill bit, or that the cutting angle of a cold chisel needs to be altered to suit different metals. But this is only the tip of the iceberg, since there are thread sizes to be considered, teeth per unit length, pitch, taps and dies, and a host of other common, every day engineering tools, with which divers must be familiar.

TOOL CATEGORIES

The tools required to be used underwater by a diver, fall into the following four basic categories:

1   Cutting tools

2 ˙ Boring tools

3   Securing/ fastening tools

4   Measuring tools

Within each of these four categories, the range of tools which will be dealt with in some detail are as follows:

Cutting Tools

a) Wood and metal cutting saws, including hacksaws and pad saws
b) Cold chisels
c) Files and rasps
d) Scrapers

Boring Tools

a) Hand drills and braces
b) Drill bits, both parallel shank, taper shank and taper sleeves
c) Reamers
d) Taps and tap stocks
e) Dies and die stocks
f) Thread gauges

Securing/fastening Tools

a) Screwdrivers
b) Spanners, open ended and ring
c) Sockets and accessories

Measuring Tools

a) Calipers
b) Depth gauges
c) Squares
d) Plug and 'go-no-go' gauges
e) Feeler gauges
f) Tape measures

Miscellaneous Tools

a) Scribers
b) Punches
c) Hammers
d) Grinding wheels

CUTTING TOOLS

WOOD AND METAL CUTTING SAWS

The working principle of all types of saws, regardless of the material they are designed to cut, is identical, with the prime considerations being;

1   The material from which the saw blade is manufactured.
2   The "pitch" or number of teeth per lin. or 25mm.
3   The "set" of the teeth on the saw blade.

Considering each of these points in turn, the material of which a saw blade is made will be determined by the maker, who had a particular use in mind, so that a wood saw will have a blade manufactured of a softer type of steel than, say, a hacksaw blade or metal cutting blade. It is therefore important to choose the correct type of blade for the job, which is more important in metal cutting than in wood.
Wood saws are seldom used underwater, but when the need arises, always choose a stiffish blade where possible, to give the best chance of a straight cut, and a coarse pitch to prevent clogging of the teeth. Most timber which has been underwater for some time will have a soft exterior, which will cut easily, but on entering the heart material, cutting can then become difficult, particularly if the timber happens to be one of the hard-woods, such as green-

heart, mahogany, or lignum vitae, the 'wood of life'. With soft woods, a standard carpenter's saw blade with a pitch of 5 teeth per 25mm (1inch) will be quite adequate, but the use of a smaller saw, such as a tenon saw with perhaps 12 teeth per 25mm will only cause "binding" in the cut and is unsuitable. For the very hard timbers, a hydraulic or air driven underwater chain-saw should be considered if the task is to be completed quickly; otherwise the diver should use a coarse bladed "cross-cut" saw with something like 3 or 4 teeth per 25mm only. The width of the blade itself make it almost impossible to achieve a straight cut underwater.
A wood saw will become blunt and make cutting slow and difficult once the face of the leading edge of the teeth becomes rounded and worn. At the same time, the "set" of the teeth will alter, causing the blade to stick or clog in the cut, and can only be remedied by "re-setting" the teeth using a re-setting tool, and then re-sharpening each tooth by use of a hand file of a triangular form.

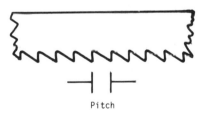

Pitch

Set

Fig 14.1 Top, saw tooth pitch; bottom, saw tooth "set"

Fig 14.2 Wood saw teeth shape

Fig 14.3 Metal cutting saw teeth
         shape

Fig's 14-2/3 above clearly illustrate
the difference in design of a cutting
saw for wood and metal. With the wood
saw, there is no clearance face on
the back of each tooth, neither is it
necessary to introduce a curve between
the back of each tooth and the lead-in
to the next. This is due to the fact
that particles of wood break off
during sawing easier than metal, and
will not normally clog the teeth.
    An enlarged outline of a single
tooth on a hacksaw blade is shown in
Fig 14.4 in which a chip of metal is
shown being cut from the surface. A
design feature of metal cutting
blades is the 25mm length of "rake"
on the back of each tooth. Without
this feature, the tooth would lack
strength, and not offer a smooth
cutting action. Hacksaw blades are
manufactured in many grades, with
special purpose blades for different
hardness metals, and a range of pitch.

The Hacksaw

Where small cutting tasks have to be
performed, the standard hacksaw is
the chief tool. Most hacksaw frames
have either an adjustable wing-nut
or similar tensioning device at the
point furthest from the handle, with
a second matching blade pin at the
handle. Most modern frames are designed to accommodate both 250 and 350mm
blades and to allow them to be used
vertical to the frame, or at an angle
of 90°. Blades may be of carbon or
high-speed steel, and with the cutting
edge only hardened, or they may be
hardened right through. Whilst the
high-speed steel blades are more
prone to breaking and more expensive
than their soft-backed counterparts,
the latter are not so efficient, and
in terms of useful working life, the
high-speed ones are more economical.
    In choosing a blade for a part-
icular task, it should be remembered
that at least three teeth should be
in contact with the thickness of the
work at any one time, otherwise the
teeth will be stripped from the blade.
This is an important consideration
when sawing pipe, for example. The
following is a rough guide to the
pitch of a blade for cutting certain
metals:

1.5mm pitch – general all round work,
               including cutting mild
               steel
1.75mm "   – Solid brass, copper
               and cast iron
1.00mm "   – Silver steel, cast
               steel rods, thin
               section structures
0.75mm "   – This sheet metal and
               steel, copper and
               conduit tubing

Blades should be secured in the frame
as taut as possible, but using fingers
only to tighten the tensioning device.
Cutting strokes should be firm and
steady, at about 45/50 per minute,
lifting the blade slightly on the
return stroke. The blade should be

fitted with the teeth pointing away from the operator, and solid metal should be cut with some pressure on the frame; light materials and tube require only light pressure.

Blades will be broken as a result of:
Erratic or too rapid strokes.
Too much pressure applied.
Blade loose in the frame.
Twisting the blade in the cut.
Binding of the blade due to an uneven cut.
The work not held securely.

Pad Saws

Pad saws are small metal handles designed to take whole or shorter lengths of hacksaw blade. They are an ideal way of utilising broken pieces of blade, and are often the only tool suitable for bolts flush with a surface. The blade is usually held in place by either a screw or a pair of screws (one on each side), and may require a screwdriver to tighten same. The biggest disadvantage of pad saws are that since the blade is not under any tension, it can easily break if not steadied with the other hand.

COLD CHISELS

The cold chisel is an important basic cutting tool for the diver. Unlike wood chisels, they do not have a handle, and apart from being graded by length, there are four basic types:

1 Flat chisel
2 Cross-cut chisel
3 Half-round chisel
4 Diamond chisel

Chisels generally are manufactured from octagonal section cast tool steel, the largest from about 30mm diameter down to the smallest of 10mm.

Fig 14.5 illustrates how the cutting edge is ground to an angle to suit the metal being worked on, and the edge should not be square to the body of the chisel, but given a slight bow or curvature as indicated. Rake and clearance are important, and assuming that the point of the chisel has been ground symmetrical, then the rake and clearance will depend upon the angle of inclination (A) between the chisel and the work. Generally speaking, a clearance of some 10° is adequate, so that for a 60° point angle, the chisel must be held with angle (A) equal to 10° + 30° = 40°, in which case the rake would be 90° − (40° + 30°) = 20°. Hard and brittle materials require less rake than softer, so that the chisel angle must be less for the softer materials and greater for the hard. The following table gives some suitable angles for grinding:

Cold Chisel Grinding Angles

Metal to be cut		Angle
Mild steel	−	55°
Cast iron	−	60°
Cast steel	−	65°
Brass	−	50°
Copper	−	45°

Of the four types of chisel mentioned earlier, the flat chisel would be chosen for standard underwater cutting tasks. The main use of the cross cut chisel is for making or enlarging keyways or slots; half round chisels and diamond point chisels are used for groove work such as cleaning out a bearing oil-way, or grooving an incorrect start for a drilled hole.

FILES AND RASPS

In keeping with other cutting tools, files and rasps have a series of teeth, which are generally cut on manufacture to give a point angle of 55 or 60°. If the face of a file or rasp has a series of such cutting teeth grooved in one direction only, then it is known as a "single-cut" tool. If the face carries grooves of teeth cut in two different directions, then it is known as a "cross-cut" tool. In making a file, the first series of grooves are cut at an angle of about 45° relative to the edge of the file, and if it is to be a "cross-cut" finish, the second set of grooves will be at 70° to the same edge.

The result is to produce teeth representing small pyramids, with rounded faces, facing in the direction in which the file is designed to cut. It is an interesting point that when files were manufactured by both hand and machines, the former were found far superior, since the slight irregularity of those hand-made, offered a better cutting efficiency than the "perfect" machine made tool. Irregular spacing in the grooving has since been introduced into file manufacture, but it is not obvious to the naked eye.

The main types of hand file in use, excluding the very fine files (Swiss files) used for instrument making etc, are:

Hand Files

Probably the most common file likely to be used by a diver underwater. This file is parallel in width, but is very slightly tapered towards the "square" end, furthest from the "tang" or pointed end, designed to take a wooden or pvc file handle. Cross-cut on both faces, with one edge single-cut, the other left plain.

Flat Files

Unlike the "hand" file, this version is parallel for only about two-thirds of its length, after which it tapers both in width and thickness. Cross-cut on both faces, single-cut on both edges.

Ward Files

Similar to a flat file, except that it is thinner and carries no tapering in its thickness.

Pillar Files

Similar to hand files, but are smaller in width, but still very much rectangular in cross-sectional area.

Square Files

Square in cross-sectional area for two-thirds of its length, then tapers but retaining its square shape. Cross-cut on all four faces.

Round Files

Also known as "rat-tail" files, these are similar to square files in that they taper, but still retain their shape. Round files over 150mm of both rough and bastard grades are usually cross-cut; under this size, rough, bastard and second cut grades, plus the smooth files, are single-cut only.

Half-round Files

Although the name suggests a semi-circular profile, this type is only part of a circle, and in keeping with the previous three types, tapers in both width and thickness. The flat side is always cross-cut, but the rounded face may be single-cut on smooth and second-cut types, otherwise cross-cut in all others.

Three -square Files

More popularly known as tri-angular files, these also taper in both planes, and are cross-cut on all three faces.

Mill Files

Very similar to the pillar file, except that its width and thickness is parallel throughout. One or both edges may be rounded, to assist in filing the radius on saw teeth. Single-cut on all faces.

Rasp Files

Used to remove greater quantities of material due to the coarse nature of its teeth, than with other files. The teeth are made by a punching action, rather than the more conventional grooves of normal files. Can be used on most soft materials, ie. non-ferrous metals, wood, pvc and non-metallic substances.

Grades of Files

Files are graded by length, and type of teeth size, viz:

Rough - Bastard - Second-cut - Smooth and Dead Smooth.

Using Files

A file should never be used without a file-handle fitted, since there is a real risk of serious hand injury from the unprotected "tang" or point.

When using a file, bear in

mind that its teeth point away from the "tang", and that it is the "pushing" action of the file that achieves the cutting effect. No amount of pressure on a file will achieve a cutting action on the "return" stroke. Always use two hands on a file, force down on the 'tip' on the forward stroke, then relax the weight or even lift it clear of the work for the return stroke. It is possible to use a file correctly by the method of "draw" filing, ie. gripping the body of the file at both ends, and using it to work at right-angles to the job.

The consequences of using the incorrect grade of teeth on a soft material will be to "choke" or clog the teeth, rendering the cutting face smooth and useless. If this happens, then a special wire-brush, with very short teeth, known as a "file-card", must be used. It is recommended that all files are cleaned in this manner after use, and in the case of use underwater, the file should be scrubbed under a fresh water tap, blown dry with an air jet, and then lightly oiled with a thin machine lubricant. The use of a thick oil will only cause clogging of the teeth as it dries, or hold particles when next used. Ideally, files should not be oiled at all. A file cannot be readily sharpened when it becomes blunt, and if wire brushing does not improve the cutting ability, it may have to be discarded.

Files in general are made from a hard material, and are brittle due to the heat treatment involved. They will shatter if dropped from any height on to a hard surface, are subjected to a bending action, or are hammered.

SCRAPERS

There are many tasks which may confront a diver in which grinding or filing is either impractical, or would remove more metal than is required. A typical example would be in the case of a bearing or bush, which may be only a fraction of a centimetre too large to accommodate a shaft or pin. To achieve this, there are two types of scraper

available:

a) The Flat Scraper:
A tool representing a hand-file in general shape, except that it is slightly flared out at the cutting end. used for the removal of small amounts of metal from flat surfaces, to remove flaws, chips, burrs etc. and leave a smooth finish. In fact flat scrapers are often made in the workshop from old blunt files, by use of a grinding wheel.

b) The Half-round Scraper:
Used solely for working on internal cylindrical surfaces such as the inner face of a bearing or bushing etc.
It should be stressed that the use of a hand scraper is a long and tedious operation, requiring much patience and no small degree of skill. The tool must be kept sharp, using an oil-stone.

BORING TOOLS

HAND DRILLS

The use of hand drills by divers should only be contemplated in circumstances where a hole of 12mm diameter or less has to be made in metal. Even this size of hole will require a considerable effort, and a hydraulic or pneumatic drill should be used where possible.
There are 3 basic types of hand drill suitable for use in an underwater situation:

Hand Brace
The standard hand brace has a 3 jawed chuck, hand tightened, which will usually accommodate up to a 10mm parallel shank drill bit. It requires two hands to operate: one holds the drill in the required position, whilst the other rotates the handle and hence the chuck, through mechanical gearing.
After underwater use, and especially if in salt water, the tool should be washed in fresh water and

dried with an air jet, after which the
chuck assembly must be stripped and
well cleaned and lubricated, otherwise
the delicate spring mechanism and chuck
jaws will quickly rust, rendering the
tool unserviceable.

<u>Breast Drill</u>

Similar to the hand brace except
that the body is fitted with a curved
end plate, by which pressure can be
applied by the operator, whilst one
hand holds the side handle and the
other rotates the handle, and hence the
drill bit. As with the hand brace, the
chuck is designed to take straight or
parallel shank drills of the smaller
sizes, and should be serviced after
"in-water" use in the same manner.

<u>Ratchet Brace</u>

This can take the form of what is
often called the carpenter's wood brace,
ie. a hand brace or drill designed to
take only wood boring "bits" for use
with timber, or the special ratchet
brace used in engineering for drilling
metal.

The wood brace is also a two-
handed tool, with a cranked arm, a two-
jaw chuck, and a ratchet facility plus
direct drive. These are designed to
accept only the square ended, wood
boring bits, which range in size from
about 6mm to 50mm. Easy to operate by
a diver and quick in action, the after
use care in order to keep the tool
serviceable is the only drawback (see
page 14.1).

Engineering ratchet braces are
ideal for one handed use by divers, but
require an appropriate surface above
the place of work as a back plate,
against which pressure can be exerted
to force the drill bit to cut. A hexagon
feed nut on a shaft, operated by a
spanner, allows pressure to be maintained against the work as the drill bit
progresses, hence also correct align-
ment. Although much slower than a
breast drill, these are suitable for
larger diameter holes, and the length
of feed can be from 60 to 90mm

Fig 14.4 Hacksaw blade tooth shown
removing a chip of metal,
illustrating the need for
clearance in tooth shape

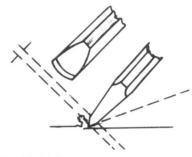

Fig 14.5(a) A cold chisel in the
action of cutting, with
typical cutting angles
shown, also the curvature
of the cutting edge

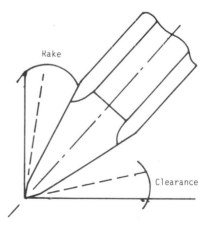

Fig 14.5(b) Rake and clearance illustrated relative to the
cutting edge of a chisel

depending on the size of unit. Smaller
models require straight drill bits,
whilst the larger models may take taper
shank bits or even special square shank
bits. The device is very slow, since
the ratchet allows only for a half-turn
rotation of the bit at each stroke.

The same after use care as
recommended for other ratchet devices
is necessary.

Fig 14.6 A breast-drill

DRILL BITS

Drill bits or twist drills are cutting
tools designed to make round holes.
They can be likened in many respects
to a cold chisel, in that they have
the same necessary "rake" and "clearance" angles, but instead of cutting
by a straight forward cutting action,
they achieve the same function by
rotation about an axis point. It is
important that the cutting action of
a twist drill is understood, in order
to be able to re-grind twist drills
when they become blunt or damaged.
This aspect will be dealt with later
in the Chapter.

Twist drills or bits are categorised by the nature of the end by
which they are held, known as the
"shank". Drills may be taper-shank,
parallel-shank or "jobber's" drills
as shown in Fig 14.7. Taking each

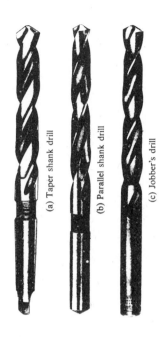

(a) Taper shank drill

(b) Parallel shank drill

(c) Jobber's drill

Fig 14.7 Types of twist drills

category in turn, from the smaller
sizes to the largest:

Jobber's Drill Bits

Usually confined to sizes up to a
maximum of 12mm, above which sizes
advance in 5mm steps. These bits
are usually shorter than the other
types, the average maximum being
100mm, although it should be mentioned that there are available a
specially "long" range of jobber's
drill bits known as "long reach"
drills of 152mm. The size of these
drills is stamped on the shank, but
in use, due to slippage and abuse in
drill chucks, these often become
obliterated or illegible, and hence
a drill gauge becomes necessary.
Drill bits of unknown or doubtful
size can then be checked in the
various holes until the matching size

is identified. The gauge shown below in Fig 14.8 changes in 1mm steps from 1mm to 15mm.

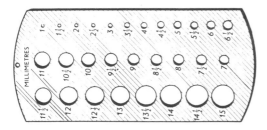

Fig 14.8 Standard drill gauge

Taper Shank Drills

Unlike the other two types of drill bit, the taper shank drill tapers off in what is known as a Morse taper, ending in a flat tongue known as the "tang".

When the taper shank is fitted into its socket, or directly into a mach- ine, this tongue engages in a suitable slot. Thus both the friction between the tapers and the tongue itself offer driving force to the bit. The smaller sizes of drill bits, with their corr- esponding small tapers, may not fit certain large machines. In such circ- umstances, it will be necessary to fit a special taper sleeve to the required drill bit, to make up the difference in size. The different Morse tapers used on various drill sizes are shown in the table below:

Morse Taper No 1
     Drill bit sizes up to 14mm

Morse Taper No 2
     Drill bit sizes from 14mm uo to 24mm

Morse Taper No 3
     Drill bit sizes from 24mm up to 32mm

Morse Taper No 4
     Drill bit sizes from 32mm up to 50mm

Morse Taper No 5
     Drill bit sizes from 50mm upwards to maximum

Once fitted into a drilling machine taper socket, or into a taper sleeve, the drill bit can only be removed by the use of a proper taper drift, which bears on top of the drill tang. A sharp tap with a light hammer will cause the tapers to separate, and allow the drill to be removed.

Parallel Shank Drills

Apart from a slight difference in finish on the portion of the drill held by a chuck, parallel shank drill bits are the same as jobber's drills, except that the former are obtainable in a range of much larger sizes, both in length and diameter. Since it is impractical to drill holes over 12mm in metal using hand held drills, larger holes usually require mechan- ical drills which will accommodate the larger range of parallel shank drill bits.

All drill bits for general use are made of either carbon steel or else high speed steel. Carbon steel drills are far cheaper, but suffer from the fact that their "temper" is qucikly drawn if they are allowed to overheat, hence become soft and quickly blunt. A sure sign that the operator is applying too much press- ure on a drill bit. that the drill is operating at too high a speed, or there is a lack of lubrication, will be "smoking" from the work, and the tip of the bit turns blue. When this happens, the only remedy is to grind off the blue portion completely, and form a new point higher up the drill by grinding.

High speed drill bits are more expensive, but will, as the name suggests, work at much higher speeds without going soft. They do have the disadvantage of being brittle, and snap easily if subjected to bending or shock.

The flutes of a drill bit are always manufactured with a right-hand twist to them, so that coupled with the right-hand or clockwise rotation of a drilling machine, chips of metal or other material are forced up and out of the hole. At the same time, the helix also allows the entry of any necessary lubricant into the hole, and hence to the point of actual drill contact.

Drill Bit Grinding and Sharpening

Unless the tip of a drill bit is correctly ground, it will neither cut efficiently nor evenly, resulting in a hole possibly oversize to that required, in a time far longer than necessary. The ability to recognise an incorrectly ground drill bit and rectify matters is therefore an important skill for a diver to understand and master.

In order to understand the requirements of drill grinding, the cutting angles etc. must be appreciated. Reference to Fig 14.9 shows the tip of a drill, looking at the point from the side. The surface A-B is the cutting face of one side of the point, and the angle of 12° is the necessary clearance, without which the cutting edge could not function properly. Fig 14.10 shows the angle of rake in a twist drill bit, which is incorporated at manufacture and cannot be altered.

As well as the clearance at the drill point or tip, achieved by correct grinding, there are in fact two other forms of clearance incorporated into a drill bit, which may not be so obvious. In manufacture the body of a drill bit is made very slightly less than its overall cutting diameter, which gives a narrow "land" running down the front of the flute of each helix face. This is referred to as the "body-clearance", and can be seen in Fig 14.11. The additional clearance is a very small taper in the overall diameter of the drill bit as a whole, from shank to tip, amounting to about 1:1000 units of length, so that the cutting end is slightly larger than the shank. This prevents any possibility of binding in a hole, between the body of a drill and the work material.

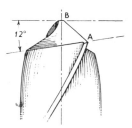

Fig 14.9 The point of a twist drill showing the "clearance" angle of 12°

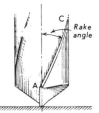

Fig 14.10 Rake angle on a drill bit

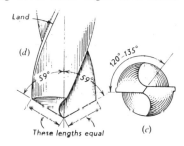

Fig 14.11 "Land" incorporated into the helix of a twist drill bit, also the necessary angles and uniformity of the cutting faces of the actual point

When correctly ground, the drill point should be central, and the cutting faces equal, see Fig 14.11. Note that in the illustration on the right, the so called "point" of the drill is in fact a "line" or "edge", which should be positionwd as shown.

Typical mistakes in drill bit grinding are as follows:

1   Cutting faces of unequal length

2   Cutting faces at unequal angles

3   Both above defects combined

In all cases the work of cutting will be unequal for each face, so that the hole drilled will be oversize, as indicated in Fig's 14.12 and 13, part- icularly in cases where the cutting faces are of different lengths.

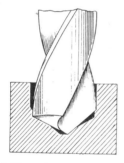

Fig 14.12 The effect of incorrect drill bit grinding, in which the cutting faces are at different angles.

Fig 14.13 Another typical fault in drill grinding, in which the faces are of a different length, giving a very much oversize hole

A simple gauge is advisable to check drill angles, especially if grinding is to take place by hand. Grinding attachments are available for use with machines, but even so, a gauge

is a useful indicator as to the serviceability of a drill bit and essential if an attachment is not available. A suitable gauge, which can easily be locally made or purchased, is illustrated in Fig 14.14

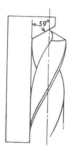

Fig 14.14 Gauge for checking cutting angles of drill bits

An additional gauge can be made by bending up a piece of mild steel to a right angle, of sufficient height to take the longest drill to be sharpened or "ground". Fit a pointed screw into the base on which the plain end of the drill bit can stand and pivot. By chalking the vertical face of the gauge level with the drill tip, a line can be drawn with the drill, first with one lip, then the other. They shoule be equal, indic- ating whether or not the cutting faces are of equal length.

Caution must be exercised when grinding drills not to overheat the tip and destroy the temper. The tip should be dipped into a container of cutting "fluid", very thin oil, or water at frequent intervals, both to cool the tip, and give a measure of lubrication during the grinding process.

The grinding action by hand is to feed the tip against a medium or fine grinding wheel, one face at a time, and in equal rotation, as if the drill were being fed into work; that is, a twisting movement of the bit accompanies a lifting action of the right hand, with frequent inspection and gauging.

REAMERS

The purpose of reaming is to improve the finish or accuracy of a previously drilled hole, or to slightly enlarge an existing hole of insufficient size. A reaming tool will not correct mistakes in a hole as regards its position or, for what matter, its direction, since a remaer can only follow an existing hole.

Reamers are available in the following variations:

1   Straight fluted hand reamers

2   Spiral fluted machine reamers

3   Chucking reamers

4   Tapered reamers for both hand and machine use

5   Expanding reamers

Of these, a diver is only likely to be required to use the hand operated versions of either the straight fluted or taper reamers. Typical requirements underwater might be a circumstance in which a bolt hole has been damaged to the point it will not accept a bolt, or an existing hole has to be enlarged to take the next sized bolt.

Hand reamers will be used with a tap wrench fitted on the square end of the tool. All reamers have a slight taper, the extreme tip usually being some 25mm less than the actual stated reamer size. At the same time, the shank of the reamer will be a few hundreths of a mm less than the diameter of the cutting flutes. The amount of metal which can be removed in this manner is very small, and something like 0.25mm would be a typical maximum. Since such tools are slow in operation, they can be manufactured from cast steel. Taper reamers can be obtained in "rough" and "finishing" grades, which allow for the bulk of the metal to be removed, after which a smooth finish is imparted.

Expanding reamers are unlikely to be considered for use underwater, due to their construction, which would require considerable maintenance after use, to prevent the internal threads from rusting.

Details of different types of reamers are shown in the following illustrations:

Fig 14.15 Types of reamers:
A - Straight fluted hand tool
B - Spiral fluted machine tool
C - Taper pin reamer
D - Chucking reamer

A worn reamer, unsuitable for a particular size, can be ground down to the next smaller size, but this should be considered only in an emergency.

THREADING TOOLS

TAPS AND TAP STOCKS

A "tap" is a specially hardened bolt, with suitable grooves cut along its length, with cutting edges, so that when screwed into a suitable hole of an appropriate size, it will cut a

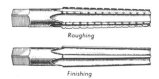

Roughing

Finishing

Fig 14.16 Taper reamers

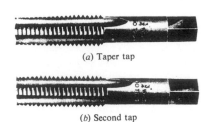

(a) Taper tap

(b) Second tap

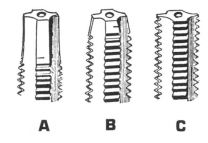

(c) Plug tap

Fig 14.16 The three taps of a set, all 3/4in Whitworth thread

thread of an internal nature, as indicated on the shank of the tap itself. Taps are usually made of high-carbon or high-speed steel, with a square end to accommodate a special holder, known as a tap wrench.

Taps are normally made in sets of three for each thread size. These are most commonly known as:

taper – intermediate – bottoming; or else:

taper – 2nd – plug.

The first tap to be used in the process of cutting an internal thread will be the taper tap; this has its leading end tapered for some 8 or 10 threads, allowing it to enter the hole in the metal, and commence cutting the thread. The 2nd or intermediate tap follows and is similar to the taper, except that only perhaps 2 or 3 threads are tapered, after which it follows the same line as the taper. Should the required hole be open at both ends, then there will be no need for the plug or bottoming tap, since the 2nd tap can be run right through, from both sides if necessary. If the hole is a blind one, that is, it is open at one end only, then the plug tap must be employed. This has a full thread cut right to the very end, and will cut a thread all the way to full depth.

Tapping a Hole

Having drilled a suitable sized hole, which in theory should be exactly the "core" diameter of the required thread,

Fig 14.17 Details of the ends of the taps in a set, being: A – Taper; B – 2nd; C – Plug

in practice is usually drilled very slightly larger, to make the task of tapping easier, without unduly weakening the thread itself. First, a suitable taper plug tap is chosen. This is then held in the jaws of a suitable tap wrench, and placed just inside the pre-drilled hole, square with the top surface of the work. It is most important that great care is taken to get the tap accurately in line with the centre line of the hole, before cutting commences. After a few rotations of the wrench and tap, a certain resistance will be felt, at which point the squareness should

once again be checked. Some suitable
lubrication should be added at this
stage, and the tap advanced in the hole,
half-a-turn at a time, after which the
action should be reversed by the same
amount. This enables the tap to clear
away the cut particles, and prevents
seizure. If anything more than mild
stiffness is encountered, forward
rotation should cease, and the tap
should be worked back carefully, clearing out the swarf as it goes.

On reaching the bottom of the hole,
or having passed clean through the work,
the operator should now proceed to
repeat the process using the 2nd tap,
followed by the plug, if necessary. With
the latter, used in "blind" holes only,
care must be taken not to mistake stiffness for the fact that the tap may have
reached the bottom of the hole. In this
circumstance, if pressure continues to
be applied, the plug tap may shear off
in the hole, leaving it blocked.

Blunt taps can readily be re-
sharpened, using a suitable thickness
and specially shaped grinding wheel,
whose edge is a radius compatible with
the grooves in the body of the tap. It is
then only a matter of carefully running
the grinder up and down each groove in
turn, with frequent visual inspection.

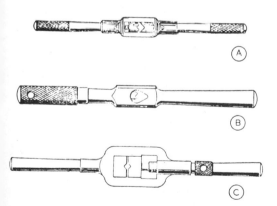

Fig 14.18 A variety of tap wrenches, all
adjustable, and suitable for hand use. The
hole in the 'knurled' portion of (B) and
(C) is to accommodate a "tommy-bar", to
assist in tightening the grip of the jaws.
Also a useful point for a wrist-lanyard.

DIES AND DIE STOCKS

Used for cutting threads on the
exterior faces of round bar or tube,
the "die" is a sort of hardened
steel "nut", with regular portions
of its internal thread removed, so
as to provide cutting edges. As with
taps, dies have a special tool
holder known as a die-stock.
Dies are of three basic types,
namely:

1 Die nuts; hexagonal devices, with
   regular spanner flats, used to
   restore existing damaged threads,
   but not to cut a thread from new.

2 Solid dies; similar to die nuts,
   but suitable for the cutting of
   new threads, but have no adjustment for 1st and 2nd cut.

3 Split dies; similar to solid dies,
   but with a split cut in one side,
   which allows for the split to be
   opened or closed slightly by means
   of pressure from screws in the
   tool holder.

All die stocks are fitted with screws,
either one, two or three in number,
which serve to hold the die in place,
and make adjustment of the cutting
tension.

Cutting an External Thread

The action of cutting an external
thread on a piece of bar or pipe,
is similar to the action of tapping,
except that even greater care must
be exercised in making sure that the
tool is square to the work. Although
the first one or two threads in the
die are chamfered, to make starting
a little easier, this does not offer
the same advantage that a pre-
drilled hole offers when using a
taper tap. It is therefore recommended that where possible, the
operator should file an additional
small chamfer on the end of the
tube or bar being worked.
The secret of using a die is

to keep it perfectly square as the first few turns of thread are being cut. Once started correctly, there should be no further trouble, and by rotation of the stock, half a revolution at a time, followed by the reverse action, will keep the die clear of particles. Lubrication is recommended for all metals, particularly ferrous materials. For pipe work, certain types of dies and stocks have specialguides incorporated, which make thread cutting much easier and accurate, especially where a fine thread is being cut on a large diameter, such as with the BSP and "gas" threads.

It is recommended that the first cut is made with the adjustment screws in the stock such that the "split" in the die is wide open. The second and subsequent cuts should then be made with the "split" under less tension, until the required diameter is reached.

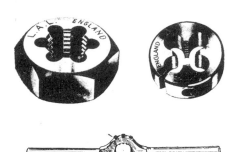

Fig 14.19 A typical die nut, split nut, and die stock

Thread gauges

Several international attempts have been made to standardize screw threads, but to date this has not been achieved. A situation therefore exists in which something like eight different thread forms can be encountered in engineering and manufactured products. It is not the intention of this Chapter to do anything other than outline the basic details of screw-threads, and make the diver aware of the appropriate tables and gauges available, in order to correctly identify a particular type and size of screw thread.

Both external and internal threads use a basic terminology, since one is the potential counterpart of the other. The basic terms use are:

Thread Angle

With reference to Fig 14.20, it will be seen that the angle created by the two inclined faces of the thread make up the "thread angle", which over the entire range of the many thread forms varies only between 47.5° and 60°.

Pitch

From the same illustration "pitch" will be seen to be the distance, measured in inches or millimetres, between the centre line of one thread, to the centre line of the next. It is also a common practice to talk of the pitch of a thread as the number of "threads per inch" or "threads per centimetre". This can be taken as the pitch measurement, expressed as a fraction and inverted for imperial threads. For example, a pitch of 1/8th inch would then be said to be 8TPI; or a pitch of 1/4ins = 4TPI., and so on.

Core Diameter

The core diameter is the diameter of the screw thread, less <u>twice</u> the thread depth (see Fig 14.21).

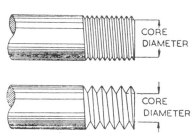

Fig 14.20 Pitch and thread angle

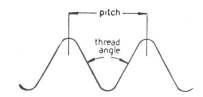

Fig 14.21 Core diameters

THREAD FORMS IN COMMON USE

British Standard Whitworth (BSW)

First standardised by Sir Joseph Whitworth in 1841, to have a thread angle of 55°, and that the roots and crests should be rounded.

British Standard Fine (BSF)

A shallower thread which in Gt Britain has for the most part superseded BSW, since its finer pitch makes for more accurate adjustments.

British Standard Pipe (BSP)

A pitch finer than that of the Whitworth form, used widely in industry and now offshore. When considering BSP nominal diameters, this refers to the bore of the pipe and not its external diameter.

British Association (BA)

BA thread angle is 47.5° with both roots and crests of the thread form rounded off. Used largely in instrument and fine engineering practice, but now not so widely used a before. BA will be specified where the diameter required is less than 6mm.

International Standard Metric (SI)

Incorporates a thread angle of 60°, with a flat crest to the threads to give clearance where crests and roots meet on mating surfaces.

American National Threads

Includes to standards, the American Coarse (NC) and American Fine (NF), the latter being better known as AF.

There are of course, many other thread froms not included in the above, details of which can be studied in most workshop manuals.

Thread Pitch Gauge

In the case where the nature of a particular screw thread form being unknown, use should be made of a "thread gauge", in order to determine the pitch. This information, coupled with an accurate measurement of both maximum and minimum core diameters of the thread in question, will allow the type of thread and size to be determined, by the use of screw thread tables.

Fig 14.22 Typical pitch gauge

SECURING TOOLS

SCREWDRIVERS

Since screwdrivers are liable to gross abuse generally, not only on the surface, but underwater, the best type are those with a solid synthetic handle, generally made of nylon or some sort of high impact pvc material. These offer the best resistance when hammered, their handles are less likely to split or break, and are unaffected by immersion.

It is important that the tip of a screwdriver is regularly ground square, otherwise the working face will quickly loose its shape, and cause distortion and mis-shaping of screw heads. After use in water, screwdrivers should be soaked in clean, fresh water, then placed in an oil bath, before wiping dry. Screwdrivers intended for regular underwater use should have a 6mm hole drilled through the handles, clear of the main grip area, to accommodate a wrist lanyard made of suitable cord or line.

SPANNERS

Spanners are available in sets to match all the many thread forms, ie. metric, Whitworth, AF, UNC, UNF etc, and these can be open ended tools, or ring spanners.

Open ended spanners are usually double ended, with a different sized jaw at each end, either one size up or down from each other, and seldom if ever, of completely differing sizes, except where provided by manufacturers of a particular equipment, as part of a tool kit. Made from cast steel, spanners will withstand a great deal of abuse, but many of the cheaper imported brands are very brittle, and break easily. Generally speaking, only special sized spanners are manufactured as single ended tools.

It is important to use the correct size spanner for a particular hexagon nut, otherwise the corners of the nut or bolt will become rounded off, offering less working surface on which a spanner of the correct size can work and offer a purchase. If an incorrect size spanner continues to be used, eventually there will come a point when it is impossible to remove the nut or bolt by conventional means, and it may then take some time to cut it free, after which a replacement item will be necessary.

If a spanner is "flogged", that is additional purchase or shock is applied by hitting the tool with a hammer, then this can only result in the width of the jaws of the spanner spreading open and becoming distorted, so that it will no longer fit its particular size. The size of a spanner is generally stamped or cast on the flat face at each end, or else on the shank between faces. Wrist lanyards can be fitted by drilling a small hole in the shank, but care must be taken not to weaken the tool as a result.

After use care consists of washing in fresh water, then oiling and wiping dry.

Ring spanners, as their name suggests, have appropriate size "rings" at each end instead of the conventional open jaw of the plain spanner. They are much stronger and give a superior purchase and grip on a nut or bolt head, and are less likely to damage by abuse. Their design is such that they give an equal tension on each corner of a hexagon device, and provided the correct size is used, are less likely to damage or "round-off" the corners.

Ring spanners are also available in a "split" or semi open-ended form, allowing them to be fitted over a shaft and then slid up to the nut, offering a combination of the advantages of both the ring and open ended spanner.

SOCKETS AND ACCESSORIES

Sockets are normally purchased in sets in the smaller range sizes, ie. up to about 50mm, after which they are usually purchased individually as work requirements demand, due to their high cost. A socket is a precision made, cast steel "tube", with one end machined with a deep square orifice, designed to take one of the many drive accessories included in kits, whilst the other is cast to accept a nut of a particular size.

Such sockets are available in the same full range of thread forms and sizes as spanners, except for the very small ranges, where "tube" spanners are available. These are mild steel tool of a tubular form, whose ends are heat houlded into an internal hexagonal form, to fit over nuts and bolts, with differerent sizes at each end, or merely one end only. Purchase is achieved by the use of a "tommy" bar, inserted through a pre-drilled hole in the tube.

Sockets are normally stamped on the out face with its size and thread form, ie ½ins AF, or 20mmUNC etc. Sockets are much preferred in industry to spanners, since they give better purchase, with little chance of damage to nut and bolt heads.

Accessories in a socket set will include a full range of drive shafts, and an operating handle, which may be plain or ratchet operated. Also included in most sets will be a cranked handle, a little like a carpenter's hand brace, but with a square end. This will fit the hole in the ends of all the sockets, and is a useful additional tool. Other devices may include flexible drive shafts, for working at akward angles, also special extension drives etc.

With some of the very large nut sizes, particularly in the offshore industry, a combination "socket-cum-ratchet" spanner tool is available. These may have shafts up to 1.5metres (5ft) long, in which the ratchet device is incorporated into the head itself. These, and any other ratchet devices used underwater, demand careful and thorough servicing after use to prevent salt water corrosion.

MEASURING TOOLS

CALIPERS

As a measuring tool , the caliper is probably amongst the oldest devices known to man, having been in use thousands of years B.C. They are available in two basic forms:

internal and external, as illustrated in Fig 14.23. They may also be "firm-joint" calipers, or "Spring" calipers.

Such measuring devices are ideal for underwater use, except that a diver may have some difficulty in taking an accurate reading from calipers himself, and may have to bring or send the tool to the surface for someone else to measure with a rule or scale. In such instances, care must be taken that the calopers do not get knocked or altered in transit.

When taking outside diameter readings of a shaft for example, the caliper is hand set to a size slightly larger than the work to be measured, then one leg of the tool is gently tapped against the task, one tap at a time, then tested over the shaft, until the two points are

felt to make light contact. The degree of contact should not be too heavy, otherwise the caliper legs may be under some tension, will spring back when removed from the task, and give a false measurement reading. The caliper is then placed on an engineer's steel rule of preference, with one leg touching the outside face of one end of the rule, whilst the reading is taken from the inside face of the other leg (Fig 14.24). The operator should never attempt to take a caliper measurement by holding one leg in each hand, and forcing them together across the item to be measured; this can only result in a false reading.

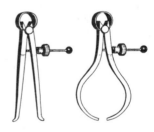

Fig 14.23(a) Firm joint calipers

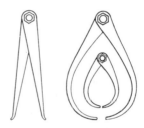

Fig 14.23(b) Spring calipers

DEPTH GAUGES

In an underwater situation in which an accurate measurement of the depth of a hole or fitting has to be taken, a depth-rule is probably the best tool. This consists of an accurate, steel, engineer's rule, probably 150 -300mm long, with a sliding cross piece, fitted with a small knurled locking device, which can be set to accurately indicate the required measurement. Since the body of the device is only some 6mm in width, it is very versatile.

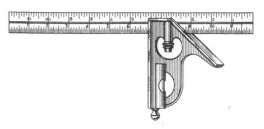

Fig 14.25 Combination square

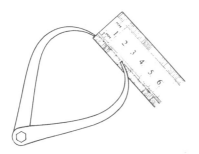

Fig 14.24 Taking a measurement reading from outside calipers

SQUARES

The "try" square is the most common tool for checking the squareness of work, and as a tool is probably even older than the caliper. In engineering terms, a square is an accurate precision instrument, which should be treated with care. In diving situations this degree of accuracy and care is not reasonable, nevertheless, squares are in need of some attention, and should not be used as scrapers, or held by the blade whilst the other portion is used as a hammer !

For general diving purposes, the combination square shown in Fig 14.25 is the most suitable, being all metal construction, fitted with a "level" bubble. Provided they are maintained after use, they will remain serviceable for a long time. The tool can be made into a perfect square, by loosening the securing screw on the arm, and sliding the arm - in this case to the far end of the rule on the left.

A combination square version of this is available with a protractor fitted, which will allow for accurate angle measurement, but except in very good conditions of underwater visibility are not really suitable for diving use.

An alternative useful tool is the carpenter's bevel, which can be used to check work angles, and then brought to the surface for comparison with a source of more accurate measurement, or else, set up on the surface, and then taken down to the job. These usually consist of two arms, held under tension by a nut and bolt with a spring washer. They are cheap, simple to use, and require only the basic after use care of washing and oiling.

PLUG, AND "GO-NO-GO" GAUGES

Measurement and gauging are different in that some tool or other instrument is used to measure something, whereas gauging is the comparison of work with a gauge of known dimensions.

In this brief section, only the principle of gauging will be covered, since it is a common practice to manufacture special gauges for many types of work, and the diving industry is no exception. Such gauges are often discarded once the task has been completed.

In many situations, where a certain object has to fit accurately into a given space, there is a possibility that either the object itself, or the receptacle, may be over or under size. The purpose of gauging is to quickly establish if this is the situation, and then to determine by how much. Examples might be a drive shaft in a bearing; a bearing in a housing; the distance between the hub of a ships propeller and the rope-guard etc.

There are many types of engineering gauges which can be purchased, but it is often the case that a special gauge must be made up in a local workshop, or even by the diver himself, to suit a special requirement. The "plug and plate" gauges shown in Fig 14.26 are either single ended,which offer a turned shaft of known diameter, or else are double ended. In the latter case, they become "go-no-go" gauges of a particular dimension, the difference between the "go" and the "no-go" ends being perhaps as little as0.030ins for example.

Such gauges are readily turned up on a lathe in any workshop, although they may not be as mechanically hard as those manufactured by instrument makers.

Shaft Gauges

Shafts and similar units are generally checked using a caliper gauge. These may be plain, as illustrated in Fig 14.27, with a "Go" - "No-go" step inside the working faces, or can be obtained with small adjustable anvils, which protrude on each side, offering a single tool which can be made to fit a wide range of tolerances. Most of these gauges are manufactured from cast steel, with the working faces hardened in order not to wear too quickly.

After use care is as for similar tools, and in the case of gauges in particular, tools placed away should be examined from time to time, to ensure that they are not rusting.

FEELER GAUGES

An essential tool, both inside and outside the workshop, by which very small gap or clearance measurements can be made. The tool consists of a holder, with approximately 10 blades of hardened steel, each of a different thickness within a particular range; for example, 5 to 60 thousandths of an inch, or similar fractions of a millimetre. Individual blades in the set will give accurate measurementsalone, or, as is common practice, several blades are used at the same time together, to arrive at a greater thickness measurement than any individual

blade can offer. Used to check the running clearances in shafts and bearings; gaps between face plates; gaps in timing devices; igniters; spark-plugs; and many other applications.

Feeler gauges are prone to rusting if not looked after correctly, and each blade, whether it has been used or not, should be wiped dry and oiled after each use of the tool. Individual blades carry an indication of their respective thickness etched into one face, and the holder the overall range and the units used.

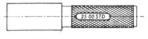

(*a*) Standard plug gauge

(*b*) Limit plug gauge

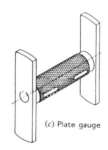

(*c*) Plate gauge

Fig 14.26(a) Plug and plate gauges

Fig 14.26(b) Taper plug gauge

Fig 14.27 Shaft gauge

TAPE MEASURES

Accurate measurements over any distance
underwater are unlikely to be within
less than ± 6mm when using a tape
measure. Nevertheless, they are in
common use, and all divers should be
familiar with their use and some of the
difficulties.

Metal tape measures such as sold
for general handyman use on land, are
not suitable for use underwater, simply
because it is impossible to dry out the
sealed container, and hence they would
quickly rust solid. Where possible,
tapes should be either plastic coated
material, nylon or a special patented
meterial called Feblon, none of which
are affected by immersion, neither do
they stretch under tension. British
tape manufacturers, such as Rathbone,
offer a wide range of tapes suitable
for use by divers, which can be marked
in metric, imperial or a combination
of both, and on one or both faces. There
is usually a choice of red or black
lettering and markings, and of these the
latter should be chosen, since red will
appear as black to the human eye when
deeper than about 16m.

Where possible, a nylon or pvc
reel or holder should be used, and there
are a number of readily adaptable cable
reels on the market for electrical
extension leads. In use, make certain
that the tape is not twisted, since this
will give an inaccurate measurement;
also ensure that you understand whether
your tape measures from the end of the
folding metal ring, or not. The difference could be a matter of some 2cms !
After use, wash the tape and reel in

fresh water, having pulled the tape
out to its full length, then hang
it up to dry.

MISCELLANEOUS TOOLS

SCRIBERS

Any short length of hardened steel
rod, up to about 6mm diameter,
ground to a point at one or both
ends, and used to mark steel or
other metal surfaces, is called a
scriber.

Manufactured scribers are
generally around 150mm long, have
the centre portion knurled, so as
to give a better gripping surface,
and offer one end straight, the other
bent over at right-angles and also
pointed. It is important that the
points are maintained sharp, usually
by an oil stone or fine grinding
wheel, but at the same time does not
lose its hardness, otherwise it may
turn out to be softer than the metal
it is required to mark.

Useful underwater to make a
temporary indication of measurement,
for marking the outline of a cutting
operation, the position of a hole
to be drilled etc.

PUNCHES

These are available in three basic
forms:

1   Centre punches

2   Parallel pin punches

3   Taper pin punches

The centre punch is used where an
accurate location is required to
mark where a hole is to be drilled,
or to outline the shape of something
by a series of "dot" marks. The
tool itself is a round or hexagonal
piece of bar, ground to a taper at
one end, which is then finsihed off
by a sharp point. Since repeated
blows at the opposite end in use
will cause it to "splay", it is

normal practice to give it a shallow
bevel, as with a cold chisel, which
should be reground at frequent intervals.

As with scribed marks made on
metal underwater, due to rusting or
corrosion, these and punch marks soon
become obliterated, and should not be
relied on for more than one or two days
without being remarked.

Parallel pin punches are made from the
same basic stock material, but for
almost half their length, are turned or
ground to a smaller, parallel shaft of
a particular diameter. These are used
to assist in the removal of pins which
often hold fittings to shafts etc. Care
should be exercised in use to ensure
that the size of the pin punch relates
to the actual pin to be removed; also
that the pin may well be tapered, in
which case it can only be driven out
from one direction. Use of the wrong
size punch, or one whose end has
become splayed, can result in the hole
being damaged, or the end of the pin
enlarged to the point whereby it can
only be removed by drilling. Such
punches, when the ends become splayed
or chipped, should have the damaged
portion ground away square to the axis
of the tool, and a slow reduction in
length as a result must be accepted.
Parallel or taper pin punches
are widely used in the servicing of
diving equipment, and on rigid diving
helmets in particular.

Taper pin punches are, as the name
suggests, tools whose shafts are
ground at manufacture to match a
particular taper. Their use is the
same as that for parallel punches,
except that as they are reground, the
diameter of the minimum taper size
increases. All punches are manufactured
from cast steel, which is then hardened and tempered.

HAMMERS

Whilst the hammer is probably taken for
granted, it is still the most commonly
used tool in the workshop, and underwater by divers. There are many
variations of this basic item, and
the ones most likely to be encountered by divers are as follows:

Sledge hammers
Mason's or "clump" hammers
Engineer's ball pein hammers
Claw hammers
Chipping hammers

The difficulty of achieving real
work with a hammer underwater, is
best overcome by employing a mason's
or clump hammer, which offers a
considerable mass of metal on a
short handle. The face of such
hammers are also larger, making it
less likely that the user will miss
the tool and strike his hand. Such
heavy hammers are ideal for use with
a cold chisel, but really too heavy
for centre punching, and certainly
too heavy for pin punching, unless
the pin is 12mm diameter or over.
Sledge hammers are seldom
used underwater, since water resistance prevents full use of the swing
potential of their long handles and
very heavy heads.
Engineers ball-pein hammers
are illustrated in Fig 14.28, and
are generally classified by the
weight of the head itself. This
weight is generally cast into the
metal, underneath the head, for
easy identification. They are hence
known as $\frac{1}{2}$lb, 1lb, 2lb (or $\frac{1}{2}$kg, 1kg
etc). The back face of such hammers
is known as the "pein", and can be
rounded off (ball-pein) or wedge-
shaped (cross or straight pein).

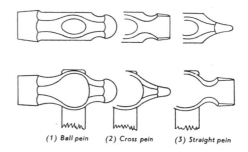

(1) Ball pein   (2) Cross pein   (3) Straight pein

Fig 14.28 Engineer's hammers

As with all hammers, the working faces will eventually "splay", which should be removed by grinding

GRINDING WHEELS

With frequent use, even by a skilled fitter, or misuse by an unskilled person, all tools with a sharp edge will eventually become dull or chipped. Others may become distorted or splayed in appearance. Tools cost a great deal of money, and there is a very considerable capital outlay involved, and to let tools rust, remain blunt, or just lie around in a damaged condition for the sake of maintenance, is a bad working practice.

Blunt tools, left in that condition, may well be taken out on the next job, possibly causing it to take far longer to complete. Damaged tools may be taken without examination, and lead to the cancellation of work, or even a contract, when they are found unusable.

All divers should make a point of learning as quickly as possible the art of regrinding the cutting aspects etc of the various tools of his profession, and in particular drill bits, cold chisels, punches etc. especially where a grindstone can bring a tool back to its original condition.

Grinding wheels, which were originally made from sandstone, are today a composition of carborundum and other materials, pressed into shape and made suitable for mounting on a drive shaft of an electric motor.

Dependent on the physical size of the carborundum particles, a grinding wheel will be designated as coarse; medium; or fine, with many variations in each category. It is now an HSE (Health and Safety Executive) requirement, issued through the Factory Inspectorate, that each workshop with a mechanical grinder has a named person, designated and qualified to change and fit grinding wheels, since there have, in the past, been many unfortunate accidents - some fatal, when this operation was carried out by well-meaning but unskilled persons.

Should a grinding wheel break-up or disintegrate on its shaft whilst at speed, the fragments can easily prove fatal, hence the need for some control.

The use of a grinding wheel is best learnt by practice, but under supervision, the following points being observed:

1   Do not use a grinding wheel on any type of soft material such as brass, copper, aluminium, lead, wood, PVC, nylon, leather etc. To do so will only choke the small gaps between the particles of the wheel, make it unusable for other materials until the wheel has been "re-dressed" by a qualified person. More important though is the overloading of the wheel which will take place as it 'takes on' more material and weight, and is a classic cause of disintegratin.

2   Do not continue to use a grinding wheel in such a condition that permanent grooves become a feature of its surface. In time, these will weaken the strength of the wheel, as well as reduce the potential working surface for other users.

3   Learn the value of lubrication when grinding tools, and that it is possible to grind either with a continuous stream of water flowing over the work, or with no water at all. As tools are ground, so heat is generated, and a flow of water will conduct this away. Grinding without water is acceptable provided it is done gently, and any heat is conducted away through the tool before it overheats and softens.

CHAPTER 15

POWER TOOLS: COMPRESSED AIR AND HYDRAULIC

HYDRAULIC POWER TOOLS

Although few power tools have beenspec-
ifically designed and produced for underwater use, most hydraulic and pneumatic
surface tools can be modified for use in
water.

Comparison tests between pneumatic and
hydraulic tools have indicated that
the hydraulic tools are superior in
many ways, including:-

1 Increased power to weight ratio.

2 Versatility and lower maintenance.
   Since hydraulic tools run on a
   closed system, tool life is longer
   and routine maintenance involves
   only external cleaning and lubrication.

3 Finer control and adjustment in
   terms of R.P.M. and torque.

4 The depth capability of hydraulic
   tools is just about limitless,
   ,whereas, most pneumatic tools
   reach their limit at around 61m.

5 No exhaust bubbles are produced
   to hinder the diver's vision.

6 Hydraulic tools are quieter in
   operation.

PRINCIPLES OF OPERATION

For shallow work the system is very
similar to that used for pneumatic
tools i.e. a pump on the surface supplies pressure to the tool via flexible hoses. There is, however, one
important addition: whereas exhausted
air is allowed to escape back to
atmosphere via the surrounding water,
this is obviously not acceptable when
using oil because of waste and pollution.
Therefore, a closed circuit must be used.

If the system only comprised a pump
and hoses it would be inefficient
because of heat, friction and bubbling in the oil or hydraulic fluid.
To minimise these losses a reservoir
is placed in the system, in it heat
dissipates and bubbling or foaming
takes place rather than in the hoses
or tool.

Friction is more difficult to combat
and is proportional to the length of
the hoses. In shallow depths the
design of the system is such as to
ensure that the pump pressure is
sufficient to overcome it, and still
provide the correct pressure to
operate the tool. However, at depths
where hoses from the surface would be
unmanageable and friction losses
really significant, it is possible to
link the pump (which by its nature is
waterproof) to an electrically driven
submersible motor. Hydraulic hose
lengths can then be kept to a minimum
and the electrical supply provided
either from the surface direct or
via the diving bell.

Fig 15.2

Submersible
hydraulic
power pack

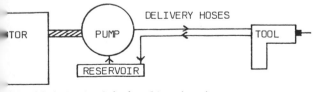

Fig 15.1 Typical hydraulic circuit

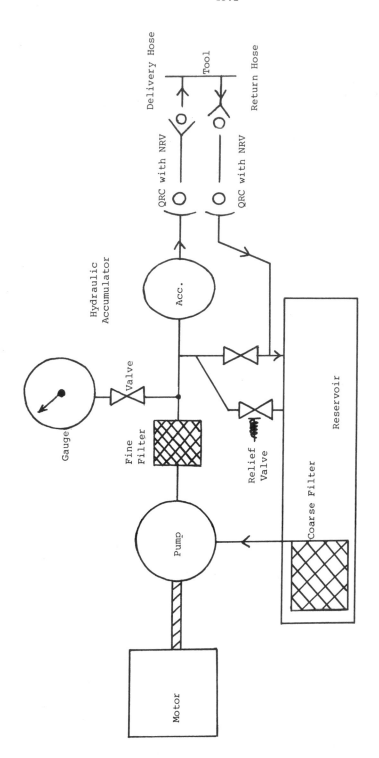

Fig 15.3 Typical hydraulic power-pack circuit

Friction losses can also be reduced somewhat by making the diameter of the return hose greater than that of the supply hose which makes some allowance for expansion of the fluid passing through the tool.

It is important to realise that the hose lengths and pump unit are matched i.e. the pressure supplied by the unit is that required by the tool plus the calculated losses due to the length of the hose. If shorter hoses were fitted then the units relief valve setting would have to be reduced to avoid over pressurising the tool.

OPERATION (Fig 15.3)

Oil is drawn through a coarse filter to the pump and then passed through a fine filter (10 micron) on to a pressure gauge. It then continues through an accumulator (or shock absorber) which is a small high pressure steel cylinder with a built-in flexible neoprene liner. The space between the liner and the cylinder wall is filled with nitrogen and charged to about 100 bars. The high pressure oil fills the bag and compresses the nitrogen, movement of the bag absorbs pulsations in the oil flow, and a relief valve is also included in the circuit to limit the maximum pressure.

After the accumulator is a quick-release coupling (QRC) with a non-return valve (NRV).

Connecting the tool and hoses completes the circuit and the oil returns to the reservoir.

TOOLS

Below is a selection of hydraulic tools available for underwater use.

When using quick release coupling you must ensure that the tool is connected independently to the hoses by a suitable lanyardd.

Impact wrench

Drill

Grinder

Cut-off disc grinder

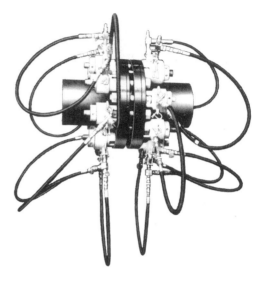

Hydratight bolt tensioner

Hydraulic
pump

Rotary reciprocating hammer drill

Fig 15.4 An assortment of hydraulic
       tools suitable for use
       underwater

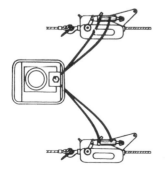

Hydraulic Tirfor

The "Select-a-Torque" side drive wrench

Peanut grinder

MAINTENANCE

TOOLS

The tools themselves require very little maintenance as they are completely sealed and continually lubricated. No stripping down is necessary, and after use servicing consists of washing, lightly oiling, inspection for wear or damage (especially the hoses) and wiping clean before putting away.

HOSES

Periodic inspection for wear and damage is all the hoses themselves require. The quick release couplings should be kept clean, oiled and protected by either connecting the ends together or covering them with polythene bags when not in use.

NOTE: The hoses and tools are always full of oil due to the non-return valves in the quick release couplings.

Marine growth and general descaler

HYDRAULIC UNIT (DIESEL DRIVEN)

A typical engine oil is Rotella TX 10/20, and an hydraulic fluid "Shell Tellus". The latter should remain usable for several years, subject to remaining uncontaminated by particles or water.
taminated (salt water).

The 10 micron filter should be changed once a year.

Friction losses approx:-

0.4   PSI/FT in 3/4 hose (0.9 Bars/m)

1.0   PSI/FT in 5/8 hose (0.226 Bars/m)

1.67 PSI/FT in 1/2 hose (o.375 Bars/m)

STARTING ROUTINE

1 Check oil levels.

2 Check fuel level.

3 Open gauge and bypass valves.

4 Start engine - warm up for 2-3mins.

5 Connect tool and hoses.

6 Close bypass (gauge reads 30/70 bars due to friction in hoses).

Equipment is now ready for use. When tool is operating pressure will rise to approximately 140 bars.

NOTE: When using impact tools close gauge valve except for initial and occasional pressure checks to protect gauge.

STOP ROUTINE

1 Open bypass.

2 Disconnect hoses and tool (only if no longer required).

3 Continue to run engine for 2-3mins if possible at half speed.

4 Stop engine and note running time.

5 Top up fuel and clean down equipment ready for storage.

HYDRAULIC BRUSHING MACHINE

Hydraulic driven rotational brushes are available singly or in 'banks', for the fast and efficient cleaning of marine growth from ships' bottoms or submerged offshore structures.

During operation an adhesive and propulsive effect is created which considerably reduces diver fatigue.

The manufacturers of such units claim that one diver can clean up to 300 sq metres per hour.

The unit illustrated overleaf is actually ridden by the diver during the cleaning operation.

Fig 15.4 "Brush Kart" underwater hull cleaning machine

15.8

PNEUMATIC POWER TOOLS

Since compressed air as a source
of power, is probably the most
readily or practically available on
a dive site, its use for pneumatic
tools is widely accepted. The air
driven "road-drill" is probably the
best known of air tools, and its
use underwater is even more difficult
and uncomfortable for the diver, but
generally, apart from maintenance
problems, the use of air tools is
easier than on the surface.

AIR SUPPLY

Pneumatic tools require a high
volume of air at medium pressure.
This is best supplied by a rotary
vane compressor (positive displacement).Rotary compressors usually only
have one stage in which air is compressed by the action of a rotor in
an eccentric stator.

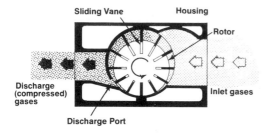

Fig 15.6 The sliding vane rotary
        compressor

The most readily available is a normal
road compressor such as the type you
may find on a building site. These
are normallly diesel driven, delivering
between 120 and 600cfm at approximately
100 psi depending on the size of machine.

These compressors, since all types are
suitable, are normally referred
to by the number of tools they are
capable of supplying i.e. a two tool,

four tool, etc.

The air is delivered via a flexible
rubber hose which is available
in varying lengths.s.

HOSES

These are of rubber construction
and have an external diameter of
48mm. They are available in 3,7
and 15m lengths. The end fittings
are known as "Chicago
couplings" these being of the push
together and 1/4 turn type. These
merely push into the hose and the
hose clamps around it. In the
coupling is a soft rubber washer
which effects the seal. A screw
fitting is also available; therefore
it is important when ordering your
air compressor that the machine
and the tools are compatible; if not,
modifications must be made to enable
operation.

TOOLS

The range of tools is wide and varied
but whatever the individual characteristics of the tool, all fall into
one of four basic categories:-

1 Rotary tools

2 Reciprocating tools

3 Rotary-reciprocating

4 Others i.e. air lifts and lifting
   bags

1 Rotary Tools

The title describes all tools where
the action is simply rotational, i.e.
augers, drills, saws, impact wrenches
nut runners, abrasive and grinding
machines.

The air forced into the body of the

tool passes over a series of vanes, the shaft of which in turn passes through a gear box, to drive the tool attachment. The used air is then passes to the exhaust ports.

2 Reciprocating Tools

These are tools where the action is punching i.e. needle guns, rock breakers and chisels.

The punching action is achieved by air entering a barrel and driving down a piston. The piston drives and vibrates the attachment. As the piston moves down it passes an exhaust port allowing the piston to rise back up the barrel and the next stroke commences.

The tools in this category are generally quite large and heavy and require considerable effort if used underwater.

3 Rotary-Reciprocating

This type of tool combines both of the following principles and is used primarily for boring into rock or masonryy where neither a rotary or reciprocating action alone is enough. It allows a combination of both drilling and hammering at the same time. Examples of these principles are found in all hammer drills.

When air enters the tool both actions are completed in one stroke.e stroke. This comes about by air passing over a rotational ratchet which starts the drilling action. The air passes on to the piston hammer (Fig 15.7) which is splined and rotates as it slides down through the driving block. As each cycle is completed the piston hammer returns to the top of the chamber and the next cycle begins.

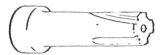

Fig 15.7 Piston hammer of a rotary
reciprocating pneumatic tool

The drill bit on a hammer drill normally has a hardened steel tip. The bits come in various sizes up to a maximum of 32mm. The drill shaft is also variable in length up to approximately 1.8m. Through the drill shaft and bit is an airhole to remove swarf from the hole during drilling and a lever to direct the flow of air into the borehole to clear it out called a "Pawl shifter". When this is operated the air supply completely by-passes the operating mechanism for as long as the lever is held in this position. Examples of pneumatic tools using the three principles mentioned are as follows:

Impact wrench

Diver using a pneumatic drilling machine
to work a hull-cleaning brush

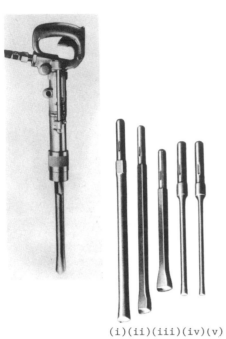

(i)(ii)(iii)(iv)(v)

Light utility hammer drills

Chipping hammer

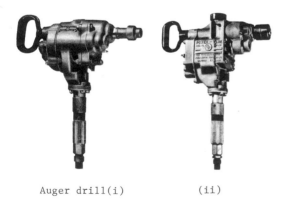

Auger drill(i)   (ii)

Needle gun

Angle or cut-off disc grinder

Underwater ship's hull cleaning brush

Fig 15.8 Pneumatic tools

METHODS OF CONTROLLING THE TOOL

Basically there are two methods for turning the tool "on" and "off" underwater.

The first and obvious one is to have a quarter turn valve at the inlet to the tool and so stop or control the air on entry.

The main disadvantage of this is that when you turn the air off the air left inside the tool will escape via the exhaust to the surface. With the subsequent absence of air pressure inside the tool, water will enter the chamber and so expose the working surfaces to corrosion. This can also cause an hydraulic lock when the tool is turned on again because the air is unable to force the water out of the tool.

If we remove or permanently open the inlet valve to the tool, and place a quarter turn control valve on the exhaust side, we can effectively stop the flow of air through the tool. In this way air is present ay in the tool at all times, provided the supply from the surface is maintained.

EXHAUST

When an air tool is submerged, as with the diver, it is subjected to ambient water pressure. The exhaust on a normal pneumatic tool is open to the water and is subject to this pressure. Therefore, as depth increases the efficiency of the tool will decrease.

If, however, a return hose is connected to the exhaust running towards or even all the way to the surface, the pressure to which the exhaust is to be dumped is being reduced, thus reducing the back pressure and so reducing the loss of efficiency. Also, the absence of exhaust bubbles at the diver will help to reduce the noise level and improve communications and comfort.

LUBRICATION

Because the tools are used underwater they will need regular if not continuous lubrication. There are several methods of introducing this lubrication.

A From the Compressor
Some compressors have a facility
for oiling the air before it
leaves the pump. This is in the
form of an oil-filled gauze pad
over which the air flows. Ensure
the pad remains lubricated at all
times during operation.

B In-Line Oiler
A length of air line is available
with a built-in gauze pad filter.
This is attached to the machine
and the additional lengths of
hose to reach the tool. Again, ed
care should be taken to ensuretaken
the pad remains lubricated.   i-
cated.

C Operation of Tool with no Automatic Oiler
Using this method it is necessary
to remove the tool from the water
during each oiling operation.
Having removed the tool from the
water, turn off the air supply
and disconnect the air hose
coupling next to the compressor.
Pour about 280ml of waste oil
or diesel down the hose toward the
tool. Reconnect the air hose and
turn on the air supply. Remember
to run the tool on the surface
for 10 or 20 seconds before
lowering it to the diver. This
ensures that the oil or diesel
has not caused a hydraulic lock.
This operation should be carried
out at least once every 45 minutes
that the tool is in use underwater.
The operation must also be carried
out at the end of each day.

Starting Procedure

Check all levels i.e.:

- Fuel, water, oil, battery

- Open drain valves (power take offs)

- Turn valve to "compressor off load"

- Push in/out cold start (when
  required)

- Start engine

  Allow engine to run off load for
  2-3 mins and close outlets before
  turning compressor to on load.

D Others
This section covers air tools for
underwater use which do not fall
into the categories previously
described, e.g. air lifts, lifting bags
and pneumatic suction pads.

AIR LIFT

An air lift is a simple but efficient
underwater tool for the removal of mud
and silt etc, mainly used for the
excavation of small areas where the use
of a dredger would be prohibitive. A
diver using this tool can move several
cubic yards of seabed per hour.

It is basically an underwater vacuum
cleaner. Compressed air at approximately 100 PSI is introduced low down
in a length of pipe of normally
between 100 and 400mm diameter (see
Fig 15.9).

The air supply is important with regard
to the volume of air supplied to the
air lift; the larger the volume of
air required to run it, i.e. a 100mm
diameter air lift will run efficiently
using a 250cfm road compressor, but a
250-300mm may require as much as 600
cfm but will of course, move a far
greater quantity of debris per hour.

The air having been introduced into
the pipe via a quarter turn valve,
immediately rises towards the surface,
the decrease in pressure causing
expansion of the bubbles within the

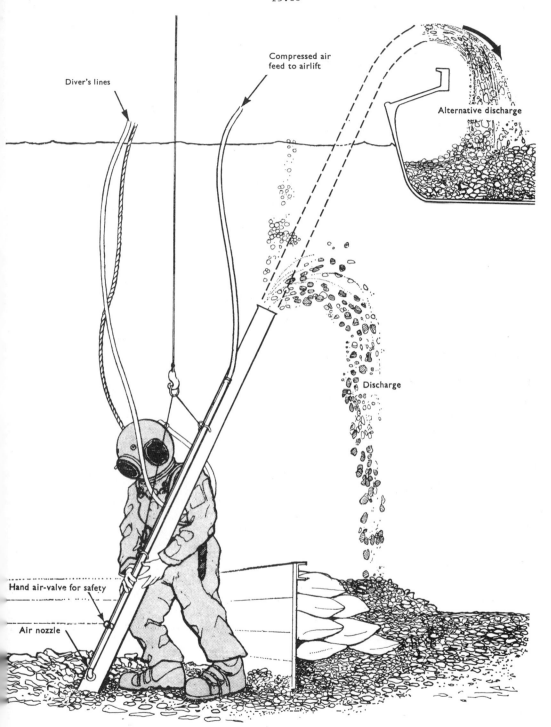

Diver's lines

Compressed air
feed to airlift

Alternative discharge

Discharge

Hand air-valve for safety

Air nozzle

Fig 15.9 Operation of an air lift underwater in foundation construction work

pipe. This increasing expansion causes a partial vacuum in the pipe which in turn causes a sucking action at the bottom of the pipe. As long as the air is contained in the pipe and continues to rise and expand, it will continue to draw up the soft seabed over which it is directed. Because of the suction effect created it is normally necessary to weight the lift to prevent it from rising off the seabed. Also, should debris become blocked in the end of the pipe the lift will attempt to rise quickly to the surface. Therefore, the operator should keep hold of the air control valve at all times.

A flexible hose connected to the air lift will ensure that the spoil is either directed away from the diver or into a surface skip.

LIFTING BAG

The use of buoyancy for lifting and salvage underwater is a simple principle which has become a major underwater tool. Lifting bags are used to support small items such as impact wrenches,to lifting 20,000 ton North Sea Oil platforms. Any container which can be inverted and filled with air can be used to lift objects underwater including oil drums, diesel and petrol cans and upturned work bags, provided they will hold air. However, the most efficient method is with a properly manufactured lifting bag. They are available in a number of different sizes which are normally indicated by the weight they will safely lift, e.g. 50kg, 1000kg 3000kg etc. These bags are provide with 'dump' valves which can be operated either by a lanyard or a valve on the top of the bag. Some are open at the bottom and others are totally enclosed, depending on their application.

The enclosed bags are fitted with relief valves to prevent explosion on ascent.

Fig 15.10 Small lifting bag - note the diver operated dump valve

Lifting bags are also provided with webbing straps with which to attach them to the object being lifted, in order to spread the loading and ensure a balanced lift.

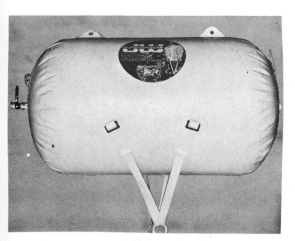

Fig 15.11 Totally enclosed lifting bag.

PRINCIPLES OF BUOYANCY APPLIED TO

LIFTING UNDERWATER

Since 1 litre of fresh water weighs 1kg,
then displace that amount of water with
air, and 1kg of buoyancy will be achieved:

density of fresh water = 1000kg M^3

density of seawater = 1030kg M^3

Therefore, in order to obtain 1kg of lift
in seawater, it is necessary to displace
rather less than 1 litre of water, i.e.
0.97 litres.

Example:

Question.
How much free air is required to lift
an object weighing 500kg from the
seabed in 40m, using lifting bags ?

Absolute pressure at 40m = 5 bars
Density of seawater = 1030kg M^3

$\therefore$ 0.97 litres of air provides 1kg
of lift in seawater

0.97 x 5 absolute pressure = 4.85lts
of free air which will provide 1kg
of lift at 40m

$\therefore$ 4.85 x 500 = 2425 litres

Answer - 2.425 litres of free air

LIFTING

When selecting lifting bags to carry
out a specific job the following
points should be borne in mind.

1 When carrying out lifts from the
   seabed to the surface always use
   the correct size bag. If a bag is
   only partially inflated on the
   seabed when the object being lifted
   gains positive buoyancy, the air
   in the bag will expand during ascent
   increasing buoyancy as it accelerates
   to the surface out of control.

   The use of the correct size bag or
   a number of small ones will eliminate this problem. As the full
   bag ascends the excess air will be
   vented out around the skirt, or in
   the case of an enclosed bag, out of
   the relief valve, not increasing
   the buoyancy.

2 Always bear in mind when lifting an
   object like a boat etc, which has
   considerable volume, that the distribution of weight within it will be
   uneven and try to support the
   heaviest area with a large number of
   the bags.

3 Again if you are lifting a craft
which you hope to bail or pump
out once it has been recovered
to the surface, remember to
place the bags as far below the
gunwales of the vessel as possible,
in order to lift it as far out of
the water as possible.

Fig 15.12 Lifting a fishing vessel by
means of lifting bags
Marine)

4 As diver's never "ride" the lift,
they must remain clear. If using
surface-demand, or wearing a lifeline, ensure that there is no
possibility of fouling. If it is
necessary for diver's to be in
the water during the lift, limit
the number where possible to one
person only.

5 Always be aware of the position
of surface support craft during
lifting operations. Several
embarrassing incidents have
occurred when lifting bags have
broken loose, or the lift has
left bottom prematurely, upturn-
ing or damaging vessels above.

TESTING

From the calculation previously
discussed it will be seen that it is
possible to test a lifting bag by

filling it with its rated lifting
capacity equivalent in water. During
this operation it should be suspended
by its lines and should not break
or leak in any way.

WATER POWERED CLEANING TOOLS

LIMPET SUCTION PADS

These are water energised suction pads
with a wide range of uses as attachments to underwater structures. They
may be used as an individual holding
device for divers and equipment on
any regular or flat surface.

Fig 15.13 "Windak" underwater limpet

Limpets are currently used on a wide
range of manned and unmanned submersibles and for underwater inspection
work, especially where concrete
structures are involved.

SPECIFICATION

Description - a two-piece suction
device with replaceable pads.
Pads - Three-fond, composed of open
cell rubber sponge, 310mm diameter.
Power supply - water, 1.2 bars over
ambient at 9 litres/minute. Water is

supplied by hose or submersible pump
Holding surface - flat and rough
surfaces.
Holding power - 300kg. Pads are fitted
with a lever to release the suction.
Operation is possible at any depth.

H.P. Water jets

The principle of using high pressure
water jets (3,000 to 15,000 PSI) for
cleaning has been used on the surface
for many years. However, their
adaption for underwater use is a
fairly recent development.

Diver held high pressure water jets
with balancing retrojets are being
used extensively for the removal
of general marine fouling, and for
the intensive bright metal cleaning
of offshore structures for detailed
inspection. They can also be used
for cutting concrete.

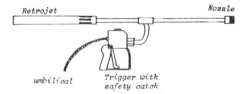

Fig 15.14 H.P. water nozzle with retrojet
       suitable for underwater use

Conventional means of cleaning such as
brushing, scraping, chipping and needle
guns will remove the coating of weed,
barnacles etc, but will remove paint
coatings and may close up the cracks
which are being investigated.

A diver is virtually a free floating
mass, and the jetting lance has to
be designed to counteract the jet
reaction. This is simply achieved
by jetting a reverse jet the same
size as the working jet, simultaneously.

It has been found that by injecting
the retrojet inside a perforated
tube, water sucked in through the
perforations gives sufficient turb-
ulance and diffusion at the exit point,
to almost nullify the otherwise lethal
exhaust stream. Several serious injuries
have been caused by the retrojet. Great
care must be exercised in the use of HP
jetting equipment, for which there is
now a Code of Practice.
The performance of the gun is sensitive
to equipment design and operating
parameters. The efficiency of hand
held units depends on several factors,
including stand-off, nozzle design and
impingement angle. Productivity is
diminished by -

- 50% loss of power, due to
  the retrojet

- Diver fatigue

- Umbilical entanglement, drag and
  rigidity when operating

- Diver awareness of physical injury
  that can be incurred

In poor visibility conditions a tubular
cage is used for the appropriate stand-
off distance for a particular job, so
that the diver knows when the end of
the cage is touching the structure and
that he is at the correct distance to
commence jetting.

Fan jets giving a 40° angle with a
50-75mm stand-off are most effective
for surface cleaning sweeping a band of
50-75mm at a time. Average times on
complex shapes are difficult to
quantify, except to say that they are
six to eight times faster than other
methods.

The reversing jet, while carrying out
an essential task does use half the
horse power, being developed at the
pump. With pump pressures now exceeding 15000 psi, pumps have become

very large, at least 120Kw.

There is a considerable pressure drop through the delivery hoses and a balance has to be drawn between the size of hose that can be easily handled by a diver in weight and stiffness and the pressure loss that is suffered. The compromise size is normally 12mm bore.

Pressures over 450 PSI can damage a man's skin and pressures of at least 3,000psi are required to remove the lightest of marine growth. Although some jets will remove worm casts and protective coatings, in order to remove hard materials in a single pass the operating pressure has to be raised to beyond present levels (approx 20,000 PSI) or, alternatively an abrasive can be entrained into the jet stream. However, some companies are concerned that grit will damage the steel's surface if an inexperienced operator is using the gun.

SAFETY CONSIDERATIONS

The use of HP water is inherently a dangerous operation. The situation is made worse because of the effect of the associated turbulence and noise on the vision and communication of the diver. Future increases in operation pressures or the addition of abrasives will aggravate the situation.

Adequate training and appreciation of the hazards are, therefore, very necessary.

OPERATIONAL HAZARDS

1 Diver must take care not to operate water jets in the splash zone where it is possible to get the retrojet in air and the main jet in water.

2 Jetting guns are activated by a trigger mechanism. Holding the trigger for long periods of time rapidly causes hand fatigue, so there is a temptation to 'modify' the system to relieve this. One serious accident occurred recently when a diver working in the splash zone tied back the trigger in the 'on' position to relieve his fatigue. The diver lost his hold on the gun and it turned on him.

L.P. WATER JETS

Low pressure water jets are used underwater for trench excavation and for clearing areas of light silt. They have a distinct advantage over pneumatic air lifts, in that they can cut into compacted mud or seabed forming a trench for laying pipe or cable. The loosened soil may then be removed by air lift if required.

Low pressure water jets operate on the same principle as a fireman's hose, except that the pressure of water leaving the

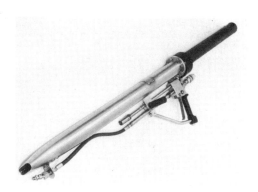

Fig 15.15 H.P. water jet

nozzle underwater is quickly absorbed; therefore, its effective range is limited. They are available in different sizes and pressures, dependent on the pump specification. The larger the volume and the higher the pressure of water passing through the nozzle, the greater the back pressure that will be produced. This can cause problems for the diver; therefore, as with the HP water jet a retro must be fitted to balance the jet. Unlike the HP water jet retro which is taken over the diver's shoulder,

the LP retro is normally a number of balancing jets in the nozzle itself which counterbalance it. Combination jets are available which use both water and air combined to give greater efficiency, when working in heavy clay etc, the air helping to aerate and loosen the material more easily.

The pumps are rated by the size of hoses and the number of gallons per minute they will pump. A typical example is a "Spate" pump, which will lift water from approximately 3m, but requires priming when commencing operations. Aletrnatively, water may be provided by a dock or ship's fire ringmain.

Fig 15.16 "Spate" 100mm induced flow pump

CHAPTER 16

UNDERWATER CUTTING AND WELDING

There are at least ten general techniques in current use for cutting underwater. Choosing the most suitable technique for a job, whether it be construction, maintenance or demolition, is more a consideration of operating conditions and the quality of the cut required, than anything else, although cost is a very relavent factor. Similarly, with welding underwater, there are two basic methods, known as "wet" and "dry" welding, both of which have their respective merits.

This chapter will deal only with the three basic cutting methods employed underwater, namely gas cutting, oxy-arc and thermic cable, which are the skills normally practised during diver training. The principles, methods of operation and safety precautions of underwater electric arc "wet" welding are also covered, with some reference to habitat or "dry" welding, but it is stressed that it takes years of practice to become proficient in this skill.

UNDERWATER CUTTING

GAS TORCH CUTTING

The basic principle of cutting metal underwater by means of a gas torch, is essentially the same as that employed on the surface, except that the equipment has to be modified, and hydrogen gas substituted for acetylene as the "fuel". Oxy-acetylene can be used underwater, but only at very shallow depths, ie. a maximum of 7m, since acetylene cannot be compressed to overcome the water pressure deeper than 7m. Instability of an acetylene flame underwater is a further disadvantage, whereas oxy-hydrogen cutting equipment can be used down to 37m.

OXY-HYDROGEN CUTTING

With this method, a special torch allows a mixture of oxygen (O_2) and hydrogen (H) to burn, generating sufficient heat to melt the material to be cut. This flame is directed at the metal until a small molten puddle is obtained known as the "hot-spot", after which the diver causes a jet of pure oxygen to be directed into the puddle, causing the metal to oxidise or burn. The pressure of oxygen in this jet is then sufficient for the oxidised metal to be blown out of the cut, sometimes known as the "kerf", after which it falls to the bottom as globules.

If the diver now moves the head of the torch, at a slow uniform rate in the direction of the desired cut, the continuous process of heating, oxidisation and blowing away of metal, will achieve the desired result. In most cases, divers under training will have some difficulty in obtaining a "hot-spot" or else maintaining a uniform cut without "bridging", but this is only a matter of practice and experience.

Although underwater gas torch cutting is seldom used in the offshore Industries, the equipment has many advantages over other methods, particularly regarding portability and the very neat, clean cut obtained.

The cutting torch most commonly used in this country is the Kirkham Sea Vixen Mk 2, which was designed specially for underwater use, and requires only a two-hose supply of oxygen and hydrogen, with a single core electrical cable as an addition, if the torch is required to be lit underwater. This torch originated as the Kirkham Seafire, designed in 1945, which has been in use by the Ministry of Defence almost to the present day. Technical changes modified the original design, after which it became known as the Vixen Mk 1 and Mk 2, the latter sometimes being known as the Vixen Salvage torch, simply because it was capable of cutting steel up to 150mm thick. The Sea Vixen Mk 2 is designed to have a maximum cutting capability of 100mm(4in), but will in fact cut metal much thicker.

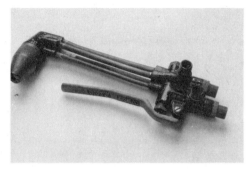

Fig 16.1 Sea Vixen Mk 2 oxygen-hydrogen underwater cutting torch

Setting up procedure

To avoid blockages due to grit or small particles entering the torch jets, it is important that the complete system is flushed through with high-pressure gas before connection. The following is the standard procedure:

1 Clear the cylinder connections of any foreign matter by briefly opening and closing the valves of both the oxygen and hydrogen cylinders, known as "cracking" the cylinders.

2 Fit the oxygen (O^2) regulator; this is usually colour coded black, and the hose connections will be right-handed.

3 Connect the blue or black hose, with right-handed threads, to the regulator, and open the cylider valve. Adjust the regulator control to flush gas through the system, then return control to the point where the gas flow ceases.

4 Fit the hydrogen (H) regulator; this is usually colour coded red, and the hose connections will be left-handed.

5 Connect the red hose, with left-hand

threads to the regulator, and carry out the flushing operation detailed in (3) as for the oxygen.

6 Fit a 'blow-back' preventer non-return valve at the torch end of each hose.

7 Connect the blue/black and red hoses to their appropriate fittings on the torch, and then tighten all connections with a spanner.

8 Close the torch valves; open the regulator controls, increasing the pressure reading on both regulator output gauges to the maximum anticipated working pressures and check for leaks. The torch can be submerged in a bucket of water, or lowered over the side of the craft as convenient for this operation.

9 Fit the striker plate and connect the leads to the torch frame, and the battery.

The torch is now ready to be lit.

Ignition procedure

Turning 'ON':

a. First turn on the oxygen (O^2), black regulator, to give a suitable gas pressure for shallow cutting.

b. Next turn on the hydrogen (H), red regulator, to give a suitable gas pressure for shallow cutting.

c. Turn on the oxygen knob (black) of the torch - 2 full turns

d. Turn on the hydrogen knob(red) on the torch - a $\frac{1}{2}$ to 1 turn

e. Light the torch

Turning 'OFF':

a. Turn off the hydrogen (red) knob, on the torch

b. Turn off the oxygen (black) knob, on the torch

c. Turn the two regulator controls

"off", hence cutting off the gas supply

It is important to note that hydrogen is a highly inflammable gas and as such very dangerous, and must be turned on AFTER the oxygen, and off BEFORE the oxygen.

STRIKER PLATE

The purpose of the striker plate is to enable the diver to light the torch underwater. This is of considerable advantage, since it allows the operator to light or extinguish the torch at will as work progresses, and be a considerable saving on gas consumption. The alternative is to light the torch on the surface each time, and either lower it to the diver, who may not easily locate it in bad visibility, or for the diver to return to the surface and collect the torch.

The striker plate consists of a serrated brass plate casting, connected through a water-tight lever switch, to the positive (+) terminal of a 12v DC source on deck. The negative terminal is connected to the body of the torch itself.

To light the torch underwater, the diver opens up his torch gas valves the correct number of turns, and in the correct sequence. He then closes the striker plate swith with one hand, whilst drawing the cutting nozzle of the torch itself across the serrated plate with the other. As the negative polarity torch rubs across the positive plate, the voltage will allow current to flow, and violent sparking will result in the gas being ignited.

The diver must remember to push the torch away from his body across the plate, in order to protect his diving suit from the somewhat violent ignition which will result. It is also advisable that the diver should wear gloves, to prevent any accidental burning of the skin. As soon as the torch has been lit, the diver can release the striker plate switch, which should isolate the positive (+) 12v connection from the plate.

In practice, the striker plate

switch and electrical connections require frequent servicing, to renew seals, remove corrosion etc, otherwise the switch will short out due to water ingress and the plate will remain at 12v positive potential for the duration of the dive. This will cause a permanent short-circuit, with the result that the voltage source, assuming it to be battery, will quickly drain to zero volts as the current flows from the torch, through the water, to the plate.

Transfer of a Lit Torch

If a striker plate is not being used, or it has become unserviceable, then the torch must be surface lit and passed to the diver within a maximum of 5 seconds, otherwise the copper shield will be burnt due to the excessive heat without cooling.

For testing or demonstration purposes, provided the outer gas shield is unscrewed and removed, then the torch can be surface lit and allowed to burn for as long as is necessary, even being used to carry out cutting work. However, once the shield is fitted, it must immediately be immersed in water.

Transfer of an Unlit Torch

If a striker plate is being used, it is essential that no water is allowed to enter the torch body before it is lit.

Before the torch is allowed to enter the water, the diver must be instructed that the surface have opened the torch oxygen valve about half a turn. This should be sufficient to allow a steady escape of gas from the torch nozzle. If, due to depth, the flow of oxygen is obviously insufficient, then the attendant must increase the flow by valve adjustment.

This trickle of gas should continue until the torch is lit, and should the diver extinguish the flame underwater, he must leave sufficient flow of oxygen to prevent water from entering the torch chambers or hose.

Cutting Nozzles

The copper alloy cutting nozzles used with the Sea Vixen torch, are precision made, complex and costly units, consisting of a series of concentric cylinders, each with accurately drill gas metering holes at both ends. For this reason, they demand careful attention, and a nozzle should never be used with which to hammer or knock an obstacle, and the nozzle jets will require frequent cleaning with special wire 'prickers'.

Nozzles are available in 4 grades, and the size (1 - 4) will be stamped on the side.

No 1 For mild-steel plate up to 19mm(3/4in) thick

No 2 For plate up to 38mm(1½in) thick

No 3 For plate from 38 to 51mm (1½ to 2in) thick

No 4 For plate from 51 to 102mm(2 to 4in) thick

Cutting Procedure

Fig 16-2 is a Table of Pressures indicating the pressure of both hydrogen and oxygen required with regard to both depth, and the size of nozzle fitted to the torch. For example, if a No 4 nozzle were fitted, the left hand arrow shows that this will cut metal from 2 to 4in thick. If the diver anticipates cutting 3in metal, then the gas pressures required would be 35lb per sq ins, to which must be added the depth allowance of an additional 11b of gas pressure for every 2ft of water depth. If in this case, the diver was working at a depth of 60ft(18m), then the depth allowance would be an extra 30psi, so that 30 + 35 = 65psi gas pressure necessary of both oxygen and hydrogen.

The diver, having lit the torch, or having it passed down in a lit condition, places the cutting shield in contact with the metal at the point where cutting is to commence, which can be an edge, or the middle of a piece of plate. There is no necessity to put any pressure on the head, but merely to hold the "tubular" section of the torch in one hand, and the base and cutting lever with the other.

Before cutting can commence, the metal must be pre-heated to the point whereby combustion can start. This should only take some 2-3 secs, after which white oxide sparks should be evident below the shield. As soon as these are seen, the diver should gently depress the cutting lever, and at the same time, commence to draw the torch at a slow, steady and uniform pace across the work in the required direction. If the torch is moved too fast, the cut will be broken and result in gaps, which are difficult to remove. If the cutting speed is too slow, this will only result in a wastage of gas.

The speed of cutting will vary accordingly with the thickness of the steel being cut. Material up to 1in thick can safely be cut at a rate of about 1in per 5 seconds, but only after some practice.

As penetration is achieved, so the sparking and volume of gas bubbles will reduce, since they will now be passing down and out through the cut. If during use, the flame and bubbles increase, and a loud "banging" noise is heard when not actually cutting, this is an indication that the torch is alight inside itself, and the hydrogen valve should immediately be closed, which will extinguish the flame. If this situation arose in cutting equipment not fitted with "blow-back" preventers, it is possible for the flame to travel back up the hose to the surface, and possibly cause a major explosion.

After Use Maintenance

Following use, the torch should be washed off in fresh water, warm if available, Before being disconnected, oxygen should be flushed through the system, after which the torch is removed and dried.

The shield should then be unscrewed, the nozzle removed by unscrewing its locking ring, and all three components wire brushed with great care. Any obstructions in the nozzle holes should be removed only with the correct size pricker tool. The torch should then be re-assembled, but with the various components removed left only finger tight.

Accessories

For safe and efficient cutting underwater, the following additional equipment should be considered:

A pair of gloves, and of choice those with a gauntlet 'sleeve' which offer some protection to the wrist seals of suits

Diving helmet or full-face mask

Diver communication

Staging or similar platform on which the diver can stand or sit to work

Underwater lighting, where possible

Safety Precautions

No oil or grease should be use on the regulators, hose fittings, cylinders or cutting torch

Surface attendant to monitor gas pressures and consumption

Beware of a build up of hydrogen gas in 'pockets' in a confined space

Follow the recommended procedure for turning a torch "ON" and "OFF"

Fault Table for Sea Vixen Operation

Torch will not light:

Insufficient electrical supply voltage; poor electrical connections; blocked jets in the cutting nozzle; leaks in the hose connections.

Torch lights, but diver unable to obtain a "hot-spot":

Incorrect technique; wrong supply pressures; jets blocked; wrong nozzle; diver holding cutting lever depressed before a "hot-spot" can be achieved.

Hot-spot achieved, but torch will not cut:

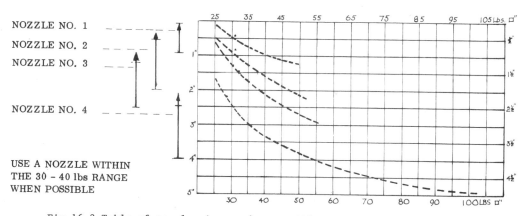

KIRKHAM
VIXEN Mk2. TABLE OF PRESSURES

Table of Surface Pressures to cut steel up to a recommended thickness of 1″. Add 1 lb pressure for each 2′ depth of water.

NOZZLE NO. 1
NOZZLE NO. 2
NOZZLE NO. 3
NOZZLE NO. 4

USE A NOZZLE WITHIN THE 30 - 40 lbs RANGE WHEN POSSIBLE

Fig 16-2 Table of nozzle sizes and gus cutting pressures

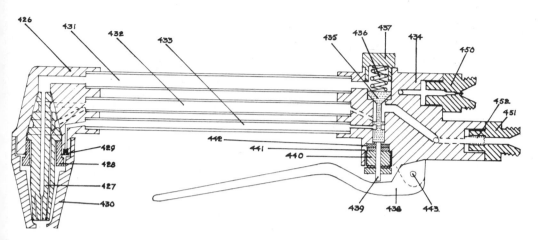

Fig 16-3 Cross section of a Sea Vixen torch, with part numbers

Manufacturers Part Numbers

50425	Vixen torch complete	429	Shield feed restricter screw
426	Head casting	430	Shield nozzle
427	Nozzle	431	Oxygen cutting supply pipe
428	Nozzle retaining nut	432	Heating oxygen or hydrogen pipe

(Part Numbers continued on page 16.7)

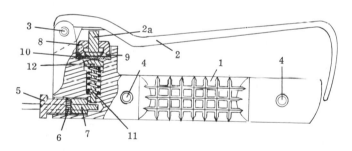

Fig 16-4 Sea Vixen torch electrical striker plate

Manufacturers Part Numbers

02962500	Striker plate complete	506	Cable gland
501	Striker plate body	507	Insulated contact
502	Switch lever	508	Cap nut guide
502a	Switch lever plunger	509	Diaphragm washer
503	Switch lever screw	510	Diaphragm
504	Clip screw	511	Switch contact spring
504a	Clip (not shown above)	512	Switch contact
505	Cable gland nut		

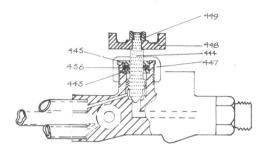

435   Oxygen chamber valve
436   Oxygen chamber valve spring
437   Spring cap nut
438   Cutting lever
439   Cutting lever plunger
440   Cutting gland nut
441   Cutting plunger gland
442   Cutting plunger washer
443   Cutting lever screw
444   Supply valve (oxygen or hydrogen)
445   Supply valve washer
446   Supply valve gland
447   Supply valve gland nut
448   Supply valve control wheel
449   Control wheel nut
450   Hydrogen inlet nipple
451   Oxygen inlet nipple
452   Oxygen filter

Fig 16-5 Sea Vixen valve assembly

Manufacturers Part Numbers (cont'd):

433   Shield supply pipe
434   Body casting

Metal unsuitable for cutting using a Sea Vixen torch; incorrect gas pressures; blocked centre jet; shield jet blocked; incorrect technique.

Torch stops cutting:

Tilting the torch on work; rough surface causes loss of hot-spot; falling gas supply pressures; lever not depressed; general blockage; nozzle burnt out.

When fully serviceable, the torch is very reliable, but any of the faults listed can usually readily be eliminated.

General Notes on Operation

The actual amount of gas being passed by the torch is controlled by the surface regulators, not the control valves on the torch itself. The torch valves are fitted only to allow gas metered by other means to reach the nozzle, and to shut off the flame.

Do not depress the cutting lever until pre-heating has been achieved, otherwise the additional flow of oxygen will only serve to cool the area.

The pressure readings on the surface will fall slightly when actually cutting, due to the additional gas consumption. This fall should not be corrected.

It is impossible to cut heavily rusted plate, or that covered with barnacles or other marine growth. In such cases, pre-cleaning must be undertaken.

Non-ferrous metals and stainless steel cannot be cut with a Sea Vixen torch.

If the cut is "lost", move over to one side of the original line, as close as possible, and start again.

OXY-ARC CUTTING

For most underwater cutting tasks, oxy-arc is more cost effective than gas-torch cutting, for the following reasons:

1   Less skill is required on the part of the diver, to achieve the same results.

2   Although more oxygen will be

consumed, this will not cost as much as the hydrogen content of gas cutting.

3 Greater thicknesses can be cut for the same effort.

4 Oxy-arc does not require the same degree of surface cleanliness as does gas cutting.

There are, however, disadvantages, as follows:

1 A considerable bank of oxygen cylinders will be necessary for prolonged tasks, or even the provision of a bulk oxygen supply.

2 The high amperage necessary, which must be "direct current" and not "alternating current" which can generally only be produced by a diesel driven generator, hence the power source is bulky and heavy.

3 The quality of the cut obtained is such that grinding may be necessary, if the remaining surface is to be flat. In gas cutting, by comparison, a very clean surface would remain.

The principle of the oxy-arc underwater cutting process is the utilisation of the intense heat created by an electric arc between the work, and a hollow steel or carbon electrode passing a current in the order of 200 amps, whilst at the same time, the arc is supplied with an oxygen flow.

The oxygen is supplied to a specially designed and fully insulated torch holder, and allowed to flow through a hollow electrode to emerge at its tip. Once an arc has been struck between the work and the tip of the electrode, the diver opens the oxygen control valve, by means of a lever, and the resultant flow of high pressure gas causes the base metal to oxidise, which is then blown clear of the cut. Since no pre-heating is required, the cutting process is instanteneous.

The heating energy available in

an arc is much greater than that of any gas generated flame, hence it is possible for the oxy-arc torch to cut non-ferrous materials.

Control of the Oxygen Supply

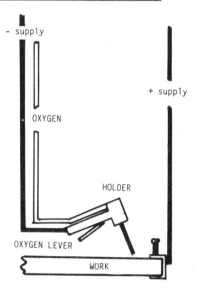

Fig 16-6 Manual oxygen control

With manual oxygen control, the necessary gas pressure is set up under "flow conditions", ie. with the torch cutting lever fully operated. For the duration of the task, the diver then has full manual control, and has only to press or release the cutting lever to start, or stop work.

An alternative method of oxygen control is illustrated in Fig 16-7, solenoid valve control of the cutting gas. Although possibly less economical that manual control, this method has the advantage of being almost trouble free.

With solenoid oxygen control, the cutting torch has no control lever, and relies purely on the current flow created by the arc, to energise a solenoid valve, which in turn opens, and allows gas to flow.

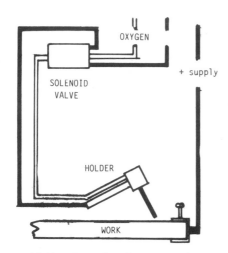

Fig 16-7 Solenoid valve control

As soon as the diver ceases work, with no current flowing, the solenoid valve de-energises, and the oxygen flow is cut-off. This method allows the diver greater concentration on the job, but otherwise its advantages are minimal.

Fig 16-8 Arc-Air underwater manual, oxy-arc cutting torch

Power Supply

It has already been mentioned that the power sourse must be DC (direct current),

and a diesel driven machine producing 80v, 300 to 400amperes is ideal. Such generators are bulky and not readily available on a hire contract basis, other than from specialist suppliers. On no account should an AC (alternating current) generator be considered, or even tried as an experiment, since the diver will experience severe electric shocks which could well prove fatal.

An oxy-arc cutting torch will operate as low as 150amps, but as the current falls, so the cut will become rough, and more difficult to maintain, and the higher current levels are recommended.

Polarity Switch

With oxy-arc cutting, the work is almost always maintained as the positive (+) electrode, and the actual cutting electrode/torch as the negative (-). A polarity switch which is a normal feature of most DC generators, will allow the polarity to be reversed if necessary.

Polarity Testing

If there is an uncertainty as to which output cable from a generator is positive polarity, the following test can be carried out, assuming that a DC voltmeter is not available.

Connect a small metal plate to one cable, and immerse the plate in a bucket of water. Insert a cutting electrode in the torch holder, and attach the other cable to the torch connection. Place the tip of the cutting rod about 2in from the plate whilst both are still submerged.

With the current supply turned on, a heavy stream of bubbles should rise from the electrode tip if the torch is negative, and the plate positive. If this result is not achieved, then reverse the leads and repeat the test.

Having determined the polarity, the ground clamp should then be attached to the positive (+) lead, suitably marked, whilst the negative lead is attached to the electrode holder. The connection of the latter should be well insulated.

Safety Switch

A quick-acting "knife-switch" must be included in any oxy-arc cutting circuit, in order to safeguard the diver, surface operator, and the equipment. Only by this means can a diver have complete confidence that the electrical power is "ON" when he requires ir, and "OFF" at all other times.

Operation of the switch can be the task of the surface diving tender, who should be aware of the hazards involved, and instructed only to operate the switch on receipt of instructions from the diver.

For this reason, it is almost impossible to work satisfactorily with oxy-arc cutting equipment without a full communication system, since the diver will need to instruct the surface support to "make it hot", ie. close the switch, and provide current into the circuit; or "make it cold", ie. open the switch, and break the supply.

The attendant controlling the switch then takes the necessary action, and acknowledges with the reply "torch is hot", or, "torch is cold", as appropriate.

Since the diver should have stopped cutting before the switch is broken, and should not restart until it has been made, there should be no arcing across the terminals of the knife switch. Nevertheless, the surface operator should be aware that arcing can occur, and that he should not look directly at the switch as it is changed over, to avoid the possibility of "arc-eye".

General Power Supply Notes

The following precautions should be taken when operating a high amperage power source, as would be required for underwater cutting:

1 Ensure the machine frame is well earthed, and that neither positive or negative terminals are allowed to touch the frame, and that all connections are clean and secure.

2 Where possible, ensure the power source is well insulated from any free flowing water, as for example might be found on the deck of a ship.

3 Keep welding cables as dry as possible and free from oil and grease.

4 Where possible, hang cables clear of any steel decking, but offer them support since when drawing heavy current, they will commence to sag as the copper conductors heat up.

Welding Cables

The cutting torch and "earth" lead must be completely insulated over their entire length, both on the surface and underwater. Current leakage underwater due to cracked or cut insulation will only result in a reduced work potential, and is often difficult to trace.

Sections of cable that are uninsulated and come into contact with any grounded metal fittings will cause arcing, melting the conductor, and breaking the circuit.

Long lengths of cable are both heavy and difficult to handle, and when being lowered or raised over the side of a diving craft are subjected to a great deal of strain, particularly at the joints. Any damage to the insulation resulting, should be rectified immediately.

For cutting operations in deep water, loss of current flow due to the increased resistance of the cable can only be overcome by using cable with a larger cross-sectional area.

All joints must be insulated with proper sleeves, and these can be given some support by taping the length of welding cable to a length of rope, rather like an unbilical.

Earth Clamp

The earth clamp must be well secured to the work task, which should first be wire brushed or scraped "shiny" clean. The cable should have sufficient slack to ensure that it is not accidentally pulled free, and must be of the same gauge material as the lead to the actual cutting torch.

Oxygen Supply

The oxygen consumption is not critical, and satisfactory results can be achieved over a wide range of pressures. Fig 16-9 shows a recommended range of oxygen gas pressures, but is intended purely as a guide only:

Cutting Electrodes

In oxy-arc cutting, work is performed at the expense of the cutting electrode, which is slowly consumed. Depending on the current setting, a steel electrode will last for about 40 to 60 seconds. The most common commercially available oxy-arc cutting or burning rod is made from 5/16in diameter steel tube, with a 1/8in bore, some 14in in length.

Another common type of oxy-arc cutting electrode is the copper coated, carbon graphite rod. Shorter in length, but greater in diameter, these maintain an arc far easier than steel rods, but are very brittle and break easily. They also require a higher amperage, in the order of 400amps.

Electrodes are covered with a flux which produces a gas bubble at the point of contact with the work, within which the arc burns. This bubble stabilises the arc, and prevents the heat generated from dissipating too rapidly into the surrounding water. Electrodes are also waterproofed, to protect the

Fig 16-9 Table of operating values for oxy-arc cutting

Depth in Feet	Current in Amps	OXYGEN PRESSURE FOR PLATE THICKNESS															
		1/8"	1/4"	3/8"	1/2"	5/8"	3/4"	7/8"	1"	1⅛"	1¼"	1⅜"	1½"	1⅝"	1¾"	1⅞"	2"
10	350	30	33	35	40	50	60	70	80	90	100	110					
	470	20	22	24	30	40	50	60	70	78	87	98	107	115	120	125	130
20	350	34	36	38	43	53	63	73	83	93	103	113					
	470	23	25	27	33	43	53	63	73	81	91	101	110	118	123	128	133
30	350	38	40	42	47	57	67	77	07	97	107	117					
	470	27	29	31	37	47	57	67	77	85	94	105	114	122	127	132	137
40	350	43	45	47	52	62	72	82	92	102	112	122					
	470	32	34	36	42	52	62	72	82	90	99	110	119	127	134	137	142
50	350	48	50	52	59	68	78	88	98	108	118	128					
	470	38	40	42	49	58	68	78	88	96	105	116	125	133	138	143	148
60	350	55	57	59	66	75	85	95	105	115	125	135					
	470	45	47	49	56	65	75	85	95	103	112	123	132	140	145	150	155
70	350	63	65	67	74	83	93	103	113	121	132	143					
	470	53	55	57	64	73	83	93	103	111	120	131	140	148	153	158	163
80	350	72	74	76	83	92	102	112	122	130	139	152					
	470	62	64	66	73	82	92	102	112	120	129	140	149	157	162	167	172
90	350	82	84	86	93	102	112	122	132	140	149	162					
	470	72	74	76	83	92	102	112	122	130	139	150	159	167	172	177	182
100	350	93	95	97	104	113	123	133	143	151	160	173					
	470	83	85	87	94	103	113	123	133	141	150	161	170	178	183	188	193

flux material from becoming soft and
falling off. It also serves to insulate
the rod itself from current leakage..

Since the flux coating is both
thin and brittle, if the cutting task
is likely to require the rods to suffer
some rough handling, it is well worth
the time and effort to wrap them with
one layer of pvc tape. Should the flux
become badly chipped whilst working in
a deep cut, the diver will notice the
rod commencing to arc out sideways.

Damaged rods can also be over
wrapped with tape, but it should be
remembered that the steel rod will
burn down quicker than the pvc coating,
and will leave a tape sleeve in its
wake.

Cutting rods should be checked
before being taken underwater to
ensure that the centre hole is not
blocked, and that the uninsulated end
to be gripped in the collet is both
clean and free from burrs. Of all the
problems likely to be encountered
whilst cutting underwater, the most
frustrating is the number of stub
ends of rods that 'stick' in the
electrode holder. For this reason
alone, it is recommended that divers
should carry a pair of pliers whilst
cutting, which will at least save the
time it would otherwise take to pull
the torch to the surface, to have
the collet cleared.

Technique of Oxy-Arc Cutting

The diver can either take down the
cutting torch, ground cable and clamp,
plus a supply of rods, or else they
can be lowered after he has made
bottom. On reaching the work site, the
first task is to clean the point of
contact for the ground clamp, then make
a secure connection ensuring that good
electrical contact is achieved. The
clamp should be positioned so that it
is in front of the diver when he is
cutting. If it were placed in such a
position that the diver was positioned
between the ground point and the work,
then his body and all his equipment
would act as an anode from the electrolytic point of view. In such a situation, even after only a short period of

time, extensive damage will be caused
to helmets and fittings. It may even
be necessary for the diver to move
the ground clamp from time to time,
to ensure that this situation does
not arise.

Using carbon-graphite rods:

1 To start the cut, hold the electrode
perpendicular to the surface to be
cut, at the same time allowing the
tip to touch the work. If manual
control is employed, the diver then
opens the oxygen valve, calls to
the surface to "Make it hot", and
withdraws the rod slightly from
the contact to start the arcing
process. After that it is only a
case of maintaining a slow steady
arc as the cut progresses.

2 To advance the cut once started,
drag the electrode along the
desired line of cut, keeping the
rod either perpendicular or else
with a slight leading angle in the
direction of travel. The tip of the
electrode should continue to
lightly touch the working surface,
the diver maintaining pressure
inward to compensate for electrode
consumption, and forward to advance
the cut. With graphite rods, only
the minimum amount of contact with
the work is necessary.

3 Should the cut be incomplete at
some stage, due to a fault, or
control of the torch, this will
generally be indicated by a "back
flare", which will be visible even
in the worst of underwater visibility conditions. Should this
situation arise, the diver should
lift the electrode out of the
present area, go back along the
cut a few inches, and renew the
cutting process.

When the cutting electrode
reaches the point at which it has
been used to within about 2in of
the holder head, cease cutting,
call for the torch to be "Made
Cold", then remove the stub, and
fit a new electrode. Since some

rods are not insulated, it is most important that the torch is held in the cutting position until the surface acknowledges that the current has in fact been disconnected from the circuit.

Failure to observe this simple safety precaution can result in the diver receiving a severe, even fatal shock, as his body conducts current through to ground.

Using Tubular Steel Rods

The following technique is for the cutting of steel plate over 6mm in thickness.

1 Commence the cut in the same manner as for carbon/graphite rods.

2 Advance the cut in the same manner, except that the electrode is maintained in contact with the work without attempting to hold an arc, and always perpendicular to the work surface.

3 An incomplete cut will be indicated in the same manner as for carbon electrodes, and should be treated exactly the same.

4 The same safety precaution to avoid unecessary electrical shocks to the diver should be observed.

Technique for Cutting Steel Plate Less than 6mm Thickness

A slightly different technique is employed in the cutting of thin steel plate from that already described, which is for thicker material.

Instead of maintaining the electrode tip in the cut, and pressing against the lip of the advancing work, the end of the rod should barely touch the work surface as it progresses forward.

An alternative technique, to be used where underwater visibility is poor, is to increase the effective thickness of the plate. This requires the electrode to be held angled towards the operator , in the direction of the cut at an angle of approximately 45°. The electrode thus

"sees" the work as being of greater thickness, and normal pressure can be applied.

Technique for Piercing Holes in Steel Plate

Piercing a hole in steel plate, to accommodate a wire strop, to fit a shackle or a "strong-back", is readily accomplished using oxy-arc equipment.

The technique is as follows:

1 Touch the rod lightly on the steel plate at the desired position of the hole. The oxygen supply is turned "on" and the current applied to the electrode.

2 The diver holds the electrode stationery, withdrawing it momentarily if necessary to permit melting of the steel rod back inside its covering.

3 Ease the electrode slowly inwards into the hole until the plate has been pierced. Steel up to 75mm thick can be pierced by this method without any real difficulty.

Technique for Cutting Cast-Iron and Non-Ferrous Materials

Cast-iron and non-ferrous metals are not readily oxidised, so that underwater cutting of these is more of a melting process.

In such instances, no benefit is derived from the oxygen supply except that it physically blows the molten metal out of the cut. It is recommended that compressed air should be substituted for oxygen when cutting these metals, and the technique requires a different approach.

The diver should manipulate the tip of the electrode in and out of the cut, since melting will only take place in the immediate vicinity of the arc.

For thin materials, such manipulation may not be necessary, and it may cut as if it were thin steel.

Since successful cutting is a pure function of the amount of heat in the arc, it is recommended that 400 amps current is used, or at least the maximum available if less than that figure.

Safety Precuations

Since the use of electricity underwater can be extremely hazardous, it is important that precautions are taken to provide adequate protection for the diving personnel. The following are considered the basic minimum precautions which should be observed:

1   The welding power source must be grounded to the parent vessel on which it is mounted.

2   No part of the electrode holder or submerged lengths of power cable, including joints, should be left uninsulated.

3   A spring-loaded, quick action knife switch should be incorporated into the circuit, connected such that its operation will 'make' or 'break' the current to the electrode holder held by the diver.

4   The position of the diver in relation to the "grounded" work clamp should be such, that at no time does he or his equipment become part of a secondary circuit.

5   If cutting inside a compartment or a similar confined space, adequate provision must be made to ensure ventilation, to prevent hydrogen gas released by the cutting action from accumulating in a pocket.

6   Avoid the use of any grease or lubricants in areas where they may come in contact with high-pressure oxygen.

7   The diver should never hold a cutting torch in such a manner that the rod or electrode is pointing at either himself, or snother diver.

8   The diver should always wear a pair of gloves made of an insulating material.

9   No attempt should be made to remove or change the used stub of a cutting electrode, until confirmation has been received from the surface that the supply current is "OFF".

THERMAL LANCE/ARC CUTTING

The limitations of oxy-arc cutting, already outlined, but summarised, include:

Requirement for a bulky, heavy duty, DC welding generator.

Limitations with regard to the thickness of steel that can be cut, and that other metals may cause some difficulties.

Inability to cut concrete, rock or protective coatings.

Requirement for the frequent replacement of the cutting electrode.

Electrical hazards generally.

A development which overcomes most, if not all of these limitations, is the use of "thermal lance" equipment underwater, and a more recent improvement from a diving point of view, the "thermal arc".

The thermal lance has been in use in industry for a very long time, but its use underwater was not fully appreciated until the late 1960's. It works on the principle that a special mild steel electrode, fed with a continuous supply of oxygen, will generate an arc of sufficient intensity (some manufacturers have claimed temperatures as high as 5000°C) that it will burn almost any substance.

A thermal lance consists of a length of mild steel tube, usually in the order of 3.2m and of some 9mm diameter, fitted at one end with a screw threaded connection. To this is attached the oxygen supply hose. The interior of the tube is filled with a series of small diameter, solid metal rods, tightly packed but with sufficient space between them to allow the passage of high pressure oxygen gas. The rods used to fill the tube of a thermal lance may be mild steel, a steel alloy, aluminium, magnesium or other materials, depending on the nature of the task.

The lance must be ignited by a secondary source of heat, which can be a gas burning torch, blow-lamp, or oxy-arc equipment. Once ignited, the thermal lance can only be extinguished by depriving it of its oxygen supply; even after removing the oxygen flow, it will continue to burn for several seconds. Hence a lance must be turned "OFF" when at least 300mm of tube is left, otherwise it will continue to burn back through the threaded holder connection, into the oxygen supply hose.

Because of the physical problems of handling long lengths of thermal lance underwater, the high consumption rate of oxygen, and the obvious hazards involved, its use by divers is limited. It is, however, of particular value in the cutting of reinforced concrete, or steel of considerable thickness, which no other cutting equipment can handle.

A thermal lance will cut through almost anything, including all steels, non-ferrous metals, rock, and all forms of concrete. With heavy shafting, such as propeller shafts on wrecks, a thermal lance will cut through 300mm of steel per minute, consuming some 200 to 300mm of lance. A complete 3.2m length of lance will therefore probably last some 6 minutes. The quality of the cut is very rough compared with oxy-arc, and less skill is required, but no diver should attempt to use a thermal lance underwater, without considerable surface practice.

The risk of explosions "in the hole" when cutting non-ferrous materials in particular, are very real, causing serious "blow-backs".

Thermal Arc Equipment

Many of the problems associated with the thermal lance underwater were resolved by the development of a flexible version of the rigid thermal lance, by Clucas Engineering Ltd, a British company based at Hull.

Known as Kerie cable, the thermal arc equipment can be likened to a conventional 6 or 7 stranded length of wire rope, which has had the "heart" core removed, and the outside sheathed in a pvc material. In this manner a flexible "lance" has been produced, which allows oxygen to fed through the centre, the strands of the wire rope taking the place of the wire rods packing a lance.

Supplied in 30m rolls, and available in both 6 and 12mm diameters, Kerie cable burns at an average rate of 27m per hour, or about 0.5m per minute. The burning temperature is in the order of 2700°C, which is sufficient to cut non-ferrous metals. The cut produced is still much wider and rough compared with oxy-arc, but not so rough as with the thermic lance. The same basic safety precautions should be observed as for oxy-arc cutting underwater, except that greater attention must be paid to safety clothing, and protection of diving suits.

STEEL TUBE

Fig 16-10 Cross section of a typical thermic lance rod

Equipment for Thermal-arc Cutting

A complete system, as purchased, although it is stressed that the surface control panel could be of local manufacture, consists of:

Oxygen reducer; a flexible manifold for 3 oxygen cylinders; a 30m

length of electrical cable; a 30m length
of oxygen hose; Kerie cable; a pair of
heavy duty cable cutters; insulating
sleeves and spares.

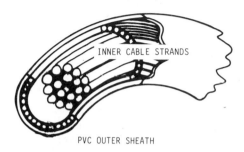

Fig 16-11 Cross section of Kerie
thermal arc cable

Fig 16-12 Clucas thermal-arc control
panel, showing supply and
reduced oxygen pressure
gauges, ammeter, knife
switch and control valve

Preparation for Use

Connect 3 full oxygen cylinders to
the HP manifold supplied, and the
common connection to one end of
the 3m length of oxygen hose. The
other end of this hose connects
to the position marked "HP O^2 IN".
    Connect one end of the 30m
electrical cable to the terminal
marked " -NEG AMPS OUT TO CUTTING
CABLE",amd the 30m length of oxygen
hose to the position "LP CUTTING O^2
OUT".
    Two 12v lead acid batteries of
at least 20AH each should then be
connected in series (ie. the +ve
terminal of one, to the -ve terminal
of the other). Then connect the main
battery negative (-ve) terminal to
the control panel position " NEG AMPS
IN", and the positive side (+ve) to
the work task with a ground clamp.
    The other end of both the
oxygen hose and the electrical cable
are then connected to the Kerie
cutting cable. The Kerie cable is
supplied in individual coils, tightly
wound and should be unpacked and
recoiled in large loops on the deck,
similar to the manner in which a
diving umbilical is stowed to prevent
kinking. Make sure than one of the
red, double insulating sleeves
provided, is slipped over the joint
at the cable end of the oxygen hose.
    The equipment is now ready for
surface testing.

Testing the Equipment

First turn "ON" the oxygen cylinder
valves, then set the control to
give a gauge reading on the panel of
200psi output pressure. Turn the
control valve marked "ON/OFF/VENT"
to "ON", close the knife switch on
the panel, and touch the tip of the
Kerie cable on the work test piece.
    Provided there is sufficient
bared metal to make contact the
cable should immediately ignite.
Break the knife switch the moment
that ignition takes place.
    Proceed to cut the test piece

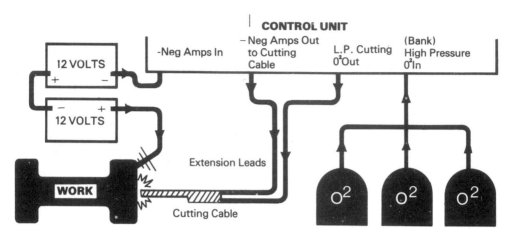

Fif 16-13 Connections and lay out of Thermal Arc cutting equipment

from one edge. To stop the process, the Clucas system offers a choice of methods, either by turning the oxygen control valve to the "CUTTING O^2 OFF" position, or to the "CUTTING O^2 OFF AND VENT" position.

In the first of these, the cable will continue to burn until all the oxygen in the line has been consumed, which may take some 5 seconds, or in the alternative position, not only is the oxygen supply cut off, but the hose is vented to atmosphere, hence extinguishing the flame almost immediately. This latter method is far safer, but is very wasteful on oxygen, and should be considered as an emergency procedure only. Should this method be employed whilst the equipment is still underwater, the entire remaining length of cable will become flooded, and cannot be relit until blown clear by the oxygen flow.

It is important to use the special 3m length of hose joining the panel and the cylinder manifold. This is an electrically "insulated" length of hose, designed to prevent the cylinder bank from become "alive".

Cutting Underwater

The cutting cable should be passed to the diver, and taken down with a sufficient oxygen flow to exclude water from entering the bore. The pressure of gas need only be that necessary to compensate for depth, (ie. at 30m, about 60 - 70psi).

On reaching the place of work, the diver, when ready, should signal or call for the oxygen pressure to be increased before attempting ignition. This is most important, since should ignition take place with the oxygen pressure too low, the cable will commence to burn inside itself. When full pressure is then applied, it will cause the flame to burn out sideways along the length of the cable in a series of "blow-holes", which can be very dangerous.

The surface operator should be made aware of this danger, and can assist by delaying the closing of the knife-switch for some 20 seconds after the application of full cutting-gas pressure. This will give time for the oxygen pressure to build up along the full length of the cutting cable.

The panel ammeter will give a reading as the diver attempts ignition, which will then fall back to zero as the burning cable retreats back inside its pvc coating. Once it is obvious that ignition has been successful, the diver should inform the surface, who will then open the panel knife switch, isolating the ignition circuit.

If it is necessary to relight the cable for a second or third time underwater, the limitations of lead acid batteries should be taken into account. After calling for the oxygen to be switched "OFF" at the end of the previous cut, the diver should continue to rub the end of the cable against the work, to keep the pvc coating clear of the inner cable, hence ensuring a good electrical contact when re-lighting. Should the end of the cable be badly burnt or distorted, then some 150mm should be removed using the cable cutters and discarded. If cable cutters are not available, beating the end with a hammer will often break up the burnt pvc, and expose sufficient bare wire to complete the circuit and allow re-ignition.

Although lead acid batteries are the accepted source of ignition, the output from a DC welding generator can be substituted, in which case, with a much higher current source available, re-ignition can be achieved merely by rubbing the pvc fused end on a rough surface.

In the event of neither a DC generator nor batteries being available, or the battery bank has been 'flattened', Kerie cable can be surface lit and taken down burning, but great care is necessary. Force a small plug of fine wire wool, about the size of a finger tip, down the end of the cable. Apply oxygen pressure of about 5psi, and set light to the wire wool with a match or lighter. Then hold the end of the cable against a block of wood, and increase the oxygen pressure to about 50psi, allowing the cable to reach a satisfactory burning temperature.

The cable is then passed to the diver, who calls for full cutting gas pressure as soon as he has full control of the situation, and before he leaves the surface. If full pressure is not applied until he reaches his task on

the bottom, water pressure may cause the cable to burn back inside itself.

Oxygen Cutting Pressures

The following is a general guide only, and should be altered to suit local conditions. The normal cutting pressures for a depth of 18m (60ft), with the two sizes of Kerie cable are:

12mm cable - 340 to 380psi

6mm cable - 250 to 300psi

An increase of approximately 11psi of oxygen pressure per 0.3m(1ft) of depth, should be applied over 18m.

As a general guide, 3 x 240 cubic ft cylinders of oxygen will cut approximately 1.8m length of 50mm thick (6ft x 2in) plate at that depth.

Thermal arc equipment will not cut concrete or rock, either above or below the surface. It should not be used on non-ferrous materials, as experience has shown that this can result in a very violent explosion, which could be fatal.

Cutting Very Thick Steel

The cutting of thick sections of steel should be carried out working around the circumference, withdrawing the cable from the cut every 2 or 3 seconds, to allow water to enter.

A brushing or stroking action in the direction of the cut should be employed, and under no circumstances should the work be allowed to become a deep seated inferno, since it is this situation that can lead to an explosion. The 12mm Kerie cable is recommended for cutting thick metal; the 6mm for thin material, wire rope or cable and general light work. 6mm cable is supplied in 15.25m lengths instead of the 30m lengths for 12mm, due to the restriction in oxygen flow.

Using Kerie cable deeper than 43m

When thermal arc cutting is to be carried out deeper than 43m(150ft), it is recommended that 12mm cable only is used, reduced to lengths of 15.2m(50ft) to assist the flow of oxygen through the core.

Thermal arc equipment has been used at 91m (300ft) depth, and possibly deeper.

Protective clothing

Thermal lance or thermal arc equipment should not be used on the surface without special attention to the protection of the operator. Fire proof material coveralls should be worn, with any pocket flaps done up, and the suit closed up to the neck. Asbestos or leather gauntlet gloves are essential for the hands, and a protective helmet with a full visor for the head and face. Footwear should be industrial boots, and care taken that sparks or globules of molten metal are unable to fall inside or get "stuck" to socks.

Underwater, similar consideration must be afforded the diver. It is strongly recommended that only rigid helmet equipment is used; that thick, gauntlet type gloves are worn, with thick rubber bands around the tops to prevent slag from falling inside. The helmet faceplate should be protected by a clear plexiglass or perspex screen, to prevent slag pitting.

The cutting arc is not so bright that glass filters are necessary to protect the eyes, neither is there the danger of electric "arc-eye".

Maintenance

Very little maintenance is required, but the following points should be observed:

Break all the electrical connections after use, clean, dry and coat them with a silicone compound.

Treat all the oxygen connections in a similar manner, ensuring that no oil or grease it used.

If the "blades" of the knife-switch show signs of arcing or corrosion, clean well with a fine emery paper to restore the bright copper surface, and smear with silicone compound.

Tape up the ends of all hose, manifold connections and the unused Kerie cable, to exclude dirt and dust. and prevent any oil contamination.

Should a leak develop on the oxygen control valve, remove the handle or knob, and gently tighten down on the gland nut until the leak stops. If this has no effect, replace the entire gland seal with a new item.

If the seat of the nylon valve in the oxygen reducer should develop a leak, the LP cutting pressure will continue to build up until the safety valve blows off at 500psi. To change this seating, unscrew the control panel, remove it from its box and turn over. Remove the hexagon cap nut from the reducer, and fit a new seat with the recessed brass ring uppermost. Replace the piston, spring and cap nut, and refit the panel back in the control box.

The manufacturers of the Clucas Thermal Arc Cutting Equipment are:

Clucas Diving and Marine Eng Ltd
Sandiacre
Dunswell Road
Cottingham
North Humberside

USA agents for the equipment are:

Taylor Diving and Salvage Co Inc
795 Engineers Road
Belle Chasse
Los Angeles   70037
California

BROCO ULTRA- THERMIC CUTTING RODS

The American Company "Broco" have miniaturised the thermic lance, in such a manner that it can be used as conventional oxy-arc cutting equipment.

Slightly longer than the

conventional oxy-arc cutting rods, the
Broco electrodes are 460mm in length
and available in a range of diameters,
the most commonly used being 9.5mm.
Since the normal oxy-arc cutting electrode is 7.5mm, a special collet will be
required to adapt the standard torcch.

Broco rods are ultra-high temperature melting (1600 to 2500°C) and
will cut or melt most conventional
materials such as steels, non-ferrous,
rock and concrete.
As with conventional thermic lance rods,
the Broco version is a steel tube packed
with steel rods, some of which are high-
tensile material, the outer tube being
pvc tape wrapped for insulation purposes.

These rods can be lit in the same
manner as thermic-cable, or when striking
an arc with oxy-arc, but will of course
consume a far greater quantity of oxygen
than conventional oxy-arc cutting. For
this reason, the manufacturers recomm-
end that any sealing washers inside the
electrode holder should have a central
hole of at least 7mm diameter, to assist
the flow of oxygen.

Field experience with Broco rods has
shown that the most common difficulties
are directly related to:

a) Current setting too high
b) Insufficient or blocked oxygen flow

POWER SETTING

Length Of Power Cable		Cable (Double Length) Amperage Setting		
Ft.	M	1/0	2/0	3/0
150	46	155	152	150
200	61	157	154	152
250	76	159	156	154
300	91	161	158	156
350	107	163	160	158
400	122	165	162	160
450	137	167	164	162
500	152	169	166	164

Fig 16-14 Current requirements

GAUGE SETTINGS FOR DEPTHS

Depth		Pressure Gauge Setting		Depth		Pressure Gauge Setting	
Ft.	M	psi	atm	Ft.	M	psi	atm
33	10	115	7.8	200	61	209	14.2
40	12	118	8.0	210	64	214	14.6
50	15	122	8.3	220	67	218	14.8
60	18	127	8.6	230	70	222	15.1
70	12	131	8.9	240	73	227	15.4
80	24	136	9.3	250	76	231	15.7
90	27	140	9.5	260	79	236	16.1
100	30	155	10.5	270	82	240	16.3
110	34	159	10.8	280	85	245	16.7
120	37	163	11.1	290	88	249	16.9
130	40	168	11.4	300	91	264	18.0
140	43	172	11.7	310	94	268	18.2
150	46	177	12.0	320	98	272	18.5
160	49	181	12.3	330	101	277	18.8
170	52	186	12.7	340	104	281	19.1
180	55	190	12.9	350	107	285	19.4
190	58	195	13.3				

Fig 16-15 Oxygen pressure settings
for various depths

When the equipment is to be used at
depths in excess of 106m(350ft),
oxygen gauge pressure can be
calculated as follows:

For every 30m(100ft) required, add
10psi to the 90psi necessary at the
rod tip. In addition, add 10psi for
every 100ft of depth of hose.

Example: Assume a working dive of
170m(560ft); what would be the
pressure of oxygen required ?

Requirement = 90psi above ambient
pressure

Ambient pressure = 560ft x 0.445psi

= 249.2psi + 90psi

= 339.2psi

Plus 560ft of hose x 10psi for each
100ft length used= 56psi

Answer: Pressure = 395.2 psi

Precautions

Cutting with Broco rods requires
little skill or practice. Divers
qualified and experienced in either

underwater oxy-arc cutting or arc welding, will experience little difficulty
in its operation. Surface practice is
recommended for those not familiar with
either techniques.

Protective clothing should be worn as
recommended for both surface and underwater operation of thermic lance and
thermal arc equipment, plus the need
for a welding visor, with at least a
No 10 protective lens fitted.

Broco rods, as with other thermal arc
type equipment, can only be extinguished
by cutting off the supply of oxygen. It
is therefore recommended that rods should
not be allowed to burn down to less than
75 - 90mm length, to protect the holder,
and avoid a "blow-back" situation.

UNDERWATER WELDING

Until some 10 years ago, all underwater
welding was "wet" welding, in which the
diver/welder took all the necessary
equipment to the task, and carried out
the work completely in a submerged, wet
situation. Since then the technique of
"dry" or habitat welding has been
introduced, a number of companies and
diving contractors have made a special-
ity of the art, and "wet" welding has
become accepted more as a "first-aid"
treatment, than a reliable repair.
    With "dry" welding underwater, the
diver is provided with either a special
welding "habitat" or "box", within which
the water is evacuated by pressure of an
inert gas which removes the risk of an
explosion, which would otherwise result
from an oxygen rich atmpsphere. The
complexity and cost of dry, habitat or
as it is sometimes known, "hyperbaric"
welding, is such that this will normally
only be carried out by divers who are
also coded welders, in order that the
insurance companies involved can have
total confidence in the work performed.
    Wet welding is an accepted and
simple approach to a great many types
of underwater repair, but has the
disadvantage that due to the instantaneous quenching of the deposited
metal by the surrounding water, the

weld must be inferior to dry welding.
Wet welds are therefore of less
impact strength, with increased
porosity and hardness, even when
carried out by a skilled welder. It
is therefore important that divers
should attempt to acquire as much
surface welding practice as possible,
in order to better equip themselves
for "wet" welding, but, at the same
time accept that it takes years of
work experience to become proficient,
and longer to become "coded" by one
of the inspection authorities.
Only in recent years has the practice
of "wet" welding become generally
accepted by Lloyds, DNV and American
authororities, and then only within
certain boundaries.

The following terms, techniques and
equipment details, are intended only
to give the diver who may be unfam-
iliar with welding practice, a basic
appreciation of the equipment.

The Welding Arc

An electric arc is nothing more than
a prolonged spark, maintained
between two terminals of an electrical circuit. The arc, or spark,
which creates a temperature of some
4000 to 6000°C, is concentrated in a
relatively small area, and is sufficient to instantly melt a small area
of the work surface and the tip of
the metallic rod or electrode.
    As the tip of the electrode
melts due to the intense heat, small
globules of metal are formed, which
are forced across the arc and deposited into the molton pool on the
work side.

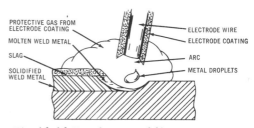

Fig 16-16 Metal arc welding

It is important to appreciate that these globules do not just fall or drop due to gravity, but are forced by current flow, hence making overhead welding possible.

Electrodes

The electrode or rod supplies the metal which will join the two surfaces together, and to a large extent, the strength and quality of the weld will depend on the composition of the wire rod material, and its "flux" coating.

The all important coating performs the following functions:

a) Stabilises the arc, and allows an AC (alternating current) to be used.

b) Causes impurities present on the surface of the work area to be "fluxed" away.

c) Forms a slag coating over the weld. This in turn protects the molten metal from contamination whilst it is cooling, and reduces the rate at which this cooling takes place. At the same time, slag smooths out the wave formation on the surface of the weld.

Welding electrodes are available in lengths of 9; 12; 14 and 18in, with 14in being the most common. The size of the electrode refers to its core diameter, ignoring the flux coating.

Diameters can range from 1/16 to 1/4in and are usually expressed in SWG (Standard Wire Gauge), or else in millimetres.

Almost any welding electrode can be used underwater, but without waterproofing the flux coating will quickly become saturated and flake off. Should this happen to an electrode, it must be discarded, and certainly not used for welding purposes. To waterproof an electrode, they can be given two coats of paint, a coat of plastic spray covering, dipped twice in molten paraffin wax, or any combination of these. Where possible, welding electrodes manufactured specifically for underwater use are recommended, since these will have been specially coated, but when not available, a diver should be prepared to coat and waterproof his own surface electrodes.

COMMON TERMS APPLIED TO A WELD

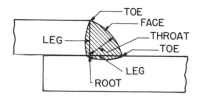

Fig 16-17 Weld terminology

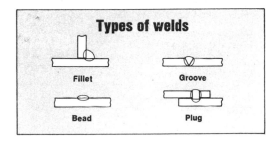

Fig 16-18 The four basic welds

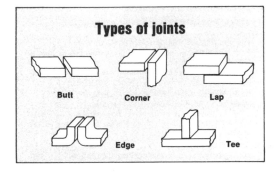

Fig 16-19 Basic welding joints

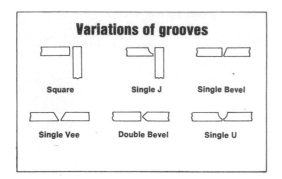

Fig 16-20 Preparation of joint faces

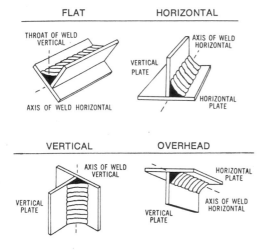

Fig 16-21 The four basic welding
positions

Electrode Holders

Electrode holders for underwater use
differ only from their surface counterparts in their element of insulation,
and the method of holding the rod.

Underwater holders are designed
with a simple "twist-grip" action to
remove and fit new rods, which can be
located in the one position only, ie.
at 90° to the axis of the handle.

Surface holders are usually
spring loaded, and allow for both a
45° and a 90° position for rods.

Holders designed for underwater
use should never be used for surface
work, since they are designed to be
cooled by the surrounding water,
and would otherwise quickly overheat. Some oxy-arc cutting torches
can also be used as welding holders,
after the collet has been changed
for the correct size rods. In general,
these are somewhat heavy for welding
purposes, and most operators prefer
the light-weight, underwater
"stinger" as it is sometimes called.

Power Sources

A DC welding generator or rectifier
with a 300 amp output capacity, is
sufficient for all underwater
welding tasks. It should be fitted
with a polarity switch if possible,
in order that the work connection
can be reversed if necessary.

External to the generator,
there must be a quick-action knife
switch, which can connect or disconnect current from the underwater
circuit both quickly and safely.

It is usual to connect the
output of the generator with the
positive (+) lead to the work clamp,
and the torch holder as the negative
(-). If used in the reverse mode,
electrolysis will quickly eat into
the metal parts of the electrode
holder and the diver's equipment,
particularly his helmet.

Protective Clothing and equipment

Rubber gloves for the diver are
essential, but apart from an anti-
glare shield fitted to the helmet
or mask, no other items are essential.

The shield offers the diver
protection from the glare of the
welding arc, although the water
between the diver's eyes and the
work task will already have cut
down on the harmful ultraviolet
rays radiated from the point of
electrical contact.

Such welding shields are
normally hinged, so that the diver
can swing it up out of the way, or

down prior to striking an arc. Welding
glasses are normally rated from No 1
to 12, with 10 the most common for
diving purposes, which should be
changed for a No 12 in conditions of
very poor underwater visibility.

<u>Safety Precautions</u>

All the safety precautions for oxy-
arc cutting apply to underwater
electric arc "wet" welding. The only
observation is that a much lower
level of DC current will be used,
normally about 180 amps.

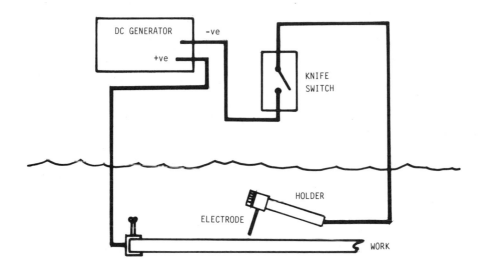

Fig 16-22   Circuit and connections for underwater "wet" welding

CHAPTER 17

UNDERWATER CONCRETING

There are two basic approaches to the problem of forming concrete underwater either the concrete is mixed in the conventional manner and then placed by special methods, or the special process of grouted aggregate is used. In addition, concrete bagwork is still used for small jobs and special purposes but its applications are relatively restricted. It is discussed separately after the more important basic methods.

In many respects the rules and recommendations for underwater concrete are the same as those for conventional concrete placed in the dry. Properly mixed concrete is a stable material with a density more than twice that of water. Once it is in position it will remain unaffected by the water in which it is immersed unless it is subjected to agitation or other movement while it is setting. Cement sets as a result of a chemical reaction-not by drying out-so concrete hardens as quickly underwater as in the dry and it generally behaves in a normal manner once it has been successfully placed. Most of the recommendations which follow are therefore directed towards solving the problem of placing concrete in these conditions without damage.

Mass concrete can be placed successfully underwater in most circumstances where de-watering is either impracticable or uneconomic. Reinforced concrete can also be formed underwater but there are substantial difficulties in ensuring sound results.

Inspection is more difficult on underwater work than it is on work in the dry and the same applies to the repair of defective work.

Partly for these reasons and partly because of the characteristics of the mix and the conditions of placing. It is unwise to design for high compressive strengths in concrete that it to be placed underwater. The highest strength normally specified is about 22.5 MN/m^2 (3000lbf/in^2).

CONCRETE PLACED UNDERWATER

When a mass of fresh concrete moves through the water, or when water flows over the surface of fresh concrete, some of the cement is washed out from that part of the mix which comes into direct contact with the water. Thus the aim, when placing concrete underwater, should be to keep as much as possible of the concrete out of direct contact with the water and to avoid any rapid movement or agitation of the exposed surfaces.

The principal methods of placing concrete underwater are:

(a) by tremie

(b) by skip or similar device

PLACING THE TREMIE

The tremie is a steel tube, suspended vertically in the water, with a hopper fixed to the upper end to receive the fresh concrete. The tube or pipe must be watertight and joints, where necessary, should have watertight meeting faces. It should be smooth-bored and have adequate cross section for the size of aggregate to be used. A diameter of 150mm (6") is commonly regarded as the minimum for 20mm (¾") aggregates and 200mm (8") as the lower limit for 40mm (1½") aggregates. The hopper acts as a reservoir to convert an intermittent supply of concrete into a steady flow down the pipe, and

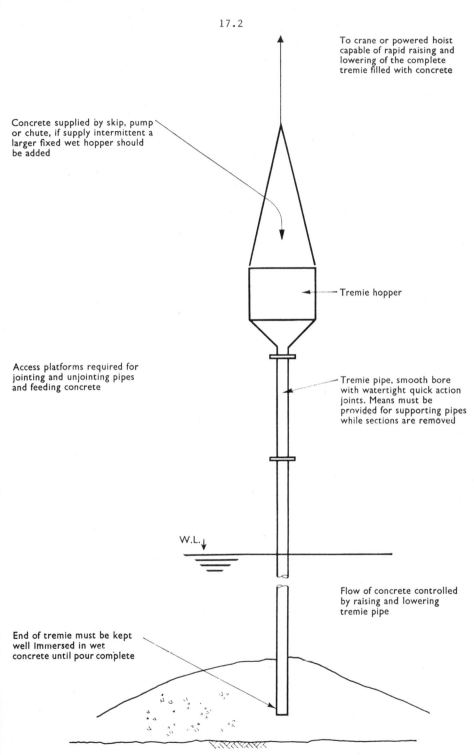

To crane or powered hoist
capable of rapid raising and
lowering of the complete
tremie filled with concrete

Concrete supplied by skip, pump
or chute, if supply intermittent a
larger fixed wet hopper should
be added

Tremie hopper

Access platforms required for
jointing and unjointing pipes
and feeding concrete

Tremie pipe, smooth bore
with watertight quick action
joints. Means must be
provided for supporting pipes
while sections are removed

W.L.

Flow of concrete controlled
by raising and lowering
tremie pipe

End of tremie must be kept
well immersed in wet
concrete until pour complete

Note: for large operations a frame or gantry can be used in conjunction with two or more tremies

Fig 17.1 Typical arrangement of tremie concreting unit

it should be of such a size that will enable the level of concrete to be maintained generally within its depth. The assemble pipe and hopper must be provided with a means of rapid raising and lowering when charged with wet concrete. Simple blocks and tackle, unless power assisted, are generally inadequate for this purpose.

CHARGING THE TREMIE

The tremie is erected vertically over the area to be concreted with the lower end of the pipe resting on the bottom. Various methods can be used for sealing the bottom of the pipe to keep out water and to enable the pipe to be filled in the dry, but it is difficult to provide a means of opening the bottom which is reliable and at the same time does not obstruct the flow of concrete or the removal of the pipe after use. Furthermore the flotation of an empty pipe can be a nuisance when the assembly is being placed in position. For these reasons, it is now common practice to place a travelling plug in the top of the pipe as a barrier between the concrete and the water. The water in the pipe is then displaced as the weight of concrete forces the plug to the bottom. Cement bags or sacks, folded into shape, are most commonly used for the travelling plug, but foamed plastic plugs and inflated balls have made an appearance in recent years. Purpose-made buoyant plugs are expected to extricate themselves from the concrete and rise to the surface, otherwise plugs are generally not recovered and if they are buried in the depths of the concrete normally placed by tremie, their effect is insignificant. More damage may be caused by attempting to remove plugs than by allowing them to remain in place.

PLACING THE CONCRETE

After the pipe has been filled with concrete it is raised a few inches off the bottom and the concrete begins to flow, quickly burying the end of the pipe.

Thereafter, the flow of concrete should continue to feed the interior of the heap of placed concrete. At the same time, the level of the top of the concrete should be maintained within the hopper as far as possible. It is particularly important to maintain an adequate head of concrete in the pipe when minimum pipe diameters in relation to aggregate sizes are in use. The flow of concrete must always be gentle so that air is not trapped within the concrete in the pipe.

When it is necessary to reduce or increase the length of the tremie pipe during concreting, the joint used should be of a simple type with a fit accurate enough to preserve the smooth bore of the pipe and make watertight meeting faces. When the pipe lengths are being removed or added, the concrete must be allowed to fall to just below the level of the joint being broken.

BROKEN SEALS

If the bottom of the tremie pipe ceases to be immersed in the body of wet concrete the seal will be broken, allowing the concrete in the pipe to rush out and in its passage through the water it will almost certainly segregate and lose its cement. Such concrete is worthless and may have to be removed completely before the tremie is recharged and work resumed. In addition, the rapid discharge of the concrete will often cause serious disturbance of unset concrete already in place and this concrete, too, may have to be removed before placing is resumed.

It is emphasised that the best insurance against such mishaps is to produce

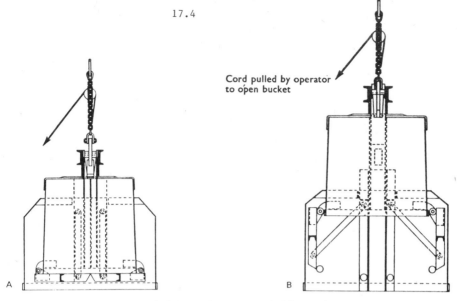

Cord pulled by operator
to open bucket

Bottom opening skip with skirt 'A'(above) closed 'B'(right) open

Canvas flaps to protect top
surface of concrete

Fig 17.2 Typical bottom-opening skip

concrete which is workable enough
to flow down the pipe and distri-
bute itself in situ with the minimum
of assistance. It is found that
most broken seals occur when attempts
are being made to clear blockages.
Blockages and broken seals do occur,
however, and if a large quantity of
concrete has already been placed it
is almost impossible to determine
the extent of the damage. Attempts
at this stage to remove the suspect
areas can often result in further
damage and the best procedure is to
discontinue concreting for the day
and allow the concrete to set before
inspection.

PLACING BY SKIP

THE SKIP

The skip should be of the bottom-
opening type possessing the following
essential features:

a) It must have bottom-opening
   double doors which may be
   operated automatically or
   manually. The doors should
   be arranged to open with the
   minimum disturbance to the
   flow of the concrete, and so
   made that they cannot be
   opened until the weight of the
   skip is on the bottom or
   embedded in the previously
   placed concrete.

b) There must be no restriction
   of the outlet when the doors
   are open, the latch mechanism
   must be outside the skip with
   the hinges set so that the
   doors swing clear of the bottom
   opening.

c) It should be straight-sided,
   perfectly smooth and vertical
   inside with no taper at the
   bottom.

d) It should be equipped with a top
   cover consisting of two loose
   overlapping canvas flaps. The
   water pressure keeps these flaps
   in close contact with the top
   surface of the concrete during
   placing; this prevents turbulence
   of the water inside the skip from
   washing out the cement.

e) The skips should be as large as
   possible, consistent with the
   work in hand.

f) In addition, skirts are sometimes
   fitted at the bottom. These may
   be an advantage in some circumstances by confining the concrete
   while it is being deposited.

PLACING THE CONCRETE

Skips must be completely filled before
the top covers are placed. They must be
lowered slowly, particularly when
entering the water, to avoid disturbance
of the concrete under the top cover,
and again when nearing the bottom, to
avoid excessive disturbance of the
previously placed concrete.

After it settles on the bottom the skip
must be lifted gently and slowly so
that the released concrete causes no
turbulence in the water around it. The
aim is to deposit fresh concrete from
the skip into the body of previously
placed concrete and to displace the
existing sloping surface of the mass
forward in the formwork.

Except for pours in very confined spaces
it is desirable to have a diver to
control the placing of the skips, even
when the release mechanism is automatic.

CHOICE BETWEEN TREMIE AND SKIP

The choice between placing by tremie or
skip is usually based on economics and
on the plant and skills available.

Placing by skip is slower, so the tremie is usually preferred for large pours. The tremie may also be preferred where there are obstructions underwater. Skips are more practicable for thin pours and for work requiring a screeded finish. They are also useful for handling small volumes of concrete; but if the job is small and there is little repetition it is often cheaper to rig up a tremie than to provide an expensive bottom-opening skip. The intermittent nature of skipwork and the way in which the pour is built up from a number of individual discharges must subject a greater proportion of the concrete to the risk of local washing out and the chance of trapping silt or slurry is more likely than would be the case in properly executed tremie work. However, such defects as may occur are likely to be small in extent and acceptable in relation to the total volume. Properly executed tremie concrete is more homogeneous and therefore better but on the other hand, the effect of a single badly executed deposit from a skip is usually much less disastrous than that of a single broken seal with a tremie pipe.

Successful operation of both methods requires a continuous supply of concrete at the correct consistency; delays in delivery of over 10 minutes are undesirable.

OTHER METHODS OF PLACING

TOGGLE BAGS

Re-usable, bottom-opening canvas bags, sealed at the top, sometimes known as toggle bags, can be used for small pours and for depositing small, discrete quantities of concrete. The bags are lowered into the water mouth downwards with the open ends tied by a chain or rope and secured by a toggle. Exactly the same principles apply for placing with toggle bags as for using bottom-opening skips.

PUMPING

Recent improvements in the design of concrete pumps have made it possible to consider them for the direct placing of concrete underwater. Experience to date is limited and the following observations are based on the filling of bored-pile shafts underwater. It may well be that with experience, pumps will be more widely used in future.

Pumping the concrete under pressure directly into the mass cuts out the necessity for frequent lifting of the pipe and ensures the desirable constant flow of concrete into the mass. Before pumping commences the pipe should be adjusted to give a few inches clearance above formation, and a sponge rubber ball, or other suitable plug, inserted in the pipeline adjacent to the pump.

This plug travels in front of the concrete and stops it dropping freely down the vertical pipe. Concreting should proceed at a fast rate, especially during the initial stages when the bottom of the pipe is being buried. It is desirable to pump for as long as possible at a time, lifting the pipe only when necessary. The depth of concrete which can be placed between lifting operations will be a matter of experiment, because it depends on the area of the pour, the characteristics of the concrete being used, the size of the pipe, and the pressure which it is possible for the pump to generate. Caution must be exercised however, as excessive lengths of buried pipe in the mass, coupled with a slow rate of pour, can result in new concrete being pushed up underneath concrete that has already begun to stiffen.

The more workable concretes suitable
for pumping can be used for pumping
directly into the mass, or for
tremie work, but the converse is not
necessarily true. The concrete will
need to have a slump in the region of
125 mm (5"), but the slump test, while
a good test for workability, does not
indicate the other desirable qualities
required. Good flowability and cohesion without stickiness are also necessary. These qualities are common
requirements for both tremie and pump
concretes.

BAGWORK

Although formerly used extensively
for both permanent works and repairs,
bagwork is now rapidly being relegated
to use for temporary works such as
sealing, expendable formwork and miscellaneous work where high structural
standards are not required.

The bags are usually made of hessian
and are half-filled with a very
plastic concrete mix. Full bags
tend towards a cylindrical shape which
are difficult to bed down properly, but
half-filled bags can be well trodden
down into position to give a large
area of contact. Adhesion of the
concrete takes place between the weave
of the hessian. The bags, which are
laid in typical brick bond fashion
should interlock to form a sound
structure. Dry mixes should be avoided
and the aggregate sizes should be
reasonably small.

Fig 17.3 A method of bagging

MIXING CEMENT

Ordinary Portland cement is normally
used, and the decision to use sulphate
resisting or other special cements
should be based on the same criteria
that would apply to any concrete in
the same environment.

AGGREGATES

The usual rules and standards apply to
the selection of aggregates but it
must be remembered that an especially
high workability is required. Thus,
where there is a choice between rounded
gravel and crushed stone, the decision
should be based on the same criteria
that would apply if concrete with
high workability were being produced
for ordinary purposes. Crushed rock
fine aggregates should generally be
avoided because the gradings are usually
poor and the particle shape unsuitable.
Where their use is necessary, as in
areas devoid of suitable natural sand,
or where the natural sand is poorly
graded, it may be necessary to supple-
ment the 'fines' by addition of
imported material. Increasing the
proportion of fine material and/or
the cement content can often help the
situation and should be checked first.

MIXING WATER

Fresh water is normally used for mixing,
but there is usually no objection to the
use of seawater for mass concrete,
provided that it is free from contamination by organic or other deleterious
matter.

ADMIXTURES

These are not normally necessary but
in certain circumstances can be used
with advantage to change the flow
properties, cohesion and rate of
setting and hardening. In deciding
whether admixtures should be used and
in choosing the type, the same criteria
should apply as for concreting in the
dry. (see 'The Concrete Society Technical.

Report Admixtures for Concrete'
TRCS 1-52.015.)

MIX DESIGN

The mix design should be carried out
in the same way as it would be for
work in the dry, while bearing in mind
the following special requirements.

(i)   Aggregates generally should
      not be larger than about 40mm
      (1½") for normal tremie work
      because of possible arching in
      the pipe, but where large concrete
      pours are being placed under-
      water and especially large
      diameter pipes are contemplated,
      aggregates should then be chosen
      in relation to the pipe diameter
      and the workability of the mix.

(ii) Especially high workability is
      required and the concrete should
      be wet by normal standards - when
      the concrete is tested in the
      dry slump exceeding 125mm (5")
      is essential. Underwater con-
      crete of the proper consistency
      is unlikely to stand at a slope
      greater than 5⁰ from the hori-
      zontal when being placed in situ,
      nor is it desirable that it
      should do so. In the interests
      of workability the mix should
      be over-sanded rather than under-
      sanded.

High strength concrete is not normally
required and the working conditions
make it very difficult to provide.
Because of this, detailed mix design
and trial mixes are inappropriate. A
common method of arriving at the mix
proportions is to take those which
are known to give the required strength
at the workability normally used in
the dry and because of the higher
workability required increase the
cement content by about 25%. This is
done for two reasons:

a) To produce comparable strength
   and durability with the increased
   workability and without the aid of
   mechanical methods of compaction.

b) To provide a margin against the
   loss of cement from exposed
   surfaces.

It should be noted that there is little
scope for placing lean concrete underwater, even when working stresses are
low, because the criteria is workability - not strength. Mixes containing
less than 330kg of cement per m^3
(550lb|yd³) are unlikely to be suit-
able. Admixtures which improve
workability may be used.

TESTING

The quality of the concrete in place
cannot be tested satisfactorily, so
that good control during placing must be
relied upon to ensure sound results.
Cores may be drilled but they are not
necessarily representative of the mass
of concrete which, because of the nature
of the placing techniques, is likely
to vary considerably in quality. Concrete test cubes taken at the mixer
should only be regarded as a check on
the consistency of the mix, the results
cannot be expected to represent the
strength in situ, but only the highest
theoretically attainable. It is not
practicable. to take satisfactory cubes
underwater.

DESIGN AND CONSTRUCTION

FORMWORK

Formwork may be made of timber or steel.
Steel is. preferable because of its
weight; if timber is used it will require
to be weighted down. Forms should be
robust enough to be assembled securely
without fussy bracing and fixings and
they should be as simple as possible to
assist the divers when fixing and striking.

Sandbags are usually used to seal forms to the bottom, but where an improved seal is required a skirting of plastic sheeting round the forms and loaded with sandbags usually proves satisfactory. Corbels and similar features are undesirable in underwater concrete work and should be avoided. Foundations should be kept simple in shape and forms made in large units. Through-bolts which interfere with the pouring of concrete, should be avoided wherever possible.

PRESSURES ON FORMWORK

The effective pressure on the formwork is that due to the submerged weight of the concrete only. It is usual when designing formwork, however, to allow for pressures as if the concrete were being placed in the dry, and to ignore the effects of submergence. This results in practical design, robust enough to be fabricated in the large sections required and to withstand the extra demands of underwater conditions.

REINFORCEMENT

Within the obvious limitations imposed by working underwater, placing reinforcement is possible, but placing the concrete is not as certain a process as in the dry so the results obtained may often be suspect. Good results have been obtained however. If it is necessary to use reinforcement simple details are required. Congested reinforcement must be avoided because even nominal steel may impede the concrete flow, causing voids with consequent deficiencies in bond strength. Where possible the reinforcement should be assembled in the dry and lowered into position as a cage. In some cases the reinforcement may be fixed to the formwork before this is lowered into position.

TOLERANCES

If necessary, the tolerances for underwater concrete can approach those for concrete in the dry, but this can only be achieved with much greater effort and expense. It cannot be emphasised too strongly that underwater concreting work is carried out under very difficult conditions, often by divers working by touch only because lighting is ineffective in cloudy water. Tolerances must be set with due regard to the requirements of the work and the particular conditions under which it is being constructed.

PREPARATION OF BASE

The usual rules of good practice for work in the dry apply to the cleaning and preparation of the area to be concreted. When depositing concrete on a soft bottom or in silty conditions it may be necessary to arrange for the removal of silt at the far end of the forms as it becomes displaced and squeezed up by the advancing face of the concrete.

SCREEDING

Screeding widths of up to 6m (20ft) are possible in good conditions with experienced divers but a lesser width is to be preferred. The screed, which must be heavy, is manageable by two divers - it is essential to use two because they must operate clear of the concrete. The screed is usually worked off the top of the forms which should be designed with this in mind. When screeding concrete underwater it is essential to have an adequate surcharge of concrete ahead of the screed so that no slacks or hollows can form because it is difficult or impossible to place extra concrete to fill these in. Skip-placed concrete is generally more suitable for screeded work because the right amount can be delivered to the divers where they require it. A level surface must be produced in a single pass, re-working is impractical underwater because it results in the formation of laitance. It is possible for divers to achieve finishes to quite good accuracies, but whenever possible, tolerances should be generous compared with those for a similar class of work in the dry.

PREPARATION BETWEEN LIFTS

Horizontal construction joints should be avoided wherever possible but where the volume of concrete makes them necessary, the greatest care must be taken to clear laitance which forms on the top surface of the lower lift however carefully the concrete is poured. As soon as the concrete has hardened sufficiently, the laitance should be removed by means of hoses, shovels, brooms, air-lifts etc, until a clean and hard surface is reached. It is useless to attempt to grout this surface before placing the next lift.

MAKING GOOD

Satisfactory repair of underwater concrete is virtually impossible and where concrete is defective it may be necessary to cut out a relatively large section to ensure that it can be replaced properly. Alternatively, in certain circumstances, it may be possible to extend the work to achieve the equivalent result. Pneumatic tools are necessary for the removal of hardened concrete and air-lifts can be used to remove laitance or plastic concrete.

GROUTED AGGREGATES

In the grouted aggregate process the forms are filled with coarse aggregate which is then grouted so that the voids are completely filled.

The grout is introduced at the bottom and any water present is displaced upwards as the grout rises.

Patented processes are used to achieve the necessary penetration of grout and the work is normally carried out by the proprietors or licensees of the particular process. It is important that the work should be carried out by specialist firms, or at least by operators and supervisors who have adequate experience of the particular process being used. First-class concrete will result if the work is carried out properly. Prejudice undoubtedly exists against the grouted aggregate process, at least to the extent that conventional concrete is preferred wherever it can possibly be used, but this prejudice is usually traceable to previous experience of bad results produced by indifferent operators.

WHEN TO USE GROUTED AGGREGATES

In deciding between conventional concrete and grouted aggregates the following factors should be considered:

(i)   Grouted aggregate is most useful in situations where the physical conditions impede the placing of conventional concrete, as for instance in some underpinning work.

(ii) Grouted aggregate is often an advantage where flowing water is concerned. The aggregate can usually be placed in the forms without too much difficulty and without its being washed away after placing. Once it has been placed, the frictional resistance of the voids is such that the velocity of flow of the water through the aggregate is reduced to a level at which grout can be introduced without any serious washing out.

An important property of the grouts is that they are almost twice as heavy as water and they are not easily diluted without mechanical mixing. Because of this the grout, even without the protection afforded by the coarse aggregate, has some resistance to scour by flowing water.

(iii)   Grouted aggregate should not be used in conditions where silt-laden water or algae can seriously contaminate the aggregate in the interval between placing the aggregate and carrying out the grouting.

(iv)   The pressures on forms from grouted aggregates are similar to those from conventional concrete. Greater attention to joints is required to ensure that they are grout-tight (though not necessarily water-tight) because seepage is not self-sealing as tends to be the case with concrete.

(v)   Special plant and trained supervisors are needed for grouted aggregate work.

MATERIALS

COARSE AGGREGATE

For underwater work the minimum size of coarse aggregate should be over 40mm (1½in), i.e. not more than 10% passing a 37.5mm (1½in) test sieve.

The maximum size of stone is governed only by the circumstances of placing and the grading above the minimum size is important only to the extent that a reduction of voids saves grout. The shape of aggregate is not very important and even slate can be successfully.grouted, although stone of the quality used for normal concrete is to be preferred. The aggregate should be clean and free from dust when it is placed because it will not be subjected to any mixing action which might otherwise remove traces of dirt.

FINE AGGREGATE

Any clean sand which is suitable for normal concrete may be used in the grout. The maximum particle size will usually lie between one-sixth and one-sixteenth of the nominal size of the coarse aggregate. The grading of the sand is important and will depend on the particle shape of both the coarse and fine aggregates. Field tests should normally be carried out to ensure that the grouting operation runs efficiently with the selected sand.

CEMENT

Ordinary Portland cement is normally used but blast-furnace slag or pozzolanic cements may also be used.

ADMIXTURES

Admixtures, such as fly ash, set accelerators or retarders, water-reducing admixtures, air-entrained admixtures, expanding agents and some others, may be advantageous in some instances as determined by the nature of the work.

Fly ash (PFA) is a common admixture and when high early strength is not required it is convenient to improve the fluidity of the grout by increasing the amount used.

The quality of the fly ash is important. It should be obtained from electrostatic precipitators in power stations and should have minimum fineness of $300m^2/kg$. Fly ash with a carbon content in excess of 5% by weight increases the demand for mixing water and leads to loss of strength.

Water-reducing admixtures are frequently added to grout to improve its physical properties. Such aids help to keep the sand in suspension in the grout, to prevent bleeding of the mixing water and to produce a colloidal effect. Intrusion aids and fly ash generally reduce the laitance on the surface of the grout.

THE GROUT

MIX PROPORTIONS

Water/cement ratios of about 0.5 are common and for underwater work the mix proportions should be approximately 1 part of cement to 1½ parts of sand by dry weight. Where pozzolana or fly ash is used it must be considered as cement.

MIXING

Grout must be thoroughly mixed in a special high-shear mixer so as to produce a colloidal-type fluid before pumping. It is essential to pass the grout through screens of about 6mm (¼in) mesh to remove foreign bodies or lumps which might otherwise choke the grout pipes.

CONSTRUCTION

FORMWORK

The formwork should be designed bearing in mind the same considerations which apply to any underwater work. The pressure from grouted aggregate concrete is the sum of the pressure from the aggregate and the fluid pressure of the grout in the submerged condition. The pressure from the aggregate is calculated using one of the well-known formulae, such as Rankine's for granular materials. This may give a pressure higher than for normal concrete but the difference is not often significant.

CLEANING FORMS

It is necessary to ensure the complete exclusion of silt from the forms because silt chokes the voids in the aggregate and interferes with the flow of grout.

If left adhering to the aggregate it may also reduce the bond between the aggregate and the grout. A 75mm (3in) layer of sand or pea gravel will usually exclude silt from the coarse aggregate if the bottom is dirty. Air lifts provide the most satisfactory means of removing silt if it is present in objectionable quantities.

Before the forms are inspected all measures should be taken to ensure that the periphery of the form is effectively sealed to prevent leakage of grout or the ingress of silt or other fine materials.

GROUTING

The aggregate should be placed and grouted as soon as possible after inspection of the base. If any possibility of contamination exists, ungrouted stone should not be allowed to remain in the forms overnight or until the next tide.

The grout is pumped from the mixer into grout tubes which are set in the forms before the aggregate is placed. To lubricate the pipelines the first mix of the day should be a neat cement grout with a water/cement ratio of 0.45.

Depending on the area to be filled, one or more grout tubes will be necessary, and the sizes and spacing of the tubes will be related to the depth of aggregate and its size and grading. The grout generally travels through the aggregate at a slope of about 1 in 7. It is important that the tubes to be used first are at the lowest point to be grouted. This ensures that the grout works its way upwards - never downwards through the voids.

It may be necessary to raise the bottom of the grout tube to limit the maximum pressure at the pump but a reasonable pressure must be maintained to indicate that the bottom of the tube is below the level of the grout. If the bottom of the tube is raised above the surface of the placed grout, the grout will flow downwards and when this happens the stones can act like the slates on a roof, shedding the grout diagonally and leaving voids directly beneath the point of introduction.

During grouting, the level of grout should be continually checked using slotted indicator tubes, about 50mm (2in) diameter, placed about half way between the grout tubes. These should be set at the same time as the grout tubes, before the aggregate is placed. The grout level is checked by soundings, either with an electric grout level indicator, or with a simple sounding cord carrying a float/weight with a specific gravity greater than unity but less than that of the grout (about 2). One suitable material is coal which has a specific gravity of about 1½.

TEST CUBES

When making test cubes the best results are obtained by using moulds with 3mm (1/8in) thick base plates perforated by 4 holes, 15 mm (½in) diameter. Ideally the size of the cube should be about four times the nominal maximum size of the aggregate. The moulds are filled with aggregate and stacked on top of one another. Grout is then pumped in from under the lowest mould in the stack until it appears at the top. It is necessary to clamp the moulds together in the stack because they tend to float as the grout finds its way up the stack. After 25 hours the moulds can be struck and the cubes cured under water at a temperature of 20°C in the normal way.

It should be noted that both of the following procedures will produce poor crushing results:

1 Filling a 150mm (6in) cube with grout and then 'seeding' it with coarse aggregate. This destroys the point-to-point contact of the stones and as the stone is usually stronger than the grout the test cube may fail under a smaller load than it should.

2 Filling a 150mm (6in) cube mould with stone and then pouring on the grout until the cube is full. This results in voids forming under some of the stones.

When fly ash is used in the grout, temperatures below 20°C prolong the hardening process while at 5°C hardening is practically halted. Because of this slow hardening it is customary to test cubes at the age of 90 days in addition to the 7 and 28 day tests when fly ash is used.

SPEED-CRETE

Speed-crete chemically cured concrete is manufactured by Acoustic Chemical Company Ltd and is available in 50lb steel kegs. It involves no skill in mixing or application.

It is ideal for all-purpose bonding and patching of concrete. However, it is fairly expensive and only small quantities can be handled easily underwater by the diver.

Speed-crete sets in 1½-5 minutes, has a compressive strength of 1800psi. in 24 hours and exceeds 5000psi.   in 28 days, with no appreciable volume change. It has three times the normal bonding strength of normal Portland cement 1:2 grout. Speed crete has been used underwater at depths below 9m (30ft). It has remained effective when applied at or below freezing point in refrigeration chambers, and in sea walls.

SPECIFICATION

1) Speed-crete should be used as
    supplied with no addition other
    than water, unless directed.

2) Water should be clean, and can
    be either fresh or salt.

3) Mixing

    a) A typical mixture should
        contain 4.5 - 5.1 litres, or
        4 - 4½qt of Speed-crete to
        1.1 litres (1qt) of water.
    b) The mixer should not take
        more than 1½ to 2 minutes
        to perform the operation.
    c) Mix only quantities that
        can be used immediately.
        Speed-crete hardens in
        4 to 8 minutes (usually
        less than 5 minutes).
    d) Too much water will result
        in a weaker mix. Do not add
        more water to soften har-
        dening mix.
    e) Water for mixing purposes
        may be from fresh, brackish
        or sea sources. It must,
        however, be free from
        industrial chemicals, i.e.
        tannic acid, sugar, detergent.
    f) The Speed-crete and water
        should be thoroughly mixed
        to the consistency of medium
        soft glazing putty.
    g) You should not attempt to
        retemper hardened mix.

PROPERTIES

Speed-crete as described above will
obtain its initial set in 4½-5 minutes.
Final set is approximately 30 minutes.
Speed-crete has a minimum compressive
strength of 1800psi. in 24 hours
and a minimum of 5000psi. in 28
days.

VOLUME CHANGE: at end of 24 hours
0.11% expansion.

BONDABILITY: Speed-crete bonds to
clean concrete stone, masonry and
steel.
BONDING STRENGTH: three times that of
1:2 Portland cement grout.
DENSITY: 120lb per cubic foot.
WATER ABSORPTION: 15 days - 1.73%.
PERCENTAGE OF CALCIUM CHLORIDE: None

NOTE: The above properties of Speed-
crete are identical for underwater and
surface use.

PLACING

-   All loose, scaly, oily material
    should be removed prior to placing.
    Speed-crete.
-   For out of water use, the area to be
    covered should be moistened with
    water immediately prior to placing.
-   Underwater the diver should carry
    the speed crete to the work site
    in a bag. This will prevent unneces-
    sary washing out of the mix prior to
    placement.
-   Speed crete should be placed in a
    firm manner to ensure complete bond
    to the area being covered.

FINISHING

Out of water Speed-crete can be finished to a smooth even surface by hand
or machine trowelling.

CURING

For out of the water use Speed-crete
less than 12mm (½in) in thickness should
be cured after 16 hours with damp sand
or sprayed with an approved curing
compound.

Underwater curing is unnecessary.

CHAPTER 18

EXPLOSIVES UNDERWATER

The use of explosives underwater has greatly increased as the technology of the offshore oil and gas industry has expanded, and explosive devices are now in common use for "constructive" purposes, whereas in the past, their use has always been associated with destruction only. Explosive charges are placed and fired deep beneath the seabed in drilling operations, to open up fissures in the rock; to cut off steel pipe or casing, to cut trenches in which flow line will be laid, to remove old structures, and countless other applications. Explosive bolts or similar shear devices can be actuated at a distance to release something as simple as a marker buoy, or control the launching of a multi-million pound platform into deep water, or shaped charges will sever wire hawsers or a 48in diameter pipe-line as easily and neatly as a knife cuts butter.

Most of these applications call for the use of pre-prepared devices, which only require connection to their triggering device, and there may be little call for a diver to actually make up a charge, fuse, place and then detonate it, except when it comes to general salvage and civil engineering contract work. These are both areas in which large quantities of explosive material may be detonated, and hence every commercial diver should have an appreciation of explosives, how they are detonated, why they detonate, how to achieve the best results from an explosive charge, handling and general safety precautions.

The subject is extremely technical, and many years' experience will be necessary before a diver could say with confidence, that he was fully competent, or "expert", but the contents of this Chapter certainly cover more than the basics.

EXPLOSIVES AND THE LAW

Regulations

The potential destructive power of any explosives substance, coupled with the need to ensure that it is handled only by competent, trained individuals, who have a regard for the public safety, makes it necessary for strict regulations in order that such materials can be purchased only by authorised individuals.

All users of explosives or explosive materials, or those who store explosives, other than certain government departments, must hold a valid Police Explosives Licence or Certificate appropriate to their operation.

It is the responsibility of the retailer of explosives that he does not make it available to unauthorised persons, and therefore it follows that the relevant documentation must be produced, before explosives are allowed to change hands. Co-operation in this matter between supplier and purchaser is essential, as with fire-arms licences and the purchase of ammunition, and each party in any, transaction has a separate and legal responsibility, with heavy penalties for failing to observe them. Particularly at a time when explosives are the main weapon of terrorist factions, the control of explosives and their associated components and accessories, in particular high explosives and detonators, has assumed a high level of importance.

All users of explosives, other than those who purchase materials under an "Immediate Use" police certificate,

must observe the regulations regarding storage, the various categories of which
are as follows:

Type of store	Quantity of explosives permitted
1 Private use	10lb nominally (metrication has caused the makers of explosive materials to supply in 5kg minimum packs, which represents 11.023lbs of high explosive, or 30lbs(14kg) blackpowder; plus up to 100 detonators, and 5 coils of safety fuze.
2 Registered Premises	
Mode "A"	60lbs explosives, including blackpowder and detonators, or 200lb blackpowder only.
Mode "B"	15lbs explosives, including blackpowder and detonators, or 50lb blackpowder only.
3 Stores	
Division "A"	150lb explosives, including blackpowder and detonators
Division "B"	300lb explosives, including blackpowder and detonators
Division "C"	1000lb explosives, including blackpowder and detonators
Division "D"	2000lb explosives, including blackpowder and detonators
Division "E"	4000lb explosives, including blackpowder and detonators
4 Magazines	Varying quantities but generally in excess of those permissable under Stores Division "E", the exact quantity being dependent upon the requirements laid down by HM Inspector of Explosives, who is responsible for the examination and approval of magazines.

NB: The explosives weight of detonators for Storage Class 2 to 4 above, should
be calculated at 2.25lb per 100 detonators. The explosives weight of
Cordtex and Superflex in Storage Class 1 to 4 above should be calculated at
16lb per 1000ft of Cordtex and 40lb per 1000ft for Superflex fuse.

Application to purchase explosives, and then store them in the relevant catgory of 1-3 above, should be made to the local Chief of Police. Application for permission to construct, erect or operate a magazine should be addressed to the Health and Safety Executive, HM Inspector of Explosives, who have the power to refuse an applicant a licence. The holder of a magazine licence does not also require a Police certificate or Licence.

Certification

Explosives certificates and licences are free, and valid for a period of 12 months from date of issue, with the obvious proviso that the Chief of Police has the power to withdraw or revoke any such authority at immediate notice, should circumstances dictate.

Police Explosives Certificate

Required to purchase any high explosives, electrical detonators and Cordtex.

Police Explosives Licence

Required for the purchase of black-powder, safety fuse and plain detonators only.

Police "Immediate Use" Certificate

Where explosives are required for immediate use in larger quantities than the existing authorisation allows, eg. a private user with an Explosives Certificate who requires 120lb of high explosive for a particular "one-off" job - or where the intending user is considered competent, but does not hold a Police certificate or Licence, the Chief of Police is authorised, at his sole discretion, to issue an "Immediate Use" Certificate.

This will be valid for the one purchase only, on a specific day, for a specific task. Should the material not be used on the day of purchase, or a quantity remains unused after, then the police issuing authority must be informed, with details of the quantity of explosives, current whereabouts, and the circumstances, plus measures being taken to ensure the safe and secure storage, whilst a decision is taken regarding their future.

It is accepted that circumstances of mechanical breakdown of craft or plant, bad weather, sickness, and other factors may bring about a situation in which explosives purchased for "Immediate Use" cannot be used as planned. Provided the circumstances are reported, then alternative arrangements can normally be made.

Application for permits

In order to be issued with any of the authorising documents mentioned, and it should be remembered that an individual person may hold both a Police Certificate and a Licence at the same time, the applicant must, in the opinion of the Chief of Police be a "fit" person to purchase, store and use explosive materials. There is no definition of the word "fit" in this context, or of a persons "fitness", either in the Explosives Act or any relevant Act of Council.

HM Inspectors of Explosive consider that that one of the conditions is that a Chief of Police must be satisfied that the applicant will take such precautions as will afford all necessary security for the public safety.

Application should be made on the appropriate form, to the Chief Constable of the applicant's home county, or Crime Prevention Officer of his home town or city, nearest to his normal place of residence. In most cases an interview will follow, at which the applicant will be expected to satisfy questions related to the intended use of the materials, where they will be stored, the type of materials likely to be purchased, and what experience or training the applicant has received.

There is normally a short delay whilst certain enquiries are made, and a visit may be necessary to see the place of storage, which may also entail the local Fire Prevention Officer. There may be other requirements, which will vary from place to place, depending on the local circumstances, and Chief Constables are free to impose such requirements as they see necessary.

In general, proof of some form of recognised training, with some subsequent practical experience under the supervision of an existing qualified Certificate or Licence holder, a character reference, proof of a permanent address and stable background, are the minimum requirements. Whilst it is not possible to be specific, applicants under the age of 18 years are unlikely to be issued with an explosives Certificate or Licence, and a criminal record or history of abnormal behaviour would be likely to debar the applicant.

Renewal

Renewal, if desired, of Certificates and Licences can take place, free of charge, on the expiry of 12 months from issue, or earlier. It is recommended that such applications be made some weeks prior to expiry of previous documents, in order to give time for any difficulties to be resolved, and in order to prevent the situation where an individual finds that his authorisation has expired, but he is now unlawfully holding a stock of explosive materials. Application for renewal will entail the completion of another application form, which should be forwarded, along with the expiring documents, to the original issuing authority. Application can be made elsewhere, since the Certificate or Licence is normally valid for use anywhere in the United Kingdom, but there may be certain restrictions or endorsements on an individual authorisations to the contrary.

STORAGE OF EXPLOSIVES

Details of the various classes of store have already been outlined, but a few notes of explanation are necessary.
There are no legal restrictions on the method in which explosives should be stored under the category of "Private Use", other than those imposed by the certification authority, but it is recommended that the maximum amount of explosive allowed under "Private Use", ie. 10lb (4.5kg) or 30lb (14kg) of blackpowder, and up to 100 detonators, should be kept in a secure, locked box, clearly marked "Explosives", and stored well clear of children, in such a place, that it could readily be removed to a safe place in the event of fire. The method of storage must satisfy the Chief of Police concerned.
Applications from individuals living in "bed-and-breakfast" type of accommodation; "shared" accommodation, or blocks of flats, are likely to be refused.

REGISTERED PREMISES - Mode A

This type of Store requires a building constructed substantially of brick, stone, concrete or iron, or a securely constructed fireproof safe, wholly detached from any dwelling house by a distance laid down in Statutory Instrument 1951, No 1163, as well as being not less than 15yds from any public place of work or thoroughfare. A registeration fee is payable, and the premises subject to inspection by the local Fire Prevention Officer.

REGISTERED PREMISES - Mode B

May consist of a properly constructed fireproof safe or other substantial container such as a locked cupboard, box or drawer, kept inside a shop, house, office or warehouse.

STORES

If the quantity of explosives and detonators to be stored exceeds 60lb (200lb if blackpowder only is to be kept), the explosives must be kept in a properly constructed building, licensed by the local authority. There will be an annual fee, and application should be made on HM Stationery Office Form No 1.

MAGAZINES

If the quantity of explosives to be stored is greater than that permissable under a Store, Division E (4000lb), and it is not convenient to erect two Stores, then an application for a Magazine must be made to HM Inspector of Explosives.

CARRIAGE OF EXPLOSIVES

The handling and conveyance of explosive materials by road is covered by the Explosives Acts of 1875 and 1923 and subsequent Statutory Orders.
Vehicles carrying explosives fall into two categories:

1 Specially constructed road vehicles

2 Motor vehicles not specially constructed.

Category 1 vehicles above are those
constructed in accordance with Home
Office Regulations in mind, which
differ for:

a) Petrol-driven vehicles
b) Diesel-driven vehicles

The regulations should be consulted if
more than 500lb of explosives is to be
carried, but less than 8000lb since
these are the maximum loads of both
types of vehicles in Category 1.
       Briefly, two men must accompany
the vehicle; there must be a fire-
resistant screen between the cab and
the body; the fuel tank must be in
front of the screen; a quick action
fuel "cut-off" must be fitted in the
fuel line, plus other regulations
relating to fire extinguishers, the
type of lamps carried, floorboard
material and security.

Category 2 vehicles are required where
the quantity of explosives exceeds
100lb, but is under 500lb. Again, the
regulations specify the exact vehicle
requirements, which include that the
outer package of explosive materials
must be an approved metal cylinder;
all such cylinders must rest on the
floor; two men must accompany the
vehicle, and other requirements.

Category 2(b) vehicles can have a
maximum permissible load of 100lb,
and can be any mechanically driven
vehicle, not carrying or plying for
public passengers, provided that the
conditions of O.S.S. No 11 are met,
and all due precautions are taken
for the prevention of accidents.

CLASSES OF EXPLOSIVES

By definition, there are three
categories of explosives, which are
as follows:

Low Explosives

These include non-shattering, lifting or propellant explosives,
examples of which are gunpowder,
blackpowder and cordite. By reason
of their chemistry, or the manner
in which they are used, they are
incapable of detonation, neither are
they affected by shock. Initiation
is by flame, flash or spark only.

High Explosives

Due to the rapid chemical changes
that occur, these are described as
"shattering". Typical examples are
dynamite, TNT, Amatol, RDX, Torpex,
and all plastic explosives or those
with a nitroglycerine content. These
can all be initiated by shock.

Primary Explosives

Are those materials which under the
stimulus of mild shock alone, will
detonate easily, ie. fulminate of
mercury; lead azide etc, all of
which have a molecular structure
which makes them unstable. Such
materials are normally used in
limited quantities only, and form
part of what is known as the
"explosives train" in providing the
shock necessary to detonate high
explosive materials.

Examples of explosives available to
the public:

Explosives manufactured in Gt Britain
will have originated from either
the ICI (Nobel Division) or E & C.P
Ltd (Explosives and Chemical Products). Examples of the wide range
of material available include:

a) Nitroglycerine gelatines

    Includes all gelatines and gelig-
    nites.
b) Nitroglycerine semi-gelatines and
    powders

    Belex, Rockite, and dynamite

c) Non-Nytroglycerine Powders

Trimonite, Nobelite, Anobel etc.*

d) Slurried explosives

Supergel, Powerfil*

* These are trade names used by the ICI
(Nobel Division) Company.

CHEMISTRY OF DETONATION

The expression "explosives train" refers
to the chain of events which once initiated will cause the detonation of an
explosives substance. It might at first
sight appear a matter of some simplicity
to initiate an explosion, whereas in
fact it is a complex process, which
should be fully understood to obtain
the best results, and avoid misfires.

A low explosive such as blackpowder
requires only a flame, flash or spark to
initiate combustion, which then consumes
the powder converting the material into
gas, accompanied by heat.

On the other hand, high explosive,
which is purposely made insensitive, and
hence difficult to detonate, requires a
considerable amount of physical shock
only. In the case of blackpowder,
practical initiation of the "train" is
by precussion, chemical or slow burning
fuse. With high explosives, a small
subsidiary charge of a more sensitive
nature is needed, usually referred to as
a "primer" which contains a "primary"
explosive compound.

Exactly how shock initiates high
explosive is not perfectly understood;
the effect may be purely mechanical in
that it secures molecular breakdown, but
an alternative theory, known as the
"Hot Spot" theory is equally convincing.
This supposes that the necessary heat
derives from the inter-crystalline
friction arising from the application of
a sudden shock. This makes sense if it is
remembered that most high explosive
materials have ingredients added in the
form of particles which improve friction,
and that a sensitive explosive can be
made less sensitive by the addition of
wax, which appears to have a lubricating
effect.

Hydrodynamic Detonation

In an explosion, the chemical reaction is one of molecular breakdown and recombination, and this
reaction proceeds through the mass
of material at a finite rate. Consider
as an example, a small quantity of
explosive material in which the reaction is developing. Now imagine
it divided into a series of thin
layers perpendicular to the axis along
which the reaction is developing. The
gas pressure resulting from the interaction will be least at the layer
furthest from the initiating point,
and at a maximum further back where
the reaction is just completed. The
gas pressure produced is achieved so
suddenly, that in any layer it causes
adiabatic compression of the gases in
the next layer, hence raising the
temperature of that layer and causing
the reaction to proceed faster.

This naturally causes even
greater pressure to be developed
which continues to compress the gas
and increase the pressure at each
layer until the furthest layer is
reached. The result is a shock wave
known as the detonation wave. The
pressure of the wave in a detonating
explosive may be in the order of
150,000 to 250,000 atmospheres, which
is reached in a matter of micro-
seconds, with an average temperature
increase to between 3000 and 4000°C.

In an explosion, the detonation wave travels through the explosive at a determined rate, the
terminal velocity being reached when
the energy produced is absorbed
completely in compressing the
material ahead; this rate is known
as the "velocity of detonation".
Typical examples of this velocity
are:

RDX	= 8639m/sec
Nitroglycerine	= 8060 "
PETN	= 8150 "
TNT	= 6480 "
Blasting gelatine	= 7900 "
Gelignite	= 6520 "

The high pressure associated with the detonation wave has already been mentioned. Any situation which relieves this pressure will discourage the propagation, so that it is necessary to have an adequate amount of confininement. If such confinement is not possible, then an explosive material must be used that will maintain detonation under favourable conditions, ie. an HE. with a high velocity.

EXTERNAL EFFECTS OF EXPLOSIONS

These fall into two categories, namely the shock wave, followed by the expansion of the resulting gas. The detonation wave passes through the explosive material, reaches the extremities and passes into either air, earth or water. Due to the "streaming" effect of a detonation wave, the effect is strongest at the terminal end of the cartridge of explosive. If the explosive is confined, as for example in a bomb case, or down a shot-hole drilled in rock, then far more energy is passed into the surrounding media.

UNDERWATER EXPLOSIONS

Explosions underwater are a very special circumstance, since the surrounding water achieves full and complete confinement or "tamping" more efficiently than ever would be achieved on the surface artificially. If such an underwater explosion could be slowed down and observed, the following sequence of events would be seen to occur:

a) On detonation the shock wave is transmitted through the water, and will be seen on the surface to give an immediate "flattening" effect, followed by the noise of detonation.
b) A rapidly expanding bubble of gas is produced, which in effect does the actual "work".
c) This gas bubble expands until its maximum diameter is achieved, which will be governed by its internal gas pressure becoming equal to that of the surrounding water, after which the natural cooling effect will lower the temperature of the gas bubble, decrease its pressure, and the water pressure will cause the bubble to collapse inward upon itself.

d) In collapsing, the pressure of the gas will rise as it becomes confined into a smaller space, as a result, its temperature will rise, and at a certain point the gas pressure will once again exceed the surrounding ambient pressure.
e) The gas bubble will now expand for a second time, performing "work" for a second time, until again water pressure, assisted by its cooling effect, prevents further expansion, and the bubble again collapses.
f) This oscillation continues until the gas is entirely dissipated through heat losses, after which the remnants will slowly bubble towards the surface. The "target" is therefore subjected to a number of repeated "blows", each weaker than its predecessor, as the gas expands and collapses. This is a situation which cannot be achieved on land, and hence allows work to be achieved in an underwater situation, using far less material than the same task would require in a dry situation.

Shallow-water Explosions

It follows that should explosives be detonated in water sufficiently shallow for the first expansion of the gas bubble to break the surface, giving a "depth-charge" effect, then no further compression of the gas is possible, and the advantage has been lost. This circumstance may prove unavoidable, in which case the size of the charge may need to be reduced, and consideration given to the surface effects of the shock wave and noise, particularly near buildings or structures.

"Safe" and "lethal" distances For Divers to Underwater Explosions

Submerged explosive charges should never be detonated with a diver knowingly underwater, nor in the vicinity of surface swimmers or public beaches where people may be partially or wholly in water.
    There is no such thing as a "safe" distance from an underwater

explosion, and the guidance that follows is only that gained by the armed forces during two world wars, in which there were opportunities to record certain incidents. If it is intended to carry out blasting operations underwater, then it is the responsibility of the appointed diving supervisor to ensure that no lives are placed at risk.

This may entail the co-operation of other diving contractors in the area, and it must be accepted from the outset that there may be delays, even to the point of withdrawing or defusing charges already laid, or even cancellation of the entire operation. The alternative is the risk of possible fatalities, injury, legal action, and the possible withdrawal of the authority to use explosives.

Planning of blasting operations is therefore essential, with full consultation regarding local authorities, the police, public services, harbour authorities and others. The safety and welfare of the public must always be the prime consideration. The golden rule is always - IF IN ANY DOUBT - WAIT.

"Safe" distance for a diver

The so called "safe" distance = 40 x the TNT equivalent weight of explosives, measured in pounds, where the distance is measured from the point of detonation in feet.

Example: What would be the "safe" distance for a diver, if a charge weighing 50lbs (TNT) were detonated underwater ?

40 x 50lb = 2000ft

"Lethal" distance for a diver

The so called "lethal" distance = 7 x the TNT equivalent weight of explosives, measured in pounds, where the distance is measured from the point of detonation in feet.

Example: What would be the "lethal" distance for a diver, if a charge weighing 50lb (TNT) were detonated underwater ?

7 x 50lb = 350ft

Typical Working Calculation

Example: A contractor wishes to detonate charges underwater, to carry out demolition work, but due to the circumstances, can only guarantee an area with a radius of half a mile (nautical), to be free of divers. What is the maximum weight in pounds, of the charge he can "safely" detonate at any one time ?

Answer:

1 x international nautical mile
= 6076ft
therefore half a mile = 3038ft

$$\text{Weight (lb)} = \frac{\text{Distance (ft)}}{40}$$

ie: $\text{Weight (lb)} = \frac{3038}{40}$

= 75.95lb

To nearest lb   = 76lbs

Fig 18-1 Typical surface disturbance following a shallow water explosion. Note the fuel storage in close proximity

Types of Explosives

Military:

TNT.(Trinitrotoluene)

Made by digesting toluene, which is obtained from the fractional distillation of coal-tar, with nitrating acid (ie. a mixture of nitric acid and sulphuric acid). There will be an incomplete combustion on detonation, due to a deficiency of oxygen in the TNT molecule, and the resulting uncombined carbon gives rise to a thick black cloud, typical of an unbalanced explosive detonated in air. Pale yellow in colour, can be poured or moulded hot, changes to light or dark brown when cast; poisonous.

RDX (Cyclonite)

Manufactured by treating hexamine with a cold concentration of nitric acid. Hexamine itself is made by combining formaldehyde with ammonia. More sensitive than TNT, it is a white crystalline powder with a very high melting point. Normally mixed with TNT, which then allows it to be poured. Can be mixed with a plasticiser to make a plastic explosive. The nitric acid content will eat its way through containers that are not lined or varnished.

Amatol

A mixture of ammonia-nitrate and TNT in the proportions of 60/40. The nitrate provides the necessary additional oxygen for the complete combustion of the TNT. The mixture melts at 80°C and readily absorbs water. Causes serious corrosion when damp and in contact with steel or non-ferrous materials, forming "bluesalts" or picric acid crystals in the case of the latter, which are extremely sensitive to shock. Amatol expands when hot, and at 30°C can be as much as 5%, causing containers to burst open.

Minol

An Amatol mixture of explosives, to which aluminium powder has been added, usually in the proportions of TNT-43%, aluminium powder-20%, ammonium nitrate-37%, making a more powerful material.
100lb of Minol 0 150lb of TNT

RDX/TNT

A mixture of 60% RDX and 40% TNT, to which wax has been added as a lubricant. Known as Cyclotol in the U.S.A.

Torpex

Another version of RDX/TNT in an aluminised form, the aluminium being added at the expense of the RDX to increase its power. More sensitive than TNT alone.

Plastic Explosives (PE-2/PE-4)

Manufactured by incorporating RDX with oil and gelatine, so as to reduce the RDX content to about 88%.

Commercial Explosives

Nitroglycerine

The most important sensitiser for commercial explosives. Made by reacting purified glycerine with a mixture of nitric acid and sulphuric acids, with water. Readily initiated by impact or shock. It is a viscous yellow fluid, which can be frozen at 13.2°C, to make a sensitive solid explosive. In order to prevent unwanted freezing when part of another explosive mix, ethylene glycol (anti-freeze) is introduced.

PETN

Pentaerythrito-Tetranitrate, an explosive material sensitive to friction and mechanical shock. Used as the dry white powder filling for Cordtex and Superflex.

Nitrocellulose

Used to thicken nitroglycerine during the preparation of both gelatine and semi-gelatine type explosives, the basic raw material being cotton. Normally handled wet during manufacture, nitrocellulose contains 30% water, and in such conditions is non-explosive, ie. when the nitrogen content does not exceed 12.6%. When more highly nitrated, it becomes "gun-cotton", and as such is very sensitive, even when wet. Dry nitrocellulose is an extremely dangerous material.

Gelatines

The main constituents are nitroglycerine, nitro-cotton, sodium nitrate and cellulose materials. Gelatine explosives are of high density, malleable (within reason), offer good water resistance, are free from fumes and store well. The normal range comprises strengths from 45 to 75%, which meets the requirements of most underwater, mining, quarry and tunnel work.

Special Gelatines

So named since they contain a proportion of ammonium nitrate in manufacture. Other ingredients are the same as for plain gelatines plus absorbents. Since ammonium nitrate readily absorbs moisture, cartridges of this explosive are either dipped in wax, or packed in a special manner to prevent ingress. Opened cases should not be exposed to the atmosphere longer than necessary before being resealed.

Two-part "Mix" Explosives

Developed in the United States, these are conveniently pre-packaged, two component, high-explosive "mix" kits. Consisting of a coarse blended solid, sealed in an anti-static pvc container, which can be bags, bottles, or pre-shaped charges, and a thinner liquid substance, neither component being an explosive material by itself, nor are they classified as highly-inflammable.

When the activating liquid component is added to the semi-solid, an explosive compound with a 40-60% power equivalent of commercial dynamite is produced. Although a relatively low yield explosive, the advantages of storage, transportation etc far outweigh its disadvantages. Since neither component is classified as explosive, it readily overcomes many of the restrictions and regulations which relate to the conventional explosive materials.

As yet, this development has not had any great impact on the UK market, and in any case, has lost some of its flexibility by being classified in accord with other explosives, for obvious reasons.

DETONATORS

It has already been stated that certain combinations of chemicals will form explosive compounds, which can only be initiated by shock. ie. high explosives and primary explosives. This "shock" is normally obtained by the use of a detonator, which itself contains a sensitive primary explosive, and hence should be treated with the greatest respect.

There are a wide range of types of detonator, which can be classified under the headings of "plain" and "electric".

Plain Detonators

These comprise of an aluminium tube, approximately 1.25in length, open at one end, the sealed end of which holds a base charge of high-explosives, overlaid with a priming charge. A typical base charge would be 0.24g of PETN, compressed into place at a pressure of 4000psi. On top of this will be placed an initiating charge of dextrinated lead azide and lead styphnate in the proportions of 2:1.

Plain detonators are designed specifically to be used with safety fuse.

Electric Detonators

Instantaneous electric detonators consist of a copper or aluminium tube, similar to plain detonators, except that they are fitted with a pair of either tinned iron or copper "lead-in"wires, which are insulated with a pvc sleeving.

Their construction is as shown below:

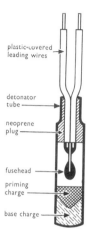

Fig 18-2 Section of an electric
detonator, showing components

Neoprene plug:

This holds the "lead-in" wires in place,
and forms a watertight seal at the
point where the tube is crimped, which
compresses the plug in place.

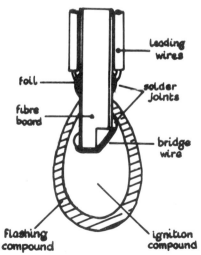

Fig 18-3 Construction and components of
a fuse-head

Fuse-head

Fig 18-3 shows the construction and
components which make up the fusehead. The metal foil strips make the
electrical connection between the
lead-in wires and the "bridge" wire.
When a current in the order of lamp
is passed through the "bridge", it
heats this small section of high
resistance wire, which glows white
hot before burning out. During the
peak of the intense heat generated,
it automatically ignites the ignition
compound, which in turn fires the
flashing compound, so setting in
motion what has already been described as the "explosive train" of
initiation.

The sequence of events in firing
an electric detonator is shown
diagrammatically in Fig 18-4

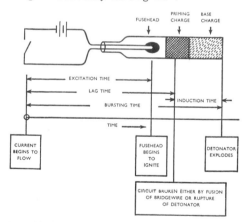

Fig 18-4 Sequence of events in
firing an electric detonator

The electrical resistance of the
fuse-head alone, without the lead-
in wires, is usually kept between
the limits of 0.9 to 1.6ohms, and
a current flow of 0.5amps applied
for 50 milliseconds is the minimum
necessary to start the cycle of
initiation. This figure is for a
single detonator, and with a multi-
detonator firing circuit, a
greater current flow will be necessary, as outlined later in the Chapter.

Since the reliability and standard of
detonators is of the utmost importance,
each stage of the manufacture is carefully controlled, so that characteristics and performance are consistent
throughout.

Detonators for Underwater Use

The standard electric detonator is not
suitable for any "in-water" use except
at very shallow depths. For deep water
or "long soak" conditions, ICI in
particular manufacture a special
submarine detonator range known as
"Hydrostar" underwater detonators, which
have a copper body tube, slightly
longer and wider than a conventional
surface elctric detonator, plus blue
pvc insulated "lead-in" wires.

These are designed to operate in
water, to a maximum pressure of 1000psi.
Details of the range of electric
detonators available is given later.

Delay Detonators

Certain blasting operations may require
a number of charges to be fired, but
with a suitable interval between each
explosion, perhaps to reduce the
shock wave, or deliberately, to
produce a "ripple" effect.

Typical examples of this would be
"trenching", or the firing in sequence
of charges in a rock face, particularly
where personal or private property
might be affected.

The construction of a delay detonator is shown in Fig 18-5. The assembly
is that of a standard electric detonator,
except that an additionalsection is
added, which gives the delay element
between the fusehead and the priming
composition. In some detonators, the
fusehead may be enclosed in a tubular
neoprene insulating sleeve, as an added precaution against the possibility of
static discharge between the fusehead
and the tube wall, which might cause a
premature initiation.

The actual delay element consists
of a thick walled tube loaded with a
suitable delay composition. The delay
period is controlled by the nature of

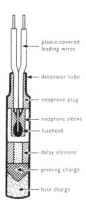

Fig 18-5 Components and construction
of a delay detonator

this material, and the amount enclosed in the tube.

Due to the nature of their
manufacture, all delay detonators
can be used in "wet" conditions,
being able to withstand water pressure of at least 60psi (equivalent to
a depth of 132ft). Delay detonators
can be wired in series or parallel,
in the same manner as ordinary electric detonators. The fusehead of
each unit will ignite as the firing
current flows through the circuit,
but actual initiation of the base
charge will occur only after the
respective delay element has burnt
through.

The actual delay time is
indicated by a coloured pvc tag
attached to one of the "lead-in"
wires, which will bear a number.
With ICI products, these tags are
colour coded as follows, but these
should be checked before use:

No 1 - Yellow
No 2 - Blue
no 3 - White
No 4 - Red   :and so on.

This aids identification, and greatly facilitates the checking of shot-
firing circuits, after the connections have been made.

Range of Delay Detonators Available

Half-second Series

In the half-second series, there are 13 detonators, numbered 0 to 12, each with a nominal time interval of 0.5sec between consecutive numbers. No 0 acts instant-eously, ie. it has no delay.

Short-delay Series

There are 19 detonators in this range, numbered from 0 to 18, with No 0 being instantaneous. The nominal delay between successive numbers from No 1 to 4 is 0.025secs; from No 5 to 12 inc. is 0.05sec,
and from No 13 to 18inc. is 0.07sec. Short delay detonators are of particular value for blasting operations in quarries and open cast work where ground vibrat-ion must be kept to a minimum. They improve blasting efficiency, and give better rock fragmentation.

"Carrick" Short-delay Series

These are specially designed for use in coal mines, since they incorporate a new type of fusehead and a special delay element which eliminate the risk of fire-damp ignition. The range is from No 0 to 10, with an interval of 0.025sec between each.

"Hydrostar" Underwater Short-delay Series

Available in a short series from No 0 to No 3 only, with a nominal delay of 25milli-seconds between each consecutive number.

Electric Powder Fuses

Designed specially for the electric shot firing of blackpowder. Each consists of a thick paper tube containing blackpowder, with a conventional electric detonator fusehead fitted at one end. On firing, this ignites the powder in the tube, which in turn ignites the main charge. The charge weight in each tube is in the order of 5 grains, and they are not waterproof.

SAFETY FUSE

The flexible, waterproof, textile covered "tube" containing black-powder, that is used to fire plain detonators. Supplied in lengths of 24ft(7.3m), each known as a "coil" of fuse, or spooled in longer lengths of 3000ft(914m).

The construction and manufac-ture is such that safety-fuse can be relied on to burn at a uniform rate, so that a carefully measured length cut from a coil, will act as a "time-delay" fuse to ignite a blackpowder charge, without the use of a detonator. Or, if inserted in-to the open end of a plain deton-ator and crimped in place, will initiate high explosives. A typical "burning" time would be 1ft per 30 seconds, but other times are available.

On purchase, and prior to its use in connection with a charge, it is recommended that after cutting off and discarding the first 4-6in (100-150mm) of a coil, a 1ft length is measured and cut, and the burning time tested.

Due to physical compression by water pressure at any depth, "safety fuse" burns faster the deeper it is employed, and over 60ft(18m) will have risen to 3.5ft (1m), and is therefore recommended for shallow water use only.

Safety fuse is ignited by any form of heat or flame, and should be stored in a dry atmosphere. This type of fuse is known sometimes as Bickford fuse, after the naval officer that invented it.

CORDTEX DETONATING FUSE

Cordtec is the trade name for a highly efficient, flexible, cord-like fuse with a very high detonat-ion velocity, being in the order of 21,000ft per sec.

It consists of a core of PETN explosive, enclosed in a tape wound "tube", reinforced by textile

yarn, the whole enclosed in a white
pvc sheath.

Cordtex is initiated by either a
detonator taped parallel and as close
and tightly in contact as possible, or
else, by enclosing one end inside a
single cartridge of high explosive. In
either case, it is sympathetic detonation which causes the Cordtex to be
initiated.

Its tensile strength is 180lb,
which coupled with the tough pvc outer
covering, makes Cordtex highly resistant to strain and abrasion, and is
particularly suitable for underwater
use to considerable depths. At temperatures down to -10°C Cordtex will
remain flexible, but below this figure
will stiffen, and cracking may occur.
Used as an instantaneous fuse between
charges of high explosive, hence
allowing any number to be linked
together, simply by passing the Cordtex
through the centre of each charge, and
on to the next.

It offer a considerable financial
saving in that possibly only one
detonator will be required, the risk of
electrical misfires are greatly
reduced, and charges can be linked over
great distances. Cordtex can be used to
form any number of "branch lines,
provided that these are made correctly,
and that the "streaming" effect of
Cordtex is taken into account. Such
"branch" junctions, which can be made
by binding with wire, tape or string,
should be over a minimum distance of
4in(100mm).

Since on detonation there is a
tendency for the detonation wave passing
down a length of Cordtex to continue on
in a straight line, sharp kinks or bends,
with a radius of less than 4in(100mm)
should be avoided. Neither should Cordtex
fuse be allowed to lay across itself. In
both cases, the fuse is very likely to
be severed at the point of crossing or
bend, and misfires will result.

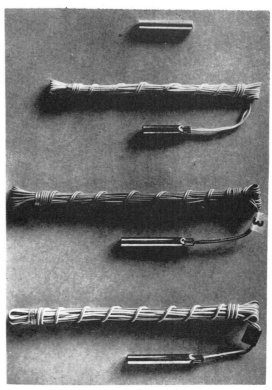

Fig 18-6 Detonator types, showing a
plain detonator (top), an electric
detonator, followed by two electric
delay detonators with tags showing

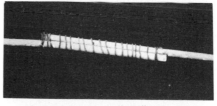

Fig 18-7 Cordtex "lap" joint

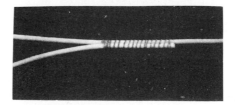

Fig 18-8 Cordtex "Y" joint

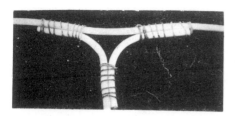

Fig 18-9 Cordtex "double L" joint

Fig 18-10 Cordtex "Clove-hitch" joint

Cordtex Used Underwater

Particularly valuable in an underwater environment, Cordtex reduces the time taken to lay charges, and reduces the actual number of electrical connections the diver would otherwise have to make.

In bad visibility this can be a great advantage, and the only consideration necessary, other than that of joints and bends, is the possibility of water ingress of the PETN core of the fuse. Underwater, a "free" end of some 4-6ft(1.5-2m) is desirable, and if there is the possibility that the fuse may be left submerged for a matter of days, or weeks, then the free ends should be sealed with special blank "caps", obtainable from the manufacturers, or else a plain detonator.

It is essential that the portion of fuse at the point of detonation is dry, after which satisfactory initiation will continue from dry to wet Cordtex, provided they are in the same section or length. If the Cordtex used for a branch line is wet, then the initiation wave will not pass into that branch, and a misfire will result.

If circumstances are such that all the Cordtex available is wet,

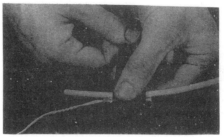

Fig 18-11 Attaching an electric detonator to Cordtex with adhesive tape. Note the amount of fuse left as an overhang, to allow for possible water ingress.

then it can still be used in conjunction with a commercial waterproof primer unit.

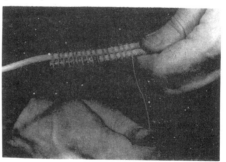

Fig 18-12 An alternative method of attaching a detonator using wire binding with a "plain" detonator and a length of safety fuse. Note that the streaming effect of the detonator is the reverse of that shown in Fig 18-11 above

Cordtex is available in rolls of 500ft(152m), which contain 3.5lb (1.65kg) of high explosive, which must be taken into account when considering purchases and storage allowances of explosive material.

SUPERFLEX DETONATING FUSE

This is a special high-energy detonating fuse developed for the initiation of slurry type explosives. Similar in construction to Cordtex, it also contains PETN but

Fig 18-13 A roll of Cordtex fuse

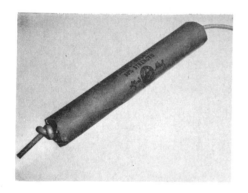

Fig 18-14 A cartridge of high explosive,
primed with Cordtex

Fig 18-15 Safety fuse, in both coil and
reel form

in a larger cross-sectional diameter. It initiates at approximately 21,300ft(6500m) sec, and is easily identified by its bright red pvc outer sheath.

PLASTIC IGNITER CORD

The greatest disadvantage of using safety fuse, is the time taken to "light! a given number of branches in a multi-shot circuit, and the difficulty in ensuring initiation in the desired sequence. Also, in damp or severe weather conditions, the operator runs a serious risk of being exposed to the effects of blast, since the physical "lighting" of each length of safety fuse can prove difficult. This can be overcome by the use of "Fast" or "Slow" igniter cord, which burns with an intense flame progressively along their length once ignited. Used in conjunction with "Beanhole" connectors, they offer a safe and reliable alternative to the "manual" method.

"Fast" igniter cord burns at not less than 1.5 sec/ft(4.9sec/m) and "Slow" igniter cord at a nominal 10sec/ft(33sec/m). Both have excellent water resistance.

If manual initiation of the plastic igniter cord is not suitable, an electric igniter can be used. These have the outward appearance of copper electric detonators, but have a filling of a burning composition, and are slotted to allow for easy crimping on to the cord.

BEANHOLE CONNECTORS

These are similar in appearance to "plain" detonators, except that they are manufactured with a slot in one end, and have a "flashing" type compound fitted between the slot and the open end. Designed to be used as a means of igniting safety fuse from plastic igniter cord, the former is placed and crimped into the open end, and the

18.17

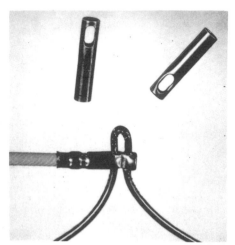

Fig 18-16 Bean-hole connectors, showing
method offitting safety fuse,
and plastic igniter cord

igniter cord into the slot.

EXPLODERS

Although there are alternative ways of
firing an electrical explosives circuit,
the use of an approved exploder offers
a number of safety factors.

It has already been stated in
the section dealing with electric
detonators, that a minimum of 0.5amp
is required to "ignite" the fusehead
and initiate the base charge; this can
be obtained from a small lead acid
battery, such as used in a car, or even
some of the larger dry-cells, but none
of these offer the portability, safety
or reliability of an exploder.

Exploders usually take the form
of an AC generator, built into a
suitable carrying case, and fitted with
a "safety" device regarding the method
of firing. The majority have some sort
of detachable handle, without which
the device cannot be operated. This
handle may be the means of operating
a gear-train, which in turn winds up
the generator, or cause a circuit to
charge up a capacitor. Both in turn,
provide an output of sufficient
voltage and current to meet the minimum
rated output of the particular model.

Exploders are generally rated as
being "2 shot" or "100 shot" or
what ever capacity stated, which
means they are designed to initiate
as a minimum, 2 electric, or 100
electric detonators in series
connection. They may well fire more
than the minimum number, but are
not designed to do so.

The detachable handle or
similar "safety" device, ensures
that the exploder is incapable of
being used until it has been re-
fitted, and should be retained by
the person in charge of blasting
operations, until it is required for
use.

SHOT FIRING CABLE

This is the cable used to join the
exploder to the detonator initiation
circuit. It should be well insulated
to prevent short-circuits between
the wires, and of choice should be
twin cable, in the order of 300ft
(100m) in length, and with an electrical resistance of about 2.5ohms
per 300ft length per single conductor.

Resistance greater than this
will lead to a serious voltage drop,
and hence current flow, and may give
rise to misfires, especially if an
exploder is being used at, or close
to, its top capacity rating.

In use shot-firing cables often
suffer cuts and abrasions, and should
be inspected before each firing to
avoid the time wasting business of
misfires etc. The end connections
should frequently be re-made, to give
good electrical contact.

Recent developments, particularly in
the United States, make full use of
the electronic chip, and these
exploders include a circuit tester,
which can be used to check the continuity of the firing circuit, even
with a detonator included. Whilst
such circuit testers are not a new
idea, their incorporation into the
exploder is, but none of the devices
illustrated in Fig 18-17 are thus
fitted.

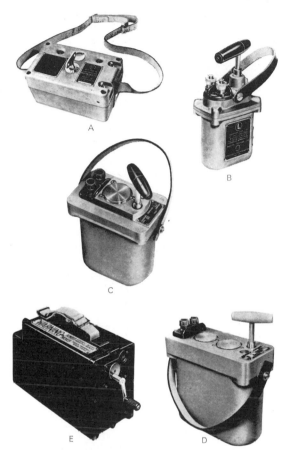

Fig 18-17 Types of exploder

A - ME12 (12 detonator)
B - Schaffler Type 350
    (25 detonators)
C - Schaffler Type 750
    (100 detonators)
D - Schaffler Type 770
    (200 detonators)
E - Beethoven Type Mk 2
    (100 detonators)

PREPARING TO FIRE CHARGES, USING ELECTRICAL DETONATORS

Check that the following minimum equipment and accessories are available at hand:

1 Explosive charges.
2 Detonators, in sufficient quantity to complete the task, allowing for the testing of firing circuits and possible misfires.
3 Firing cable, or sufficient length to reach from the "safe" firing position, and the place of work, with sufficient extra to allow for the cutting back of damaged cable.
4 Exploder, or sufficient capacity to fire the maximum number of detonators to be used at one time. NB: If it incorporates an internal battery, or has a re-charging facility, ensure that a new battery has been fitted, or the unit fully charged.
5 An aluminium or brass pricker tool, with which to pierce the cartridges and insert the detonators.
6 A sharp knife.
7 A roll of adhesive tape.
8 Spare single core connecting wire.
9 Suitable containers in which to store the explosives and detonators, separate from each other.
10 A suitable "red" explosives warning flag.
11 A whistle or other warning signal.

The serviceability of the firing cable and the exploder can be tested at the same time. Connect both leads of one end of the cable to the exploder terminals, and an electric detonator across the other end, some distance remote, and either with the detonator inside a steel pipe, or buried in the ground. Operate the exploder. At sea, it is the accepted practice to lower a weighted detonator to about 30ft(10m) depth, well below the keel of the craft, and clear of any fittings.

Charges are then prepared as required, being made up as individual small charges, larger quantities as "bundles", or even complete cases. Packets or cartridges can well be placed inside pvc bags and taped, or lashed together. Such charges should not have the detonators fitted – an act known as "priming" – until required for use, but kept stored in a safe place. Whether or not charges are completely prepared on the surface and taken down with the detonators fitted, or the detonators are fitted after placement, is a matter of choice, and circumstance. Provided that the bared ends of every detonators lead-in wires are short circuited by being twisted together immediately the detonators are removed from their container, and the charges are handled carefully, there should be no risk involved.

The priming of a charge is achieved by piercing a hole in a packet or cartridge of explosive using the pricker tool. This hole should be of sufficient depth to allow the detonator to be completely "buried" in the substance, thus ensuring close proximity contact, but not so deep set that the end of the detonator protrudes out the other side. After the detonator has been implanted, the lead-in wires are either "hitched" around the outside of the cartridge, or left secured by tape or string, to ensure that it cannot be accidently withdrawn after placement.

After ensuring that the shot firing cable is not connected to the exploder; that the inboard ends of it are shorted together, and that the "safety" handle has been rendered "safe", the business of connecting the detonator wires together can commence.

Choice of Circuits

Electric detonators can be connected up as parallel, series, or series/parallel circuits. Since many blasting operations will require a number of charges to be fired at the same time, it is common practice to use a simple series circuit. When firing with an exploder, a series circuit should not be used when the number of detonators exceeds thirty.

When firing a number of charges in series, remember that as a safeguard a minimum of 1.5amp should be passed through the circuit.,The actual voltage necessary to ensure this

current flow can be calculated by Ohm's Law, ie. the voltage required equals 1.5amps multiplied by the total resistance of the circuit, in ohm's. This includes the resistance of the firing cable "there and back", plus the lead-in wires, plus the resistance of the individual fuse-heads in the detonators.

In practice such calculations are not necessary, since exploders are "rated" by the number of detonators they will fire, which takes into account typical resistance values as above, based on the following figures:

Firing-cable resistance "there and back" should be in the order of 5ohms per 100yd(100m).

Lead-in wires and fusehead of an electric detonator is in the order of 2 ohms.

A parallel circuit will greatly reduce the possibility of a misfire due to insufficient current. In a series circuit insufficient current may cause the most sensitive fuseheads to fire, but break the circuit before they have all received sufficient current to achieve complete initiation. In similar conditions in a parallel circuit, the most sensitive fuseheads may still fire first, but the others will remain in circuit with all the remaining current available.

Parallel circuits also reduce the possibility of misfires due to current leakage. The resistance of a series circuit is often of the same order as that of a leakage path, and therefore a considerable amount of current may travel down this path. Also, in parallel circuits, the overall resistance is very low to that of a leakage path, and hence current will choose the desired detonator path rather than that of the leakage path.

Firing Charges Using Plain Detonators and Safety Fuse

Although safety fuse with plain detonators will provide a safe means of iniitiating high explosives, in most operations, and particularly underwater work, it is better to employ electric shot-firing methods, for the following reasons:

a) The ignition of safety fuse in open water conditions is not easy, and at sea in strong winds or pouring rain may be almost impossible.

b) Safety fuse, once ignited, offers a delay which can prove dangerous, since in the period between ignition and eventual detonation of charges, circumstances may change, but it would then be unsafe or perhaps impossible to stop the "explosive train".

c) Should a misfire occur with safety fuse, the accepted practice is to wait a period of 30 minutes before approaching the area of the charge to ascertain the cause. This may prove unacceptable at sea in certain weather or tidal circumstances.

The use of safety-fuse and a plain detonator on the surface, to initiate an underwater charge via Cordtex, should therefore be considered only as an alternative to normal electric firing, perhaps in the event of an exploder becoming unserviceable, or the loss of the firing cable.

In such circumstances, the surface end of the Cordtex is securely lashed or taped to the upper side of a piece of timber, sufficiently large enough to take the drag without sinking. The plain detonator and safety fuse are then mated and crimped together, secured tightly along the line of the Cordtex, and when ready, ignited. Considerable surface noise and disturbance should be anticipated when using this method, whereas electric firing is considerably more discreet.

SHAPED CHARGES

The ability to accurately focus an explosive charge in any particular direction, will greatly enhance the amount of work achieved for a certain weight of explosive. This can be achieved by building up explosives into a cone or pyramid, with the least amount of explosive material furthest from the target, and the initiating detonator set in the very top, pointing straight at the target surface. Whilst the results will greatly exceed that produced for an equal weight of explosive, placed in a conventional manner, a far greater effect can be achieved by taking advantage of the "Munroe" effect.

The enhanced effect of a hollow gunpowder charge was first noticed by Davey as far back as 1790, and an American named Munroe developed the theory of hollow charges in Washington in 1885, but little practical use was made of this phenomena until the Second World War. Today, the effect of shaped charges feature in a number of commercial and military fields, and pre-charged, shaped charges are now available "off the shelf" for a number of offshore applications, including pipe-cutting.

If a cone, normally of metal, and of a pre-determined thickness, is backed by an explosive charge initiated from the rear, and if the base of the cone is "stood-off" from the target by a suitable amount, on detonation, a deep narrow hole will be produced. The technique is often called the "cavity", "hollow" or "shaped charge" effect, and its success is determined by a number of factors, all of which can be calculated.

The nature of this special effect has been closely studied by X-ray flash photography, which indicates that on detonation, the metal liner of the cone collapses towards its apex. From this collapse emerges a needle-like stream or jet of particles along this axis, which exceed the velocity of detonation at the tip, decreasing gradually towards the rear. This initial stream is followed by somewhat larger fragments and finally by a "slug" of metal moving at a lower velocity, which is the remains of the cone.

The exact nature of the enhanced effect of a shaped charge is still not fully understood, but it is accepted that the stream of jet particles strike the target area with a pressure in the order of 200,000 atmospheres, ie: in the order of 3,000,000 psi with the result that the material of the target is pushed aside, leaving a neat round hole.

Bearing in mind the effect, it will now be clear that the thickness of the conical liner, the "stand-off" height, which allows the jet to develop, and the amount of explosive, are all critical factors.

Conical liners must be made of a uniform thickness material, and the internal angle of the cone must be exactly 80°. Any form of obstruction along the axis of the intended particle jet will prevent its correct formation, so that for a cavity charge to be effective underwater, the space between the charge and the target must be an air space, free of all water. Once the particle jet has been correctly formed, it will equally well penetrate steel, concrete or hard materials generally.

The manufacture of such devices demands a high degree of mechanical accuracy, especially if they are intended for use underwater at considerable depths, where external pressure effects could well distort the outer case and hence alter the shape.

SAFETY PRECAUTIONS

Unless suitable precautions are taken, electric detonators could be initiated accidently by:

1 Electrical energy entering the firing circuit from an outside source, ie:
Lightning
Static electricity
Stray currents
Electromagnetic radiation

2 Sympathetic shock from an outside source, ie:
Other explosive detonations

In the case of lightning or electric storms, it is strongly recommended that all work using explosives should cease, and that the materials are stowed away under cover. Should lightning strike a firing circuit, detonation is likely to take place regardless of what precautions are taken. It has even been known for a circuit to be initiated accidentally by lightning several miles away.

The best protection against static electricity is to ensure that the ends of all detonator lead-in wires are shorted by twisting them together, and that the shot firing cable is treated in the same manner.

Stray currents are only likely to be found in the immediate vicinity of portable power machines, motors, generators and the like. Where possible, all such machines should be stopped on board when handling any explosive charges, and to ensure that lead-in wires are not allowed to trail on the deck, touch such machinery, their mountings or accessories.

Although very rare, premature initiation of firing circuits has been known as a result of induced currents in closed circuits from high-power radar equipment and radio transmitters. Portable radio sets should not be allowed within 30ft (10m) of a site in which explosives are being handled.

Accidents

In the event of an accident in which explosives were involved, all unused material should be collected and impounded awaiting examination.

A report and statement of events should
be sent to the Health and Safety Executive (Inspector of Explosives), and if
physical injury has resulted, the police
should also be informed.

Failure to take these common sense
actions could lead to a suspension of an
explosives license or certificate, and
possible withdrawl completely.

Misfires

In good explosives practicem misfires
should not occur, especially if the
equipment is kept in good order, and
circuits are checked. Nevertheless,
misfires do happen, sometimes for
inexplicable reasons.

Since the chances of a defective
detonator as regards its manufacture
are almost impossible, misfires can
almost always be accredited to incorrectly connected electrical circuits,
badly made joints, unsuitable materials,
wet fuse or defective exploders. It is
a sensible practice to spend sufficient
time before leaving base, to carry out
the appropriate physical checks on all
explosives material and accessories,
since the necessary tools and cleaning
gear will then still be readily available.

Do not approach a circuit in which
safety fuse has been used until a minimum
of 30 minutes has elapsed, or an electrical
circuit for 5 minutes. The first action
should then be to remove any detonators
in the circuit, prior to any closer
examination as to why the misfire took
place. Suspect detonators or lengths of
safety fuse should not be reused, but
discarded in a safe manner, or destroyed
by being wrapped around a charge which is
to be detonated.

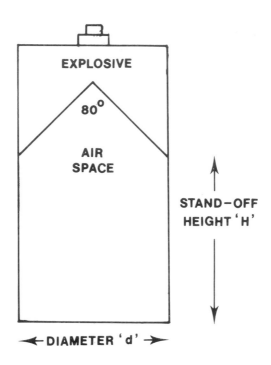

Fig 18-18   Outline of typical shaped charge showing
ceitical dimensions

Weight of explosive	Cone material thickness		Diam d	Height H = 3/4d	Thickness of concrete cut		Thickness of mild-steel cut
0.25lbs	0.058"	16swg	2.125"	1.625"	9	– .12"	2.75 – 3"
0.50lbs	0.073"	15swg	2.375"	2.00"	12	– 15"	3.75 –-4.25"
1.00lbs	0.092"	13swg	3.375"	2.50"	15	– 20"	4.75 – 5.25"
5.00lbs	0.158"	8swg	5.625"	4.25"	24	– 32"	7.50 – 8.25"
10.00lbs	0.198"	6swg	7.125"	5.375"	33	– 40"	9.00 – 10.5"
100.00lbs	0.427"		15.50"	11.50"	75	– 85"	20.00 – 21.5"

Fig 18-19 Table of dimensions for shaped or hollow charges

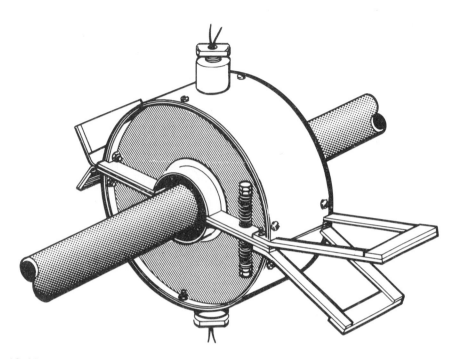

Fig 18-20 Shaped charge explosive unit, for cutting heavy cables underwater,
or small pipes. Hand positioned by divers, with a maximum depth
rating of 1000ft

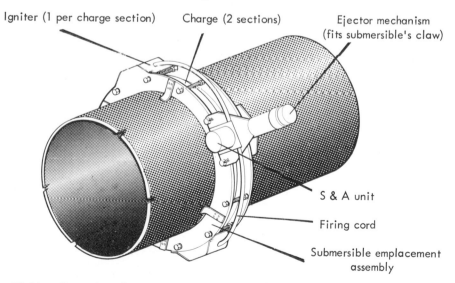

Igniter (1 per charge section)   Charge (2 sections)   Ejector mechanism
(fits submersible's claw)

S & A unit

Firing cord

Submersible emplacement
assembly

Fig 18-21 A "Euroshore" roughcut shaped charge for pipe cutting underwater,
specifically designed for submersible vehicle placement

CHAPTER 19

SALVAGE

It is almost impossible to work as a commercial diver, without at some time finding valuable objects on the seabed. Such items may range from small, low value personal property, such as rings, watches, jewellry, money, handbags, tools or outboard engines, all typical shallow water finds in harbours and anchorages, to broken or even intact vessels. In the case of finding a complete ship, this may be of some historic importance, or of high value with regard to its cargo or materials, or a potential hazard should it contain toxic or explosive substances.

Within territorial waters around the United Kingdom, regardless of the value of the object, if material is removed from the sea, unless the salvor is the rightful owner - or has the permission of the rightful owner to retain what he has salvaged - it must be declared to the appointed representative of HM Govern, ment, generally known as the Receiver of Wreck. In short, whilst at first sight it might appear unjust, it is the long established law in Gt Britain and most other western nations, that something lost in the sea remains the property of that person, or their heirs, for all time. If the rightful owner cannot be traced, and the statutory period given for this in law is " a year and a day", following display of public notices etc, then full ownership reverts to the Crown, who will determine and offer a suitable reward to the salvor.

This is of course a simplificatin of the law of salvage, which is very complex, but it is a general summary of the content of Part 9 of the Merchant Shipping Act of 1894. This concerns itself mainly with legal ownership of property. Items found apparently abandoned in the sea are therefore not the property of the finder, simply because he stumbled across them. In the same way, the finding of a wallet full of money in the street does not make it the property of the finder. If in fact the wallet was retained and the money spent, having deprived the owner of his property for all time, the finder would be guilty of "stealing by finding". In both cases, the law states that the rightful owner is entitled to receive back his own property, and if he has been deprived, then an offence has been committed.

It is therefore in the general interest of all divers to have an appreciation of the law of wreck and salvage, both to avoid the chance of prosecution and to be able to obtain the best financial return for a situation, assuming that a return is likely. This chapter is therefore a summary of the basic principles, written in layman's terms, and will cover the following:

1 Definition of Wreck
2 Voluntary salvage
3 Declaration of Wreck goods
4 HM Receiver of Wreck
5 Disposal of declared goods
6 Historic wreck finds

By definition, "Wreck" is anything foreign to the sea, recovered from the bottom, found floating on the surface, or washed ashore below high water marks. Originally, wreck meant just that, parts of a ship, its stores or lading, but has since been enlarged to include aircraft, hovercraft, balloons, satellites, watersport equipment - even dead animals such as cows and sheep, that fall over cliffs. There are of course certain "grey areas" in the law, but basically if the object is not "natural" to the sea, then it is classified as wreck.

Regarding the extent of coverage of the Merchant Shipping Act in this context, it applies to all tidal waters, below the highest point to which the tide normally flows, ie. high-water springs. Hence the law is applicable in the mouth of most rivers and for some distance

upstream. It is perhaps worth comment-
ing on the age old custom of beach-
combing, which is in fact an offence,
unless the finder declares the items
he, or she recovers.

Mention has already been made to
lawful ownership. If a person recovers
something from within tidal waters to
which they do not have ownership, if
a lawful owner then appears, they have
full right of their own property, and
the salvor may receive nothing. It is
also the law that even if a salvor is
operating with the consent of a lawful
owner, recoveries have to be declared
to the Receiver of Wreck, to avoid any
conflict at a later date.

VOLUNTARY SALVAGE

It is important to consider the position of someone setting out to salvage
something from the sea. If that person
has title, or the permission of the
owner(s) to retain what he recovers,
then apart from an obligation to
report the nature of what is salvaged
to the Receiver of Wreck, there are no
problems.

If,however, the salvor does not
have title, then the work is defined
as "voluntary" salvage, which means
that it is carried out fully aware of
the financial gamble involved. The
reader may well ask, "what risk" ? At
the worst, a lawful owner may appear,
and in law has entitlement to all the
goods recovered, even though he may
have made no contribution to the
salvage work entailed. He is, after
all, only taking back what rightly
belongs to him. In such cases, whether
the salvor gets only a reward, a
percentage of the true value, or no
more than a polite "thank you", is the
gamble entailed. In such circumstances
the salvor is entitled to nothing.

The solution is therefore to
establish ownership before salvage
commences, or at least determine that
it is very likely that the Crown are
the owners by default. Since the
Department of Trade, who advise on
wreck, almost always offer a minimum
of 50%, and usually more, in the case

of unclaimed wreck, this financial
return is preferable to the alternative.

DECLARATION OF WRECK GOODS

The law requires that salvaged goods
shall be declared to the nearest
Receiver of Wreck, at the point of
landing, at the earliest possible
opportunity. Since there is no
definition of what is meant by "the
earliest possible opportunity", it
is a matter of discretion on both
sides. If a salvor was at sea for
two months, carrying out recovery
work, and only came ashore briefly
in that time for fresh provisions or
fuel, then that would be reasonable
as an excuse; but if a salvor lay in
harbour for two months without
making a declaration, then there
would be little exucse.

It may not be necessary for
the salvor to actually take the
salvaged goods to the receiver of
Wreck, but this is at the receiver's
discretion.. It may be sufficient to
make a declaration only, and then
surrender the goods at a later date,
but the items must be out of the sea
and on dry land, or at least accessable for the receiver to see if he
so wishes. A typical situation in
which the goods are not surrendered
immediately would be where the goods
were bulky, ie. a 10 ton propeller,
or where there was some hazard, ie.
barrels of chemicals etc.

In the case of perishable items,
such as fruit, meat, carcases of
animals etc, the Receiver of Wreck is
empowered to dispose of the item by
sale immediately, but will then
retain the proceeds for the statutory
period of time. In circumstances where
items of historic value or interest
have been recovered, the Receiver is
empowered to allow the salvor to
retain same temporarily, whilst
conservation work is carried out. A
typical example of this would be in
the case of a bronze cannon suffering
from bronze-disease, which would
require immediate treatment, if it

were to be left untreated, this could greatly reduce its potential value. In such cases, the salvor will be required to sign a document, agreeing to indemnify HM Receiver should the goods not be produced when required at a later date.

The action of declaration is the completion of form WR5, giving details of the salvaged goods, time, place, vessel from which they came, if known, plus the names, addresses and signatures of all the relevant salvors. In return, the salvor will receive a Salvor's Warrant. This is the receipt for the goods handed in, or declared, which will have to be produced at the end of the statutory period, or when demanded, if earlier.

Following declaration, and an agreement as to whether the goods are to be held by the Receiver in the "Queen's Warehouse" or by the salvor, details of the recovery are then forwarded to the Department of Trade, Marine Division, in London. The local Receiver will place a public notice outside the Customs House, or at some other suitable location, advising of the nature of the recovery, but does not identify the salvor by name. This notice serves as an invitation for any owner or other interested party to come forward, and declare their interest.

There is of course a breathing space of twelve months, during which the salvor may be able to locate the rightful owner, and reach agreement.

H.M. RECEIVER OF WRECK

The receiver of Wreck is usually an officer of H.M. Customs and Excise, who will perform this and other duties. In certain remote areas of Gt Britain, in which there is no Customs House, it is usual for someone else in authority to be appointed to the position, such as a police officer, school teacher, solicitor etc.

Since offences against the Merchant Shipping Act are not civil offences, prosecutions have to be brought by H.M. Customs and Excise and not the civil police, except in special circumstances.

DISPOSAL OF DECLARED GOODS

If, during the statutory period of one year and one day, a legal owner to the salvaged goods lays claim, provided appropriate legal right has been established to the Receiver's satisfaction, then the claim will be noted, but usually no decision will be made until the end of the period. If the claim is upheld, then after payment of any expenses involved, the goods will be handed over. Any consideration of a reward between the owner and the salvor then becomes a personal matter, but it is stressed there is no obligation for the owner to pay anything.

In circumstances in which no rightful owner appears, which is more often the case than not, the Department of Trade arrive at a value for the goods, based on market prices, antique, valuation, or otherwise, and offer the salvor a certain percentage. This will be communicated to the salvor through the Receiver in writing; in turn, the salvor can either accept or refuse the offer, provided there seem to be reasonable grounds for so doing. Awards for straight forward salvage of scrap metals will vary between 50 and 100% usually, but there would appear to be no rules. In the case of coin or bullion, then 75% is usually the minimum offered, and for artifacts or items from declared historic wreck sites, 95 to 100%, less expenses seems to be the current level.

If it is the D.T.I's decision that the goods are to be sold or auctioned, then the salvor(s) have every right to bid for their own material. Should the items be sold elsewhere, then the salvor(s) will receive the percentage offered of the sum realised. Expenses will include auctioneer's commission, the Receiver's expenses, and VAT.

Should the goods in question be of outstanding historic value, then a third party, such as the Tower of London, or British Museum, may be invited to purchase, in which case the salvor would still receive his percentage of the purchase price.

HISTORIC WRECK FINDS

An amendment to the Merchant Shipping Act now allows the Secretary of State

to designate any underwater site as being
of particular historic value, or in the
case of dangerous wrecks, to designate
them as unsafe. When a site or wreck
receives such designation, in the case
of an historic site, only the licensee
and the named diving team are allowed on
the site. It should be noted that there
is no such offence as trespass underwater
under normal circumstances, and in law,
anyone can dive on any wreck, even to the
point of removing items, provided they
are declared in the usual manner.

In the case of designated sites, for
what ever reason, historic, hazardous, or
otherwise, trespass alone, provided it can
be proven, becomes an offence, as does the
removal of items from that site, and is a
civil offence, so that designation offers
real protection, but the policeing of a
site is a difficult problem.

There are certain restrictions and
obligations on licensee's when a site is
designated, and whether or not a potential
salvor would wish to assume these is a
matter of personal choice. If a salvor
were considering making application for
site designation, they should talk to the
nearest receiver of Wreck, and possibly
contact the Department of Trade and
Industry for guidance. Printed leaflets
oytlining the scheme are available.

CHAPTER 20

BASIC UNDERWATER PHOTOGRAPHY

Most people are capable of taking an acceptable photograph in ideal conditions, particularly since the modern generation of cameras have been introduced. These offer automatic exposure setting, range finding, focus control, and other electronic assistance, so that the taking of ordinary photographs demands very little skill or thought. Even in poor conditions, a fair proportion of the public can obtain reasonable photographic results, but could of course not guarantee them, which summarises the difference between the amateur and the professional.

The professional photographer is expected to produce good results every time, regardless of the conditions, and for the professional underwater photographer, this is no mean task. Respecting the fact that it takes years of experience to become a professional photographer, all divers should have sufficient knowledge of the subject to at least be capable of attempting to take photographs underwater, and hopefully bring back acceptable pictures. This Chapter is therefore a summary of the art only, intended as a basic coverage of the function of the camera, how it should be used, the problems of photography underwater, and the special equipment involved.

THE CAMERA

It is important to understand the terminology associated with cameras. The camera is a device which allows the operator to focus an image onto a photosensitive surface, in a controlled manner. It will have a lens system, which can be controlled so that the incoming light image is in focus when it strikes the film, also the amount of light is regulated.

Focus is a matter of physical movement of the various glass elements which go to make up the lens, in that they are moved closer or further apart to achieve a sharp image.

The amount of light which the lens passes is controlled by an iris diaphragm, the aperture of which can be altered; the larger the opening, the more light passes, and the smaller the "f" number. A smaller opening means less light, and consequently the "f" number increases.

A mechanical shutter mechanism, probably either an iris-diaphragm, or a focal-plane shutter, controls the admission of light, and hence the actual taking of the picture.

Hence, a combination of focus, aperture and shutter control, dictate completely the light image that will fall onto the film. Provided that the operator has used the viewfinder correctly, so that the required image was in the required position when the shutter control was operated, the result should be a perfect reproduction. This end product is of course, exactly what the client is paying the photographer to achieve, usually because he is unable, for what ever reason, to see the subject for himself (ie. due to time, location or distance etc) or simply to obtain a permanent record. This aspect and attitude of mind when taking photographs is very important. A photographer looking at prints which he himself has taken, has the very distinct advantage of having seen the original, but the question he must ask himself is, "Will my client see the same picture, not having had the benefit of seeing the original ?"

THE CAMERA LENS

Even the cheapest and most basic "box" cameras will have at least two elements in its lens construction, and expensive camera may have as many as twenty.

The advantage of such complex lenses, as for example is used in the 300mm Auto-Nikkor Zoom, is that these compound lenses as they are called, are a combination of simple positive and negative elements which tend to cancel out each other's optical defects. These defects, which are minute imperfections found in the very best lenses, are known as " aberrations ", and can only be eliminated by cancelling them out.

Another error is known as "chromatic aberration", and this is an optical error brought about by the fact that in the spectrum of light, each colour will come into focus as a different point behind a simple lens. Since each of the seven colours has a different wave length, then without correction, they would fall onto a film with different points of focus, hence giving a general "fuzzy" outline. Lenses which are designed to overcome this are known as "colour corrected", and in which any of the colour wavelengths are guaranteed to be in sharp focus at the "focal-plane".

This is the point behind the lens in a particular camera, on which all the rays of light fall, to create a photographic image. Hence the focal length of

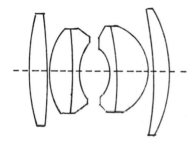

Fig 20-1 Compound lens elements

a lens is the distance of the optical centre of the lens, from the focal plane of the camera when the lens is set to focus at infinity. This is always expressed in millimetres, and can usually be found as an engraved number on the barrel of the lens.

APERTURE

The admission of light through the lens of a camera is very carefully controlled by means of an aperture device as shown in Fig 20-2.

Fig 20-2 Control of aperture by the use of an "iris" diaphragm device

It functions in the same manner as the control of light to the human eye, by means of the pupil. It is protected by being incorporated between the lens elements, and consists of a series of very thin metal leaves arranged around a central point. The action of pushing or pulling on these leaves alters their position, and they then close or open the diameter of the aperture orifice.

Movement of the aperture control is usually by a series of fine "click" stops, known as "f" stops. These, for example, on a simple camera could be:

f/4, f/8, f/16, f/22

On a more expensive camera lens, for example, one would expect to find a much wider range, such as:

f/1.4, f/2, f/2.8, f/4 and so on.

The "f" is merely a symbol of the word "fraction", which denotes a mathematical relationship. This relationship is the ratio or fraction between the focal length of a lens and the diameter of the lens aperture. The "f" stop is therefore only a measurement of the lens opening, or the effective aperture presented to the incoming light.

A lens with a 50mm focal length, and an aperture opening of 25mm diameter, would indicate a maximum "f" stop of f/2. Hence to determine the diameter of the aperture of any "f" stop, it is only necessary to divide the focal length of that lens by the "f" stop number: eg: 50mm ÷ 2 = 25mm

Hence the lowest "f" numbers relate to the largest of the aperture diameters, and vice versa.

APERTURE/LENS SPEED RELATIONSHIP

For conventional surface photography, a fast lens would, in most situations, be an unnecessary luxury, only adding to the cost of the camera, and there are seldom many "low-light" situations. Underwater, however, the diver photographer is more often in a "low-light" situation than not, due either to depth or visibility.

In this case, the speed of a lens is a measurement of the intensity of light reaching the film, and the greater this degree of intensity, the "faster" the lens. As a measure of "speed" in this sense, the larger the aperture diameter in proportion to the lens focal length, the greater its speed.

At first glance, it might appear that since f/11 is twice the diameter of f/22, the f/11 setting would pass twice the amount of light as f/22, but this is not true. The amount of light passing through an aperture does not double   simply because the aperture diameter has doubled. In fact, a setting of f/11 will pass four times the amount of light of f/22.

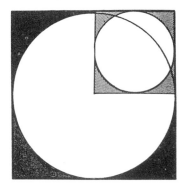

Fig 20-3 Aperture relationship

The above illustration should clarify this point. The two circles are in proportion to the two squares in area, and since the area of the larger square is

four times that of the smaller, but the diameter is only twice, if these diameters are considered as f/11 and f/22, it will be seen that f/11 passes four times as much light.

The following table indicates the " x2" and " x4" relationship*

f x2	=	f x4	=	f
1.4		2		2.8
2		2.8		4
2.8		4		5.6
4		5.6		8
5.6		8		11
8		11		16
11		16		22
16		22		-

It is important that this is fully understood.

THE SHUTTER

There are basically only two types of shutter, these being the front leaf shutter, working on the "iris" principle already described, and the focal plane shutter.

With both types, the energy to move the shutter is derived from a spring-loaded mechanism, which today, in most cameras, is controlled by an electronic timer, capable of accuracy to within one millisecond (1/1000th of a second). The speed of the shutter is in fact not determined by the total time it is open, but by the interval between the "half open" - "half closed" position. This time interval in fact exposes the major portion of the film, the actual opening/closing interval contributing little to the actual exposure time. As an example, a shutter speed set at 1/500th of a second, which is 2 milliseconds, will in fact be open for 3 milliseconds to achieve the shorter time. It will in fact take 1 millisecond to fully open; another 1 millisecond to fully close, with 1 millisecond fully open time interval.

Most 35mm cameras, and the

Nikonos underwater camera in particular, utilise a focal plane shutter mechanism. This consists of two parallel, light-tight metallic or special cloth-type "curtains" which move across the plane of the film, one a set time and distance ahead of the other. Hence the width between the "curtains", and the time it takes the gap to pass in front of the film, determines the amount of light reaching the film. These focal plane shutters may travel vertically, as with the Nikonos, or horizontally, as with the Leica.

Each "curtain" is wound on a roller, under spring tension, which is normally achieved as the previous exposure is "wound-on" by action of the wind on lever. Having selected the shutter speed required, when the release is triggered, the leading curtain is released, followed after a measured interval by the trailing curtain. Light therefore strikes and exposes the film in a "band" which moves across the film, creating a series of exposures in the one frame. The focal plane shutter speed is therefore the length of time that each section or band of the film is subjected to light, and not the total time for the "slot" to travel right across the film. Short exposures are achieved by narrow slits in the curtains; longer exposures by wider slots.

The focal plane shutter, being incorporated actually inside the body of the camera, and not inside the lens itself, offers a number of advantages, namely:

1 A wider variety of cheaper interchangeable lenses

2 Through-lens focusing and view finding

3 A range of faster speeds over the iris diaphragm

Shutter speeds

A quality 35mm camera would be expected to at least offer the following minimum range of speeds:

1 sec; 1/2 sec; 1/4sec; 1/8sec; 1/15sec; 1/30sec; 1/60sec; 1/125sec; 1/250sec; 1/500sec, and 1/1000sec.

It is normal for the 1/60sec speed to be that selected for synchronisation with an electronic flash unit. In addition, the speed selection control may show positions marked "B" and "T", with possibly "R" as well. These are: "B" for 'brief' or 'bulb', in which the shutter is held wide open until the trigger is released; "T" is for 'time', to offer time exposures, and "R" is the position to which the control must be set for rewinding the film, before removal from the camera body.

There are of course a few disadvantages with the focal plane shutter, namely:

1 It cannot be synchronised with electronic flash units at the slower speeds.
2 The focal plane shutter is more noisy in operation, and is sufficient to "scare" off fish and other marine life underwater.

DEPTH OF FIELD

An understanding of "depth of field" is essential, if the diver photographer is to produce good results, which are consistently in focus.

It will be appreciated that every object has "depth", ie. some portions are closer to the camera than others. With small subjects, for example a short length of weld, or a ringbolt, the depth of field is small, with perhaps only 100mm difference from front to back. But with a complete "node" on an offshore platform, or a 2 metre section of ships bilge keel, there is a considerable difference, and there is a high probability that either the part nearest or furthest away from the diver will be out of focus when his photographs are processed.

From the point of view of a camera lens, the focal length determines its depth of field. The shorter the focal length, the greater the depth of field, and the longer the focal length, the shorter the depth of field. As the lens aperture is reduced in size, so the light reflected by the subject entering the lens becomes limited, and image blurring is prevented.

As examples of depth of field measurements, if the lens of a camera is opened up to f/2.5, at a distance of 1.8m (6ft) the depth of field is reduced to roughly 100mm (1ft). Hence any object within the range 1.5 - 2.1m (5 - 7ft) can be photographed and remain in focus, but outside of this, the background will be blurred. If now the same 1.8m (6ft) distance is maintained, but the aperture is now stopped down to f/22, everything within a range of 0.9 - 9m (3 - 30ft) will be in sharp focus. Controlling the depth of field is therefore only a matter of real choice, when the ambient light is sufficient to allow such a wide change in "f" settings.

Underwater, where lack of natural light becomes a very real problem, the larger lens openings mean less depth of field, which will put both the fore and backgrounds out of focus. If this is unacceptable, and the amount of light ia insufficient to allow for a small aperture, then the photographer must resort to artificial light.

FILM SPEED

Whilst there are a number of standards in the world for the speed rating of films, the one most commonly used is that of ASA (American Standards Assoc- iation). This is based on film stand- ards set by the American National Standards Institute, and is now used internationally, appearing on the out- side of most film cartons, and on film cassettes themselves.

The speed of a film is an indic- ation as to its sensitivity to light. Film with a low ASA number or "rating", usually described as a "slow" film (ASA 50), will require a lot of light, whereas "fast" films require a great deal less (ASA 200). Choice of film speed is therefore a matter of either experience, or anticipation as to the conditions regarding light levels, at the place where the film is to be exposed. This decision is best made

by the use of a light meter.

As an indication of film speeds, and the type of film they represent, the following table may be of some assistance:

ASA rating	Film type
50	Slow speed
100	Medium speed
200	High speed
400	Super high speed

It is worth remembering that with each doubling of the ASA rating, the film will require either one less "F" stop, or the shutter speed can be halved. This will be clear from the table below:

Changing the aperture

ASA	f stop	shutter
50	f8	1/30
100	f11	!/30
200	f16	1/30
400	f22	1/30

Changing the shutter speed

ASA	f stop	shutter
50	f8	1/30
100	f8	1/60
200	f8	1/125
400	f8	1/250

Regarding quality, the slower speed films offer excellent quality in the photograph, but require a lot of light, or the use of artificial light such as a flash unit. Fast films can be used at low light levels, but tend to produce a 'grainy' photograph, and cannot match the quality of slow films.

OPTIMUM EXPOSURE

Having established the variables
connected with photography, it must
now be established how they affect
each other.
  Optimum exposure can be defined
as being the correct combination of:

1 'f' stop
2 Shutter speed
3 ASA film rating

Changing any one of these three items,
will involve a change in one or both
of the other two.
  If we assume a constant ASA
film rating in a particular situation,
it can be seen that it is possible to
change both the 'f' stop and the
shutter speed together to give the
same exposure. The difference would
then be in the "depth of field" and
the ability to "freeze" moving objects.

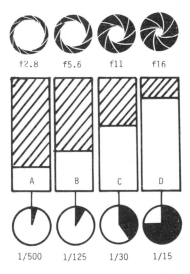

f2.8   f5.6   f11   f16

A   B   C   D

1/500   1/125   1/30   1/15

Fig 20-4 Identical exposure achieved by
a combination of aperture and shutter
speed

Example "A" above would offer a poor
depth of field, due to the large aperture, but an excellent "freezing"
ability for fast moving objects.

Example "D" offers a poor "freezing"
action, but an excellent depth of
field.

Choice of Film

For underwater use, colour film is
nearly always specified, with the
additional choice of either colour
transparencies (35mm), or negatives
(2 1/4ins square).
The two favoured films are:

Ektachrome - X (known as EX-36)
          film speed = 64 ASA

High Speed Ektachrome (EH-36)
          film speed = 160 ASA
This can be rated as high as 320
or 640 ASA with special processing.

ARTIFICIAL LIGHT UNDERWATER

Although flash units are still
available which take individual,
throw-away flash bulbs, these have
almost completely disappeared in
favour of the electronic "strobe".
The strobe device is contained
either in a special built-in unit
with the camera, or else as a completely separate, self-contained
unit, with only a "triggering" lead
or cable connected to the camera
itself. Their function, on being
switched 'on', is to rapidly charge
up a capacitor to a high voltage
level. On operating, or 'firing'
the flash, an action synchronised
and operated by the shutter release,
the capacitor discharges across a
special 'discharge tube', full of
gas, which promptly ionises, and
gives a brief but brilliant discharge
of light, lasting about 1/1000 sec.
  To achieve the desired result,
the discharge of the flash must
synchronise with the opening of the
shutter, to give the correct exposure.
With many cameras, this is 1/60 sec,
and it is usual for this speed to be
marked in red numerals on the cameras
shutter sdjustment control knob. With
other cameras, this may be 1/125 sec.

FLASH GUIDE NUMBERS

All flash-units or strobes are given
a guide number, which is a measure of
their light output. This guide number
is then used to calculate the 'f' stop
setting for optimum exposure. In order
to achieve this, it is only necessary
to know the distance between the flash
and the subject.

The following simple formulae is
then used:

$$\frac{\text{Guide number}}{\text{Distance}} = \text{f stop}$$

The guide number is based on a film
ASA number allocated by the manufacturer.
If the film used is different from this,
then a further simple calculation will
give the necessary new guide number:

$$\frac{\text{New film ASA}}{\text{Original film ASA}} \times \text{original guide No.}$$

$$= \text{new guide number}$$

For simplification, most flash-units
and strobes have a handy conversion
table of film speed guide attached in
the form of a printed table.

Underwater flash units have also
a filter factor, which takes into account
an average water visibility condition.
This gives a lower guide number than if
used on the surface. Guide numbers
should be checked before use, to see if
it is still applicable underwater.

Used singly or in pairs, flash-
units underwater should be positioned
such that they will illuminate the
subject from an angle of approximately
45 - 60°, thereby reducung the back-
scatter effect of particles in
suspension in the water.

Underwater cameras

Very little professional use is now made
of conventional 35mm cameras contained
in special waterproof housings, but the
larger, more expensive cameras such as
the Hasselblad and Rollei still utilise
special cases, and the work of some of
the top underwater photographers using
this equipment, is testimony to their
quality.

The most popular 35mm underwater camera today is the Japanese
Nikonos, Models I, II, III. IV and
IV-A, which was the first 35mm
camera to be built completely water
and pressure proof, to about 61m
depth. Whereas 35mm cameras had
previously been accommodated in
what were basically waterproof
containers, with sealed controls to
allow operation from outside, the
Nikonos range have all their controls
and openings fully "O"-ring sealed.
The alternatives to the 35mm range
already mentioned earlier, such as
the Hasselblad, Rollei and Bolex, are
all single-lens reflex housings, in
a completely different price range.

Since the commercial diver not
employed as an underwater photographer
is more likely to be required to use
one of the Nikonos range cameras,this
is the one that will be dealt with in
some detail.

Fig 20-5 The Nikonos Mk II camera

The Nikonos range of underwater
cameras are manufactured from die
cast aluminium alloy, impregnated
with plastics to seal any small
imperfections or blowholes in the
casting process. Weighing only 540g
or 20ozs, the camera housing
measures only 3.9 x 5.1 x 1.9ins
(99 x 129 x 47mm) and can be taken
safely to 61m water depth.

Fig 20-6 The Nikonos II with special
underwater view finder frame

Fig 20-8 The UW-Nikkor 15mm f/2.8N
camera, with optical viewfinder

The lens construction of this new
model of camera has 12 elements in
9 groups, including the watertight
front cover glass, giving a picture
angle of 94°. Focusing scale is
from infinity to 0.3m (1ft) in
optical distance underwater. There
are two pointers coupled to the
aperture knob, which serve as depth
of field indicators, indicating
near and far limit. Overall weight
on land is 1265g.

Fig 20-7 The Nikonos IV-A camera body,
with 35mm f/2.5 W - Nikkor lens and
the SB - 101 Nikonos Speedlight u/w
flash strobe unit attached, on a
special mounting 'tray'

Fig 20-9 Seacor 21mm Sea-Eye lens

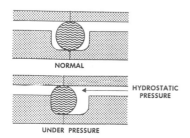

Fig 20-10 "O" ring sealing method

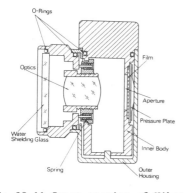

Fig 20-11 Cross section of Nikonos II

a – shutter speed dial
b – safety lock
c – film-advance/shutter release
d – accessory shoe
e – viewfinder
f – depth-of-field indicator
g – distance scale
h – aperture knob
i – aperture scale
j – focusing knob
k – rewind knob and rewind crank

Fig 20-12 Controls and components

Fig 20-13 Film advance and shutter control lever. Also shown is the "safety-catch", with the letter "O" in white on the handle of the lever, visible when in the "operate" position. Note the exposure counting indicator to the left

Fig 20-14 Details of the shutter speeds available (see 20.4 regarding "B" & "R")

The Nikonos camera film advance lever and shutter are incorporated in the one control, which is unusual but extremely convenient, especially underwater.

Provided the safety-catch locking device has been slid across to the left, exposing the white engraved letter "O" or "operate" indicator, the photographer need only apply light finger pressure inward towards the camera body, in the direction shown in Fig 20-13 to operate the shutter mechanism. As pressure is taken off the lever it will spring out to the position shown in Fig 20-13 and remain there until pressure is again applied in the same direction. This will then advance the film one frame, the exposure counter will record the fact, and the shutter mechanism will be re-cocked for the next exposure.

Function of the Other Controls

Accessory Shoe

This will accept a wide range of view and optical finders, plus other accessories made specially for this camera.

Depth of Field Indicator

A depth-of-field indicator is incorporated behind the plain glass cover of the lens. Two pointers, coupled to the focus and aperture controls, readily indicate the depth-of-field available.

Distance Scale

The Nikonos is basically a compact camera, with no real focusing facility. It is therefore necessary for the operator to estimate - or physically measure the distance between the camera and subject, and set this figure on a scale, by means of the knob (j). An attachment now available, is a fixed distance and frame finder, which made of pvc coated wire, is fixed to the lens, and is then offered up against the subject, giving a guaranteed 'stand-off' distance.

Aperture Scale

Adjustment of control knob (h) alters the iris diaphragm, and hence the aperture setting.

Rewind Control

Once the film has been exposed, it will be impossible to reset the film advance lever, which will be left sticking out (see Fig 20-13). The exposure counter should confirm that the correct number of exposures have been taken (ie. 20 or 36), so that it necessary to rewind the film back into its cassette for processing.

First set the shutter control to

position "R" (rewind). Then lift the rewind knob (k), unfold the crank rewind lever, and wind the film in the direction indicated by the arrow. When it is obvious that the film is well clear of the camera body, and in its cassette, remove the lens assembly complete. This is achieved by holding the body of the camera in one hand, the lens mounting in the other, then push in and twist the lens in relation to the body. The lens assembly can then be withdrawn, and should be placed in a safe position.

Double check that the film is fully re-wound into its cassette, then using the 'built-in' fittings, lever the camera top unit up away from the body, exposing the cassette and shutter mechanism. Remove the cassette.

Fig 20-15 Rewinding procedure after film has been exposed. Set shutter control to the position "R"

Fig 20-16 Lift up the rewind crank lever; turn until the mechanism engages, then wind gently until a change in tension indicates the film has disengaged. Wind a further few turns, then "split" the camera

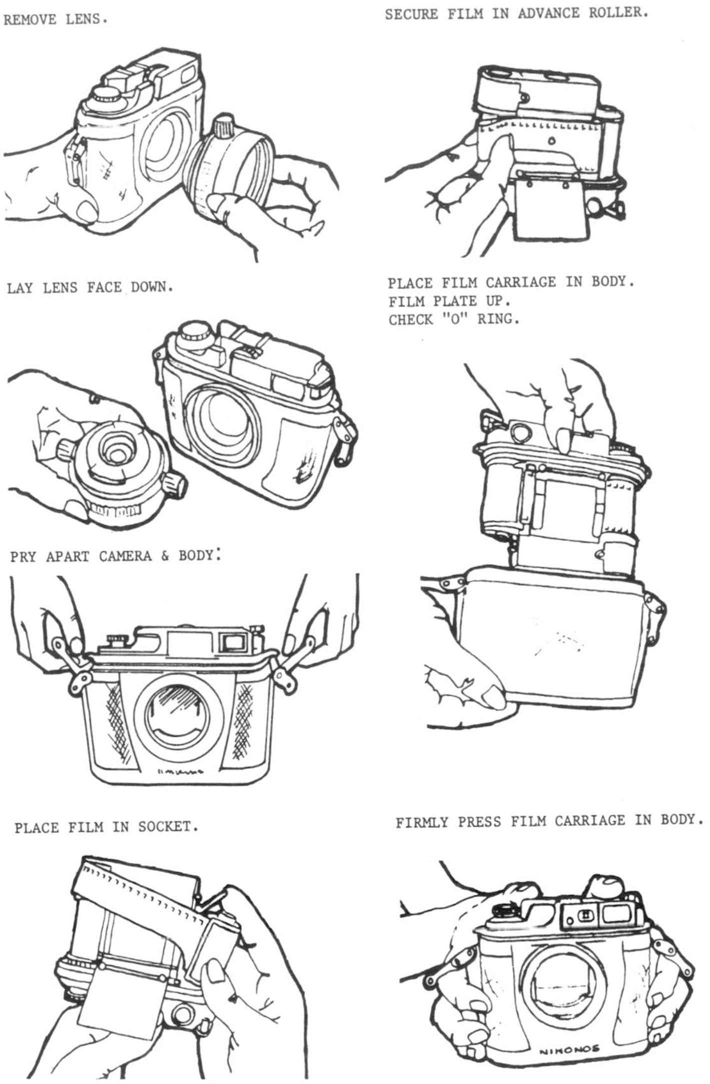

REMOVE LENS.

SECURE FILM IN ADVANCE ROLLER.

LAY LENS FACE DOWN.

PLACE FILM CARRIAGE IN BODY.
FILM PLATE UP.
CHECK "O" RING.

PRY APART CAMERA & BODY.

PLACE FILM IN SOCKET.

FIRMLY PRESS FILM CARRIAGE IN BODY.

Fig 20-17 Procedure for loading a 35mm film cassette into a Nikonos camera. Great care is necessary when inserting the camera mechanism back inside the body casing, since the film-plate may easily over-ride the back plate; if even minimal force is then applied, it will badly damage the plate and hinge. All the "O"-ring seals should be wiped clean, and coated with a silicon compound from time to time. nb. Some Nikonos cameras, particularly the later models, may have a different back-plate assembly.

Dealing with a flooded camera

1   Remove the film in the normal manner, since film is not seriously affected by salt or fresh water, and it may well be possible to save the photographs taken already.

2   Having removed the mechanism of the camera from its body, if surgical alcohol is available in sufficient quantity, completely submerge the camera unit and leave to soak. Turn the camera from time to time, to allow trapped air to escape and to let the alcohol penetrate every corner, and for water to be fully displaced.

3   If alcohol is not available, wash the camera under a tap of fresh, luke-warm, running water, turning all the time for the reasons given above. Repeat the operation several times, but do not leave to soak for any length of time, since rusting will commence.

4   Remove the camera from the alcohol or fresh water, shake off surplus fluids, turning as you do so, then dry with a very low pressure air jet. Continue to operate the controls from time to time, shaking and turning the camera over.

5   Place the camera in an open, warm oven, and very gently heat to about 48°C (120°F), removing from time to time to check that it is not over-heating and to operate the controls.

6   Either lightly oil the mechanism and controls, operating all the time to allow penetration, or else lightly spray with a water repellant aerosol such as WD-40. Shake out the excess fluid, and dry with a lint-free cloth.

Most cameras can be saved in this manner, provided treatment is not delayed, and is carried out in a thorough manner.

Keep the camera in a dry place, operate the controls from time to time, and check their functioning. As long as salt water was not allowed to dry inside the camera, then the controls should not seize or fail to operate correctly. If trouble is experienced, soak the camera in a bath of WD-40 or similar water-repellant, reassemble with a quantity of the fluid inside, seal the package and return to any Nikonos agent operating a "flooded-camera" service. Do not forget to include written details of any treatment or stripping already attempted.

Fig 20-18   Sub Sea electronic flash unit (Mk 100)

Video Cameras and CCTV

Underwater television, both mono and colour, offers the obvious advantage of live picture transmission, immediate interpretation, recording, and the fact that any number of others can view proceedings on the surface. This cuts out the delays and frustrations of waiting for still or cine films to be processed, with the attendant possibility that the pictures are unacceptable, or that the photographer was even filming in the wrong place!

Television and video recording are currently in very wide use throughout the diving industry. The systems allow for prolonged inspection of fault areas, until such time as the engineer or expert is satisfied. Such areas can be viewed from different angles, some basic work can be carried out and then reviewed, measurement scales can be introduced and moved around, plus many other advantages. In particular, the TV camera shows a "real time" picture underwater, on the surface, or at some location remote by thousands of miles. Such cameras can be hand held by divers, carried by a submersible, or permanently installed on the seabed or on a component, in which case it can be remote controlled.

There are three ways of recording details from a CCTV system[2]

1 By photographing the actual TV screen.

2 By combining the TV camera underwater with either still or movie cameras.

3 By recording the live TV sequences on a magnetic video tape recorder.

Until recent years, monochrome television was the normal standard, but with the development of very small colour cameras, most underwater television work today is done in colour, and this has proven to be invaluable in NDT inspection (Non destructive testing), where marine growth may have to be identified etc.

Television cameras used for diving purposes are all "closed-circuit", in that there has to be an umbilical to the surface, through which power and signals are passed. Some models of CCTV will have miniature diver's "monitors", small screens, perhaps only 75mm square, on which the operator can see exactly what the TV camera can see. This is particularly useful in a training situation, but greatly increases the cost of the equipment, and is an additional feature to go wrong.

Camera Handling Techniques

The following points regarding the camera are important, in order that the data required is seen as quickly and clearly as possible by the viewer.

Orientation

The camera should be mounted such that it is always held in a vertical position, that is, there should never be any confusion in the mind of the viewer, which items are vertical and which are horizontal. Control handles should always point "down".

Focus

Television is not capable of "freezing" fast movement. Therefore movement when "panning" must be slow, with due regard that the focus may be changing all the time.

The diver must be patient with his surface support, since wave or tidal movement may cause no end of problems, of which the camera operator can be blissfully unaware. In the same way, the surface must be patient with the diver, who may have all manner of unseen problems, ie. trailing cables becoming foul, breathing or diving equipment problems, cold, exhaustion, marine life etc.

Commentary

It is likely that the surface controller will "talk" the diver through the entire inspection sequence, with a continuous stream of instructions, such as "pan left", "more left", "more still", "stop", "hold it right there", "alter your focus", "more", "dolly in", "closer", and so on. The controller will call for close-up's of various objects, or different angles, inclusion of scales etc. as work progresses.

Camera movements

Instructions from the surface will include the following[2]

"Pan" - either left or right, which is a call for the camera to be swung left or right as the diver faces the objective, until clearly told to stop panning. The only mistake an

operator make here is to move the TV
camera too quickly in a particular
direction, or jerkily. It must be
remembered that the surface support
may wish to see every inch of object
in front of the camera as he "pans left"
or "pans right". The instruction means
literally, move from your present
position to another left or right, but
nice and slowly, not to "jump" from the
existing subject to a new area.

"Dolly" - either in or out from the
subject, so that on the instruction
"Dolly out", the camera is slowly pulled
back away from the subject, increasing
the field of view, until told to stop.

One last word of caution when operating
an underwater television camera; never
point the lens of a TV camera directly
at the sun. The intense light will
seriously damage the light cells, and
render the camera unserviceable.

CHAPTER 21

BASIC NON-DESTRUCTIVE TESTING UNDERWATER

All engineering products need to be checked for defects during manufacture, and at subsequent intervals thereafter, having been put into service. Cars, motorcycles, washing machines, all items with which we are familiar, become unserviceable if not regularly inspected and maintained. Despite the difference in size and cost, exactly the same philosophy applies to all fixed and mobile marine installations, such as offshore structures, sub-sea pipelines, drilling rigs, ships' hulls, piers, jetties etc, all of which are subject to thorough inspection during fabrication and periodically during their service life.

Such engineering structures are inspected by either or both of the following methods:

DESTRUCTIVE TESTING

This requires a sample of a particular material, process, fastening or fitting, which is then bent, twisted or otherwise subjected to testing which will destroy its usefulness for any further service. A typical example might be a particular type of high-tensile bolt. Such an item is likely to be subjected to stress tension testing until it shears, after which of course the bolt can no longer be used, but at least the quality of other bolts manufactured in the same batch is assured.

This type of testing is expensive, and limited to a small percentage of batch items, and assumes that those items not tested are of an equal quality.

NON-DESTRUCTIVE TESTING (NDT)

This method determines the quality of a component without altering or changing its physical qualities or usefulness. Unlike destructive testing, by this method the item is fully inspected without damage to its physical structure.

OFFSHORE STRUCTURES

It is estimated that there are probably between 2,500 and 3,000 offshore fixed oil installations around the world. Included are steel and concrete production platforms, flare structures, buoyant storage towers, loading buoys, sub-sea structures and thousands of miles of underwater pipeline.

In the North Sea alone, it is predicted that by 1985 there will be about 130 oil and gas platform installations, representing a £10 billion investment in capital equipment. The marine environment is extremely harsh, imposing loads on offshore installations which may result in the formation or propagation of unacceptable defects both above and below the surface. These often start as inconsequential, even acceptable flaws, that grow to become potentially dangerous faults. Early warning of such small defects is therefore very desirable, both from the point of view of the owner, user and insurer.

The role of the diver as an underwater inspector and NDT (Non-Destructive Testing) technician is therefore of vital importance, since it is he who will have to provide reliable and valid data on defects, from which qualified engineers will assess the sub-sea condition of the structure. Alternative inspection techniques are being developed to save cost, such as structural monitoring, remote controlled methods and internal examination of risers, all of which are aimed at dispensing with the diver. To date, few of these advances have proven to be satisfactory or cost-effective, and it is unlikely that the diver-inspector will be supplanted in the immediate or even forseeable future.

For offshore structures, and to a lesser degree, vessels and inshore installations, a regular programme of inspection is necessary to satisfy the following requirements:

1 To obtain a certificate of fitness, or continuation of an existing certificate from a certifying authority (eg: Lloyds, Bureau Veritas, DNV, etc.)
2 To give the operator assurance that the structure or vessel is sound, safe and functional.
3 To assess the structural condition following repair.

At present, most inspection work falls into the first two categories, but as structures become older and repair work becomes necessary, it can be predicted that the third category will assume a greater importance.

For North Sea structures, the level and nature of inspection is agreed between the certifying authority and the operator. This normally follows a five-year cycle, backed up by a programme of annual inspections. It will therefore be obvious that the whole aspect of underwater NDT inspection is of considerable and necessary importance. It also offers all commercial divers a highly technical field of work, with regular employment, potential for initiative, which is still expanding. The object of this chapter is only to outline the basic principles of underwater NDT techniques, and is not intended to embrace the syllabus for an inspection diver.

Details of such qualifications, with an indication of the standard required, has been included at the end.

SUMMARY OF DEFECTS

It is obvious that those engaged in underwater inspection must be capable of detecting and, more important, identifying the types of defects likely to be encountered. Such individuals must know how defects are formed, how they manifest themselves, and their significance to the qualified surface engineer, since it is he who has to interpret the data provided, and therefore they must work closely together.

A broad classification of underwater defects is illustrated below:

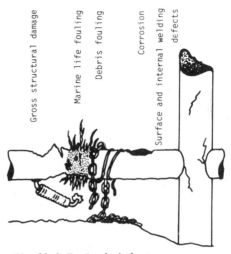

Fig 21-1 Typical defects

Gross Structural Defects

These are obvious defects which are discovered during general visual inspection, or are high-lighted by structural monitoring techniques. These would include:

Serious dents, buckling, and deformation.

Missing members, components, lost and badly corroded anodes.

Paint coatings or monel cladding removed or damaged.

Damaged cabling and ducting.

Cracked pile grouting.

Unstable foundations, scouring or settlement.

Spalling of concrete from the surface of a concrete structure.

Bolts missing from assemblies.

Lost or misplaced instrumentation

such as reference electrodes, wave monitors, acoustic emission sensors, pressure transducers, CCTV cameras etc.

MARINE GROWTH FOULING

The underwater inspector will have to contend with marine growth as part of his every-day life, and much of his work will entail its removal. Unfortunately, this is estimated as accounting for some 80% of inspection work, and is hence a costly operation. It is therefore important that the diver inspector is aware of the ways in which marine growth can affect structures.

The effect of fouling by various types of weed and marine growth can be classified as follows:

Increase in deadweight, wave loading and drag.

Exaggeration or lessening of corrosion of the structure.

Concealment of metal surfaces, features, and defects from normal visual inspection.

Blockage of seawater intakes.

Fouling of moving parts.

Fouling of instrumentation.

It is necessary at this point to differentiate between hard and soft fouling:

Type	Distinction
Soft	Density approximately the same as seawater; includes bacteria, seaweed, anemones, sponges etc.
Hard	Density approximately 1 to 4 times that of seawater; includes tube worms, limpets, mussels, and barnacles.

Effects of Fouling

Significant levels of hard fouling, especially mussels, will add considerably to the weight of a structure, as well as increase its cross-sectional area. This in turn will increase the wave loading and impact, simply

because there is more surface area on which to act. The depth and thickness, as well as accurate identification of this sort of loading is essential, if a critical level is not to be reached. Failure to do so could lead to the collapse of part or all of the structure, resulting in loss of life, a possible oil spill or fire, and enormous cost.

Fouling and Corrosion

It is currently not possible to predict with any certainty the effect that marine growth will have on the corrosion of a structure, but the possibl effects are as follows:

Enhancement or deterring of corrosion on steel surfaces.

Influencing the efficiency of a cathodic protection system.

Mechanical damage to anti-corrosion coatings.

Corrosion of the piling.

Apart from its physical effect on the structure itself, marine fouling will prevent the diver inspector from carrying out most, if not all of the usual techniques involving close-up photography; ultrasonics; eddycurrent techniques and MPI (magnetic particle inspection).

MARINE DEBRIS FOULING

Large quantities of material of all kinds are to be found on the seabed surrounding offshore and inshore platforms and structures. Divers will be familiar with the profusion of wire hawsers, rope, ladders, paint pots, crockery and tools to be found beneath or around piers and jetties, but they may not be prepared for the volume of debris found offshore.

Although most platform operators prohibit the disposal of material in this way, "out of sight, out of mind" is an attitude which still prevails, and it is all too easy to throw things over the side. In fairness, a great deal is lost accidentaly, and typical "scrap" on the sea bed will include steel girders, railings, pipework, scaffolding, electrical cable, wire, complete cranes, Portacabins, and the like.

This presents not only a hazard to the divers, but a danger to the complete structure in the following manner, so often overlooked or forgotten:

Additional steel touching part of the structure places an additional load on the 'built-in' cathodic protection system, which is incapable of any discrimination between scarp and structure.

The unwanted material may set up or enhance galvanic corrosion action, aggravated by any physical fretting movement due to tide or weather.

Debris may foul important guide wires or controls on seabed equipment, and heavy items may even cause physical damage.

Other problems associated with structures, which form part of the overall inspection programme include "scour" and "coating" defects.

CORROSION

The majority of offshore installations are made partly or entirely of steel. Steel is prone to many forms of marine corrosion, the most familiar of which is rust. In simple terms the reason for this is that the iron from which the steel was made was originally a natural ore, the most common of which is haematite. In turning it into steel, heat was used to separate the oxygen from the iron, but the resultant alloy is always trying to revert back to its natural state, hence it reacts with oxygen and forms rust, which is chemically very similar to haematite.

The most important forms of corrosion

encountered offshore are:

a) General and pitting corrosion
b) Fretting corrosion
c) Galvanic corrosion
d) Crevice corrosion
e) Erosion corrosion
f) Corrosion fatigue
g) Biological corrosion

Taking each of these in turn, their cause snd effect is as follows:

General and Pitting Corrosion

If corrosion proceeds around a steel surface in a uniform manner, this is classified as general corrosion. This is the easiest form of deterioration to predict, and for which full allowance can be made during design. If the corrosion proceeds the anodic areas of the surface, these will shift from place to place, until the entire surface has been anodic at some time. The result will be a regular thinning of the material overall.

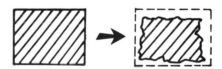

Fig 21-2 Pictorial effect of general corrosion

Sometimes the anodic areas of a steel structure remain stationary, in which case pitting corrosion takes place instead of a general thinning, which cannot be detected by visual inspection, and can be very serious in components.

Fretting Corrosion

This occurs where two metal surfaces are rubbing against each other, assuming that one or both are prone to corrosion. Even slight fretting will abrade the surfaces, cause any corrosion that has formed to be removed, and hasten more corrosion. Riser clamps and mooring chains are particularly prone.

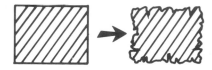

Fig 21-3 Pictorial effect of pitting corrosion, in which the deterioration is not uniform

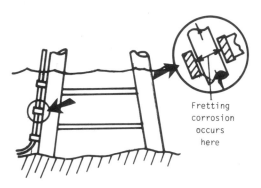

Fretting corrosion occurs here

Fig 21-4 Example of fretting corrosion on a riser clamp

Galvanic Corrosion

Dissimilar metals, or alloys of the same metal, in electrical contact in an electrolyte, will cause the less noble metal to act as an anode, and be corrosively attacked. The metal nearest to the active end will corrode away, and that closest to the noble end will act as a cathode and be protected. In most cases, metals from one group can be utilised with metals from the same group without severe galvanic corrosion.

A typical example would be a brass stud in an aluminium casting. The stud being more noble than the casting, the aluminium would be sacrificed and slowly eaten away, particularly if immersed in salt water which would hasten the action.

Crevice Corrosion

Rivet lap joints are typical areas in which crevice corrosion may occur. This form of corrosion may be generated by differences in the environment (electrolyte) and not the metals. Within a crevice some metal will dissolve, assuming it is immersed in salt water, and go into solution as metallic ions. remote from the crevice, the relative amounts in solution will result in a lower concentration outside the crevice than within.

The metal just outside the crevice will attempt to reduce this imbalance, and commence to go into solution at a more rapid rate. If, as with salt water, the solution is in motion, the metallic ions will be carried away as it dissolves, preventing equilibrium and speeding up further attack.

Erosion Corrosion

A typical offshore example of this problem is the wear found at the base of riser pipes, where the rapid flow of the product, plus its entrained particles, causes one wall of the pipe to become very thin.

Corrosion Fatigue

Metals that fail as a result of cyclic stress are said to fatigue. Failure is normally due to the formation of a single fatigue crack, and when cyclically stressed in a corrosive environment, the combined actions intensify the damage. Marine structures are continually under cyclic stress, due to:

1   The action of the sea, causing the structure to oscillate in the direction of the waves

2   Vibration due to the running of heavy machinery

Cracks

Linear fractures in the weld metal

of joints are generally caused by excessively high current, insufficient pre-heat, incorrect bevel angle, or highly restrained joints. Cracks due to defective welding during fabrication will have been detected, and removed during surface inspection. It is therefore reasonable to assume that any weld cracks found underwater at a later stage must be service cracks. The detection of cracks in welds underwater forms a major part of inspection work.

UNDERWATER CLEANING

There are two basic types of cleaning carried out, depending on the required finish:

a) General cleaning, to reduce drag and wave loading. Marine growth is removed in bulk.

b) Precise cleaning, to allow detailed visual and NDT inspection. A bright metal finish will be required, hence protective coatings and all corrosion must be removed.

There are four standard methods by which this cleaning can be achieved:

1 Hand tools - including wire brushes, hand scrapers, and wire strops. The latter are wrapped around members, and with one end in each hand, the diver see-saws the strop over the area to be cleaned. All hand cleaning is very time consuming and labour intensive.

2 Needle guns - pneumatically operated, these have a set of needle pointed rods encased in a barrel, which oscillate under power, causing a rapid vibration action, which quickly removes marine hard growth and corrosion.

3 Power driven wire brushes - can be pneumatic, hydraulic or electric. Effective only for marine growth.

4 HP water jets - hand held tools with balancing retrojets, working at between 3,000 and 12,000 psi. Now being used extensively for the removal of fouling and corrosion products down to bright metal. Grit can be entrained in the water flow.

Very dangerous in the hands of the inexperienced, and have been the cause of a great many accidents, some resulting in severe physical injury to the diver/operator.

BASIC NDT TECHNIQUES

The following are the techniques employed underwater in carrying out NDT inspection work, each of which will be followed by a brief resumé of the principle and the equipment involved. It is stressed that a great deal of detail has been omitted, since this is only intended to be a summary, to give the trainee diver an outline of the subject, and no more.

Visual Inspection

Although various optical aids are used extensively on land in NDT work, the underwater situation does not lend itself to the use of mirror probes, endoscopes, magnifiers and the like. Visual inspection for divers is therefore limited to the human eye, the inspector making use of a rule, calipers, feeler gauges and camera as appropriate.

Magnetic Particle Inspection

Known generally as MPI, this technique operates on the principle that if a ferromagnetic specimen containing a crack at or near the surface is magnetised, the lines of magnetic force will be confined within the material, apart from where they jump the gap made by the flaw. The leakage field is sufficiently strong to attract magnetic particles, and thus reveal the presence of the defect. MPI is used for the detection of surface or near surface defects in ferromagnetic materials at low cost. Non-magnetic stainless steels, and of course non-ferrous metals cannot be inspected by this method. It is difficult to use on rough surfaces, and elongated defects parallel to the magnetic field may not give a pattern. It is therefore sometimes necessary to apply the field from two directions, preferably at right angles to each other. The crack defect becomes visible to the eye by application of a magnetic particle rich 'ink', which is retained after surplus has been wiped or washed off.

The technique of MPI requires skill in the proper interpretation of indications, and the recognition of patterns that are irrelevant.

Underwater, MPI is used extensively on nodal welds for the detection of surface cracks. Permanent magnets, electro-magnets, current prods and parallel conductors are used to magnetise the test area. The inks used are fluorescent magnetic, activated by the use of an ultraviolet lamp.

Magnetographic Tape

This principle is similar to MPI. Since a defect will cause flux leakage at the surface, if a magnetic tape is laid over the surface, a permanent record is then obtained. The tape can be "played back" on a special tape recorder, and either shown on a CRT display screen, or on a record chart.

One particular advantage of this method is that a permanent record is obtained, which can be interpreted by skilled technicians on the surface.

Disadvantages are that the tape is difficult to handle, and the process requires two divers. There are also some doubts as to the sensitivity of the system when rough surfaces are involved.

Ultrasonics

Thickness and lamination measurements are possible, by making use of the principle that pulses of high freq-

uency sound energy can be transmitted through certain materials, which will be reflected back by the far boundary or by an internal flaw. The total transit time can be measured and may provide an indication of the location of the reflecting surface.

Ultrasonics are best suited to the detection of planar defects. In steel, sound has great powers of penetration, enabling examination of extremely thick sections of metal. In addition, access to only the surface of the test area is necessary. For flaw detection and sizing, the technique requires a high degree of skill to interpret the data, and any permanent record is not easily obtained.

Radiography

X-rays are utilised on the principle that certain materials, such as steel, are translucent. If the specimen being subjected to X-rays is irregular in shape and not homogenous in composition, a variation in the weakening of the radiation will occur as it penetrates the specimen. These variations can be recorded on a photographic plate placed behind the target.

The irregularities may be changes in shape, thickness or surface condition, and volumetric flaws such as voids or inclusions may be present. Depending on their nature, these features will either impede or assist the transmission of X-rays or gamma rays through the specimen.

X-rays are not used underwater as yet, and gamma radiography is not widely employed. Apart from operational problems, there are few qualified diver technicians authorised to handle the radio isotopes underwater.

Eddy Current Testing

If a coil carrying an alternating current is brought close to a conducting metal surface, the AC magnetic field from the coil induces eddy currents in the surface of the metal. These eddy currents produce magnetic fields which alter certain measurable properties of the coil.

Hence, changes in metallic composition, defects in or near the surface and surface coatings modify the interaction between the coil and the conductor. This effect can be detected by the use of suitable equipment, but requires a highly trained operator.

STRUCTURAL MONITORING

The two most relevant methods of structural monitoring are:

a) Vibrational analysis

b) Acoustic emission

Vibrational analysis relies on the principle that if a structure is vibrated it will oscillate in a specific manner, which would depend on rigidity and geometry. Should part of that structure now become damaged, it will oscillate in a different way, producing changes which can be monitored by the use of accelerometers.

Platforms continually vibrate under the influence of wind and waves. If for example a member fails, it will cause a change in the stiffness of the structure, resulting in a different frequency and magnitude of signal. Periodical inspection to obtain a "finger-print" is often carried out on both steel and concrete platforms, using divers to position and remove the accelerometers.

Acoustic emission relies on the high frequency sound which will result from defects etc. in metal components when they are stressed. When monitoring a platform for structural defects, wave action provides the necessary stress for analysis. A series of sensors are placed around the structure, both above and below the surface. The nature and location of discontinuities can then be monitored. Divers may be involved in this work, positioning the sub sea sensors.

Corrosion Potential Measurement

This technique is widely used underwater. When two dissimilar metals are connected and then bridged by a suitable solution able to conduct charged ions, an electrolytic cell is formed. An electrical potential then arises which can be measured on a potential meter. As an example, assume that it is necessary to measure the degree of corrosion on a buried pipe-line. If a reference half-cell (usually silver/silver chloride) is then connected to the pipe-line, and placed in contact with the soil around the pipe to complete the circuit, a potential will be generated, which at any moment represents the state of corrosion of the pipe. As the corrosion advances, so the potential reading will change.

Cathodic Protection (CP)

There are four essential components in a corrosion cell. These are:

1 An anode that corrodes
2 A cathode that is protected
3 An electrolyte which allows a current to flow by the passage of charged chemical ions
4 Electrical contact between the anode and the cathode

If any of the components are reduced to the point of insignificance, isolated, or removed, the corrosion cell is destroyed and corrosive attack will cease. The principal methods of prevention of control of corrosion are:

*   Cathodic protection
*   Application of protective coatings
*   Metal sheathing and concrete encasement
*   Treatment of the electrolyte
*   Attention to design

Cathodic Protection Methods

Consider a bare steel surface immersed in salt water. If it were possible to study the surface of the steel at a microscopic level, it would be found that there were innumerable anodic and cathodic areas forming individual corrosion cells. A method of preventing this corrosion is to connect an external anode, inducing an equal or greater current to flow from this anode to the structure, which consequently becomes a cathode.

This process is called cathodic protection, but can only be effective on the submerged parts of the structure. Protection will only occur as long as the external anode works properly. It will be seen that the system is equivalent to a corrosion cell. There is still the cathode (the structure), an anode, electrolyte (sea water), and a metallic connection. It is most important that there is a good connection between the anode and structure. Protection can therefore be achieved by one of two methods:

1 Sacrificial anodes

2 Impressed current anodes

Sacrificial Anodes

With reference to a table of the galvanic series of metals in sea water, it will be seen that if steel is connected to any metal that is below it in the series, then the steel will become cathodic and be protected. The anodic metals are normally aluminium, zinc, magnesium and their alloys. Since these corrode and are generally consumed, such anodes are called sacrificial anodes. If they are to function properly, sufficient cross-sectional area must be available, and there must be a good electrical connection to the steel structure.

Often the inspection diver will be required to check the condition of the anodes for pitting; to measure their diameter, and generally ensure they have a firm fixing on the structure.

Impressed Current Anodes

The principle of cathodic protection is to induce a current from an external anode thereby making the steel cathodic. The current can be induced by feeding a surface generated D.C. (direct current) to an external anode through a heavy duty electrical cable. This would then be called an "impressed current" system. The anodes can be expendable, and made of ordinary mild steel. These will require periodic replacement, and hence are only used in coastal applications.

Anodes used offshore are more or less permanent, being usually platinum, platinum sheated titanium, niobium or other materials.

There are two types of impressed current systems which may be used offshore, namely:

1 Local anodes which are attached directly to the structure, but insulated from it by "stand-off" insulators.

2 Remote anodes, placed at a suitable distance from the structure to provide an overall blanket protection.

For inspection purposes, the tendency or potential to corrode can be obtained using a reference half-cell, built into a portable corrosion test meter. The steel of the structure acts as one half of the cell, contact being made by means of a probe; the other half of the circuit is the reference half-cell, which will give a reading in millivolts.

TRAINING AND CERTIFICATION OF DIVER INSPECTORS IN UNDERWATER NDT

Lloyds and CSWIP

Divers interested in obtaining training and an appropriate qualification in NDT, should write to CSWIP, requesting full details for the CSWIP Phase 7 Group 3.1U and

3.2U Requirement for the Certification of Diver Inspectors, and a list of approved courses:

The Secretary
CSWIP
Abington Hall
Cambridge CB1 6AL

Telephone: 0223 - 891162 Telex: 81183

Candidates wishing to take the CSWIP Phase 7 Group 3.1U examination, are required to furnish proof of :

1 The possession of a minimum diving qualification of HSE Part 3 Diver, with at least 60 hours logged commercial diving experience.

2 A valid diving medical certificate.

3 The successful completion of an approved training course for Group 3.1U Inspection Diver.

On acceptance, candidates will be required to take the necessary written and practical examinations for Group 3.1U, in those subjects covered by the appropriate syllabus, copies of which are obtainable from CSWIP.

The examination will be conducted at an approved examination centre, which may or may not be the place at which the candidate undertook approved training.

Successful candidates will be awarded a Certificate of Proficiency for Group 3.1U Inspection Diver, a copy of which will also be forwarded to the company or organisation paying the certification fee. Duplicate certificates to replace those lost or destroyed will only be issued after exhaustive enquiries, and the payment of another standard certification fee.

Such certificates will be valid for 1 year from the date of completion of the original test, and may be renewed upon application to CSWIP annually without further test, up to a maximum of 5 years. Candidates whose certificate expire at the end of the maximum 5 year period of validity, will be required to take a 5 year renewal test, details of which can be obtained from CSWIP. Candidates who fail the 5 year test will be required to follow the procedure as for a new certificate.

To qualify as a full CSWIP Phase 7 Group 3.2U Certified Diver NDT Inspector, candidates are required to furnish proof of:

1 Possession of a minimum diving qualification of HSE Part 3 Diver.

2 A valid diving medical certificate

3 Having held a Group 3.1U for a minimum of 12 months, during which the diver has completed a minimum of 30 hours, relevant and logged underwater inspection work
4 The successful completion of an approved training course for Group 3.2U NDT Inspector

On acceptance, candidates will be required to take the necessary written and practical examinations for Group 3.2U, in those subjects covered by the appropriate syllabus, copies of which are obtainable from CSWIP.

The same conditions apply as for passing or failing the Group 3.1U examination, also validation and renewal of certificates.

Unsuccessful candidates and the organisation paying the certification fee will receive a standard form from CSWIP setting out the reason for non-acceptance for examination, or failure of an examination, as appropriate. Such individuals may attempt a "retest" of the failed part(s) provided such tests are completed within 16 weeks of completion of the initial tests. After that they will be treated as new or initial candidates.

CHAPTER 22

BASIC ENGINEERING DRAWINGS AND REPORT WRITING

Whilst the purpose of all engineering drawings is to provide a permanent and accurate record of an object, they also serve less obvious but equally important functions, namely:

Provide sufficient information to allow exact replicas of the original to be made.

Provide sufficient information to allow individuals who may never have seen the original object, or talked to the designer, to fully understand the nature of the object, its size, function, details of component parts, the materials used, degree of finish, and tolerances.

Provide sufficient information to allow anyone to readily identify component parts, in order to be able to order spares or replacement parts.

Those with a technical work background prior to entering the commercial diving field, may well be familiar with engineering drawings, their interpretation and use. Others, without a technical background, may find them quite difficult to understand.
    It is a requirement of all candidates for HSE. Part 1 Diver qualification, that they be capable of reading at least a simple engineering drawing, and in fact all commercial divers should be able to interpret same, for the following reasons:

1   There will be many underwater tasks which will require careful study of drawings before work commences, in order to appreciate complexity, position, orientation, related materials, obstructions, hazards etc.

2   On completion of any dive, the dive supervisor, foreman or client may require the diver to indicate on a drawing the nature of a defect, or progress of work. In the case of damage for example, the information would entail the limits, position, component parts affected, and any relevant aspects regarding the rectification work.

3   A diver may be required to produce at any time, an engineering sketch, or something more accurate, to accompany a report, or to be sent to a workshop, remote from the dive site, who will be required to manufacture a component part, or provide a spare.

    In all these examples, there is no room for error, and the ability to read and understand engineering drawings will stand a diver in good stead. This chapter details the types of drawings likely to be encountered and their identification; symbols and other conventions used in drawing, and other basic but relevant aspects. It is recommended that those not familiar with the subject should practise interpretation, using actual engineering drawings, seeking professional assistance where necessary.

TYPES OF DRAWINGS

Drawings are produced at various stages of development or production to suit various requirements, and it is important to appreciate their significance.

Design Lay-out Drawings

These are usually "sketchy" drawings on detail paper, but should include calculations and sufficient information for further work to be carried out on the project, without much reference to the designer. These are not intended to be accurate detailed reproduction drawings.

Tabulated (Collective) Drawings

These are used for similar parts or assemblies, possibly such items as nuts, screws, springs, bolts, washers etc. Such drawings will show the part in question, with dimensions lettered, and a table giving the actual dimensions relevant to each component part listed under the appropriate letter.

Assembly/Sub-assembly Drawings

Such drawings will show the actual arrangement of component or adjacent parts as they form part of the whole. Dimensions are not normally shown, except those that may affect fitting or location. Assembly drawings usually have a parts list, quoting the identity and quantity of the parts required to make up the assembly.

General Arrangement Drawings

These show the complete object, machine, structure or project in outline, giving overall dimensions, fixing and details, but not individual component information.

Jig and Tool Drawings

Intended for one-off or small batch quantity production; jig or tool drawings may take the form of combined drawings with the assembly, parts list and details all on one sheet.

Operation Drawings

A drawing of a component as it appears at a particular stage of manufacture, with only those dimensions and tolerances relevant to the particular operation being carried out. Within this category could be extrusion drawings, showing one extrusion from which several parts may be made, casting, forging drawings etc.

LAY-OUT OF DRAWINGS

With reference to Fig 22-1 which shows a typical drawing lay-out, it should be noted that the following information should be included:

a) Name of firm or company
b) Description and title
c) Drawing number, and/or part number (this will normally appear twice)
d) Draughtsman's identity
e) Checker's identity
f) Date
g) Scale and units
h) Revision and modification record
i) Projection used

Other information which may appear on manufacturing drawings will be:

Material process(es) employed

General tolerances used

Key to machine finish

References to similar parts

Reference to assembly drawing

It should be noted that there is no "national" or "international" standard lay-out for engineering drawings. There are many variations employed, but provided any drawing contains most or all of the above detail, there really are no special problems involved in interpretation.

IDENTIFICATION OF DRAWINGS

All drawing offices maintain a methodical system of numbering drawings, in order to assist identification at a later date.
If, as a result of a change or modification, so that a part now becomes non-interchangeable with the original existing design, then a new part has been created, and hence would have a new number and drawing. If a modification was so minor that interchangeability was not affected, then the drawing number would remain the same, but the ISSUE

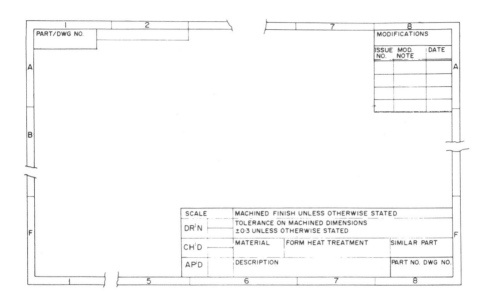

Fig 22-1 Typical lay-out for manufacturing drawing

NUMBER of the drawing would be altered.

When new drawings are issued as a result of changes or modifications, then a modification note will be issued, and noted in the box (see top right, Fig 22-1) so that the person reading the drawing knows how up to date his material is.

PROJECTIONS

Basically, the difference between an artist's impression of an object, and an engineering drawing, is that the artist draws those aspects which he can see from one particular viewpoint. On the other hand, the draughtsman who produces "orthographic" drawings presents different faces of the object in order to demonstrate all its physical features. In other words, the engineer shows the object from many viewpoints, so that nothing is hidden and there are no mysteries.

In order to achieve this to the best effect, it is necessary for the "trade" to have some sort of "standard", so we know from which viewpoint he was viewing the object when the drawing was made. In many instances it is perfectly obvious from which angle the drawing was made, but with complicated items or components it may be far from obvious, and cannot be left to chance.

The welded, fabricated bracket in Fig 22-2 is relatively easy to understand, but even then, its proportions have changed dramaticslly when viewed from another "artist's" angle as in Fig 22-3. But in neither instance are we quite sure that there is not some hidden detail behind the back plate with the single hole. In neither of these projections is it possible for the artist or the engineer to give a true picture.

It has therefore become the accepted "standard" to use certain conventions when it comes to drawings. Known as orthographic projections, there are only two, "First angle" , and "Third angle".

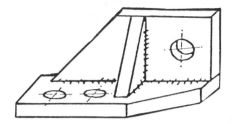

Fig 22-2 Oblique view of a fabricated, welded bracket

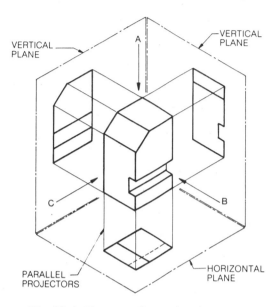

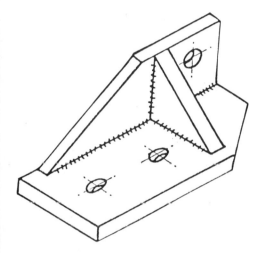

Fig 22-3 Isometric view of the same bracket

Orthographic Projections

First angle

Fig 22-4 shows a pictorial view of a block with a groove milled across the front face, and its top left hand corner removed. Imagine two vertical planes at right angles to each other and parallel to the sides of the block, with an additional horizontal plane beneath. The three arrows are used to observe each face of the block in turn, and then project the image on to the surface behind the face. The arrows must be assumed to lie at right angles to each face of the block.

The view in the direction of "A"

Fig 22-4 First angle projection

on the horizontal plane shows us what the "top" of the block looks like, and is known as the "plan view". Any hidden detail such as the slot, which may be obscured from above, is indicated by a dotted outline.

Arrow "B" indicates what is known as the "front elevation", and "C" gives us the "side" or "end" elevation. Presented as a draughts-amn's drawing, the result would be as shown in Fig 22-5.

Since the object has six sides or viewpoints, it would be possible to draw all six, as shown in Fig 22-6, but this is unecessary of course in a case where the object is of little complication. It is also worth noting that of course, many objects do not have a top, back or front, so we have to rely on the draughtsman to show the important faces.

Note that it is conventional in drawing terms to refer to the different views as "elevations", so that the view from the side ("C"), would be the "side elevation" and so on.

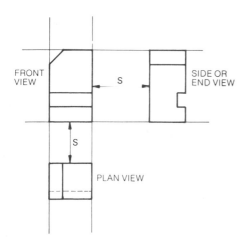

FRONT VIEW

S

SIDE OR END VIEW

S

PLAN VIEW

Fig 22-5 Engineering drawing of the block - First angle

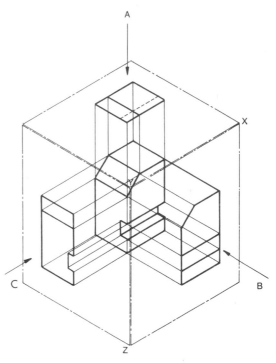

Fig 22-7 Third angle projection

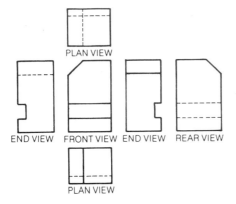

PLAN VIEW

END VIEW FRONT VIEW END VIEW REAR VIEW

PLAN VIEW

Fig 22-6 All six faces of the block on one drawing

Third angle

In this alternative method of indicating "viewpoints", as shown in Fig 22-7, imagine that the block has three panels of glass around it, and that we are viewing it through the glass.

If a felt tip marker pen was then used to outline the view seen from the angles A,B and C, assuming that the

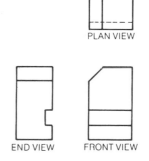

PLAN VIEW

END VIEW FRONT VIEW

Fig 22-8 Engineering drawing of the block - Third angle

arrows are all at right angles. then the result would be the three views shown in Fig 22-8, which is of course different from that in Fig 22-5,

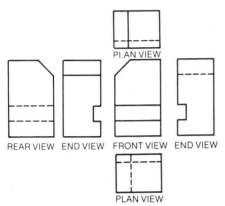

PLAN VIEW

REAR VIEW   END VIEW   FRONT VIEW   END VIEW

PLAN VIEW

Fig 22-9 Six faces of the block on one
drawing, compare this with Fig 22-6

and that a drawing of all six sides
would appear as in Fig 22-9 above.
These then are the differences betwen
First and Third angle projections,
and provided the drawing indicates
which of the two projections was uses,
and the "reader" knows the difference
between them, there should be no
problems.

DRAWING SYMBOLS

The First angle projection is the
convention most widely used in Europe,
and the Third angle that used in the
United States of America. In order to
prevent any misunderstanding, each
projection has been given a distinct-
ive symbol.
        The symbols represent drawings
of tapered cylinders, and it can be
seen that these have to be turned a
certain way to obtain the required
views.

Standard projection symbols

Fig 22-10 First angle

Fig 22-11 Third angle

DIMENSIONS

Dimensions relating to a particular
part or feature should be shown
just the once, and not repeated on
other views, and if possible all
details on the one view. Unnecessary
dimensions or an abundance of dimensions should be avoided, provided
there are sufficient to allow interpretation.
        Where dimensions are such that
they affect the function of a part,
they should not be left as the sum or
difference of other dimensions, but
actually specified. Overall dimensions
should always appear, and it must
always be borne in mind that the stated
tolerance overall for the drawing
applies to every dimension.

TOLERANCES

A degree of tolerance is necessary to
allow for inaccuracies in manufacture,
or between different manufacturers of
the same item.
        A tolerance can be defined as
"differences in a dimension to allow
for unavoidable imperfections in
workmanship", and these can vary from
whole inches or tens of centimetres,
to thousandths of an inch, or millimetre. The extreme tolerance allowed
a particular dimesnion is called its
"limit", which would be expressed
thus:

                    + 0.010mm
Tolerance on 20mm of
                    - 0.010mm

would result in an allowable limit
of:
            20.010mm
            19.990mm

Welding symbols B S 499

Weld	Section	Symbol	Dimensions	Comments
Fillet			T < 5, l = 3 5 < T < 8, l = 5 8 < T < 16, l = 10	No edge preparation
Square butt			T < 5 g = 3	Thin sheets only (12 max)
Single vee butt			a = 60°−100° T < 10, g = 2-5 T > 10, g = 3-6	For use with thicker plates with access on one side only
Double vee butt			As above	Access req'd from both sides uses less electrode but more preparation req
Single U butt			g = 3−6 T < 12, t = 2 T > 12, t = 4 r = 3a > 15° r > 5a > 10°	More prep. than vee butt; less distortion occurs
Double U butt			As above	
Single bevel butt			a = 20°−30° T < 10g = 3-6 T > 10g = 5-8	
Double bevel butt			As above	
Single J butt			a = 20°−30° g = 3-6, r = 5(min) T < 12, t = 2(max) T > 12, t = 3(max)	Use only when access is limited to one side
Double J butt			As above	
Edge				
Seal				

Fig 22-12 The above are the welding symbols recommended in British Standard BS 499

Weld	Section	Symbol	Dimensions
Sealing run			
Backing strip			
Spot		(N) d (S)	d = diameter N = number of welds S = spacing
Seam		d	d = diameter
Mashed seam	Before After		
Stitch			
Mashed stitch	Before After		
Projection		N WPS S	WPS - see Weld Procedure Sheet for projection dimensions N = no. of projections S = spacing
Flash		(L)	L = Upset travel
Butt		(L)	l = total loss of length
Stud		(N) C	N = no of studs C = centre dist
Full penetration butt weld			

Component	Code	Followed by
Bolt hex head	MBX	
Screw hex head	MSX	
Socket cap	MUC	dia. in mm : Length in mm.
C S K head	MSK	
Grub cone point	MUGSC	
Grub cup point	MUGCP	
Nut thick	MNT	
Locknut	MNL	dia mm
Self locking	MNSL	
Washer plain	WP	Bore in mm : O/D in mm
Taper pin	TP	Pin no. followed by length in mm

Fig 22-13 Abbreviations used for locking devices

All screws to be prefixed by 'SM' followed by diameter in mm			
Length of thread(mm)			
Code for head type			
Code for material			
Code for finish			
e.g. SM 0830 A/01/03 means hexagonal−headed screw (metric thread) chrome finish on brass 8mm dia. X 30mm lg			
Type of head	Code	Material	Code	Finish code
Hexagon	A	Steel	00	Natural 00
Round	B	Brass	01	Drill nickel 01
C sunk	C	Copper	02	Bright nickel 02
Socket cap	D	Aluminium	03	Chromium 03
Socket grub	E	Dural	04	Cadmium 04
Grub cup point	F	Nylon	05	Anodised 05
Grub cup point	G			Blued 06

Fig 22−14 Abbreviations used for
          screws, including head
          type, material and finish

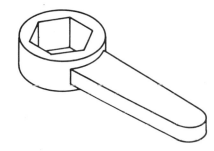

Fig 22−15 Isometric view of a tool

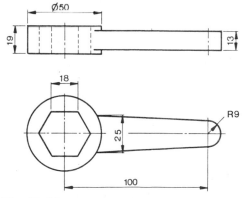

Fig 22−16 An acceptable engineering
          of the same tool, less
          details of tolerance etc.

Report writing

Report writing and the preparation
of reports is a regular aspect of
commercial diving activities, and
all divers should be conversant with
the principles.
Regardless of whether the report
relates to observations made during
an inspection dive, the actual
progress of a job, an accident, or
merely to the breakdown of a piece
of equipment, the same basic criteria
apply.
    The reason for reports is all
too often neglected, and instead of
communicating the actual information
required, reports often become something of a monument to individuals,
perhaps trying harder to impress
than carry out their actual work task.
    The purpose of a report can be
summarised as follows:

1 It informs others not present at
   the time the event occurred

2 It provides a permanent record for
   the future

3 It summarises the whole sequence
   of events, and extracts information which would otherwise
   become either "hazy" or forgotten

4 It brings together in one place
   and at one time, information,
   comments, drawings, photographs,
   tapes, film and other data, which
   might otherwise become scattered
   information

5 It reflects the degree of not only
   care and detail given to the task
   by the individuals concerned, but
   also the professionalism, and may
   well reflect on future employment

An extension of the above are the
purposes for which a report may be
used, namely:

a) Making decisions resulting from
   information contained in the
   report.

b) Expenditure relating to any action
   necessary.

c) The call for further information,
   more detailed investigation etc.

When making out the rough basis of a
report, the following elements are
essential:

Sufficient information relating to the
subject of the report

Organised presentation

Clarity of expression

Legibility

Photography

Drawings, sketches and maps etc.

Lack of sufficient information, sketches
and photographs are probably the most
common failing of otherwise good reports.
Photographs and other illustrations
convey far more information in less space
than any drawn or written information.
      Whilst it is difficult to summarise
all report writing in a few words, the
following are the accepted categories
around which the report should be based:

1 The contract, agreement, working
   situation or circumstances leading up
   to the submission of the report.

2 A summary of the equipment, gear,
   manpower, individuals, time, weather,
   location, conditions prevailing and
   relevant exclusions.

3 The actual "meat" of the report, free
   from extraneous information or any
   "padding" or repetition of information
   already furnished.

4 Supporting information, ie. eye-witness
   accounts; sources of additional
   documentation; other or related
   reports; previous history of component
   inspection, purchase, work, modification
   etc. Sketches and photographs well
   marked.

5 Conclusions and summary

Finally, send sufficient copies of
the report, and retain spare copies
for later use. If there is even the
remotest chance that the report may
be delayed or lost in transit, it
is advisable to send copies of the
report by different routes, postal
collections, or different days. The
receipt of duplicate reports is far
better than no report at all !

CHAPTER 23

DIVING REGULATIONS AND STANDARDS

Following the introduction of the "Diving Operations at Work Regulations 1981" by the Health and Safety Executive on 1 July, that year, a period of 6 months grace was afforded all existing commercial divers, during which time they were required to obtain a certificate of diving competence. This required a minimum of 2 years' previous commercial diving experience in the grade sought, which was required to be supported by log-book evidence, plus current medical fitness. Those with less than 2 years' experience were required to produce proof of approved training.

As from 1 January 1982, the termination date for the acquisition of such certificates (except in special circumstances), it became law that no person should be employed as a diver within the United Kingdom in any diving operation unless:

a) That person has a valid certificate, issued prior to 1 January 1982, or has a valid certificate of training issued by either the Manpower Services Commission (Training Services Agency or Division), or the H.S.E.

b) That person has a valid certificate of medical fitness to dive, issued by an approved "diving doctor".

c) That person has a divers' log book, containing his photograph, and a record of medical fitness.

d) That person is competent to carry out safely the work which he is called upon to perform in that operation.

Divers who by previous experience and/or training, and who have been working abroad or in some other situation, whereby it was not possible for them to obtain a recognised certificate of diving competence, may still apply direct to the Health and Safety Executive, forwarding proof of diving experience, training, medical fitness, references, etc for consideration.

Newcomers to diving as from 1 January 1982, are now required to furnish proof of having undertaken a course of approved training, and attained satisfactory completion. Full details of the availability of approved training can be obtained through the Health and Safety Executive, either at an area office, or the public enquiry point:

Health and Safety Executive
Baynards House
1 Chepstow Place
London W2 4TF
Telephone: 01 - 229 - 3456

Currently, approved air diver training courses for the three grades are available at the following establishments only, which cater to the general public on a commercial basis:

Prodive Limited
Services Area
Falmouth Docks
Falmouth
Cornwall
Tel: Falmouth (0326) - 315691
Telex: 45362

Plymouth Ocean Projects Limited
Fort Bovisand
Plymouth
Devon PL9 0AB
Tel: Plymouth (0752) - 42570/45641
Telex: 45639 (quote P27)

Underwater Centre Limited
Inverlochy
Fort William
Inverness-shire Scotland
Tel: 0397 - 3786/9
Telex: 779703

HSE DIVING QUALIFICATIONS

There are currently four diver qualifications obtainable in the United Kingdom,
three of which relate to "air" diving,
and one to "mixed-gas/saturation" diving.
The apparent anomaly in the numbering
system, which might suggest that the HSE
Part 1 qualification was higher than that
of Part II, is a result of earlier
legislation. Introduced at a time when
there was no Part's IV and III qualification, Part I was designated the "air"
qualification and Part II the "mixed-gas".
Although the order may be changed in due
course, the qualifications, from the
lowest upwards are, Part IV, Part III,
Part I, Part II. Any change in the system
now could well entail the alteration of
several hundred, if not thousands of
existing diving certificates.

HSE Part IV

The basic air diving qualification,
suitable for scientists, inspection personnel, engineer's, and those required to
dive commercially to a maximum depth of
30m (98ft) using self-contained diving
apparatus where no surface compression
chamber is required on site. This qualification calls for no trade skills or tool
training as part of the syllabus, although
the use of basic hand-tools is normally
included. Additional training will be
necessary if the diver seeks endorsements
to allow him to dive deeper, down to a
maximum of 50m (165ft). The training is
intended to meet the requirements of
inspection diving only.

A typical training course would be
of 3 to 4 weeks duration, depending on
the applicants previous sport diving
background and qualifications.

HSE Part III

This qualification can be obtained either
as a training "module" from Part IV Diver,
or by successful completion of the appropriate training course, which will be in
the order of 6 weeks duration. Intended
for those wishing to work as divers in
the civil-engineering/inspection industry,
who are required to dive to a maximum

depth of 30m (98ft) using self-
contained or surface-supplied/
surface-demand equipment, where no
surface compression chamber is
required on site.

The qualification calls for
no tools or skills training, apart
from basic hand tools. If the
diver seeks appropriate endorsements to be allowed to dive deeper,
down to a maximum of 50m (165ft),
or to use power tools or undertake
the use of other skills, then
additional training will be required.

Neither Part's IV or III
qualifications are acceptable offshore in the oil and gas industry,
for which a Part I qualification is
the mandatory minimum standard.

HSE Part I

The highest air diving qualification
obtainable, which can be achieved as
a series of "modular" progressions
from Part IV, through Part III, with
the appropriate training and work
experience, or obtained by the
successful completion of the training course laid down in the "Basic
Air Diving Training Standard" of
the MSC's Training Services Division.
Such a course will be approximately
10 to 12 weeks duration.

It is the only air diving
qualification acceptable in the offshore industry, and is rapidly
receiving international recognition.
Those holding this certificate are
considered competent in both self-
contained and surface-demand/surface-
supplied equipment to 50m (165ft).

Training includes power tools
operation, both hydraulic and pneumatic, underwater cutting, bolt-
punching and other work related
skills.

An HSE Part I certificate is
essential if a diver intends to
progress, at a later date, to mixed-
gas/saturation diver training.

HSE Part II

This is the mixed-gas/saturation
diving qualification, required by

the regulations for those wishing to be employed in "deep-diving" in the UK
offshore industry. At least 12 months regular and varied diving work experience
is required as a Part I Diver, before enrolment for training. The training course
is approximately of 4 weeks duration.

Basic Air Diving Training Standard – in accordance with Schedule 4, Part I,
Diving Operations at Work Regulations, 1981

In 1975, the Manpower Services Commission set up a voluntary system of
certification for trainee divers as part of a programme to improve the quality
of training in commercial diving and underwater working. Concurrently, two
training standards covering Basic Air Diving and Underwater Working (ISBN
0 9504011 2 9) and Mixed Gas Diving (ISBN 0 9504011 3 7) were developed, in
co-operation with the diving industry and other government departments, and
published by the Manpower Services Commission.

   The certification arrangements involved a system of approval of establishments to run courses to the training standards, and to monitor courses to ensure
standards were being maintained. In the period September 1975 to June 1981, a
total of 1013 trainees successfully completed courses to the requirements of the
Basic Air Diving and Underwater Working Standard at five approved diving
schools, and were awarded MSC certificates. The diving schools were:
Directorate of Marine Services Diving School, H.M. Dockyard, Rosyth, Scotland;
Fort Bovisand Underwater centre, Plymouth; Prodive Ltd, Falmouth Docks, Cornwall;
Royal Engineers Diving establishment, Southampton, and the Underwater Training
Centre, Fort William, Scotland. Courses at the five diving schools were of 12
week's duration, and course programme and assessment methods were similar, but
not identical.

   In November 1980 the Health and Safety Commission agreed to establish the
Certification Board for Diver Training, and the Diving Operations at Work
Regulations 1981, SI 1981 No 399, came into force on 1 July 1981.

   The Standards, Aims and terminal Objectives of Air Diver Training for all
three Grades of Part IV, III and I are contained in the Basic Air Diving Training Standard mentioned above, and in order that those in training, or those
contemplating becoming professional commercial divers appreciate the standard
required, the following is a full and complete extract from that document.

   This clearly outlines the Terminal Objectives in each section of training,
plus the Training Objective, and for simplicity, to which diver qualification
this applies. Copies of the Training Standard are available from:
The Chief Diving Inspector, Department of Energy, Thames House South, London SW1

Branch F16, HM Factory Inspectorate, Health and Safety Executive, 25 Chapel Street,
London NW1 5DT

Manpower Services Commission, Moorfoot, Sheffield, S1 4PS

BASIC AIR DIVING TRAINING STANDARD

Aims and terminal objectives

1 The aims are brief statements of the purpose of the training standard, and the
  terminal objectives describe what the trainee must be able to do on completion
  of training.

2 The wording and interpretation of the terminal objectives are very important

as they are used to produce the topics to be included in the training programme. It is realised that there are difficulties in expressing clearly and precisely the level of competence to be developed in the trainee.

Aims

3 To train underwater workers for the Diving Industry to operate safely and competently to depths of 30m(98ft) using self-contained, and to 50m(165ft) using surface supplied diving equipment in accordance with Schedule 4, Part I of the Diving Operations at Work Regulations 1981, SI 1981, No 399.

4 To provide a knowledge of the underwater skills required by the industry and the application of basic skills in order to complete a range of underwater taska safely and efficiently.

5 Before considering the terminal objectives, two important aspects of the aims need to be stressed. These are safety and health and team training.

Safety and Health

The safety and health of the diver and the development of safe working practices MUST be integrated into all aspects of the training course.

Team Training

The training, particularly in practical diving and underwater working, needs to be directed not only towards developing individual competence but also to develop the trainee to think and act as a member of a team.

Terminal objectives

The terminal objectives have been grouped under ten headings:

Table 1	Diving Theory	Table 6	Underwater hazards
Table 2	Use of diving equipment	Table 7	Air compressors
Table 3	Seamanship	Table 8	Compression chambers
Table 4	Diver communications	Table 9	Physiology and first aid
Table 5	Underwater tasks	Table 10	Legislation and guidance

Terminal objectives can be classified into two groups: those whose purpose is to develop some degree of competence, and, those limited to developing an appreciation of, or acquaintance with a particular piece of equipment or a procedure.

To which HSE Grade applicable	Terminal objectives	Training objectives

Table 1 - Diving theory

To which HSE Grade applicable	Terminal objectives	Training objectives
1/3/4	Relationship between pressure and volume (Boyle' Law)	Calculate the volume changes with changing depths
1/3/4	Relationship between pressure and temperature (Charles's Law)	Calculate the pressure changes with changes in temperature
1/3/4	Partial pressure of gases (Dalton's Law)	Calculate the partial pressure of gases at different depths
1/3/4	Solubility of gases in solution (Henry's Law)	Explain the solubility effect of gases in liquids and the need for decompression
1/3/4	Buoyancy (Archimedes' principle)	Calculate the buoyancy of various objects at different depths
		Explain the effect of salt and fresh water on buoyancy

Table 2 - Use of self-contained and surface-supplied diving equipment (including rigid helmet with free flow primary air supply)

To which HSE Grade applicable	Terminal objectives	Training objectives
1/3/4	Dive safely and competently using self-contained diving equipment in sheltered and open water in varying bottom conditions and water visibility	Dive, act as a diver's attendant and stand-by diver in diving operations using self-contained diving equipment
3/4	Dive safely and competently using surface supplied diving equipment in sheltered and open water in varying bottom conditions and water visibility	Dive, act as a diver's attendant and stand-by diver in diving; operations using surface supplied diving equipment
1/3/4	Dive safely and competently to a depth of 30m using self-contained diving equipment to the reserve limit of the breathing set	Explain the function and operation of reserve systems currently available Operate the reserve safely
1	Dive safely and competently to a depth of not less than 40m (131ft) using two types of surface supplied diving equipment, one of which must be a rigid	Act as a diver, diver's attendant, stand-by diver and panel operator in diving operations involving the use of bandmask/demand helmet and free flow helmet to a depth

	helmet with free flow primary air supply	of not less than 40m
1/3/4	Carry out emergency drills applicable to self-contained diving equipment	Explain the procedure to be followed in the case of: Trapped diver Unconscious diver Broken face plate Explain current SCUBA emergency procedures, eg. equipment sharing, use of inflatable life jacket and buoyancy aids etc.
1/3	Carry out emergency drills applicable to surface supplied diving equipment	Explain the procedure to be followed in the case of: Broken helmet/face plate Blow up Trapped diver Unconscious diver
1/3/4		Carry out at least one simulated rescue of an unconscious diver using self-contained diving equipment when acting as diver and stand-by diver
1/3		Carry out at least one simulated rescue of an unconscious diver using surface supplied diving equipment when acting as a diver and a stand-by diver
1/3/4	Dress and undress divers using self-contained diving equipment	Explain safety procedures. Carry out pre- and post-dive checks
1/3	Dress and undress divers using surface supplied diving equipment	Explain safety procedures. Carry out pre- and post dive checks
1/3/4	Perform user maintenance of self-contained diving equipment, and prepare equipment for use	Dismantle and reassemble self-contained diving equipment Explain the function and operation of masks, SCUBA and associated diving equipment Explain the testing procedures to check equipment for defects Identify worn and damaged parts
1/3	Perform user maintanance of surface supplied diving equipment, and prepare equipment for use	Dismantle and reassemble surface supplied diving equipment Explain the function and operation of masks, helmets, and associated diving equipment

		Explain the testing procedures to check equipment for defects
		Identify worn and damaged parts
1/3/4	Perform repairs and tests on diving suits	Explain the principles of porosity testing of dry suits and perform user maintenance and repair of diving suits

In-water Training Times

The following <u>MINIMUM</u> in-water training times must be achieved. In-water time should include some decompression stops. Trainees may require more than the minimum time to achieve the terminal objectives.

Depth in metres	Equivalent feet	In-water times in minutes
0 - 19m	0 - 62.3ft	1600 (with a minimum of 400 minutes in the depth range 11 - 19m)
20 - 39m	65.6 - 128ft	250 (with a minimum of 100 minutes in the depth range 30 - 39m)
40 - 50m	131.2 - 165ft	150 (with a minimum of 3 wet dives each of which must have a bottom time exceeding 10 minutes)

Note: In very special circumstances the certification authority MAY accept compression chamber dives of up to 50 minutes at a depth of 50m (165ft) as counting towards the 150 minutes minimum.

Table 3 - Seamanship

1/3/4	Outline the pattern of tidal movements and how to determine the depth of water and tidal direction in a given place at a given time	Calculate predicted depth and tidal movement using a chart and tide tables
1/3/4	Recognise the standard symbols used on charts and how distance, position and direction are determined	Plot the course on a chart between two points and measure direction and distance Use a chart to calculate distance and position
1/3/4	Outline the principles of handling a small craft in harbour and at sea in varying sea conditions	Explain precautions to be taken when navigating in confined waters and at sea with respect to other vessels, natural hazards and structures

1/3/4	State the essential safety equipment to be carried in a small craft and its use	Explain the use of essential safety equipment
1/3/4	Handle a small craft under supervision	Perform the following operations and manoeuvres: Start and stop the engine Launch and recovery Anchoring Recovery of a floating object Picking up a buoy

Table 4 - Diver communication systems

1/3/4	Recognise, identify, interpret and correctly respond to hand and rope signals, from diver to diver, diver to surface and surface to diver	Explain the principle of tending a diver. Explain and use hand and rope signals Act as a diver and attendant in a diving operation where rope signals are the primary means of communication
1/3	Outline the basic principles of underwater communication and diver intercom systems	Explain the differences between two and four-wire telephone systems Perform a functional test on a diver intercom system Explain the principles of through water communication systems
1/3	Use underwater communication and diver intercom systems for communication from diver to surface, surface to diver	Act as a diver, telephone operator and linesman in a diving operation where a diving intercom system is the primary means of communication with a diver
1/3	Carry out user maintenance of underwater communication and diver intercom systems	Perform user maintenance, eg. change earphones, microphone, check connections and battery, recharge battery Perform a test on a communicatin system and isolate a fault in a helmet, cable, or box Explain the precautions to be taken to protect the equipment

---

Table 5 - Underwater tasks

1/3/4	Outline current underwater search methods and locate an object using two of them	Explain at least three current methods of carrying out underwater searches
		Locate an object underwater using at least two different methods
1/3/4	Produce a report based on an inspection/survey of an underwater structure or natural feature	Explain the principles of producing a clear, concise and well laid out reports
		Explain the essential points to be included in briefing for a survey/inspection
		Perform an underwater inspection/survey and prepare a report
1	Outline the basic principles of various underwater inspection and measurement techniques, including video inspection	Explain the elementary principles of various underwater inspection and measurement techniques including:
		Tape measurement Recording and writing Still photography Video inspection
1	Explain the basic principles of non-destructive testing	Explain the basic principles and techniques of current non-destructive testing, including:
		Ultrasonics Magnetic particle Cathodic protection measurement
1	Handle safely and efficiently cordage, wire, ropes, blocks and tackle, chain hoists, associated winches, Tirfors, and working stages on the surface and underwater	Tie basic knots used in diving
		Handle ropes and wires
		Rig a working stage for a practical diving task
		Use blocks, tackle, chain-hoists, associated winches, and Tirfors on the surface and underwater
		Explain the principles of mechanical advantage
		Explain the main purposes of current legislation concerning the use of lifting appliances applicable to diving operations

		Perform user maintenance of blocks and tackle, chain hoists and Tirfors
1/3/4	Complete underwater tasks safely and efficiently using a range of hand tools, eg. spanners, hammers, chisels and hacksaws	Complete a range of underwater tasks to the required standards using a range of hand tools
		Act safely and competently in a diving operation involving the use of a range of hand tools
		Perform user maintenance of hand tools
1	Outline the methods of operation and safety requirements of compressed air and hydraulically operated tools, eg: jack hammers, impact wrenches, drilling machines, grinders and cut-off discs	Explain the safety precautionn to be taken when using compressed air and hydraulic tools
		Explain the principles, operating procedures and limitations of compressed air and hydraulic tools
1	Complete underwater tasks safely and efficiently using a range of compressed air and hydraulic tools	Act as a diver in a diving operation using a range of powered tools
		Complete a range of tasks to the required standards.
1	Perform user maintenance of compressed air and hydraulic tools	Perform pre- and post-dive checks and user maintenance
1	Outline the principles, methods of operation and safety requirements of high and low pressure water jets, air lifts and lifting bags	Explain the principles of water jetting equipment, air lifts and the use of buoyancy for lifting and the safety precautions to be taken
		Calculate the number of lifting bags and determine the procedures required to lift a given object
1	Use a low or high pressure water jet, air lift and lifting bags safely and efficiently	Complete underwater tasks to the required standards using a low pressure water jet, air lift and lifting bags
1	Carry out user maintenance of water jetting equipment, air lifts and lifting bags	Perform post-use maintenance
1	Outline the principles of operation of underwater bolt-guns and the safety precautions to be taken when using the equipment	Explain the principles of operation and demonstrate how to load a bolt gun
		Explain the action to be taken in the event of a misfire

		Select the correct ammunition for an appropriate task
1	Outline the principles, method of operation, safety requirements and uses of thermal arc cutting equipment	Prepare thermal arc cutting equipment for use
		Calculate appropriate oxygen pressure
		Explain alternative methods of ignition
		Explain safety precautions to be taken on the surface and under-water
1	Outline the principles, method of operation and safety precautions to be taken when using oxy-arc cutting equipment	Prepare equipment for use
		Calculate appropriate oxygen pressure
		Explain safety precautions to be taken on the surface and under-water
1	Use oxy-arc cutting equipment safely and efficiently to cut flat steel plate up to 25mm (1in) thickness and complete one other cutting task	Perform pre- and post-dive checks
		Perform cutting tasks to the required standards
		Change cutting rods underwater
1	Perform user maintenance of oxy-arc cutting equipment	Perform post-dive maintenance of cutting equipment including:
		Generator
		Knife switch
		Cables
		Torch
1	Outline the principles, methods of operation and safety prec-autions to be taken when using current methods of underwater electric arc welding	Prepare equipment for use
		Explain safety precautions to be taken on the surface and under-water
		Explain different types of electrode and appropriate current settings
1	Outline the types of explosives currently available for under-water use, their common usage and relevant statutory regulat-ions	Explain the procedure for the safe handling of explosives
		Explain current methods of initiation and procedures to be used in case of a misfire

		Explain the use of explosives accessories, tools, exploders
1	Outline the use of explosives and the setting of firing circuits and their initiation using electrical and non-electrical methods and handle equipment under classroom conditions	Explain the correct placing of explosive charges, parallel and series electrical circuits
1	Outline the elementary principles of construction methods and practices associated with underwater structures, and interpret relevant simple engineering drawings	Explain how to set up scaffolding underwater, and the use of various techniques including concreting, sand bagging, shuttering and bolt tensioning Interpret a simple engineering drawing

NB Some of the power tools must be used at a minimum depth of 35m (115ft), and a substantial majority of the tasks must be completed using surface supplied diving equipment. At least one of the dives to a minimum depth of 35m should involve an underwater task that an average diver would need at least 20 minutes to complete.

Table 6 - Underwater hazards

1/3/4	Outline the hazards to divers of water flow around and through underwater structures (including gates, culverts, sewers and intakes) and explain the safety precautions to be taken	Explain the safety precautions to be taken before undertaking diving operations where hazardous flow conditions may exist Explain the principles of differential water pressure and the operation of sluice gates and intakes.

Table 7 - Air compressors

1/3/4	Outline the principles, method of operation and health and safety requirements of high and low pressure air compressors	Explain compressor air flow, and volume requirements for particular diving operations Explain the relevant requirements of statutory provisions
1/3/4	Operate safely and efficiently and carry out user maintenance of high and low pressure air compressors	Operate high and low pressure air compressors Perform all checks and user maintenance including checking oil and water, and draining filters

1/3/4	Transfer gases into and out of high pressure air banks safely and efficiently	Explain the main safety precautions to be observed concerning the use of high and low pressure air vessels and compressors and the siting of air intakes
		Explain the principles of decanting
		Explain the procedure for charging and charge air cylinders directly from a compressor and from an air bank
1/3/4	Operate and carry out user maintenance of associated air filtration equipment	Explain the purpose of a filtration system, including the components of a filter and its replacement and the siting of air intakes
		Use a simple analyser kit to determine air purity

Table 8 – Compression chambers and therapeutic decompression

1/3/4	Outline the lay-out of a two-compartment compression chamber, safety and fire precautions, emergency procedures, method of operation, control panel, air supply and oxygen breathing system	Explain the purpose and operation of services to the chamber including the function of all components.
		Explain the need for oxygen cleanliness and the safety precautions to be observed
		Explain the main provisions of the staututory regulations concerning pressure vessels
1	Perform use maintenance of a two-compartment compression chamber	Perform pre- and post-dive checks
1	Operate a two-compartment compression chamber	Pressurise, flush through and decompress a two-compartment compression chamber
1	Complete a test dive to 50m (165ft) in a two-compartment compression chamber	Complete a simple dexterity or comprehension test at a depth of 50m (165ft)
1	Prepare a two-compartment compression chamber for therapeutic treatment	Perform functional tests of all appropriate systems including communications equipment
		Ensure appropriate fire precau-are taken and fire prevention equipment is available

		Ensure appropriate first aid and personal supplies are available for the patient
1/3/4	Interpret and apply air de-compression tables	Calculate the correct de-compression schedules for single/ repetitive dives using current decompression tables
1	Outline and perform surface decompression drills under simulated conditions	Explain the principles and procedures for surface decompress-ion
		Perform a surface decompression drill transferring from the water to a two-compartment compression chamber
1/3/4	Understand the use of therapeutic tables	Explain the use of air and oxygen therapeutic tables

Table 9 - Diving physiology and First Aid

1/3/4	Outline the respiratory, circul-atory, basic skeletal and nervous systems of the body	Explain briefly the function of the following:
		Skeletal system; heart, blood vessels and circulation of blood; properties of blood, lungs and airways including control of respiration and simple gas exchange; brain; spinal cord and nerves
1/3/4	Outline the basic need for and problems associated with maintaining the normal body temperature of the diver	Recognise signs and symptons of hypothermia and hyperthermia and how to treat these conditions
1/3/4	Describe the dangers and symptoms caused by breathing too high or too low a concentration of oxygen or too high a concentration of nitrogen	Explain briefly the effects on the brain and lungs and what is meant by oxygen pulmonary toxicity
1/3/4	Apply first aid treatment in typical diving emergencies	Explain the causes, signs, symptons and treatment of:
		Decompression sickness; squeeze; "ears" and sinuses; reversed ears; drowning; vomiting under-water; cold exposure; carbon dioxide poisoning; carbon monoxide poisoning; nitrogen narcosis; pulmonary barotrauma; air embolism

1/3/4	Apply first aid treatment to minor injuries	Explain the signs, symptons and treatment of shock, burns, bleeding (both external and internal), wounds and fractures including long bones and spine, electrocution, high-pressure jetting injuries
1/3/4	Apply first aid treatment to an unconscious person	Explain the causes, signs, symptons and treatment of asphyxia
		Demonstrate external cardiac massage and artificial maintenance of respiration

Table 10 - Relevant legislation and guidance

1/3/4	Outline the relevant statutory provisions and associated guidance notes as they relate to air diving operations appropriate to Schedule 4, Part 1, Diving Operations at Work Regulations 1981, SI 1981, No 399	Explain the main duties of the employer and employee under the Health and Safety at Work Act 1974.
		Explain the main duties of the diving contractor, the diving supervisor, and the diver under the Diving Operations at Work Regulations 1981
		Explain the main purpose of other current statutory provisions and associated Guidance Notes as they apply to air diving operations using surface supplied and self-contained diving equipment.

CHAPTER 24

CONVERSION FACTORS AND TABLES

The international nature of diving will bring individuals in contact with both the Imperial and Metric system of units, and whilst certain basic units and conversions may already be second nature, there will be frequent need to make calculations regarding conversion of pressure, capacity, distance etc. The following basic tables and conversions will not only meet the requirements of diver training courses, but also the majority of diving situations.

DISTANCE

1 inch	=	2.540 centimetres
1 foot	=	0.304 metres
1 yard	=	0.914 metres
1 fathom	=	1.828 metres
1 statute mile (5260ft)	=	1.609 kilometres
1 nautical mile	=	1.853 kilometres
1 centimetre	=	0.393 inches
1 metre	=	3.280 feet
1 metre	=	1.093 yards
1 metre	=	0.546 fathoms
1 kilometre	=	0.621 statute miles
1 kilometre	=	0.539 nautical miles

VOLUME

1 cubic inch	=	16.378 cubic centimetres
1 cubic foot	=	0.028 cubic metres
1 cubic foot	=	28.317 litres
1 cubic yard	=	0.764 cubic metres
1 cubic centimetre	=	0.061 cubic feet
1 cubic metre	=	35.314 cubic feet
1 cubic metre	=	1.308 cubic yards
1 litre (1000cc)	=	0.035 cubic feet

CAPACITY

1 pint	=	0.568 litres
1 gallon	=	4.546 litres
1 litre	=	0.22 gallons
1 litre	=	1.76 pints
1 U.S. gallon	=	3.785 litres
1 U.S. quart	=	0.946 litres
1 Imperial quart	=	1.136 litres

WEIGHT

1 ounce (troy)	=	31.103 grammes
1 ounce (avoirdupois)	=	28.35 grammes
1 pound (1b)	=	0.4536 kilogram
1 pound (1b)	=	453.6 grams
1 ton (of 2240lbs)	=	1.016 metric tonnes
1 ton (of 2240lbs)	=	1016 kilograms
1 gramme	=	0.03215 ounce troy
1 gramme	=	0.03527 ounce avoirdupois

```
1 kilogram                    =    2.2046 pounds
1 metric tonne                =    0.9842 ton (of 2240lb)
1 metric tonne                =    2204.6 pounds
```

PRESSURE
```
1 pound per square inch       =    0.0703 kilogramme/sq.cm
1 kilogramme/sq.mm            =    1422.32 pounds/sq.in
1 kilogramme/sq.cm            =    14.223 pounds/sq.in
1 kilogramme/metre            =    7.233 foot/pounds
```

WATER
```
1 cubic ft fresh water        =    62.5lb
1 cubic ft salt water         =    64lb (average)
```

TEMPERATURE

     To convert degrees Fahrenheit to degrees Centigrade
          subtract 32, and multiply by 5/9

     To convert degrees Centigrade to degrees Fahrenheit
          multiply by 5/9, and add 32

NAUTICAL MEASUREMENTS
```
1 fathom                      =    6ft
1 shackle                     =    15 fathoms (90ft)
1 cable                       =    608ft (100 fathoms approx)
10 cables                     =    1 nautical mile (international)
1 nautical mile (int'nl)      =    6076.12ft or 1852 metres
```

CONVERSION TABLES

To convert	into	multiply by
Atmospheres	ft of sea water (4°C)	33.9
	kg/cm^2	1.0333
	kg/m^2	10332
	lbs/in^2 (psi)	14.7
	tons/ft^2	1.058
Bars	atmospheres	0.9869
	kg/m^2	10200
	kg/cm^2	1.02
	lbs/ft^2 (psi)	2089
Feet of water	atmospheres	0.0295
	kg/cm^2	0.03048
	kg/m^2	304.8
	lbs/ft^2	62.43
	lbs/in^2 (psi)	0.4335
Centimetres	inches	0.3937
	feet	0.0328
	yards	0.01094
Metres	inches	39.37
	feet	3.281
	miles (nautical)	0.0005396
	miles (statute)	0.0006214
Kilometres	feet	3281
	yards	1094

	miles	0.6214
Feet	millimetres	304.8
	centimetres	30.48
	metres	0.3048
	miles (nautical)	0.0001645
	miles (statute)	0.0001894
Miles (statute)	centimetres	160900
	metres	1609
	kilometres	1.609
	feet	5280
	yards	1760
	miles (nautical)	0.8684
Miles (nautical)	metres	1853.248
	kilometres	1.853248
	feet	6080
	yards	2025.4
	miles (statute)	1.1516
Cubic centimetres	cubic ins (in^3)	0.06102
	cubic ft (ft^3)	0.00003531
	cubic yds (yd^3)	0.000001308
	gallons (U.S.)	0.0002642
	litres	0.01
Cubic metres	cubic ins (in^3)	61023
	cubic ft (ft^3)	35.31
	cubic yds (yd^3)	1.308
	gallons (U.S.)	264.2
	litres	1000
Cubic inches	cubic cm (cc)	16.39
	cubic ft (ft^3)	0.0005787
	cubic metres (m^3)	0.00001639
	cubic yards (yd^3)	0.00002143
	gallons (U.S.)	0.004329
	litres	0.01639
Cubic feet	cubic cm (cc)	28320
	cubic ins (in^3)	1728
	cubic metres (m^3)	0.02832
	cubic yards (yd^3)	0.03704
	gallons (U.S.)	7.48052
	litres	28.32
Callons (imperial)	cubic cm (cc)	3785
	cubic ft (ft^3)	0.1337
	cubic ins (in^3)	231
	cubic metres (m^3)	0.003785
	litres	3.785
	lb of water	8.33
	gallons (U.S.)	1.20095
Gallons (U.S.)	gallons (imperial)	0.83267
Kilometres/hour	centimetres/sec	27.78
	feet/minute	54.68
	feet/second	0.9113
	knots	0.5396
	metres/minute	16.67
	miles/hour	0.6214

Miles/hour	centimetres/sec	44.7
	feet/minute	88
	feet/second	1.467
	miles/minute	0.1667
	kilometres/hour	1.609
	kilometres/minute	0.02682
	knots	0.8684
	metres/minute	26.82
	metres/second	0.447
Pounds/in^2(psi)	atmospheres	0.06804
	feet of sea water	2.250482
	kilogramme/metre^2	703.1
	pounds/ft^2	144
Tons (short)	kilogrammes	907.1848
	ounces	32000
	pounds	2000
	tons (long)	0.89287

COMPARISON TABLE FOR DEPTHS - Feet/metres

Feet	number	Metres	Feet	number	Metres
3.28	1	0.30	98.43	30	9.14
16.40	5	1.52	101.71	31	9.45
29.53	9	2.74	114.83	35	10.67
32.81	10	3.05	121.39	37	11.28
49.21	15	4.57	131.23	40	12.19
59.06	18	5.49	147.64	45	13.72
65.62	20	6.10	150.92	46	14.02
75.46	23	7.01	164.04	50	15.24
82.02	25	7.62	328.08	100	30.48

CYLINDER PRESSURES - COMPARISON TABLE

Pounds sq/ins (psi)	MN sq/metre	Atmospheres	Bars
1800	12.4	122	124
2000	13.8	136	138
2250	15.5	153	155
2500	17.2	170	172
2650	18.2	180	183
3000	20.7	204	207

BEAUFORT WIND SCALE

Beaufort number	Mean wind in knots	Descriptive term	Deep sea conditions	Approx. wave height (m)
0	Less than 1	Calm	Sea mirror-like	—
1	1-3	Light air	Ripples without crests	—
2	4-6	Light	Small wavelets, not breaking	0.15

3	7 - 10	Gentle breeze	Large wavelets, crests beginning to break	o.60
4	11 - 16	Moderate breeze	Small waves, fairly frequent white horses	1.00
5	17 - 21	Fresh breeze	Moderate waves, long, many white horses	1.80
6	22 - 27	Strong breeze	Large waves beginning, white foam crests	3.00
7	28 - 33	Near gale	Sea heaps up, breaking waves blown in streaks	4.00
8	34 - 40	Gale	Moderately high seas, with foam blown in streaks	5.50
9	41 - 47	Strong	High waves, dense streaks of foam, crests topple	7.00
10	48 - 55	Storm	Very high waves, sea takes on a white appearance	9.00
11	56 - 63	Violent storm	Exceptionally high waves, crests blown to froth	11.30
12	64 plus	Hurricane	Sea completely white, air filled with foam and spray	13.70

GENERAL INDEX